EIGHTEENTH CENTURY ENGLAND

A HISTORY OF ENGLAND

General Editor: W. N. MEDLICOTT

* *Already published*

EIGHTEENTH CENTURY ENGLAND

DOROTHY MARSHALL

LONGMAN

Longman Group UK Limited
Longman House, Burnt Mill, Harlow
Essex CM 20 2JE, England
and Associated Companies throughout the world

*Published in the United States of America
by Longman Inc., New York*

© *Dorothy Marshall 1962*

First published 1962
Seventh impression 1970
Second edition 1974
Eighth impression 1993

ISBN 0-582-48316-6

Produced by Longman Singapore Publishers (Pte) Ltd.
Printed in Singapore.

INTRODUCTORY NOTE

ONE of the effects of two world wars and of fifty years of ever-accelerating industrial and social revolution has been the growing interest of the citizen in the story of his land. From this story he seeks to learn the secret of his country's greatness and a way to better living in the future.

There seems, therefore, to be room for a rewriting of the history of England which will hold the interest of the general reader while it appeals at the same time to the student. This new presentation will take account of the recent discoveries of the archaeologist and the historian, and will not lose sight of the claims of history to take its place among the mental recreations of intelligent people for whom it has no professional concern.

The history will be completed in a series of eleven volumes. The volumes will be of medium length, and it is hoped that they will provide a readable narrative of the whole course of the history of England and give proper weight to the different strands which form the pattern of the story. No attempt has been made to secure general uniformity of style or treatment. Each period has its special problems, each author his individual technique and mental approach; each volume will be able to stand by itself not only as an expression of the author's methods, tastes, and experience, but as a coherent picture of a phase in the history of the country.

There is, nevertheless, a unity of purpose in the series; the authors have been asked, while avoiding excessive detail, to give particular attention to the interaction of the various aspects of national life and achievement, so that each volume may present a convincing integration of those developments—political, constitutional, economic, social, religious, military, foreign, or cultural—which happen to be dominant at each period. Although considerations of space will prevent minute investigation it should still be possible in a series of this length to deal fully with the essential themes.

A short bibliographical note is attached to each volume. This is not intended to supersede existing lists, but rather to call attention to recent works and to the standard bibliographies.

W. N. MEDLICOTT

CONTENTS

Chapter 4

The Struggle for Power   101

Chapter 5

The Ascendancy of Walpole   131

Chapter 6

Walpole and the Opposition   150

Chapter 7

The Fall of Walpole   168

Chapter 16

Domestic Success and Colonial Disaster

Chapter 17

The Influence of the American War of Independence on Domestic Politics

Chapter 18

Social and Economic Developments

Chapter 19

Peace Overseas and Conflict at Home

MAPS

ACKNOWLEDGEMENT

We are grateful to J. M. Dent & Sons Ltd. for permission
to include extracts from the Everyman's Library edition of
John Wesley's Journal.

PREFACE

Anyone who attempts to write the history of eighteenth-century England at the present time is rushing in where more cautious people fear to tread. During the last thirty years research into this period has revolutionized many traditional interpretations. 'George be a King' has gone. So has the concept of Sir Robert Walpole as the prototype of the modern Prime Minister, and the belief that whigs and tories can be equated with the organized party system of the nineteenth century. Yet this research is still very incomplete. Small patches have been covered in great detail, as for instance by the late Sir Lewis Namier in his epoch-making study, *The Structure of Politics at the Accession of George III*. In the same way J. Owen's *The Rise of the Pelhams*, J. Brooke's *The Chatham Administration*, Professor Herbert Butterfield's *King George III, Lord North and the People*, and I. R. Christie's *The End of North's Ministry* 1780–82, all concentrate on a few years. Biographies, such as J. H. Plumb's two volumes on *Sir Robert Walpole* and B. Tunstall's *William Pitt, Earl of Chatham*, are available only for some of the leading actors in the eighteenth-century scene. The only major exception as yet is the recent volume, *The Reign of George III* by J. Steven Watson in 'The Oxford History of England' series. As a consequence anyone rash enough to cover the entire century in one volume is faced with narratives so detailed and so subtly analysed that the task of reducing their essence to a few pages is bound on the one hand to lead to the falsification of over-simplification, and on the other to the hazard of applying the new interpretations to those periods which have not yet been subjected to this detailed scrutiny.

This volume has been written to provide some kind of guide through this morass, where between the tussocks of modern scholarship still lies the vast bog of ignorance and tradition. It is intended, like the other volumes in this series, mainly for those readers who are attempting a serious study of the period for the first time. I hope that the university student, and those readers who are looking for a reasonably comprehensive introduction to this most fascinating of centuries, either out of general interest or as a base for more specialized later reading, will find it useful. For this purpose a narrative treatment seemed to me to be the most appropriate. It is after all necessary to know what happened before it is possible to speculate intelligently on why it happened. The complaint has often been made to me that historians are too apt to take for granted a greater degree of factual knowledge on the part of their readers than they possess. People are not born knowing the date of the Septennial Act, or even that of the accession of George III, and may never have studied the period at school. For many readers, therefore, a framework of fact is essential and almost inevitably this leads to giving a certain priority to political history. The rise and fall of ministries, war and peace, between them make the main sequence of events, though the social and economic historian may argue, in my opinion legitimately, that unless this is accompanied by an adequate knowledge of the structure of society and the economic resources of the country, political events can only be very partially understood. In as far, therefore, as space has permitted, I have woven social and economic threads into my political pattern.

I have tried to write a narrative which will incorporate the results of recent scholarship, and at the same time provide a certain amount of background for the reader unfamiliar with the century. With this aim I have written two introductory chapters, sketching in the social and economic framework, and the conditions of political life, both essential material for an understanding of the narrative that starts with the accession of George I in 1714. In subsequent chapters, in addition to a further social and economic survey on the eve of the Seven Years War, I have used the device of the organized digression to provide the background necessary to understand events as they are reached in the narrative. In this way much social and economic information has been incorporated. For example when Ireland first figures on the English political scene in connection with Wood's Halfpence, there is a short description of its relation with England. In the same way the account of the passing of the Septennial Act is accompanied by an analysis of its importance and influence on political life, which will contribute to a fuller understanding of subsequent events. My hope is that by so doing readers will find the information they want at the moment that they are conscious of the need for it, without having to refer to other chapters. In adopting this method I am conscious that some repetition is apt to creep in. When the same basic situation occurs repeatedly, as it does in the relations between ministers, the Commons and the Crown, repetition is difficult to avoid.

As in the other volumes in this series my footnotes are not usually intended for the specialist, who will be familiar with the sources I have used and the references I have given. They are intended to perform two main functions. The first is to supplement the 'Note on Books' at the end of this volume, and to lay a foundation for further study by indicating some of the books that should be consulted for fuller details on particular topics. The second is to introduce readers to easily available printed source material, in the hope that the extracts chosen will not only illuminate the text but encourage students to consult the original authorities for themselves. In order to facilitate this, when possible I have used editions that are easily available in reprints, as for instance the 1959 edition of Defoe's *Tours* edited for Everyman by G. D. H. Cole. In the same way I have supplied page references to documents to be found in *English Historical Documents* rather than to the originals. It has not of course been possible to confine my footnotes exclusively to such sources, but later collections of printed materials, such as the new edition of the Burke *Correspondence* now appearing under the general editorship of Professor Coupland, and even earlier collections such as the Hardwicke papers, can often be consulted without much difficulty.

I should like finally to add a word of apology to all those scholars whose researches I have so freely used, for what must often seem to them the distortion of their work. To summarize for the non-specialist in a few pages a detailed monograph is an all but impossible task. My earnest hope is that my readers will correct any such misconceptions as may have arisen, by subsequently consulting those works to which this volume owes so much. In addition there is one last inconsistency which I must explain. Having lectured for long in Wales I have become conscious that to many people in this island England is not Britain and English is not the equivalent of British. Yet because I am English and because many of my readers will be accustomed to hearing Britain called England, I have sought refuge in inconsistency and used both interchangeably, thereby probably pleasing no one!

I should like also to express my thanks to Professor Medlicott, the general editor of this series, for all the help and encouragement he has given me and, though convention dictates that no one person shall be particularized, to those members of Longmans who have borne so patiently with those failings of mine of which, by now, they must be even more conscious than I am. I am also most grateful to Mrs. Alice Colburn and Mr. Warren Wager of Wellesley College, Massachusetts, who have extended to me, a visiting colleague, the great kindness of reading my proofs.

D. M.

University College of South Wales and Monmouthshire,
   Cardiff.

PREFACE TO THE SECOND EDITION

So much work has been done on certain aspects of English eighteenth-century history since this book was published in 1962 that a new edition has become necessary in order to bring it into line with recent scholarship. In doing so I have tried to make as little change in the original format as possible and the new material has been dovetailed into the existing text. Sometimes this has entailed re-writing several pages, sometimes merely a couple of sentences. Where possible I have drawn attention to new material or new views in footnotes rather than in making alterations in the text. My major structural alteration has been to split chapter 10 into two, dealing only with colonial issues in what is now chapter 10 and transferring the sections dealing with social and economic developments to a new chapter 18, which allowed me to follow these up to 1780 instead of stopping at 1754. This I hope readers will find an improvement.

Finally I must express my deep gratitude to John Carswell and Professor I. R. Christie for their very generous help in suggesting new material which I might have missed, in reading those parts of my text which lay within their own specialist periods and by their very helpful criticism in saving me from at least some of those slips and inaccuracies which so often result from having to write about complicated specialist issues in the limited space which a wide survey entails.

D. M.

Old Hutton,
Kendal.
August 1973.

INTRODUCTION

IF the years from 1784 can be described as 'The Age of Improvement' it would be equally appropriate to describe the period from 1714 to that date as 'the Age of Challenge, Contrast and Compromise'. The element of challenge was an inheritance from the tumultuous seventeenth century, which had undermined men's faith in most of the fundamentals in which they had previously believed. Man was no longer the centre of the universe: his world was no longer under the close and personal control of God the Father and redeemed by Christ the Son. Instead it had become a part of Newton's vast, impersonal system. Religious doctrine too, in the narrower sense, had been challenged. The Anglican Church had been temporarily deposed from its position as an established church by the powerful protest of Dissent. Political certainties had also gone. No longer was the monarch the divinely ordained governor of the land; no longer was God the 'only ruler of princes'; Parliament was now claiming to share that control. In both Church and State, therefore, beliefs which in previous ages had been questioned only by the daring individual mind were now matter for argument for most thinking men. Even in the economic sphere the same element of challenge appeared. The seventeenth century had created a new empire of trade in India, of settlement in the West Indies and on the American mainland, which profoundly influenced the pattern of trade and the growth of wealth in England. Added to this stimulus were the new techniques in industry and agriculture. The use of coal as a factor in industrial prosperity and growth, the invention of an elementary steam engine (puny though Savory's steam pump was), new crops with their promise of more food for beast and man, all presented a new challenge to the social and economic pattern of the past. It was symptomatic of the new age that Swift should put into the mouth of the King of Brobdingnag the oft quoted sentiment that 'whosoever could make two Ears of Corn, or two Blades of Grass to grow upon a Spot of Ground where only one grew before; would deserve better of Mankind, and do more essential Service to his Country, than the whole Race of Politicians put together'. Contrast was the inevitable consequence of such circumstances. Because there was no unity of belief as to the nature of man there was no basic standard of behaviour. The acceptance of the traditional view of the reality of original sin jostled with new optimistic philosophies as to human perfectibility. The freethinker, who could accept a vague Deism but who turned in intellectual revolt from a personal Saviour, argued interminably with the champions of traditional Christianity. In the world of politics similar contrasts of opinion were to be found, some men still upholding the theory of the divine right of the hereditary succession, others the contractual basis of the monarchy as developed by Locke. The same element of contradiction and contrast permeated the economic and social life of the community. The squire, managing his estate on traditional lines, contrasted bitterly his narrow fortune with the wealth of the new merchants and relished Pope's lines 'Get money, money still! And then let Virtue follow if she will'. Viewed in a wider historical framework there is nothing particularly novel in this antagonism between the country squire and the rich citizen. The sixteenth century, a period of rapid economic and religious change, was very familiar with it, and even medieval England was not unacquainted with the man who made money and used the scaling ladder of opportunity to penetrate into the castle of class. But the increasing openings, particularly in trade, were making the process almost automatic, and the multiplicity of instances increased the resentment of men whose lives were still lived within the traditional social and economic framework of the past. Increasing wealth sharpened social contrast in other ways. Not only the aristocracy and the wealthy but the middling sort were coming to adopt a higher standard of comfort in their everyday life. Their new houses, which were everywhere being built, are still among the most pleasing features of the English country town. But the streets were filthy, dead dogs were found in the conduit heads from which water was drawn, and the poor for lack of conveniences had to relieve themselves when and how they could. In individuals the same contrast is to be found. An education based on the classics, and completed by the civilizing influence of the Grand Tour, gave to the nobility and to wealthy gentlemen sophistication and polish. It did not prevent them from attending a public execution or glorying in the mangling ferocity of fighting cocks. Against the bestial nature of the mob must be put the sobriety and sense of decency that characterized not only Dissenters and Quakers but the majority of the solid middling sort. Alike in individuals and in society dramatic contrasts abounded. In political life independence and subservience, honesty and corruption, jostled each other; in private life debauchery and sobriety, philosophical argument and brutalizing sport were found cheek by jowl; physical comfort alternated with the physical endurance inflicted by exhausting transport and ignorant doctors. Many of these contrasts were not new, and indeed to some extent are to be found in every age. Even so, rapid improvement in so many spheres throws them into even sharper relief in the eighteenth century.

Out of challenge and contrast must come some measure of compromise if the community is to remain healthy and to grow. The particular contribution of the eighteenth century was to take the old and blend it with the new in such a way that serious breaks in political and social development were avoided. Because it succeeded in doing this it is sometimes, in contrast with the revolutionary activities of the seventeenth and the rapid economic, social and political changes of the nineteenth century, labelled as an age of stability. This word can be misleading unless it is realized that the stability comes from the balancing of tensions, not from inertia. It is this balancing of tensions that makes it an age of compromise. It was not, of course, complete or equally successful in every sphere. In spite of Pope's valiant attempt in his *Essay on Man* to have his cake and eat it, the doctrines of a personal salvation and of Deism, of original sin and human perfectibility, were too far apart for reconciliation, and a dichotomy of thought on such issues continued through the century and beyond, though rather more successful attempts were made to reconcile God and Newton. In the sphere of the Church, too, the compromise achieved was incomplete. The dilemma of the High Churchman was that of either acknowledging a hereditary monarch who belonged to the alien Roman Church or recognizing the Hanoverian King whose title was purely parliamentary. For most clergy the compromise was made, but at a considerable cost. The backwoodsmen remained Jacobite and tory in sentiment without being actively seditious, thereby diminishing seriously any political influence they might have exercised. Moral authority remained largely with the non-jurors. Their more latitudinarian brethren, by co-operating actively with the new dynasty, laid themselves open to the charge of having sold their birthright for a mess of pottage. In many cases this was manifestly unjust. Edmund Gibson, who became Bishop of London in 1723 and who has been described as 'the third subject in the state in point of political consequence', was a staunch churchman, a puritan in morals, and an efficient administrator of his diocese, and he saw his duty in terms of reconciling the ordinary clergy to the new dynasty. Nevertheless for many of the clergy this compromise seems to have resulted in some loss of spiritual fervour. It is easy to exaggerate the deadness of the Established Church in the eighteenth century; but, apart from the non-jurors, it was not a body of martyrs.

Englishmen are popularly regarded as being more successful in dealing with practical than with theoretical issues, and it can certainly be argued that the most brilliant achievement in the field of compromise was in politics. The 'Glorious Revolution' of 1689 had left England with a virtually unworkable constitution. Essential powers of final authority had been taken from the Crown without being transferred to any other body: the balance between King and Parliament was too complete. Without compromise, deadlock was inevitable and deadlock could only produce stagnation, inefficiency, and a despair that might breed further revolution. From all these evils the eighteenth century was saved by the growth of a system of influence and patronage, which compromised by acknowledging the theory of parliamentary control, and by combining it with the practical leadership of the King and the ministers chosen by him. The political history of the reigns of the first three Georges is essentially the history of the working out of this compromise. Like all compromises it was at times bitterly criticized and bitterly opposed. By the last third of the century there were signs, such as the emergence of the Foxite whigs, that it could not provide a permanent solution of the constitutional problem. Nevertheless, for the greater part of the century it gave Great Britain a stable and reasonably efficient government.

The greatest rejection of compromise came not in the domestic but in the imperial and economic sphere. As wealth increased, and with it the complexity of trading and the tangle of vested interests, the mercantilist framework of the late seventeenth century proved inadequate to contain them. This was most dramatically illustrated in the case of the American colonies. Here the points of view were diametrically opposed, and neither side was willing to compromise. Both believed themselves to be in the right; both had solid grounds for their belief. The result was armed conflict. Yet the age of compromise did not end completely with the Treaty of Versailles, which in 1783 recognized the independence of the United States of America. Pitt's India Act of 1784 was essentially based on a compromise which endeavoured to harmonize the responsibility of His Majesty's government with the commercial interests of the East India Company. In the sphere of domestic politics also, owing to the skill of the younger Pitt and to the need which he and George III had for one another, the age of compromise lingered on. Even so the growing demand for some measure of parliamentary reform, and the slow emergence before the end of the reign of something that was beginning to look like a two-party system, were indicative of a slowly rising tide of criticism of and dissatisfaction with a solution that earlier in the century had served the country well. In the world of economic theory the same wind of change was blowing. In 1776 Adam Smith had published *The Wealth of Nations*. Though its immediate impact was confined to a small circle, and what he had to say has been frequently misinterpreted and over-simplified, it too encouraged men to turn their backs on the practices and theories of the past. The Age of Compromise was almost over; the Age of Improvement was at hand.

I

THE ECONOMIC AND SOCIAL BACKGROUND
OF THE AGE

1. The Countryside and the Agricultural Interest

WHEN George I ascended the British throne in 1714 he became the King of a country which had just reached the status of a first-class power. In spite of the great disparity of populations the economic strength and naval resources of England had played a major part in subduing the France of Louis XIV. If this part had not been quite so large as contemporary Englishmen were inclined to suppose, at least the negotiation of a separate peace between England and France had been sufficient to force the other allies to come to terms. In spite of the frequent cries of 'ruin' raised by the opponents of the war of the Spanish Succession, England had withstood the strain remarkably well. By the beginning of the eighteenth century the foundations of her economic prosperity had already been laid and, though occasional setbacks and years of crisis occurred, never again was her population to be drastically reduced by famine and disease. Indeed, there is no greater proof of her progress during this century than the fact that an increase in national wealth prevented the pressure of a considerable and rapid growth of population[1] from driving down the general standard of living. Compared

[1] It is not yet possible to speak with any certainty about either the rate or the causes of the growth of population in the eighteenth century. It is fairly generally accepted that England and Wales had a population of about 5½ million at the end of the seventeenth century, and ended with one of just over 9 millions. The increase was not, however, a steady one. There may have been an absolute check in the 1720s and 1730s, which were marked by a good deal of smallpox and a series of influenza epidemics, and there was no rapid increase until the latter part of the century. For a fuller discussion see

with the centuries that had gone before, the eighteenth was one of national well being, and it was upon this foundation that the achievements both at home and overseas were based. In every branch of her economy a new awareness of the opportunities to be seized was apparent. Agriculture, under the impetus of the scientific revolution of the seventeenth century, was increasingly influenced by new methods and new ideas. As the population grew and the political importance of land made its possession more and more socially desirable, landowners turned with growing enthusiasm to new methods to recoup themselves for its enhanced price. Though the possession of land was a social asset, and though agriculture can be described as a way of life, it was also a great industry calling for the expenditure of much capital, on which an adequate return was expected. The man who combined some subsistence farming with the practice of a craft might still, of course, find the techniques of his forefathers sufficient. Even at the end of the century Crabbe writes of

> Creatures no more enlivened than a clod,
> But treading still as their dull fathers trod,
> Who lived in times when not a man had seen
> Corn sown by drill, or threshed by a machine.

But a man who required more from his land was under constant pressure to apply to it less inefficient methods. By the beginning of the eighteenth century English agriculture was marked by 'enterprise, experiment, mobility'.[1] In this her agriculturalists could hardly be described as pioneers, for in the Low Countries, where a shortage of land had long made it a commodity too precious to be used wastefully, the rotation of root and grain crops had long been practised. Nevertheless the attention given to the growing of new crops in the seventeenth century was for England something of an innovation. Most, if not all, of these were intended as fodder for animals, and therefore only indirectly for the consumption of man. More clover, more lucerne and sainfoin, above all supplies of

H. J. Habakkuk, 'The English Population in the Eighteenth Century' (*Econ. Hist. Rev.*, 2nd ser., vol. VI, no. 3, 1958), and 'The Economic History of Modern Britain' (*The Journal of Economic History*, vol. XVIII, 1958), Thomas McKeown and R. G. Brown, 'Medical Evidence related to English Population Changes in the Eighteenth Century' (*Population Studies*, vol. LX, 1955–6, pp. 119–41). J. T. Krause, 'Changes in English Fertility and Mortality 1781–1850' (*Econ. Hist. Rev.*, 2nd ser., vol. XI, no. 1, 1958).

[1] T. S. Ashton, *An Economic History of England: The Eighteenth Century* (1955), p. 32.

turnips, meant more winter feed, more fresh meat, less salt food, and less scurvy. Even by the beginning of the century the raising of such crops had passed the stage of the experimental[1] and in many parts of Norfolk a fine field of turnips would have called for no undue comment.[2]

The demand for agricultural products came from many quarters. The most obvious was for food. Increased industrial efficiency meant increased division of labour: though the population as a whole was growing, that proportion of it which produced its own food was declining. Moreover the non-producing element was beginning to possess more purchasing power, which meant an increased demand for wheaten bread, for barley for malting, for butter and cheese, for beef, for mutton, and for poultry. Where this increased demand was concentrated in towns of some size it, in its turn, encouraged specialization in the producing areas. This was particularly true of London. Defoe pointed out how the 'whole kingdom, as well the people, as the land, and even the sea, in every part of it, are employ'd to furnish something, and I may add, the best of everything, to supply the city of London with provisions'.[3] Cheshire, Wiltshire and Suffolk concentrated on dairy farming, in Leicestershire and Lincolnshire graziers bred and fattened cattle, Sussex and Surrey reared geese and capons, Suffolk sent turkeys, East Kent and Worcestershire specialized in orchards and hops. Much of the Midlands grew wheat, other counties, such as Cambridgeshire, Hertfordshire, Berkshire, produced barley, northern counties went in for oats. In the West, Bristol exerted the same kind of influence.[4] Wheat came from the Midlands, barley from West Wales and Gloucestershire, oats from Cardigan and Carmarthen, peas and beans also from Gloucestershire, cider from Devon

[1] A. H. John, 'The Course of Agricultural Change 1660-1760' in *Studies in the Industrial Revolution* (ed. L. S. Pressnell, 1960, p. 130): 'An impressive list can be compiled of the counties in central and southern England in which, by 1700, clovers, the new grasses, and root crops were in use. What is not known is the extent to which these crops had been adopted.'

[2] J. H. Plumb, 'Sir Robert Walpole and Norfolk Husbandry' (*Econ. Hist. Rev.*, 2nd ser., vol. V, no. 1, 1952), and E. Kerridge, 'Turnip Husbandry in High Suffolk' (*Econ. Hist. Rev.*, 2nd ser., vol. VIII, no. 3, 1956).

[3] D. Defoe, *A Tour through England and Wales*, edited G. D. H. Cole (Everyman edn., 1959, vol. I, p. 12).

[4] W. E. Minchinton, 'Bristol Metropolis of the West in the Eighteenth Century' (Alexander Prize Essay, *Trans. R. Hist. Soc.*, 5th ser., vol. 4., pp. 73-74).

and Herefordshire, butter from Pembroke, Glamorgan and Somerset. Wiltshire sent eggs, milk, and poultry; cheese came from Cheshire. Everywhere concentration of demand was leading to concentration of effort. In consequence there was a considerable interregional trade. By the time that George I became King a picture of a restricted and local agriculture would be quite false, though most areas produced enough food to meet local demand, and many small hidebound unprogressive subsistence farmers were to be found.

The second great source of demand was for the raw materials of industry. The most obvious of these came from the clothing manufacture, which, in spite of considerable imports from Spain, was largely dependent on the home clip. Another vitally important contribution provided by the sheep was the tallow made from its fat—the raw material for the candles burnt by the labouring poor. Though wax candles and whale oil illuminated the houses of the better off, the labourers' homes depended largely on the tallow candle and even the dipped rush, and this alone provided a large demand. Nor did illumination exhaust the uses to which the fat of beasts could be put. The soap boilers used it extensively and, though the use of lubricating oils was limited, cogs and wheels that required grease had to be supplied from this source. Sheepskins and hides were required by the tanners, who in turn supplied shoe makers, glovers, breeches makers, for the countryman's breeches, like those of the Austrian peasant to-day, were made of leather.[1] Harness too was a great devourer of leather. From the bones of the animals came glue, while horns could be fashioned into handles by the cutlers. Thus, though the market for meat was important enough for sheep and cattle to be raised in the more remote and barren regions, and taken on the hoof to the richer pastures of the Midlands and East Anglia for fattening before being sold at Smithfield market, there was a substantial market for the remainder of the carcass. A growing population needed clothes and shoes even more than the augmentation of its diet by fresh butchers' meat, and more regular slaughtering meant not only more fresh meat in winter but more regular supplies of its raw material to many important industries. Nor was industry supplied in this way only by the animate products of the farmer. Grain was widely used by many industries in the various

---

[1] H. J. Wilkins, *The Poor Book of Westbury-on-Trym* (1910, p. 282). Here the overseers provided one man with 'a pair of lather breekhes'—a rather pleasant misspelling of leather in the circumstances.

processes of their crafts. Wheat was the raw material of the starch makers. The making of beer and the distilling of gin were widespread and both depended on the barley producing counties.[1]

Markets of this size could only be supplied regularly by adequate investment and well-organized effort. Neither was likely to be provided by the small open-field farmers. In consequence throughout the century the pressure was for larger farms and for the extinction of common rights. At its. beginning perhaps half the arable land was still held in the commingled strips of the open fields, but everywhere progressive landowners were enclosing where they could. As yet enclosure by Act of Parliament was unusual, but where a parish was in a few hands, so that few heads had to be convinced of its utility, or where the owner of a large and compact estate was able to convert copyhold into leasehold, and buy out any enclaves of small freeholders, the tendency was to enclose. Once enclosed it could be let out in substantial farms, well equipped with buildings, for seven, fourteen, or twenty-one years. From an arable farm of from 200 to 300 acres a tenant farmer with a lease of some such period could hope to make a comfortable living. The landowner too benefited by the more regular payments of his rents, the removal of the uncertainty as to when he would again get the possession of his farms, and the cutting of his overheads. That the agricultural section of the community should prosper in this way was of great importance to the government, and what it could do to foster the Landed Interest by way of legislation it did. The import of wheat was burdened with heavy tariffs while, when the domestic price fell below a certain statutory level, a bounty was paid on its export. Whatever the effects of such legislation, and economists have been divided on this issue, its intention was clear.[2] This was not, however, as has sometimes been supposed, merely the effort of a selfish legislature composed of landowners to protect their own interests. In time of war the Land Tax was the chief means of raising supply, while many of the other products of agriculture provided taxable commodities. A malt tax was a favourite device and even cider did not escape. English overseas expansion and her position as a great

[1] P. Mathias, *The Brewing Industry in England 1700–1830* (1959), p. 387, points out that 'Wheat, the queen of cereals, has exercised a far wider dominion over the text books of farming than she has ever enjoyed in the fields', and emphasizes the importance of drink corn in the eighteenth century.

[2] For a discussion on this point see E. Lipson, *The Economic History of England* (vol. II, 1931, pp. 455–9) and T. S. Ashton, *op. cit.*, p. 49.

power were closely linked with her agriculture, and the student who would understand the politics of eighteenth-century England can never afford to disregard its fortunes.

2. THE COMMERCIAL INTEREST

A knowledge of her trade is equally essential.[1] After the uphill struggles of the sixteenth century, and the varied fortunes of the seventeenth, by the close of the War of the Spanish Succession England had become one of the great trading and colonial powers of the West. Agricultural wealth alone could never have supported the great strain of the late wars, and contemporaries were well aware that the prosperity of the country was bound up with the prosperity of her trade. To her politicians this was no airy generalization but a matter of great financial importance. Administrations needed both steady revenue and temporary financial accommodation until taxes came in. Both these the merchant community, either directly or indirectly, supplied. Apart from the Land Tax and some excise duties the main sources of revenue were the import and export duties, levied on both raw materials and finished goods. When loans had to be raised it was again the merchants and their near fellows, the financiers and bankers of the City, who had the liquid capital to take them up. In time of war, too, merchants with their overseas connections could remit money abroad to pay for armies and subsidize allies. For all these reasons trading interests had to be fostered jealously: this in turn affected foreign policy vitally. Mercantilist thought dominated most people's attitude towards trade, and it was generally assumed that if one party gained as the result of a transaction it was at the expense of the other. As most of the economic advisers, if one can use so modern a term, of the European statesmen argued in this way, commercial concessions became a matter for diplomatic bargaining. It was necessary to be on good terms with those countries which provided valuable markets or which, like the Northern powers, controlled some commodity vital to English interests. Often commercial concessions could only be obtained in return for political support. Spain in the uneasy period after the Peace of Utrecht used this bait in an effort to get British help against the Emperor. In the middle of the century it was colonial rather than European issues which finally

[1] For a general survey of English trade and its antecedents in this period see G. D. Ramsey, *English Overseas Trade during the Centuries of Emergence* (1957).

caused the outbreak of war between England and France, just as earlier the problem of the free navigation of the Caribbean had produced the war of 'Jenkins' Ear'. A knowledge of England's commercial interests is therefore necessary for an understanding of much of her diplomacy.[1] It was an issue which seemed relatively unimportant to the first two Hanoverian Kings but of great moment to certain sections of the House of Commons, and ministers were frequently forced to steer an uneasy course between the interests of a King who thought in terms of a continental ruler, and those members of the House of Commons who had constituted themselves the champions of British trade.

This trade was composed of three interlocking parts, European, Eastern and Colonial. The European was the oldest and it has been calculated that at the opening of the century about 53 per cent. of the imports of England and Wales, and as much as 78 per cent. of her exports were due to this trade.[2] Much of it was concentrated in a few great continental ports.[3] From the sixteenth century Antwerp had been the pivot of English overseas transactions. From it came both the luxuries of the East and the commodities of Germany and Italy, and to it went cloth. With the commercial decline of Antwerp, Amsterdam and Rotterdam had become increasingly important as emporiums. Once the struggle with the Hanse had been victoriously settled in the early seventeenth century, Hamburg in turn had attracted English merchants; throughout the eighteenth century it continued to act as the base for her German trade. A good deal of business was also done through Lisbon and Oporto: Portugal had been an ally in the War of the Spanish Succession, and the Methuen Treaty of 1703, which facilitated the export of English cloth there in return for an import duty on Portuguese wines one-third lower than those levied on their French rivals, had fostered commercial relations between the two countries. Not all the European trade was centred on these few great ports. Partly due to the policy of the Navigation Acts vital supplies of timber and naval stores came directly from the Baltic. French trade, though limited

---

[1] *The New Cambridge Modern History* (vol. VII, edited J. O. Lindsay, ch. 2) 'The Growth of Overseas Commerce and European Manufactures' provides a useful, brief survey of some of these developments.

[2] T. S. Ashton, *op. cit.*, p. 154.

[3] Charles Wilson, *Anglo-Dutch Commerce and Finance in the Eighteenth Century* (1949), says: 'Exports to Holland were, for the larger part of the eighteenth century, the biggest item on the British export account.'

by national rivalry and made less officially necessary by that great eighteenth-century industry, smuggling,[1] was to some extent a direct, cross-Channel one, though considerable quantities of French goods came via the ports of the Low Countries.

The Eastern trade was very largely the concern of the East India Company. Founded in 1601, and torn by dissensions and rivalries and the threat to its charter at the close of the century, by 1709 it had emerged as the United East India Company. It was to play an extremely important part in the commercial, financial and political history of the next hundred years. As yet it was purely a trading company with factories, as its local headquarters were called, in India—at Calcutta, Madras and Bombay. With its internal affairs, and with its relations with the Indian rulers, within whose territories it operated, the State had no concern. Organized as a joint stock company, shares to the value of £500 entitled the owner to a vote in the Court of Proprietors. No shareholder was entitled to more than one vote, however large the holding. These facts were to be of considerable importance in the second half of the century, when the affairs of the East India Company became entangled in the political struggles of the day, but in 1714 they were of concern only to the shareholders. The day-to-day business of the Company and the management of its finances belonged to the Court of Directors, elected by the Court of Proprietors, and to some extent dependent on the confirmation by them of its major decisions and appointments. These men were drawn from the wealthy merchants and financiers of the City; the aggregate of their fortunes was very considerable. India and China both lay within the monopoly of the Company. Richard Savage boasted of

> Ships, with gilded palaces that vie,
> In glittering pomp, strike wondering *China's* Eye;
> And then returning bear, in splendid State,
> To Britain's Merchants India's eastern Freight.
> India, her treasures from her western Shores,
> Due at thy Feet, a willing Tribute pours.

From them they imported pepper and spices, indigo and saltpetre, but especially silk and printed cottons and, from China, tea.

---

[1] 'A very conservative estimate in 1733 put the share of smugglers in English commerce with France and Holland as equal to a third of the legitimate trade.' G. D. Ramsey, 'The Smugglers' Trade' (*Trans. R. Hist. Soc.*, 5th ser., vol. II, 1951, p. 135).

Though mercantilist theory demanded that imports be paid for by exports, the East India Company was never able to do this directly. The climate was against the widespread use of English cloth and though the Company did export a certain amount of copper, lead, tin, iron and steel, most of its imports had to be paid for with silver. As British currency was still bimetallic, and silver therefore legal tender, this was considered to be a drain on her monetary resources. It was to rebut this charge that the Company's apologists developed the theory that by re-exporting Indian and Chinese goods to European markets it created a favourable balance of trade, that measuring rod of eighteenth-century national prosperity. The writers of the eighteenth century, like our own, were apt to believe that if an assertion were repeated often enough, and firmly enough, it would come to rank as a self-evident truth. Not all the goods which the Company exported from India, however, came to Europe. Raw cotton, opium, pepper, sandalwood, ivory were all acceptable merchandise in Canton and could be exchanged there for the precious cargoes of teas.

During the eighteenth century England became a great tea-drinking country. By 1765 ninety families out of every hundred were estimated to drink it twice a day.[1] This minor social revolution in the habits of the masses caused considerable disquiet among their betters, characteristic of which was Jonas Hanway's 'An Essay on Tea considered as Pernicious to Health, obstructing Industry, and impoverishing the Nation'. In the course of his tirade he declared that 'the vast consumption and *injurious effects of tea*, seemed to threaten the lives of the common people equally with *gin*',[2] and that '*suicide* would not be so frequent, nor held in so little detestation, if a better diet than *tea* were in fashion'.[3] For its enormous popularity the smugglers were largely responsible. In the shops the average price of the ordinary leaf was five shillings a pound in 1733, and as in that year the legal duties alone amounted to four and nine pence, it is clear that most of it had by-passed the revenue authorities.[4] Against this evasion the revenue men waged an unremitting but largely unsuccessful battle. Landed illegally from the East Indiamen or smuggled from the Continent, the tea, contained in small waterproof bags, was carried by night to London and there

---

[1] Neville Williams, *Contraband Cargoes* (1959), p. 97.
[2] Jonas Hanway, *An Essay on Tea* (1777), p. 88. [3] *Ibid.*, p. 77.
[4] N. Williams, *op. cit.*, pp. 94–96.

hidden in cellars, in stables, even in the Fleet prison itself. It has been estimated that for every pound of tea seized three hundred-weight escaped.

The third great area of trade was that provided by the British colonies and Ireland. The latter had indeed a somewhat unenviable position of her own. According to the accepted Laws of Trade she was neither the equal of England, Wales and Scotland, nor was she quite a colony. Had she been allowed to develop her economic resources fully it was thought that she might be a serious rival to English interests. In consequence she was not allowed to export her raw wool to any of the latter's trading rivals. Nor was she allowed to export her cloth except to England, where it was burdened with heavy duties, and had to meet English competition. In compensation she was permitted to develop her linen industry, which strengthened the Protestant population of Ulster as against the Roman Catholic South. Denied most industrial outlets, Ireland had been forced to turn her energies to the production of butter and cheese, cattle and meat, which, as these were her only means of paying for the manufactured goods that she required, meant that the Irish peasant was forced back on to a diet of potatoes. Irish provisions went both to England and to the colonies, and were important in the victualling of the ships that called at the south Irish ports, before undertaking the long Atlantic crossing. The position of the majority of the colonies was rather different, as most of them could be fitted into the British economy without any obvious major threat to purely English interests. This was because, with the exception of the New England colonies, they needed large supplies of manufactured goods, and produced such crops as sugar and tobacco and rice, which provided English merchants with some of their major exports. The trading posts of the Royal African Company dovetailed smoothly into this pattern, for from them came the slave labour necessary to work the plantations.

3. ENGLAND AND HER COLONIES

The apparent harmony which existed between the three great branches of British trade, that with Europe, with the Far East and with her colonies, was not due to the free play of economic forces. Trade was far too vital a national interest to be left to the unknown; by the eighteenth century a complex mass of legislation, embodied in the Navigation Acts,[1] and sometimes alluded to as the Laws of Trade, had been evolved. The Navigation Acts of the seventeenth century had originally been sponsored as a means of protecting English shipping against foreign, at that time largely Dutch, competition. For this purpose certain branches of trade had been assigned to English, Welsh and colonial ships built and manned within these areas. These acts also contained other clauses, which prevented colonists from sending certain important commodities to any countries outside the Empire, and which made it necessary for them to purchase the manufactured goods which they required via England. By the beginning of the century the situation was roughly as follows. European goods, except for certain enumerated commodities, such as timber and naval stores from the Baltic, or the goods imported by the Levant Company, could be brought freely to this country by any ships. Enumerated goods had to come either in English, Welsh, Scottish or colonial ships, or in the ships of the country producing the goods. Before the Act of Union, Scotland as well as Ireland had been excluded and freedom to trade had been one of the baits that had induced her to assent to that measure. If, however, goods did come to this country in foreign bottoms they paid additional, alien, duties. The trade with the Far East was the monopoly of the East India Company, and need not therefore be considered in this connection. Colonial trade was barred to foreign countries. All imports and exports to and from the colonies had to come in British or colonial ships. By the terms of the Staple Act of 1663, manufactured goods imported into the colonies had to come via England.[2] This did not make it impossible for them to get such goods but it certainly made them more expensive, and, by making England an entrepôt for the trade, placed it largely in the hands of British, and in practice English, merchants. Important crops like sugar from the West Indies, tobacco from the southern colonies, rice from South Carolina and Georgia, were all on the list of enumerated commodities which could only be sent to Britain.

Such restrictions may sound harsh to the modern reader in an age when 'colonialism' has become 'a dirty word' but they were the common practice of eighteenth-century colonial powers. It was

[1] See L. A. Harper, *The English Navigational Laws: A Seventeenth Century Experiment in Social Engineering* (1939).

[2] *English Historical Documents*, vol. IX, *American Colonial Documents to 1776*, edited Merrill Jensen, (1955), p. 356.

argued that the parent country had spent resources in establishing the colonies and was still responsible for defence and administration. It would be wrong to dismiss the system as one of sheer exploitation. Colonial produce coming to England received preferential treatment in the shape of lower duties, and when re-exported could claim a draw-back. Colonial ships and colonial merchants received the same protection from the Navigation Acts as their British fellows. Indeed the shipbuilding of New England was a serious rival to that of the mother country. In the same way New England merchants, driven by the need to earn enough currency to settle their debts with England, were often to be found in competition with her merchants. That colonies should provide a market for British manufactures and supply the raw materials that she required did not seem to either party an unequal arrangement in such circumstances. In other ways too the predominance of the mother country was accepted without question: British rights were in no sense limited to legislating for the empire as a whole on matters of trade and navigation. As Englishmen the early colonists had taken with them certain political rights. Each colony had an elected Assembly which granted taxes and assumed pretty much the same functions as the British House of Commons. But the Governor and certain other officials were appointed by the Crown which, though for all practical purposes it had lost the use of the veto at home, could still disallow laws passed by the colonial assemblies, when these seemed to conflict with British law, or to be against the common interest. Much of the responsibility for advising the Crown as to how these powers should be used lay with the Commissioners of the Board of Trade. Such a wide trading area, which offered the geographical advantages of a foreign country, but which was an integral part of the British economy was naturally most attractive to merchants: throughout the century, until the breakaway of the American colonies, the tendency was for the proportion of British trade that was done with the colonies to grow steadily.

4. THE ORGANIZATION OF TRADE

This extensive trade was largely in the hands of individuals or of small partnerships, often composed of members of the same family or their connections by marriage. After the Revolution of 1688 the unpopularity of monopoly had cost many of the older trading companies their exclusive privileges, and, with the exception of the

Far East and the Levant, merchants could trade where they would. In the early decades of the century four-fifths of this trade was still centred on London, thus contributing much to the wealth of the City. Already, however, there were signs that London's almost exclusive control of trade had reached its peak. Between 1710 and 1721 Liverpool was equipping itself with new dock facilities, an indication of the increasing cargoes of cotton that were coming to that port. The expanding colonial trade was bringing increased business also to Bristol, well situated for sending out its slaving vessels to the West African coast, and bringing back cargoes of sugar from the West Indies with the money earned by their sale. The increasing volume of trade brought with it an increasing differentiation of function between those men who continued to call themselves merchants. Many began to busy themselves not with actual trading but with the services which the merchants needed. Overseas trading was still a dangerous and hazardous business. In time of war losses to the enemy were heavy, and throughout the century there was much war at sea. In times of peace storms could still do extensive damage. Ships might be utterly lost or have their cargoes ruined by sea water. A great trading nation needed underwriters and marine insurers to bear the financial burdens of such disasters.[1] As the number of ships leaving London and the outports grew, middlemen to arrange cargo space, or to put owners in touch with underwriters and marine insurers, were essential for the smooth working of the system; from this need grew groups of specialized brokers. Nor did the direct employment given by trade end here. A horde of humbler men were needed to pack goods and load ships, while each business house needed its clerks and invoicers. Among so many enterprises serving so many markets there were inevitably sufficient problems and difficulties for astute opposition politicians to raise the cry 'Our trade in danger' and to gain a following.

Because the importance of overseas trade was so clearly recognized it is easy to underrate that which was carried on internally. Yet this also provided a livelihood for a multitude of people who contributed greatly to the smooth working of the economy. Middlemen were to be found in every branch of trade. The corn merchant

[1] A. H. John, 'The London Assurance Company and the Marine Insurance Market of the Eighteenth Century' (*Economica,* vol. XXV, new ser., May 1958, p. 126), points out that 'the growth of marine insurance facilities represents one of the major developments in the history of English commerce during the eighteenth century'.

bought the grain when the harvest was in and resold it to the miller, or stored it until the lean months just before the new crop was ready, thereby making a profit for himself and evening out supplies and therefore prices. The drover bought cattle in the poorer grazing areas, brought them to London, or to other big towns, on the hoof, then sold them to the fattening grazier, if the drover did not also undertake this function. Then as fat cattle they were sold to the wholesale butcher, who in turn sold the carcass to the retailer, the hides to the tanner or to a dealer in hides, the bones to the glue maker. In the same way dealers had contacts for buying cheese and butter from the dairying counties. Nor were the functions of the middleman confined to the handling of food. Wholesalers bought cloth locally from markets or fairs, or through their agents, and resold it either for export or to the drapers in the towns. Iron-mongers did the same service for the craftsmen who worked in that metal. The list could be greatly extended. By the eighteenth century shopkeeping was increasingly supplementing, where it was not supplanting, the older fairs and markets. Often a man combined the function of both wholesaling and retailing. Where, however, he was completely a retailer the wholesaler was his main source of supply, except for commodities which he could obtain at first hand locally. In these ways a chain of middlemen served the domestic market as well as providing a link between English manufacturers and the merchants who sold their wares overseas.

5. INDUSTRY

By the beginning of the eighteenth century Britain's industry too was far from negligible. It was able to supply most of the home demand for consumer goods, as well as providing a substantial contribution to the export trade. From medieval times, though her largest export had been wool, some of her cloth had gone abroad and by the sixteenth century this had become her major export. Since then the character of the cloths she made had changed con-siderably to meet the changing demand of her overseas markets, but the woollen manufacture still absorbed her major industrial ener-gies.[1] Though it would be difficult to find any part of the country

[1] After stressing the unreliable nature of contemporary estimates and the available statistics, Phyllis Deane in 'The Output of the British Woollen Industry in the Eight-eenth Century' (*Journal of Economic History*, vol. XVII, 1957, p. 212) writes: 'We have some precise evidence for a fairly marked increase in the real output of the woollen

where some cloth was not woven, much of it was for local consumption. But those districts which served foreign markets, and the more exacting sections of the home demand, had already become specialist areas. The finest cloths came from the West, which had been the old centre of the broadcloth manufacture, and from East Anglia. The coarser ones came from the North, particularly from Yorkshire. Even by the beginning of the century the growing cotton manufacture of Lancashire was causing some uneasiness to the older woollen industry.[1] The growing vogue for the gaily printed cottons which the East India Company imported had shown how dangerous this new manufacture might be. Because the clothiers were able to gain the ear of Parliament as representing the major export industry, they had been able to get in 1701 a law prohibiting the wearing of East Indian prints in England. If, however, the Lancashire men could produce the calicoes, and if calico printing, which was already just beginning to develop in the London area where unprinted Indian cottons were easily available, should establish itself firmly in the North, then the older industry might find itself faced by an extremely vigorous competitor.

No other industries provided anything like the same volume of goods for export. Small quantities of specialized manufactures went abroad, but apart from the textiles the demand was for primary products, copper from Cornwall and coal from the Northumberland and Durham coalfields. Even this, at the beginning of the century, was not large. Apart therefore from textiles, most English production was for the home market. Except for cotton, which had to be imported, the raw materials were indigenous. English industry can therefore be divided into two sections: that providing the raw materials, the coal, the copper, the lead, the stone, the iron; and that engaged in working up either these, or imported raw materials, into consumer goods for domestic consumption. The provision of the raw materials often called for considerable capital and was, for obvious geographical reasons, localized. Copper was mined in Cornwall and to some extent in the North. Lead mining was important in Cumberland. In Northumberland and Durham, in the

industry in the first four or five decades of the eighteenth century, although a fall in the value of wool and probably (though to a less extent) of average earnings and prices of the final product meant that there was only a small increase in money terms.'

[1] A. P. Wadsworth and J. de Lacy Mann, *The Cotton Trade and Industrial Lancashire 1600–1780* (1931).

Midlands and in South Wales, coal mining was already well developed;[1] by 1700, the annual output of the United Kingdom may have been in the region of two and a half million tons. Iron was worked where supplies of ore were to be found in areas which could supply the necessary charcoal. Though Abraham Darby seems to have discovered the method by which some types of cast iron could be made by coking coal as early as 1709,[2] this had little practical bearing on the location of the iron industry in the early decades of the century. Quarrying too was important. Increasing trade called for better roads, and a rising standard of living, together with new concentrations of population, called for more houses. It is understandable therefore that apart from the activities of the agriculturalists many Englishmen should have been engaged in producing primary products.

A rising standard of living, a growing population and an expanding demand from the colonies provided a market for a wide variety of consumer goods. These too tended to be localized. Some grew up round ports which imported raw materials from abroad, or where great markets like Smithfield in London attracted some commodity whose by-product they used. It was natural that tanners and glue makers should congregate round Smithfield, and that distillers and starch makers and brewers should be established within easy reach of the great grain markets of London. When as in the London area there were the facilities of a great port, the necessary supplies of water to drive mills, or scour and steep hides, and the concentration of demand, it was inevitable that almost every variety of craft and industry should come together.[3] The process was that of a snowball. Industries started because the raw material and the facilities for working it were available. Next came the men who made the tools for the industry, then came those who supplied their daily needs, 'the butcher, the baker, the candle-stick maker'. As wealth grew so the demand for luxury goods grew, for elaborate coaches, for elegant clothes, for jewels, for wigs—the list could be extended indefinitely. Other ports too, though in a lesser way, attracted secondary industries. So did towns in areas where specialized industries already

---

[1] T. S. Ashton and J. Sykes, *The Coal Industry of the Eighteenth Century* (1929), p. 13.

[2] Fragments of his accounts show that he was selling small quantities of pots and kettles as early as 1707-9—A. Raistrick, *A Dynasty of Iron Founders* (1953), p. 7.

[3] *Vide* M. D. George, *London Life in the Eighteenth Century* (1925), ch. 4, 'The People and Trades of London'.

existed. Manchester grew with the cotton manufacture, Leeds and other Yorkshire towns as cloth-making expanded, Birmingham with the metal industries. At the beginning of the century all these places were small compared with their size at the end; nevertheless even when George I became King a noticeable start had been made.

Other industries were still more localized in relation to the markets they served, and belonged to the traditional economic framework of the past. Villages were not solely agricultural communities in the sense that most of their inhabitants worked on the land. They too had their local craftsmen, catering for local needs. Wheelwrights, blacksmiths, and farriers were needed for the business of farming. Thatchers were in constant demand. Often there were small rural industries employing a handful of workers and supplying the wants of a few neighbouring parishes. Most villages had their ale house or beer shop, even if they did not rise to the dignity of a village inn. Where the necessary water power was available, especially where grain crops predominated, there was often a miller to whom the open-field farmer could take his wheat. Goods that could not be supplied by the village were provided by the nearest small town. Many of these had a weekly market, to which the country folk brought their surplus products, buying with the proceeds such necessities as shoes and clothing, and such minor luxuries as they could afford. In consequence most towns had enough craftsmen to provide for the normal needs of the area that they served. Such towns created additional needs of their own. The shoemaker had to buy his bread, the miller his beer. Often too there was a small nucleus of better off families. In the clothing counties the clothier, the pivot of the organization, was often a town dweller. Merchants mainly engaged in local trade had their headquarters in the town. The vicar or rector might be a man of some substance. Lawyers often found profitable business both among the neighbouring gentry and among the urban businessmen. Sometimes there was a doctor, more often an apothecary. In addition certain country towns were socially important. Difficulties of transport, and to some extent limitations of income, made visits to London impracticable: some convenient town had to provide a social gathering point for the county. Though luxuries might be sent for from London, the mantua-makers and milliners of Norwich had to supply much of the necessary finery of the ladies of Norfolk. In an age when the horse played so large a part in transport, coaches, carriages and harness were in constant demand and in most cases locally made. From even so brief a survey it is clear that with the exception of textiles the English economy was still in the stage of either producing primary products, or of serving a number of limited and linked local markets with the commodities of everyday life. To think too exclusively in terms of the export trade, or even of a metropolitan market, is to ignore the activities in which most English craftsmen were engaged at the beginning of the eighteenth century. To them local demand was still the major factor.

The methods by which industry was organized varied according to both the character of its technical processes and the nature of the market it served. The larger and the more distant the market the more elaborate the organization required. A clothier or linen draper who concentrated on the export trade needed a considerable amount of capital to purchase the raw material, to pay his workers, and to wait for a return on his money. It was not uncommon for these men to have several hundred people in their employ as spinners, weavers, finishers, dyers, packers. But because the machinery for cloth-making was simple and traditional—spinning wheels and looms substantial, long lasting and not difficult to acquire—and because they were as yet operated completely by hand, there was no need to concentrate the workers in their employer's buildings. As a result one man might give employment to families whose homes were scattered over a wide area. Though this method reduced the investment in building and equipment, it was wasteful of time and manpower. Intermediaries were necessary to give out the wool or the cotton, and to take back the yarn or the cloth, but these could only operate from certain focal points and many weavers had to walk considerable distances or lose many working hours, for which they received nothing. It was difficult, too, to check the purloining of the raw material and eliminate faulty workmanship. This so-called Domestic or Putting Out system was not confined to the export industries. In the Black Country the nailers, whose wares were much in demand, were organized in the same way. Each family had its small workshop but depended on the wages paid by some large-scale manufacturer. Such a system was almost infinitely flexible. In some areas the weaver or the nail maker was an independent craftsman, buying his material on credit and selling the finished product to a merchant. So long as he remained out of debt he was free to buy and sell where he pleased, and might, if he were hard-working and thrifty, in time have other people working for him. Some families combined industry with a little subsistence agriculture, some worked partly independently and partly for an employer. It is probable that in industries organized on the Putting Out system where the demand, whether national or international, was extensive, the wage earner predominated, but even in these industries there were plenty of independent craftsmen to be found.

The small independent master was, however, better suited to serve the limited and conservative needs of the smaller towns and villages. Sometimes he worked alone, sometimes with two or three apprentices or helpers. He was known personally to his customers and had a secure place in the community in which he lived. Much of his time was employed on special orders made to individual requirements. Often his level of attainment was high in the sense that he produced solid, durable, well made goods. Had he not done so in a small community where news travelled fast his earnings would have dwindled rapidly. Scattered up and down the country today are many pleasant pieces of furniture made locally for the neighbouring gentry by the cabinet makers of Queen Anne. It was men of this type who provided the things needed for everyday living, and their combined contribution to the nation's productive capacity must have been considerable. It was, however, limited to those goods which could be made by hand in a confined space. Even in the early eighteenth century there was a long list of articles which, by their very nature, could not be made in these conditions. For these a different organization was required.

Commodities of this kind can be divided into two groups. One is composed of primary products—the output of the extractive industries. It is obvious that coal mining, on however small a scale, cannot be carried on in the back yard. Neither can the production of iron, the mining and smelting of tin or copper, the refining of salt, the digging of clay. All these and kindred industries involve employment away from home. The second group comprises those commodities which need some kind of power, or team work, or space for their production. The refining of sugar, the making of bricks, or of glass, the manufacture of ropes and sails, the processing of copper or brass into rods or sheets, the finishing of cloth, are all examples of this second group. Here, therefore, though the capital involved and the number of workers employed in each business might be small, there is an essential difference from the Putting Out system. Fixed capital has to be invested in mines and equipment, or in plant and buildings. Management and supervision have to be provided on the spot. Workers normally become hands. This was not, however, universally the case, especially in mining, where groups of miners often worked together on a contract basis, thus retaining a semi-independence. It was in enterprises of this kind that the largest aggregates of capital were to be found. This was particularly true of coal mining, especially that which centred on the Tyne and the Wear, and of the production of copper and brass. In 1689 the two companies of Mines Royal and Mineral And Battery lost their monopoly and rapid investment in mining concerns followed. By 1714 the Cheadle company was displaying all the characteristics of a modern integrated concern. It dug the ore, refined it, and had rolling mills and wire works for processing it. Another important group was the Quaker Lead Company.[1]

6. Transport

Thus, though agriculture was the greatest single employer of capital and manpower, England's industrial activities were important and substantial. To her traditional export of woollen goods she was adding, though as yet on a small scale, that of cotton. She made the major proportion of the goods consumed by her own people. Her industry, by eighteenth-century standards, was reasonably efficient. Already areas were specializing in those commodities which they produced best, and in enterprises where considerable capital had been invested there was often an awareness of the value of specialization of function within the plant. Nevertheless, much of her industry remained small-scale and local. For this the inadequacy of transport was largely responsible. The sea was still the highway of commerce and for that reason many industries had grown up round the ports.[2] It was comparatively easy to refine sugar in the neighbourhood of Bristol or London and then re-export it to continental markets. Cornish ore could be shipped to South Wales and refined in furnaces heated with coal that had come down the Severn.

[1] A. Raistrick, *Quakers in Science and Industry* (1950), pp. 171 seq.

[2] 'Industry was dependent upon the coasting trade for at least a proportion of such raw materials as wool, alum, dyes, leather, timber, iron, lead, tin, copper, clay and coal as well as for the carriage of part of its manufactured goods either for consumption within the country or for export.'—T. S. Willan, *The English Coasting Trade 1600–1750* (1938), p. 190.

Coal could be brought by sea from Newcastle for industries established near east coast ports. It was easier to sail round Wales than to send goods between Shropshire and Whitehaven over land. For this reason many a now deserted wharf and silted up small harbour was once a scene of busy trade. Nevertheless, even areas that could be linked and supplied in this way faced certain difficulties. Small ports meant small ships with the double disadvantage of limited cargoes and little capacity to face winter storms. Fragile cargoes could be tossed and broken, or spoilt by sea water. Mariners could be pressed for the Royal Navy. In time of war enemy privateers were a constant danger. Even so, a port was a better location for industrial development than an inland town unless the latter had some very special advantage.

Nearness to a navigable river could confer the same advantages as a favourable position on the coast, but in the early eighteenth century few rivers were satisfactory from this point of view. Too many people made too diverse demands on them. Milling was an important and widespread industry, and millers built dams across the stream. Locks were as yet non-existent and it was only by the favour of the miller that a flash of water could be got to carry the vessel over the obstructing weir. Already, however, a movement had been started for improving the inland waterways. By the end of the previous century this had hardly got beyond the stage of paper planning and persuasion, but in the brief period between the wars of William III these plans began to take more concrete shape. Then came the long struggle over the Spanish Succession, and it was not until 1717 that groups of investors, often local men, were prepared to subscribe money and form a company for the improvement of those rivers whose waters were needed as an outlet for some growing industry. In 1721 a project to make the Irwell and Mersey navigable illustrates the growing need of Lancashire for better links with the sea. A similar scheme was being applied to roads. These had long been quite inadequate for the traffic they were being increasingly called upon to carry. Contemporary road maps are misleading. The country was well provided with tracks of a kind that linked town with town, but in many cases the drainage was non-existent and the surface lamentable. In wet weather many of those that crossed the clay belt were impassable for wheeled traffic. In theory, as embodied in the Highway Act of 1555, parishes were responsible for the upkeep of the roads that ran through them;

but the obligation of parishioners was limited to a few days' forced labour in the year and, lacking both technical knowledge and enthusiasm, the contribution that most of them made was altogether insufficient.

It was to remedy this situation that the device of the Turnpike Trust was first employed. The idea was the basically simple one of forcing the users of the road to pay for its upkeep by levying tolls. This right seems first to have been conferred on the justices of Hertford, Cambridge, and Huntingdon, through whose counties ran the Great North Road. In this case it was an attempt to improve a much used road without placing an undue burden on the parishes through which it went. Little advantage was taken of this precedent until the problem of traffic on roads like that running between London and Holyhead emphasized the need for tapping new financial resources. The result was the Turnpike Trust. Here the initiative came largely from local enterprise. Landowners wanted to get their agricultural produce to market. Farms let for higher rents if transport facilities were improved. Sometimes, too, some industry needed a better road to reach the nearest river. The solution was to form a group of local notables into a board of trustees, empowered to borrow money with which to improve and keep up a certain stretch of road, to erect toll houses and levy tolls on all vehicles and animals passing along it. By 1706-7 the first of these trusts had been set up and its success ensured a rapid creation of new trusts. Bad, therefore, though the roads were in 1714 there was some reasonable hope of improvement.

Until this could be achieved, English industry could make no spectacular progress. Cloth, which, both in its raw state as wool and in its final form, could be moved by packhorse, presented no great problem. Neither did the growing cotton industry. Heavy goods or fragile goods were a different proposition. And even for goods that were neither fragile nor heavy the expense of carriage was a considerable item. It was cheaper to manufacture locally what was to be consumed locally. In such conditions only a few commodities were likely to sell outside their own immediate area, and the average unit of production was necessarily small, though even in the early years of the century such institutions as the Royal Arsenal at Chatham showed that large-scale production was not beyond the capabilities of the age when the demand was there. A further result of the scattered nature of industry was that the political influence of the manufacturers was less than their contribution to the national economy would have justified. Petitions in plenty on economic matters were presented to the Commons, but these plead the case or state the grievances of individual towns or of the clothiers of the West, or of a group of Yorkshire towns, never those of an industry as a whole, though in certain cases the aggregate of such petitions had almost that effect. Yet, in spite of factors which seemed to be limiting industrial expansion and holding it back, it was rapidly accumulating capital, skill and experience. The previous century had been one of technological progress which had encouraged men to experiment, and already these experiments were contributing to increased industrial efficiency. Though as yet the basic crafts of spinning and weaving were untouched, the first tentative steps towards the smelting of iron with coal had been taken. If demand continued to rise, and if the bottleneck of transport could be broken, the prospects were good for further industrialization along the path of increased investment, growing specialization—both between areas and within industries —and further technical developments. By the beginning of the eighteenth century there was nothing inherently improbable in the transformation, known as the Industrial Revolution, which was starting to take effect by its close.

7. The Aristocracy and Gentry

The society which this economic structure supported was both simple and complex: simple in that it was a class society composed of four main layers: complex in the composition of these layers and in the relations between them.[1] In spite of the number of people who got their living from manufacture or trade, fundamentally it was a society in which the ownership of land alone conveyed social prestige and full political rights. Whatever the source of his wealth, as soon as he could a man bought land. Landowners alone might sit in the House of Commons. In the counties the parliamentary franchise was confined to the forty shilling freeholders. The Justices of the Peace, except in the corporate towns, were chosen from the ranks of the landowners. The apex of this society was the nobility. In the eyes of the Law only members of the House of Lords, the peerage in the strictest use of the word, were a class apart, enjoying

[1] For a fuller account of eighteenth-century social structure see my *English People in the Eighteenth Century* (1956).

special privileges and composing one of the estates of the realm. Their families were commoners: even the eldest sons of peers could sit in the House of Commons. It was therefore in the social rather than in the legal sense of the word that English society was a class society. Before the law all English people except the peers were in theory equal. Legal concept and social practice were, however, very different. When men spoke of the nobility they meant the sons and daughters, the brothers and sisters, the uncles and aunts and cousins of the peers. They were an extremely influential and wealthy group. The peers and their near relations almost monopolized high political office. From these great families came the wealthiest Church dignitaries, the higher ranks in the army and navy. Many of them found a career in law; some even did not disdain the money to be made in trade. What gave this class its particular importance in the political life of the day was the way in which it was organized on a basis of family and connection. At the head of each great group was the peer himself, usually the owner of large estates, sometimes concentrated in one area but often widely scattered. An important peer might own land, and therefore possess parliamentary influence, in half a dozen different counties. Though, because of primogeniture, these estates went to the eldest son, they were often burdened with settlements for mothers or daughters or aunts. There was in addition an accepted obligation to further the fortunes both of younger sons and brothers, and of other kinsmen, who in return owed their political loyalty to the head of the family. These groups were further linked together by marriage. In consequence, in eighteenth-century politics men rarely acted as isolated individuals. A man came into Parliament supported by his friends and relations who expected, in return for this support, that he would further their interests to the extent of his parliamentary influence.

Next in both political and social importance came the gentry. Again it is not easy to define exactly who were covered by this term. The Law knew nothing of gentle birth but Society recognized it. Like the nobility this group too was as a class closely connected with land. Indeed, the border line between the two classes is at times almost impossible to define. A family though originally descended from some noble house must with the lapse of time come to be numbered with the gentry. In discussing the internal relations within this class it is convenient, as in the case of the nobility, to make some distinction between the heads of families and their cadet members. The former were landowners, often Justices of the Peace, sometimes Members of Parliament for the county, or for some pocket borough. They represent that segment of society usually described as the 'Country Gentlemen'. Their relations, on the other hand, had to make their own way in the world. Though connected with the land they owned little or none. These men also, in competition with the cadets of more aristocratic houses, hunted for preferment in the Church or filled family livings. They secured commissions in the army or navy. They were called to the bar. Some of them became members of the College of Physicians, which was open only to graduates of Oxford, Cambridge, and Trinity College, Dublin. They became one of the great sources of recruitment for the growing professional class. Many went into trade, particularly in the early part of the century when fewer openings in the professions were available. Those whose families had the necessary funds to pay the stiff apprenticeship fees demanded by successful merchants concentrated on the various branches of the overseas trade.[1] Not all were successful in the careers that they chose, and the sons of poor gentlemen in stagnant agricultural areas had sometimes to be apprenticed to masters whose trades seem to have been of a very humble nature. The sons of such men might in time lose even that last remnant of their social heritage, the right to be described as 'gentleman' on their tombstone. Others, making a fortune in trade or at the bar, might buy an estate of their own or marry one, and so again enter the charmed circle of the landed gentry.

Often these men are described as the squirearchy, this term being used to cover the major landowning families in every county who were not connected by birth with the aristocracy. Between them and the local nobility there was often considerable jealousy. The country gentleman considered himself well qualified to manage the affairs of his county without aristocratic interference, which he resented. When prices for agricultural products were low and rents difficult to collect, envy caused by the fatter purses and more lavish way of life stimulated this antagonism further, a factor which political managers busy constructing parliamentary majorities before an election had to consider carefully. Even within their own ranks

---

[1] See W. E. Minchinton, 'The Merchants in England in the Eighteenth Century', *The Entrepreneurs: Papers presented at the Annual Conference of the Economic History Society*, April 1957, p. 23.

there was considerable financial inequality. Wealthy squires might have an income of as much as £2,000 from their estates while a neighbour had to struggle along on between £800 and £300. In their habits and outlook, also, considerable diversities were to be found among them. Some might be the rude squire of caricature and fiction, deep drinking, hard riding and with a mentality as limited as his activities.[1] But others were builders of minor country seats, collectors of libraries, improvers of their estates, and by no means incapable of listening intelligently to the arguments of the politicians in the Commons. The part that they played in parliamentary life was an interesting one: indeed they can almost be described as the jury to whom both ministers of the Crown and their opponents appealed. It is sometimes said that the highest political offices were reserved for the nobility and, like most generalizations, there is some truth in the statement. Grafton would never have become First Lord of the Treasury had he not been a duke. But though rank and connection was an enormous help the lack of it was not an insuperable bar. Walpole with only one respectable face card in his hand—his early connection with the Marquis of Townshend—by his outstanding ability became one of the most powerful ministers of the century, though to the end he retained the outward characteristics of a Norfolk squire. If the country gentlemen as individuals played little part in high politics, this was due to lack of inclination as well as lack of opportunity. Active as many of them were in local affairs and county politics they had no desire for office, preferring the independence of the uncommitted member to the drudgery of the professional politician.

8. THE MIDDLING SORT

The next great layer in society is perhaps best described by the contemporary term 'the Middling Sort'. As with all eighteenth-century

---

[1] Describing the country squire Le Blanc writes: 'He is naturally a very dull animal; perhaps his food is the cause of it. He eats nothing but salt beef, cold mutton, cabbage, carrots and pudding; which last is his favourite dish; and that which is heaviest he likes best. His drink is ale, coarse Portugal wines, and now and then a little of the strongest brandy. He drinks two favourite healths at his meals, which is perhaps the only rule he observes; the first is to all honest fox hunters in Great Britain, protestant or catholic without exception; the title of hunter reconciles them all; the second bumper is confusion to the minister.'—Le Blanc, *Letters on the English and French Nations* (1747), p. 279. The impressions of foreign visitors should not be taken too seriously, but the above is a good contemporary description of the traditional eighteenth-century squire.

groups it is difficult to draw a clear line of demarcation between them and their social superiors and inferiors. No economic line is possible, for a man with no pretensions to gentility might well be more prosperous than many a small squire. There was even on the fringe between the two classes some overlapping of activities. One merchant might be a gentleman born, another the son of a yeoman who by his skill had won an equal fortune. A gentleman might be called to the bar, so might the son of a middle-class attorney.[1] Here the dividing line was one of manners and behaviour. The ambitious upstart who bought an estate and spent his income as a gentleman, might be either cold-shouldered by his better-born neighbours or treated by them with a certain contemptuous politeness. If however his daughters were presentable and well dowered, and if his sons received the education considered suitable for gentlemen, the next generation would see the obliteration of whatever distinction still remained. The solid mass of the middling sort had however no such aspirations, or considered them beyond their reach. They can perhaps best be described as comprising all those families whose income came from some non-manual occupation but who, by their way of life and attitude of mind, had no claims to be ranked with the gentry. They, too, were by no means a homogeneous group: the difference in their income levels and in their ways of life were very great. In the country districts they were the substantial tenant farmers, the smaller freeholders, the millers, the innkeepers. In the towns they controlled most forms of economic activity; they were traders, shopkeepers, middlemen. Most of the internal trade of the country was in their hands. So was most of its industrial production; they were clothiers, ironmongers, linen drapers. As industry grew their numbers grew with it. In addition they were invading the lower ranks of the professions: they became apothecaries, attorneys and men of business, school masters, clerks and civil servants, customs and excise men.

It was these people who made up the solid backbone of the country and who were largely responsible for running its day-to-day economic life. Many of them were very prosperous and had more

---

[1] Robert Robson, *The Attorney in Eighteenth Century England* (1959), p. 58, points out: 'The professions, in which individual merit may count for more than inherited status, have always been one of the bridges across the gulf which tend to separate society into classes. For many in the eighteenth century the profession of attorney was an accessible social bridge.'

money to spend than the poorer gentry. The control of urban life was largely in their hands and, at least in parliamentary boroughs, some outward deference to their wishes had to be paid by the local gentry and nobility. Politics at a national level meant very little to them, and at the beginning of the century there is no indication that votes were either asked for or given on this basis. But local politics and local welfare meant a great deal. A borough monger had to be prepared to use his influence to favour the fortunes of the men whose votes he was soliciting. He had to spend money locally, to court popularity, and to be ready to pay some attention to the economic interests of the borough. Doubtless even so the opinions of the majority of the middle class went for nothing. Some of the most rapidly growing towns like Manchester and Birmingham had no Members of Parliament. In others a restricted franchise cut out all but a handful of voters. As yet, making money was the main activity of the middle class: those that made enough passed into the ranks of the gentry: the failures went to swell the numbers of the labouring poor.

9. THE POOR

This term was widely used to designate the great mass of the manual workers. Within their ranks differences of income and of outlook were as varied as those that characterized the middle class. Once again the line of demarcation is hard to draw. The skilled artisan might easily become a small shopkeeper, selling his own and other men's wares, or a small employer of labour. The prosperous craftsman might enjoy a higher standard of life than the poor clerk. In discussing the general characteristics of this great class, generalization is made a little easier if a distinction is first drawn between the urban and the rural workers. This in the eighteenth century is a more satisfactory dividing line than that between agriculture and industry. Many people employed in industry were to be found in villages and in communities too small to be dignified by the word town. Sometimes these were engaged in purely rural crafts in so far as they were smiths, wheelwrights, farriers, thatchers. Often they were following some small local industry; the villages round Northampton, a county of graziers where hides were plentiful, were full of shoe makers. Everywhere there were weavers. Sometimes the local industry was nail-making, or the fashioning of buckles or belts, as in the villages of the Black Country. Not all these people were wage earners. Some were independent craftsmen buying their raw material and selling their finished products. Sometimes they were able to take advantage of a village common, or they might rent a cottage with a scrap of land attached. In time of hay and harvest they could make additional money by acting as labourers. The specialist agricultural labourers were probably in a minority. Many farmers, especially in the open-field areas, were able to work their farms with the help of their family, paying for an occasional odd day's work when more labour was needed. Only the bigger farms required a full-time ploughman or cowman or dairymaid, and in the beginning of the century these usually lived in the farmhouse. For most of these rural workers, whether independent or wage earners, life was hard but not impossibly so except in time of scarcity. When prices soared then most of the income had to be spent on bread. But in the years of low or average prices which marked the early years of George I's reign, there was money for a sufficiency of food, though it lacked variety; meat was still a luxury unless the family could keep a pig. Clothes were durable and solid and lasted for years and few of these people were without a little finery for high days and holidays. Housing was bad; cottages were still very simply made, often of daub and wattle, with clay floors and low roofs. Much depended on the local building traditions: where stone was plentiful, stone walls and stone floors made a more substantial dwelling. But everywhere there was overcrowding, for the influence of the Poor Law was to prevent the building of cottages that might harbour paupers. This indeed itself was a commentary on how near to subsistence level most of these rural workers lived. While they had their health and strength and times were not hard they could manage. But they had no reserves and no means of acquiring any. This was partly because wages and earnings were too low, but also because there was no incentive to save, and nowhere except a stocking for savings. Everywhere there was a certain recognized standard of life to which the worker was supposed to be entitled: what was earned over this went to the beer house. As a result illness, ill luck, or old age pushed most workers over the line that divided the labouring poor from the pauper. The Poor Relief administered by the parish became their only refuge.[1] It was understandable therefore that parishes should try to limit the number of potential paupers

[1] For this aspect of social history see my *The English Poor in the Eighteenth Century* (1926).

by limiting the cottages in which they could live. Even so, each village contained a sprinkling of paupers or those whose working days were over, those of sub-normal intelligence or strength, who were never able to support themselves completely, orphaned or deserted children.

There was a larger range of incomes and ways of life to be found among the urban workers. Particularly in London, but to some extent in the more important ports, and in those towns which acted as the social centre for the local gentry, there was a demand for highly skilled craftsmen, for coach makers and cabinet makers, for jewellers and watch makers, for engravers and printers. These men had served a long apprenticeship and their handiwork could command good money. Their work was in itself of such a character as to give them notions of comfort that were quite outside the experience of the rural craftsman. They were the aristocrats of the working world. The majority of the urban workers were less well placed. The more fortunate had some steady trade. They might work in tanyards or brickyards, or be tailors or shoe makers or bakers. Many were carpenters or builders' labourers. Many were porters or lightermen. The ladder is one of many gradations from skill to strength. For those at the bottom life was hard. Much of the work they did was seasonal. Storms might prevent ships from arriving or bad weather hinder building. Sometimes Court mourning could ruin the employment of a host of tailors and seamstresses. Food was a matter of bread and beer eked out by the doubtful wares of the poorest street hawkers. A family to a room was the usual housing of the poor, and for the very poor a common lodging-house, or a mere corner in which to sleep. Their cooking facilities were never more than the open hearth and, unlike the rural poor, they had no free fuel. Catering had to depend on the oven of the baker where the more prosperous had their Sunday dinner cooked, or a nearby cook house. It is not surprising that the beer houses were the clubs of the poor. More desperate than all the hardships of the poorer workers was the position of those dregs of society—ill, old, half-witted or reckless and depraved—that were to be found in every big town. London in particular had an underworld of pimps and prostitutes, of thieves and receivers who, in the absence of any police force more powerful than the parish constable and the watch, were a constant menace to the more law-abiding sections of society. It was from these dregs, leavened by a more respectable element of desperate workers when employment was scarce or prices high, that the eighteenth-century mob was drawn. This was something that the propertied classes feared most profoundly. The eighteenth-century worker had no political rights and though the Law recognized his legal equality with his social betters, lack of money made legal rights little but a mockery. In prison a poor man starved while the man able to pay for comfort could make his position tolerable enough. But though he had nothing else he had the weapon of violence with which to terrify his masters. When prices were high markets were stormed and millers attacked. Unpopular laws that threatened to put up the price of food or give advantages to foreign wares often produced mob violence; though a demonstration might be staged by the respectable, the temptation to riot called out all that was most violent in the eighteenth-century worker and a sense of injustice combined with the love of destruction. On 7 July 1740 'A Rabble at Norwich began to be tumultuous, and affix'd a Note on the Door of every Baker in the City, in these Words, *Wheat at sixteen shillings a Comb.* . . . About 8 in the Evening the Mayor committed 3 or 4 disorderly fellows to Prison, which so incensed the Mob that they broke open the Prison and released their Companions, and still growing more furious, provok'd some to fire among them, whereby 3 Men, 2 Women, and a Boy were killed, and many more dangerously wounded. At Derby, Northampton and Wellington the Populace rose also.'[1] At Newcastle, disliking the decisions on the scarcity taken by the authorities, 'the Rabble then fell upon the Gentlemen in the Hall, wounded most of them, ransack'd the Place, and the Court and Chambers, destroying the Public Writings and Accounts, and carried off near 1800*l* of the Town's Money. After this they patroll'd about the Streets, all the Shops being shut, and threatened to burn and destroy the whole Place'.[2] Episodes such as these, which were in no sense unique, explain the eighteenth-century fear of a mob.

10. Education

To put too much stress on such incidents can be misleading. Though education varied according to the needs of different social classes it played an important part in the life of the country as a whole. For a gentleman its basis was still the humanities. These were studied either with a private tutor or at one of the ancient grammar schools. Most of these were non-residential and catered

[1] *The Gentleman's Magazine*, July 1740, p. 356.   [2] *Ibid.*, p. 355.

for local boys; but a few, such as Winchester, Westminster, Eton, and rather later Harrow, were acquiring national prestige. Boys who went there might make useful friends. They had, however, serious disadvantages for the boy living away from home. Discipline was at once lax and brutal and the system of supervised boarding houses only grew slowly out of the need to secure suitable lodgings for non-scholars in the town. In such conditions the herding together of a mass of boys could give rise to many abuses, and some parents preferred to employ a tutor at home. Often a year or two at Oxford or Cambridge followed, but the man who was not forced to earn a living by academic attainments seldom proceeded to a degree. For him the university was merely the prelude to the Grand Tour, and he did as little or as much work as his fancy dictated.

Financially the same type of education was also available to boys who had no pretensions to gentility, because the grammar schools were endowed institutions. For a tradesman's son or the boy of middle-class parents the utility of such an education, unless he were hoping to go on to the university and follow one of the professions, was strictly limited. What he needed was a more modern and practical education to fit him for business. This was increasingly provided first by the Dissenting Academies, originally set up to cater for the needs of those excluded by religious tests from the endowed schools, and later by the private fee-paying school. For the craftsman the ability to read and write and do a little arithmetic was an advantage in his daily life, and these elements of education were provided in various ways. The traditional dame's school that taught reading and sometimes writing for a couple of pence a week, the efforts of some of the clergy, and the charity schools between them produced a higher standard of literacy than is always realized.[1] Even among the labouring poor, especially in the towns, there were enough people who could read, and retail to their fellows what they had read, to give the broadsheet, the pamphlet and the press a varying but never negligible importance in shaping popular prejudices. The education available for women was much more sketchy and haphazard as they were eligible neither for the endowed school nor for the university. In families that

[1] Diana McClatchey, *Oxfordshire Clergy 1777–1869* (1960), gives a brief account of the parochial day schools in that county (pp. 150–51). See also M. G. Jones, *The Charity School Movement. A Study of Eighteenth Century Puritanism in Action* (1938).

employed a private tutor some crumbs of his attention might fall to the sisters of his pupils. Most girls were taught at home the elements of reading and writing, often by their parents. Some, encouraged by book-loving fathers and with libraries available, became scholars in their own right; the bluestocking is a figure of the eighteenth-century social scene. But for most gentlewomen their competence was restricted to the reading of novels, the writing of letters, and the casting of household accounts. Later in the century the private boarding school, with its stress on deportment and such accomplishments rather than a solid education, catered for 'young ladies'. The tradesman's wife, and often his business assistant, needed some knowledge of reading and writing, perhaps arithmetic; the labouring woman needed none, though many urban charity schools taught their girls the rudiments of reading so that the Bible was open to them.

Hanoverian society is not something about which it is easy to generalize: it is too marked by those contradictions which are so characteristic of the eighteenth century. Class distinctions were important and gave form and order to everyday living, but created no insurmountable barrier to either economic or individual progress. If in many ways it was an age of violence it was also an age in which Englishmen of all classes boasted of the rule of Law. Though it was an age of patronage and subservience, when men could write bitterly

> God help the man, condemn'd by cruel fate
> To court the seeming or the real great.
> Much sorrow shall he feel and suffer more
> Than any slave who labours at the oar.
> (Charles Churchill, *Night*)

it was also an age in which men prided themselves on their independence and felt a pitying contempt for their continental neighbours as the victims of absolute power. In some ways there was a great respect for authority, in others none at all. The same contradictions ran through its religious and cultural life. An age that seemed dominated by the debauchery of the rich and the ignorance and brutality of the poor, saw the formation of the Society for the Reformation of Manners. It was a vigorous, often violent, but fundamentally healthy and progressive society over which the Georges ruled. Though only a small proportion of their subjects enjoyed political rights, and government was the affair of

the minority, the student of history must never become so absorbed
in the activities of the politicians as to forget the hopes and fears,
the prejudices and the pleasures of the people whom they governed.
It was the people who provided the funds that the statesmen spent
and it was they who suffered from the blunders that were made.
When Walpole failed to carry his Excise bill and feared to increase
the Land Tax, ordinary people had to pay more for their salt to
bridge the financial gap. When England went to war the press-
gang was active in her ports. Political, social and economic history
are one and indivisible.

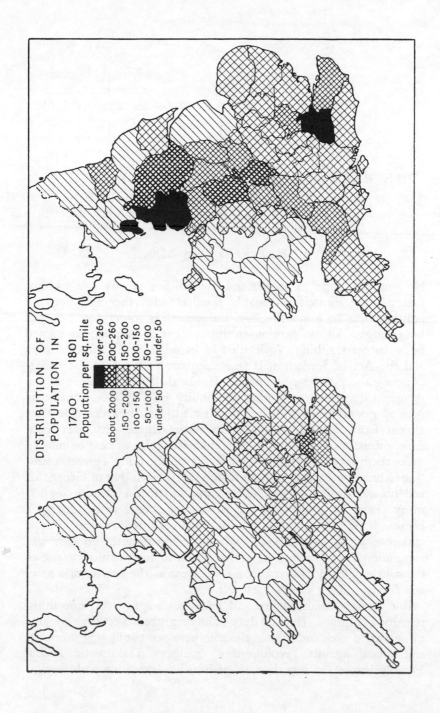

DISTRIBUTION OF
POPULATION IN

1700   1801
Population per sq. mile

■ about 2000   ■ over 260
▨ 150-200   ▨ 200-260
▨ 100-150   ▨ 150-200
▨ 50-100   ▨ 100-150
□ under 50   ▨ 50-100
                □ under 50

2

THE BACKGROUND OF POLITICAL LIFE ON THE ACCESSION OF GEORGE I

1. Measures and Men

No one can hope to understand the politics of any age without first making himself reasonably familiar with the conditions of political life. To know the legal framework is something, but it is not enough. 'A little learning' in this context, as in most, can indeed be 'a dangerous thing'. A detailed knowledge of the Bill of Rights and the Act of Settlement is an inadequate preparation for understanding the politics of Georgian England. This is because of the dangerously outward-seeming continuity of English institutions. Names go on unaltered, but the institutions they describe vary almost from decade to decade; in some degree they vary even from ministry to ministry, as each man struggles as best he may to make them serve his purpose in carrying on the King's government. The Cabinet of Anne worked very differently from that of George II, and no description pinpointed in time will retain its accuracy for many years. To understand the pattern of events when George I became King it is necessary to look, however briefly, at the political structure which he inherited. Only by seeing how the country was run under Anne is a student of the period in any position to notice the subtle differences that become apparent as the impact of a new, and foreign, King makes itself felt.

But though circumstances and resources might vary, one thing remained constant. The first duty of any eighteenth-century government was to keep order, hold the ring between conflicting interests, and guard against revolutionary changes in domestic affairs. Equally important was the task of handling relations with foreign powers, so that British prestige and British wealth might be increased. If, as was not uncommon, diplomacy slipped over the brink into open war, ministers had to face their most serious test. A war mismanaged, or, however brilliantly managed, prolonged until it became unpopular, was the one thing no administration could survive. This limited conception of the functions of government meant that such policy as it had was largely shaped by immediate problems and short-term views. Throughout the century, with a few vital exceptions, who should do things remained more important than what should be done. Only in moments of crisis, such as the need to bring the war of the Spanish Succession to an end in 1713, or to make peace with the revolted American colonies in 1783, were measures more important than men. Certainly no minister taking office was expected to know what he would do if some hypothetical event took place. Sufficient unto the day as yet were the politics thereof.

In any case at the beginning of the century the responsibility for determining policy lay in practice, as well as in theory, with the Crown. The royal choice still determined who should hold office, though the need to choose men who could work together in tolerable harmony, and who could persuade the House of Commons to grant the necessary supplies for the policy they advocated, was beginning to impose practical restrictions on his choice. William III plainly found this irksome, but no one doubted that he was the head of the executive. It was his business to make policy: the great officers of state, as heads of departments, were responsible for carrying it out within their own spheres. The King could take counsel where he would: but his was still the co-ordinating hand. With Anne her sex, her character, her interests, modified the rôle of the Crown. Unlike William III, who had been forced since his youth to grapple with the problems of war, administration and supply, Anne had received little training in statecraft. When she became Queen there was much business which she felt herself unfit to handle. That she should rely on her ministers more than William III had done was inevitable. The extent to which the sovereign controlled the executive and framed policy depended therefore on the accidents of personality rather than on any clear constitutional theory. Ministers were servants, disguised tutors, or even masters, according to the play of personalities and the circumstances of the time.

2. The Executive and the Armed Services

Nevertheless, by the eighteenth century some offices were recognized as carrying with them special distinction. The Lord Chancellor, the Lord Keeper, the President of the Council, the Lord Privy Seal, the Lord Treasurer, and the Secretaries of State were all coveted offices. None, however, yet gave the automatic cachet of being the chief minister of the Crown, though in Anne's reign the staff of the Lord High Treasurer, having been held for so long by Godolphin, and then by his rival Oxford, seemed to carry with it a certain claim to special importance. Indeed it has been suggested that it was this fear which, on Bothmar's advice, made George I adopt the seventeenth-century device of putting the Treasury into commission, lest a powerful Lord Treasurer should 'become troublesome for the King himself'.[1] Lord Halifax, who had expected the Treasurer's staff, was much displeased by this arrangement, which he almost regarded as a personal slight. The office of Lord High Admiral was similarly treated. Another of the great offices of state, the Lord Lieutenancy of Ireland, in spite of its dignity, was not popular with ambitious politicians. This was because it entailed absences from England, which put its holder at some disadvantage in the constant struggle for power, while the task itself was no easy one. In the earlier part of the century appointments to this office are therefore illuminating in assessing the rising or falling fortunes of any politician or group.

In order to understand what government could, or could not, achieve in the eighteenth century it is necessary also to look at the working of the great administrative departments. The historical chaos of their past accounted for much of the administrative inefficiency of eighteenth-century governments. There was no single department which was solely responsible for the financial business of the country, for the control of the Treasury was far from complete. For instance the expenses of the Household, with its subsidiary departments, such as the Board of Works, were met from the Civil List, as were the salaries of the judges, and sundry other government officials. Though the Treasury had some control over military expenditure, at least as far as to be able to demand estimates

---

[1] Wolfgang Michael, *England under George I. The Beginnings of the Hanoverian Dynasty* (1936), p. 92.

See H. Roseveare, *The Treasury: The Evolution of a British Institution* (1969), for an account of its growth and functions in the eighteenth century.

from the fighting services, the fact that the Secretary at War could go directly to the House of Commons to ask for additional supplies made Treasury checks ineffective. In the same way the Admiralty and Navy Board could deal directly with the House of Commons over matters of supply. In such circumstances all that the Treasury could hope to attain was a certain formal check on payments and receipts. Even here, though the Board was active in pursuance of these duties, it was terribly hampered by the archaic organization of the office. It was not only that Roman numerals, court hand and tallies were still used. There was also much overlapping of functions between officials, some of whom had originated in the Exchequer and some in the Treasury. Also so many minor departments—as for instance the Commissioners for the collection of Excise, of Land Tax, of Customs—were in theory under Treasury supervision that, hampered by limited staff and old-fashioned methods, the Board was quite incapable of exercising an efficient control.

This is important for the understanding of political life. Money handed out to the spending departments might not be audited for years. As a result the ministers in theory responsible for it could use the balances in their hands for their own speculations, diverting to their own private purses any interest that accrued. The fortune that Sir Robert Walpole made has never been fully explained, but there is little doubt that this slackness in handling public money must have given him opportunities which a more watertight system would not have afforded. Of all the offices which handled public money that of Paymaster-General offered the greatest scope for the acquisition of a private fortune, and it was this office which he took in 1714. The inadequacy of Treasury control was also reflected in the numerous motions of members anxious to harry the ministers of the day. It was so very easy to raise the cry of unnecessary placemen, when so many public officials seemed to serve no purpose save that of creating confusion of function. It was equally easy to raise the cry of corruption when the accounts of the Treasury for years past were in arrears or where, as could well happen in an emergency, expenditure had not been properly authorized. All these cries were the stock-in-trade of any opposition. Waste and corruption were things which the country gentlemen were convinced did much to raise the Land Tax, and an effective rejoinder on the part of the government was often impossible. Figures, it is often said, can prove anything: the lack of figures provided by the eighteenth-century Treasury was the source of many a fierce parliamentary debate.

The figures produced by the Treasury may have been inadequate, but the House of Commons had no control at all over the expenditure of the Household, which was the personal concern of the sovereign. The Civil List was granted at the beginning of each reign and it was only when the royal debts had become unmanageable, so that Parliament had to be asked to discharge them, that there was any chance of criticism. Such criticism was hampered by some respect for the Crown, and even more by the lack of adequate information as to how the money had been spent. Estimates were not prepared and the King refused to allow his accounts to be produced. So, though there was often much sound and fury in the debates, and occasionally some very straight speaking, in the end there was little the House could do but provide the necessary money. The Civil List was in fact rarely sufficient to meet all the charges made upon it. There was also ground for criticism in the organization of the Household, which was antiquated and traditional beyond belief. That a footman in the royal service, from his perquisites of unburnt candle ends, should have been able to found the modest shop that afterwards became world famous as Fortnum and Mason, is some measure of the waste that was sanctioned by tradition. It was a system, however, which neither the King nor his ministers had any inducement to reform. Between them the honourable, the useless and the duplicated offices of the Household made up a mass of patronage which, judiciously used, was most valuable in creating a favourable majority in Parliament.

The control of the Household, inherited from Anne, continued unimpaired under George I. The other focus of his interest in English affairs was the army. The magnitude and extent of the wars in which Britain had been involved since the accession of William and Mary had made the organization and supply of the army a matter of increasing importance. English feeling was predominately anti-military, and a standing army was regarded as a perpetual threat to liberty. Nothing had made Marlborough more distrusted than his demand that he should be created Captain General for life. Almost as popular with the country gentlemen as the cry against waste and corruption was that against the maintenance of a standing army.[1] Yet in view of our expanding trade and our growing colonies, no responsible minister would dare to dispense with, or even economize too far on, a permanent military force. Even after the peace of Utrecht and the accession of George I this remained true. Foreign affairs for some time continued to be difficult and George I was, both from temperament and because of his Hanoverian territories, personally interested in this aspect of his government. Yet important as the army was, both as a factor in foreign policy and as a defence against Jacobite invasion, its organization was far from efficient. Conditions of service were so hard and punishment so barbarous that only the desperate or the stupid were tempted to enlist. Commissions were sold, and colonels expected to make a profit from the bounties and allowances to which they were entitled. The administrative side was also weak. The Commons had made good their claim to control the force it feared to the extent of providing, usually after fierce debate, the money necessary for its upkeep, based on yearly estimates. They also, by the annual Mutiny Act, gave a legal basis to military law, by which discipline was maintained.

The link between Parliament and the army was the Secretary at War. As the head of an administrative department he was responsible for recruitment, billeting, supply and the hundred-and-one details of day-to-day business. As a politician he had to pilot the army estimates through Parliament and handle any other matter that concerned its administration. Here his functions stopped. The planning of campaigns and the movement of troops fell to the Secretary of State, the command in the field belonged to the Commander-in-Chief. As if this division of authority were not enough the army received its pay through the Paymaster's office, and was furnished with ordnance and military stores by the Board of Ordnance. In addition, the engineers and the artillery were regarded as a separate branch, connected with ordnance rather than with the infantry, and therefore also under the control of that Board. George I, who was deeply interested in army matters, was able to make some improvements in this ramshackle organization, but traditions, departmental jealousies, and privileges went deep. Indeed, it is

---

1 The following typical illustration is taken from *The Craftsman*, 26 January 1733-4, 3rd edition, 1737, p. 395: 'It is certain then that if ever such Men as call Themselves *Friends to the Government* but are *real Enemies to the Constitution*, should prevail, They will make it a Capital point of their wicked Policy to keep up a *standing Army*.'

something of a mystery how, with so much overlapping and in-efficiency, Britain ever put an army in the field. With Marlborough in command, and with the support of Anne and Godolphin at home, miracles had been achieved during the war of the Spanish Succession. That miracles cannot be performed at will by lesser men the history of the years between the dismissal of Marlborough and the emergence of Pitt as a war organizer was to make plain.

Though England was proud of her navy, and money for its upkeep was more willingly granted than for the army, it was almost as weak on the administrative side. Like the army, general orders for the movement of ships came from the Secretary's office. The Board of Admiralty were responsible for seeing that the ships were fit for service and were supposed to supervise in detail the carrying out of the Secretary's orders. They in turn had also to work with and through the Navy Office, the Treasurer of the Navy and the Commissioners of the Royal Dockyards, a task of co-ordination and control that could at times prove difficult. Much indeed depended on the abilities and personality of the First Lord of the Admiralty. During the early part of the century it was customary to appoint an admiral to this office. The Earl of Orford, who had won his title for his naval prowess, was First Lord in 1714, and was succeeded in 1717 by the Earl of Berkeley, another competent seaman.

It is something of a relief to turn from this picture of departments smothered in tradition and privileges to the office of Secretary of State. If the Justices of the Peace could justly be described as the maids of all work of the Tudors, the Secretaries of State seem to qualify for this description in the eighteenth century.[1] Because they had no medieval past, and had always been the medium through which the royal will had been expressed, their office had remained more personal and more fluid than that of any of the other great offices of State. They were the channel through which negotiations with foreign powers took place. If war broke out they were closely concerned with the general direction of strategy. When peace had to be made negotiations passed through their office. Because they were in theory the mouthpiece of the King they were able to link together other departments, nominally independent, in a way that none of the other ministers could do. Though much of their

[1] For details of this office see Mark A. Thomson, *The Secretaries of State, 1681–1782* (1932).

attention was given to matters concerned with foreign policy, they were also responsible for internal order, in so far as its maintenance created problems that were beyond the competence of the magistrates to handle. Linked with the preservation of public order was the need to track down dissatisfaction, to investigate the actions of suspicious characters, who might be Jacobite agents, and generally to take the appropriate action that any internal emergency might demand. Had their departments been larger the personal influence of the Secretaries might have been less, but the Secretariat was quite small, around a score in all. As a result the Secretaries really had to conduct their own correspondence and deal with the miscellaneous business that arose. In spite of the abundance of sinecures in some sections of the administration, and the duplication of unnecessary functions in others, the number of clerks and active working personnel in important offices, such as those of the Secretaries,[1] or of the Secretary at War, remained fantastically low. The surprising thing is not that business was often delayed or neglected, but that so much was accomplished.

In addition to a shortage of staff a further difficulty arose from the slowness of communications. When, as happened constantly, one Secretary was with the King in Hanover while the other was left to conduct the business of his office in London, this slowness of communications could result in misunderstandings which, on occasion, were to have politically disastrous consequences. It had early been found that the multifarious activities which fell to the Secretaries were too much for any one man to handle and by 1714 there were always two Secretaries. This arrangement, though easing pressure in one way created possibilities for friction in another. This was because their duties were divided on a purely geographical basis. As foreign policy could not be so neatly divided into self-contained areas it was not a good arrangement. In practice, however, personality came to count for more than theoretical responsibility, the more forceful of the two Secretaries taking the lead in the general direction of foreign affairs.[2] Much depended on where the danger spots seemed to be in any particular period. In

---

[1] *Ibid.*, pp. 128–48, for an account of the staffing of the office and the position of the Under Secretaries.

[2] *Ibid.*, p. 19: 'When a Secretary aspired to be a chief Minister he usually strove to have an undistinguished colleague.' cf. D. B. Horn, *The British Diplomatic Service 1689–1789* (1961), pp. 2–11.

the early years of George I the more important politician took the Northern Secretaryship. This was held successively by Townshend, Stanhope and Sunderland. By the middle of the century the Southern Secretary, to whose sphere the colonies and Ireland belonged, had to deal with the more urgent problems: it is worth noting that William Pitt took the Southern Secretaryship in 1756. Not until 1782 was the more logical division of business into home and foreign affairs adopted. In addition to the two permanent Secretaryships, for most of George I's reign there was an additional Secretary for Scotland, and for a time in the reign of George III, one for the colonies.

A large-scale war, however, could not be waged successfully, indeed it could hardly be waged at all, so long as the great officers of State acted in a vacuum, each responsible for his own department. Even an effective and active head of the executive, such as William III, needed the co-operation of his ministers, acting as a group, if both the framing and the executing of his war plans were to be successful. This was even more true in Anne's reign, since she was less able to act as a co-ordinating agent. From this fact arose the great importance of the Lords of the Committee, whose business it became to work out the detailed running of the war, as well as to attend to the domestic business of the country. In Anne's reign its composition was still fluid.[1] All the great offices enumerated earlier carried the right to attend, but other offices depended on the personal importance of the holder. The Earl of Shrewsbury, when Lord Chamberlain, attended regularly: the Marquis of Kent, who had held the same office previously, did not. During the war years of Anne's reign this committee met regularly to hammer out problems of strategy and supply. In some ways it was as much an information-collecting body as a policy-making one; or rather, to it were entrusted the first steps in framing a policy—namely, the collection of information. Commissioners of transport, admirals and generals about to undertake a new expedition, junior ministers, ambassadors, were all summoned or invited to its meetings, which were usually held in the senior Secretary's room at the Cockpit. Indeed it was only by interviewing those immediately responsible for each phase of an operation and dovetailing their resources, that complicated military or naval expeditions could ever get away, or diplomatic missions be

[1] See J. H. Plumb, 'The Organisation of the Cabinet in the Reign of Queen Anne' (*Trans. R. Hist. Soc.*, 5th ser., vol. 7, 1957).

briefed, or negotiations for treaties be set on foot. It was in these meetings of ministers that the practical details of politics could be adequately discussed.

Such a committee could explore possibilities and suggest a tentative policy on its findings: it could not take final decisions or give orders. For its policy to be implemented it was necessary that its members should leave the Cockpit for one of the royal palaces and there, meeting as a Cabinet, in the presence of the Queen, submit its recommendations to Her Majesty. To some extent its work, when sitting as a Cabinet, was more formal than the deliberations of the same ministers meeting at the Cockpit. For example, letters drafted by the Lords in Committee were approved and signed by the Queen. But its functions were always wider than to approve of what had been settled previously. Fresh considerations might be submitted. Sometimes it almost appeared as if vital information was deliberately kept back until the more important meeting and fresh arguments used where opinion had been divided.[1] Not until Anne had been won over could the business be concluded. George I therefore inherited a reasonably effective machine for collecting information and advising him on policy, a machine which the King could dominate if he wished, but which, except for formal business, could function quite effectively without his presence.

3. PARLIAMENT

If, however, policy-making was still a matter for the Crown and for those ministers who had the royal confidence, the money to carry it out was provided by the votes of the Commons. It is true that the Civil List provided the King with a revenue for routine expenditure. But the money required for the upkeep of the army and the navy, and for any extraordinary expenditure, had to be granted by Parliament, which in practice meant the House of Commons. One of the great problems of eighteenth-century ministers therefore was to harmonize the views of the sovereign on foreign policy with the prejudices of that House. This fact provides one of the main clues to the behaviour of politicians throughout the century, but particularly before 1760, when public opinion was highly suspicious of the royal attachment to Hanover. The dilemma that faced them was clear. If they failed to get supplies to give substance to the royal policy they were of no use to the King: if on the other hand they

1 *Ibid.*, pp. 152-3.

were suspected of furthering non-British interests they jeopardized their control over the House.

It was this which made the composition of Parliament of such vital importance in the politics of the century. In the House of Lords the Crown had a good deal of influence, even though it was largely a hereditary chamber. During the greater part of the century a large proportion of the ministers were members of the Upper House. This gave them the opportunity of explaining the royal policy very fully, for, though a judicious distribution of Court offices and royal favours might incline men to support the King's ministers, its members were far removed from a rubber-stamp mentality. More effective was the control of ministers over the non-hereditary elements. This was supplied by the bishops and the representative Scottish peers. While Anne lived, the former were appointed with some care as to their suitability and their churchmanship, though ministers did their best to see that political reliability was not forgotten in the search for more spiritual qualities. After her death bishops were chosen more and more from Broad Churchmen, whose whiggish sympathies would provide the administration with a solid block of dependable voters.[1] A politically unsound cleric had therefore very little chance of being raised to the episcopate. If however an independently minded cleric tended to stray from the ministerial fold the great differences in the revenues of the various sees gave ministers a most effective weapon against him. It was the practice, when a man first became a bishop, to appoint him to a see where the income was hardly equal to the expense of that dignity. Then, if he proved reliable, he was translated as opportunity offered, to a wealthier bishopric. As it was well understood that the consequences of defiance were likely to be fatal to future promotion it is not surprising that the Crown could depend on the votes of the bishops.[2] The other non-hereditary group, the Scottish representative peers, also had the reputation of voting solidly with the administration.

The problem of controlling and managing the House of Commons, so as to harmonize its various interests and make them serviceable to the Crown, made the composition of that House a matter of vital importance. On the accession of George I there were

---

[1] A popular print depicting Walpole as a quack doctor declared that 'he has cured a whole Bench of Bishops of Religion': quoted M. D. George, *English Political Caricature* (1959), vol. 1, p. 83.

[2] Norman Sykes, *Church and State in England in the Eighteenth Century* (1934), pp. 61–65.

558 members—489 English, 24 Welsh and 45 Scottish. This large proportion of English members made them the key to the situation, and it is on them that attention must first be focused. Here the traditional division of members into the knights of the shire and the burgesses representing the urban constituencies is important, because the problem of controlling and influencing elections varied with the type of elector and the size of the electorate. In the counties the voter was the forty shilling freeholder. In theory his freehold was the guarantee of his independence. The knights of the shire were apt to preen themselves on the fact that they represented the least corrupt and corruptible group of voters. Reality was often at variance with this idealized picture. Many freeholders were poor and very amenable to pressure from above. Men do not fall into mutually exclusive categories of freeholders and tenants. Many leased land which they farmed together with their freehold. Many were craftsmen or traders dependent on the approval and patronage of the local gentry. Moreover, there was a more subtle sense in which they were not free. Living in an area where the Walpoles or the Townshends or the Stanleys had always been the recognized leading family, men unversed in political issues would feel that they owed the courtesy of their vote to him, or to his nominee. This local loyalty was not necessarily subservient, but it was a very real factor in eighteenth-century politics. In any case votes had to be publicly cast: this meant that the local magnates knew pretty clearly on whose support they could rely. In their hands the county representation really rested. It was a matter of very nice calculation and compromise to know what combination of influence would be strong enough to carry a candidate to Westminster. Here the size of the electorate was of great importance. Rutland with 609 voters might be manageable from a electioneering point of view: Yorkshire where 15,054 voted in 1741, was a very different proposition. Probably the average voting strength of an English county was about 4,000.[1] Even this number, scattered over a wide area, where several important families struggled jealously for supremacy, was far from easy to organize politically. While the technique of electioneering was still imperfectly developed, and the ruinous expense of fighting only half realized, bitter conflict between local families to secure the success of their faction was common. Later in the century the counties less often

[1] Sir Lewis B. Namier, *The Structure of Politics at the Accession of George III* (2nd edition, 1957), p. 65.

went to the polls. Instead, intrigue was centred on securing the nomination. Sometimes the interests of the leading county families could be so nicely calculated that a compromise between them was possible. Sometimes one of the two seats went to the nominee of a locally important peer and the other to the chosen candidate of the local gentry. When compromises of this character took place it is misleading to speak of the independence of the forty shilling freeholder; in practice such manœuvres meant that he had been disfranchised.

The very diverse franchises of the boroughs gave more scope for electioneering. Each had its peculiarities. To place the pieces correctly in the parliamentary jigsaw it is necessary to know both who had the right to vote and the size of the electorate. Most boroughs fell into one of three main categories, though there were endless variations within them. The first of these was based on some sort of residence, the qualifications for which ranged from the simple possession of a hearth on which to boil one's pot to the payment of local taxes. Secondly there were the boroughs in which the right to vote was attached to certain freeholds, in some cases the right belonging to the occupier, in others to the owner. In the third type the vote belonged to those men who had some special status in the borough, either because they were freemen or because they were members of the corporation. Here again there were many variations. In some forty of the boroughs the right to vote was rigidly restricted to the members of the corporation.[1] In others the corporation could co-opt an indefinite number of free burgesses, which gave a good deal of elasticity to the franchise. In the 60 boroughs where the right to vote was vested in the freemen the same variations existed.[2] Where honorary freemen could be created by the corporation, and where such honorary freemen were allowed to exercise the franchise, the dominant group in any corporation could create them in such numbers as to secure the return of their favourite candidate. In such boroughs, where two factions fought for control, with success swinging first to one side and then to the other, the number of such honorary freemen could become considerable. Many boroughs, however, excluded the honorary freemen from the franchise: in these, voters would tend to be fewer. But a freeman did not necessarily have to be resident. In some boroughs the

[1] Robert Walcott, *English Politics in the Early Eighteenth Century* (1956), p. 15.
[2] *Ibid.*, p. 18.

eldest son inherited his father's rights and these non-resident freemen, who were no longer swayed by local considerations, were particularly open to the temptation of disposing of their vote for a consideration, and might well be the deciding factor in any election.

To the patron nursing a borough the type of franchise, and even more the number of the electorate, was important. To gain votes in a borough where only those burgesses voted who paid 'scot and lot' —that is, who paid the ancient local taxes—it was necessary to play on the special interests of a majority of the voters regarded as individuals. One might be won over by a social attention, another by a direct bribe, a third by promotion or a place, either for himself or for a member of his family. In other boroughs where the vote was attached to a particular freehold, the burgage franchise, the obvious solution was to buy up as many of these burgages as possible. In consequence, as the rewards of controlling a borough became more and more apparent with the growth of political management, many were the fierce struggles of opposing local families to secure by purchase such desirable property. When George I became King the results of many of these local fights in the 43 boroughs where the franchise was of this type were still undetermined. In only about half of them were they safely in 'the pocket' of any one family. Among this half was Old Sarum, already the pocket borough of Diamond Pitt. But as the century progressed, persistence and wealth brought more and more of them under the control of a patron. Even the ownership of the coveted burgages did not always give a simple, straightforward control. In those where the vote belonged not to the owner but the tenant the patron had to create fictitious tenancies, so that his dependents could exercise their vote in accordance with his directions. Such tenancies were conferred by deed, appropriately known as 'snatch papers', since as soon as the election was over they were hastily reclaimed by the owner. Where the vote was confined to the corporation, or to the freemen, willingness to look after the interests of the town, as well as to win over individual members of the corporation, or of the freemen, was often necessary. One such deal was uncovered by the investigations of the House of Commons, an inquiry obviously undertaken more to embarrass the ministry than to secure the purity of elections. On the occasion of a by-election in Banbury in February 1722, Sir Francis Page, a baron of the Exchequer, had agreed with the corporation to pave the streets, enlarge the vicarage and build a school, in return for their support for his candidate.[1]

The size of the electoral roll was as important as its nature. It might seem that a borough in which every man paid scot and lot was less likely to fall under the control of a patron than one in which the right was attached to certain burgages. This depended, however, largely on the number of the residents so qualified. The idea that even in these boroughs all payers of local taxes were entitled to vote is erroneous. Only those who lived within the confines of the ancient town, the parliamentary borough, enjoyed this privilege: the growing suburbs were usually excluded. As a consequence 30 out of the 39 boroughs that fell into this category had less than 200 voters.[2] Even 200 was formidable when compared with the 13 voters in Buckingham or the 14 members of the corporation of Banbury. But though it might seem easier to influence thirteen or fourteen men than a couple of hundred, in practice this was not always so. Each elector had a scarcity value which he was not slow to exploit. Also a wealthy rival might find it easier to undermine the loyalty of seven or eight electors than that of a hundred and one. Where the number of the electors was greater each man had to be content with less, but even so he was able to guard against a too unremunerative purity. In the large open constituencies, like Southwark with 4,000 electors or Westminster with 9,000, different methods had to be employed. These ranged from oratory, through free beer to a species of gang warfare. So numerous an electorate was unusual: only in three were there more than 4,000 voters. Boroughs with a voting strength of 1,000 or more were commoner, making up about one-eighth of the total. But nearly two-thirds of the borough members were returned by less than 500 voters each and over forty per cent by less than a hundred.[3] This meant that most of the 203 boroughs at the beginning of the century were susceptible to management of some kind. Even so it was a tricky business: few patrons could relax their efforts even when their influence was apparently safely established. Also even when parliamentary management was at its height not all boroughs whose electoral structure made them susceptible to influence did in fact fall under outside control. At least 28 of those where the franchise was vested in the freemen seem to have kept some degree of independence. In addition, on the rare occasions

---

[1] J. H. Plumb, *Sir Robert Walpole* (1956), vol. 1, p. 373.
[2] R. Walcott, *op. cit.*, p. 13.   [3] *Ibid.*, pp. 24–25.

when any deep feeling on national issues was widespread, even the more venal boroughs could become restive. Because management, influence and the customary deference paid to local important families all played a part in the choice of members, it would be unwise to assume that the borough vote represented only subservient Englishmen on the make.

The character of the House returned by this electorate remained remarkably stable throughout the century, though minor changes in the proportion of the groups did occur. Since Anne's reign there had been a property qualification for members, but even without this it would have been predominately a House of landowners. In the last Parliament of William III, before the Act of 1710 had fixed the qualification as land to the annual value of £600 for a knight of the shire, and £300 for a burgess, it had been calculated that, out of 489 members representing English constituencies, 350 owned either a manor or a sizeable part of one, and spent at least some of their time managing their property. Many of these men, it is true, had other interests, which makes it a little misleading to describe them as mere landed proprietors. But even when those M.P.s who can be placed in more than one category are excluded, there were still 270 who must be regarded as representing the land and its interests. That the House of Commons should contain men with practical knowledge of trade, and especially of overseas commerce, was a matter of importance when these matters came to be discussed. In the Parliament of 1701 there were no fewer than 43 merchants and financiers and an additional 18 members who represented other diverse manufacturing or commercial interests. The connection between business and politics was close. Rival interests in the City were active in seeking the support of influential politicians and in creating parliamentary 'lobbies' for their various projects. The services accounted for another 48 members. The legal profession, including some of the law officers and a good many Recorders, who sat for their own boroughs, made an even larger group, some 62 in all. The motives which members had for desiring a seat were obviously varied. The eldest sons of peers, of whom the Commons always contained a considerable number, looked upon a few years in that House as a useful preliminary training for their future responsibilities in the Lords. Country gentlemen, without ambition for an active political career or office, regarded a seat as a public acknowledgement of their position within their own county, or sat for a borough which they themselves controlled. Merchants made useful contacts that led to government contracts. Financiers were interested in the floating of loans. Officers in the fighting services and lawyers both hoped that political influence would bring professional advancement. Men whose ambitions were purely social hoped that loyal support of ministers would lead to a peerage. Except for the country gentlemen nearly everybody wanted something.

The practical problem that faced every eighteenth-century monarch was how to weld this heterogeneous collection of men into a stable support for government. Like Gilbert later they too felt that

> The prospect of a lot of dull M.Ps. in close proximity
> All thinking for themselves is what
> No man can view with equanimity.

In theory the Crown had a claim on their support, based on their duty and loyalty but, as every ruler found, fundamental loyalty might well be combined with a degree of criticism and obstructionism of the royal ministers and the royal policy that made government extremely difficult. On more than one occasion William III would have returned to Holland, rather than struggle with hostile Parliaments, had he not needed English help so badly in his struggle with Louis XIV. There seemed very little stable on which to build. For the better part of a hundred years English political life had been a series of crises; there had been Civil War, the beheading of Charles I, constitutions had been drawn up, had collapsed and been reshaped by Cromwell, even the restoration of Charles II had resulted in a further struggle for power between King and Parliament. Finally James II had been driven into exile and his daughter Mary, with her Dutch husband, though himself of Stuart blood, had become Queen and King by the will of the Convention Parliament. The so called 'Revolutionary Settlement' which followed, as embodied in the Bill of Rights, was essentially negative. It merely laid down a list of expedients which any monarch struggling to strengthen the executive might no longer employ. Political stability seemed as far off as ever.

Clashes over religion continued after 1660 as Anglicans struggled to avenge the treatment meted out to them during the Interregnum by the triumphant Dissenters, who now in their turn were fighting for survival. The tug of war between King and Parliament remained unresolved. Meanwhile a new dimension was given to the clash of opinion by a marked increase in the politically conscious section of the nation. The population was growing, though anything like statistical proof is lacking and, which is perhaps even more important, this increase was accompanied by an expanding trade and flourishing agriculture which in turn was swelling the numbers of the middling sort, merchants, middlemen, prosperous artisans, all types that had been encouraged to think for themselves during the upheavals of the century. In the boroughs in particular, but in the counties also, these men were creating a new as well as a more numerous electorate which, because of the tendency during the Interregnum to widen the franchise in the boroughs, combined with the growth in the numbers of the forty-shilling freeholders in the counties due to the fall in the value of money, may have amounted to some one-thirtieth of the population. This introduced a new element into English political life. Whoever wanted to control Parliament within the framework of law, whether it were the monarch or the aristocracy, must first win the support of this electorate. Two factors, namely the existence of issues about which men cared deeply and the existence of an electorate that held the key to power, namely the selection of members of the House of Commons, combined to create a situation very favourable to the fostering of political parties.

Once the euphoria of the Restoration had evaporated, therefore, Charles II could no longer depend on a complaisant Parliament. In the Commons cleavages appeared. Office holders and their friends, or members who had a reasonable chance of profiting by government influence, could be depended upon to give a general support to the ministers of the Crown and, since the Restoration, had often been known as the 'Court Party'. In contrast the 'Country Party' was composed of two different types of members. The majority of them were not so much antagonistic to the Court as independent of it.[1] These members were the country gentlemen, who sat for the counties, or represented boroughs which they or their friends controlled. They were often critical of ministerial policy, especially when it involved heavy spending, but they were not generally unfriendly. They were however the raw material out of which more active and hostile politicians might hope to create an anti-ministerial

---

[1] Sir Lewis B. Namier, *Monarchy and the Party System* (1952), points out that 'not playing for office, they were not bound to factions', and that to have accepted it would, as a rule, have destroyed their local standing (p. 17).

group as their special *bêtes noires* were extravagance and corruption. Active and hostile politicians were also to be found in the ranks of the Country Party. They were the ambitious, the disappointed, the greedy for office who saw that their best chance for getting it lay in making a nuisance of themselves by criticism, and often by mis-representation, that might lead to an anti-ministerial revolt among the country gentlemen.[1]

Despite the skill with which Lord Danby strove to build up a solid group of 'King's Friends' Charles found his 'faithful Commons' difficult to handle, but it was the conflict over the proposal to exclude the Roman Catholic Duke of York from the throne which finally divided both Parliament and the electorate into two bitterly opposed factions, labelling them with the names by which hereafter they were to be known throughout the eighteenth century. The petitioners in favour of exclusion were nicknamed 'whigs', the abhorrers of such exclusion, 'tories'. By the death of Queen Anne in 1714 the rivalry between them had come to dominate both political and social life. Whigs and tories moved in separate sets, frequented different coffee houses, patronized different clubs, while rival presses poured out a stream of propaganda pamphlets and news sheets in an attempt to win over what today would be described as 'the floating voter'.

It is a truism that in essence politics are concerned with the struggle for power. Before the Revolution the issue had been whether Parliament should be controlled by the aristocracy and landed gentry, in order to protect their own social and economic interests, in other words to shape society to their liking, or by the King in the interests of the executive. Temporary victory had gone to the Crown which had used it to decrease and curb the power of the new elector-ate by remodelling borough charters in order to make them more amenable to government pressure. With this end in view men on whom the King could not rely were dismissed from key local offices. The result was bitter local resentment and the Revolution had been used to reverse this process. After 1688 the fiercest electoral battles had been between whig and tory, each struggling to get a grip on the Commons which in turn would secure the solid fruits of power, pickings, places and patronage and commercial advantages

---

[1] For full and stimulating analyses of the political situation between 1688–1725 see J. H. Plumb, *The Growth of Political Stability in England, 1688–1725* (1967), and G. Holmes, *Politics in the Age of Queen Anne* (1967). Both are indispensable for this period, and the following pages have been largely based on these two works.

for their adherents. Opportunities for conflict increased still further when the whigs forced William III to concede the Triennial bill, by which no Parliament could last for more than three years. Between 1688 and 1714 there were twelve general elections. In the rest of the century there were only thirteen.

The result seemed to be an almost inbuilt instability in the political life of the nation because neither party was able to dominate Parliament for long enough to give the Crown a sufficiently firm base for its policy. Yet somehow the monarch, as head of the executive, had to continue to finance and run a major war, first against France and later against both France and Spain. This resulted in the necessity of a balancing act. The close links between the executive and the legislature were only as yet in the process of formation and though probably fundamentally strong enough under William III to do so, the Crown had not yet built up a strong and reliable body of supporters who would put loyalty to the King above loyalty to party. This meant that William III, and afterwards Anne, though to a lesser extent, had to work with whichever party seemed at the moment strong enough to support the royal policy in Parliament. As the electoral fortunes of whigs and tories fluctuated, or as leading politicians changed sides, the Crown had to give office and show favour to each in turn. When the parties were evenly balanced coalitions were inevitable. At first, hampered by the backlash of the Revolutionary Settlement, William III, conscious of how little he could rely on personal popularity or loyalty, was hesitant to use the very considerable influence which the control of patronage gave to the Crown. By the accession of Anne the situation was changing in her favour. To run successfully a war on the scale of that on which Britain had embarked in 1701 meant building up a new administrative machine. The consequent expansion of the Treasury, the army and the navy had greatly increased the patronage at the disposal of the Crown; so did the growth in the personnel of the Customs and Excise, which had to administer a host of new taxes imposed to finance the war. These were the spoils for which the parties fought; these were the lures which the Crown could use to bind men to the executive.

With this changing situation the parties also were changing. Originally the whigs had been the anti-court faction. By tradition they were highly suspicious of the autocratic power of France, full of fears that Charles II was aiming at a similar regime in Britain; they were deeply Protestant, tender towards Dissent, anxious to clip the power of the executive and to secure the independence of Parliament from the royal control. In contrast the tories had supported, at least to some degree, the theories of divine right; they were less prepared to challenge the prerogative, though loyal Anglicans they were less suspicious of the Stuart penchant towards Rome. Nevertheless, widely though the members of Parliament differed in their political philosophy, socially they were a homogeneous body, deeply devoted to property rights, whether these took the form of land, or office or privilege. Fundamentally they were committed to upholding the Protestant religion. When therefore James II removed respected local persons from office and reshaped the borough charters he outraged these basic tenets and the propertied classes closed their ranks and ignored those aspects of their political creeds which dictated a blind loyalty. After the Revolution, therefore, though party conflict remained, the issues over which they fought had altered with the altered circumstances. Political life was now dominated by almost continuous years of war, broken only by the uneasy peace that followed Ryswick. During Anne's reign the whigs became identified with the policy of continuing the war until Philip V had been driven from the throne of Spain, whereas the tories began to press for the conclusion of peace. Being committed to the war transformed the old whig party. To wage such a war successfully the executive had to be able to control Parliament and to develop a partnership with the major financial and commercial interests. Broadly speaking this was a policy that appealed to the wealthy, the powerful and the self-confident, and to their followers, offering as it did all the power and pickings that went with the control of the wartime establishment. But to the smaller landed gentry war brought more kicks than halfpence. Taxation was a heavy burden and their chances of competing with the wealthy for the favours of government became less as these became more and more worth having. Because a seat in the Commons was the key to advancement the competition at elections became more frantic and more expensive, so that a man of moderate fortune could no longer afford to fight one. Yet while the war continued there seemed little chance of curbing the executive in favour of a House of Commons devoted to defending their traditional interests.

Nevertheless to describe the whigs as the war party and the tories as the peace party is to oversimplify the situation. English political life was lived on two levels, the national and the local; for many people the local was the more important. The struggle for power within a county or a borough could be exceedingly fierce when, like the Montagues and Capulets, rival families fought for domination. When families fought an election they fought as local rivals, not as whigs or tories in the sense of being concerned with national issues. It was sufficient for one to be a tory for the other to fight under the whig banner. The fight was about power not policy. Nevertheless though local politics explain local politics more accurately than party labels the latter were still meaningful, particularly with regard to the problem of the succession on the death of Anne who, after Gloucester's death, had no heir to succeed her. The whigs were stoutly Protestant and firm for the Hanoverian succession, the tories, though equally determined to defend the established church, looked more favourably on the pretensions of the Old Pretender, provided his succession did not imperil the Protestant religion. To have the support of the Crown was to wield power and to enjoy all its fruits; and that each party should have its own candidate for the throne is easily understood. There was, however, rather more than a mere struggle for power to characterize the two parties; they looked to a different path of constitutional development. The whigs now wanted a closely integrated relationship with the Crown based on the acceptance of aristocratic domination. The tories, reversing their previous role, aimed at securing the freedom of Parliament from executive control in the interests of the landed gentry. They resented the power of the aristocracy and the political corruption and jobbery of which they felt themselves to be the victims. Whigs on the other hand had no objection to a strong executive so long as they could control it. Whigs and tories therefore had pretty clearly defined attitudes, though the use of the word 'party' to describe them may seem premature when compared with the tight organization of the modern parliamentary party. There were no whips, no Central Office, rarely a recognized party leader. Nevertheless it is the opinion of a distinguished modern historian that 'however much their methods of organization may have lacked the normal manifestations, the professionalism and some of the accepted techniques of a modern party machine, they were frequently flexible enough, and at times rigorous enough, for the purposes for which they were designed.'[1]

Until the death of Anne party rivalries continued with undiminished bitterness. For the last years of her reign the tories had the

[1] G. Holmes, *op. cit.*, p. 321.

better of the conflict. They enjoyed the personal support of the Queen; peace was popular with the country gentry; the trial of Dr. Sacheverell illustrated the almost hysterical support for the High Church party. Yet within ten years all was changed. There was a new dynasty; the whigs dominated politics to such an extent that for forty years Britain was to enjoy the placidity of a one party state; the conditions of political life had been transformed as party rivalries gave place to managed Parliaments. In this change fortune favoured the whigs but it was not to fortune alone that they owed their success. From the days of the Junto they had stood firm behind the Hanoverian succession and had shown themselves capable of a solidity of action that had increased rather than been broken by their late reverses. Among their numbers they had some excellent politicians who had grasped the principle that if they did not hang together they would hang separately. The tories too included in their ranks some brilliant men; Harley was an able politician, Bolingbroke intelligent and ambitious. But the rivalry between them came to a head too late for either of them to take effective action on Anne's death. Nor did the tories speak with a united voice. To many of them the Old Pretender, if he could be persuaded to renounce the Roman faith, was more attractive than the whig candidate, the Elector of Hanover. The result of this flirtation, combined with the support of the Crown, and the expertise of whig politicians, such as Robert Walpole, was to besmirch the tories as Jacobites. As a result the next ten years were to witness the elimination of the tories as a practical fighting force, and the establishment of what was in effect a whig one party state.

This led to considerable changes in political life. The King and the whig magnates now worked together to control and manage Parliament but, because there was never enough pasture for the sheep, never enough offices, places and pensions for all the ambitious, politically minded whigs, they too split into factions, rather like rival clans fighting for the booty of office, rather than for any clearly expressed principles, which were in fact no longer an issue. If to the ministers of the day the challenge from any one group seemed dangerous the normal practice was to buy them off with office. Gradually therefore a new pattern of parliamentary management established itself as normal. The Crown had much to give: it need not appeal empty-handed to the loyalty of either the peers or its faithful Commons. The use of patronage in this way had much to justify it.

The Crown needed servants to administer its affairs. Until the death of Anne there was nothing to prevent a man from being both an M.P. and what to-day we should describe as a civil servant rather than a politician. In the House of Commons of 1701 there were eight men holding high and responsible office and twenty-five more who were all but full-time administrators. To these must be added men who held legal positions, or were military governors of garrison towns, together with all those who held household posts or sinecures or who received pensions. In all, the office holders in the Commons in 1701 totalled 113[1]—quite a sizeable group out of 513, though nowhere near a majority. All of them had an interest in maintaining those ministers who had been responsible for their appointment. In many cases they owed their seats in the House to the influence exerted locally by some government department; there were boroughs near dockyards or garrison towns where the administration was strong enough to return the candidate of its choice. With the accession of George I the clause in the Act of Settlement, originally intended to exclude placemen from the House of Commons, and modified in 1705 so as to permit a wide range of office holders to stand for re-election, made the position of the placeman in the Commons a little more difficult, or rather more expensive. It was generally understood that such placemen would support any minister who had the confidence of the Crown. This was not mere subservience: it was to their interest that administration should be supported so that the King's government, of which they were a part, should be carried on as smoothly as possible.

The placemen in themselves were not, however, numerous enough to give ministers sufficient support. In order to reinforce them, therefore, the usual procedure was to attach two or three groups of active politicians to the administration by giving office to their more important members. A detailed study of the political life of the entire century illustrates how much of the business of politics actually turned on just how little a particular group would accept in the shape of office, titles, sinecures or pensions in return for its support. Such negotiations if successful would give the ministers a very solid nucleus, though still not a majority. There were never enough distributable favours to do this. Such deals both bought off dangerous opponents and supplied useful speakers and henchmen. But for their majority every administration had to rely on

[1] R. Walcott, *op. cit.*, p. 171.

winning the support of the independent members. Most men, at least in theory, were willing to give a general support to ministers who had the confidence of the Crown. But this could never be taken for granted. Ministers might induce the solid block of merchants to support them by a careful attention to the welfare of British trade. The country gentlemen were always very sensitive to changes in the Land Tax. When Anne died no one could describe her House of Commons as a rubber stamp assembly. If carefully managed, if pressure was kept on the placemen to secure not only their votes but those of their friends or relations, if the most powerful groups, or a large enough selection and combination of lesser connections, were admitted to office, and if skill were used in handling the independent members, then all would be well. But none of these things by itself would suffice. Ministers had to argue, persuade and convince as well as manage the members. It is a commonplace that eighteenth-century administrations did not lose their elections; it is sometimes forgotten how often they were defeated in the lobbies. No one who has studied the fight put up by Walpole in the chaos that followed the collapse of the South Sea Bubble will suppose that government influence invariably secured a smooth passage for ministerial policy.

4. THE PRESS

In this struggle for power the press played a considerable part.[1] In 1702 London got its first regular daily paper, *The Daily Courant* followed in 1706 by *The Evening Post*. Social conditions encouraged these new ventures, particularly in London, where men with similar interests met regularly in coffee houses to discuss the news of the day. For many this was a necessary ingredient in business success: war and peace, the rise and fall of stocks, the safe arrival of shipping concerned them deeply. For others, politics with its rumours, its scandals, its hints of intrigue was part hobby and part an opportunity for profit, through the securing of contracts, the floating of loans, the giving of places. There was in addition a demand for information for its own sake, information that ranged from sound antiquarianism and scientific experiment to the relation of the bizarre and the incredible. This appetite for the printed word was

[1] See L. Hanson, *The Government and the Press* (1936), and for the later part of the eighteenth century I. R. Christie, *Myth and Reality: The British Newspaper in the later Georgian Age* (1970).

almost inevitably exploited by the political journalist. His main instruments were the weekly or monthly news-sheets, and the pamphlet on any topic that had temporarily captured public attention. In them truth was often subordinated to creating interest or belittling an opponent, and these verbal duels, as pamphlet answered pamphlet, were as bitter as, and often more deadly than, those which were fought with pistol and steel. Not infrequently indeed one led to the other. Over the century the number of these pamphlets was enormous and their range very varied. The agricultural crank with a theory to expound, an industrialist hunting concessions, the merchant intent on the remission of a duty or the securing of a protected market, the politician anxious to pull down a rival, all wrote, or hired hacks to write, a suitable pamphlet. Most of them were written under fictitious names drawn from the classics or the armoury of patriotism: Catos and True-born Englishmen abound. This was in part because such work was considered somewhat disreputable, though men of the calibre of Dean Swift and Dr. Johnson occasionally used their talents in this way.

With the appearance of *The Tatler* in 1709 the periodical essay became one of the favourite literary vehicles of the century. Not all of them were political; both *The Tatler* and *The Spectator* aimed at entertainment and edification; but by the accession of George I many of them exhibited a consistent pro- or anti- ministerial bias. There was still much anti-Hanoverian feeling in the country and periodicals such as *Mist's Weekly Journal* made a practice of recording every scrap of scandal that reflected unfavourably on the Court. The influence of such periodicals was not confined to London. In August 1721 it was reported that in Warwick and Coventry 'In every Alehouse People have the London Journal in their Hands, shewing to each other with a kind of Joy, the most audacious Reflections therein contained'.[1] *The London Journal* was at this time actively engaged in attacking the administration for its handling of the South Sea Bubble crisis, though in 1722 Walpole apparently bought control over it and used it to defend government policy. Such victories were only temporary. All administrations were forced to defend themselves by seizing the offending journals and

[1] C. B. Realey, 'The London Journal: Its Authors', *Bulletin of the University of Kansas Humanistic Studies*, vol. 5, no. 3, (1935), p. 10.

prosecuting their printers and publishers for seditious libel, or by subsidizing rival journals to refute the charges of their opponents. That this was considered necessary is interesting. With so small an electorate, and one moreover that was highly susceptible to management, it is difficult to assess the importance of extra-parliamentary public opinion on the shaping of policy and the position of ministers. By itself a smear campaign, however skilful, was powerless to pull down a minister in whom the King had confidence, but in conjunction with an unsuccessful policy it could be dangerous. *The Craftsman* undoubtedly contributed to the unpopularity of Walpole, as did *The North Briton* to that of Lord Bute, and *The Letters of Junius* to that of the Duke of Grafton. Throughout the century ministers showed themselves particularly sensitive to this kind of attack and an account of the conditions of political life that ignored their existence would be incomplete; though in themselves few merit any special study or even mention, in the day-to-day struggles of political life they must never be forgotten.

5. LOCAL GOVERNMENT

It would be even more misleading to ignore the importance of local government.[1] In 1714 England was in a very limited sense a nation. To many men what happened within their own county and their own town was of much greater importance than what happened at Westminster. This in turn reacted on national politics and ministerial strategy. Each county had its quota of families whose local influence was considerable and between whom ancient feuds had produced long traditions of rivalry. Because of this, men who had no ambition to play an active part in national politics yet considered it a very great honour to represent their county at Westminster. The main field of their activities lay however in local government. Here a sharp distinction must be drawn between that of the towns and that of the countryside. In the latter the gentry were supreme. At their head stood the Lord Lieutenant of the County, who was normally a peer, and whose business it was politically to exercise his local influence in support of government. As however the royal choice was by normal usage limited to a few

---

[1] See Sir David L. Keir, *The Constitutional History of Modern Britain 1485–1950* (1953) pp. 312–15. I. R. Christie, *op. cit.*, points out that in a society where there were ample opportunities for political criticism government could never operate in a closed circle of immunity.

great families in each county, it was not always possible to confer this honour on a friend of the administration. Very occasionally a Lord Lieutenant who had identified himself with a factious opposition was removed for political reasons as a sign of the King's displeasure, but this was not the normal practice. The main responsibility both for administration and 'the punishment of wickedness and vice' lay with the Justices of the Peace. They were appointed from among the leading gentry of the county by the Crown, usually on the recommendation of the Lord Lieutenant, and endowed by virtue of their commission with extensive administrative and judicial powers.

The full weight of their authority was exercised at Quarter Sessions. Here county rates were levied, parishes were presented for nuisances (such as failing to keep their roads in repair), settlement cases tried, regulations made for the holding of markets, and action taken on the hundred-and-one problems of local government. Its judicial power was almost as extensive. By their commission they could try all crimes and felonies except treason, though in practice offences which involved the death penalty were remitted to the Assizes. Between the meetings of Quarter Sessions individual Justices, either acting alone or—in rather more serious matters— with a fellow Justice, played a large part in the affairs of their own divisions. These activities ranged from the punishment of petty crime to the authorizing of parish rates, and the appointment of the Overseers of the Poor. Within the orbit of his influence the Justice was responsible for order; it was he who had the occasionally dangerous task of reading the Riot Act to unruly mobs, requiring them to disperse. He had to examine suspicious characters, and issue warrants of removal for persons 'likely to become chargeable to the parish from which they had come'. In his own area he was the local autocrat, benevolent or bullying according to his temperament; for though his powers were strictly limited by law, reinforced as they were by the possession of property and by social prestige, few men were prepared to challenge them. That men with so much power should be politically reliable was highly desirable. When George I became King the names of many men whose sympathies were known to lie with the old régime were struck out of the commission, and until 1760 the tory gentry complained bitterly that they were denied their legitimate place in the control of county business.

Urban local government was less uniform, though most towns fall into one of two categories, those with charters and those without. Most towns of ancient origin belong to the first, others which, like Birmingham and Manchester, grew into importance only with the growth of late seventeenth- and eighteenth-century industry, to the latter. In the former, administration was in the hands of a mayor and corporation and only their freemen enjoyed full rights of citizens; many of them also had the right to return two Members to Parliament. Such towns were separate civil entities, where civil and criminal jurisdiction within their boundaries was exercised by specially appointed Justices of the Peace with the Recorder at their head. Within this general pattern there was much variation of detail, both in the selection of the corporation, in its rights and obligations and in the position of its freemen: variations which we have already seen reflected in their parliamentary franchise. The position of the non-corporate towns was very different. Manchester in the eyes of the law was no more than a village, coming like other villages under the jurisdiction of the Quarter Sessions for the county and dependent on the officials of the manorial Court for the regulation of its local affairs. Such towns were dependent on the local magistrates, the nearest of whom might be some miles away, for the maintenance of order and for the supervision of their poor relief, and on the member either for the county or for some nearby borough to represent their economic interests in the House of Commons. There were, however, some counterbalancing advantages in that the inhabitants of such towns were free to develop their economic resources unhampered by the monopolistic privileges of the freeman. New industries, therefore, were likely to be attracted to them, with the result that by the end of the eighteenth century some of the most important centres of industry and population were to be found among their number. This in turn meant that parliamentary representation became less and less in line with economic realities, which in turn helped to produce a clamour for reform which finally found expression in the Reform Act of 1832.

In the first half of the eighteenth century this dichotomy of national and local government worked reasonably well because it still accorded with the economic and social framework of the country. In the absence of good communications and a large and well-trained civil service, the responsibility of local magnates for local concerns was a reasonable solution. Later, under the pressure of a growing population and the increasing complexity of economic and social changes, it was to prove less satisfactory. By the end of the century it was not working well and it was clear that, like the national government, it was in need of substantial reform. While, however, ministers were dependent for their parliamentary support on an unreformed House of Commons they were well aware that they could never venture to disregard local politics, for it was on them that their majorities in that House so often depended.[1] Though the direct control of the central administration over local government might appear slight, the interaction between them often holds the key to the understanding of much of the political manœuvring of the period. It is to the story of this that we must now turn.

[1] See E. N. Williams, *The Eighteenth Century Constitution* (1960), for stimulating comments on the various aspects of local government (pp. 256–8).

3

THE SECURING OF THE DYNASTY

1. THE RECONSTRUCTION OF THE ADMINISTRATION

THE accession of George I was bound to alter the conditions of political life profoundly. This was more immediately apparent with regard to persons than institutions. When, at the Privy Council on 30 May, Bolingbroke, fresh from his victory over Oxford on the 27th, made no protest at the offer of the coveted Lord Treasurer's staff to Shrewsbury, it was clear that the day of those politicians who had held power during the last years of Anne's reign was over. Immediately on her death the Council of Regency, which had been provided for by the Act of 1706, took over responsibility for the affairs of the country until George I could arrive from Hanover. By its provisions the seven great officers of State were included, but it was significant for the future shift of political power that the eighteen members named by the Elector were all men who had either long paid ostentatious court to Hanover, or had been opposed to the making of the Peace of Utrecht. It was on this ground that Lord Nottingham, who must be regarded as a tory if he is to be classified by his almost fanatical devotion to the High Church party, was included. Rather surprisingly Marlborough, who had been bitterly opposed to the peace, and who had found it pleasanter to live in exile than to stay in an England dominated by Oxford and Bolingbroke, was not included. Perhaps his reputation for intrigue with the Old Pretender, and his great influence with the army, made him seem a dangerous choice at a time when anything might have happened. Sunderland was similarly omitted: so was Lord Somers. On the other hand the Earl of Anglesea, who represented the Hanoverian tories, was given a place. Loyalty to the idea of the

Hanoverian succession, and soundness on the question of the peace of Utrecht had obviously been the deciding factors: for these more whigs than tories qualified, but there was as yet no rigid determination to exclude everybody who could be considered a tory. So far, then, the Hanoverian tories had a modest hope that their unpopular foreign policy might be overlooked in view of their undoubted loyalty to the Protestant Succession as fixed by the Act of Settlement.

Much would depend on the new ministerial appointments. Only in the case of Bolingbroke did the Council of Regency make drastic changes before the arrival of the King. But in his case George I was disinclined to leave a man so tangled up with the Old Pretender and the French alliance as Secretary of State. The other ministers—even the other Secretary, Bromley, and the Lord Chancellor, Lord Harcourt, though the loyalty of both was suspect—were allowed to continue in office for the time being. George I's arrival was to be the signal for a major reconstruction of the ministry, but the vital decisions had been taken before. The new King was not unfamiliar with the personalities of British political life. During the later years of Anne's reign there had been a steady stream of discontented whigs to the Electoral Court. More important still was the knowledge gained by Bothmer,[1] the Hanoverian envoy in London, because to him had fallen the task of attempting to organize the whig resistance to the hated Treaty of Utrecht. As a result he had a first-class knowledge of the men who were now clamouring for office. Most of them realized the extent of Bothmer's influence. Later many of them came to resent the way in which he interfered in British politics, but while he was the channel through which their hopes, ambitions and protestations of loyalty must be conveyed to George I, politicians competed anxiously for his favour. It was not only whigs who had contacts with him. Lord Nottingham, whose resistance in the Lords to the Treaty of Utrecht had allied him with the malcontents, was also ready with his plans and advice.

As Bothmer was a shrewd judge of both the men and the situation, George I's first ministers were well chosen. Lord Cowper, one of the few whigs Anne had seen go with regret in 1710, and an able lawyer, again became Lord Chancellor. Lord Halifax became First Lord of the Treasury. He was a competent financier and had had

[1] W. Michael, *op. cit.*, pp. 104-5.

close connections with the Hanoverian envoys in London, but he felt that merely to be appointed First Lord instead of Lord High Treasurer, was to give him less than his due. Even the grant of an earldom and the Garter left him touchy and difficult, and political life became easier when he died in 1715. Most of the prominent men who had supported the continuance of the late war came back. Edward Russell, created Earl of Orford by William III, became First Lord of the Admiralty. The Marquis of Wharton got the Privy Seal, Shrewsbury, who had resigned the Treasurer's staff in October, retained his office of Lord Chamberlain. Lord Somers, too frail now for active office, was summoned to Cabinet meetings. Marlborough was reinstated as Commander-in-Chief, but, with no war to fight, his days of great influence were over. The fact that Nottingham became Lord President of the Council showed that at first George I had no intention of choosing his ministers only from the whigs. These men were, however, very much the old guard: in a few years most of them were dead.

More interesting from the point of view of the future were the appointments of the new Secretaries of State. Standing highest in the royal favour was Charles, Viscount Townshend, who became responsible for the Northern Department. His previous career had not been outstanding but his obstinate, unimaginative bargaining with Louis XIV during the Gertruydenberg negotiations had been in line with the Elector's own views. In other respects he had much to recommend him. He came from an old Norfolk family, and after the Restoration his father had been created a peer. In addition, since the death of the Duke of Norfolk in 1701 he had been Lord Lieutenant of that county, a fact that gave him considerable parliamentary influence. On the personal side he had some attractive qualities. He was loyal to his family and his friends, his standard of morality, both with regard to women and the pickings of office, was high. In public business he was hard-working and efficient. Unfortunately he was also proud, quick-tempered and inclined to hasty, angry speeches. He was also very obstinate in his opinions, and without the fluidity of approach that diplomatic situations at times demand.

These defects might have been of less importance if he had been in sole command of foreign policy. But the Secretary for the Southern Department, responsible for France, Spain, Portugal, Italy, Turkey, Ireland and the colonies was no nonentity. James Stanhope was one of the most interesting of the new ministers.[1] He was in his early forties, and had already a distinguished military career behind him, gained in that most heartbreaking of all the campaigns of the late war, Spain. At first glance the choice of a general might seem a little unusual for the Secretaryship, but Stanhope was a man of many parts. He had as wide a knowledge of international affairs as any politician in England. Because his father had been ambassador first at The Hague and then at Madrid he had had the advantage of long periods of residence abroad and spoke fluent Spanish and French. In addition he had wit and personal charm, except in moments of exasperation, when his manner became hard and overbearing. Such qualities, when combined with considerable intellectual power and a willingness to take responsibility, made him a formidable colleague. In conjunction with Townshend's obstinate and touchy nature, particularly as the latter regarded him as a comparative newcomer to the world of diplomacy, Stanhope's temperament and high abilities were not likely to make for a smooth partnership.

Other important offices went to men who were soon to cut great figures in the political world. One of these was Robert Walpole the new Paymaster-General.[2] His political record from the Hanoverian point of view had always been sound. While General Stanhope had been winning the battle of Saragossa in Spain Walpole had been Secretary at War. When Harley and St John won the Queen's confidence for their peace policy, Walpole, who had opposed them, lost first this office, then the Treasurership of the Navy, which he had also held. Finally, to put him out of political action, he had been expelled from the Commons, now controlled by his enemies, and committed to the Tower on a charge of peculation. In handling public money Walpole was no more scrupulous than his contemporaries, but in this case the verdict had been a purely political one. There is no evidence that as Secretary at War he had gone beyond the lax standards of his day. He had suffered because he had supported the war and been an unwavering Hanoverian: now his reward had come. His abilities were greater than

---

[1] See A. F. B. Williams, *Stanhope, A Study in Eighteenth Century War and Diplomacy* 1932), for details of his previous career.

[2] Later Lord Hervey wrote of him: 'He had a strength of parts equal to any advancement, a spirit to struggle with any difficulties, a steadiness of temper immovable by any disappointment.'—John, Lord Hervey, *Some Materials towards Memoirs of the Reign of King George II*, ed. R. R. Sedgwick (1931), vol. I, p. 17.

those of Townshend,[1] with whom his connection was close: the latter had been the ward of Walpole's father, and later was to marry as his second wife Walpole's favourite sister Dorothy, but his social position was less. The Walpoles, like the Townshends, were an old Norfolk family but unlike them had not yet moved out of the country gentleman class. When his father died in 1700 Walpole had inherited an estate worth some £2,000 per annum gross (though there were many charges on it) and the right to the nomination to the seat of Castle Rising, which his father had represented. His fortune, though ample for that of a private member, was by the eighteenth-century standards an inadequate foundation for a great political career. But from the beginning Walpole was to show that ambition and a love of power were two of his most prominent characteristics. With the aid of Townshend he had rapidly made connections with the whig politicians of his day, Lord Orford in particular proving himself a useful friend. By spending far beyond his income, by his ability to be a good companion, and by his capacity for hard work and affairs, he had won the right to be considered one of the most promising of the younger politicians. In 1714 he was in his late thirties. Why then did he merely receive the office of Pay-master-General?[2] The reasons were various. That he was not a peer had some influence, though this had not prevented General Stanhope from being made Secretary. That he was away in Norfolk when the spoils were being distributed may have had something to do with it, especially when so many places had to be found for so many faithful supporters of the House of Hanover. Also he was not really popular: in spite of his cheerful bonhomie, the lust for power that underlay his actions, and the success that he had, how-ever briefly, obtained between 1700 and 1710, had made many people jealous of this jumped-up Norfolk squire. It is possible, however, that he was well content with his new appointment. The fortune which he seems to have accumulated from his previous term of office had been dissipated by his years in opposition and by his defiant refusal to adjust his expenditure to his modest fortune. By 1714 his finances were in an embarrassed state. The Pay Office carried with it many chances of making money and considerable patronage. His friendship with Townshend gave him ample oppor-tunity to get near to the heart of government, so his love of power

---

[1] For details of Walpole's early career consult J. H. Plumb, *Walpole*, vol. I (1956).
[2] *Ibid.*, p. 204.

was in no real sense frustrated. For a time he was content to re-establish the basis of his political power in Norfolk, to make money and to wait.

In the apportioning of offices Charles, Earl of Sunderland, had a greater grievance than Robert Walpole. As the candidate of the Junto and the son-in-law of Marlborough he had been forced on Anne as her Secretary of State in 1706. Just as his appointment had marked their triumph, so his dismissal had heralded their fall in 1710. With the accession of George I he had expected to get his old office back. Instead he was offered, partly through Townshend's influence, the Lord Lieutenancy of Ireland. It is doubtful if he ever forgave the latter for this slight, for which he suspected him to have been responsible. Outwardly complying with the royal command he dallied in London, cultivating Madame Schulenberg, the royal mistress, and Bothmer, now Hanoverian minister to the Court of St. James's, Bernstorff and Robethon.[1] Though proud, arrogant, and as ambitious as Walpole himself, he was a man of considerable charm, and his attempt to win the support of this inner German Court circle was successful. When Lord Wharton the Lord Privy Seal died, Sunderland succeeded him in August 1715. By now his influence with the King was growing and a year later he was able to pay Townshend back in his own coin. For the time being however the Townshend-Walpole combination was able to hold its own, for death, by removing with impartial efficiency the Earl of Halifax, made it possible in October for Walpole to become Chancellor of the Exchequer and First Lord of the Treasury. Of the less important offices William Pulteney, as yet Walpole's friend though later to be his enemy, became Secretary at War. Aislabie—pushing, ambitious, but basically stupid and to be deeply involved in the scandal of the South Sea Bubble—became the new Treasurer of the Navy.[2]

2. PROBLEMS OF THE NEW REIGN

With the removal by death of the older statesmen four men —Townshend, Stanhope, Walpole and Sunderland—became the nucleus of the administration. Though George I's accession had been

---

1 Count Bernstorff had entered the service of the Elector in 1705 and acquired great influence over him. Jean Robethon had left France after the repeal of the Edict of Nantes, and became private secretary to William III. After his death Robethon became connected with Bernstorff and became private secretary to the Elector in 1705.

2 John Carswell, *The South Sea Bubble* (1960), p. 50.

unexpectedly peaceful, intelligent men must have known that there
were many difficulties ahead. The warm welcome given to the new
King when he reached England at the end of September was com-
pounded of the relief that civil strife had been avoided, the excitement of a new reign, with its hidden prospects and promises for
every individual in touch with the Court, and the love of the people
of London for any kind of spectacle. But even during the elections
for the new Parliament, which met in March 1715, there were
riotous meetings and threatening incidents, which showed that
material existed for a pro-Jacobite campaign. To this the personality
as well as the nationality of the King undoubtedly contributed.
Foreign rulers have never been popular in England and the foreign-
ness of George I was all too obvious. For the popularity of the new
dynasty it was unfortunate that Anne had managed to survive by a
few months the Electress Sophia. Unlike her son, Sophia had a
vivacious personality and a sense of the dramatic. Even at eighty-
four she would have been a colourful Queen, a Queen moreover
who could and would have str:ssed her Englishness. Her command
of the language, which she had spoken since a child, was fluent,
whereas her son never achieved more than a smattering.[1] To the
end of his reign important documents had to be translated into
French for him. Had she reigned even for a few years she might have
collected a little popularity for her dynasty.

George I had none: it would have been difficult even for the
modern propagandist press to have built him up as a figure of
romance. Even his two official mistresses were unattractive and
greedy. Probably too much should not be made of his failure to
master English. French was still the language of diplomacy, and
most peers and ambitious politicians had a working knowledge of it.
It was his personal behaviour that was responsible for the lack of
enthusiasm for him felt by most English people. The royal levees
were no longer occasions: he had no taste for dressing in public. He
preferred a quiet game of cards, or a visit to the opera or the theatre
with a few friends, to public hospitality and display. People felt
cheated of the pageantry of monarchy.

But the problems presented by his un-Englishness went deeper
than mere trivialities. The men in his inner confidence were Hanoverians not Englishmen. The Act of Settlement had tried to guard
against this by the proviso that no foreign-born person 'shall be

[1] W. Michael, *op. cit.*, p. 114.

capable to be of the Privy Council or a Member of either House of Parliament or to enjoy any office or place of trust either civil or military'. But no statute could prevent the King from discussing what he would with whom he would. Nor could reasonable objections be made to the presence of Hanoverians at his Court. George I of England was still the Elector George Lewis of Hanover, and it is significant that in his Electorate he remained George Lewis. He was not any the less the Elector because he was now also a King. As Elector he was entitled to have his Hanoverian ministers, such as Bernstorff, in attendance. In the same way he took an English minister with him on his visits to Hanover. In his double capacity Bothmer could even be accredited as the Hanoverian agent of George Lewis to the English Court of George I. This situation made it difficult for the English ministers to prevent the Electoral servants from meddling in English domestic affairs, for to antagonize the King was to lose Closet favour to a more tactful rival. In so far as these facts were known, or at least guessed, they could not fail to be resented. Yet there was little that could be done, and the clue to the changing fortunes of ministers in the years 1715–22 is often to be found in the inter-relationships between them and the Hanoverians.

If Hanoverians interfering in British politics was a problem, the link between the two countries was an even greater one. That George I should hope to use the resources of the King of England to help the Elector of Hanover was inevitable. To some extent it was even possible to argue that the two countries had much in common. Throughout William III's reign, and for much of Anne's, England's traditional alliances had been with the United Provinces and the Empire against France. There was still plenty of support for a return to that policy. As the Elector had also supported the Emperor, in their main outlines the foreign policies of both countries were not incompatible. Unfortunately in detail and in timing this harmony was often less. There were occasions when the friendship of France seemed more attractive than that of the Emperor and trading interests in Spain of much greater importance than those concerned with the German markets. In consequence English ministers were constantly in a quandary. Even the suspicion that British resources were being used to further Hanoverian ends was enough to cause an angry debate to flare up in the Commons. Country gentlemen were not prepared to risk an increase in the

Land Tax for so alien a purpose. Yet unless the House of Commons could be either hoodwinked or cajoled, the necessary funds for the army and the navy, on which in the end all foreign policy depended, would not be forthcoming. This was something which George I found very difficult to understand, and which he resented when he did. It was not his idea of loyalty to a King: it was not the way things were done in Hanover. English ministers, well aware of these difficulties, were forced to be cautious. Often they were driven to badger and argue and persuade, or to stonewall, until the King and his Hanoverian advisers began to wonder whether another group might not be more pliant. In this way the interests of Hanover led to interference in purely English ministerial appointments, which again caused resentment and often a fresh alignment of political groups. Thus indirectly Hanover was a further factor in the instability of English politics, at the same time providing up to the accession of George III opposition groups with an endless supply of verbal, if repetitive, material for attacks on their successful rivals.

In the first months after George I's accession, however, it was to the joint interests of Hanoverian and English ministers to act together. To Bernstorff and Bothmer and Robethon those whig politicians who had been in opposition to the possibly Jacobite ministers of Anne's last years were the only men who could be trusted with office. Naturally these men seized the opportunity to strengthen their hold as far as they could over the machinery of government, local as well as national. Probably most of the so-called tories who had supported Anne's peace policy were completely loyal to the new dynasty, but the political interests of the present administration made a purge necessary. They and their supporters had been in the wilderness too long: now offices and places held by tories were needed to reward their loyalty. But there was more to it than a simple redistribution of the spoils. The old Parliament was dissolved in January 1715 and if ministers were to secure a friendly House of Commons they could not leave their critics in key positions in local government. Cowper, Stanhope and Townshend went through list after list, studying every man's record and replacing tories by whigs. Nothing was more calculated to alienate the tory country gentry, hitherto loyal if unenthusiastic, but the ministerial strategy was immediately successful. In the new Commons they could depend on a solid majority. This was not surprising as, apart from the redistribution of offices, electors were given a strong hint as to the royal wishes. In his Proclamation calling the new Parliament George I said that he hoped they would have 'a particular regard to such as shewed a firmness to the Protestant Succession, when it was in danger'. It may be that this clear indication of the royal wishes was due to Walpole's suggestion, for as soon as the new Parliament met he showed a ruthless determination to ruin his late opponents. In the Commons, moving the address he declared the ministerial intention 'to trace out those measures wherein he [the Pretender] placed his hopes and to bring the authors of them to punishment'.[1] Such a pronouncement heralded the impeachment of the late ministers. Bolingbroke hesitated no longer. After a theatre performance on 26 March he slipped unobtrusively out of London and over to France. In reality he had little choice. True his treason might be hard to prove, but he realized that the attack on him was political not legal. He and Walpole had long been enemies. Both men must have remembered that in 1710 Walpole had been sent to the Tower on charges of peculation for which there was even less proof. Moreover, it was far from certain that France might not act as a springboard for his return, while once in the Tower he would have nothing left with which to threaten or bargain. Yet his flight could not fail to give some advantage to his enemies, for in itself it could be, and was, used as a confession of treason. Henceforth whigs, arguing fallaciously, could say, 'Bolingbroke was a traitor, but Bolingbroke was a tory, therefore all tories are traitors'. There are times when false logic can be good politics.

In April a select committee, of which Walpole was chairman, was appointed to study the evidence which had been collected on the late peace negotiations. The mere reading of this report on 9 June took five hours. For the House to digest it quickly was an obvious impossibility. It was also politically dangerous, for in places the ice was thin. Therefore on 11 June, Walpole, rejecting all opposition arguments for its fuller consideration, persuaded the Commons to vote for Stanhope's motion that Bolingbroke be impeached. Motions to impeach Oxford and Ormonde followed. Faced with this threat Ormonde too escaped to France, where he and Bolingbroke entered the service of James II's son, the Old Pretender. Oxford was tougher or more indifferent to his fate. He stayed to face impeachment and was committed to the Tower: Ormonde and Bolingbroke in their absence were attainted for treason.

---

[1] W. Michael, *op. cit.*, p. 212.

3. THE FIFTEEN

By the end of August it was clear that the administration had to face more important problems than the guilt of the late ministers, for Scotland was on the verge of revolt. The bitter discontent aroused by the late purges in tory circles now bore fruit. Without this wave of hostility and criticism it would have been more difficult for the Pretender to gather even the rudiments of an expedition against England. So far outwardly Louis XIV's position had been correct. He would have been glad to see the Stuarts restored, but not at the price of another war with England. Relations between the two countries, however, had remained strained. By the terms of the late peace treaty the defences and facilities of Dunkirk, a notorious nest of pirates and raiders, were to be destroyed, but it was known that the French were already making a new naval base at Mardyke. When the British ambassador in Paris, Lord Stair, remonstrated he was blandly told that the new work was necessary to deal with flood water. This excuse drew forth from George I the caustic comment that the only difference between Dunkirk and Mardyke was that the former had been a round and the latter would be a long harbour.

News of the general dissatisfaction in Britain now made it seem that it might not be a hopeless, or even a costly, operation to give the Pretender some substantial backing of an unofficial kind. That he had a chance, if only a gambler's chance, the action of Bolingbroke seemed to show. When he had first fled to France he had been careful not to become entangled with the Pretender, but by July he decided that James Edward's chances were good enough to risk entering his service. By then it had become clear to Lord Stair, from the attitude of the French Court towards him, that something was being planned. In this fog of uncertainty the English ministers, alarmed by Stair's report, took decisive action. In Parliament whigs and tories both proclaimed their loyalty, pledging their support for any measures that the ministers might think necessary. Fresh troops were raised; arrangements were made with the Dutch for further help if necessary; arms and horses of Roman Catholics, especially in London, were seized; from the beginning of the month an English squadron was ordered to cruise along the French coast looking out for any suspicious movement. In Scotland plotting was obviously going on, though the Earl of Mar, whose political career as Secretary

of State for Scotland had been brought to an end by the accession of George I, did not raise the standard of the Pretender at
Braemar until 6 September. Stanhope and Townshend bore the main
burden of deciding on plans to meet the threatened dangers. Whatever happened in Scotland both agreed that their first task was to
see that Jacobite supporters in England were given no chance to
organize.

While an invasion by the Pretender seemed as yet in the balance
Louis XIV died on 1 September. What effect this was likely to have
was not immediately clear. The Duke of Orleans was successful,
with the help of the Parlement of Paris, in ridding himself of the
restraints imposed upon him by the will of Louis XIV and, as Regent
for the young Louis XV, he became the effective ruler of France. If
the new King should die the nearest heir by blood was Philip V of
Spain, who had renounced his claim to the French throne by the
Treaty of Utrecht. If this treaty were strictly enforced it seemed
therefore possible that the present Regent might become the future
King of France. That Philip V would acquiesce in this arrangement
was unlikely and should he determine to renounce the Spanish
throne in favour of that of France he could be sure of the support of
a good many Frenchmen. The Regent's attitude to the Pretender
tended to be influenced therefore by two things, the strength of the
Spanish party in France and the strength of the Jacobites in England.
If George I were going to keep his throne, and if the Spanish party
were formidable, then Orleans had everything to gain by a friendship with England based on a firm adherence to the terms of the
Treaty of Utrecht. If on the other hand the Hanoverian hold was
slipping, if, with a reasonably cautious amount of aid to the Pretender, George I could be replaced by James III while the Spanish
party within France could be held in check, then the Regent could
combine his own dynastic interests with what most Frenchmen
thought was the best policy for France—namely, the subordination
of England to French influence. In these circumstances the attitude
of France was changeable and uncertain.

Apart from such encouragement and underhand help as had come
from France, the Pretender and his friends had to fight alone. The
main events of this sorry enterprise are soon told. The rift had not
yet developed which was to break the friendship between Stanhope
and Townshend, and the two Secretaries worked harmoniously,
and with great energy, together. Both were convinced that the

essential thing was to keep England quiet and so prevent any kind of outbreak which might act as a focus for armed discontent. It was not until September that the first open act of rebellion took place. Indeed, critics of the government were beginning to declare the threat of invasion a mere scare, designed to give ministers the opportunity to increase the armed forces and get rid of their political enemies. The raising of the Stuart standard by the Earl of Mar at least proved that the government was not shouting 'wolf'. The support Mar received was patchy. The Mackintosh clan seized Inverness, and most of Scotland fell to the rebels. But they were neither well led nor well armed. They failed to take Edinburgh, and such success as they had was due to the paucity of the royal troops. These were under the command of the Duke of Argyll and were concentrated on Stirling, but were too few to prevent Mar's forces from breaking through to the south. For a time therefore the stalemate continued, with Argyll in Stirling, the gateway to the south, and Mar based on Perth, the gateway to the Highlands. Somewhere in the intervening thirty miles it was clear that the deciding battle would have to be fought.

At the end of September ministers received, first from Stair and then from one of the men involved in the plot, news of an intended rising in the west. How real or serious the danger was it is impossible to say. The administration acted promptly by arresting its presumed leaders, and when Ormonde appeared off the Devon coast he did not even receive enough encouragement to induce him to land. In the north the rebellion did manage to flicker into a little precarious flame. In Northumberland, Thomas Foster, a Member of Parliament, hearing that a warrant was out for his arrest, joined with the Lords Derwentwater and Widdrington. Having raised a straggling force from their tenants and sympathizers they tried to take Newcastle, and, failing, crossed the Border to join forces with the Lords Kenmure, Carnwath and Wintoun. There was a good deal of rather aimless marching and counter-marching. Eventually Foster and his friends recrossed into north-west England, with the idea of gaining the support of the counties of Cumberland, Westmorland and Lancashire where Roman Catholics were strongest. To deal with this threat Stanhope sent two of his fellow officers from Spanish days, General Carpenter and General Wills. Between them they cornered the insurgents at Preston on 12 November and after some sharp fighting Foster surrendered next day. The leaders and some 1,600

of their followers were taken prisoner. This was the end of any
serious danger in England: ministers could now concentrate on
bringing the rebellion in Scotland to an end.

There the situation was confused. On 13 November, Argyll and
Mar fought an indecisive engagement at Sheriffmuir[1] where, to quote
a contemporary song—

> There's some say that we wan, and some say that they wan,
> And some say that nane wan at a', man:

At all events the stalemate continued, so that the Pretender when he
finally reached Scotland at the end of the year wrote to Bolingbroke,
'I find things in a prosperous way.' It was wishful thinking based on
inadequate knowledge, for by then English preparations had been
made for the kill. Cadogan was sent north with reinforcements, the
rebels were driven back to the Highlands and in February, realizing
that his presence could only ruin his supporters' remaining chance of
making terms with George I, James Edward sailed for France. By
April the last resistance had been crushed: Scotland was as quiet as
England. The rebellion of the Fifteen was over.

Though the rebellion was over its aftermath was important.
The Hanoverian dynasty had not only survived: it had tested the
very great measure of support on which it could count in the country
in spite of the personal unpopularity of the King. Men had no more
love for George I after the rebellion than before, and his eagerness to
return to his beloved Hanover, as soon as it was safe to do so, was
not likely to increase their affection for him. Even so he was preferred
to a Roman Catholic King. To some extent the failure of the exas-
perated tories to rise was due to apathy. As Stair wrote, 'There are
very few among them whose love for the Pretender goes so far as to
make them lie three nights under a hedge in November.'[2] If by
rising they could have embarrassed and overthrown the whig politicians who were monopolizing power, without jeopardizing the
Church of England, more might have been tempted to take up arms,
though some credit for maintaining almost unbroken peace in
England must be given to the effective and early measures taken by
the two Secretaries. Even so, from September 1715 to the spring of
1716 there had been danger. If France had been prepared to take a

---

[1] J. Bayne, *The Jacobite Rising of 1715* (1970), is of the opinion that more energetic
action by the Jacobites in October might have toppled the throne, but that after
Sheriffmuir the best chance of this ever happening was lost.

[2] W. Michael, *op. cit.*, p. 169.

more active part then that danger might have been great. This was something that ministers remembered. It was something that was to have a considerable influence on Anglo-French relations for the next two decades. If her success in crushing the revolt made England seem a safer ally, English ministers could not forget that an actively unfriendly France might have swung the balance the other way. An examination of Stanhope's foreign policy until his death in 1721 makes this abundantly clear.[1]

Calling for more immediate attention, however, were the political repercussions of the rebellion. The government held a good many prisoners, including most of the leaders: how were they to be treated? On this question there was considerable disagreement between those like Walpole, who favoured the death penalty for men who had deliberately upset the peace of the realm and threatened the Protestant Succession, and those like Nottingham, who favoured clemency. The latter's feelings were shared by many of the tories, who may well have felt that they 'but for the grace of God' might have found themselves in danger of the scaffold or the gibbet. This different attitude was clearly seen in the behaviour of the two Houses. In the Commons, Walpole moved the adjournment until 1 March, by which time the rebel leaders would be dead and the House be spared the pressure of the petitions for mercy that were threatening to pour in. In the Lords, Nottingham's influence was sufficient to prevent their following a similar course, and their Address petitioned for a respite and mercy for such as the King 'judged might deserve it'. Eventually only Kenmure and Derwentwater were executed: Wintoun, Nithsdale and Foster all managed to escape, the rest were reprieved. Nottingham, however, suffered for his intervention; he, his sons, and his brother Lord Aylesford all lost their places.

This was politically important. Though the whig groups had managed to collect the major offices of State, Nottingham and his friends had not been excluded, and so long as there was a solid block of Hanoverian tories in the Commons, the prospect that men with tory connections might still hope to enjoy the King's favour seemed not unlikely. Indeed, a skilful tory leader, able to gather supporters under a pledge of loyalty to George I, might come to have considerable value in his eyes. It would enlarge the groups from which ministers could be selected, and prevent the monopolizing of political power by a few aristocratic families and their friends. Of this

[1] Readers unfamiliar with the period will find an excellent introduction to the background of foreign affairs in J. H. Plumb, *Walpole*, vol. II (1960), ch. 1.

danger the present ministers were well aware. No tory leader was to be allowed to emerge: office was to be the prerogative of the whig groups. That the tories had supported the Act of Settlement, had offered no resistance to the Hanoverian succession, had backed the measures which the administration had taken to crush the late rebellion, were all ignored. Once the danger was over their petitions and speeches in favour of mercy could be used as evidence that they were a bunch of Jacobite sympathizers. In this the whig ministers were successful, indeed so successful that the possibility of a two-party system developing out of a more or less permanent alignment of the, as yet, fluid whig and tory groups was cut short.[1] In consequence, whatever meaning the term whig and tory had previously borne disappeared. Just as it was necessary for every barrister to be called to the bar before practising, so every active politician who aspired to office had to call himself a whig. For a time a residual group, under the leadership of Sir William Wyndham and William Shippen, still possessed some political importance. This was because, whatever men called themselves, the struggle for power went on as fiercely as ever. Though only whigs could now hope for office, not all whigs could achieve it: there were too many of them. Also, though Townshend and Walpole, Sunderland and Stanhope, might agree on the fundamental importance of maintaining the Hanoverian succession and the Church of England, yet on the best way to do this, and above all on the vital issue of foreign affairs, genuine disagreements as well as personal rivalries soon split them into opposing groups. When this happened the leaders of the rival whig groups within Parliament were haunted by the fear that their adversaries might secure control of the Commons by acting with the tories in that House. This was precisely what Walpole did when he was forced into political opposition two years later.

4. The Septennial Act

The aftermath of the rebellion was also responsible for an important piece of legislation. This was the Septennial Act. This received the royal assent in May 1716 and extended the legal life of that and

[1] 'The original principles on which both these parties were said to act altered so insensibly in the persons who bore the names, by the long prosperity of the one, and the adversity of the other, that those who called themselves Whigs arbitrarily gave the name Tory to any one who opposed the measures of the administration.' J. Hervey, *op. cit.*, vol. I, p. 3.

subsequent Parliaments from three to seven years. There were sound political reasons for this. Under the Triennial Act the next election was due in 1718 and it was feared that this might revive the smouldering elements of Jacobitism in the country. Such an argument was persuasive but there were others which ministers were less anxious to avow. Once the danger of a successful Stuart rising was past, and parliamentary opposition could no longer be equated with treason, they feared that a new House of Commons might be more difficult to control. But apart from purely temporary considerations there was much to be said for longer Parliaments. The Triennial Act had not worked well. In practice three years was too short for the maximum life of a Parliament. The first year was spent in hearing election petitions, the last in preparing for a new election, leaving only a year in which the Commons could be regarded as supplying a stable basis for government. The absence of any modern party system merely intensified these difficulties, for the organizing of support for the administration took time when the inclinations and attitudes of groups had to be 'managed' by the ministers of the day. The 1716 act met serious opposition in both Houses, the chief arguments against it being that no Parliament had the right to prolong its own life and that longer Parliaments could only lead to increased corruption and the undermining of the Commons' independence. In spite of the campaign against it, it was passed by 60 votes to 36 in the Lords and by 264 to 121 in the Commons. Twenty-four of the tory peers entered a protest against it and for the next half century a demand for its repeal was regularly made by opposition politicians. There were, however, fewer reasons for taking exception to the new Act than are sometimes conceded. The Triennial Act was not an ancient enactment, being less than twenty years old. Moreover that Act had altered, by curtailing, the legal life of Parliament without reference to its electors. Was there a legal difference between curtailing and prolonging, particularly as the latter was merely permissive, giving the King the right to extend its life if he so pleased?[1]

Nevertheless its opponents were correct in supposing that the Septennial Act would alter the conditions of political life, though they were wrong in supposing that the King and his ministers would be the main beneficiaries. This was because it soon came to be regarded not as a permissive measure, which gave the Crown some room for manœuvre, but almost as a measure which ensured to each

[1] Betty Kemp, *King and Commons 1660–1832* (1957), p. 40.

Parliament a life of seven years. Thus eight of the eleven Parliaments between 1716 and 1783 lasted for between six and seven years. Of the remaining three one was automatically dissolved on the death of George I in 1727. Only in the crisis year of 1780 did George III deliberately use a dissolution for a political purpose, though that of 1747 was certainly intended to discomfort the followers of the Prince of Wales.[1] Superficially the fact that the royal influence had only to be built up afresh every seven years might seem to imply that the Septennial Act had strengthened the royal control over the Commons. In one sense that is true. A seat which was secure for almost seven years was obviously more valuable than one that could be retained only for three. But the men who really benefited by the new arrangement were those with borough influence whose bargaining power *vis-à-vis* the Crown had been correspondingly strengthened. As far as individual ministers were concerned the change was less important because there was no connection between a general election and a change of administration.[2] The normal practice was for administrations to be reshuffled, rarely more than two or three ministers being changed at a time, as they lost the favour of the King or were unable to do his business in the Commons. When an election did take place it was a matter of bargaining and adjusting between various groups. It was not, as a modern election is, an appeal to public opinion to replace one set of ministers by another. The choice of ministers was still the responsibility of the Crown. Whatever the intention of the Act it seems likely that it did come to give the House of Commons a considerable degree of independence both against ministers and against the electorate. For seven years the independent and the venal member alike were safe.

5. FOREIGN POLICY[3]

In 1716, however, its chief value seemed to be that it had secured the continuance of power in the hands of the four ministers who had acted so competently together in the late crisis. But once the danger was over the harmony which it had induced, and which in the case of Townshend, Stanhope and Walpole had been cemented by private friendship and long association, began to give way to a bitter struggle for power between them. This was due partly to differences of temperament, partly to the difficulties of reconciling the dual dignitaries of George I as King of England and Elector of Hanover.

[1] *Ibid.*, p. 38. [2] *Ibid.*, p. 77.

[3] See D. B. Horn, *Great Britain and Europe in the Eighteenth Century* (1967), for the background to foreign policy throughout the period.

The occasion for the split came when he left for Hanover, taking Stanhope as his Secretary in attendance and leaving Townshend and Walpole, who was now First Lord of the Treasury and Chancellor of the Exchequer, to handle affairs in Britain. Its cause was a radical difference on foreign policy. The Treaty of Utrecht, and particularly the way in which it had been negotiated, had left great bitterness behind it. The United Provinces, after having been spurred on to exhausting efforts by the bait of the Barrier Treaty of 1709, had been forced to accept much less favourable terms by the final settlement. A Protestant Britain was still necessary to them, but little enthusiasm could be expected from their statesmen for giving her more support than was strictly necessary. The Emperor had been equally disillusioned. He was still quite unreconciled to the loss of Spain: he refused to recognize Philip V as its rightful King and, though there was no fighting, technically the two countries were still at war, which might easily flare up again. Meanwhile Britain was isolated.

It was not an easy task to win back the confidence of the Emperor Charles VI. The problem was further complicated because he and the Dutch were profoundly irritated with each other over the Barrier fortresses. These in theory were to be the advance points of Dutch defence if France should attack again. This right had first been given to the United Provinces in the time of the weak Spanish Netherlands, though, as Louis XIV's swift advance had proved in 1701, these fortresses had not afforded the protection expected from them. Nevertheless the United Provinces were now claiming what were practically enclaves in the Austrian Netherlands. In addition they expected such privileges and financial arrangements as would throw the burden of their maintenance on the Emperor. It is little wonder that he was unenthusiastic and had so far refused to implement any sort of Barrier Treaty. Clearly it was going to be difficult for Stanhope to re-create harmony between Britain's late allies. The Provinces, knowing that their support was important to the new dynasty, raised their terms. Charles VI, though not unfriendly to George I, was unsure that he would be able to establish himself securely on his new throne. It was characteristic of Stanhope's impetuous and direct methods that he decided to accompany Lord Cobham, the new British ambassador, to Vienna. As Secretary of State he was in a position to negotiate at top level, and he hoped that his friendship with Charles VI, with whom he had fought in Spain, would be useful in influencing Austrian policy. In this he was partially successful. He managed to wring some concrete proposals out of the Austrian Court on the settlement of the Barrier problem, which at least made a basis for a final year of haggling between the United Provinces and Vienna, with Britain acting as a go-between and mediator.

To the English ministers, and to Stanhope in particular, the restoration of friendly relations between the United Provinces and the Empire was only a necessary step in the rebuilding of the old alliance between the Maritime Powers and the Emperor. Here Stanhope's mission was less productive. Charles VI was willing enough for an alliance with Britain which would further his own ends, namely a fleet in the Mediterranean to ensure his keeping Majorca and gaining Sicily, whose acquisition by Savoy he had much resented. He was not, however, anxious to guarantee the Hanoverian succession, or risk another war with France. The British alliance therefore mainly had value in the imperial eyes in so far as it could be used to further his vendetta against Spain. Stanhope, however, knew that any commitments which threatened English trade with Spain, and through Spain with her American possessions, would be most unpopular in England. From the angle of parliamentary management this was important, for though foreign affairs were the sphere in which the King's actions were least fettered, the financial obligations incurred could only be discharged by the House of Commons. This dual control was responsible for much of the outward-seeming concern for trade shown by ministers when debating problems connected with foreign policy in the House. The liquid resources which could be mobilized for war were under the control of the City of London, and money was likely only to be forthcoming when trading interests were apparently being fostered. This co-operation with the City was particularly important because the independent member of a toryish complexion was opposed to any war, which necessarily increased the burden of taxation, unless it seemed to him that a foreign power was threatening English independence or interfering in English affairs. Without the support of either the commercial classes or the country gentlemen no administration, however skilfully it organized its patronage and marshalled its placemen, could finance and fight a war. In addition it was widely believed that a flourishing trade was vital to build up national resources. As one eighteenth-century pamphleteer wrote,

'The Interest and the Commerce of the *British* Empire are so inseparably united, that they may well be considered as one and the same.'[1] Knowing the popularity of such views, and aware of the anti-Spanish slant of the imperial policy, Stanhope can hardly have thought that the prospects for the kind of alliance he had in mind were very promising.

His wisdom in refusing to embroil England with Spain was vindicated even before the end of the year. The immediate results of the Treaty of Utrecht on Anglo-Spanish trade had been disappointing. The Spaniards were particularly skilful at conceding the shadow and withholding the substance. How much this was due to design and how much to inefficiency and bureaucracy in her trading machinery even contemporaries found it difficult to decide, but certainly British trade was hampered on every side. Suddenly in the autumn of 1715 Alberoni, Philip V's chief minister, decided that his personal ambitions, the dynastic hopes of Elizabeth Farnese, (the King's second wife and a powerful influence over Spanish policy), and the national interests of Spain, would all be best served by an accommodation with Britain. Everything that she had been demanding was apparently to be conceded. Customs duties were to be no higher than those authorized in the Treaty of 1667; her traders were to be put on the same footing as Spanish ones; irregular exactions were to cease. For good measure even the Asiento Treaty, which permitted the British to export a limited number of negro slaves into the Spanish West Indies, was to be revised, and a new version was signed in May 1716. It all seemed too good to be true, as indeed it was. In spite of the new treaties, as soon as Alberoni discovered that the English ministers were not prepared to back his ambition unreservedly all the old obstacles came back and British merchants received little benefit from this seeming diplomatic success. Its effect on foreign relations was more important. Because it was negotiated while the Fifteen was still a threat in Scotland, it demonstrated that at least one great European power believed in the stability of the Hanoverian dynasty. This impression was confirmed when the Dutch renewed their Treaty of alliance and guarantee with Britain in February. Now that she was no longer isolated, both the Emperor and the French Regent began to revise their opinions as to her worth as an ally. After this Stanhope was able

[1] John Campbell, *The Present State of Europe* (1750): quoted *English Historical Documents 1714–1783*, edited D. B. Horn and M. Ransome (vol. X, 1957, p. 851).

to negotiate from a position of strength and the pattern of his diplomacy became clearer.

Further success was secured when on 25 May/5 June 1716 the Treaty of Westminster was concluded between the Emperor and Britain on a basis of a mutual guarantee of their existing honours, dignities and rights. Stanhope could now claim that the pre-Utrecht diplomatic framework had been restored. These negotiations had finally been hurried on without waiting for the dilatory Dutch, because both Stanhope and George I had wanted the matter completed before they set out for Hanover in July. This, the King's first absence from England since his accession, is important for many reasons. The King, as effective head of the administration, could not be absent for long periods without causing complications at a time when the speed of communications depended on sail and horse, on weather and roads. These difficulties were increased by the opportunity which they gave for personal intrigues and jealousies. This was because on his visits abroad the King was accompanied by at least one of his important English ministers, usually one of the Secretaries of State. Whoever was chosen for this honour was brought into very close personal contact with the King and almost inevitably began to look at the problems of foreign policy through continental rather than insular eyes. Moreover, separation from the prejudices of Englishmen made it easier to minimize the difficulty of getting the House of Commons to accept some policy that had now come to him to seem desirable. This situation was to arise again and again. Its first victims were Stanhope, Townshend and Walpole. Sunderland can hardly be so described. He seems to have fomented trouble in pursuit of his own ambitions, and in revenge for the attempt of Townshend and Walpole to fob him off with Ireland earlier.

These difficulties in themselves contained dangerous material but there were others equally explosive in the tensions within the royal family. This too was to be a recurring factor of great importance in British politics throughout the century. George I was jealous of his son and made no secret of his lack of affection for him. The Prince of Wales had indeed some outward advantages that his father lacked. Chief among these was the possession of an attractive and clever wife. Princess Caroline knew how to gather people round her and gain popularity. She had also the tact to guide her husband along the same path. As a result the gayer, the younger, and the

more purely English gathered round the Prince and Princess of
Wales, who spoke English easily, though the Prince's accent
remained thick and guttural. Because of this parental jealousy,
when George I left for Hanover, the Prince, his nominal deputy, was
so hemmed in by restrictions that he had little actual power. In
particular he was excluded from taking decisions on foreign affairs,
which remained with George I and with Stanhope as his minister
in attendance.

Here there were two major issues to be decided, which at first
looked like separate problems but eventually became interdepen-
dent. One was the wish of the French Regent to make an alliance
with England and Holland to protect himself against Philip V if
young Louis XV died. The other arose out of the entanglement of
Hanover in the Northern war between Charles XII of Sweden, and
Denmark, Poland and Russia. Of the two problems the Northern
war was the older. Because England depended to an embarrassing
degree on the Baltic countries for naval stores, this war was highly
inconvenient for her. In these circumstances it was not to her
interest that any one power should dominate the Baltic, though
the powers that controlled the Sound were the greatest danger to
her trade. Therefore when the war flared up again with the return
of Charles XII from his sulking exile in Turkey, England had
legitimate interests to defend. They were not such as would normally have led to war. But the issue was complicated by George I's
Electoral ambitions. He was anxious to use the opportunity to
possess himself of the long-coveted duchies of Bremen and Verden,
which would have given Hanover an outlet to the sea. In 1712
they had been conquered by Denmark, but in November 1714
George I, in his capacity as Elector, had succeeded in getting
Frederick William of Prussia to recognize his own claims to them.
In the following May, in return for money compensation and the
prospect of an alliance with Hanover, Denmark also agreed to hand
over the duchies. As a consequence, in October 1715, Sweden
declared war on Hanover. England on the other hand was still
bound by a Treaty of 1700 to aid Sweden against her enemies.
The commitments of George I as King and Elector would clearly
be difficult to reconcile.

This was the problem that faced Townshend and Stanhope
throughout 1715. Hanover itself was not a strong military power.
Moreover, what Denmark and Prussia particularly needed was

naval help. If they made treaties that furthered the ambitions of the Elector of Hanover, what they wanted was assistance from the King of England. Outwardly this could not be given. In the first case the Act of Settlement had specifically forbidden British resources to be used for the non-British possessions of the King; in the second the House of Commons would undoubtedly refuse the necessary funds. The difficulties were both legal and practical. This was something which more autocratic rulers found difficult to understand. When, therefore, the expected British naval help was given in a half-hearted, clandestine manner, Denmark and Prussia felt cheated and deceived, an attitude that added fresh complications to George I's foreign policy. Townshend and Stanhope were between the devil and the deep blue sea: the royal favour was vital, so was the support of the House of Commons. In the circumstances they were forced to play an underhand game. The dangers and wrongs of British merchants in the Baltic were stressed, and in 1715 and again in 1716 Admiral Norris was sent with a squadron to protect British shipping. He was furnished with public instructions that were unexceptionable, and private ones intimating that he was to give the Danes every assistance that was in his power.[1] So far Townshend had collaborated actively with the Hanoverian ministers to carry out the King's wishes, and it was as a result of the appearance of the British fleet in the Baltic that in October 1715 Hanover had finally gained possession of the duchies. To some extent Swedish anger at British interference had even played into George I's hands, for the Swedish ambassador in London, Count Gyllenborg, started to intrigue with possible Jacobites, and his correspondence, which was seized late in 1716, showed that he had been actively plotting against the country to which he had been accredited. In spite of diplomatic custom he was arrested, his papers seized, and the Commons informed of the intrigue. Foreign interference in domestic issues was something that even the country gentlemen resented. That it had come as a retaliation for the use of the British fleet against Sweden might be suspected, but the instructions given to Norris had been so carefully framed that nothing could be proved. Moreover, British ministers had been careful wherever possible to act with the Dutch who, to protect their own trade in that vital area, had also

---

[1] D. B. Horn, *op. cit.*, p. 245, is of the opinion that he did in fact concentrate on furthering British trading interests.

dispatched a squadron. On the surface Britain, too, had merely been protecting her trade.

In the handling of the problems connected with the Northern war there had been little divergence of opinion between any of the English ministers. During the King's absence, however, the desire of the Duke of Orleans for an English alliance, which started as a separate scheme, became entangled with the Hanoverian interests in the North in such a way as to lead to the break up of George I's first administration. During the troubles of the Fifteen the Regent had blown now hot, now cold. But once it was clear that George I was in secure possession of his throne, that English relations with Spain had improved, and that both the Dutch and the Emperor had accepted the British alliance, Orleans, fearing for his personal authority in an isolated France, began to work for a triple alliance between England, Holland and France. For this purpose he used his old tutor, the Abbé Dubois as a negotiator. Dubois went to Holland secretly and there contrived a meeting with his old acquaintance Stanhope, who was on his way to Hanover. Stanhope himself was uncertain whether he welcomed the idea of a treaty with France: his general attitude was still pro-Austrian. Moreover an alliance with France, as one of the keystones of English diplomacy, seemed to contradict all previous whig notions. His conversations at The Hague went far to change his opinion and it was arranged that Dubois, still strictly incognito, should follow the Court to Hanover after having reported back to the Duke of Orleans. After six weeks of negotiations, during which Dubois remained a voluntary prisoner in Stanhope's house, preliminaries were settled to the extent that the Abbé could come out of hiding and be publicly received by the King. Arrangements were then made for the signing of the new treaty at The Hague by France and England, and if possible, by the Dutch. All was not yet plain sailing. The Emperor, suspicious of England's new policy, was ready to influence the Dutch against co-operating. Also the Regent was under such pressure from the anti-English elements in the French Court that it needed all Dubois' persuasiveness to keep him steady. That these irritating delays suddenly assumed more serious proportions was the result of fresh developments in the Northern war.

The basic trouble once again was due to George I's dual role. As Elector he had already secured Bremen and Verden but his failure as King to throw his full naval power into the scale had led to some cooling of relations with his allies. Also Peter the Great of Russia had quartered his troops in Mecklenburg. This alarmed George I both because of his immediate interests and because it suggested an ominous change in the balance of power in the Baltic. In addition his leading Hanoverian minister Bernstorff owned several villages in Mecklenburg, which encouraged him to stiffen George I's resistance to this threat of Russian penetration. To Stanhope and the King the situation held ugly possibilities, especially as the Tsar seemed ready to make terms with Sweden, where Charles XII, antagonized by British action in the Baltic, was planning to help the Jacobites. Frederick William of Prussia was also acting in co-operation with Peter. It therefore began to look increasingly possible that George I would be left with Denmark, now so exhausted by the war that she was more of a liability than a help, as his sole ally, that Peter would dominate the Baltic, and that Sweden would actively champion the Pretender. This gave a quite new value to the French alliance, for France had considerable influence with Sweden which could be used in favour of her new ally to damp down Jacobite plots. Accordingly Stanhope wrote urgently to Townshend stressing the vital need for completing the treaty with France in the shortest possible time.

To Townshend and Walpole in London the situation appeared rather differently. There was undoubtedly a good deal of resentment in English political circles at the way in which the Hanoverian advisers of the King were allowed to interfere in English affairs. Stanhope's stroke of policy in coming to terms with France, though it was later to be the basis of Walpole's own diplomacy, was as yet hardly appreciated. Haste to sign looked too much like seeking French favours before promises about Mardyke and the removal of the Pretender had been in any way implemented. Also the Dutch were still hanging back and Walpole, whose brother Horatio was now the English ambassador at The Hague, had assured them that England would not sign until they were ready to come in. The urgency of the King's demands seemed to stem from Hanoverian interests. Townshend and Walpole therefore were unco-operative and unimpressed with the need for haste: to George I they seemed frankly obstructive. Had it been possible to discuss the situation, agreement might have been reached, for in this case English and Hanoverian interests were not in conflict. To have had Bremen and Verden in friendly hands would have assisted English merchants to

increase their hold on the important German market. Nor, for commercial reasons, did it seem wise to allow Russia to dominate this
area. Future events were to show that George I and Stanhope were
wise to insist on haste. But separated as they were by a distance
which communications were slow to bridge, neither party to the
argument could see the other point of view. In consequence the
situation became explosive.

6. MINISTERIAL RIVALRY

There were plenty of people eager to exploit the King's growing
irritation with his ministers in London. Foremost among these was
the Earl of Sunderland. Scruples he might lack, but not ambition or
intelligence. Soon after the King's departure he discovered that his
health made it imperative to take the waters at Aix. Having obtained
permission to leave England he rapidly made his way to Hanover,
where he used his influence against Townshend and Walpole. Once
there it was not difficult to play on George I's suspicions of his son
which had already put the latter in a delicate position. They had, as
Walpole wrote in a letter to Stanhope, to manage so 'that neither
they who would misrepresent us to the King for making our court
too much to the Prince, nor they who would hurt us with the Prince
for doing it too little, can have any fair advantage over us, but this
is a game not to be managed without difficulty',[1] a remark which he
was to find events abundantly justified. The Prince still attended the
formal meetings of the Cabinet; he was the acting deputy for his
father and could not be ignored. At first 'the brothers' as they were
often called, had expected him to make their position difficult;
instead they met 'with civil receptions'. Here was a situation which
Sunderland could handle to his own advantage; Walpole and Townshend, it could be hinted, were already paying court to their future
King. When there were delays and difficulties in furnishing Horatio
Walpole with full powers to sign the treaty with France, it was
decided to by-pass promises made to the Dutch by arranging for
Cadogan to sign alone. Then his credentials were discovered not to
be in order and there were further delays. Not until the end of
November did he and Dubois finally sign. For these delays George I
blamed the active malice in his London ministers. In this his worst
suspicions were probably not justified, though it is difficult to believe
that Townshend, who was a competent man of business, had exerted

[1] J. H. Plumb, *Walpole* vol. I, p. 229.

himself to the full to comply with George I's demand for haste. An additional aggravation lay in the fact that when Horatio Walpole was sent to Hanover to explain the difficulties he took with him the suggestion that if the King did not intend to return to England soon the Prince of Wales should be given authority to open Parliament. Few more unwelcome pieces of advice could have been offered and George I's answer was a definite 'No'.

A ministerial crisis could not be long delayed. A few days later George I decided on the transfer of Townshend from his post as Secretary of State, though the King was prepared to soften this action by offering him the Lord Lieutenancy of Ireland. This seems to have been the King's own decision. Such indeed was the impression that Stanhope tried to give Walpole when he sent a covering letter to him in an attempt to reconcile him to the rearrangement. Walpole felt that Stanhope, with whom he had been bound by old ties of friendship, had leagued with his enemies. Stanhope was not by nature given to intrigue, though Sunderland was, and it seems unlikely that he had deliberately used his opportunities with the King to undermine Townshend and Walpole. He had, however, been convinced that speed in signing the French treaty was essential if both Hanoverian and English interests were to be preserved in the Baltic, and he was never a man to take opposition to his plans lightly. The decision may have been George's own, though the fact that the brothers had lost the support of the Hanoverian group, and that Sunderland was at the royal elbow to pour poison into his ear, no doubt helped; but it seems likely that Stanhope agreed. As he wrote, 'His Majesty has been more uneasy of late than I care to say: and I must own, I think he has reason.'[1] To Walpole these excuses rang hollow and he wrote a bitter reply. For a time, however, it looked as if the breach might be healed; following a suggestion made by Walpole, the question of Townshend's accepting the Lord Lieutenancy was deferred until the return of the King in January. Certainly neither Stanhope nor George I had any desire to meet a Parliament in which a resentful Walpole in the Commons and an aggrieved Townshend in the Lords might stir up opposition against Hanover and hamper the business of supply. How powerful their friends were, who would follow them in opposing the Crown, neither Stanhope nor Walpole really knew. In an attempt to smooth over the trouble George I was civil and friendly in his reception of

[1] Quoted A. F. B. Williams, *Stanhope*, p. 244.

Townshend, who did consent to accept the office of Lord Lieutenant, and for a time outward harmony was restored.

4

THE STRUGGLE FOR POWER

I. Townshend and Walpole in Opposition

Townshend's behaviour soon made it clear that this outward accord could not continue. His dissatisfaction expressed itself by voting against such essential legislation as the Mutiny Bill; and by going to the length of registering a formal protest against it he deliberately defied the rest of the administration, and even the King himself. On 9 April he was dismissed from his office as Lord Lieutenant and Walpole resigned next day. Some of his friends, including William Pulteney, Paul Methuen, the Duke of Devonshire and the Earl of Orford, followed his lead. Other less eminent supporters were ignominiously dismissed in a drive to destroy the political influence of the rebels, and to underline the fact that disloyalty to the King's ministers carried with it the penalty of the political wilderness.[1]

Why did Townshend act in this headstrong way and why did Walpole follow him into opposition? If the episode were merely an undignified squabble among ministers it would merit little attention. It is because of the light that it throws on the conditions of political life that it is worth consideration. Party, even in the eighteenth-century sense of a loose acceptance of certain broad principles, had nothing to do with it. Townshend and Walpole never ceased to call themselves whigs, though they acted with the tories in their efforts to bring about the fall of Stanhope and Sunderland. It is true that there were some genuine differences between them, but these were more of emphasis than of basic direction. Stanhope inclined towards George I's wider continental outlook; Townshend and Walpole

---

[1] In this Walpole had a precedent for the dismissal of his opponents after the failure of the Excise Bill in 1733.

thought in terms of the House of Commons. But both agreed that the maintenance of British influence in the Baltic was important. Even after his resignation Walpole voted for the necessary supplies for this. Personalities counted for more than principles. Basically it was a struggle for power. Both men had lost face by Townshend's transfer to the Lord Lieutenancy of Ireland. This they ascribed to the malice of Sunderland, and the near treachery of Stanhope, previously one of their closest political associates. Could they remain as the weaker group in the administration? Would not this deprive them of all real political power? If they were known to have little influence over patronage their personal following would soon dwindle. They were unpopular with the influential Hanoverians for their opposition to a pro-Hanoverian foreign policy, and the Duchess of Munster loathed Townshend. Older political families regarded them as upstart intruders into their exclusive circle: Walpole's frank lust for power and his enjoyment of it had more than offset any advantages that his surface conviviality might have gained for him. Their position could hardly get stronger and might well get weaker. Might it not be wiser therefore to force the issue while they still had a reputation and a following? Temperament too, no doubt, played its part. Townshend was proud, hot tempered and not good at dissembling his feelings; moreover as a wealthy peer he could afford to indulge his resentment. Walpole had more to lose: power, which he loved; the opportunity to play a great part in affairs for which he knew himself to be supremely capable; the opportunities for wealth which office brought. It must have been hard to relinquish these for the doubtful chances of a triumphant return. But, apart from any question of loyalty to his brother-in-law, there was nothing else he could do. If he had stayed, and it has been suggested that the scene in which George I pressed him to do so is a figment of Horatio's ageing memory, he would have been out on a limb alone, distrusting his colleagues and cut off from his friends. Once Townshend went he had no option but to resign also.[1]

Just as party had nothing to do with the break up of the ministry, so it had little influence on the struggle that followed. It is impossible to describe the parliamentary history of the next two years in terms of a whig ministry and a tory opposition; the contest was between opposition groups of various complexions and the Court. There were still some tories of repute in the Commons—men

[1] J. H. Plumb, *Walpole*, vol. I, p. 241.

like Sir William Wyndham, whose Stuart sympathies during the Fifteen had led to his arrest, and William Shippen, 'honest Will', whose attacks on the Crown had earned him more than one sojourn in the Tower, where he had been committed by a loyal and scandalized House. These men had their followers. Moreover the mass of the country gentlemen, though not sufficiently politically minded to do more than wear their traditional family party label lightly, tended to follow the tory leaders, in so far as they were against war, against high Land Tax, anti-Dissent, and pro-Anglican. Walpole had a following of whigs but not enough seriously to discommode the administration, particularly as the danger of internal war had been so greatly diminished with the friendship of France and the consequent checking of Swedish intrigue. If he adopted the tactics of a middle party, now opposing, now supporting the ministers' measures on what seemed to be their merits, he would neither be valuable as a friend nor feared as a foe. The struggle for power necessitated his acting with the tories, whether he approved of their measures or not. He had to embark on full-scale, factious opposition: nothing less would serve his purpose. Later, he too suffered from the same type of opposition, which in the end clawed him down; but it was he who showed the possibilities of such tactics and made it into a naked contest for power, quite divorced from party labels. Not party principles, which in any case were too fluid to bind men together, but personal ambitions and personal followings were to dominate the behaviour of opposition politicians for decades to come. This again was probably inevitable: too much must not be ascribed to Walpole's example. Office was the gift of the King. However great the outcry against a particular piece of legislation might be, there could be no genuine appeal to the electorate. The convention that each Parliament had a right to the full seven years of its legal life, together with the fact that even when an election was due to take place the opposition groups rarely had enough borough influence to prevent the Crown from winning its elections, meant that these groups had no outside tribunal to which they could successfully appeal. All that even outstanding politicians in opposition could do was to be such an obstacle to smooth government that the administration had to be perpetually on its toes, and to be prepared to suffer the occasional defeat in Parliament when its enemies caught it off its guard. All this the behaviour of Walpole in the next two years made abundantly clear.

At first, however, he acted with restraint. To some extent this was due to the fact that while Stanhope and Sunderland had been in Hanover he had been busy with a project for reducing the National Debt. In the early years of George I's reign this had not yet been accepted as a necessary part of the national economy; men were worriedly asking how it could ever be paid off. Lenders, seeing the fate of loans in non-parliamentary countries, were wondering how far it was safe to lend. Walpole's proposal was to raise a new loan at five per cent. With it he intended either to redeem or convert outstanding loans on which a higher rate of interest was being paid. During the war this had been seven, eight, or even nine per cent. Now money could be had for five per cent. and such a conversion was plainly in the national interest. What was new in his bill was that in addition to the raising of a new loan, and the provision of taxes to service it, certain taxes were to be ear-marked for debt redemption and paid into a sinking fund. As this was not to be raided without parliamentary sanction it was hoped that in time the accumulation in the sinking fund would extinguish the National Debt. By devising this scheme Walpole aimed at enhancing his reputation with the City and with the country gentlemen, two birds not normally easy to kill with the same stone, and also at carrying through a useful administrative reform.

Though Walpole had been forced by Townshend's impatience into resigning before he could pilot the measure through the Commons he was not prepared to attack it when Stanhope, in his new role of First Lord of the Treasury, introduced it, declaring that it would not fare the worse for having two fathers. Even so the two fathers nearly came to blows over their joint offspring later in the debate. Nor did he exercise his skill in arousing the anti-Hanoverian prejudices of the country gentlemen when the necessity of providing funds for possible action against Sweden was being debated. His intention of harrying the ministers was first apparent when his friend Pulteney moved that an inquiry should be set up into the rumour that there had been serious mismanagement of the money allotted for the transportation of the Dutch troops to England in the Fifteen. When the papers were laid before the House in June the ministers had considerable trouble in rounding up their supporters and even then only scraped home with ten votes. On one occasion Sir William Wyndham, with the co-operation of Walpole, even managed to carry his motion that Dr. Snape, the High Church head of Eton, should be asked to preach to the Commons at St. Margaret's, Westminster. The issue was not important and the vote a snap one, but it drove home the fact that Walpolian whigs and Wyndham tories might be a formidable combination. Equally revealing was Walpole's behaviour over the trial of the Earl of Oxford. When the question of his impeachment had been first discussed in 1715 Walpole had been relentless in his insistence on impeachment and had played a leading part in sending Oxford to the Tower. There the earl had stayed awaiting trial while the ministers had been absorbed first in suppressing the rising of the Fifteen, and then in the complications of the Triple Alliance and the Northern War. Now, with his enemies divided, Oxford asked that his case might be heard. Stanhope, probably in the hope of embarrassing Walpole, got him appointed to his old post of chairman of the committee for impeachment. Walpole made no protest but behaved with masterly inactivity in the Commons, while in the Lords Townshend and Harcourt engineered a quarrel between the two Houses. The impeachment was never completed, and eventually the Lords declared Oxford not guilty. It was a severe snub for the ministry, and an even greater indication of the dangerous nature of an opposition inspired by Walpole.

2. ANGLICANS AND DISSENTERS

If Walpole saved Oxford, his erstwhile enemy, he was equally inconsistent in his dealings with the problems of religious toleration. The question of Church and Dissent was dangerous for any politician to handle. In the deeper sense the great majority of the English people in the eighteenth century were not devout. To such as were, the period seemed one of moral squalor. Men like Bishop Gibson deplored the laxity which threatened to engulf society. From this kind of consciousness, either religious or social, sprang such movements as the Society for the Reformation of Manners, and that for the provision of Charity Schools, where poor children could be trained in religious knowledge and be taught a responsible attitude towards society. They were, however, like good deeds in a naughty world. People who tried to enforce the older laws against drunkenness, lewd behaviour and bad language, found themselves condemned as spoil-sports and hypocrites; the ability to read proved a two-edged weapon, which made the chapman's wares as easily available as the Bible. Also there was truth in Defoe's contention that the laws against vice were cobwebs in which to catch small flies only: the upper and middle classes were too powerful to be disciplined in this way.

Yet religion, in the sense of attachment to the Church of England, remained one of the important political forces of the day. Though in the early seventeenth century the Anglican Church had been regarded as a pillar of the despotic monarchy, the pro-Roman tendencies of Charles II and James II had transformed it into one of the bulwarks of English liberties, in spite of its own predilection for the theories of divine right. The resistance of the seven bishops to James II's second Declaration of Indulgence was more widely remembered than the fact that the majority of them later became non-jurors, unable to accept a King whose rights were based on Parliament and were not hereditary. The Church had become symptomatic of the English way of life, and, as such, was treasured even by those who had little personal regard for either religion or morals. Part of the price which the Church paid for this identification was that she became an integral part of the State, but in the role rather of a handmaiden than a superior or even an equal partner. Bishops were appointed for their political soundness to support the ministers of the day. Hoadly, Bishop of Bangor, in a sermon given before the King in 1717, even attacked the very basis of the Church's claim to doctrinal and disciplinary authority, thus weakening it against the State and starting what came to be known as the Bangorian Controversy. The Lower House of the Convocation of Canterbury, composed as it was of clergy nurtured in the High Church school of Anne's reign and encouraged in the Upper House by Atterbury the Jacobite Bishop of Rochester, found his thesis so distasteful that to avoid their protests Convocation was prorogued. It did not meet again until 1741, and then only briefly. The Convocation of York, though less aggressive in its attitude, suffered the same fate.

In spite of the fact that the doctrines and authority of the Church were being challenged in this way, with the result that theology became almost a fashionable topic of conversation,[1] in spite of the deadness of much of its spiritual life and the political latitudinarianism of most of its bishops, politicians alleviated the hardships of non-Churchmen at their peril. The grudging toleration given to the

[1] Dr. Samuel Johnson in his poem *London* (1738) declared bitterly that 'here a female atheist talks you dead'.

Dissenters in 1689 had been diminished by the Act against Occasional Conformity in 1711, which made it difficult for a conscientious Dissenter to hold office of any kind. This Act had been designed to destroy their political influence in the boroughs, and had been followed by the Schism Act of 1714, which made a bishop's licence necessary for the setting up of a school. The position of the Dissenters in the Community was an interesting one. Their religion, because it placed them apart from their fellows, was more likely to be an integral part of their lives; why otherwise should they accept the disadvantages of being excluded from office, from the grammar schools and from the universities? Cut off from temptations to waste time and money, Dissenters tended to be serious, responsible and hardworking, town dwellers rather than countrymen. Socially most of them were to be found among the solid middle classes or respectable artisans. Because they were debarred from so many activities both Quakers and Dissenters frequently turned their energies into the opportunities offered by industry, and later by banking.[1] Here steady application brought rewards: many of them acquired considerable influence in the communities in which they lived. In politics they tended to the whig position, finding latitudinarian bishops less troublesome than those of the High Church party. Yet, though their Protestantism was unquestioned, and their acceptance of the Hanoverian Succession much more wholehearted than that of many of the country clergy and their flocks, there was a widespread feeling that to admit them to the status of full citizens was dangerous.

Though the administration might be whig, a great part of the country was not; most members might be described as having a back-bencher mentality, which was shared by the majority of their constituents. Also many disliked the Dissenters because they were different and did not conform to the established norm. Some resented their stricter moral outlook, with its implied condemnation of their own laxer code. Others were jealous of their worldly success. Quaker helped Quaker: frequently their relations with their employees were more friendly than those prevailing between the Anglican master and man, so that work was better done.[2] As a result Quaker and Dissenting businessmen tended to prosper. It was perhaps their condemnation of loose living, combined with

[1] T. S. Ashton, *Iron and Steel in the Industrial Revolution* (1924), pp. 211–12.
[2] A. Raistrick, *Quakers in Science and Industry* (1950), p. 33.

this prosperity, that inflamed the mob against them. To storm their meeting-houses and to break their windows with the cry of 'The Church in danger' was a delightful occupation: such opportunities for unrepressed, half-organized hooliganism gave an outlet for all that was worst in the eighteenth-century mob. It and the country gentlemen in conjunction provided a formidable, if not over-intellectual, defence for the Church, and made the relief of Dissenters a tricky business.

When in the winter of 1718 Stanhope decided to repeal both the Act against Occasional Conformity and the Schism Act he placed Walpole in a difficult position. By this time the latter had become convinced that only outright opposition would serve his turn, and this would mean attacking a measure of which he basically approved. Faced with this dilemma Walpole adopted the implausible argument that Stanhope's policy of repeal covered a deep-laid plot to introduce toleration for Romanists and so reverse the Revolution.[1] Such argument could deceive nobody. Indeed, one of Stanhope's motives for introducing his bill had been an apparently genuine apprehension of a rising tide of Roman Catholicism in Europe, and by his opposition to it Walpole had improved neither his reputation nor his political position. Later in the session Stanhope was able to ease the position of the Dissenters further by an Act for 'Quieting and Establishing Corporations', by which a member of a corporation who had not qualified for office by taking the sacrament, but whose omission to do so had not been challenged for six months, was to be left in quiet enjoyment of his office. In towns where nonconformist influence was strong this provision opened a reasonably effective back door to office.

3. STANHOPE'S FOREIGN POLICY

If Stanhope's handling of this matter was skilful, his reputation was even more enhanced by his foreign policy. Though he had taken over Walpole's offices, leaving Sunderland and Joseph Addison, the essayist, as the two Secretaries of State, he had found the management of the Commons and the responsibility for domestic and financial affairs a distasteful business. It was therefore with relief that in March 1718 he had changed offices with Sunderland and gone to the Lords in July as Lord Stanhope. The state of diplomatic relations in Europe at this time needed the most skilful

[1] J. H. Plumb, *Walpole*, vol. I, p. 296.

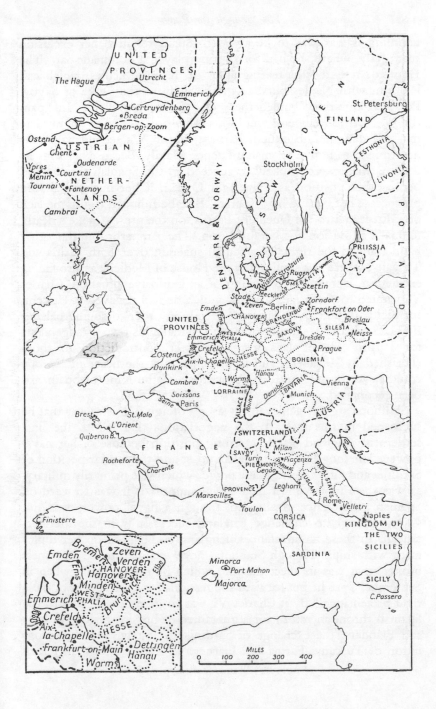

Inset (top left)

UNITED
PROVINCES
The Hague• •Utrecht
•Emmerich
•Gertruydenberg
Breda•
Bergen-op-Zoom
Ostend•
Ghent• AUSTRIAN
Ypres• •Oudenarde
Menin• •Courtrai NETHER-
Tournai• •Fontenoy
LANDS
Cambrai

Main map

FINLAND
St. Petersburg•
ESTHONIA
S W E D E N
LIVONIA
POLAND
PRUSSIA
Stockholm•
D E N M A R K   &   N O R W A Y
Wismar•Stralsund
•Rugen•
Mecklen• POMERANIA
Stade• Stettin•
•Zeven Berlin• Zorndorf•
Emden• HANOVER •Frankfort on Oder
UNITED WEST Elbe BRANDENBURG Breslau•
PROVINCES PHALIA SAXONY SILESIA
Emmerich• Crefeld• Dresden• Neisse•
Ostend• Aix-la-Chapelle• HESSE Prague•
Dunkirk• •Hanau BOHEMIA
Cambrai• •Worms BAVARIA Vienna•
Soissons• Rhine Danube •Munich
Seine LORRAINE ALSACE AUSTRIA
Brest• •St.Malo Paris•
L'Orient• SWITZERLAND
Quiberon B.• SAVOY •Milan
Rocheforte• F R A N C E Turin• •Piacenza
PIEDMONT PARMA
Charente Genoa• TUSCANY
PROVENCE Leghorn• PAPAL
Marseilles• •Rome STATES
C.Finisterre• Toulon• •Velletri
CORSICA Naples•
KINGDOM OF
THE TWO
SICILIES
Minorca• SARDINIA
•Port Mahon
Majorca• SICILY
C.Passero•

Inset (bottom left)

Bremen• •Zeven
Emden• •Verden
Ems HANOVER
Minden• Elbe
Emmerich• WEST Brunswick
PHALIA
Crefeld• HESSE
Aix-
la-Chapelle• •Dettingen
Frankfurt-on-Main •Hanau
Worms•

Scale

MILES
0   100   200   300   400

handling if war was to be avoided. Spain resented her exclusion from Italy, where she had for so long played a dominant part. The Emperor resented the tearing apart of the two Sicilies, which had left him with Naples but had given Sicily to the Duke of Savoy. Personal ambitions fanned these discontents into flame. In Spain the plebeian, intelligent, ambitious Alberoni, acting with his late master's daughter, Elizabeth Farnese, Philip V's second wife, was determined to revive Spanish influence in Italy. Because her sons by this marriage were unlikely to succeed to the Spanish throne, and because her position as a dowager Queen, if her husband should predecease her, would be desperate, Elizabeth hoped to use the lack of a direct heir to the Duchy of Parma, on the present duke's death, to make provision for her own son. The Emperor on the other hand claimed the rights of a feudal suzerain over both Parma and Tuscany, where in a similar way the House of Medici was also facing extinction. Here was the making of an explosive situation. Charles VI wanted to exchange Sardinia, which he had received at Utrecht, for Sicily, to take over Tuscany directly in order to counterbalance France's advantages in Lorraine, and to make his own arrangements for Parma. These plans were in direct contradiction to those cherished by Elizabeth, and it was clear that the peace of Europe could never be safe until the Emperor and the King of Spain had been reconciled.

Stanhope's great achievement as a Foreign Minister was that he succeeded in this task. In the negotiations that led to the final settlement England was in a strong position because of her naval power. The long line of the Italian coast and the insular position of Sardinia and Sicily meant that a power which was primarily military, as was the Empire, must have naval support if it was to ward off Spanish interference. Spain also, though a naval power, was not strong enough to challenge England successfully in the Mediterranean. In these circumstances, England could back up her diplomacy with ships. Though Stanhope never claimed to be an honest broker, that was in effect the role which he hoped to fill when in September 1716 he put forward suggestions for a settlement of these rival pretensions.[1] By it Charles VI was to give up all claim to the Spanish throne in return for a guarantee of his possessions in Italy and Flanders, the exchange of Sardinia for Sicily, and the recognition of Tuscany, Parma and Piacenza as imperial fiefs. In return

---

[1] A. F. B. Williams, *Stanhope*, p. 276.

for accepting these arrangements Philip V would be secured from any imperial claim to the Spanish throne, and the personal ambitions of Elizabeth, whose influence over her uxorious husband was immense, were to be met by the promise to institute Don Carlos, her elder son, in the Duchy of Parma on the death of the reigning duke. It was a tidy and workmanlike scheme, though Alberoni did later call it paring states as if they were Dutch cheeses. Unfortunately for Stanhope, personal blunders and miscalculations bedevilled it. Both Spain and the Emperor tried to obtain further advantages, while Dubois, acting for the Duke of Orleans, found it difficult to overcome the slant towards Spain that marked French public opinion. Before anything could take final shape, Molinez, Philip's minister at the Papal Court, on his way back to Spain was arrested by the imperial governor. Such an insult neither Philip V nor Elizabeth could endure; and though Alberoni was dismayed by their demand for immediate action, because he knew that Spain desperately needed further time for preparation, he turned to the task of carrying out their wishes with all the energy and resources at his command. As a retaliation for the Emperor's act the Spanish fleet seized Sardinia: Spain had now revived the war and Stanhope had lost one of his bargaining pieces.

He did not allow himself to be unduly disconcerted by this rash act. Indeed, in some ways it helped his plans because it emphasized to the Emperor his need for a British fleet in the Mediterranean. So long as England and France acted together there still seemed a chance of inaugurating a period of peace in Europe. This Stanhope conceived to be a vital English interest in view of her expanding trade and dislike of military expenditure. It was therefore not only as a good European that he aimed at getting a little sense, by either persuasion or force, into the heads of Philip V and the Emperor. In November 1717 a conference was arranged at Hampton Court where Stanhope, acting as a negotiator between Dubois and the imperial envoy, attempted to hammer out a possible compromise. Spain, elated after her success over Sardinia, refused to join these discussions. Therefore the procedure followed was first to arrive at a preliminary understanding, which was to be submitted to the Emperor and, if it received his assent, was afterwards to be presented as a joint demand to Spain. Stanhope also hoped that the Dutch would co-operate with England and France in this matter. Here his aim was probably not so much the additional strength which they would bring to the alliance as a precaution that, if there were to be trouble with Spain, the Dutch should be equally involved with ourselves and not, as neutrals, use our difficulties to extend their trade. Whatever his aims he was unsuccessful. The United Provinces never committed themselves to a direct refusal but contrived by procrastination to keep clear of any obligations involved in this attempt to keep the peace in Europe.

Any brief account of the events that followed must inevitably produce a false air of simplicity, an impression which would be rapidly dissipated by a more detailed study of the negotiations. Charles VI continued to make extravagant demands, or to raise formal quibbles. Negotiations were protracted shamelessly: for instance, the English envoy Schaub was kept dawdling for nearly three months on one occasion before he could get an answer. In France the Regent, torn between the counsel of ministers trained in the anti-English school of Louis XIV and the pro-English realism of Dubois, was a constant anxiety. In Parliament Walpole was carping in detail at the size and composition of the army, and sniping at Stanhope wherever he could. Also it must be remembered that in the early stages of these negotiations Stanhope was not officially in charge of foreign policy, having succeeded Walpole as First Lord of the Treasury and Chancellor of the Exchequer. This fact, which is often overlooked, is an interesting one. In theory each minister was responsible to the King only for his own department: there was as yet no widespread recognition of the overriding responsibility of a prime minister. Yet Stanhope continued to direct foreign policy without any departmental claim to do so until March 1718, when, as has been seen, he changed offices with Sunderland and again resumed the Secretaryship. The explanation lies in the empirical nature of the English government and the overall control exercised by the King. Stanhope had the threads in his hands; he had the confidence of George I, and Sunderland and Addison were content to be guided by him. In view of all these circumstances, both foreign and domestic, it is not surprising that the negotiations were lengthy. By February, however, the preliminary draft was ready to be submitted to the Emperor, though he did not assent to it, even in principle, until April. Once this had been gained Admiral Byng was sent to the Mediterranean, this having been the bribe that had at last coaxed a decision out of the imperial court.

Next the Regent began to cause difficulties and in June Stanhope travelled to France to argue him out of them. Meanwhile Spain had not stood idly by while others decided her fate. Throughout the winter of 1717/18 Alberoni had been making tremendous efforts to strengthen and re-equip the navy, which, sailing under secret orders, swooped down on Sicily at the beginning of July.[1] Now both Sardinia and Sicily were in Spanish hands. Before this fresh development had become known, for news travelled slowly, Stanhope, having successfully ironed out the difficulties with the Regent, made a brief visit to Spain. Unfortunately whatever chance he might have had of persuading the Court there to accept his settlement vanished when the news of this new success arrived during his visit. It was lucky for him that the news of Admiral Byng's virtual destruction of the Spanish fleet off Cape Passaro did not arrive until after his departure.[2] Stanhope was indeed criticized, and not only by the Spanish Court, for going to Madrid at all as an ambassador of peace when in the previous May he had furnished Byng with instructions that must have led to hostilities in the Mediterranean if Spain attempted further adventures there. That he should have done so is one more illustration of his belief that in the end Spain would be forced to accept the terms of the Quadruple Alliance, and one more proof that a commercially-minded England above all demanded peace with Spain. On this occasion British merchants suffered as a result of Stanhope's high-handed action in using the fleet to bring Spain to terms, however desirable this might be in the long run for British trade. In spite of a previous understanding that, even after a formal declaration of war, English traders should have time to settle their affairs and depart unmolested, many of them were imprisoned and their goods confiscated. Later Spain's action was to play some part in the outbreak of the War of Jenkins's Ear in 1739. Meanwhile, though Spain and England were not officially at war, English merchants were in Spanish gaols and Spanish troops were bottled up in Sicily by an English fleet. All of which furnishes another illustration of the way in which formal diplomacy creaked after events. Nevertheless the situation had advantages: hostilities could be allowed to smoulder locally while the diplomats continued to search for the most effective fire extinguisher.

This was found in the secret clauses of the Quadruple Alliance which stipulated that if Spain did not accept the proffered terms

[1] 1 July 1718 (N.S.).   [2] 11 August 1718 (N.S.).

within three months force might be used against her and that she should forfeit some of the concessions initially made to her. The diplomatic machine moved slowly. France was reluctant to declare war against a Bourbon prince, Holland kept putting off a final answer, while Charles VI waited in anticipatory glee for the additional pickings in Italy, which he thought would be his as a result of Spanish delay. While the powers hesitated Alberoni, as usual, acted. Everywhere he tried to stir up trouble for his enemies. He hoped to prevent the Turks, who were at war with the Empire, from making peace, in order to keep up the pressure on Charles VI's eastern frontier; he tried to reconcile Russia and Sweden, and to use the latter as a base for a new Jacobite attack on England. In furtherance of this scheme the Old Pretender was invited to Madrid and Ormonde was supplied with ships and men to use against England. All his schemes miscarried. Charles XII of Sweden was killed at Frederikshald on 16 December 1718. In the following March a violent storm destroyed Ormonde's expedition. Meanwhile formal war had been declared, by England on 16 December and by France twelve days later. In both countries Alberoni's ingenious schemes recoiled on him. To help the Pretender was to range the English Parliament behind Stanhope, in spite of anything that Walpole might say. In France the discovery that the Spanish ambassador was plotting to overthrow the Regent could be used to justify a military expedition which, as a sop to Bourbon solidarity, was declared to be not against Philip V but against his minister, who was keeping Europe in turmoil. This was unjust. Alberoni would have played a more skilful waiting game if his ambitious, impatient mistress had let him. The dispatch of a French army under the Duke of Berwick in April 1719, and the action of the British fleet in continuing to isolate Spanish troops in Sicily, brought this tragi-comic war to a close. Alberoni, on the advice of the Duke of Parma whose house he had so faithfully served, was dismissed in December. Even so, it took another year of haggling and another visit of Stanhope to Paris to buttress Dubois and to re-assert his influence over Orleans, before peace was finally secured by the acceptance of the allies' terms. Finally in February 1720 Philip V's representative accepted the Quadruple Alliance without reservations. It was apparently a great personal triumph for Stanhope. Only a few years after Utrecht, England had emerged from her isolation, restored her alliances and even extended them, and retrieved, by this settlement, the reputation that she had lost by her methods in making peace in 1714. Now she had both France and the Empire as her allies, her relations with Spain had been restored, and she could hope to extend her trade in a peaceful world. Unfortunately the future was not to be so rosy or so easy. At a conference held at Cambrai to work out the details of the broad settlement which had been reached in February, both Spain and the Empire, by the difficulties they made, illustrated again the old proverb that it is easier to lead a horse to the water than to make him drink. But by then Stanhope was dead and it fell to Walpole, his most relentless critic, to continue his work of safeguarding the peace of Europe.

In the north Stanhope's efforts to end the war continued. The situation was a complicated one. Since his return from Turkey Charles XII had been fighting fanatically against his ring of enemies, Denmark, Hanover, Prussia and, most formidable of all, Russia. To the first three Sweden had lost most of her territory in Germany, to the last her Baltic provinces of Esthonia and Livonia. To some extent the very completeness of her losses gave her some bargaining power, if Charles XII could persuade himself to make concessions. Neither Denmark, Hanover, nor Prussia could be happy at the prospect of the Tsar as a near neighbour. They might therefore be prepared to support Sweden in an attempt to win back her Baltic provinces if she would resign herself to the loss of her German lands. This policy would also commend itself to Charles VI, who had no desire to see Russian influence spreading. Peace on these terms would be welcome to Britain. It would secure Hanover from Russian threats and recognize her legal right to Bremen and Verden, thereby preventing her interests from further complicating British diplomacy. Genuinely British interests would also benefit by a restoration of friendly relations with Sweden. On the principle of 'better the devil you do know', Britain, with her great dependence on the Baltic trade, had no wish to see the balance of power upset in favour of Russia. At last it seemed that Charles XII had some room for manoeuvre.

This he refused to use. While he lived, diplomacy continued to be shattered against his iron determination not to recognize Sweden's losses; but after his death in December 1718, his younger sister, elected as Queen in the following February, accepted the fact that peace, with its attendant losses, was inevitable. This was the moment for which Stanhope had been waiting. The first requisite for success was that France and England should agree on the terms to be pressed on the belligerents. This caused some difficulty. France, anxious to retain her traditional influence with Russia and Sweden, wanted terms as favourable as possible to these countries. Dubois realized that Hanover must have Verden and Bremen, and he was willing to concede Stettin to Prussia, but he argued that Sweden should at least keep Rugen and Stralsund, which Denmark wanted, and that Russia should be brought into the general treaty, even though this meant her retaining Livonia, Esthonia, Ingria, Carelia and most of Finland. Eventually Stanhope was successful in persuading him to accept a less ambitious settlement which would compose Sweden's quarrels with her German and Danish neighbours, while leaving her quarrel with Russia for a separate settlement. If this policy were to have a real chance of success it was necessary first to detach Prussia from Russia, and this he had managed to do. In September a treaty between Prussia and Hanover, and another between England and Prussia, was signed on the basis of George I getting his duchies and Prussia Stettin. This was to some extent dividing the skin of the lion before it was dead: not until Sweden agreed could these terms become operative. That her consent was obtained was due partly to the pressure of events and partly to the skill of Stanhope's representative in Stockholm, Lord Carteret.[1]

This was the first appearance as a public figure of a statesman who was to play an important, if intermittent, part in English politics for the next twenty-five years. At this time he was nearly thirty, a man of charm and wit, with a gift for languages and a liking for the classics: a contrast in every way to Walpole, with whose career his own was to be so often entangled. At the Swedish Court he had personal success, and showed a gift for diplomacy and a capacity for making decisions which more than justified Stanhope's choice. His task was to persuade the Queen and her Consort, Prince Frederick, who became King in March 1720, to agree to the concessions outlined by Dubois and Stanhope, the bait being the hope that their mutual mediation later might lead to the recovery of the Baltic provinces. After protracted negotiations a series of peace treaties was finally secured along these lines. Denmark gave up her claim to Rugen and Wismar and in return Sweden renounced her claim to a share in the tolls levied by the former in the Sound. To this extent Stanhope's diplomacy had been successful; in his hope of checking

[1] A. F. B. Williams, *Stanhope*, pp. 369–70.

Russia he was less so. The British fleet, under the rather unenter-
prising Norris, failed to make much impression on Russia, and after
Stanhope's death it was French mediation, backed up by an invasion
of Sweden by Russia, that brought the long war to a close in 1721 by
the Treaty of Nystad. By it Peter gained practically everything he
had wanted, though Finland remained Swedish. Peace had at last
come to the North and peaceful trade could be resumed in its
entirety. Earlier fears that Russian domination in the Baltic would
be detrimental to English interests there proved unfounded. In
addition, in spite of the bitter charges that British interests had been
sacrificed in backing those of Hanover, the Hanoverian ports of
Bremen and Verden gave England useful channels of communication with Germany. In this sphere of diplomacy the alliance of
France and England, Stanhope's child, had produced useful results.
While it continued unbroken the two countries proved capable of
giving peace to Europe. For his part in the re-organization of peace
after the bitterness left by the Treaty of Utrecht Stanhope must be
regarded as one of the great Foreign Ministers of the eighteenth
century.[1]

4. RECONCILIATION OF TOWNSHEND AND WALPOLE

There was little danger of Stanhope's position being successfully
challenged while he could conduct so brilliantly a foreign policy in
harmony with the King's wishes, and while he could rely on the
support of Sunderland. Nevertheless neither minister could feel
happy about the situation at Westminster. Since his resignation
Walpole had been acting in close co-operation with the Prince of
Wales, who was engaged at the time in a public quarrel with his
father, and the ministers' state of mind can be compared to that of an
occupying force in unfriendly territory. They knew their resources
were sufficient for the task in hand but they could never feel completely safe: tomorrow they might run into a dangerous ambush:
next week the enemy might gain allies that would destroy their
supremacy. It is not surprising that by 1719 Stanhope and Sunderland were feeling a sense of strain. It was probably this that drove
them to try to strengthen their control in the Commons by a series of

[1] Later Henry Pelham told Lord Hardwicke that his brother 'always had a
partiality and regard for the late Lord Stanhope. I know he thinks that no minister but
him has made a great figure in the two reigns.'—*Life and Correspondence of Philip Yorke,
Earl of Hardwicke* (edited P. C. Yorke, 1913, vol. II), p. 12.

measures which sought to cut the ground from under their enemies' feet and which, as so often happens when men are driven on by a sense of insecurity, undermined their own position. A year later Walpole and Townshend were back in office.

The first of these measures was the Peerage Bill. This was first introduced by the Duke of Somerset on 28 February, dropped owing to opposition, and re-introduced in the autumn of the same year. . The hereditary principle in the House of Lords was to be strengthened by replacing the sixteen representative Scottish peers by twenty-six with permanent seats. New creations were to be limited to six. Once that number had been reached new members could only be added to the Lords when an old peerage became extinct except in the case of members of the royal family. Had it passed it could have made a decisive change in the balance of the constitution because the House of Lords would have become a body whose political intransigence could never have been overcome by the creation of new peers, as had been done to secure its approval for the Treaty of Utrecht. Its immediate objective was, however, purely political, not constitutional. Six further creations, carefully chosen, would have put Townshend, Devonshire, and their friends in a permanent minority from which the Prince of Wales on his accession would have been unable to rescue them by new creations.

The other part of the ministerial plan was designed to supplement the Peerage Bill. Stanhope and Sunderland toyed with the idea of repealing the Septennial Act, though to do so without reviving its predecessor, the Triennial Act, would again mean Parliaments with an indefinite life. Whether this was offered as a bribe to present members to pass the Peerage Bill, or whether they thought that a House of Commons with an indefinite life would be easier to control, is difficult to say. Owing to the arguments of the Duke of Newcastle the reactions of the Commons were never tested. This young man was coming to play a definite, if minor, part in the politics of the day. Immensely wealthy since his inheritance in 1711 of the vast estates of his maternal uncle the Duke of Newcastle, he had been rewarded for his support of the Hanoverian dynasty by the revival of the dukedom in his favour in 1715. In 1718, as a reward for having supported Stanhope and Sunderland against Walpole, he was appointed Lord Lieutenant of Middlesex and Nottinghamshire. No one has ever described Thomas Pelham Holles as brilliant but when it came to the realities of political life he was shrewd enough. To repeal the Septennial Act might seem a clever stroke to men of imagination like Stanhope and Sunderland, but he knew it would not do. Already he was beginning to realize how the Commons could be 'managed' and that electoral influence, not perpetual Parliaments, was the answer.

The third part of the ministerial programme was the reformation of the universities. The tories, divided and discredited though they were, were still a potential danger. Walpole's alliance with them was enough to show that. Too many independent country gentlemen found their attacks on foreign policy, or on a standing army, congenial. When so many members remained unattached to any political group it was important for smooth and efficient government that they should be well affected to the Court and whiggish in their views. Here the influence of the local clergy was important. Though the Crown was in the position to select as bishops men whom it thought politically reliable, it had less control over the choice of the beneficed clergy because so many livings were in the gift of private individuals. At this time most of the clergy seem to have been tory in their outlook, an attitude reflected in the opposition of the Lower House of Convocation to the attempts of Hoadly and his colleagues to sponsor a theology which would have placed the Church in the leading reins of the State. The response of the administration had been the negative one of ceasing to call it. This was not, however, a complete answer to the problem, for, though the clergy could no longer express their views as a body, a local rector or vicar could fulminate from his pulpit against the ministers of the day with considerable effect. The only effective remedy seemed to be to cut off the supply of High Churchmen by obtaining greater control over the universities which produced them. Had this been done the threat to liberty of thought might have been serious, though it could have been represented as an anti-Jacobite move and a further bulwark to the Hanoverian succession. The failure of the Peerage Bill forced Stanhope and Sunderland to give up the idea; to touch the universities might be too dangerous.

Unpopular though the terms of the Peerage Bill were, it might have passed had it not been for the determined opposition of Walpole, for the whig peers were in a defeatist mood and thought that little could be done. Here, he realized, was at last a topic on which he could rouse the Commons against the ministers. Moreover, for once he could speak with utter conviction instead of, as so often he had done in the last two years, being forced to attack what he would much have preferred to defend. The debate on 8 December was a great personal triumph, but there is little doubt that the feeling of the House was with him when he rose to speak. Too many of the men present saw service in the House of Commons as a gateway to a peerage, for either themselves or their relatives, to view with pleasure any attempt to limit the power of a grateful King to reward his supporters in this way. The bill was rejected by 269 to 177 votes, plainly underlining the fact that there were limits to ministerial management and royal control in an eighteenth-century House of Commons. But a defeat of this kind did not, as it would to-day, lead to the resignation of the ministers concerned. All that an occasional triumph on the part of Walpole and his friends could do was to make Stanhope and Sunderland less secure *vis-à-vis* the House of Commons. Nevertheless Walpole's victory came at an awkward time for them, as Stanhope's determination not to allow Bernstorff to interfere in English foreign policy had led to a cooling of relations between him and the Hanoverian group.

Townshend and Walpole had next to exploit their success in view of these more favourable circumstances. A frontal attack would obviously gain them little. Clearly Stanhope and Sunderland were too well entrenched to be driven out, but it might be possible to bring them to terms. The way in which this was done is not altogether clear. A paper fell into their hands which seemed to reveal a scheme on the part of the affronted Hanoverian group to use their influence with the King to reshuffle his ministers in such a way as to give the predominance to Townshend and Walpole and relegate Sunderland and Stanhope to second place. It has been suggested that this was in fact a carefully prepared 'leakage' designed to frighten the present ministers into a more co-operative frame of mind.[1] If so it succeeded. To leave Townshend and Walpole not only as allies of the tories, but as possible collaborators with the Hanoverians was too dangerous. It seemed wiser to bring them into the ministry in a subordinate position where they could be controlled. Other reasons contributed to this change of heart and may even have been more important in producing it. Secretary Craggs seems to have taken the initiative in enlisting Walpole's help in bringing about a reconciliation between George I and his son. It is significant that at this time, 9 April, he was already deeply involved

[1] J. H. Plumb, *Walpole*, vol. I, p. 283.

in the South Seas conversion scheme. Also the debts on the Civil
List had piled up. It would obviously be easier to get the Commons
to authorize the one and discharge the other if Walpole was no
longer in opposition. Walpole and Townshend may therefore have
been manœuvring to take a position that had already been abandoned.[1] Whatever the combination of causes, during April negotiations along these lines were under way. On the twenty-third the
Prince made a reluctant and sulky apology. Less than a fortnight
later Walpole handled a tricky financial deal in the Commons which
wiped out the royal debt.[2] On 11 June he returned to office as Paymaster-General; Townshend became President of the Council. It
was only a modest success.[3] The brothers-in-law were back in office,
but the solitary friend whom they managed to bring back with them
was Paul Methuen, who became Comptroller of the Household.
William Pulteney was passed over, a matter of some future importance, as from this disappointment sprang his later furious dislike of
Walpole. Apparently Stanhope and Sunderland were stronger than
ever: the Hanoverians had been circumvented, trade was booming,
the City was happy, South Seas stock was soaring. Cynical observers
wondered how long the reconciliation would last once Stanhope
and Sunderland had sucked its orange dry. Though all four dined
and wined together in outward bonhomie the old harmony between
Walpole and Stanhope was not restored and Sunderland's dislike
was unabated.

5. THE SOUTH SEA BUBBLE

It was that dramatic episode in British history, the South Sea
Bubble, which reversed their roles.[4] It is interesting, if unprofitable,
to speculate on what would have happened had Walpole still been in
opposition when it broke. In June when he achieved office the price

[1] J. Carswell, *The South Sea Bubble* (1960), pp. 128–31.

[2] The debt was funded and serviced by a duty of 6*d*. in the pound on all pensions,
annuities, charged on the Civil List, and on salaries and offices of profit granted by the
Crown. J. E. D. Binney, *British Public Finance and Administration 1774–92* (1958),
p. 73.

[3] R. Sedgwick, *History of Parliament, 1715–54* (1970), says that Walpole's failure to
get the Treasury was due to the failure of a plan to secure the resignation of Marlborough
as Captain General so that Stanhope could succeed him, thus leaving the Secretaryship
of State vacant for Sunderland.

[4] The best and most up-to-date account of this complicated affair is to be found in
J. Carswell, *op. cit.*

of its stock was high, and prosperity seemed there for everyone's asking. By November, when Parliament reassembled, a discredited ministry appeared hardly able to stand against the howls of fury that assailed it from every side. It is one of the ironies of history that Walpole should have gained his derisive title 'the Skreen Master' as a result of his battles on behalf of Sunderland and his friends. The story of the Bubble is complicated, curious and highly characteristic of the early eighteenth century, a period of both great achievement and great potentiality. Within thirty years England had survived a great war, given peace to Europe on something like her own terms, and secured her own liberties by a bloodless revolution. During the same period her wealth had become apparent. Despite the strain of war there was money for trade, money for investment, money for building. The itch for material improvement was everywhere: undeterred by his political misfortunes Walpole had been altering and rebuilding Houghton, and in this he was typical of his age. Land was being enclosed and improved, great houses were being modernized. Everywhere men were living and spending lavishly, too lavishly often to be sustained by traditional methods of finance. Men wanted to get rich quickly and Law's gigantic financial operations in Paris convinced them that they could. Wars had been financed by credit and loans even more than by taxes. Quite how this miracle had been performed few men understood, but they had the faith that moves mountains, even mountains of facts. It was against this background of hope and credulity that the Bubble must be studied.

When George I became King there were three great financial corporations in the City—the Bank of England, the East India Company, and the South Sea Company. All three had received their existing privileges in return for making substantial loans to the government and for taking over large blocks of government debt. Among their directors were to be found the wealthiest merchants and financiers in England. Of these companies the youngest was the South Sea Company which had only received its charter in 1711. Its origin is an illustration of the close connection that was growing up between the politicians and the City. In 1711 Harley needed allies if he was to carry through his peace negotiations with France, and the foundation of the South Sea Company was his answer to the support which the Bank of England had given to his political opponents. By it, holders of £9,000,000 of unfunded government debts were forced to exchange their securities for stock at par in the new company. Its commercial basis was to be monopoly rights of trade in the South Seas, to be wrung from Spain on the conclusion of peace. Though the offer was made more attractive by this provision its promoters were never genuinely interested in its commercial activities. The transaction of 1711 was essentially a conversion loan and the South Sea Company a financial corporation.

In France shares in the Mississippi Company, which had been given a monopoly in 1712 to exploit the French possessions in North America, were soaring as a result of John Law's skilful manipulation of public credit. The English were as eager to buy as the French, and by November 1719 the directors of the South Sea Company were planning to take advantage of this wave of speculation to make their company the most influential corporation in England and to destroy the predominance of the rival Bank of England. The scheme was to launch a gigantic conversion operation. It was clear that the government would welcome such a move, for they were paying some £1,500,000 per year interest on annuities and a mass of other financial obligations, legacies from the late war. The directors now proposed to take over this enormous debt, which for book-keeping purposes was calculated as representing a capital of £31,000,000 in return for an annual payment of five per cent. As the debt had originally been contracted when interest rates were higher, this in itself would represent a substantial saving to the government. As an additional sweetener they also offered £3,000,000 as a free gift for the privilege, and agreed after seven years to reduce the annual interest to four per cent. There was nothing altruistic in this apparently generous offer. The directors intended to offer stock in the South Sea Company in return for the surrender of the government securities. The acceptance of this proposal was to be voluntary and the terms on which the exchange was to be made were deliberately left vague. The mechanism of this tremendous financial deal was simple. The Company was authorized to create £1 of new stock for every £1 of debt it took over. Because of the exaggerated expectations entertained as to the profitability of its monopoly of the South Seas trade it expected to exchange its shares at well above par. It would therefore have additional stock to sell in the open market. From this source would come the £3,000,000 promised to the Treasury and ample profits for the Company. On

22 January 1720 Aislabie, the Chancellor of the Exchequer, who with the Secretary (Craggs the younger) was deeply involved in the scheme, laid it before the House of Commons. In the flurry of debate and negotiations that followed there is nothing to suggest that Walpole criticized the scheme because he was convinced of its unsoundness.[1] His chief aim was to protect the interests of the Bank of England, whose directors were among his friends, and to secure for them an opportunity to outbid their rivals. The Bank's proposals were presented on 27 January and were promptly outbid by the South Sea Company. The administration were determined that these should be accepted and the independent gentlemen, enchanted by the idea that the burden of debt would be so painlessly reduced, agreed on 1 February without a division.

From this point the story of the Bubble becomes fantastic. The directors could only hope to make a profit and cover the large bribes which, in the form of fictitious holdings, had been given to prominent politicians and courtiers (including the royal mistresses), by driving up the market price of their shares. To do this Sir John Blunt, the most influential of the directors, contrived a series of pump-priming operations. A subscription for stock in the Company was opened on 14 April, and the fact that it was heavily over-subscribed immediately forced the old stock up to 325. To furnish the market with funds for fresh buying, and the incentive to buy, the Company then offered to loan money against stock deposited on what was really the instalment plan. £100 stock entitled its depositor to a loan of £250 at 5 per cent. Three times this operation was repeated until at last its efficiency failed. As an additional precaution for insuring that the money so released flowed back to the company in the shape of fresh purchases of stock, the directors secured the passing of the so called Bubble Act, which made companies without a charter illegal. Its long-term were greater than its immediate effects. Not until the nineteenth century was easy incorporation available to direct large capital into industrial development.[2] Its immediate consequences were probably small; there were sufficient chartered companies who regarded their charters with such elasticity that they could be made to cover a multitude of projects. The conversion scheme went through, annuitants being offered stock

[1] For Walpole's attitude towards the scheme see J. H. Plumb, *Walpole*, vol. I, pp. 302–9.
[2] J. Carswell, *op. cit.*, pp. 183–4.

at under the market price to induce them to exchange their government securities for it. In the meantime complicated manipulation had driven up the price of stock to £1,000 by the end of June. Throughout July the fever of speculation was scarcely abated, though the cautious and the wise were now selling.

By August every expedient to keep up the price of stock had been exhausted. The Fourth Money Subscription was a failure and the promise of the directors to pay a 50 per cent dividend for the next ten years merely brought home to investors the probable modest yield on their investment. The period of capital gains was over and the price of stock fell rapidly: by the middle of September the situation was desperate. Paper fortunes disappeared overnight and men who had purchased stock on the instalment plan, or who had covenanted to buy when prices were high, were faced with commitments which might mean ruin if honoured. The result was a furious demand for revenge and a bitter attack on ministers. This was not merely because they had sponsored a scheme which had proved to be calamitous; it was widely believed, and with good cause, that their advocacy had been bought with blocks of stock, allotted when prices were low and redeemed as they soared, and that even such purchases were often fictitious. The Prince and Princess of Wales, the royal ladies, even the King himself had gambled heavily in South Sea stock. When Parliament met on 8 December everyone knew that it would be a stormy session and that ministers could not hope to get through unscathed.

6. THE TRIUMPH OF WALPOLE

Walpole at last was to have his chance. Politically his position was strong. He had been in opposition both when the South Sea Company had been originally chartered in 1711, and in the early part of 1720 when the new scheme was being negotiated. Also he was less associated with the Bubble than most public men. He had left London in July, and apart from a brief visit in September, when with other ministers he was engaged in trying to arrange for the Bank of England, in the so-called Bank Contract, to come to the rescue of the South Sea Company, he had the political wisdom to stay in Norfolk until George I returned from Hanover in November. But the story of the wise man who warned the country against the dangers of the Bubble, made a fortune for himself when his advice was disregarded, and who finally, as a financial wizard, was called to extract the country from its troubles to be rewarded with twenty years of political power, has been exploded.[1] Walpole did not make money out of South Sea stock. On the contrary he lost a great deal. Between January and March his holdings, which were considerable, had all been sold, possibly as a gesture to its rival the Bank of England. Had he held on for two or three months and then sold he would have made a fortune. In June, when stocks were almost at their height, he bought again, and indeed even contemplated buying in the unlucky Fourth Subscription in August. From this last folly he was saved by luck and the good sense of his banker, Robert Jacomb. Even so his losses were heavy, though to some extent offset by other investments he had made, particularly in insurance during the boom.

Walpole's main asset in the weeks that followed was his shrewd appreciation of the financial and political position once the Bubble had broken. The ministerial problem was twofold. Confidence and stability had to be restored to the City and for this purpose the South Sea Company had to be rescued and made capable of once again resuming its normal functions. Secondly the reputation of the ministry had to be protected, if possible, from the attacks converging on it from every side of the House. In both these Walpole was to play a predominant part. His share in the financial rehabiliation for which he has received more than adequate recognition, was not very impressive; even the idea on which it was based he seems to have owed to Jacomb. But politically his timing was perfect.[2] Walpole kept to himself the information that the Bank had no intention of ratifying its earlier proposal to take over large blocks of South Sea stock at 400, and, once the full effect of this dismaying news had chastened directors and ministers alike, Walpole stepped in with his own privately negotiated proposals. This did something to reassure the City, though the scheme in question was accepted without enthusiasm and had to undergo considerable modification in 1721/2. More effective in restoring stability was the steady improvement in trade. Money could still be made, though not in bubble schemes, and as men settled down to make it in older, traditional ways, confidence returned. The exuberant age of credit expansion was over.

---

[1] See J. H. Plumb, *Walpole*, vol. I, ch. 8, for a full discussion of Walpole's part in the Bubble, on which that book has thrown an important new light.

[2] J. Carswell, *op. cit.*, pp. 203–6.

But though confidence returned to the City, nothing could put back into people's pockets the money they had gambled away. Revenge, and perhaps a few crumbs of compensation to be retrieved from the personal fortunes of the directors, seemed to be the only satisfaction obtainable by the dupes of the scheme. It was in dealing with these demands that Walpole was to show himself a first-class handler of crises. His task must often have been distasteful to him, for it involved saving the reputations, or if not the reputations then at least the pockets, of the very men who had so lately been his avowed enemies and who were still, underground, his political rivals. Sunderland seems to have been deeply involved; so were Aislabie, the Chancellor of the Exchequer, both the Craggs and Charles Stanhope. It must have been a temptation to leave them to their fate and sit mutely watching their attempts to extricate themselves. It was not his generosity but his shrewdness that made Walpole the champion of the men who had used him despitefully. If the full dealings of the ministers with the directors were uncovered much else might come to light, including the King's own buying and selling of shares and that of his mistresses. Such revelations would hardly have strengthened either the Hanoverian settlement, to which Walpole was sincerely attached, or his own personal influence with George. Moreover, it is possible that some of his own financial transactions during the boom might be difficult to explain. His activities for the next few months were therefore directed to riding out the storm, helped by a judicious jettisoning of the less valuable cargo and passengers from the ship of State, and bringing the Court and its favourite Sunderland to safety.

Being a realist Walpole knew that there would have to be victims. The House of Commons when it met in December demanded an inquiry and the punishment of the guilty and, judging that opposition at this stage would be useless, Walpole made no determined effort to prevent the sending for the directors, together with their books and papers, on 15 December. A little delay was secured by the presentation of Walpole's scheme but when Parliament re-assembled after the Christmas recess ministers could no longer circumvent the demand for an inquiry into the affairs of the Company. Since the committee appointed was largely composed of enemies of the ministry, what they might uncover was disquieting. As a preliminary to justice being done, a bill was rushed through both Houses, forbidding the directors to leave the country or alienate their estates.

Then the committee, with Thomas Brodrick as its chairman, settled down to serious investigation. The first check came when, after two searching examinations, Robert Knight—the man most conversant with the underhand dealings of prominent persons—fled abroad taking with him such relevant papers as he could. The committee was more fortunate in dealing with Sir John Blunt, who seems to have felt that his best course was to throw himself on its mercy and tell the truth. This put Brodrick's committee in the possession of some very damaging evidence and placed the ministry in an extremely difficult position. By 18 February the House had enough evidence to condemn the directors for a gross breach of trust and to sequester their estates for the benefit of their victims.

The next step taken by the committee was politically more dangerous, being a deliberate attack on the ministry. Already the charges of corruption had claimed one notable victim, for in the Lords Stanhope had replied so vigorously, and with such heat, to aspersions cast on his personal honour, that his excitement brought on an apoplexy from which he died. In the Commons his cousin Charles Stanhope, Secretary to the Treasury, and Aislabie, Chancellor of the Exchequer, were both accused of corrupt practices. Walpole might leave the directors to the fury of the Commons, but he could hardly abandon his colleagues in the same way. Moreover, if the authority of the Crown and the ministry was to survive, the time had come to make a stand. By every pressure and artifice, by exploiting every particle of doubt, Walpole just managed to prevent Charles Stanhope's condemnation by a mere three votes. It had been a near thing, and the evidence against Aislabie was too strong for even so slender an acquittal to be likely to be repeated. If a ministerial victim had to be provided, then he seemed the best candidate for that honour, and Walpole made no move to prevent his being sent to the Tower. There was little doubt of his guilt and he deserved small sympathy. Doubtless, too, Walpole hoped that it would blunt the demand for revenge before the Commons debated the guilt or innocence of Sunderland. There was a good deal of evidence against him. Yet Walpole and Henry Pelham managed to discredit Blunt, the chief witness against him in the absence of Knight the cashier, and to secure the rejection of the charges by 233 to 152 on 15 March. On the previous day the elder Craggs died, probably through a self-administered dose of laudanum. His death removed the possibility of another damaging investigation, for the Postmaster-General had been deeply implicated in the scheme from its beginning. As his son, the handsome and popular Secretary of State, died of smallpox, which was raging then, the committee was balked of the last of its prominent ministerial victims.

Once the storm had blown itself out, Walpole exerted himself to save what he could from the wreckage, even for the condemned men. By long fighting and wearying rearguard actions he secured reasonable living allowances for the directors from their forfeited estates. Even Aislabie was allowed to keep those he had possessed before being Chancellor of the Exchequer. When Parliament was prorogued at the end of the summer session the crisis was over. Individuals had suffered, but the economic strength of the country and the political strength of the Crown were unimpaired. It was more than reasonable men might have expected a year before. Much of the credit must go to Walpole's iron nerve and imperturbability in face of defeat after defeat in the Commons and bitter abuse in the country. By now, to most of his countrymen he was not their saviour from chaos but the Skreen Master, who had come between them and their revenge. To have to defend corruption, peculation, dishonesty, may be a political necessity, but it can never be an attractive performance. Revenge would have caused infinite damage to the structure of credit, for the directors of the South Sea Company were men of many interests. It might have brought down the ministry and damaged the monarchy, so making way for a Stuart revival. Walpole prevented revenge taking its full course but he brought down on himself infinite abuse.[1]

At the same time he gained his first genuine chance of power. That it was a chance and not a certainty throws an interesting light on the working of the eighteenth-century political machine. Though Sunderland had resigned his office as First Lord of the Treasury[2] and been succeeded in April by Walpole, who combined this office with that of the Chancellorship of the Exchequer, his predecessor had not lost the confidence of the King. As Groom of the Stole he retained the right to attend the Cabinet, and was probably still the most influential and powerful man in the ministry. He still kept control of the Secret Service money, always the touchstone of power, and

1 'There can never have been a Prime Minister who rose to power in such a welter of denigrations.'—J. H. Plumb, *Walpole*, vol. I, p. 353.

2 The importance of the Treasury was that it gave control of patronage (Roseveare, *op. cit.*, p. 85).

though Townshend again became Secretary of State on Stanhope's death, James Craggs was succeeded by Carteret, Stanhope's able representative at Stockholm during the late peace negotiations there. It was widely known that the co-operation between Walpole and Sunderland was neither loyal nor friendly, and the outcome of their rivalry was by no means certain. Walpole had skill in managing the Commons; but he was not well liked, nor was Townshend in the Lords. Sunderland and Carteret had the royal favour. For the rest of the year a slow underground struggle was being waged. When the election of March 1722 took place, each man was desperately engaged in trying to secure the return of friendly candidates. Their behaviour was that of political opponents, not colleagues, as each strove not to go down in defeat before the other. Then, with the issue still undecided, on 22 April Sunderland died of a sudden attack of pleurisy. Within two years death had removed both Stanhope and Sunderland. However much George I might dislike Walpole and distrust his lust for power, there was now no one else to do his business. Walpole had arrived. At last one man was to combine control of the House of Commons and, eventually, the confidence of the King. With his accession to power a new chapter in English political history had begun.

5

THE ASCENDANCY OF WALPOLE

I. MINISTERIAL INFLUENCE IN THE COMMONS

ROBERT WALPOLE loved power and he loved the trappings of wealth. He had struggled long for both and now, with the aid of a little luck, they were his. His determination to keep what he had won is the key to the political history of England for the next twenty years. It was not to be easy and he was never to be able to relax, but in spite of moments of physical and mental weariness he enjoyed the game itself, as well as the prizes that it brought. That he held his position as the most effective man in English politics for so long, against all comers, is a tribute to his grasp of the situation. Of vital importance was his standing in the Closet. George I had stopped attending Cabinet meetings after his quarrel with the Prince of Wales and the breakdown of the administration in 1717, probably in order to prevent his son, who had acted as his interpreter, from passing on information to his opposition friends. But this had done little, if anything, to lessen royal control over policy. Foreign affairs, appointments, ministerial changes, parliamentary business, military decisions, were all still discussed in the Closet. Both George I and George II had very definite ideas, particularly where diplomacy or the army were concerned. If a minister were not to be a mere tool he needed skill, address, and patience in persuading his royal master against some injudicious or unpopular policy while still retaining his favour. Again and again when his rivals were hopeful of pulling Walpole down, rumour would fly round that he had lost favour in the Closet, that the King was only waiting for an opportunity to dismiss him, for everybody in the world of politics knew that if that were true his days of influence were over.[1]

Royal favour, though essential, was not the sole ingredient in political success. If it had been, Walpole would not have fallen in 1742, for George II parted with him reluctantly. By the eighteenth century the control of supply by the House of Commons had made the support of that body equally essential. Indeed one of the major qualifications for royal favour was that the minister in question could do the King's business for him in Parliament.[2] It is sometimes assumed that this was easy, that the royal power to influence through the use of patronage was enough to assure a smooth passage for his measures, but this is not true. Management was an art in which Walpole, and later his loyal servant the Duke of Newcastle, excelled, but there were very definite limitations to its usefulness. As has been previously pointed out, the direct power of the Crown to bribe was insignificant in relation to the number of men who would have to be bought. It is true that its favour was a very valuable instrument; ecclesiastical preferment, commissions in the fighting services, offices, contracts, all went to persons who in some way could influence Members of Parliament. But even these favours were in short supply, and many were more tokens of royal approval than of much financial importance. They might incline a member to give his vote to the Court, other things being equal, but be quite insufficient to outweigh his serious convictions on a specific topic when feelings ran high. In every Parliament there was a solid band of placemen whose ties with government were sufficiently important to ensure their voting with a minister as long as he had the royal support,[3] but by themselves they were not numerous enough to provide a majority. For this, Walpole, like any other minister, had to depend on the so-called independent member. It probably did not matter very much whether he regarded himself as a whig or a tory; both were in general equally ready to admit that the King's business must be carried on and that a loyal subject should support the royal ministers. But a

---

[1] In this connection it is interesting to compare contemporary gossip with the actual situation as revealed to later historians by a study of the papers and correspondence of the persons concerned.

[2] Lord Hardwicke stressed as essential for the success of any administration 'the *general* principle, that there must be a minister *with the King* in the House of Commons'.— *Hardwicke Correspondence*, vol. II, p. 245. The same conviction occurs repeatedly in all the political correspondence of the period.

[3] J. B. Owen, *The Rise of the Pelhams* (1957), pp. 56–57.

general disposition to support in theory could be combined in practice with a good deal of tiresome opposition. On matters vital to the ministry a favourable vote could be secured but it was wise not to have to exert such pressure too often. Again and again Walpole would avoid pushing to a division matters on which resistance was likely to be pronounced, or would give considerable latitude, even to placemen, to vote as they pleased. This was particularly so when a general election was pending. Walpole did not want to create difficulties for his supporters in their own constituencies. For though the franchise was undemocratic, public opinion was far from indifferent as to how members voted. A county M.P. was very aware of the sentiments of his fellow gentry; a borough member had to please the narrow clique that returned him. If necessary the Lords could usually be depended upon to reject an inconvenient measure when it reached them.

When discussing the royal control over Parliament it is sometimes forgotten that the influence which depended on patronage was not the monopoly of the Crown. In order to assess the importance of patronage it is necessary to define it carefully. Into the first category fall all offices in the administration, the Church, the army or the navy, which were in the direct gift of the Crown. The second is made up of the patronage which a great landowner could dispense—parliamentary boroughs which he might control,[1] livings within his gift, the economic dependence of local tradesmen on his favour, his influence as a landlord, and as a great employer of local labour. Patronage of this kind could be, and very often was, placed at the disposal of the government in return for office and political favour for its possessor. In such cases, of which the Duke of Newcastle is an example, public and private interest were fused together, and used to strengthen the ministers of the Crown. But against this must be put the territorial influence of the great landowner who was a member of an opposition group. Such patronage as he commanded was used against and not for the administration; and it could be very extensive, as witness that possessed by the Marquis of Rockingham in the second half of the century. An M.P. who represented the interests of an opposition peer was in no kind of danger when he voted against the ministers of the Crown; patronage made him independent rather than subservient. Walpole was well aware that it was impossible to ride roughshod over the House of Commons,

[1] *Ibid.*, p. 55.

even though he dispensed the loaves and fishes for the Crown. Such an assembly needed handling with care: some topics and some policies were always dangerous.

Most explosive of all were the problems connected with foreign policy. Here many conflicting interests were involved. George I and George II were both interested and both competent to express an opinion. Indeed it can be argued that they were more competent to do so than Walpole. But though well informed they were biased, and could hardly avoid viewing the problems of Europe through the eyes of German princes, rather than through those of an insular British King. Because royal favour was essential for his power, Walpole had to contrive either to carry out the royal policy or persuade the King to act against his personal inclination, without leaving invincible resentment in his stubborn Hanoverian mind. It was equally dangerous to go contrary to the wish of the House of Commons, which in matters of foreign policy was a suspicious watchdog of what it conceived to be British interests, though hardly a watchdog with an undivided mind; too many interests were represented in the House for such simplicity.

The attitude of the country gentleman, whether he stood for a county or a pocket borough, was fairly straightforward. He objected to the weight of war taxation, which, in its direct incidence, fell most heavily on him, and resented the fact that it might be used to promote Hanoverian rather than British interests. Indeed, on this point he was so suspicious that he was usually ready to believe the opponents of the ministry when they attacked any policy that benefited Hanover, even if a more sober judgment could see that the interests of the two countries were not mutually exclusive. But he was not necessarily a peace-at-any-price man: skilful propaganda could produce in him a most bellicose attitude. Fear of France was ingrained, despite the fact that since the Triple Alliance she had been an ally. Fear of foreign interference in the Protestant Succession could always be aroused. Fear that other nations were twisting the lion's tail, stories that English sailors were languishing in Spanish gaols, that Spanish coastguards were cutting the ears off gallant English captains, could always be counted upon to produce howls of fury. But though violently patriotic the country gentleman was anti-militarist. He regarded a standing army in time of peace, however necessary it might be as a weapon in reserve to give weight to British diplomacy, as a threat to British liberties and a waste of the nation's money. To many members a war that could not be fought out at sea was the kind of war in which England should never become involved.

The trading interests in the House were inclined to take the same view, as of necessity British trade was seaborne. On this subject the House had every opportunity of being well informed, having many merchants, financiers and government contractors among its members. They did not, of course, speak with one voice. Members whose business was with Spain did not necessarily see eye to eye with the West Indian lobby; South Sea Company directors might be at variance with those of the Bank of England; members of the East India Company had problems of their own. Each group had its particular axe to grind: each represented its well-being as identical with that of the nation. Here again was matter for ministerial caution. If Walpole tried to meet the needs of the West Indian lobby, as he did over the Molasses Act in 1733, New England merchants were aggrieved. Whatever interest he sponsored, political rivals could point out how much more vital was the one he was neglecting. In addition trade was a matter on which public opinion was particularly sensitive, and a skilful politician could mobilize it against a minister. The method was to use the constitutional right to petition the House. For instance, in the crisis over the Excise Bill in 1733, and again when the opposition were attempting to push Walpole into war with Spain in 1738, petitions were organized and presented from ports and commercial towns, and gave constant opportunities to raise the matter in the House. A tender regard for British trade was therefore one of the most useful weapons against a minister. He could be accused of making a peace that sacrificed British interests, of not making a war that would safeguard them, of failing to negotiate a favourable commercial treaty, of not protecting her ships at sea, of favouring the Bank, of lining his own pockets: in short of being a disaster for British prosperity by his incompetence, blundering and dishonesty.

The diplomatic game seems to have had little fascination for Walpole. He believed above all in the value of peace, and was more inclined to pour oil on troubled waters than to fish in them. His almost obsessive fear of Jacobitism played a large part in this, for in turn an unfriendly France, Sweden and Spain had each tried to assist that ineffective and pigheaded young man, the Old Pretender. But it is doubtful, even if there had been no Pretender, if

Walpole's policy would have been greatly different. He respected material things and loved wealth: that they should be destroyed by war over something which ought to have been settled round a table by the commonsense of give and take, was something that temperamentally shocked him. Moreover, war had many practical inconveniences. It was expensive and put up the Land Tax. It dislocated trade. It wasted national resources.[1] Lastly, it gave openings to jealous rivals to criticize Walpole for doing badly something in which he did not believe. Yet for the first nine years of Walpole's effective ministry the strains in Europe were such that it hardly looked as if a general conflagration could be avoided.

2. RIVALRY IN THE CLOSET

Nor could Walpole speak with much authority in these early years. The office of Prime Minister was one which he never claimed, however dominating his influence over later Secretaries of State. The accepted constitutional theory was still that each minister was responsible for his own department to the King, and Walpole, as First Lord of the Treasury and Chancellor of the Exchequer, had no right to interfere with the conduct of foreign affairs, which belonged to the Secretaries of State. It is true that considerable practical inroads had been made on constitutional theory while Stanhope had been First Lord of the Treasury. In the early twenties, however, foreign affairs were still a little outside Walpole's interests. In 1722 he had only just attained real power and was still busy consolidating his position and was in no position to ignore the two Secretaries, Carteret and Townshend. Though the understanding between the brothers-in-law was close, the 'firm' was still Townshend and Walpole, and Townshend had no doubts as to his own capacity to handle foreign policy. Over Carteret Walpole had little influence: he represented the Sunderland group, having succeeded Stanhope on the latter's death. He was a further danger in that his views on continental problems were very near to those of the King, with whom he could converse easily, as he spoke fluent German. Much, however, as Townshend and Walpole would have liked to undermine his Closet influence there was little at first that they

---

[1] For a contrary view see A. H. John, 'War and the English Economy 1700–63' (*Econ. Hist. Rev.*, 2nd ser., vol. VII, no. 3), in which he argues that in the particular circumstances of the period war was in general beneficial to the development of the national economy.

could do about it. With Spain and the Emperor still on bad terms, and with England estranged from both of them, the alliance with France remained a matter of prime urgency. Here the close connection between Carteret, as Stanhope's pupil, and Dubois was important.

In 1723 events became less favourable to Carteret. Dubois died in August and the Duke of Orleans survived him by only four months. With his successor, the Duke de Bourbon, he had fewer ties. Moreover, in an attempt to win the favour of the Countess von Platen, the King's mistress, and to demonstrate his own influence at the French Court, Carteret was busy intriguing for her daughter's marriage into the Vrillière family. The coping stone to this project was to be the conferring of a French dukedom on the bridegroom and the Regent was given to understand that this was the personal wish of George I. The go-between was Sir Luke Schaub, the British ambassador in Paris and an ally of Carteret. When Walpole's trusted brother Horatio was sent to Paris to assess the difference that Dubois' death would make to Anglo-French relations, he uncovered the plot and determined to scotch it. George I was persuaded to disavow any interest in the matter once he discovered that to grant the coveted dukedom would create difficulties for the Regent, and after a considerable delay Sir Luke was recalled and Horatio replaced him. On the surface this intrigue was a matter of little importance, but its failure was to parade Carteret's lack of influence with the Regent and the King and his position was consequently weakened. Of such things were eighteenth-century politics made. The next step towards his undoing was when he became involved in Irish affairs.

3. CARTERET AND IRELAND

Unlike Scotland, Ireland had failed to assert an equal partnership with England under the British Crown. Since the Reformation her loyalty to the Roman Church had made her suspect as a possible base for attack on Protestant England—and not without reason as events had shown even so recently as 1689. England, apprehensive of a sudden Jacobite thrust and still uncertain how much response a sudden appearance of the Old Pretender might evoke, was concerned with the subjection rather than the prosperity of Ireland. Unfortunately for that country the English manufacturers were only too anxious to use this mistrust to further their own interests.

Practical considerations were reinforced by economic theory. Ireland was considered as a particularly tiresome colony whose development must be conditioned by English needs where those conflicted with her own. Irish ships were shut out of the colonial trade; Irish woollens might be exported only to England, where they were subjected to heavy duties; nascent Irish industries were smothered by English legislation. Against this control of her economic life Ireland had no legal weapon, for, though she had her own Parliament, its life was as yet not limited by anything corresponding to the Septennial Act. Moreover, by Poyning's law, still unrepealed, no bill could be introduced into the Irish Parliament without first securing the approval of the English Privy Council. Even this fettered Irish Parliament represented only the small Protestant minority. All Ireland was allowed were the crumbs from her rich sister's table, and it can be no matter for surprise that Irish opinion, even Protestant Irish opinion, became increasingly resentful.

It is against this background that the next episode of Carteret's career must be studied. Ireland was very short of small change, an inconvenience which she shared with England. Coining was a royal prerogative and a patent to supply a copper coinage was granted to the Duchess of Kendal. This she sold to William Wood, who undertook to manufacture the necessary halfpence. The only possible grievance was that the coins, which were good and genuinely needed, were to be made in England and the modest profit was to go to an Englishman. But because it could be made to look like yet another exploitation of Ireland it gave an opportunity to all those interests which were unfriendly to Walpole to make trouble.[1] In Ireland, as in England, political life was dominated by personal and family feuds, and the struggle for office, with its rewards, was as bitter. At this time Alan Brodrick, Viscount Middleton, was Lord Chancellor of Ireland: the Brodrick family was a powerful one and its influence was opposed to that of Walpole. To them the resentment caused by the issue of the halfpence was a convenient weapon. They also had as an ally one of the most

---

[1] In a bitter satirical tract, *A Modest Proposal for Preventing the Children of Ireland from being a Burden to their Parents or Country*, Swift suggests that the chronic unemployment of the Irish population could best be solved by breeding its children as a delicacy for the English table. This savage jest reveals the depth of Irish resentment against the economic policies of England.

trenchant writers of the day, Dean Swift, the author of that once famous pamphlet *The Conduct of the Allies*, which had done so much, to swing public opinion behind the peace policy of Harley and St John in the closing stages of the War of the Spanish Succession.

Though Swift described himself as 'of the old Whig principles' he and Walpole represented opposing points of view.[1] It is sometimes implied that the latter might have purchased the friendship of the Irish Dean by a judicious gift of preferment in the English Church, and that at least part of his bitterness against Walpole came from disappointed ambition. This is probably too superficial a view.

Temperamentally and in outlook the two men were antagonistic. Swift was a moralist and a High Churchman, essentially backward-looking rather than forward-looking in his sympathies. He disliked the materialistic money-making world which Walpole's policies seemed to encourage. He disliked the enslavement of the Church to the necessities of the State. Holding such views, he found himself much more at home with the tories, both on religious and on social grounds, than with the supporters of the government. Walpole was certainly unlucky in that he failed to attract the friendship of the foremost writers and literary men of his time. This in part may have been due to his own personality: his taste was too robust and the bent of his mind too practical for him to have much patience with the subtle spinning of intellectual arguments. Past politics also played their part. Bolingbroke was deeply imbued with the new philosophical theories, he delighted in the use of words as an art, and he was in every way well fitted to attract to his circle of friends wits and men of letters. But because of the deep political antagonism between him and Walpole their circles were mutually exclusive. Men like Pope and even Swift, though on religious and moral grounds he had his reservations where Bolingbroke was concerned, found little to attract them in the new England of 'go-getters' where old standards of behaviour seemed to be repudiated or ignored in the new scramble for wealth. They were attracted neither to Walpole's person, nor to his friends, nor to his policy. As a consequence, though he regularly employed

---

[1] Kathleen Williams, *Jonathan Swift and the Age of Compromise* (1958), has many stimulating things to say about the relation of Swift and his friends to the religious, social and political problems of the period.

government hacks, the government point of view was rarely put forward with the wit and the passion that the opposition press could command. Swift soon demonstrated how formidable this could be by writing, with barely veiled anonymity, *The Drapier's Letters* against the new coinage.

Contemporary political conditions were well illustrated by Carteret's part in this business. After the snub administered by the elevation of Horatio Walpole, the struggle for power inside the ministry was intensified, and Carteret gave his open sympathy to the opponents of the new coins. Far from embarrassing Walpole and Townshend, this gave them their opportunity. The brothers got the King's permission to recall the present Lord Lieutenant, the Duke of Grafton, and to send Carteret to Ireland in his place. Earlier in his career Townshend had been demoted from being Secretary to being Lord Lieutenant; now he arranged for the demoting of another. It was a skilful manœuvre. For part of the year it got Carteret away from the Closet and at the same time faced him with the alternative of either enforcing a policy against which he had previously protested, or acting against the King's wishes. In October 1724 he landed in Ireland and, accepting his new responsibility, did his best to enforce the official policy. Opposition to the coins proved too widespread and, realizing that Irish opinion was too formidable to be overcome, Walpole decided that the hated patent must be withdrawn. He continued, however, to hamper Carteret as much as possible by acting through Hugh Boulter, the Bishop of Bristol who had become Bishop of Armagh in 1724. This politically minded prelate used his influence over the Irish Church to make Ireland as little trouble to Walpole as possible. Since in addition Carteret proved himself a successful and popular Lord Lieutenant for the next six years,[1] Walpole had to face neither trouble from Ireland nor the rivalry of Carteret in the Closet. In the next two years two more of the old Sunderland group disappeared. Lord Macclesfield, the Lord Chancellor, was impeached for corruption; the President of the Council died in March 1725.

Appointments were a safe barometer to Closet favour. The new ones showed that Walpole had at last consolidated his position as the man to whom the King listened. Sir Peter King, who had great borough influence in the West country, became the new Lord

---

[1] For an account of Carteret's activities in Ireland see A. F. B. Williams, *Carteret and Newcastle* (1943).

Chancellor, and the Duke of Newcastle replaced Carteret as Secretary of State. This appointment was in some ways a surprising one. William Pulteney would have been a more obvious choice. He had gone into opposition with Walpole in 1717 and, though something had been done for him when in 1722 he had been made Lord Lieutenant of the West Riding and in 1723 Cofferer of the Royal Household, his early friendship with Walpole seemed to warrant a more important office. He had had a good deal of previous political experience, had some knowledge of finance, was acknowledged as an accomplished orator, and—an asset that might have been very useful to Walpole's administration—was on easy and friendly terms with the wits and writers of the day. To these recommendations he added great wealth, an assured position in society, and a good deal of personal charm. Thomas Pelham-Holles, Duke of Newcastle, at least on the surface, was a mediocre person. His fussiness, his lack of method, his touchiness were apparent to all; Townshend is said to have had a considerable contempt for him as a colleague. One explanation often given for Walpole's choice is that he did not like rivals and that Pulteney, with his ability and his ambition, might have disputed Walpole's newly secured hold over the Closet. Newcastle, it is assumed, was a mediocrity and Walpole preferred that there should be only one directing mind in the ministry, his own. There were, however, other factors which at least modify this view. About Pulteney's real abilities it is difficult to be sure.[1] By his own directions the bulk of his papers were destroyed, and the historian has less material on which to base a judgment than he has for most of the outstanding eighteenth-century figures. His greatest speeches were made in opposition, and it is difficult to know how far the policies they advocated were constructive and how far intended merely to embarrass the administration. He was never tested by the continuous holding of office, though it is perhaps significant that, when his own opportunity came after years of opposing Walpole, he was a failure. Newcastle in contrast had some sound political qualities. He was a useful and frequent debater and rapidly came to be a first-class manager of

---

[1] Lord Hervey wrote of him 'he was a man of parts, but not to be depended upon; one capable of serving a minister, but more capable of hurting him from desiring to serve himself'.—*Some materials, etc.*, vol. I, p. 7. For a full discussion of Pulteney's ability and character *see* C. B. Realey, *The Early Opposition to Sir Robert Walpole 1720-1727* (1931), pp. 160-7.

patronage, no detail of which was ever beneath his notice. His own territorial, and therefore political influence was extensive. He had large estates in Sussex, Lincolnshire, Nottinghamshire and York-shire, and smaller ones in Kent, Derbyshire, Dorset, Wiltshire, Hertfordshire and Suffolk. This alone would have made him a valuable colleague. In addition, in spite of a foolish manner which called forth the caustic comments of contemporaries, he possessed considerable political judgment and, though he hated the responsi-bility of taking decisions, he was a useful member of a ministry when controlled and managed by a more commanding personality. At all events he was almost continuously in office for forty years, which implies some capacity for dealing with eighteenth-century political life.

4. THE BEGINNING OF OPPOSITION IN PARLIAMENT

Walpole's choice of Newcastle was important not only in terms of that nobleman's career; it also marked the beginning of serious opposition to Walpole. Hitherto this had been disorganized and ineffective. Jacobitism had little appeal and was represented only by 'honest' Will Shippen and a handful of adherents who still sympathized with the exiled Stuarts.[1] Sir William Wyndham led a group of Hanoverian tories. Neither represented any political danger to Walpole. Now these disorganized groups were to be reinforced by a couple of very able politicians, one in and one outside Parliament. In April 1725 Bolingbroke's estates were restored to him, though he was not allowed to take his seat in the Lords. He had had a long struggle even to retrieve so much. Since 1716, disillusioned with the Pretender, he had been negotiating with every person in the least likely to be able to help him. In 1723, largely owing to the friendship of Carteret, who exerted his in-fluence on his behalf, Bolingbroke had been allowed to return to England. As, however, he was still without estates, title or seat, he retired again to France, where he tried to make himself useful to the ministers in London, while continuing to negotiate for a full pardon. Like other men with favours to ask, he turned to the Duchess of Kendal, who used her influence with George I. Town-shend too seems to have been friendly. Walpole alone disliked the prospect of his old rival being again free to take part in political

---

[1] Realey points out that by 1725 the new opposition was 'entirely purged of Jacob-itism', *ibid.*, p. 157.

life. But as it was the King's wish that mercy should be shown, Walpole had the distasteful task of presenting Bolingbroke's petition to the House, in consequence of which a bill was brought in to restore his estates. Walpole was successful, however, in preventing Bolingbroke from taking his seat once again in the House of Lords. For this Bolingbroke never forgave him, though he did not go into immediate opposition. That would have done him no good and it seemed more prudent to wait in the hope that his good behaviour might extract further favours from the King. But when by March 1726 this hope had proved unjustified, Bolingbroke began to move openly in those circles known to be opposed to the Court.

In an equally tentative way William Pulteney, though still an office holder in 1725, was coming to take up a similar position. In April he played a prominent part in the debate on that perennial subject the payment of the debts on the Civil List, implying that it was ministerial corruption rather than royal extravagance that necessitated new demands for money. This was the preliminary skirmish that indicated that Pulteney was about to follow the tactics so favoured by eighteenth century politicians looking for advancement, namely to emphasize his nuisance value. Far from succeeding, after two years of provocative conduct he was deprived of his Coffership, which significantly was given to the Earl of Lincoln, a relation of the Duke of Newcastle. Early in the spring of the next year rumours were circulating that Pulteney and Bolingbroke were seeing a good deal of one another. Their friendship was not necessarily purely political, as they had literary and intellectual interests in common. But proximity and disappointed ambition must have played a large part in bringing the two men to the point of concerted political action. Their hopes of collecting allies were good; there were a number of disgruntled politicians who could be enlisted in any attack on Walpole. Lord Lechmere had coveted the Lord Chancellorship, vacated by Macclesfield, which Walpole had given to Lord King. Lord Chesterfield, who had succeeded his father in 1725, had lost his captaincy of the Yeoman of the Guard for making fun of the revived Order of the Bath, and was ripe for opposition. Lord Carteret, too, was anxious to exchange the Lord Lieutenancy for an office that would bring him more into the main current of political life. He was not yet in opposition, and Walpole played with him skilfully until 1730, but he was known to be dissatisfied. From 1726 therefore, particularly in the House of Lords, there was forming something almost like an organized group of men in opposition. The significant thing for the history of parties is that the individuals making up this new group were nominally whigs. Pulteney and Chesterfield never gave up their allegiance to whig principles, and indeed claimed that it was Walpole and his friends, Court whigs, who were the renegades.[1] Opposition to a standing army, opposition to the over-mastering influence of the Crown, a due regard for the liberty of the subject, these they claimed were the doctrines of true whiggery. Yet to be in any way effective, they had to act, as Walpole and Townshend had acted earlier, with the tories in both Houses. As by now these were, in their practical support or opposition to measures, but little divided from the opposition whigs, the party labels were coming to mean less and less.

If Walpole had to meet more opposition in Parliament he could console himself with the fact that his position in the Closet was improving steadily. The Order of the Bath had been revived at his instigation. It made a useful addition to the favours to be conferred in return for political support. In 1725 Walpole became Sir Robert, and next year, as a further mark of royal favour, a knight of the Garter.[2] Perhaps more significant was the fact that George I, who enjoyed informal evenings with his friends as much as he disliked the formal entertaining of the Court, dined privately with Walpole in September and October 1726.[3] Plainly, language was no barrier to their friendly intercourse: Walpole's French must have been at least adequate. It is difficult to imagine a successful evening with both men conversing gaily in dog Latin! This increasing dependence on Walpole's judgment was to strengthen the latter's hand when serious differences of opinion led to the break-up of the long political partnership of Townshend and Walpole. Once again it was foreign

---

[1] 'Modern Whiggism is only the *Practice of the worst Principles* that were ever imputed to the *Tories*.'—*The Craftsman*, 22 June 1728.

[2] In 1723 his eldest son was made a peer. In 1725 he became a knight of the newly resurrected Order of the Bath, and in 1726 George I conferred on him the Garter, a unique honour to be given to a commoner. Walpole was inordinately proud of this distinction and allusions to it appear frequently in the opposition press. Describing Parliament as a monster called Polyglott because it had five hundred mouths and as many tongues, the account continued 'His *Mane* and his *Tail* were tied up with *red Ribbons* at vast Expence; but he was usually led by the *Nose* with a *blue one*.'—*The Craftsman*, 22 July 1727.

[3] C. B. Realey, *op. cit.*, p. 195.

affairs which caused the rupture. In 1717 the brothers-in-law, then closely in touch with the feeling of the House of Commons, had been reluctant to embark on a foreign policy that might prove expensive. Now it was Walpole, still sensitive to the wishes of the House and the more so because of the growing opposition, who remained constant in this attitude. In contrast Townshend, more influenced by diplomatic considerations, now inclined towards a less pacific policy.

5. FOREIGN PROBLEMS AND TOWNSHEND'S RESIGNATION

Even before Carteret had been replaced by Newcastle it had become clear that Stanhope's policy for the pacification of Europe along the lines of the Quadruple Alliance had achieved only a very limited success. Nobody's position appeared clear cut. Spain was pressing England for the return of Gibraltar, but was at one with her in the desire to suppress the Ostend Company which was a threat to both English and Spanish merchants. England wanted a general peace for the sake of trade, but was determined to keep Gibraltar. The Emperor was not prepared to oblige his English ally by giving up the hated Ostend Company, and was determined to keep his control in Italy. In an attempt to break the deadlock Philip V decided to open direct negotiations with Charles VI and sent his chief minister, Ripperda, to Vienna for this purpose. Fresh urgency was given to his plan in February 1725. As part of the earlier *rapprochement* between France and Spain young Louis XV had been affianced to the even younger Infanta who had been sent to live in France. But the French need of an heir to the throne could not wait for the maturity of the little Spanish girl. With a distressing lack of ceremony she was bundled back to Spain and Louis XV married Maria Leszczynska. Full of resentment Philip V immediately instructed Ripperda to conclude a pact with the Emperor. The result was the Treaty of Vienna. Its public clauses were innocuous, and indeed no more than the Quadruple Alliance had designed: a treaty of peace between the two late rivals, and a Spanish guarantee of the Pragmatic Sanction, that pathetic diplomatic illusion by which Charles VI endeavoured to secure the succession for his daughter Maria Theresa. It was the secret clauses, which rarely in the eighteenth century remained secret long, that worried the British ministers. By them the Emperor promised to support Spanish claims to Gibraltar and Minorca, and Spain's agreement to recognize the Ostend Company, if really implemented, would have serious repercussions on English trade. This diplomatic revolution was to be cemented by marriages between the Spanish princes and the Hapsburg archduchesses.

For a short time the situation looked serious, particularly as Catherine of Russia (Peter's widow) had joined the Spanish-Hapsburg group. This jeopardized British trading interests in Spain and in the Baltic. Complicated and feverish diplomatic manœuvres followed. In an attempt to build up a counter block England and France managed to detach Prussia from her traditional loyalty to the Emperor, and the Alliance of Hanover was signed in September 1725. This temporary success was counterbalanced in June 1726 when Louis XV replaced the Duke de Bourbon by Cardinal Fleury, who, while still considering the British alliance useful, was chiefly concerned to repair French relations with Spain. The British position deteriorated still further when Prussia withdrew from the Alliance of Hanover which, however, received some new strength by the accession of Sweden and Denmark. In southern Europe the bellicose attitude of the Spaniards, determined to recover Gibraltar while they had the support of the Emperor, even involved England in informal war. As a precautionary measure one British fleet was sent to blockade the Spanish treasure ships in Porto Bello, and another to cruise off the coast of Spain. Undeterred, in February 1727 the Spaniards began the siege of Gibraltar, the defence of which helped to endear 'the Rock' still more to English public opinion.[1] It was a difficult position both for Walpole and for his parliamentary rivals. Even though formal war was never declared the country had to be kept in a state of readiness. Fleets, too, could not be kept on active service without vast expense. All this meant a severe financial drain and additional taxes: indeed, in April the King was given what almost amounted to a blank cheque for emergencies, so uncertain did the future seem. The situation exhilarated Townshend, who was animated by a bulldog tenacity on the subject of Gibraltar and by a deep distrust of the Emperor over the matter of the Ostend Company, and who was perhaps slightly over-confident as a result of the alliances he had negotiated against him. Walpole

---

[1] S. Conn, *Gibraltar in British Diplomacy in the Eighteenth Century* (1942), p. 97, quotes Townshend as writing 'the bare mention of a proposal, which carries the most distant appearance of laying England under an obligation of ever parting with that place, would be sufficient to put the whole nation in a flame'.

had little faith in and less liking for Townshend's optimistic schemes for dividing the Austrian Netherlands between France and Holland, who had once more been lured by this bait to join the alliance. He hated the prospect of having to finance such a war: to him negotiation still seemed the most sensible way of resolving the rival claims. Pulteney and his friends in opposition were not much happier, for in such a crisis they could hardly refuse support. All they could do was to hint at, and move motions against, waste and peculation.

In the spring of 1727, to Walpole's infinite relief, the crisis appeared to peter out. Charles VI, increasingly doubtful of the promised Spanish backing and fearing diplomatic isolation, accepted the Preliminaries of Paris at the end of May. A Congress was to meet at Soissons to deal with the international difficulties and, to the delight of English trading circles, the Ostend Company was to be suspended for seven years. Like most sudden clearings of the contemporary diplomatic sky, the respite proved brief. The Congress dragged on, nothing was settled, the danger of war was not yet over. In July 1729 Elizabeth, unable to get Charles VI's agreement to the presence of Spanish troops in Parma and Piacenza, made another of her *volte-faces* in favour of England's friendship. In November 1729 the Treaty of Seville was signed between England and Spain. In return for backing Spanish claims in the Duchies, the privileges of the Asiento were to be restored and outstanding difficulties arising out of trade in the Caribbean were to be referred to commissioners. This success increased rather than diminished the growing rift between Walpole and Townshend. To the former, European peace remained the aim of British foreign policy, to the latter the isolation of the Emperor was of paramount importance. Finally Walpole's influence over the King prevailed and Townshend resigned on 15 May 1730. He retired into private life rather than face the probability that if he remained at Westminster he would drift into opposition. The long partnership was over. So, tragically, was the long friendship.

Townshend's resignation left Walpole in effective control of foreign policy, though the vacant Secretaryship was given to Lord Harrington, the friend and candidate of Newcastle.[1] Peace was still precarious; Spain and Austria were still estranged and Charles VI

[1] Lord Hervey's spiteful comment on his tenure of office as Secretary was: 'he was absolutely nothing, nobody's friend, nobody's foe, of use to nobody and of prejudice to nobody.'—*Some materials, etc.*, vol. I, p. 174. One confirmation of his lack of self-assertion is to be found in the fact that Newcastle found him an easy colleague.

showed no sign of accepting the ultimatum of the Treaty of Seville. In the next two years Walpole carried out a diplomatic revolution of his own.[1] Since 1717 the alliance with France had been the sheet anchor of British foreign policy. Now Walpole aimed at a direct accord with the Emperor in flagrant contradiction of French policy to secure his isolation. The crisis came when the Duke of Parma died in January 1732, and the Emperor occupied the Duchy as an Imperial fief. To preserve peace Walpole offered to recognize the Pragmatic Sanction; this was decisive. The Emperor withdrew both his troops and his objections. By the end of 1732 Don Carlos was at last in possession of Parma, and had a firm promise of his eventual succession to Tuscany. With the attainment of Elizabeth's ambitions it looked as if the general peace, which had been threatened since the signing of the Quadruple Alliance, had been secured at last.

6. THE ACCESSION OF GEORGE II

Foreign affairs and the preservation of peace were not Walpole's only causes for anxiety during these years. On 3 June 1727 George I left for Hanover. On the 11th, most unexpectedly, he died. For a short time it looked as if Walpole's political power were at an end; his enemies were jubilant. It seemed as if his early political dexterity were catching up on him at last. While in opposition from 1717 to 1720 he had assiduously cultivated Leicester House. Then in 1720 he had worked his passage back into office by arranging a formal reconciliation between the irate father and the rebellious son. It was widely believed and probably true that the Prince of Wales retained a grudge against him for this. For a few days it seemed likely that he would be dismissed as George II made it clear that henceforth official business would be transacted through Spencer Compton. Newcastle, that sagacious politician, told Townshend that he thought Compton would be the chief minister, and Walpole's levee was significantly thin. However, Sir Robert's services could not be dispensed with immediately. There was Queen Caroline's jointure to be settled and the new Civil List to be negotiated.[2] For managing this type of parliamentary business Walpole's reputation stood high. In the short session between the end of June and 7 August he was able to earn the royal gratitude by pointing out, with genuine justification, that the Civil List of £700,000 had never been enough for the late King and that George II, unlike his father, had a

[1] J. H. Plumb, *Walpole*, vol. II, p. 220.   [2] C. B. Realey, *op. cit.*, pp. 215–16.

numerous family for which to provide. He therefore moved to settle a Civil List of £800,000 on the King, together with a jointure of £100,000 and some estates on Caroline if she survived him. On 7 August Parliament was dissolved: people waited to hear that Walpole had been demoted. They waited in vain. While Spencer Compton had been occupied with his duties as Speaker of the House of Commons, Walpole had made good use of his opportunities in the Closet. Compton had made the additional mistake of relying on the influence of Lady Suffolk, the new King's mistress, but Walpole had judged correctly that it was his wife on whom George II really relied. In his inelegant, agricultural language, he had 'got the right sow by the ear'.[1] Much to the discomfiture of his rivals Walpole retained power: George II merely indulged his personal predilections in minor ways. Spencer Compton was raised to the peerage as Lord Wilmington and became Paymaster; Lord Scarborough became Master of the Horse; Lord Chesterfield, whom the King liked, kept the Bedchamber and went temporarily as British ambassador to Holland. Though the years to come were to shake Walpole's hold over the Commons, to the end of his political career he was able to rely on the steady support of his royal master.

[1] *Ibid.*, p. 222.

6

WALPOLE AND THE OPPOSITION

1. THE EXCISE BILL

BEFORE 1724 the most serious opposition that Walpole had had to meet was from men who were already ministers of the Crown. It was a struggle in the Closet rather than in Parliament. Between 1720 and 1722 Sunderland had been the principal danger; after his death it had been Carteret. Then came two or three peaceful years when his power had been least challenged: his relations with George I had been happy and his opponents in the Commons ineffective. He was never to know such security again. The growth of His Majesty's Opposition as a recognized part of the machinery of government is one of the major constitutional developments of the eighteenth century. Although once Parliament had achieved some measure of independence from royal control some form of opposition was endemic, at the beginning of the century there was still no place for it in political theory. This was dominated by what today might be described as a belief in 'a one party system'. To the monarch belonged the right of choosing ministers and to Parliament the duty of supporting them on the assumption that the King would choose wisely from the available talent without regard to party or connection. The realities of politics were against this idealistic view. Increasingly office meant power for oneself and pickings for one's friends and was therefore a prize worth securing for less altruistic reasons than that of serving one's king and one's country. Because the King was still the recognized fount of power, aspirants for office concentrated on cultivating the royal favour. When success seemed improbable another expedient, as we have seen, was to acquire influence at a rival court, either that of the Pretender while there still seemed any possibility of his ousting the Hanoverians, or that of the Prince of Wales so often at loggerheads with his father. When neither held out prospects of success ambitious men had no resource but opposition, making their nuisance value serve as their key to office. Opposition of this kind was frowned upon. As late as 1751 Hardwicke described such tactics as 'the most wicked combination that men can enter into'. To provide a more respectable cloak for their activities politicians driven to adopt them formulated the excuse that the King was being deceived by evil advisers, from whose machinations they were fighting to rescue him.

Though after the fiasco of 1715, and even more after the failure of the Forty-five, party conflict was being smothered by the blanket of whig success, so that there was no longer a clear cut struggle between whigs and tories for the control of the Commons men excluded from office continued to go into something that was developing into permanent opposition. In spite of the aura of disloyalty that hung about such conduct until the end of the century, by the fall of Walpole the existence of the Opposition had come to be an accepted part of normal political life; but the conflict was no longer between whig and tory as it had been in Anne's reign. To some extent this possibly hindered the growth of a tighter party organization which might have developed more rapidly under a two party system than when all the serious contenders for office were nominally whigs. Nevertheless by 1742 the Opposition were already occupying the seats on the left of the Speaker. Up to 1727 the Opposition had not represented a serious challenge to Walpole but with the accession of George II his influence in the Closet had to be re-established, and here he had a shrewd ally in Caroline. At the same time the increasing antagonism of Pulteney and the backstage management of Bolingbroke made the Commons more difficult to handle. Increasingly, too, the delicate state of foreign relations and growing differences with Townshend had created difficulties. The latter's resignation and decision to retire from active politics brought to an end another chapter in the story of Walpole's determination to retain power. Then, after 1730, the situation changed again. The newly constructed ministry contained no rivals. Newcastle anxiously impressed Lord Harrington, the new Secretary, with their mutual obligations to Walpole. This dependable element was further reinforced when Henry Pelham, Newcastle's brother, became Secretary at War. By 1730 also George II's earlier mistrust had been overcome: for the remainder of his long administration Walpole could depend on the Closet.

The events of the next twelve years were to illustrate the dual nature of the base of political power in eighteenth-century England. Walpole had overcome opposition in the Closet only to meet it to an increasing degree in Parliament. Carteret could not be kept in play for ever, and losing hope, resigned his Lord Lieutenantship in 1730. In future his critical comments would have to be faced in the Lords, while in the Commons Pulteney's eloquence could be depended upon to put everything that Walpole did in a most unfavourable light. It was not, however, until three years later that the bitter controversy over the Excise Bill gave this growing opposition a chance to show how dangerous it could be. The interval was filled with a running, sniping engagement. With the conclusion of the Treaty of Vienna, of which Carteret had basically approved, foreign affairs sank for a time from their recent predominance. Instead, attention was focused on commercial and financial issues. Walpole was fully alive to the importance of money, and of the use that might be made of fiscal machinery to secure both political and commercial ends. As Chancellor of the Exchequer and First Lord of the Treasury much of his attention was taken up with these topics. It was a major point in his policy to keep the Land Tax at its lowest possible level, for he realized that nothing was so likely to give administration a safe majority among the independent country gentlemen in the House.[1] To do this other sources of revenue had to be found.

The first storm blew up in 1731 over Walpole's proposal to divert some of the taxes appropriated to the Sinking Fund in order to keep the Land Tax at a shilling in the pound. Pulteney attacked the proposal with righteous indignation; but since investors in the National Debt had no wish to see their loans repaid, Walpole's action was both financially sound[2] and, so long as he had the consent of the Commons, constitutionally correct. In the debate Pelham suggested that the reason for opposition protests was that 'it will please the country too much, and therefore we must endeavour to render it abortive'.[3] With this judgment the Commons seemed to agree when

[1] W. R. Ward, *The English Land Tax in the Eighteenth Century* (1953), p. 71, stresses the fact that it 'acquired a distinctive place in eighteenth-century political propaganda'.

[2] For a discussion of the financial soundness of his actions see J. E. D. Binney, *op. cit.*, pp. 108–9.

[3] William Coxe, *Memoirs of the Life and Administration of Sir Robert Walpole, Earl of Orford* (1789), vol. I, p. 371.

they approved Walpole's motion by 245 votes to 135. Walpole's next proposition was less likely to please the country, and was, in this sense, a gift to his opponents. Although in his private capacity he was not above benefiting by smuggled goods, in his official position he could hardly approve of the widespread evasion of the payment of Customs that was regularly taking place. In 1722 he had removed many of the duties on exports, partly with the idea of increasing the carrying trade, partly because simplification eased the burden for merchant and official alike. This, however, was a very negative reform and by the spring of 1732 the political grapevine reported that Walpole was contemplating further changes in the way in which duties were collected on certain key commodities.

In the previous year, finding the revenue buoyant, he had taken the tax off salt, but in the following year had judged it necessary to re-impose it in order not to increase the Land Tax. This decision gave a rallying point to the opposition, who were able to accuse him of 'grinding the faces of the poor', and in the vital debate the government majority sank to 29. This narrow margin was an indication that the imposition of unpopular duties might convert the opposition from a potential to an actual danger. Nevertheless Walpole went ahead. The two major sources of revenue leakage were smuggling and various forms of misrepresentation—even downright fraud— on the part of merchants. The battle with the smuggler went on continuously; operations were often on a major scale. Since 1723, 229 boats engaged in smuggling had been confiscated, and some 2,000 persons prosecuted; in the process 250 Customs officers had been beaten up or otherwise abused, and six had been murdered. The extent of liquor smuggling was shown by the seizure of 192,515 gallons of brandy. As it must be presumed that far more cargoes escaped capture than were ever taken it is clear that there must have been a very large leak of potential revenue. As for tobacco it was calculated that the government was defrauded of one-third of the duties it should have had.[1] Here the loss was due less to outright smuggling than to the ingenious ways in which the merchants manipulated the methods by which the duties were collected. When tobacco was landed in England, as by law it was required to be, the duty was $6\frac{1}{3}d.$ per lb. The importer could either pay this immediately,

[1] N. Williams, *op. cit.*, p. 94. 'For every ounce of tobacco the Revenue Officers impounded, a pound escaped their vigilance: for every pound of tea taken 3 cwts. got away.'

in which case he got a rebate of 10 per cent., or he might give bond for future payment. Much of the tobacco was intended for the European market, and was therefore re-exported. In that case the merchant received as a draw-back a considerable amount of the original duty paid. This provided ample opportunities for fraud. Tobacco, dry after its long voyage, weighed light for duty; but having been deliberately allowed to get damp in store, weighed more heavily when re-weighed for draw-back. Sometimes almost worthless stalks, mixed with rubbish, were weighed for draw-back and tossed into the sea before the ship in which they sailed reached its destination. Another trick was to collect the 10 per cent. for prompt payment, and on re-export claim the full draw-back. The merchant was then 10 per cent. in pocket at the government's expense.

It was generally believed that the method to be adopted would be some kind of Excise. This method of internal taxation had first been introduced into England in an Ordinance of 1643/4. During the Civil War it had been widely used and as widely hated. This resentment was partly due to the smack of foreign tyranny, but its genuine cause was the efficiency with which it was administered. Unlike the Customs men, who were largely paid by fees, the majority of the Excise men received a salary. They were also subjected to much careful checking and counter-checking in the performance of their duties. The result was a much greater degree of efficiency, which naturally recommended them to any minister anxious to increase revenue. As, however, they had the right to enter any premises on which excisable commodities were stored or sold, and as they seem to have used these rights in a very high-handed and often bullying manner, both for their efficiency and for their harshness they were much hated. But the Excise was too useful to be abandoned and though with the Restoration the number of excisable commodities had been reduced, it was with Excise duties, half of them hereditary and half renewable by a parliamentary grant at the beginning of a new reign, that Charles II had been compensated for the loss of his feudal dues. In 1723 Walpole had made a modest extension of the system by introducing a system of bonded warehouses in which tea, coffee, and chocolate imported into the country could be stored. If the goods were to be re-exported the payment of draw-back duties would be avoided; if they were intended for home consumption the duty was payable only when they were taken out of bond.

Because, however, of the unpopularity of the Excise these duties were carefully described as Inland Duties to avoid the hated name. Though, as has been seen, large quantities of smuggled tea continued to come into the country, Walpole argued that the same system could be applied with advantage to tobacco.

His enemies were right in thinking that for once Sir Robert had allowed his desire for financial efficiency to get the better of his political judgment. Indeed, for all his sagacity he was never very good at feeling the public pulse. He knew how to handle men as individuals but his touch was less sure when he had to handle them in the mass. His enemies started their campaign promptly. On 23 February, in a debate on the Sinking Fund, Pulteney dragged in an allusion to 'that monster, the Excise, that plan of arbitrary power, which is expected to be laid before this House in the present session of Parliament'.[1] Four days later Walpole announced that he was contemplating some such plan and on 7 March he moved for a committee to consider improvements in the method of collecting the existing duties on wine and tobacco. From this date the campaign against the scheme started in earnest. The rumour was spread that a change in the method of collecting the duties on tobacco was the thin end of the wedge and that the minister's real intention was to levy a general Excise. This Walpole categorically denied in a speech marked by closely reasoned arguments, in which he pointed out that the fair trader had nothing to fear; the increase in the general revenue must lighten the burden on those people who had to pay the full price for their tobacco, and meet the deficiency in the revenue caused by frauds which profited them nothing. As for the arguments of his opponents, he declared that 'whoever attempts to remedy frauds, attempts a thing very disagreeable to all those who have been guilty of them'.[2] The scheme itself was a simple one. The tobacco would be weighed at the Custom House and pay a duty of $\frac{3}{4}d$. per pound. It would then be placed in a warehouse, one key of which would be retained by the merchant, the other by the storekeeper. If eventually the tobacco was taken out for home consumption another 4d. would be paid; if it were exported it would be re-weighed and the $\frac{3}{4}d$. per pound returned.

This scheme was described by the opposition as an assault on the liberties of Englishmen. Were they, it was asked indignantly in the Commons, prepared to sacrifice personal liberty to prevent frauds in

[1] W. Coxe, *op. cit.*, vol. I, p. 383.   [2] *Ibid.*, p. 386.

the revenue, even if (which they denied) these frauds could not be remedied by a better supervision of Customs machinery as it then existed? The new scheme would let loose on the country an army of Excise men whose existence would increase the already dangerous patronage of the Crown, and jeopardize the privacy of the English-man's home with their right of search. In vain Walpole pointed out that a mere 126 additional officers would be required, and that though warehouses, cellars, shops and rooms where tobacco was kept, manufactured, or sold, would have to be registered, and would be liable to search, private premises could only be inspected by apply-ing to a magistrate for a warrant. Walpole's friends were already convinced of the wisdom of the measure and his enemies had no intention of being won over by any arguments, however reasonable, bitter, or sarcastic. Their tactics were to whip up feeling in the country. A mob, never difficult to collect, was encouraged to swarm round Westminster, so that Sir Robert was in some danger from it as he struggled to his coach. At first, in spite of the fury of the attack, the administration kept safe majorities. Then they began to shrink. Petitions organized by the opposition mobilized public opinion. Feeling in many constituencies was running high, not all of it manufactured by the politicians. A vote against the Excise Bill was a popular vote.[1]

Walpole still had the confidence of both George II and Caroline. When Lord Stair attempted to justify his opposition to the bill on grounds of conscience, his explanations drew from her the famous retort, 'My lord, speak not to me of conscience. You make me feel faint.'[2] But Walpole knew that he was losing the confidence of the Commons. A majority of 56 on 4 April had sunk to 16 on the 5th. The measure could still probably have been forced through by narrow majorities, but it was becoming increasingly clear that a very dangerous opposition was building up in the Lords, and that Walpole was losing control of that House also. Moreover, public

[1] Viscount Perceval reported on 9 April 1733 that 'The City is so inflamed that some ladies going in their coach thither were rudely stopped, and the cry was: "We know this coach, it comes from St. James's end of the town; knock the coachman down." One of the ladies having presence of mind, saved her servant by calling out: "Though we live at St James's end, we are as much against Excise as you." On which the mob said: "Are you so? Then God bless you. Coachman drive on." I heard the City have declared, pass what bill you will, they won't comply with it.—*Hist. MSS. Com. The Diary of Viscount Perceval, afterwards Earl of Egmont*, vol. I, (1920), p. 357.

[2] Hervey, *Some Materials, etc.*, vol. I, p. 141.

opinion had been whipped up so skilfully that enforcement would have been difficult. Unwilling to set a precedent for yielding to clamour outside the House, he used all his control over it to secure the rejection, unheard, of the monster petition of the City of London and then informed his friends on 9 April that he intended to abandon the measure.[1] 'He would not,' he said, 'be the minister to enforce taxes at the expense of blood.'[2] On the 10th he moved that the next reading of the bill be postponed until 12 June, by which time it was expected that Parliament would have adjourned. The effect was to withdraw the bill. The opposition and the City were jubilant. Houses were illuminated, bonfires blazed, and Walpole's enemies confidently predicted his fall. He was not to fall so easily. Pulteney and his friends moved for a committee to inquire into abuses and frauds in the Customs, and for the committee to be elected by secret ballot, but they had an unpleasant shock when Walpole carried the Court list by eighty-five votes.

The episode of the Excise Bill is interesting and important. Outwardly Walpole's power remained unshaken and his influence in the Closet was soon to be demonstrated by the dismissal from office of his opponents. Though the Excise Bill had never reached the Lords, the opposition there had made clear their enmity to him by demanding, against the wishes of the administration, an inquiry into the handling of the confiscated estates of the guilty directors of the South Sea Company during the Bubble. A motion for the relevant papers was carried against the government, its first defeat in that House for years. In addition it was notorious that members of the Lords had used their influence over individual members of the Commons to vote against Walpole's bill. Lord Chesterfield had three brothers there, all of whom voted against it. In face of this revolt Walpole rallied every scrap of influence he had, and mainly with the aid of the episcopalian vote managed to defeat a subsequent motion for the setting up of a small committee of inquiry. It had been a near thing and Walpole was determined to strike at the ringleaders before they could do more damage. From his point of view the alarming factor was that the majority of his opponents in the Lords were members of the administration, not open enemies. Except for Lord Carteret they were all holders of Court or military or minor offices—men who owed their places not to Walpole but to

---

[1] J. H. Plumb, *Walpole*, vol. II, pp. 268–9.
[2] W. Coxe, *op. cit.*, vol. I, p. 173.

the personal choice of the King. Most of them had always resented Walpole's power, and feeling secure in the royal favour, had used the opportunity of the Excise Bill to demonstrate that Walpole's ability to do the King's business had limits. It was an attempt to undermine him in the Closet quite as much as to defeat an unpopular measure, and as such he was forced to strike back or go under.[1] He struck back, and demonstrated that when it came to a choice George preferred Sir Robert to his earlier friends. Lord Chesterfield (Lord Steward of the Household), the Earl of Burlington (Captain of the Band of Pensioners), Lord Clinton (a Lord of the Bedchamber), the Duke of Montrose (Keeper of the Great Seal), the Earl of Stair (Vice Admiral), Lord Marchmont (Lord Register), Lord Cobham (Colonel of the King's Regiment of Horse) and the Duke of Bolton (Colonel of the King's Regiment of Horse Guards) were all dismissed from their offices. This is sometimes called a milestone in the development of the constitutional doctrine of the solidarity of the Cabinet, but this is to give constitutional importance to a political episode. Any minister got rid of his rivals in the Closet if he could; if he could not, he endured them. Cabinets continued through most of the eighteenth century to contain some very ill-assorted colleagues, who agreed on nothing but their dislike of one another. Walpole's action was to have two political results of importance: it affirmed his immediate hold on the royal confidence, and it created a much stronger opposition in the House of Lords than he had had to face previously.

2. THE NEW OPPOSITION

The new opposition was far more dangerous because it was composed of malcontent whigs, men of experience who had once enjoyed the royal favour and who might enjoy it again. Their tactics were indeed to emphasize their whiggery. In subsequent debates, and in articles in *The Craftsman*, the taunt was constantly thrown at Walpole that it was he who was now adopting tory principles in defiance of English liberties, and that Pulteney and his friends were now the true whigs. In this situation, in which the tories hardly existed and the parliamentary struggle was between whig and whig, party could have no meaning in the political struggle. Sir Robert's

---

[1] Hervey was of the opinion that 'it was indeed full time for Sir Robert Walpole, if he had power, to make some examples among those who distressed and opposed him at Court in order to show it'.—*Some materials, etc.* Dr. Plumb corroborates this view: see *Walpole*, vol. II, pp. 265–79.

enemies acted together as a loosely directed hunting pack: perhaps it would be more accurate to describe the chase as one in which several packs, each with its own huntsman, acted in loose co-operation to corner and destroy their quarry. In the Lords the ministers were so badly represented when faced by the brilliant debating powers of Carteret, Chesterfield and Cobham, that Sir Philip Yorke, a staunch supporter of Walpole in the Commons, was made Lord Chief Justice under the title of Baron Hardwicke and sent to the Upper House to support his friend Newcastle. These bitter enmities within Parliament meant that the election of 1734 was fought with more than usual vigour. The opposition had considerable electoral influence and hoped that in the counties and the more popular boroughs the recent episode of the Excise Bill would turn the scale against its supporters. These hopes proved false. Backed by the resources of government patronage Walpole came back with a majority of some fifty, in so far as majorities can be calculated in any eighteenth-century House of Commons. Nevertheless it had only been done as a result of great exertions on his part and on that of Newcastle.[1]

Though Walpole kept his majority in the new Parliament, he was faced by a dangerously talented collection of political opponents in the group of young men whom he mockingly dubbed 'the boy patriots'. In the main they represented Lord Cobham's influence, and were the first fruits of that nobleman's dismissal. Cobham had made Stowe one of the great political houses of his day. He had no direct heir, but one sister had married into the Grenville family, another into the Lyttletons; the latter's daughter Christian married Thomas Pitt, through whom his younger brother, the far more famous William, got his first vivid contacts with the world of politics. Because of the new talent combined against him from 1733 Walpole was on the defensive. But so long as he had the royal

---

[1] The following letter is typical of the kind of pressure used. The Duke of Richmond wrote to John Russell, 'Altho' Old Snooke has received a most pressing letter from my Lord Wilmington, in favour of Sir Thomas Prendergast: yet he will not declare and the true reason is that he wants money, which we shall certainly not venture to give: so I would have you talk to his son and tell him the ill consequence it will be to him and to all his family, if they don't vote for Sir Thomas Prendergast; for they will lose my Lord Wilmington's favour and mine entirely: whereas if they can persuade the old man and all three to vote hearty for us, it will eternally oblige us and we shall always be ready to serve them.'—M. E. Matcham, *A Forgotten John Russell* (1905), p. 46.

confidence and no issue of wide national appeal arose to swing the independent members against him, his position remained a strong one. The game was skilfully played and it was nine years (only the last three of which were bitter and dreary) before Walpole acknowledged defeat. The fight was one for power not for principles, though out of the cut and thrust of debate a new conception of British interests, or rather a new emphasis on them, began to emerge, as the younger men attempted to woo the independent members from their traditional support of the King's ministers to a wider conception of British needs. The tactics employed by both sides are reasonably clear. Walpole was defending what he already possessed. So long as he could manage the financial business of the Crown and keep order in the country, he was relatively immune from attacks, however able, and speeches, however eloquent. Only an unpopular war, or even a popular one that went badly, was likely to lead to the crumbling of this support, which in turn might convince the King that the time had come to make a change. Walpole's policy therefore could hardly have been any other than that which he followed, namely to stir up no domestic trouble and to avoid war. The taunt that he let sleeping dogs sleep far too long and far too soundly applies only to this last phase of his career. In his earlier days he was confident that snarling curs could be disciplined with a well-aimed kick.

The role of his enemies was a more spectacular one—to build up the picture of a selfish and corrupt minister, ready always to sacrifice the public good to his private pocket. He was to be portrayed as the sycophant in the Closet, who betrayed a trusting King and ruined the nation by debauching its public morals through bribery and by draining its Treasury through corruption.[1] No chance of flinging a little mud was ever neglected, no discontent outside the House

---

[1] In *A New Ballad to the tune of Bonny Dundee* he was portrayed as

> Bob of Lynn was as lusty as tall,
> His Head it was large, and his Belly not small;
> With huge goggle Eyes, and a soft fawning Grin:
> How.like you the Picture of Bob of Lynn.

> Bob of Lynn, during twenty long years,
> Directed, perplex'd and mismanaged Affairs;
> A Whig out of Place, and a Tory when in:
> And a very great Trimmer was Bob of Lynn.

A subsequent verse declared,

> He the Honour of *England* not valu'd a Pin;
> The Merchants be damn'd cry'd Bob of Lynn.

ever unfanned. Such tactics were made easier by certain weaknesses in Sir Robert's position. When he first took office his personal finances were heavily embarrassed. Since then he had rebuilt Houghton, accumulated a considerable fortune, and provided his friends and relations with offices, sinecures and pensions. Both contemporaries and historians have asked where the money came from, without getting a completely satisfactory answer. Stanhope and Townshend acquired no such wealth: Newcastle was to leave public life stripped of much of his fortune. Wealth such as Walpole's was not the automatic fruit of office. The necessities of his public role as the leading minister of the Crown also laid him open to the imputation of corruption. Parliament had to be managed and a safe majority created in the Commons. That this was done by wholesale bribery and a crude use of the Secret Service money is no longer believed by historians, though Walpole's contemporaries may have been honest in holding this view. But a skilful use of patronage there was, even if little money passed, and Walpole was not over-concerned with men's morality so long as he got their votes. His use of patronage was efficient and ruthless. Only friends, relations and those who could serve him received his favours. Men for whom he had no further use, whatever their claims on his gratitude for past assistance, were heartlessly ignored. Newcastle may have been a willing henchman and—after Walpole's quarrel with his 'pope' (Edmund Gibson, Bishop of London)—the channel for ecclesiastical patronage, but Walpole himself was the main distributor of the loaves and fishes. Though Walpole did not invent the system, with his administrative efficiency he perfected it. There was therefore some justice in his opponents' charge that 'Gold was the wisdom of Bob of Lynn' and such critics were no less honest because they used, when they came to office, the same methods of parliamentary control as Walpole had employed. There was also, in the slack and inefficient financial machinery of the Treasury and other departments, a fruitful field for suspicion. Audit of accounts was often delayed for months or even years, while records of expenditure and the authorization of expenditure were apt to get lost between departments. When the opposition speakers clamoured for details of this or that, hinting darkly that they were being withheld because of peculation, it was often quite impossible to produce figures that would stand scrutiny because they were not available. To some extent and on occasions Walpole was the victim of the departments which he supposedly controlled.

3. GEORGE II AND THE PRINCE OF WALES

Inefficiency and corruption at home and a betrayal of essential interests abroad were the charges which his enemies constantly sought to bring against Walpole between 1733 and his fall in 1742. In the course of these years circumstances provided several suitable occasions of embarrassing him. In particular, Pulteney and Carteret and their friends were able to make good use of the strained relations between George II and the Prince of Wales.[1] There seems to have been little natural affection between young Frederick and his parents, for which he could hardly be blamed. He had been brought up in Hanover and it was not until the end of 1728 that he was summoned to England. Even then he was kept in the background without an establishment of his own, and though, subject to the King's consent, Parliament had set aside an income of £100,000 a year for him, George preferred to keep him dependent by doling out half that sum from the Civil List. It was the old Hanoverian story of the jealousy of the King for his heir. The situation was made the more dangerous in that, though a young man of no outstanding gifts or character, he had a certain charm, and was willing to take trouble to ingratiate himself with both society and the ordinary citizen. With some genuine claim to understand music, and some pretensions to artistic leanings, he was naturally drawn to the company of men like Pulteney, Carteret and Chesterfield. Even without this pull a rapprochement between him and them was all but inevitable, since the Prince believed that Sir Robert Walpole concurred with, if he did not originate, the policy which kept him a helpless dependant on his royal father. To opposition politicians the Prince of Wales was a godsend because it gave them a rallying point of impeccable loyalty. Moreover he was the rising sun. However helpless he might be now, the time would come when the old men would go. Then those who had supported the Prince in his troubles might expect to benefit. Of all this George II and Walpole were well aware; it did not make them love Frederick any the better.

This was the background which made the question of the Prince's marriage important. It was desirable that he should have an heir: yet, to his father, marriage for such a purpose almost savoured of the preparation of the funeral feast before the death had taken place. Nevertheless by 1735 even George II felt that the matter could be

[1] See Betty Kemp, 'Frederick, Prince of Wales' in *The Silver Renaissance*, ed. A. Natan (1961), pp. 38–57.

postponed no longer and, without any attempt to consult his son's preference, which leant towards a matrimonial alliance with Prussia, informed him that it was proposed to negotiate for the hand of Augusta of Saxe-Gotha. Once decided upon, the matter was speedily concluded: at the end of the following April the pair were married. Augusta turned out to be a young woman of sense and some attractions, and as Frederick died in 1751 the responsibility of bringing up the future George III devolved on her. The marriage had a more immediate consequence in that it provided Walpole's enemies with further material with which to harass the Court. A most insolent speech from one of Cobham's young men, William Pitt, made it clear that they intended to use the Prince's difficulties for their own ends. Pitt, the new member for Old Sarum, in congratulating the King on the marriage, emphasized in the most extravagant and effusive terms the joy he was sure George II as a father must feel. As the relations between father and son were notorious, there could be no mistaking the irony of the performance: at the end of the session Pitt was dismissed from the cornetcy which he had earlier owed to Lord Cobham's generosity. For the young politician it was good publicity. Flaunting his poverty by driving about in a one-horse chaise, unattended by a single servant, he underlined the autocracy of Walpole and the King, and became the martyr of the Patriot group.

Such incidents did not improve relations between father and son. George II clung the more firmly to his financial control and refused to agree to a regular settlement on Frederick, though as a married man he had a claim to his own establishment. Finding complaints and requests ignored, the Prince allowed the opposition to take up his cause. In the autumn of 1737 the matter was raised in Parliament and an allowance of £100,000 demanded. This put Walpole in a difficult position. Personally he was not unmindful that something should have been done for the Prince, but the disapproval of Caroline and George II made it difficult for him to press the matter. To have the question debated in Parliament was exceedingly awkward; it put the King in a most unfavourable light, and widespread sympathy for the Prince was expressed in a vote of 234 against 204. Had not 45 of the tories, including Wyndham, refrained from supporting a motion which they considered derogatory to the royal prerogative, Walpole would have been defeated. The final breach between George II and his son occurred over the birth of Augusta's first child. When his wife's labour pains were almost on her, Frederick, with a dramatic gesture, moved her from Hampton Court to St James's Palace, rather than have his child born under the hated paternal roof.[1] Subsequent lame excuses that it was necessary to be nearer the medical resources of London were brushed aside, and the young couple were forbidden the Court. They then rented Norfolk House, and society was regaled with the spectacle of a King and a Prince of Wales at complete variance. George II even went to the length of sending the letters which had passed between him and his son to foreign diplomats, and any person attending his son's levees, or continuing in his service, was forbidden the Court. Walpole's enemies at last had a Court of their own, and the link between the Prince and the opposition was further emphasized when George Lyttleton became his Principal Secretary and Pitt one of his Grooms of the Bedchamber.[2]

The Prince of Wales's affairs were not Walpole's only anxiety. In 1736 there was discontent and rioting in London against the Gin Act. To interfere with the pleasures of the mob was always dangerous and they resented the new prohibitive duties placed on gin. At best London was a dirty, turbulent place, but during the early decades of the century its squalor and vice had been increased by a tremendous growth in the consumption of gin. At a time of low prices, the landed interest had welcomed this enhanced demand for 'drink corn', and the social evils of cheap gin had not been realized. The effects of a low Excise duty coupled with an unrestricted sale, had by the thirties reached frightening proportions, particularly in London, where the Bills of Mortality showed a steep rise.[3] The Gin Act of 1736 was almost a panic measure. It attempted to stop the trade by prohibitive duties on both the distillers and the retailers of gin: all it did was to arouse intense hostility to the government and drive the gin drinkers to the eighteenth century equivalent of the 'speakeasy' of the days of American prohibition. In despair at the lack of result, two years later illegal hawkers of gin were to be committed to the House of Correction for two months

---

[1] For a dramatic account of this episode see Hervey, *Some Materials*, *etc.*, vol. III, pp. 757–8.

[2] There is an interesting article by A. N. Newman on 'The Political Patronage of Frederick Lewis, Prince of Wales' in *The Historical Journal*, vol. I, 1958, p. 70, in which he points out that office in the Prince's household was compatible with a seat in the Commons without re-election.

[3] M. D. George, *op. cit.*, pp. 30–36.

and, before discharge, whipped until their backs were bloody. This measure was equally ineffective: some eight million gallons of spirits were distilled every year, and when Sir Robert fell from power the orgy of gin drinking was at its height. It was not until more moderate, and therefore more enforceable duties, were imposed in 1743 that the rise of production was halted, and not until distillers were forbidden to sell retail and duties were at the same time again increased, that gin ceased to dominate the social life of much of urban England.

4. SCOTLAND AND THE PORTEOUS RIOTS

In 1737 Edinburgh, the capital of the northern kingdom, provided Pulteney and Carteret with fresh ammunition. Here the trouble was not gin drinking but the execution of a popular smuggler called Wilson. Trouble had been expected, so that both the magistrates and the troops were at hand, but all was quiet until the hanging was over and the magistrates had departed. Then the mob surged forward. Eighteenth-century mobs were ugly and dangerous things, and Captain Porteous, in command of the troops, fired. Deaths followed, and the Scots, fired on by an English soldier unauthorized by the magistrates, were stirred to fury. Porteous was condemned to death, but the carrying out of the sentence was postponed for six weeks by Queen Caroline, who was acting as Regent during her husband's absence in Hanover. On the day on which the execution should have taken place the Edinburgh mob broke into the prison, seized Porteous and hanged him. The importance of the Porteous riots was that they created further difficulties for Walpole. Scottish members of both Houses, though generally regarded as a dependable body of government supporters, were quick to resent any interference in Scottish concerns. Accordingly, when Carteret and his friends forced Walpole to agree to a bill fining the City of Edinburgh £2,000 as a provision for Porteous's widow, and disabling its Provost, Alexander Wilson, from holding office, the bitterness which this measure caused in Scotland materially lessened Walpole's popularity there. The result of this manœuvre was seen in the next election, when the Scottish bloc turned against him.

But to concentrate on these more dramatic episodes is to give a slightly distorted impression of the political battles of these years. It was not a matter of a few outstanding incidents, which might be supposed to have aroused genuine sympathies, but a factious opposition, determined to take every chance of discrediting Walpole. Everything that could be done to underline the corruption of the régime was done: demands were made for the repeal of the Septennial Act, place bills were introduced, attempts to repeal the Test Acts were made. Sometimes Walpole resisted actively, defending the Septennial Act as a basis for stable government. Though he approved in principle of the abolition of the Test Acts, his argument was that the time was not yet ripe. He was probably politically wise. In 1736 when he tried to bring in a bill to give some relief to Quakers over the collection of tithe, he found the bishops against him. Edmund Gibson, Bishop of London, and hitherto Walpole's chief ally in the policy of keeping the Church loyal to the Hanoverian dynasty, disagreed with him vehemently on this matter. As a result the partnership broke down and Newcastle became manager-in-chief of ecclesiastical patronage.

5. PUBLIC OPINION AND THE CENSORSHIP OF PLAYS

In these years Walpole's main aim was to block other men's measures and to slip out of the difficulties which they created for him. When on occasion, however, he was determined to act he could still be pertinacious in getting his way. One example, which has a more than temporary interest, was his handling of the Playhouse bill. Walpole chafed continually under the jibes and sarcasms and innuendoes to which he was ceaselessly subject, and when he could he hit back at his tormentors: he had invoked the traditional powers of the Lord Chamberlain to stop the performances of Gay's *Polly*.[1] Apart from their political comment, contemporary plays often contained much that was crude and licentious, and thoughtful men were apprehensive of their effect on public morals. Consequently in March 1737 Sir John Barnard, the ex-Quaker merchant, introduced a bill to limit the number of playhouses in London. Both Pulteney and Walpole supported the bill, but when the latter tried to insert a clause which affirmed the power of the Lord Chamberlain to license plays, Sir John protested strongly and withdrew his bill, realizing that what Walpole really wanted was to stifle stage attacks on

[1] Hervey, *Some Materials, etc.*, p. 98: 'Sir Robert Walpole resolved, rather than suffer himself to be produced for thirty nights together on the stage in the person of a highwayman, to make use of the authority of his friend the Duke of Grafton as Lord Chamberlain to put a stop to the representation of it.'

ministers. But Walpole succeeded in out-manœuvring him. Shortly afterwards a play with the title of *The Golden Rump* was brought to his notice. He read the worst passages to the House to emphasize the need for action, and then brought in a bill to amend the law with regard to rogues, vagabonds and beggars in so far as it related to the common players of interludes. In the course of the debate he skilfully got the acceptance of a clause which ordered all new plays and any amendments to old ones to be sent to the Lord Chamberlain 14 days before they were performed. Breach of this regulation could lead to a £50 fine and, what was still more serious, the loss of the licence of the theatre. Barnard, too, then had his way and a second amendment restricted playhouses to the liberties of the City of Westminster and wherever the King should reside. When therefore in the late eighteenth century the demand for provincial theatres became strong, parliamentary sanction had in every case to be sought, which provided some interesting social sidelights in the subsequent debates on the propriety of encouraging the labouring poor to spend time and money on theatrical entertainment. Even here, however, enterprising managers found a way round the law; the device was to charge for a concert and throw in the play free.

7

THE FALL OF WALPOLE

1. WALPOLE'S ECONOMIC AND COLONIAL POLICY

WEARYING and persistent as the attacks of the opposition whigs were, they would only have been able to bring about Walpole's resignation or dismissal if they had won the support of sufficient of the independent members of the House to make it impossible to carry on the King's business there. So long as he could keep the country prosperous and at peace no crisis was likely to occur; both Walpole and the opposition whigs realized this. Since there seemed little likelihood of undermining him in the Closet, the country would have to be pushed into war. Almost inevitably, therefore, their political ambitions made them warmongers. That in such circumstances Walpole's skill should have been directed towards the maintenance of peace is understandable. But even if there had been no opposition to harry and vex him, it is unlikely that Walpole's policy would have differed greatly from that which he did in fact follow. Temperamentally he disliked the wastage of war and believed that the national interests could just as well be secured by patient negotiation. Moreover it could well be argued that nothing would so effectively establish the Hanoverian dynasty, and frustrate all Jacobite plots, as general contentment, and that nothing would so disturb this gainful tranquillity as war, with its heavy taxation and dislocation of trade.

Peace he knew must be accompanied by prosperity and this he made it one of his main aims to foster. The speed with which English economic life had returned to normal after the over-stimulation of the South Sea Bubble was proof of the soundness of his policy. Walpole is usually considered to have handled economic matters well. He was not an innovator and few of his projects were original: between 1723 and the famous Excise Bill of 1733, his attempts to develop London as a great free port merely aimed at giving a concrete form to projects frequently discussed since the mid-seventeenth century. In the same way his moderate reforms of the tariff had been advocated by writers such as Roger Coke[1] and Charles Davenant, who had popularized the view that moderate and intelligently applied tariffs were the best receipt for a flourishing trade. What Walpole with his practical common sense did, was to clear out some of the obstacles in the channels of trade and cut away a good deal of dead wood from the tangle of tariffs. The speech from the throne in 1721 had stressed the need to overhaul both import and export duties. Accordingly, during the session legislation provided for the removal of export duties on more than a hundred manufactured commodities. Import duties, particularly on raw materials required for the textile industry, were likewise removed. In addition bounties were given to stimulate sugar refining and the home production of such things as sailcloth and silk—all industries which had to meet severe foreign competition. In order to bring it more into line with contemporary prices the Book of Rates, which had last been overhauled in 1694, was further simplified. Nor were the special needs of the landed interest forgotten. Bounties on the export of grain were continued and agricultural produce was included in the commodities freed from the burden of export duties.

How much of the credit for these reforms is to be assigned to Walpole it is difficult to say. By the time economic legislation reaches the statute book it may appear to be the product of one controlling mind, but this is rarely true. In most cases it was rather the pressure of rival interests than any coherent plan that initiated it. Most measures of an economic character can be traced back to petitions from groups of merchants, or special towns or individual colonies. The motion that the petition be read, often moved by a member with local interests, then led to a debate in the Commons, which gave ample opportunity for any members who were in any way concerned to put forward their special interests. There were plenty of merchants in the House competent to discuss such measures. The West Indian lobby was a strong one; the East India Company

---

[1] Roger Coke, *A Treatise wherein is demonstrated that the Church and State of England are in Equal Danger with the Trade of it* (1671).

was well represented; the Baltic merchants and those engaged in the Levant all had their advocates; members from ports regularly championed the needs of their constituencies. When ministers were concerned it was usually because of the influence which these conflicting interests might have on parliamentary votes. The West Indian lobby was too powerful for Walpole, or any other minister, to risk driving it into opposition; the goodwill of the East India Company was worth retaining. When Walpole insisted on the renewal of its charter in 1730—in face of the clamours of the opposition for a regulated company—he was thinking not only of the advantages of having a strong company to control a distant trade but also of the £200,000 that the Company was prepared to contribute to the supplies for that year. To support his own practical common sense in deciding the ministerial line when economic issues were raised in the House, Walpole had access to the sensible and well-informed advice of his Treasury officials and of the Commissioners of Trade and Plantations.

Walpole's colonial policy was based on the same mixture of expediency and common sense. His primary aim was the interest of the English merchant and manufacturer: when either seemed in danger he had no scruple in regulating colonial trade. In 1732 the American colonies were forbidden to send beaver hats to this country; instead they must send the beaver skins which were required for English hat manufacturers. A well-known example of his interference in colonial trade is furnished by the Molasses Act of 1733.[1] All colonies found their balance of payments with the mother country a problem because of their dependence on English manufactured goods, but for the northern colonies, which had no acceptable crop like sugar or rice or tobacco to send in exchange, it was particularly acute. To meet it a trade had grown up by which the New England colonies sent timber for barrels, horses and provisions to the French West Indian Islands, taking in return their sugar and molasses from which they made rum. This was considered to be detrimental to the British West Indian sugar interest, faced with the competition of the lower production costs of the French islands. From 1731 the West Indian planter interest had been trying to get the trade stopped by the imposition of duties which would have been prohibitory. Here Walpole seems to have been a moderating influence, for the duty imposed by the act of 1733 of

---

[1] *English Historical Documents,* vol. IX, *American Colonial Documents,* p. 362.

6*d.* a gallon on molasses was heavy enough to ensure that the crop from the British islands would be sold first, while leaving the New Englanders free to supplement supplies from the French islands afterwards. In practice this act seems to have had little effect because of the extent to which it was evaded.[1] It does however illustrate the way in which the British Parliament had to balance conflicting colonial interests when considering economic legislation. Two examples of legislation which was intended to benefit colonial producers were the removal of rice from the list of enumerated commodities in so far as Carolina in 1730, and Georgia in 1735, were allowed to ship it direct to any country south of Cape Finisterre.[2] Previously all rice had first to be shipped to England and re-exported from there. The heavy competition of the rice grown in the south of Europe had made it difficult to find a market for colonial rice when burdened by this additional charge, and the relaxation was an attempt to meet this difficulty. The same concession was given to the West Indian islands with regard to sugar. There was therefore a certain amount of elasticity and common sense used in the application of the laws of trade. In economic matters Walpole showed a practical grasp of the problems of British merchants and colonial interests to which justice is hardly done by dismissing it with the phrase that his colonial policy was one of 'letting sleeping dogs lie'. It is also misleading in that the 'dogs', far from sleeping, were continually asking for bones: it was Walpole's task to distribute these.

In handling problems of public finance Walpole showed both greater originality and more personal initiative. In 1717 he had been anxious not to resign before he had had the opportunity of introducing his bill for the Sinking Fund. Time and time again he showed considerable dexterity in dealing with the deficit on the Civil List. It will be remembered that part of the price he paid for his reconciliation with Stanhope and Sunderland had been to arrange that the deficit should be funded. He enjoyed administration, and within the limits of the antiquated system he inherited his management of

[1] The whole problem was a complicated one which it is impossible to explain adequately here. For a full discussion see R. B. Sheridan, 'The Molasses Act and the Market Strategy of the British Sugar Planters' (*Journal of Economic History*, vol. XVII, p. 83, 1957), whose final verdict is that though the Molasses Act was 'a near failure in the application to the North American colonies, it cannot be so regarded with reference to the British Isles'. Apparently it did secure for English and Scottish merchants the monopoly of the Irish market.

[2] Walpole was personally opposed to this measure.—R. Sedgwick, *op. cit.*, p. 12.

the Treasury was good. Throughout his period of office he gave high priority to keeping the level of taxation low. One of his main objections to Townshend's tougher policy in 1727 was that it meant raising the Land Tax to what was regarded as the wartime level of 4s. in the pound. Once he had taken the control of foreign affairs into his own hands, and peace seemed assured, he had reduced it rapidly to the abnormally low figure of 1s. in the pound. Probably this left too large a gap to be filled by other sources. The re-imposition of the Salt Tax in 1732 and the Excise Bill of 1733 were both necessitated by his determination to keep the Land Tax low. Wherever he could, and for as long as he could, he preferred to tax the mass of the people and the merchant. Though Walpole's relations with the inner ring of financiers and bankers were close, there was little love lost between him and the great body of the merchants. It is sometimes forgotten that the City was not a homogeneous community.[1] The controlling element was made up of a small group of the wealthiest merchants, often directors of one of the three great moneyed companies—the Bank of England, the South Sea Company, and the East India Company—and the leading financiers. These were the men who floated government loans and secured government contracts. They were bitterly opposed by all the lesser merchants and the small fry in the City who automatically sympathized with the opposition in the Commons. In consequence Walpole found the City troublesome, and its democratic franchise prevented him from getting his own supporters returned for City offices. Having failed to get indirect control by the manipulation of its elections, in 1725 Walpole launched a frontal attack. In spite of the protests of the citizens and the parliamentary fury of the opposition, he secured the passage of the City Bill which recognized the traditional right of veto of the Mayor and Aldermen over the Common Council and disenfranchised many of the smaller citizens. Henceforth the ministers, acting with their big-business allies, had little trouble with the City. His action increased the bitterness of the ordinary citizen. This hatred his enemies did their best to exploit. Again and again in debates on financial issues Sir John Barnard, the leader of the popular party, opposed Walpole's measures in the House, or tried to force his hand by proposing measures of

[1] Lucy Sutherland, 'The City of London in Eighteenth Century Politics' in *Essays presented to Sir Lewis Namier* (1956), ed. Richard Pares and A. J. P. Taylor, is illuminating on this topic.

his own. He tried to prevent the renewal of the East India Company's charter in 1730 and pressed for the reduction of the rates of interest on certain South Sea stock in 1737—both without avail. This antagonism between Walpole and the City explains to some extent the success of the opposition in whipping up demonstrations and petitions against the Excise Bill.

2. THE WAR OF THE POLISH SUCCESSION

In spite of opposition Walpole contrived to keep England at peace until 1739, though his wisdom in avoiding any entanglement in the War of the Polish Succession has been much debated. The outbreak of the war was a symptom that the situation on which the diplomatic arrangements of the years 1717–31 had rested was changing, and changing in favour of France. By the thirties she too had recovered from the strain of Louis XIV's wars. Her King was a married man with an heir. She had no quarrel with England, and was prepared to keep and use the Anglo-French Alliance, but this was no longer as necessary to her as it had been, now that friendly co-operation between the two Bourbon Kings was again possible. England too, by the Treaty of Vienna, had to some extent returned to the old system. This was the situation when Augustus the Strong of Poland died in February 1733.

The fact that the Polish monarchy was elective made that country particularly susceptible to the intrigues of foreign powers. Its geographical position meant that neither Austria nor Russia dared allow it to be dominated by an enemy, while France regarded it as a most desirable outpost of French influence. Louis XV's marriage with Maria Leszczynska now showed that it had other advantages besides the quick provision of an heir: Stanislas, her father, had been King of Poland until driven from his throne by Charles XII of Sweden. France proposed to support his candidature, and he was duly elected by the Diet. This extension of French influence was something that Austria and Russia could not permit, and they agreed to recognize the late King's son as Augustus III. Walpole was fully aware of the difficulties which lay ahead if a general war should break out. Accordingly in preliminary conversations he made it clear that though he favoured the imperial candidate he was not prepared to enter into engagements that would involve the use of force. He even persuaded the Emperor to leave to Russian troops the active business of intervention. Faced by a Russian invasion and the threat of 6,000 Austrian troops on the frontier, a section of the Polish Diet elected Augustus III. For the rejected Stanislas France could do little, but having gained the support of Spain by the promise of help for her Italian ambitions, and of Sardinia with the bait of further territory to be seized from the Emperor, Fleury brushed aside the contention that Charles VI had not actively intervened in Poland. With her new allies France made attacks on imperial territory both in Italy and Germany. Walpole was in a dilemma. By the Treaty of Vienna (1731) he had guaranteed the Austrian possessions: now Charles VI was looking to England for help.

It is true that nothing in that treaty had committed England to back up Charles VI's ambitions in Poland, though she had encouraged them to the extent of helping to bring about an agreement between the Emperor and Saxony, by which the Elector was to recognize the Pragmatic Sanction and the Emperor to back up Saxon claims on Poland. But Poland soon ceased to be the centre of the conflict. The real danger came from French aggression in Italy and along the Rhine. George II, Lord Harrington and, to a large extent Newcastle, considered that help should be given. Walpole was determined that it should not, and used every artifice to delay a decision. He argued that the Emperor had neglected the Barrier fortresses so that the Dutch would never dare to venture war with France; but they equally with ourselves had signed the Treaty of Vienna, and without them we could not move. To his colleagues and to George II he emphasized the dangers of plunging into war on the eve of a general election, and the need to temporize until a new Parliament had been chosen and public opinion roused to the desirability of helping the Emperor against France. This argument had some justification. The storm over the Excise Bill had hardly died away and opposition to the government had never been stronger than it was in the Lords. War over Poland could be made to look like sacrificing purely English interests to the imperialist leanings of the Hanoverians. Walpole carried his point in the Closet, though not without difficulty. This episode is an interesting commentary on the realities of political life in the vital years of Walpole's struggle to retain power. Neither George II nor Harrington agreed with him. Newcastle was deeply troubled. The Closet was full of intrigue. The King and Harrington favoured schemes which might involve the United Provinces, despite themselves, in the war, while Walpole was endeavouring to get them to act with England in offering a strong joint mediation to the Emperor and France.

The bitterness of the Emperor, who had asked for arms and after nine months was offered mediation, is understandable. Walpole, he concluded, was the man responsible for his rebuff, and the Viennese representative in London began to act with the opposition. Walpole, however, was lucky in that he managed to convince Caroline that peace was essential to English interests, and it is a tribute to her influence and to his that, in spite of George II's personal preferences, Charles VI *was* offered mediation instead of arms. As the war was now going badly for him he was forced to accept the offer. With some duplicity Walpole then turned to a secret negotiation with Fleury, conducted through his brother Horatio, as to the terms to be offered to the Emperor. It may have been a practical step to make sure in advance that France would agree to the terms which Walpole would propose to Austria but, as Newcastle pointed out, it was treating our imperial ally very shabbily. On this occasion Walpole was outwitted at his own game; while professing to discuss the English suggestions, and going through the motions of hammering out acceptable terms, Fleury was also in secret negotiations with Vienna. The result was that England had no share in influencing the terms of peace as finally ratified in the Treaty of Vienna of 1738. By it Stanislas received Lorraine, which on his death was to go to his daughter, Louis XV's wife. The Duke of Lorraine, the husband of Maria Theresa, was to receive Tuscany, long disputed between Spain and Austria, while Don Carlos obtained Naples and Sicily. England had received a snub and the affairs of Europe had been settled without her, to the advantage of France and Spain and the disadvantage of the Emperor, whose main gain was France's signature to the Pragmatic Sanction.

Walpole's wisdom in standing aside was doubted by his colleagues and his King at the time and has been criticized by many historians since. He, personally, does not seem to have been much disturbed by the diplomatic rebuff: peace had been secured and England had not been involved: that his objectives should have been obtained by Fleury rather than himself seemed of no great importance. Contemporary critics were largely disturbed by the cool relations with Vienna that inevitably followed. Later critics have concentrated rather on the lost opportunity of curbing France, arguing that had England joined the Emperor in 1733 she might not have had to fight France in a major war a few years later. To Walpole the situation must have appeared somewhat different. England in 1733 was prosperous within a known and accepted framework of trade; he could hardly be expected to foresee the struggle with France in America, and the fact that the rivalry between the French and British East India Companies was to mean the gaining or losing of an empire. Moreover he had outlived so many changes in the diplomatic pattern of Europe that he might well expect the advantages gained by France at Vienna to prove transitory. Walpole was not cast in the traditional mould of a great foreign minister; prestige and the subtle manœuvring for position meant less to him than concrete results; he was apt to underrate the imponderables. His instinct was to seize the cash and let the credit go. He had little use for rhetoric and talk of national honour. As he was to observe later, 'other nations must be supposed to have honour as well as we, and all nations generally have a great opinion of their courage and power.'[1] His preference was for patient and persistent negotiation: he of all men believed in 'jaw, jaw, rather than war, war'.

3. ANGLO-SPANISH TRADE

Nowhere was this more clearly to be seen than in his relations with Spain.[2] In the early eighteenth century England's trade with Spain was far more important than that carried on with France. It touched her economic life at many points. To Spain England sent large quantities of cloth, both the finer woollen which was worn by the nobles and gentry and the coarser used as habits for Spain's large population of monks and nuns. Spain also took large quantities of dried and salted fish. In return she supplied the fine wool, so necessary for cloth manufacture, together with the soap and olive oil needed for cleansing the raw wool, and from her colonies much indigo, cochineal and logwood for dyeing it. These exchanges by themselves would have been sufficient to make the Spanish trade an important part of British commerce, but they were only half the story. Spain had a large colonial market which her own underdeveloped manufacturers could never supply. Though she forbade direct trade between any other country and her colonies she was glad to buy from England the goods needed in the New World. In return England received the commodity she most needed, gold and

---

[1] W. Coxe, *op. cit.*, vol. I, p. 576.

[2] For the general background to this problem see J. O. McLachlan, *Trade and Peace with Old Spain 1667–1750* (1940).

silver to finance her Baltic and Indian trade. This had been the pattern of Anglo-Spanish trade up to the outbreak of the War of the Spanish Succession; its legal basis was the commercial treaty of 1667 and it had worked to the advantage of both countries. Perhaps it should be added that in addition to this recognized trade a good deal of illegal trade—particularly in slaves and provisions for their support—took place between Jamaica and the other West Indian islands, and the Spanish possessions in the Caribbean Sea.

English merchants, however, had long desired the privilege of a direct trade with the Spanish colonies, and England's success in the War of the Spanish Succession seemed to give an opportunity to secure this. It was in the hope of such privileges that the South Sea Company made its loan to the Crown. In the peace negotiations of 1713 the Asiento, or right to import negro slaves to the number of 4,800, was fairly easily obtained, together with the right to send one ship of 500 tons with the annual silver fleet from Spain. In practice this eagerly sought concession proved more of a complication than a blessing. So concerned with the Asiento were the English negotiators, that Spain managed to slip into the treaty explanatory clauses which made the old established trade with Spain itself exceedingly difficult. It was not until Alberoni was seeking English goodwill for Elizabeth Farnese's schemes, that Bubb Dodington was able to secure, on paper, reasonable terms for direct trade with Spain. Moreover, the Asiento and the annual ship proved a disappointment. The South Sea Company had to pay heavy duties, £34,000 a year, on the first 4,000 negroes sold in the colonies, and their trade had been limited to the Atlantic seaboard. No British ship was to sail round the Horn or penetrate into the Pacific, though the Company was allowed to trade in slaves there in hired ships. The benefits of the annual ship proved equally illusory. It had to sail to whatever port the silver fleet went and to offer its cargoes in competition with theirs. This was a poor reality for the splendid dream of a direct and unlimited trade with the Spanish possessions, yet even this meagre concession had been accompanied by the stipulation that illegal trade between the Spanish and the English colonies should cease, which was a bitter blow to Jamaica.

Moreover, the course of trade, both that of the merchants trading to Old Spain, and that of the South Sea Company, was far from smooth in the twenties. The Spaniards had a wonderful gift for obstacles, delays and vexatious duties, which made trade expensive and slow even when Madrid and London were on friendly terms. When relations were strained, as they frequently were, almost to the point of unofficial war, they excelled themselves in hampering British merchants in every way. Indeed, their realization of the importance of their trade to England was the strongest weapon in their diplomatic armoury. As a result it was not until after the signing of the Treaty of Vienna in 1731, when Don Carlos was at last put in possession of the Duchies, that Spain set out to be accommodating. In concluding that treaty, therefore, Walpole was taking the most effective steps possible to secure for England a most valuable trade. For the next few years Spain followed a conciliatory policy, and it is not surprising that Walpole hesitated to upset the Spanish trade by joining the Emperor against France and Spain. His neutrality paid: English merchants were treated particularly well, first to prevent Britain from joining the Emperor and then, between 1735 and 1737, in the hope that English influence might be used to thwart the separate negotiation between Charles VI and Fleury which was being conducted to the exclusion of Spain. That two years later England and Spain were at war was the doing neither of Walpole nor of Madrid but of the opposition members of Parliament.

It was at once a manufactured crisis and a piece of sustained and magnificent imagination, probably beyond the compass of anything that Robert Walpole could have achieved. To be fair to both Walpole and Pitt, it is necessary to look at the facts out of which the *casus belli* was constructed, then at the vision that inspired it, and finally at the muddle and mess in the early years of the war which resulted. The storm centre was not the trade with Spain but that with the Spanish islands in the Caribbean. Madrid still thought of these waters as reserved for Spanish ships and was determined not to allow others to navigate them without permission. This monopoly Spain tried to maintain by the patrol of armed coastguards' ships. Even had these been well disciplined incidents would have been common, for though the South Sea Company tried to prevent the captains of its permitted sloops, carrying negroes in accordance with the Asiento, from smuggling, a great deal of illicit trade between the merchants of Jamaica and the Spanish islands was taking place. The patrolling was, however, far from being an easily controlled instrument of Spanish policy, for financial stringency dictated that the coastguards were rewarded, almost on a commission basis, by a share of the captured ships. They were indeed more than half-licensed pirates, eager to seize any vulnerable ship as a prize and to discuss the legality of the capture later, preferably when the cargo had been sold and their share of it spent. Nor was it always possible to decide whether a British ship had been encroaching on Spanish waters with the intention of smuggling or whether she had been driven off her course by bad weather and contrary winds.[1] Rather naturally, relations between captains who frequented Spanish waters, whether on legitimate business or not, and the coastguards were extremely bad. If the British could catch a patrolling ship at a disadvantage its crew was roughly, often brutally, handled,[2] while in the same way the Spanish crews behaved with equal violence when the opportunity came to seize a British ship as a prize. There is nothing inherently improbable in the story of Jenkins's ear, though his ship, the *Rebecca*, was not one of the original causes of the dispute.

After 1732 Spain had been behaving with surprising moderation towards British shipping on the Main, a mildness of which the Jamaican contraband runners seem to have taken full advantage until, in despair, in 1737 the Spanish colonial government fitted out a few more coastguard ships. The result was the presumed capture of some twelve British ships, and strong diplomatic representations followed. Spain's response was conciliatory. Five of the ships had disappeared without a trace and may well have been seized by bona fide pirates, three others though plundered had escaped, and of the remaining four it seems probable that they really were engaged in illicit trade. But if Spain's reply was conciliatory it was also extremely dilatory. Keene, the British ambassador in Madrid, had made his protest on 10 December 1737, but the Spanish answer agreeing to release the ships was only received towards the end of May 1738. All this time anger, carefully fanned by the opposition, was rising in England, so that in February 1738 Keene was instructed to present a further list of complaints. The details would be tedious to repeat; but, basically, opposition tactics were to dig out grievances dating from the earlier period of strained relations to buttress present claims. Jenkins's ship the *Rebecca*, for example, had been captured as long ago as 1731.

[1] R. Pares, *War and Trade in the West Indies* (1936), p. 23, draws attention to the importance of the prevailing winds, a point often forgotten in this mechanical age, on the routing of English ships in this area.

[2] Rear Admiral Charles Stuart wrote from Jamaica, 'The sloops that sail from this island on that illicit trade have more than once bragged to me of having murdered seven or eight Spaniards on their own shore.'—Quoted N. Williams, *op. cit.*, p. 143.

4. THE OPPOSITION AND SPAIN

Both La Quadra in Madrid and Walpole were anxious to arrange matters amicably, and though the West Indian merchants had been organizing petitions Walpole and Newcastle had been fairly successful in smothering discussion in both Houses. In March, however, the news reached England that the sailors taken from the captured ships had been forced to work their passage to Spain on a Spanish warship and were now in chains in a Spanish dockyard. Again there was nothing unusual in this: it was the normal treatment of sailors taken off a prize. Moreover, these particular crews seem to have been treated with more than usual leniency by the Spanish authorities. But the story made wonderful propaganda. When on 3 March 1738 a group of merchants from the plantations prayed to be heard by counsel as well as in person, Walpole suggested that the eloquence of the trained advocate was most undesirable in that it would only generate emotion. But Alderman Wilmot replied 'Seventy of our brave sailors are now in chains in Spain. Our countrymen in chains, and slaves to Spaniards! Is not this enough to fire the coldest? Is not this enough to arouse all the vengeance of national resentment?'[1] It was not an atmosphere favourable to negotiation. Nevertheless Walpole persevered. When the House demanded that the relevant papers be laid before it, he got an amendment that excluded the diplomatic exchanges between the Spanish Court and the British ministers. He warned the Spanish ambassador to pay no attention to the language of the opposition and, when forced to agree to Newcastle's sending a stern note, contrived that it should be sent with a covering letter to moderate its effect, and accompanied by a strong hint that it might be well that a reply should not be made until Parliament had risen.

Meanwhile patient negotiation was continuing for the settlement of outstanding claims. Unfortunately for Walpole's pacific policy Philip V was turning more to France, so that an original claim for £140,000 had to be reduced to £95,000 before Spain would accept it as a basis for a settlement. After much argument Walpole did get his colleagues to agree to the lower figure and there seemed a chance that he would succeed in keeping the peace. Unfortunately for his plans the negotiations now got entangled with the affairs of the South Sea Company. The financial relations between the Spanish Crown and the Company were always involved. The Company

[1] W. Coxe, *op. cit.*, vol. I, p. 575.

owed certain dues to the King in respect of its Asiento and its annual ship, and there was nothing unusual in Philip's asking the Company to settle his agreed liabilities in England out of the money that would normally have been paid to him in this way. The Company had, however, been a victim of the strained relations between England and Spain in 1718 and again in 1727. During these years of unofficial war its property had been seized, in spite of agreements which should have given the English merchants time to realize their assets and remove their goods. The Company therefore counter-claimed against Philip V. He in turn counter-claimed against it on the ground that it had been paying duties in the depreciated *real* as if its international value had been the same as its face value. It was a pretty tangle, for now the Company refused to pay the £95,000 unless its own claims were met. After desperate negotiations Walpole was able to announce in the House that the Convention of Pardo had been signed in January 1739. But the condition of signing was that the Company should pay the £95,000 in return for promises to restore its property, and as the opposition were supported by public opinion in backing up the Company's determination not to pay, the Convention lapsed. There was little hope that war could any longer be avoided.

In this sense the crisis had been a manufactured one. In 1739 Britain had probably fewer genuine grievances against Spain in the New World than she had had at any time since 1714. Yet though the English case was often quite unjustified on legal grounds, it had a core of reality. The fundamental question concerned the freedom of the seas, the right of British ships to sail where they would on their lawful occasions. This right in the Caribbean Spain steadfastly denied, conceding only the right to sail to and from the British islands there: anything else was trespass.[1] The only exceptions they were prepared to recognize were those conferred on Britain by commercial treaties such as the Asiento. In March 1738 Pulteney had moved a motion to assert the right of free navigation to any part of the American seas by a British ship, so long as it did not touch at a Spanish port, the right to carry all kinds of goods from one British port to another, the right to cut logwood at Campeachy[2]

[1] Because of this claim they argued that they were entitled to search any ship and if it was carrying Spanish products and not covered by treaty rights to seize it. England was claiming the right to sail freely.—R. Pares, *op. cit.*, p. 37.

[2] *Ibid.*, pp. 41–43.

and to gather salt at the island of Tortuga. In these four demands he mixed wide issues of policy together with extremely doubtful claims against Spain. In the debate that followed Walpole managed to concentrate the attention of the Commons on the first of these propositions. But in the Lords the ministers were less successful, and the extremely delicate question, right of search, was raised.

By the beginning of 1739 these tactics had inflamed public opinion outside Parliament and there was something which might almost be described as a general clamour that Spanish captains who had molested British ships should be punished, that Spain should disavow her right of search, that she should give up her claims to Georgia and part of Carolina, and that she should pay £340,000 compensation for previous confiscations and large sums to the South Sea Company for their losses in the unofficial wars of 1718 and 1727. When therefore Walpole announced that the settlement of outstanding difficulties had been arranged by the Convention of Pardo, and when the details of that Convention, with its whittling away of British claims, were laid before Parliament, the opposition had at last a cause that aroused the keenest interest. In the Lords it was only approved by 95 to 74, thirty-nine peers protesting. The debate in the Commons on 6 March was felt to be so important that a hundred members had taken their seats by 8 a.m., a most unusual occurrence. Walpole's speech of two and a half hours in favour of the Convention was answered by young William Pitt who asked: 'Is this any longer a nation? or where is an English Parliament, if with more ships in our harbours than in all the navies of Europe, we will bear to hear of the expediency of receiving from Spain an insecure, unsatisfactory, dishonourable convention, which carries downright subjection in every line'.[1] Lyttelton supporting him, declared that the right of search was 'the root of all our grievances' and that 'peace at the expense of rights, of essential justice, peace exposed to insults, peace exposed to injuries, is the most abject, is the most deplorable, is the most calamitous circumstance of human affairs. It is the worst effect that could be produced by the most ruinous war.' On the 9th Wyndham and his friends declared their intention of seceding from Parliament rather than be involved in so much dishonour. Pelham would have had a motion to commit him to the Tower for his insolence, but Walpole drily observing that 'I am only afraid that they will not be so good as their word, and that

[1] Coxe, *op. cit.*, vol. I, p. 601.

they will return'[1] used their absence to push through certain measures in which he was interested. One of these, a bill to permit the West Indies to export sugar in English ships direct to the continent without touching at a British port first, and the placing of additional duties on foreign sugar and molasses, may well have had the political aim of conciliating the West Indian lobby.

5. WAR WITH SPAIN

Hysterical though much of this storm of protest and invective was, Lyttelton was arguing prophetically in maintaining that Britain with vital interests in the New World could no longer submit to restrictions which previously she had been too weak to challenge. In the seventeenth century her trade with Spain, and via Spain with her colonies, had been so important that good relations with Madrid were essential. This trade was important still, but the American colonies were providing more extensive markets, and the entrepôt trade in colonial produce, and in the imports of the East India Company, were playing a larger part in her European commerce. It is significant that on the declaration of war in October 1739 stocks rose, as English merchants thought it would be an easy matter to despoil a supposedly weak Spain of her colonies. Though trade had been an important issue in the war of the Spanish Succession, that which broke out in 1739 can perhaps be described as the first of the great eighteenth-century wars which were to establish Britain as a leading colonial power. Yet it may well be that the opposition was only unwittingly co-operating with her imperial future. Much of their eloquence was intended merely to embarrass Walpole. Even Pitt may have come, through his own oratory, to the full realization of the importance of trade and empire which was to characterize his later career, though Governor Pitt may have conditioned him to being especially sympathetic to such ideas.

All was jubilation when Admiral Vernon with the six ships he had demanded captured Porto Bello in the following November. But that was the end of British success.[2] A large expeditionary force sent to the West Indies was badly commanded by General Wentworth. In spite of Vernon's considerable and able help he failed successively to

[1] Coxe, *op. cit.*, vol. 1, p. 606.
[2] For a discussion of British strategy and achievements—or the lack of them, see R. Pares, *op. cit.*, pp. 85–127.

take Cartagena, Santiago de Cuba, and Panama. Meanwhile the West Indian climate was the Spaniards' most useful ally against England's unseasoned troops. By the end of 1742 the expedition, which had been so optimistically dispatched, was recalled with even the memory of Vernon's original exploit eclipsed by the subsequent fiascos. By then, however, it was clear that England was no longer involved only in a colonial war with Spain. In October 1740, just a year after the outbreak of the Spanish war, the Emperor Charles VI died. It was a matter to concern most of Europe, for in spite of the Pragmatic Sanction the succession of a woman, Maria Theresa, seemed to offer an opportunity to acquire Hapsburg territory. Spain still had unsatisfied ambitions in Italy, so had Sardinia. The Elector of Bavaria was anxious to push his candidature to the imperial crown to the exclusion of Maria Theresa's husband Francis, now Duke of Tuscany. France was reserving her freedom of action by distinguishing between Maria Theresa's rights to the Hapsburg lands and her husband's election to the imperial throne. England, already at war with Spain, was hesitating whether to renew her alliance with Austria or not. Meanwhile in December 1740 Frederick seized Silesia, to which he proffered a nominal claim, and. then promised Maria Theresa his help against other marauders in return for a recognition of his claim. Her refusal and armed resistance meant the general alignment of the major Powers on one side or the other.

To Walpole the outbreak of the Austro-Prussian war brought fresh problems. Relations between the ministers were strained. Newcastle resented Lord Hervey's recent promotion to the office of Privy Seal, and both he and Harrington had approved the war with Spain—'your war' as Walpole bitterly called it. With its increasing lack of success the opposition, under Pulteney in the Commons and Carteret and Chesterfield in the Lords, were pressing home their attack. In general they followed the line of increasing Walpole's unpopularity by attributing to him all the failures of the war, and by harassing him with repeated motions for the production of letters and papers that might incriminate him if granted and throw odium on him if refused. In February 1741 these attacks culminated in motions from both Houses for an address to the King asking that Sir Robert Walpole might be removed from his counsels for ever. To their mortification both were defeated; in the Lords where the motion was introduced by Carteret, by 108 to 59 and in the Commons by 290 to 106. One reason for Walpole's triumph was that the opposition was even more divided than the ministers: the tories, more leaderless than ever after Sir William Wyndham's death in 1740, were profoundly distrustful of the ambitions of Pulteney and Carteret, and showed this distrust by either abstaining from voting or actively supporting Walpole.[1] It was his last great triumph.

6. THE WAR OF THE AUSTRIAN SUCCESSION

It was against this turbulent background that a decision had to be taken about Maria Theresa, who was demanding that England honour her signature to the Pragmatic Sanction. Walpole, fully alive to the difficulties of having a fresh war on his hands, argued that if she were not encouraged by the hope of British help Austria would have to come to terms with Frederick II, but the cards were stacked against him. George II's pro-Austrian and anti-Prussian feelings made him sympathize with the opposition cry that help must be given. It was a question on which there was ground for a genuine difference of opinion. Carteret was not necessarily being factious when he argued that it was dangerous to allow Austria to be weakened. It was far from clear what France would do. So far she had given Spain no active help beyond sending a fleet to the West Indies, but Englishmen were aware of her growing commercial and industrial strength. Unless there was to be a repetition of the War of the Polish Succession it could well be argued that Austria must be helped now. Bending to the royal wishes and the will of the House, Walpole moved that a subsidy of £300,000 be granted to Maria Theresa.

On 25 April Parliament was dissolved and writs for a general election issued. In June 1741 France made a treaty of alliance with Prussia, in July she agreed to support Charles of Bavaria's claim to the Empire, and in August she stirred up Sweden to attack Russia. When the new Parliament assembled it would be to face the complications of a European war. Would it still be content to accept Walpole's half-hearted leadership? Both to him and to his enemies the composition of the Parliament would be a matter of vital importance. Both sides used all their resources and both seemed sanguine as to the result. Nothing, however, could be certain

---

[1] Moreover tory principles did not countenance an attack on the King's right to choose his own ministers; see A. S. Foord, *His Majesty's Opposition, 1717–1830* (1964), p. 139.

until it came to a test of the lobbies, for many of the men who called themselves whig were enemies rather than supporters of the administration. In consequence the only way for the politicians to assess their probable strength was to study the past record and family connections of each individual member and from this to guess his probable future conduct. As the new Parliament contained 148 new members prognostication was difficult. The Duke of Newcastle thought that the administration would have a majority of 14, Walpole optimistically calculated on 40, which would have been roughly equal to his possible majority in a full House in the previous Parliament.[1] Bubb Dodington, equally optimistically, made the returns indicate an opposition majority of some 14 votes including the Scottish ones. Once the House got down to business the supporters of the administration seem to have had a majority of about 14, a number which indicates how well Newcastle's political intuition had served him. The results of eighteenth-century elections, however, reflect the strength of small organized political groups and family connections more than the swing of any general public opinion. Walpole's enemies would get in candidates pledged to attack him where they could, Walpole's friends naturally gave him similar support in the constituencies, while whoever was, either from conviction or interest, a supporter of the administration, would be prepared to act with him so long as he had the confidence of George II and could do his business in the Commons. Only a few of the more open constituencies with large electorates were likely to be much influenced by general opinion. This falling away of support from Walpole, therefore, must not be taken to imply more than the enmity of the Prince of Wales, who had used all his influence in the Cornish boroughs, and of the Duke of Argyll, who had used discontent with the fines imposed after the Porteous riots to return anti-Walpolian candidates.

A majority of 14, though small, would have been sufficient if it could all have been mobilized for critical divisions, but, without a tight party organization, there was a tendency on the part of members to dissociate themselves from Walpole in view of his increasing difficulties. It was impossible to pretend that the war, either in the West Indies or in Europe, was going well. The help Parliament had intended to give to Maria Theresa in April had proved of little use. Two French armies, nominally as the auxiliaries of the Elector of Bavaria, were now in Germany. One, under

[1] A. S. Foord, *op. cit.*, considered sixty the safe minimum for a stable administration.

Maillebois, was stationed in Westphalia with the obvious intention of exerting pressure on the United Provinces or Hanover if either attempted to intervene on Austria's behalf. The other in concert with Bavaria had invaded Austria, and was to capture Prague by the end of the year. In the circumstances George II panicked. He had gone to Hanover in May 1741 intending to supervise the sending to Maria Theresa of the Danish and Hessian troops which by treaty England was obliged to provide. But in face of the danger from France he both kept the troops for the defence of Hanover and made an agreement with France by which he secured the neutrality of his Electorate. These dismal acts were taken on George II's own responsibility as Elector, but the secrets of the Closet could hardly be revealed in Parliament, and for the general ill-success of the war it was easy to blame Walpole. When therefore the new Parliament met in December politicians of every group were watching for straws in the wind.

7. WALPOLE'S LAST FIGHT

The action of the Commons in the next weeks well illustrates the importance of the independent member. The struggle was between Walpole and his friends and the leading whig politicians in opposition, to win over the independent gentlemen in the House, whether they called themselves whigs or tories. The attack of Pulteney and Carteret was essentially against Walpole rather than against the administration as a whole and could be summed up in the slogan 'Walpole must go'. They had therefore to convince the independent members that so long as he remained the war would be disastrously handled and the national interests betrayed. Sometimes they overreached themselves in their desire to embarrass Sir Robert, demanding information which in the national interest was better not discussed. On such occasions the inclination of the independent members was to support the administration, and Walpole's majorities looked a little healthier as a consequence. The real test of his power came over disputed elections and the appointment of committees. Eighteenth-century electoral procedure gave many openings for corrupt practices, and every general election was followed by numerous petitions attempting to unseat successful candidates. No one expected them to be decided on their merits: they were regarded as a test of strength between the administration and the various groups in the Commons. The way in which they went was therefore of great importance in the new Parliament. If favourable to the administration Walpole, by protecting his friends or unseating his enemies, would demonstrate that the ultimate control of the House still lay with him. It was therefore a great blow when at the outset the opposition won a significant victory by carrying their candidate against Walpole's for the key post of chairman of the Committee of Elections and Privileges. Though the administration managed to carry the earliest petitions it was only by single figure majorities, and the bitterly contested Westminster election went against them. Walpole's slender majority began to dwindle as more and more of his erstwhile supporters absented themselves. More and more members whose main allegiance was to the Crown and to their own careers were growing aware that Walpole's days of power were almost over. If he could no longer depend on securing adequate majorities in the Commons then, even though he still had the royal confidence, George II would have to let him go.

In the Christmas recess rumours were circulating that the end was in sight but, after so many years of power, office had become almost second nature to Walpole and he could hardly realize that resignation could be forced upon him while he still held the favour of the King. Moreover, even in the struggle over election petitions, if he had suffered some humiliating reverses he could also count some gains, and his nominal majority now stood at 21. A nominal majority eroded by absenteeism was, however, likely to prove a delusive comfort. To strengthen his position and split his opponents, Walpole tried to effect a reconciliation between father and son through the mediation of the Earl of Cholmondeley acting for George II, and Thomas Secker, Bishop of Oxford, who represented the Prince of Wales. The bait was an extra £50,000 a year, the payment of his debts, and an entry once again for his friends at Court. The pill covered by this jam was to be Frederick's unreserved acknowledgement of his past misdeeds. That George II was prepared to make the offer, coupled though it was with this provision, is proof of the value that he still placed on Walpole's services. Both the jam and the pill were refused: by now the Prince was reasonably confident that his friends would soon be in office. Walpole had lost doubly by his last manœuvre. He failed to win over the support of those members who belonged to the Prince's party, and whose addition to his own friends might well have been crucial, and he was made to appear the major obstacle to a reconciliation between

George II and his eldest son. In such circumstances members who normally supported the administration and who did not want to give a direct vote against the King's minister, would be inclined to solve their problem by absence. Even so, Walpole fought toughly to the end. When on 21 January 1742 Pulteney moved for a Select Committee to examine all the papers relevant to the recent conduct of the war everyone realized that a fresh personal attack against Walpole was about to be launched. It is a tribute to the honesty and impartiality of a large part of the House that Pulteney failed to carry his motion, though only by 3 votes, after a fighting speech by Sir Robert in his own defence. But, though he could still rally his supporters in defence of the policy of the administration as a whole, he could no longer prevent those members who were luke-warm towards him personally from failing to attend what everyone now knew to be the vitally important committees on elections. On the 28th that of Chippenham was presented and when a minor point was pressed to a division and lost by one vote Walpole's friends seem to have decided that it was hopeless for him to struggle on. By the 31st he had come to agree with them and informed George II of his decision. When two days later, on 2 February, the Chippen-ham petition was carried by a majority of 16 against the adminis-tration, Walpole was already armoured against his defeat and took the opportunity of announcing his resignation.[1]

So came to an end a remarkable public career. For twenty years, ever since the death of Sunderland, Walpole had been the most powerful minister of the Crown. Under his peaceful, practical rule the economic resources of the country had grown steadily and the Hanoverian dynasty, if not much loved, was firmly established. For twenty years he had veiled the constitutional dilemma that was inherent in the 1689 settlement, namely how the right of the King to chose his ministers was to be reconciled with that of the House of Commons to refuse supplies to ministers it did not trust. His skilful handling of the royal business in the Commons, his adroit lowering of the Land Tax, his sound exposition of the adminis-tration's policy in debate, quite as much as the adroit manipulation of patronage by the Duke of Newcastle, persuaded the solid un-committed member to continue his support. On questions of foreign policy he and George II were not always in agreement and in minor

---

[1] For a full analysis of the last weeks of Walpole's administration see J. B. Owen, *The Rise of the Pelhams* (1957), ch. I, on which this account has been based.

matters Walpole could not always get his own way, yet after his initial distrust on his succession had been dissipated George II clung to Walpole. He might often try to circumvent his policy and cabal with Newcastle and Harrington to drag England into the War of the Polish Succession. Occasionally he insisted on appointments which Walpole disliked, but his actions after the Excise crisis were proof that he considered outright opposition to Walpole as tantamount to outright opposition to himself. It was because Walpole was trusted by the King and supported in the Commons that his tenure of office was so long. In no modern sense was he a Prime Minister, and to speak of him as making any great contribution to the development of the Cabinet is to misunderstand the political conditions of his day. The King listened to his arguments; so did the Commons. Like all eighteenth-century politicians he used his Closet influence to get rid of ministers whom he disliked, and in this he was more successful than most, thereby giving an appearance of Cabinet responsibility and harmony. Because he was indispensable to the King so long as he could command a majority in the Commons, other ministers had to put up with his interference and accept his domination or get out. Because he loved power he was never prepared to share it and rarely to delegate it, and in the royal counsels there was no room for men as ambitious as he was but less able. His domination was a personal one and he left no constitutional cloak for his successors to assume.

This was amply illustrated by the arrangements that were made for carrying on the administration after his resignation and retirement to the Lords as the Earl of Orford. His most important colleagues remained in office; there was never any question of a clean sweep. This was not because Newcastle and Harrington had thrown Walpole to the wolves. There seems little evidence, apart from rumour, that either of the Secretaries had betrayed their colleague. It is true that in 1740 relations between Walpole and Newcastle had been very strained. They had differed over the policy to be followed over Spain, and Newcastle had probably more sympathy with the arguments of the opposition than with those of the First Lord of the Treasury. Also the elevation of Hervey, whose sneering wit had often been displayed at the Duke's expense, had been a bitter pill for him to swallow,[1] though it seems

---

[1] Newcastle to Hardwicke, 14 October 1739: 'The world must think that for some reasons I am not, at present, to be lay'd aside, but to be made useless, and that this

that George II rather than Walpole was responsible for this particular appointment. Nevertheless, in the election of 1741 Newcastle had worked with his accustomed zeal and lavish expenditure: such seats as were lost were not lost through any failure of his. It was not Newcastle's intrigues but the hammering of the opposition on Walpole's lack of success as a war minister that finally destroyed faith in his leadership. Once that was gone nothing that either Newcastle or George II could do could save him. But, just because the attack on Walpole was a personal one led by men in whose way he had stood, and because there was no doctrine of corporate Cabinet responsibility, there was no reason why either his colleagues should resign with him or George II should demand their resignation. Obviously some of the late opposition who had the ear of the House, and who could do the King's business there, would have to be brought in, but that was the extent of the necessary changes. In the eighteenth century, administrations were patched not replaced; and there was more continuity that way. Whether one minister took a decisive lead or dominated his colleagues was more a matter of personality and accident than design, though the experience of the eighteenth century was to demonstrate that only when a minister, with the confidence of both Commons and Crown, dominated the general direction of affairs did things go smoothly.

man was brought in to have the confidence and real secret of the Ministry; for his behaviour towards me has been such that this extraordinary mark of favour to him cannot be consistent with the least remains of regard towards me: and in this light I do, and shall ever look upon this step, as it relates to myself.'—Hardwicke, *op. cit.*, vol. I, pp. 230-1.

8

THE RISE OF THE PELHAMS

1. The Reconstruction of the Ministry

THE importance of the twelve years after the fall of Walpole is more real than apparent. On the surface domestic politics were dull. In 1744 the attractive, intellectually arrogant Carteret was forced to resign from the Secretaryship of State and Henry Pelham became George II's leading minister. His was not the personality to make an impact on the pages of history: he was too universally liked and respected; men are apt to be remembered more for the unkind things their enemies said about them. It is for this reason, even more than for his long tenure of office, that his brother, the Duke of Newcastle, is chiefly remembered. Despite real integrity and solid common sense, the latter's mannerisms and foibles made him 'a whetstone for wise men to sharpen their wits on'. To readers so conditioned neither Pelham nor the Duke can provide the dramatic interest that Walpole could always afford. Foreign politics seem equally dreary and frustrating. When Walpole resigned, involvement in the affairs of Maria Theresa had been added to England's earlier quarrel with Spain. Ahead stretched the mismanaged, inconclusive War of the Austrian Succession. The Peace of Aix-la-Chapelle, which ended it, settled nothing, and the diplomacy of the years between 1748 and Pelham's death in 1754 was confused, and finally rendered meaningless by the Diplomatic Revolution.

Yet to a student of the eighteenth century these years are full of interest. When Walpole retired to the House of Lords it was impossible to say whether in his struggle for power he had stumbled on the solution of the problem posed by the Revolution as to the relations between the House of Commons and the King. His long success might have been no more than the triumph of personality impressing itself on Commons and King alike. Certainly contemporaries regarded it in that way, and hoped to have no more first ministers of his vigour and authority. If a man without his personality could succeed, by the methods he had used, in managing the King's business to the satisfaction of both Parliament and the Closet, then it is clear that new and valuable political conventions were being formed. It was this question that the next twelve years were to answer. In the sphere of foreign affairs, too, these years were to be a seed-bed for future developments. If the peace of Aix-la-Chapelle solved little, the widespread dissatisfaction felt with its terms showed that men were conscious of the problems it evaded. In India the rivalry of the French and British East India Companies continued unabated. The popularity of the 'old system' and the Austrian alliance was at its nadir. As Pelham wrote, 'the Queen of Hungary has undoubtedly lost the affection of the people. . . . They see no end of perpetually crying out "Support the House of Austria" when that House totally neglects the general view.'[1] Out of the failures and disappointments of these years a new foreign policy, later to be associated with the name of Pitt, was coming into being.

In February 1742 George II and the politicians were concerned with the practical problem of reconstructing the ministry rather than with long-term speculations.[2] Out of the welter of conflicting interests some solid facts emerge. Walpole must go and enough of the opposition be taken in to give the King's ministers a working majority in the Commons. George II still had the core of an administration; what was wanted were new allies. Newcastle, Hardwicke and Harrington still remained in office. The tory groups for practical purposes could be disregarded. George II had an aversion to them on principle, and for their part they wanted neither office nor honour from him. His choice therefore lay between the followers of the Duke of Argyll, including Chesterfield, Cobham and Dodington, and the groups attached to Carteret and Pulteney. Both on personal grounds and because of their views on foreign policy the King preferred the latter. Cobham and his 'cubs', of whom young William Pitt was one, and Lord Chesterfield had been not only bitter critics of

[1] W. Coxe, *Memoirs of the Administration of the Right Honourable Henry Pelham* (1829), vol. I, p. 283.

[2] For a detailed analysis of the politics of the period 1742–7 consult J. B. Owen, *The Rise of the Pelhams* (1957).

Walpole but were openly opposed to any foreign policy which seemed to give preference to Hanoverian interests. Carteret on the other hand spoke German fluently, and was deeply interested in, and well informed about, German politics. The next two years were to show that he and George II had many views in common. Nor could Pulteney, whose oratory had given him considerable command over the Commons, be passed over. Therefore negotiations, at first on an exploratory and informal level, were started with these men.

The problem that faced George II, Newcastle and Hardwicke was easy to state but harder to solve. The solid core of Court and Treasury whigs, together with those men who had habitually supported Walpole and had come to be known as 'the old corps' had to be retained. At the same time places had to be found for enough of the 'new whigs', the followers of Carteret and Pulteney, to draw the teeth of the opposition. In the hard bargaining that followed, the Crown showed considerable skill. Pulteney's oft expressed intention not to take office and his scorn of placemen were used to manoeuvre him into refusing the Treasury when formally offered to him. Carteret's claims to it could be more easily ignored because he had little influence in the Commons. Into Walpole's vacant office George II was therefore able to 'slide' Wilmington—in some ways an ironic choice for, as Spencer Compton, he had been intended for the Treasury by the King in 1727. The new First Lord had much to recommend him. He was personally devoted to George II, he had been at best a lukewarm supporter of Walpole, and he had been on good terms with the opposition groups. His appointment satisfied them and at the same time prevented the royal loss of 'face' that must have resulted had either Carteret or Pulteney succeeded to that office.

Carteret became Secretary of State, Harrington being moved into the vacancy created by Wilmington's promotion. Lesser offices were shuffled round to meet Pulteney's demand that he and his friends must have a majority in the Cabinet, the Treasury and the Admiralty. Places were found at the Treasury and the Admiralty for his followers and Sandys became Chancellor of the Exchequer. The apportioning of places soon showed how little unity there was in the late opposition. Pulteney had to meet a rising tide of distrust from his erstwhile allies, the followers of the Duke of Argyll, who considered that he had betrayed their interests to safeguard his own. Because of this bitterness the Court found itself in a stronger position by March

1742 than might have been expected. When the rump of the opposition, including Argyll and his friends, moved on 9 March for a secret committee to inquire into the conduct of the administration for the last twenty years they were defeated, though only by two votes.

2. THE CONDUCT OF THE WAR

The major problem which faced the newly constructed ministry continued to be that of conducting the war. Here there was considerable divergence of views between England and her allies. The main English objective was to build up German power round Maria Theresa, so that the Empire would continue to act as a counterbalance to France, who was trying to build up a coalition behind her client Charles Albert of Bavaria. If English aims were to be realized it was imperative that Maria Theresa should come to terms with Frederick II and resign herself to the loss of Silesia. This she was most unwilling to do without at least the guarantee of full compensation elsewhere, which England was anxious that she should find in Italy at the expense of Spain, and for this purpose advocated a close alliance with the ambitious and rising power of Sardinia. English policy was further complicated by the perennial problem of Hanover. At first George II had been full of warlike ardour, but we have seen that when he found the Electorate threatened by both Prussia and the French troops supporting Charles Albert he panicked, declared Hanover neutral, and gave his vote in the electoral college to the Bavarian candidate. This had the further result of making the Dutch determine to avoid all direct participation as a principal in the struggle. In the House of Commons, too, it produced difficulties, for opposition members could ask why England should make costly efforts to support Maria Theresa when Hanover refused to share the burden and the risk.

The intention of the ministry was to infuse new vigour into the prosecution of the war. George II, Newcastle and Carteret had got what they wanted, and cordiality and harmony seemed to be the keynote of the new administration. The Commons, having clamoured for a more effective policy, were now prepared to support it. A subsidy of £500,000 was unanimously granted; £200,000 of it was to go to the King of Sardinia, who in February had come to an agreement with Austria known as the Convention of Turin. In April a force of 16,000 men was sent to form part of the Pragmatic

Army of Flanders. Though there was a good deal of hopeful but not very realistic thinking behind the scheme, it looked in the spring of 1742 as if an army of some 70,000 might be used either to harass French troops in Bohemia, or to make a direct invasion of France. This is what both Maria Theresa hoped and Frederick II feared, though in fact the Pragmatic Army remained ingloriously in the Austrian Netherlands throughout 1742. This neither could foresee, while both expected some advantage to themselves from concluding an agreement. In consequence Britain was able to bring about the Preliminaries of Breslau in June 1742. It was a triumph for Carteret[1] but it left Maria Theresa resentful. She felt, not without cause, that harder bargaining on Britain's part might have secured much of Upper Silesia for herself.

With the potential threat of an English invasion and the freeing of the Austrian armies, the French forces in Germany were in danger of being cut off. From this they were brilliantly extracted by Bellisle, the French commander. With the lifting of the threat to Hanover George II determined to reduce the number of troops he had kept in the Electorate for its defence. This intention showed only too clearly that the King's primary concern was for Hanover, and was greeted with dismay by his English ministers, aware of the effect it would have on England's allies. To obviate this they arranged that these Hanoverian troops be taken into British pay. This decision, though militarily sound, was to cause future political trouble, for it could be represented as a fresh instance of the use of British money for Hanoverian convenience. In the debate sanctioning this arrangement Pitt used his finest oratory against it, declaring in an oft quoted phrase that England had now become 'a province to a despicable Electorate'. In spite of the opposition the government secured a majority of 67 votes. Pitt's oratory, like curses, came home to roost: it was long indeed before George II forgave him for this insult.

3. CARTERET AND THE PELHAMS

So far, in spite of the fulminations of the opposition, the foreign policy of Carteret, which had been partially outlined previously by Newcastle[2] and certainly endorsed by him, had achieved a fair

---

[1] But see D. B. Horn, *op. cit.*, p. 55: 'His policy has only to be reduced to its essentials to show how little Carteret deserved his reputation in England as a master of German politics.'

[2] In a memorial drawn up by Newcastle in November 1741 on The Present State of Affairs.

measure of success. But by the winter of 1742 differences of opinion were appearing between the two Secretaries on the actual conduct of operations. At first they were of minor importance only, but they revealed a difference of approach that might, in certain circumstances, produce serious strain. Such circumstances were provided by the departure of the King for Hanover immediately after the prorogation of Parliament on 21 April 1743. George II had been straining at the leash for some time, and would have crossed to Flanders in the autumn of 1742 had it not been for the united arguments of Pelham and Carteret. His going caused the inevitable inconvenience of a divided administration with its inherent possibilities of friction between ministers. When the individuals concerned were Pelham and Newcastle, Carteret and George II, difficulties were certain. Pelham, as leading minister in the Commons, was particularly aware of its aversion to heavy commitments. Newcastle was touchy of his dignity and jealous of Carteret's influence with the King. Carteret was supremely confident of his own judgment, apt to take a gambler's risks, and he loved the diplomatic game. He had a good deal of contempt for Newcastle, and affected to regard Pelham as a superior clerk, fit for drudgery but incapable of wider views. Carteret never grasped the necessity for parliamentary support while he had that of the Crown, and this flaw in his political judgment made him a particularly dangerous member of the Cabinet to accompany the King abroad.

Negotiations at Hanau, though abortive in the end, produced dissensions among the ministers which illustrate their opposed points of view. The situation was briefly this. On 15 June George II, leading the Pragmatic Army, which had finally been moved to Germany in the spring of 1743, won the Battle of Dettingen. It was a victory of courage not strategy. George II led his army into a trap, which only failed to close because of French mistakes during the battle and the steadiness of the troops under his command. No attempt was made to follow up this success. Nevertheless, as France was already withdrawing her troops from Bavaria, it looked as if her client the Emperor Charles VII would be left out on a limb. This made him anxious to come to some accommodation with the English, and put new life into negotiations which had already been opened by Prince William of Hesse at Hanau. To Newcastle the situation had dangers: he feared its effect on Maria Theresa. Carteret on the other hand thought it worth while to try to detach the

Emperor from France. The terms on which this was to be done were unexceptional in that Charles VII was to give up all pretensions to the Austrian inheritance. The difficulty was financial. Money would have to be provided from somewhere to support his imperial dignity, and Carteret was prepared to fill the gap with a subsidy which could come only from England. If Carteret and George II thought this price worth paying Pelham and Newcastle did not, and in view of their objections the proposed treaty of Hanau was abandoned.

Having failed to detach Charles VII, Carteret next tried to serve both Austrian and British interests by negotiating an alliance between Maria Theresa and Charles Emmanuel of Savoy. England had considerable trading connections with Italy, where the free port of Leghorn acted as a base, and had no desire to see the Mediterranean converted into a Spanish lake. Her apprehensions had been increased when Spain, under cover of the French fleet, had landed troops in the peninsula late in 1741. Though a reinforced British squadron had compelled Charles of Naples to recall his Neapolitan contingent and declare his neutrality by the threat of bombarding his capital, without assistance Britain could not drive the Spanish troops out of Italy. As it was also part of British policy that Austria should be compensated for the loss of Silesia by Italian gains at the expense of Spain, to strengthen Maria Theresa's position there seemed important. For this the help of Sardinia was needed. Basically Charles Emmanuel disliked the idea of either Austria or Spain establishing a strong position in Italy, but if offered a sufficiently large slice of territory he might be bribed to acquiesce. His geographical position, controlling as it did the approaches to Italy from France via the mountains of Piedmont, made it certain that offers would be made to him from both sides. Originally neither Austria nor Spain had been willing to pay his price, but, after the Spanish invasion, as a counterweight he had shown some disposition to support Austria.[1] Carteret was anxious to turn this new accord into a formal treaty. His task was to persuade Maria Theresa to accept Sardinia's terms before Charles Emmanuel reached an agreement with France, who was also angling for his alliance. Under pressure she agreed to the Treaty of Worms on 2/13 September. By it Sardinia was to get part of the Milanese, Piacenza and the right to buy Finale from Genoa. In return Charles

[1] J. B. Owen, *op. cit.*, p. 175.

Emmanuel pledged himself to support Maria Theresa and Great Britain until peace was made. In order to reconcile Maria Theresa to her sacrifices, Carteret by a 'Separate Declaration' signed the same day as the treaty, pledged English support for the securing of an adequate compensation for them. Even then she remained irate. A further grievance was that the English subsidy to Sardinia was 'tant que la guerre et le besoin durera', while her subsidy was only on a yearly basis. Accordingly she now demanded that by a 'Supplementary Convention' hers should be put on the same footing. Somewhat reluctantly, fearing that otherwise his whole elaborate diplomatic structure would collapse, Carteret agreed.

These concessions proved another source of discord between Carteret and the Pelhams. The 'Supplementary Convention' filled them with dismay. This, as Newcastle wrote, 'will go down with great difficulty in Parliament'. So nervous were they that when the King returned in November 1743 a full Cabinet of thirteen members advised George II not to ratify it.[1] Only three ministers supported Carteret. The result of this refusal was to leave Maria Theresa with a permanent sense of grievance against Great Britain. As well as antagonizing her, the Treaty of Worms had other unfortunate effects. When the negotiations at Hanau had fallen through, Frederick II had been extremely annoyed. He wanted neither a powerful Austria nor a French army in Germany, and had hoped that the less formidable Charles VII, dependent on English support, would have been a counterweight to Austria without being a danger to himself. His disappointment at the failure of the negotiations had turned to suspicion when he discovered that the Treaty of Worms contained a guarantee of the Pragmatic Sanction which did not except the territories that Maria Theresa had ceded to him by the Treaty of Breslau. This omission seems to have determined him to re-enter the war before Austria had time to regain her strength. For England the effect was similar. Louis XV, like Frederick II, alarmed at the growing strength of Great Britain and Austria, began with more cordiality to back Spanish claims both in Italy and against Gibraltar. The Treaty of Worms therefore gained a new ally for Austria only at the cost of encouraging France to enter the war as a principal, and of goading Frederick II to reopen hostilities. Carteret's diplomacy became in consequence increasingly the object of parliamentary attack. To the politically sensitive New-

[1] J. B. Owen, *op. cit.*, p. 179.

castle and Pelham it became urgent that they should disentangle their policies from those of the unpopular Carteret before they all went down in common ruin. If George II would not follow their advice in preference to that of Carteret then either they or he must go. There was no longer room for them in the same administration. This is the key to the political manœuvres of the next few months.

The Pelhams could, however, speak with rather more authority than when Carteret had left England, because on the death of Lord Wilmington later in 1742 Henry Pelham became First Lord of the Treasury. Since the early days of the administration, though still retaining his previous office of Paymaster-General, he had been one of its most influential members. This was partly owing to his own persuasive level-headed personality, and partly to the fact that, with both Newcastle and Carteret in the Lords, he was responsible for the management of the Commons. His elevation to the Treasury —an office that was coming to carry such prestige that in future even the jealous Newcastle commonly alluded to his brother as 'the Premier'—was an indication of the ever-growing importance of the Lower House. Both brothers were to need all their skill in managing this body in the coming session. Their Closet influence was still inferior to that of Carteret, and they were well aware that the latter was concerting policies likely to be most unpalatable to the Commons. Moreover, in George Grenville, George Lyttleton and above all in William Pitt,[1] the 'Cobham cubs' of the previous Parliament, they had to face critics of eloquence and ability, whose oratory and arguments combined might well prevail with the independent members if the war went badly. Indeed, so aware were the Pelhams of this potential danger that in the previous July they had attempted, though without success, to win them over by an arrangement with Lord Cobham.

The most difficult of the political problems to be faced was the future of the Hanoverian troops in British pay. Here George II's own lack of tact was partly responsible for the heat of popular feeling. At Dettingen he had gone into battle wearing the Hanoverian colours, and wildly exaggerated accounts had filtered back to England of his preference for his Hanoverian troops and the slights to which he had subjected his British officers. It seemed therefore possible that when the debate on the army estimates took place the House would refuse the necessary funds and that the issue might

[1] B. Tunstall, *Chatham* (1938), is very good.

seriously divide the 'old corps'. So worried was Newcastle by this possibility that he even considered advising the King against their retention. To do this was to risk diminishing his Closet influence still further; for George II to be forced to part with his Electoral troops would have been as bitter to him as Parliament's demand that he dismiss his Dutch Guards had been to William III. Here Orford showed some of the resource that had made him as Sir Robert Walpole so successful a handler of political negotiations. Advising Newcastle against a panic-driven decision he persuaded the leading members of the 'old corps' to support the retention of the Hanoverian troops. In this he was doubly wise. From a military point of view they and the Pragmatic Army would have been seriously weakened by the withdrawal of trained and seasoned troops. From a political point of view it demonstrated to the King that Pelham, Newcastle and the 'old corps' were too useful to be discarded. As a result of Orford's tactics the furious attacks of the opposition, led by Pitt, did no more than detach the doubtful fringe of administration supporters.

In view of the desperate attempts of opposition speakers, and of Pitt in particular, to stir up feeling on the issue of Hanover, the new session went more smoothly than might have been expected. It is difficult to estimate the effects of these tirades. His argument that as a result of Carteret's mismanagement England was faced with a Francophil Emperor, a weakened Austria, and a suspicious Prussia fell on sympathetic ears. Not even Orford's influence could keep every member of the 'old corps' loyal in face of Pitt's searing criticisms. As a result the division lists, when these are available, show considerable fluctuation in the support given to the administration by individual members. On controversial issues, when emotions were aroused or individual judgments came into play, it was common to find opposition supporters in the government lobby and vice versa. But though individuals might waver, government majorities remained satisfactory. It was not until the military defeats of 1743 that divisions in the Cabinet became a serious threat to the continuance of the existing administration. For a little time longer the Pelhams worked together in uneasy alliance with Carteret.

Meanwhile their parliamentary position was becoming stronger. The promotion of Pelham, together with several convenient deaths, had given the administration some useful patronage to distribute.

This was done in the Christmas recess, so that the new office holders could stand for re-election while Parliament was not sitting. It is very difficult in any general survey to convey the importance of such manœuvres in eighteenth-century politics. When parliamentary majorities had to be built up out of groups, and groups held together partly though by no means entirely by the hope of spoils, the disposal of each scrap of patronage could have important repercussions. It was also a barometer to Closet favour in so far as a minister was known to be able to carry his recommendations with the King. Newcastle knew, with almost a broker's exact knowledge, the value of each appointment and, like a skilful chess player, he fitted the move of even a single pawn into his general plan. It is because of this that negotiations over office, reduced by the gulf of time to a tiresome list of unimportant names, held for contemporaries the key to the rise and fall of ministers. Therefore when at the end of 1742 the 'old corps' were seen to be the chief beneficiaries of the reshuffle, the world realized that however much George II preferred Carteret in his Closet he was fully prepared to entrust his parliamentary business to the Pelhams.

Divisions among their critics also made their task easier. These became very apparent once England and France were officially at war. Though Pitt, Lyttelton, Chesterfield and Dodington were opposed to Carteret's handling of diplomacy, with its emphasis on German and Hanoverian interests, they were anxious to prosecute the war against France with vigour. The Grenvilles and Cobham were in contrast totally opposed to it in any form, and aimed at concluding a general peace in the shortest possible time. This made common action between the opposition groups more difficult and less effective. It also revealed how much common ground there was between Pitt and the Pelhams. Once Carteret went, there seemed good prospects of an accommodation between them, always provided George II could be brought to agree. The threat of a new Jacobite invasion strengthened the ministers still further. Even the tories had no desire to see the Stuarts back on the throne, and the possibility of an invasion backed by France rallied most of the House behind the government. Political opposition could only take the form of accusing the ministers of creating and exaggerating the whole crisis. By February 1743 the situation looked threatening. It was known that there were 15,000 men at Dunkirk under Marshal de Saxe, but as France and England were still formally not at war a large part of the English fleet had been sent to the Mediterranean under Admiral Mathews. Then came the news that the French fleet at Brest under Admiral de Roquefeuil was sailing up the Channel to protect the passage of transports from Dunkirk. By the 24th it had reached Dungeness. Hastily the veteran Admiral Norris (he was now 84) was sent out to intercept them. Fortunately for England the weather proved a better defence than Norris promised to be. In a terrific storm the French fleet was scattered, 17/28 February 1744, and many of the soldiers in the transports drowned. For the immediate future the danger was over, but the formal declaration of war by France made a recurrence more than likely. During this alarm the division in the ranks of the opposition was very apparent. Its more irresponsible members remained thoroughly factious, using every occasion to attack and criticize and belittle the administration. In this they did themselves little good. The House as a whole disapproved of attempts to harass ministers in these circumstances and even the suspension of Habeas Corpus went through smoothly.

But though the administration survived until the end of the session, its position was far from happy, for by the spring of 1743 it was clear that the war was going badly. In the Austrian Netherlands, Menin, Courtrai and Ypres were lost to a French army led by Louis XV and commanded by his most able general, Marshal de Saxe. Though a temporary respite was secured when Austrian forces attacked Alsace, Frederick II's re-entry into the war and attack on Bohemia meant that Austrian troops had to be hurried back for its defence. To Pelham, who had just negotiated the payment of a subsidy of £150,000 to Maria Theresa, this was a bitter blow. From every side came news of fresh disasters. Frederick II took Prague. Even the short breathing space afforded by the depletion of Saxe's forces had been frittered away by divided counsels. The Austrians were forced to retreat from Bavaria, and in the autumn Charles VII was able to re-enter Munich, though he did ease the diplomatic situation a little by conveniently dying there in the following January. In Italy, too, things were going badly. An attempt on the part of Maria Theresa to invade Naples had to be given up after the indecisive battle of Velletri, while Charles Emmanuel was threatened with invasion by a joint Spanish-French army, and complained bitterly to England of the lack of Austrian help.

These disasters intensified the divisions in the Cabinet. George II with some show of justice blamed the parsimony of the Pelhams for Maria Theresa's difficulties. The King and Carteret had long been anxious that the Elector of Saxony should be given a subsidy on condition that he should be prepared to go to Austria's assistance if Frederick II should attack again. Fearing as always the criticisms of the Commons, they refused to do this. Now George was able to say in effect 'I told you so', and the treatment that Newcastle as joint Secretary of State had to endure from George II and Carteret, reduced him to querulous despair. On 25 August he wrote, 'No man can bear long what I go through every day, in our joint audiences in the Closet.'[1] At the same time the handling of the abortive negotiations at Hanau was dragged out into the light. Frederick II, as has been pointed out, had been deeply chagrined by their failure and now proclaimed in a manifesto that the English treatment of the Emperor was one of his major reasons for resuming the war. Such a charge was peculiarly adapted to split the ministry, for each could blame the other for mismanagement. Carteret could lay the blame for the failure of the negotiations on the refusal of Pelham and the 'old whigs' to provide the subsidies to Charles VII which had been necessary to implement them. Newcastle, Pelham and Hardwicke could argue that the arrangements in question were quite indefensible from the British point of view and that Carteret ought never to have become entangled in them.

Finally the position became so intolerable that one or other of the contending Secretaries would have to go. After some discussion the Pelham group decided to take their stand on the question of Holland. For some time both in the Commons and among the 'old whigs' there had been much dissatisfaction at the way in which Britain had been left to shoulder what seemed more than her fair share of the financial burden. Now that France had declared war and the attack on the Austrian Netherlands had begun, it was felt that Holland had every reason for entering the war as a principal. She should now make definite and binding arrangements with Britain as to the size of the forces she would furnish to the Pragmatic Army and the amount of financial contributions she would make. Yet when pressed to demand satisfaction on these matters, Carteret (now since his mother's death Earl Granville) refused to make any decisive move. His reluctance, the Pelhams suspected, was

[1] E. R. Turner and G. Megaro, 'The King's Closet in the Eighteenth Century' (*American Historical Review*, vol. XLV, no. 4, July 1940).

due to the fact that Holland might well require George II in his capacity as Elector to commit Hanover in the same way. The next step agreed upon by the Pelham group was that Hardwicke should draw up a memorial embodying these views and making it clear that unless every possible effort was made to act in concert with Holland the 'old whigs' must resign from the ministry. Though the drafting of the memorial was left to Hardwicke it was submitted to the entire inner ring, consisting of Hardwicke, Harrington, Pelham and Newcastle, each of whom was briefed to make it clear in his individual interview in the Closet that he would feel it impossible to go on as long as the general direction of the war policy was entrusted to Granville. Newcastle was able to assure George II that, though they had not signed the memorial, Dorset, Argyll, Richmond, Grafton, Devonshire, Montague and Pembroke were prepared to support the policy it advocated. The memorial was, in fact, an ultimatum: George II would either have to let Granville go or find fresh support for him in the Commons. This last he tried to do, first by endeavouring to detach Lord Harrington and, when this was unsuccessful, by an approach to the opposition. As both the Prince of Wales and the King were personally attached to Granville this was one of the few occasions on which father and son were able to act together. Though it was hardly possible for George II to make a direct approach himself, Frederick, who had long been on friendly terms with their leading men, attempted on 21 November to open negotiations with the opposition on the basis of the dismissal of the 'old whigs' and a broad-bottomed administration of the opposition and the 'new whigs'.

These negotiations were probably doomed to failure in any case. Eighteenth-century politicians would do much for office and there was no doctrine of Cabinet solidarity to prevent its being composed of differing and even conflicting views. Nevertheless, it is difficult to see Chesterfield and Cobham in the same ministry as Granville, and impossible to visualize Grenville, Lyttelton and Pitt supporting the latter's policy in Parliament. But the Pelhams had made doubly sure by entering into negotiations with the opposition themselves. It was for just such an eventuality that the 'old whigs' had kept channels of communication open. William Murray and Hardwicke were both on friendly terms with Bolingbroke, and as early as August there had been exploratory talks between them. Moreover, the more responsible attitude which Pitt had been taking in the last session, and the clear distinction which, in the debate on the Hanoverians, he drew between the Pelhams and Granville, made it likely that he would not be averse to some such accommodation. Thus it was not difficult to reach agreement on the desirability of a more systematic conduct of the war and the necessity for getting rid of Granville, Bath, and the 'new whigs'. By common consent the delicate problem of reapportioning their offices among the plotters was left in abeyance until the prime object, the removal of Granville, had been secured. Much as he disliked parting with Granville there was really very little that George II could do. He had to have ministers who could do his business in the Commons. Granville had little interest there and few followers. The unsuccessful conduct of the war was generally attributed to him; his more elaborate schemes, with their trail of subsidies, were much disliked and the House had no confidence in him. Royal patronage and influence in these circumstances were not sufficient to create a majority for government business in the Commons. For the second time George II was forced to accept the resignation of a minister who still retained his confidence but had lost that of the Commons.

4. Growing Ascendancy of the Pelhams

There is no doubt that at first the King's resentment was very deep. When Walpole had resigned there had been some circumstances to soften the blow. Newcastle, Harrington and Hardwicke, in whom he then had confidence (though he never seems to have liked Newcastle), had remained and with their help he had managed to out-manœuvre the more far-reaching designs of the opposition. Moreover, the one man to whom he had been forced to give high office had been Carteret, to whose war policy George II was sympathetic. Now the King was forced to keep men with whom he was at odds and, when the new offices were distributed, appoint men whom he disliked. The following snatch of conversation between him and Hardwicke portrays well his frame of mind. *King*, 'I have done all you asked of me. I have put all my power into your hands, and I suppose you will make the most of it.' *Chancellor*, 'The disposition of places is not enough, if your Majesty takes pains to shew the world, that you disapprove of your own work.' *King*, 'My work. I was forced, I was threatened.' *Chancellor*, 'I am sorry to hear your Majesty use those expressions. I know of no force: I know of no threats. No means were employed but what have been used in all times, the humble advice of your servants, supported by such reasons as convince them that the measure was necessary for your service.'[1] In this short passage the opposing points of view are succinctly put. George II felt that he had been placed in such a situation as to leave him with no freedom of choice, that he was 'a King in toils', the victim of his ministers. Hardwicke equally felt that there had been no desire to force the King, but that in the circumstances there was no alternative way of carrying on his business while he employed a minister whom the Commons refused to support. Once again the constitutional dilemma of the eighteenth century had been exposed: unless power in the House and favour in the Closet were combined, government jammed until a fresh start could be made.

Yet this hardly justified the charge that George II was 'a King in toils' unless it is conceded that the toils were those of circumstance. Within the framework of the political conditions of the day George II enjoyed a formidable power. For several months he had retained Granville after he had lost the confidence of both his colleagues and the Commons. In the months that followed he was to show how difficult he could make it for ministers who had incurred his resentment. Even a minister like Walpole, and later Henry Pelham when he came to rely upon him, were never able to take the royal acquiescence for granted. He would listen, sometimes pettishly and with irritation, to arguments in favour of some policy or some appointment that he disliked, and if convinced would take the unpalatable advice. But he had to be convinced by argument just as the House of Commons had to be convinced by argument and was far from being a mere rubber stamp in the hands of his ministers. It is interesting to notice that in August 1745, amid the confusion of the Young Pretender's rising, Pelham, while waiting the King's return from Hanover, wrote to the Duke of Argyll, 'We must do our best; but nothing can go on right until the government has a head, which I hope it will not be long without.'[2] Indeed the difficulties which arose whenever he went to Hanover are an additional proof of the active part he played in the day-to-day decisions of government. Nevertheless, having to take good advice that was unwelcome, having to employ ministers who could manage Parliament, must often have been psychologically frustrating, and there is little room for surprise that the Elector of Hanover, with a much simpler administrative and political machine to run, often felt that the King

---

[1] W. Coxe, *op. cit.*, vol. I, p. 201.   [2] *Ibid.*, vol. I, p. 258.

of England was 'in toils' without quite analysing their nature. The autumn of 1745 and the early spring of 1746 was a period when, if his behaviour to his ministers is accepted as evidence, such thoughts were uppermost in his mind.

The dismissal of Granville had both constitutional and political importance. It underlined the fact that the King's favour alone was not sufficient to support a minister who had lost the confidence of the House of Commons, and it enabled the Pelhams to disentangle themselves from any responsibility for his policy before they too had become involved in his political ruin. Nevertheless, their troubles were far from over. Three major problems confronted them. They had to strengthen their control over the House of Commons, for their usefulness in that place was their chief recommendation to the King. They had to overcome his resentment at beir.g forced to part with Granville, for George II blamed them rather than Granville's lack of political realism for the position in which he had been placed. Finally they had to conduct the war in such a way as to induce the Commons to grant supplies without further antagonizing the King. Only if they were successful in all three could they hope to survive, for only then would the power and the favour be again united.

The more immediate of these problems was to reconstruct the ministry in such a way as to give them a comfortable working majority in Parliament. The basis of that majority must continue to be the 'old corps'; whatever favours and honours were given elsewhere they must be kept in good heart. At the same time the most formidable critics of the administration must be won over, which could only be done by providing some of them with places. This was likely to prove a delicate operation. Many of those whom the Pelhams designed to placate had been foremost in attacking Granville and his policy, and George II viewed them with hearty dislike. When Lord Chesterfield's name was first mentioned it brought forth a disgusted 'I command you to trouble me no more with such nonsense' from the irate King. The feelings of the 'old corps', too, resembled the workers in the vineyard who, having borne the heat and burden of the day, saw those men who had laboured but one hour made equal with them. With skill and judgment, however, the task was accomplished. Since places had to be found for 'the new allies' without disobliging the 'old corps', the inevitable victims were the 'new whigs' of 1742 who had come in with Pulteney and Carteret after Walpole's resignation. To justify their removal Hardwicke put forward the then novel doctrine that the dismissal of a minister carried with it a loss of office for his followers, though no political group at that time had anything like the coherence or discipline that would have justified this doctrine.[1] Previous negotiations with Chesterfield, Cobham and Lord Gower, once it had been decided that something must be done for the groups which they represented, had roughed out the most important changes. The Pelhams, however, managed to keep the vacant Secretaryship of State within their own inner ring, Lord Harrington returning to the office he had yielded to Carteret in 1742. Lord Gower once again became Privy Seal, while his son-in-law, the Duke of Bedford, took over the Admiralty from Lord Winchelsea, with his young protégé Lord Sandwich as a member of his Board. In the general reshuffle that took place, Dorset succeeded Harrington as Lord President of the Council, while his late office of Lord Steward was filled by the Duke of Devonshire. This enabled the Pelhams to work Chesterfield into the Lord Lieutenancy of Ireland vacated by Devonshire.

It is, however, among the lesser appointments that the most interesting developments are to be seen. At last two of Cobham's cubs were given places. George Grenville went to the Admiralty and George Lyttelton to the Treasury, but of all this notable group the most outstanding of them all, William Pitt, was left out. His career since 1742 had been marked by the violence of his language, some inconsistency of behaviour, and growing indications of the Pitt that was to be. On occasions his denunciations of Carteret had been almost demoniacal, as if his latent unbalance had been struggling to express itself in his hatred of the man whose policy he regarded as obstructing England's destiny. At the same time his speeches show a certain common ground between himself and Henry Pelham. When the danger from France, both in her threatened support of the Pretender in 1744 and in the invasion of Flanders, grew in intensity, Pitt was prepared to give his support to the administration. A Pragmatic Army to defend Flanders from French attack seemed to him a very different thing from an army dispatched to Germany to help Maria Theresa or to defend Hanover. France was the enemy, but even France could not be fought solely at sea, and in America and India. Unlike certain other members of his group, in some of the critical divisions in 1744 Pitt had supported the minis-

---

[1] J. B. Owen, *op. cit.*, p. 242.

ters. Had his diatribes against Hanover been less bitter it is probable that Pelham would have been disposed to find a place for him in the reconstruction that was taking place. But George II could have been brought to accept Pitt only by the application of extreme pressure. This the Pelhams were not prepared at this point to apply. For one thing they had no reserves of royal goodwill on which to draw. For another their own constitutional principles did not include forcing the King's hand unless they were convinced that it was absolutely necessary for the carrying on of his government. Office for Pitt did not, as yet, come under this category largely because, now that Carteret had gone and Pitt's friends had places, they hoped that he might give a general support to their conduct of the war. Nevertheless the changes of 1744 mark a vital stage in Pitt's career, even though he was excluded from office. Partly he found himself in more general agreement with the ministers than he had ever been before, and partly, it seems probable, he realized that he must 'work his passage'. For the next session he became the defender rather than the attacker of the administration's measures.

The other significant pointer to the future in the reconstruction after Granville's resignation was the behaviour of the tories. Four tories accepted office: Lord Gower, the new Lord Privy Seal, John Pitt, Sir John Phillips, who went to the Board of Trade, and Sir John Hinde Cotton, who became Treasurer of the Chamber. The first two of these were interested in a political career and gradually came to count as whigs, but the behaviour of the other two is more interesting. Though Sir John Phillips had accepted office he apparently felt no general obligation to support the administration; he repeatedly voted with the opposition and resigned at the end of the session. Sir John Cotton also proved unreliable and was dismissed a year later. Nevertheless, tories had once again been included in the list of office holders. Moderate tories were coming to feel that there were issues on which they could support the administration, and that office was not wholly repugnant to them. The ministers, too, showed a new desire to break down tory hostility, and went a long way to meet their desire for local influence by declaring that in future Commissions for the Peace 'proper regard shall be had to gentlemen of figure and fortune, well affected to His Majesty's Government, without distinction of parties'. Nevertheless, it is too soon to speak of a tory party as an effective force in politics. Those tories who had accepted office had no authority or even influence over the mass of tory gentlemen, who remained a collection of individuals as yet more interested in local influence than in political careers. Such support as they gave ministers was temporary, arising out of their realization of the national danger and their satisfaction that Granville had gone.

Their skilful reconstruction of the ministry considerably strength-ened the Pelhams' control over the House of Commons. It was not so easy to find an immediate solution to the problem of the royal resentment. For some time yet, the displaced Granville was to remain 'the minister behind the curtain'. Much therefore depended on the war policy of the reconstructed ministry. Somehow they had to reconcile the anti-Hanoverian policy of the Commons with a Hano-verian King, and if possible to secure a satisfactory and speedy peace. The business of the Hanoverian troops in British pay was handled by a neat subterfuge: their employment by England was discontinued, but Maria Theresa received an extra subsidy of £200,000 a year to enable her to hire them. In general the Pelhams were prepared for a vigorous prosecution of their war effort on the ground that only by so doing could they hope to attain a satisfactory peace. Opposition speakers might describe this as old measures with new men, but Pitt declared that he saw 'a new dawn of salvation to my country breaking through'.

5. THE FORTY-FIVE

The year 1745 was to be a murky dawn. At home it was to see the rising in Scotland under the Young Pretender, abroad it had to chronicle a series of disasters. In Flanders the Duke of Cumberland was in command of the allied forces, a command which he owed to the Pelhams' insistence that an Englishman should lead our troops. This appointment had, however, ruffled George's feeling still further for, though Cumberland was his favourite son, he took it as a personal slight that, despite his own known desire to lead these troops, he was passed over for his own son. To the end of his life George II always found difficulty in understanding that what was possible for an Elector of Hanover might be most undesirable for a King of England. His son, however, fared even worse than his father had done, for he failed to win even a nominal victory. On 11 May he was defeated at Fontenoy while the French under de Saxe took possession of Tournai, Ghent, Oudenarde and Ostend, the last a particularly serious loss because it made communications difficult between England and her overseas armies. In Germany, too, things were going badly in spite of the fact that Saxony, inspired by jealousy of Prussia and tempted by the offer of subsidies from the Maritime Powers, had joined a quadruple alliance in January 1745, by which, in return for a subsidy of £150,000, her Elector had promised to provide 30,000 troops for the defence of Bohemia. During the year Frederick defeated a combined Austro-Saxon force at Hohenfried-berg and again at Soor in Silesia, and by December had invaded Saxony, and taken Dresden. Even the beginning of these defeats was enough to persuade the ministers that Maria Theresa must be forced into accepting Frederick II's offer of peace on the same terms as those of Breslau.

Meanwhile at home a new crisis had arisen with the landing of the Young Pretender in Scotland. He rallied the Highland clans with disconcerting ease, seized Edinburgh and set up his Court at Holy-rood. In London everything was in confusion. In August Pelham wrote to the Duke of Argyll, 'I am not so apprehensive of the strength and zeal of the enemy, as I am fearful of the inability or languidness of our friends.'[1] Domestic political divisions increased this confusion, for the Marquis of Tweedsdale, the Secretary for Scotland, was a supporter of Granville and unwilling to act cordially with his rivals. George II remained in Hanover until the end of August, and when he finally returned his presence did little to restore harmony. He was abominably rude to his ministers, by way of underlining his lack of confidence in them, so that Henry Fox described his attitude as 'obstinate, angry, determined impractica-bility throughout'.[2] Also when Parliament met on 18 October it was clear that Pitt was once again preparing to make difficulties: a motion moved by him on 23 October for the recall of all British troops from Flanders was lost by only twelve votes. Whether this was intended as a forcing bid or not, it brought a prompt response from the Pelhams. Two days later they sounded him as to the terms on which he would join the administration. These proved too high, and both this negotiation and a similar one in November left the situation un-changed. For a time the ministers' attention was fully taken up with the danger from Scotland. On 4 December the Young Pretender reached Derby and threw London into a panic. But once he had decided on retreat they were free to concentrate on the management of the Commons and fresh negotiations were opened with Pitt. As

[1] W. Coxe, *Pelham*, vol. I, p. 258.   [2] *Ibid.*, p. 254.

in the interval he had come to modify his views on the conduct of the war, so that they were now more in line with those held by Henry Pelham, a deal was easily arranged. Pitt was to be Secretary at War, Lord Barrington was to go to the Admiralty, and James Grenville was to be provided with some place worth £1,000 a year. It was one thing for Pitt and Pelham to come to terms, it was a different matter to get the King to accept them. George II made it abundantly clear that if Pitt became Secretary at War, he would consider that he had been forced upon him and 'treat him as ill as possible' or even refuse to receive him.

6. THE TRIUMPH OF THE PELHAMS

This head-on collision between the King and his ministers produced one of the more dramatic episodes of eighteenth-century political history. Both sides were eager for a show-down. George II still resented the loss of Granville and heartily disliked the foreign policy of the Pelhams, who at Christmas had succeeded in forcing Maria Theresa to conclude the Treaty of Dresden with Frederick II. The ministers in their turn felt their position to be intolerable. Either they must have the royal confidence and be known to have it, or the King must find other servants, as indeed the political grapevine informed them he was already trying to do. In face of the pending crisis Pitt withdrew his pretensions to the Secretaryship at War, but by now he had become a symbol rather than its cause. If the King continued to be obdurate the 'old corps' decided to resign in a body. Hitherto, mass resignations had not been usual. One or two ministers had resigned and vacancies had been filled up. Now on 10 February 1746 Newcastle and Harrington resigned, followed next day by Pelham, Bedford, Gower, Monson and Pembroke. The rest of the 'old corps' made it plain that they too intended to resign. Since 1742 their patience had been sorely tried. They had seen the 'new whigs' given places, they had been forced to accept Granville's handling of foreign policy, and even after his fall they were debarred from genuine Closet influence. At last their patience was exhausted: if George II wanted Granville and Bath let him find out for himself how impractical was his idea.

This was demonstrated with humiliating speed. On the 10th Harrington and Newcastle had resigned. Next day came the resignations of their colleagues; two more days sufficed to make it clear that neither Bath nor Granville could ever hope to command the support of the 'old corps'; and by the 13th the Pelham group was in a position to present George II with its terms for resuming office. These included the dismissal of most of the erstwhile supporters of Bath and Granville who still held office, the bringing in of Pitt into 'some honourable employment', and substantial proof of the possession of the royal favour in the distribution of honours. There was little the King could do but accept. In spite of the lure of office and the high regard paid to the royal favour it had proved impossible to find enough politicians of reasonable competence to accept places in an administration in which Bath and Granville were to be the leading ministers. This tussle between George II and the Pelhams is often regarded as having great constitutional significance. The device of the joint resignation is taken as marking a new stage in the development of Cabinet solidarity. It seems more likely, however, that its real significance was political rather than constitutional. It ended the long struggle between the 'new whigs' and the 'old corps', the struggle between those who had opposed Walpole and those who had supported him. Increasingly until his death in 1754, Henry Pelham was to wear the mantle of Sir Robert. This, rather than the device of collective resignation by which it was won, is the most significant aspect of the whole episode. The House of Commons was still far from being able to dictate to the King whom it would have, but the individuals who made up its membership were quite clear that they would not accept ministers in whom they had no confidence and whose policies they distrusted. On the surface and to contemporaries it was a matter of politics, a struggle between Granville and Bath and the Pelham group for power, in which the latter was able to convince a sufficiency of members that the policies it advocated were in the best interests of the country. In this contest adroit parliamentary management certainly played its part. The agonizing care with which Newcastle bestowed every scrap of patronage, both that belonging to him and his friends and such royal patronage as he was able to influence, paid handsome dividends. By 1746, almost every politician of note had been drawn into the Pelham orbit, either by the receipt of some favour or by the hope of one to come. As politicians expounding a policy and building up their connections, the Pelhams had deserved to succeed, and by their political success they demonstrated what was coming to be a constitutional fact. Once again they had done what Sir Robert Walpole had done. They had 'managed' the House of Commons by a mixture of influence and reason. By this political dexterity they had made themselves indispensable to the King, so winning first a reluctant and then a genuine support from him. Once again the power and the favour had been combined. If the result should prove to be the smooth carrying on of the administration and the disappearance of the instability of the years since 1740, when Walpole had first lost the real sympathy of the Commons, then this must afford additional proof that Walpole's success was deeper than a mere personal triumph. When Parliament and the King both put their trust in the same men, then the ambiguities of the Revolutionary Settlement ceased to produce political crisis, and eighteenth-century government took on a deceptive air of tranquillity and even stagnation. The eighteenth-century 'rat race' was made up of politicians each attempting to achieve these twin controls.

For the next few years all was harmony in spite of the difficulties of managing an unpromising war. To this harmony Pitt made no little contribution; for some years to come his whole attitude was to be pliable and co-operative. How far this was a matter of conviction, how far of temperament, it is difficult to say. Though for years he had fulminated against British money being spent to further Hanoverian interests, he had an almost exaggerated deference for George II as King of England and, in view of the royal dislike, accepted the Vice-Treasurership of Ireland instead of the more responsible Secretaryship at War. He also realized, perhaps, that his previous line of conduct had outlived, and more than outlived, its political usefulness: it had indeed become a real liability. How long he would have continued outwardly content with his lucrative but undistinguished place historians are not forced to speculate, for the death of Winnington in April necessitated a new re-shuffle. As George II was still opposed to Pitt's going to the War Office, Pelham was reluctant to provoke a new crisis, particularly as the King was at last behaving more cordially to his ministers. Yet it was clear that Pitt's claims to more responsible office could not be ignored in the coming reconstruction. After anxious discussion it was decided that Henry Fox should have the Secretaryship at War and Pitt the Pay Office, decisions which annoyed many of the 'old corps' who felt that such plums should not go outside their ranks.

For Pitt the Pay Office might have proved a dangerous promotion. The Paymaster-General had few opportunities, other than his general contact with the other ministers, for shaping policy, but he had wonderful opportunities of acquiring wealth. That Pitt, who for so long had raged against corruption, should accept this office seemed to his contemporaries suspiciously like a deal. He, too, apparently had his price. Lampoons and caricatures appeared on every side, particular play being made on the fact that in the previous year the old Duchess of Marlborough had left him £10,000 in her will as a recognition of his attempts 'to prevent the ruin of his country'. In at least one famous cartoon her ghost haunted him for his apostasy. Yet it may be doubted whether this upsurge of bitterness against a fallen idol was in any real sense justified. Office was a necessity for Pitt if his talents were not to be completely thrown away and, just because of his past, he must take what he could get. But there was more immediate justification for his joining Pelham's administration than that. By very different paths the two men had come to hold very similar views on the war of the Austrian Succession. Pitt had been against continental entanglements because he thought Britain's real interests lay overseas. Pelham disliked them because of the weight of taxation which it was necessary to impose in order to fulfil her financial obligations to her allies. Historians are sometimes prone to bestow a condescending approval on a policy that poured out treasure in the shape of subsidies rather than manpower in the form of armies, but contemporaries were not wanting to whom a little more British blood and a little less British money would not have come amiss. By 1745, however, both Pelham and Pitt had come to think that, committed as they were, some kind of containing operation on the continent was inevitable. As Pelham wrote to the envoy at The Hague, Mr. Trevor, 'Our hasty engagements, three years ago, making ourselves principals in all the wars upon the continent, without any plan concerned, or any obligations from the parties we were serving, except it was to take our money and apply it as they pleased, have rendered this country incapable of doing what its inclination and interest always induce it to do.'[1] With such sentiments Pitt would have had no difficulty in agreeing. His conduct on becoming Paymaster swiftly disposed of the adverse criticism which his acceptance had provoked. Unlike all previous Paymasters he ostentatiously refused the pickings of his office. Balances which his predecessors had used as if they had been personal assets, he deposited at the Bank of England for the benefit of the national revenue. Percentages on payments

[1] *Ibid.*, p. 292.

and subsidies which had customarily been paid he renounced. If in the House of Commons he advocated foreign subsidies, at least there should be no suspicion that he had a private interest in so doing. How far this was a matter of conviction, how far of policy it is impossible to tell. The emoluments of his office, which were over £4,000 a year, combined with the Duchess of Marlborough's legacy, were ample for his needs. He was still a bachelor and no longer a poor man. Soon after becoming Paymaster he began to indulge his taste for building and improvements by buying his first establishment, the small estate of South Lodge at Enfield Chase. In other ways, too, office brought Pitt gratification and contentment. He took a keen delight in mastering its details; he kept in personal touch with overseas agents, cleared up arrears, saw that pensions were promptly paid and was in every way a 'very, very model' Paymaster-General. And so for a time both he and the Pelhams had peace.

Internal harmony was very desirable if the war were to be brought to any tolerable conclusion. The results of the continental campaigns continued to be disappointing. British policy was indeed labouring under considerable handicaps. The Dutch were determined not to enter the war against France as a principal, and the help they gave to the Pragmatic Army to protect the Austrian Netherlands was grudgingly given. Maria Theresa was a difficult and resentful ally. She was highly suspicious of Anglo-Sardinian relations, feeling with some justification that England was unduly tender of the interests of Charles Emmanuel of Savoy. He had certainly proved a shifty ally. The joint Austrian-Sardinian invasion of Provence with the idea, favoured by Britain, of capturing the naval base of Toulon, after initial success had to be abandoned, partly owing to the skilful pressure of Bellisle, partly owing to the revolt of Genoa against her Austrian occupiers. The hope of compensation for Silesia by increased territories seemed to be vanishing into thin air and the Treaty of Dresden to have been a useless accommodation with an unscrupulous foe. When to these difficulties were added the slowness of communications, it is not surprising that relations between Vienna and London were often strained; each thought the other unreasonable and unyielding.

Britain's main disappointments were to be found in the Netherlands. This was her most sensitive spot. Here the triumphs of the French in 1744 were repeated in the next two years. In 1745 the Duke

of Cumberland had been defeated at Fontenoy while attempting
to relieve Tournai, and in the next year the allied forces under
Charles of Lorraine suffered another defeat at Rocoux. Pelham was
most despondent. 'A good peace is every man's wish, an indifferent
one would be gladly accepted, a sad one, I am afraid, will be our
lot.'[1] Even the one success, the capture of Louisbourg, the great
French stronghold on Cape Breton, by a mixed British naval and
colonial military force, brought him little comfort. It was the one
possible card in the hands of the English negotiators, for to regain it
France might be prepared to relinquish her conquests in the Netherlands, but Pelham realized that any ministry that handed it back
would do so in the face of popular disapproval. In his opinion it
would be 'a stumbling block to all negotiations; though' he wrote, 'I
am not so taken with sound, as to venture losing my whole substance with it. But that is not the sense of the generality: they look
upon it as a most valuable possession for this country: as indeed it
is, if it did not endanger the quiet possession of what is more valuable. Gibraltar and Minorca have kept us for thirty years at variance
with Spain; I am of opinion, that Cape Breton will do the same with
France; and to speak as a financier, the balance of that account is
against us.'[2]

7. ABORTIVE PEACE NEGOTIATIONS

By 1746 none of the contestants, except possibly Maria Theresa,
had much desire to continue the war. Philip V of Spain died unexpectedly in July and his successor Ferdinand inclined towards
peace. Louis XV, despite his successes in the Netherlands, was
finding money harder to raise, British sea power an increasingly
limiting factor, and his own inclinations turned more and more
towards peace. The Dutch were more than anxious to bring the
conflict to an end. The first feelers were put out in 1746 when the
Dutch and French worked out a project for preliminaries of peace.
Cape Breton, as was to be expected, was to be restored to France,
who in return was willing to agree to a barrier for the Dutch if
they would consent to the neutrality of the Netherlands, and to
renew her treaties of 1715 and 1717 with England guaranteeing the
Protestant Succession. France was willing also to acknowledge Maria
Theresa's husband Francis as Emperor and to secure his recognition
by the other Bourbon powers, though Spain, as her part of the

<hr/>

[1] *Ibid.*, p. 283.   [2] *Ibid.*, p. 284.

settlement, was to receive the Grand Duchy of Tuscany for Don Philip, Ferdinand's half-brother. These proposals had a mixed reception from the English ministers. Harrington, Chesterfield and Pelham thought that at least they would make a basis for negotiation and that peace on almost any terms we must have. Again and again this despondent strain runs through Pelham's correspondence. Newcastle and Hardwicke were less despairing, believing that with another year's campaigning and an all-out effort at least moderate success might be secured. In consequence the Cabinet was much divided but it was finally decided that negotiations should be opened at Breda and an English representative sent. Because Pelham and Harrington were so desperately anxious that the negotiations should succeed they tended to favour the exclusion of the Austrians, at least in the early stages. To this Newcastle was opposed. Both his sense of the fitting and his traditional loyalty to the Austrian connection made him insist that plenipotentiaries from Austria and Sardinia must be included.

These tensions inside the Cabinet soon gave rise to a new political reshuffle. As always, personal factors played a large part in it. George II and Newcastle found themselves in substantial agreement, and in opposition to the views of Harrington and Pelham. In consequence the position of Lord Sandwich, the British envoy at Breda, was one of some difficulty. Harrington, as Secretary of State for the Northern Department, should have been in control of the negotiations but it was to Newcastle that George II turned for advice, and it was to Newcastle that Sandwich sent many of his confidential dispatches. There was in this something more than a conflict of views between Harrington and George II. Though earlier he had been a great favourite with the King, partly because of his brusque manner in tendering his resignation on the fateful 10 February 1746, and partly because of an earlier gaffe, he had become *persona non grata* with George II, who indeed only reinstated him as Secretary with reluctance. Now he was put in a position when it was almost impossible, despite the looser conventions of the eighteenth century, for him not to resign. This he did on 28 October 1746 to the great pleasure of the King; but his colleagues were able to secure for him the Lord Lieutenancy of Ireland in November, which he held until the Duke of Dorset replaced him in December 1751.

The new appointment was a slightly surprising one. The seals that Harrington had resigned were given to Lord Chesterfield. Once again personal factors were more important than policies; Chesterfield, like the man he replaced, was known for his pacific views. He had, however, used his opportunities since being appointed Lord Lieutenant of Ireland in 1744. Then the mere mention of his name had elicited an angry response from George II; now it was the King himself who suggested his appointment to Newcastle.

The whole episode is a revealing one, though outwardly it merely replaced a by no means outstanding Secretary by another who, whatever his social competency, was destined to have no long life in that office. Its real interest lies in the light thrown on the conditions of political life. Henry Pelham was generally acknowledged as the King's first minister. During this period Pelham's ideas on foreign policy were perfectly clear and tenaciously held: he thought that almost any peace would be better than the continuance of the war. He thought, too, that our natural ally was Frederick II of Prussia and was prepared to make considerable efforts to bring him into the circle of our diplomacy. Of Harrington his opinion was that he was 'both an able and an honest minister'.[1] Yet George II consistently took the advice of Newcastle, which coincided with the royal desire to press on with the war; he intrigued against Harrington, whose views coincided with those of Pelham; and in the reshuffle he conferred with Newcastle, not Pelham, on the new appointment. Nevertheless, there was no question of Pelham's resigning nor of the King's intending that he should. In this incident George II can hardly be described as 'a King in toils' any more than Pelham can be considered as the master of his own Cabinet. Meanwhile Chesterfield deferred to the royal wishes by assuring Newcastle that he was prepared to abandon his peace-at-any-price policy—a promise which the breakdown of the negotiations at Breda made it temporarily easy to keep.

[1] *Ibid.*, p. 341.

9

PEACE AND STABILITY

1. THE PEACE OF AIX-LA-CHAPELLE

FOR the next few months political life ran smoothly. There was virtually no opposition to ministers in the Commons and, at last, they had the confidence of the King. This was just as well for the war itself was going badly. The all-out effort envisaged by the Duke of Newcastle proved more impressive on paper than in the field. Allied contingents were not up to strength, and the Duke of Cumberland found it one thing to rout the Highlanders at Culloden and quite another to stem the French advance under Marshal Saxe. Not only was he defeated at Lauffeldt but the French, at last turning their strength against the Dutch, were able to capture the great fortress of Bergen-op-Zoom. This meant that the United Provinces now lay open to their armies. No one could foresee what disasters might happen next year, a year in which, under the terms of the Septennial Act, a general election would have to be held. Moreover, by then the ministers might have to face not only the dislike of an unpopular peace but also a reviving parliamentary opposition prepared to make the most of their troubles. By the beginning of 1747 it was clear that the almost unnatural harmony between Leicester House and St James's was breaking down, and that the Prince of Wales was beginning to collect a party round him once again. For this reason as well as because of the military situation, it seemed wise to hold new elections before the Prince could reorganize his supporters; when the session came to an end on 17 June, George II announced the dissolution of Parliament.

The news was received with dismay by the Prince, who made some rather pathetic attempts to rally tory support round him by an appeal to the prejudices of the independent country gentlemen, and

with modified rapture by the majority of M.P.s. The decision to
dissolve was undoubtedly politically wise. The Prince of Wales had
little time to organize his electoral influence and the administration
was brilliantly successful. The organization of such victories at the
polls is so taken for granted that it is easy to underestimate the elaborate planning and dovetailing of government and private interest
which it involved. Each great government supporter had his own
areas of influence, but behind them all was the patient, co-ordinating
work of Henry Pelham, who like Walpole, was his own chief election
agent. When the new Parliament met in the autumn he was able to
face the hazards of the peace negotiation of 1748 and the subsequent
post-war reconstruction, secure in the knowledge that he had the
confidence of both the House of Commons and the King. He had
indeed come a long way since the general election of 1742. Now at
last the mantle of his old chief was firmly on his shoulders.

The breakdown of the negotiations at Breda allowed the war to
drag on for another weary year. In the Netherlands the French
gained success after success but at sea Britain was slowly gaining the
upper hand. In May 1747 Anson, in an action off Cape Finisterre,
captured six French ships of the line and four East Indiamen; in
October Hawke fought another successful engagement off Belleisle;
in India Pondicherry was being blockaded by Boscawen with ten
ships. Therefore, in spite of her victories on land, France also
had some inducements to make peace. But though she was prepared
to be moderate in her demands, she was far from exhausted, and not
in the least likely to accept terms which did not include the return of
Louisbourg. Negotiations were reopened at Aix-la-Chapelle early
in 1748. The discussion of the preliminaries continued to divide the
Cabinet, and Sandwich, as the British plenipotentiary, once again
found himself acting under the immediate orders of Chesterfield,
who was anxious to smooth the negotiations by concessions, and
corresponding secretly with the Duke of Newcastle, who was not.
This in its turn led to a minor political crisis. Like his predecessor,
Lord Chesterfield felt that he was being put in an impossible position, and in February he too resigned. Views were divided on the
filling of the vacancy. Newcastle was anxious that Sandwich, whom
he flattered himself he would be able to control, should receive the
seals; but his views were shared by neither Pelham nor George II.
Instead the Secretaryship was offered to the Duke of Bedford, who
accepted.

Meanwhile the English ministers had resigned themselves to the restoration of Louisbourg to France. In April 1748 Cumberland was writing to Sandwich, 'I cannot help owning, that I think a tolerable peace is absolutely necessary.'[1] Even Pitt had come to feel that there must be a breathing space and an end to the present entanglements. These entanglements were, however, making the path of the negotiators difficult, for Maria Theresa was both furious and distrustful. Once again the Cabinet was divided in its attitude towards her. Newcastle was sympathetic and based his diplomacy on the need to maintain the friendliest possible relations with Vienna, while his brother was all in favour of a firm line. These difficulties were increased by George II's insistence on leaving for Hanover in May, the very day that Parliament was prorogued. Newcastle himself could not get away until the beginning of June. Finally, by a pressure that was very near to bullying, Maria Theresa was brought to authorize Kaunitz to sign the preliminaries in May. She had indeed very little option, for in April England had decided to agree to France's terms without waiting for the agreement of her allies. Only a detailed study of the feverish diplomacy of the months between May and October, when the treaty was signed, can really do justice to the perplexities of the Cabinet and the cross-currents between its members and the Closet. The statement that the preliminaries were signed in May and the definite peace in October sounds straightforward and simple. To the ministers involved it was a period of agonizing and complicated uncertainty.

The peace which was finally achieved was in many ways better than Pelham had expected. Louisbourg, England's sole conquest of value, was handed back to France, and provided one of the causes of the war which broke out again in America in 1754. Without it French forward policy would have been far more difficult both to conceive and to execute. But in 1748 the situation which was to develop in America had scarcely been foreseen. Meanwhile, the Austrian Netherlands had been saved from France, and the Dutch were once again to have their barrier, though Austria so bitterly resented the terms on which this was conceded that a great strain was to be placed on 'the old system'. Indeed, in these arrangements lay some of the reasons for the diplomatic revolution. The settlement in Italy made very little difference to English trading and naval interests in the Mediterranean. Don Philip was to get the Duchies of

[1] W. Coxe, *op. cit.*, vol. I, p. 409.

Parma and Piacenza, an appendage which was to remove him out of the way of Ferdinand VI. Charles Emmanuel retained most of the concessions which British diplomacy had secured for him from Maria Theresa by the Treaty of Worms. In India the status *ante bellum* was restored, though here the advantage lay slightly with the English East India Company in that French official approval had been withdrawn from Dupleix's more adventurous policy. So much had France become the main enemy in English eyes that the clauses which concerned Anglo-Spanish relations received relatively little attention. The Asiento was to be continued until 1752, but the thorny question of the right of search in the Spanish Main was passed over in silence. Even Pitt in a later speech blandly asserted that it was something which we could hardly expect Spain to concede, though the speeches of the 'patriots' in 1739 burned with the conviction that without it British trade was doomed to stagnation and British seamen to an invasion of their most sacred liberties.

2. FINANCIAL REORGANIZATION

With the securing of peace Pelham was able to turn to the reorganization of British war-strained finances. In the closing months of the peace negotiations, he had written to his brother, 'You know, I have had very little comfort in the great scene of business I have long been engaged in. I have no Court ambition, and very little interested views; but I was in hopes, by a peace being soon made, and by a proper economy in the administration of the government afterwards, to have been the author of such a plan, as might, in the time to come, have relieved this nation from the vast load of debt, it now labours under. . . . Here, I own, lay my ambition.'[1] To this project he now devoted the remaining years of his life. For the last year of the war the budget had stood at £13,000,000 plus an additional £800,000 for the Civil List, and the national debt had crept up to £78 millions. It seemed a staggering burden, but by refusing to reduce the Land Tax from its wartime level of four shillings, by retaining the Malt Tax and taking a million from the Sinking Fund, while at the same time making arrangements for the unfunded debt, he began to get the financial situation under control.[2] To carry through a conversion scheme was never easy. A reduction of interest

[1] *Ibid.*, vol. II, p. 15.
[2] L. S. Sutherland, 'Samson Gideon and the Reduction of Interest, 1749–50' (*Econ. Hist. Rev.*, vol. XVI, no. 1, 1946).

was always unpopular with the fund holders, and as the three great moneyed companies held 26 per cent. of the 4 per cents. which he was hoping to convert to 3 per cent., they were likely to make a rallying point for the dissatisfied. In preparing his ground Pelham had shown his usual gifts for moderation and conciliation. Walpole's administration had been disliked by the popular party in the City, led by the ex-Quaker merchant and underwriter, Sir John Barnard, and it had been opposed by the inner financial rings which, on the basis of a closed subscription, had floated government loans. Pelham knew that if his conversion scheme were to have any reasonable chance of success these groups must be mollified, if not completely won over. It was for this reason that he allowed early in 1746 the introduction of a bill repealing the measure of 1725, which had confirmed the right of the Court of Aldermen to veto resolutions of the Common Council. Moreover, in the following year he agreed that the necessary loan for 1747 should be raised by open subscription by which, once its terms had been settled, it should be open for anyone to subscribe to it. As the market rate was then around 3 per cent. he introduced into the Commons in November 1749 a bill to reduce the 4 per cent. interest on the Funds to $3\frac{1}{2}$ per cent. from 1750 to December 1757. After that it was to be 3 per cent. In spite of having managed to associate Sir John Barnard with the measure and of having come to some degree of private arrangement with the directors of the three great companies to advise their proprietors to accept, and in spite of the active propagandist help given by Samson Gideon, the Jewish financier, the whole transaction for a time trembled on the verge of failure. The rate of acceptances was small and slow, and the Courts in each of the three companies refused to follow their directors' advice. It was not until February 1750 that Pelham's success was sure; when at the end of the month the books were closed 64 per cent. had accepted the proffered terms. A short supplementary act then offered less good terms, namely the continuance of the $3\frac{1}{2}$ per cent. only until December 1755, to holders who now wished to capitulate. Those who still refused were to be paid out and in 1751 a million was raised at 3 per cent. for this purpose. The fact that this was not done easily makes it clear that, if Pelham had not prepared the ground so carefully and reduced opposition to a minimum, the financial interests in the City might well have been too strong for him. During the next two years he tidied up the national finances still further by consolidating various stocks, all bearing 3 per cent. interest, into one easily administered stock. In this way he left a permanent mark on British public finance for his consolidated stock became known as the 3 per cent. Consols.

Pelham's determination to economize did, however, bring him into conflict with other ministers. Newcastle was justifiably worried about the international situation. That war with France would be renewed in the foreseeable future seemed certain.[1] Once again the Netherlands would be in danger, and to safeguard these it seemed imperative that the old alliances with Austria and the United Provinces must be made serviceable. Newcastle's methods for achieving this remained those of the past, namely financial assistance judiciously applied and a careful fostering of cordial relations with Maria Theresa. Immediately after the peace there had been much discussion of her right to a payment of £100,000, which had been promised in return for an imperfectly kept agreement to supply troops. Newcastle wanted to pay; Pelham would not do so without parliamentary sanction. Newcastle also had a somewhat impracticable scheme, shared by George II, that Maria Theresa might be won over by bringing about the election of her son Joseph as King of the Romans. This would involve payments in the form of subsidies to interested parties in return for a favourable vote. Bavaria received a subsidy of £30,000 and Saxony one of £48,000 in return for promised military help should the need arise. To this expenditure Pelham remained bitterly opposed.

In 1749 both the army and the navy were drastically reduced. Had it not been for the protests of both Newcastle and the King these cuts would have been carried even further. Next year Pelham moved for another reduction in the naval forces from 10,000 to 8,000 men. This motion, too, was carried by 167 votes to 107, in spite of the protests of Pitt, Grenville and Lyttelton, who, encouraged by Newcastle's tacit approval, went so far as to vote with the opposition. It is true that next year the naval strength was again brought up to 10,000, but this figure, with a standing army of only 18,000, left very little margin when war came. The position of the armed forces

[1] A. H. John, 'The London Assurance Company and the Marine Insurance Market in the Eighteenth Century' (*Economica*, XXV, new ser., May 1958), makes the interesting point that 'the continuance of a high premium income between 1748 and 1756 suggests that the merchants, at least, discounted the prospects of a permanent peace with France after the Treaty of Aix-la-Chapelle'.

was the subject of other than financial debates, all of which throw an interesting light on contemporary attitudes. In·the autumn of 1748 a motion was debated that half-pay officers should still be subject to martial law. This was opposed on the ground that it would force many of them who 'were of good family and fortune, to exert their extensive influence in favour of ministers'. In the same session a proposal to pay 3,000 seamen a retaining fee of £10 a year, and so, by having a margin of manpower available in an emergency, to avoid the need of extensive pressing, was also rejected. Even more directly political was the motion sponsored by the opposition in the 1750-1 session to suspend the office of Captain-General in time of peace. Its aim was to decrease the influence of the Duke of Cumberland, an object of particular antipathy to Leicester House. If England seemed unprepared to meet the hazards of a new war in 1756 it must be remembered that in the vital years between the wars parliamentary decisions on military and naval matters were almost invariably influenced more by political and financial considerations than by problems of defence or offence.

3. DOMESTIC REFORMS

Other aspects of Pelham's domestic policy are less open to criticism. One change of major importance for which he was responsible was the reform of the calendar. Because Britain had refused to accept the Gregorian revision of the calendar which had been adopted by most European states, her dates had got more and more out of alignment with those of her neighbours. She was now eleven days behind and her new year still started on the 25th March. This was most inconvenient both for international trade, in which agreements had to be specified in both the old and the new style, and for diplomacy. Chesterfield, having suffered from the system in his ambassadorial capacity, was anxious that a change should be made. In this he was supported by Pelham and Hardwicke. Newcastle, as usual, was nervous of its effects on public opinion; to some extent his fears proved justified. Parliament accepted the bill without much difficulty, backed as it was by the scientific authority of the Earl of Macclesfield, President of the Royal Society, but it did lead to popular protest in the country. The elimination of eleven days between the 2 and 14 September 1752 was bitterly resented. Hence the cry, 'Give us back our eleven days'. To many people altering the dates of Saints' days smacked of impiety. It is sometimes difficult for twentieth-century minds to realize to what extent eighteenth-century society, particularly in its lower levels, was held together by tradition. Change was suspect just because it was change.

Two other reforms which Henry Pelham had at heart were dashed against the rocks of religious prejudice. One was a project for nationalizing foreign Protestants. In 1708 an act along similar lines had been passed, only to be repealed in 1711. In 1747 the idea had been revived but had been badly received by the City of London. Now, in February 1751 it was reintroduced by a Mr. Nugent with the approval of Pelham. Though leave to introduce the bill was granted, and though it got as far as the committee stage, in face of the strong protests received from the City of London and other bodies Pelham withdrew his support. In consequence it was ordered to be read again in two months' time, a polite way of shelving it, and it was not brought forward again. In view of this failure it is surprising that an attempt to facilitate the naturalization of Jews, which was made in 1753, should have had even a temporary success. It was a very modest measure, which would merely have made naturalization by private act easier in that it omitted the words 'on the true faith of a Christian' from the oaths of supremacy and allegiance, which had to be taken. Such a law had been in operation in the American colonies since 1740, where religious diversity was more readily accepted and where the need to encourage the sinking of capital was acknowledged. In the House of Lords the new proposals passed easily enough, but they were bitterly resisted in the Commons in spite of Pelham's argument that the naturalization of wealthy Jews, and only the minority could in any case afford a private bill, would increase revenue by encouraging capital investment and would do no harm to Christianity. His arguments were eminently reasonable and the bill, with his influence behind it, was passed. That the majority of members were indifferent might well be argued from the small attendances. Outside Parliament, however, it was easy to whip up prejudice, prejudice which to some extent could be explained by the fact that, while English Roman Catholics and Protestant Dissenters laboured under heavy disadvantages because of their faith, it was unfair to make life easier for the Jew. There can be little doubt that much of the uproar was fomented by those people whose financial interests clashed with those of the wealthy Jew: Pelham certainly seems sure that much of it had been deliberately manufactured. Newcastle, as usual, was much perturbed[1]—the more so on this occasion because in 1754 a new general election was due and he did not want to leave such a useful card in the hands of the opposition.

This again illustrates the sensitiveness of administrations to popular opinion, and refutes the conventional picture of Newcastle waving the wand of corruption and hey presto creating a packed and submissive Commons. In consequence the act was repealed, to the sarcastic comment of Lord Granville that had it been called a bill to prevent the profanation of the Communion by Jews nothing could have been said against it!

Though outwardly religious measures, both were promoted and attacked largely for financial reasons. The administration was also concerned with social problems, and in the period between the wars some attempts were made to deal with the licentiousness of the age. Responsible opinion seems to have been genuinely worried by the violence and brutality of the lower strata of society, particularly in the bigger towns and most especially in London.[2] It is of some significance that Henry Fielding's *Enquiry into the Causes of the late Increase of Robbers* appeared in January 1751, that Hogarth's bitter satire on the drinking habits of Londoners, 'Gin Lane', came out a few weeks later, and that in August John Fielding became a magistrate for Westminster where he joined his half-brother Henry, who had held the office for the past three years. Most people were agreed that one of the major reasons for this demoralization was that, in spite of the almost penal duties imposed by Walpole in 1736, gin drinking was as prevalent as ever. Once its attention had been released from the immediate necessities of waging war and making peace, the government was urged by a petition from the City of London to frame fresh legislation to deal with this evil. By the bill introduced by Mr. Nugent, distillers were not to be allowed to retail or to sell to unlicensed vendors, and teeth were given to the

---

[1] The Duke of Bedford, describing the incident to Rigby declared, 'His speech was if possible, rather worse than usual; his arguments, which indeed it is a great presumption ever to pretend to understand, seemed all to tend for the bill he meant to repeal; he spluttered out exclamations against evil minded people, that had endeavoured to work upon the weak but well intentioned poor multitude . . . in one thing indeed, he did greatly better than usual, he was much shorter.'—*The Correspondence of John, Fourth Earl of Bedford*, edited J. Russell (1846), vol. II, p. 138.

[2] C. Hibbert, *The Road to Tyburn* (1947), though popular in its approach, is based on reliable sources and chapter 5, 'Crime and Punishment', gives a good picture of contemporary conditions (pp. 46–62).

prohibition by the provision that debts of less than one pound were not to be recoverable at law. This automatically made the small buyer a less attractive one. Only persons duly licensed were to be allowed to retail gin, and licences were to be confined to inn-keepers, victuallers and vendors occupying premises of an annual rent of at least £10. For a second offence the punishment was whipping and imprisonment, for the third transportation. In this way it was hoped to eliminate the small fry and riff-raff who had been so active in the distribution of gin, and to leave this dangerous trade in the hands of the more socially responsible.

Gin was not the only social temptation which Parliament attempted to regulate. The statute book during these years is studded with acts against the keepers of disorderly houses, acts regulating public places of entertainment, acts aimed at the prevention of robbery and murder. Their efficiency may well be doubted; offering rewards to those who had been responsible for the capture of a convicted felon was a method open to much abuse. The thief taker, like Jonathan Wild or McDaniel and his crew, might well also be the instigator of crime.[1] Nevertheless, it was in these years that the beginning of an effective organization to deal with London crime first began to take shape. Alarmed by the wave of brutal gangs terrorizing the capital, Newcastle found time, amid all his other worries and perplexities, to consult with John and Henry Fielding, the Westminster magistrates, about the best methods of breaking these up. Under their régime at Bow Street, ably helped by Saunders Welch the High Constable, thief takers who were experts and whose integrity was carefully checked and controlled, began to pit their wits against those of the criminal. When Henry's health forced him to give up his London employments in 1754, his half-brother John took on the full responsibility. If headway was slow, at least a beginning had been made.

Another source of social abuse was the lax regulations which covered the contracting of marriages. Though since the reign of Anne marriages in churches required the publication of banns, irregular marriages performed by priests whose orders were often dubious, or whose poverty or lack of a patron had forced them into the ranks of the hedge priests, were legally binding. By the middle of the century the Fleet prison had become particularly notorious

[1] Patrick Pringle, *The Thief Takers* (1958), provides a rather chatty account of Jonathan Wild and Sir Thomas de Veil.

for the facilities it afforded for clandestine marriages. Clergymen imprisoned for debt, or those who merely posed as clergymen, did a thriving business, so thriving indeed that they even employed touts to bring them custom. At a time when marriage put a husband in full possession of his wife's money, unless it had been carefully tied up in settlements, the kidnapping of heiresses was not so much a romance as a business proposition for unscrupulous men. Prostitutes, too, made a habit of trapping unwary youths after a drunken debauch. Young people had every inducement to marry in haste and repent at leisure and the social results were often deplorable. Earlier attempts to stamp out the abuse of clandestine marriage in other recognized haunts of the practice, such as the purlieus of the Savoy and in May Fair, had merely concentrated the evil in the Fleet. It was one which Lord Hardwicke, with his great legal experience, was anxious to eliminate, and in 1753 the Marriage Act, which is known by his name, was introduced. By it, stringent provisions which are the basis of the present law were made for the consent of guardians in the case of minors, for the calling of banns and for the need of residence. Special licences were required for any deviation from the general rules, and irregular marriages were robbed of their legality. It was a piece of wise legislation, designed to prevent much misery and fraud. Social improvements are, however, seldom welcomed by a traditional society, and a parliamentary opposition looking for a vulnerable place in their enemies' defence was able to represent Hardwicke's Marriage Act as an outrage on English liberties. Opposition to the act in the House of Lords was led by the Duke of Bedford, and in the Commons by young Charles Townshend and Henry Fox. The latter's bitter attacks on the bill are often attributed to personal sensitiveness. In 1744, at the age of 38, he had eloped with Lady Caroline Lennox, the eldest daughter of the Duke of Richmond, when she was only 20. The marriage had proved a happy one and he was conscious that he owed it to the laxity of the law. But Fox's past is, by itself, hardly an explanation of the concerted disapproval with which the measure was greeted by sections of both Houses. Fox was connected with the Duke of Cumberland, Newcastle full of fears at the growing friendship between the royal Duke and the Duke of Bedford had engineered the latter's resignation in 1751. It may well be that the attempt to throw out Hardwicke's bill owed much to the earlier rift in the Cabinet between Bedford and Newcastle.

Some of the arguments used in debate cast a curious light on contemporary mentality: everywhere the stress was placed on the need to preserve personal liberty. It was feared that the new law would give too much power to guardians, that it would promote immorality, particularly among the poor, by making marriage more difficult and expensive, and that it might lead to the bastardizing of innocent children of parents whose marriage had been irregularly solemnized. Much play was made with the delicacy of women's feelings, a delicacy which it was stated would be outraged by the public reading of the banns. Ingenuous and amusing were the arguments of Charles Townshend who declared, 'A gentleman marrying a beautiful young girl of little or no fortune is generally so much laughed at by his companions, that no man would chose to have it made public beforehand . . ., and the necessity of his doing so may very probably prevent his making her happy, and induce him to render her miserable by debauching her.'[1] More serious politically was the bad blood which the debates engendered between Lord Hardwicke and Henry Fox. The latter likened the author of the bill to a giant spider. The Lord Chancellor did not forgive him, though in a subsequent speech Fox tried to smooth over his remark. 'I despise the scurrility and I reject the adulation'[2] was the reply of the indignant Hardwicke. This bitter exchange of personalities between two members of the administration, the Secretary at War and the Lord Chancellor, illustrates dramatically the degree of divergence, and even animosity, that political convention allowed to ministers in the same administration.

4. MINISTERIAL QUARRELS

These years of reconstruction and reorganization after the war provided a period of political stability. George II was content with Henry Pelham and the two men worked smoothly together, though they did not always agree on foreign policy. There were, however, two difficulties. Though the early election of 1747 had caught the Prince of Wales at a disadvantage, with the result that his supporters had done badly at the polls, the potential threat of a new Leicester House party was always present. Already the hope of dead men's shoes was exerting its attraction, for it was supposed

---

[1] *The Parliamentary History of England from the earliest period to the year 1803*, vol. XV, p. 60.

[2] Lord Ilchester, *Henry Fox, First Lord Holland* (1920), vol. I, p. 193.

that George II was unlikely to have many years in front of him. All this was made more worrying because of the personal rivalry which had developed between the two Secretaries of State. By the very nature of their responsibilities they were forced to work closely together. This was something that Newcastle always found difficult, unless his colleague was of a pliant and accommodating nature. No one could describe John, Duke of Bedford, in these terms. He was considerably younger than Newcastle, but had no intention of deferring to him, being by temperament imperious, obstinate and at times intensely irritable. But he had none of Newcastle's obsession with his office, much preferring the rural pleasures of Woburn to the drudgery of public business which, as a result, was often neglected. What alarmed Newcastle was the growing friendship between Cumberland, with his great Court influence, and Bedford. This friendship was in part due to the pleasing manners, wit and charm of Lord Sandwich, who had attached himself to Bedford. This was particularly bitter because earlier Sandwich had been Newcastle's own candidate for the Secretaryship; this was before the two men had differed over the policy to be followed at Aix-la-Chapelle. Now it looked as if Bedford and Sandwich were replacing Pelham and Newcastle in the regard of the royal Duke, and Newcastle made himself miserable with his suspicions, and wore out his brother and Hardwicke with his complaints. Once again he was determined that his fellow Secretary must be got rid of. The problem was how.

As a result of these internal strains the Cabinet spoke and acted with a divided voice. Fox, an adherent of the Cumberland group, tended to act with Pelham, while Pitt gave general support to Newcastle, though he was far from agreeing with all his policies. It may have been through his influence that Pitt again began to draw near to Leicester House. If Cumberland was indeed gathering a party round him, the Prince of Wales might prove a useful counterweight as Pitt was well aware. Chiefly, however, he seems to have aimed at playing the part of the peacemaker, soothing the anxious Duke with the flattery which he well knew how to apply. Certainly there was a need of peacemaking, for Pelham and his brother were now on such bad terms that they could not trust themselves to meet; instead they corresponded through Newcastle's secretary, Andrew Stone. Such a situation could not continue, either there must be a reconciliation or the ministry would lose all authority. Finally, through the good offices of the Earl of Lincoln, who was New-castle's son-in-law, good relations were restored between them in February.

Then, in the following March the whole political scene was altered by the unexpected death of the Prince of Wales. For the time being the nucleus of an opposition had disappeared. The heir to the throne was now a minor, and the Princess of Wales appeared willing to remain on good terms with her father-in-law. The death of Frederick did, however, produce one delicate problem, namely the need for a Regency bill. George II was nearly 70 and might die before the young George came of age. The Duke of Cumberland's friends urged his claims. He was the uncle of the new heir and, they argued, the natural Regent. He was, however, very unpopular—in Scotland because of his behaviour in suppressing the '45, in England because of his stiff manners. Rumour declared that as Captain-General of the forces and Regent he would use this combination of power to make himself King on the death of his father. In such circumstances Pelham persuaded George II that the Princess of Wales must be named as Regent, with a very carefully chosen Council to assist her. Of this Council Cumberland was to be president but, in face of the widespread distrust and also doubtless of the fears of Newcastle, his powers were to be carefully restricted. It was a decision over which the Cabinet was far from unanimous. Once again the cleavage of opinion between Pitt and Fox was marked. Fox preferred Cumberland, and won the approval of George II for the advocacy of his son's claims, though he knew that on this point it would be unwise to follow his heart rather than his head. Pitt, already sympathetic to the Leicester House group, preferred the Princess. It was a preference that confirmed Cumberland's dislike of him, which in 1757 was to have an important effect on Pitt's career. Cumberland submitted to these arrangements but retained an understandable grudge against Newcastle and Pelham, feeling that their action was taken partly in revenge for his patronage of Bedford and Sandwich.

The crisis over the Regency Bill was followed in June by a reconstruction of the ministry in conformity with Newcastle's wishes. The events of the last few months had not improved the relations between the Pelhams and Bedford; that Pelham was feeling the strain is clear from his correspondence. Finally he seems to have come to the conclusion that Bedford would have to go. As, however, it would have been difficult to persuade George II to dismiss the proud Duke out of hand, more subtle methods were employed. The King was persuaded instead to dismiss Sandwich from the Admiralty, the hope being that this cavalier treatment of his protégé would drive Bedford to resign. This subterfuge worked. Sandwich was ungraciously dismissed on 13 June and Bedford resigned next day. In their place Anson, Hardwicke's son-in-law, went to the Admiralty and Newcastle got the docile colleague that he wanted in Holderness. These appointments were each, in their own way, successful. Anson did good work at the Admiralty and friction between the Secretaries disappeared. At the same time a further reshuffle took place. Harrington, whom George II had never really forgiven for his behaviour in 1746, was dismissed from Ireland, without being given any compensating employment, and Dorset got his long-wanted Lord Lieutenancy of that country. This created a new vacancy, for his position as Lord President of the Council had now to be filled. Newcastle's choice of his old rival Granville was less surprising than, on the surface, it seems. Granville had always been two-sided, drawn to politics by his early career and success and his wide knowledge of Europe, but drawn also to literature and good living, and to all the attractions of a cultivated leisure. After the show-down of 1746 he seems to have relinquished without regret the idea of a political career. If he could not dominate he preferred to stand aside. The failure of George II's attempts to reconstruct his ministry round Bath and himself seems to have left him without regrets, a half-amused, half-indifferent spectator. Newcastle was therefore no longer afraid. When no longer a competitor for power Granville had much to offer as a colleague. His views on European policy were much nearer Newcastle's own insistence on the careful nursing of the 'old system', and he was more likely to be sympathetic on the subject of subsidies to German princes than Pelham. Indeed when, earlier, Newcastle had been pressing for Bedford's removal, he even suggested that Granville might once again become Secretary, a suggestion that Pelham negatived, even to the extent of threatening to resign. As President of the Council Granville would be a useful, well-informed and unambitious colleague and, with George II's approval, the appointment was duly made.

The last years of Pelham's administration, until his death in March 1754, were a peaceful contrast to the earlier stresses and strains. His control over the Commons was complete. Indeed Henry

Fox, writing to Hanbury-Williams on 4 December 1751 said, 'I do not foresee a debate this session, nor any difficulty to the ministers, but that of getting forty every day to make a House.'[1] Only two minor incidents ruffled this calm. One was the quarrel already discussed between Fox and Hardwicke over the Marriage Act in 1753. The other was an ugly rumour that Jacobite influence was strong in the Princess of Wales's household and that the heir to the throne was being brought up with dangerous political ideas. The government took it seriously enough to hold an inquiry and to examine witnesses, but the charges seem to have been due more to the hope of discrediting the Pelhams than to any solid basis of fact. So weak was the opposition that when Parliament met in November 1753 no amendment to the Address was even offered in either House. This lack of excitement did not mean that no useful legislation was passed in these years. Most sessions had their crop of characteristic eighteenth-century statutes dealing with specific local needs, or the problems of individual industries, or trades. These might vary from fixing the width of the wheels of wagons, to throwing open the privileges of the Turkey Company to any British subject on the payment of £20. A constantly recurring theme was the need to tighten up and improve the Customs administration in the endless war between the revenue and the smuggler.[2] A careful perusal of the statute book during Pelham's long ministry would reveal a steady interest in the fostering of the economic interests as well as the social morality of the country as a whole. But such legislation, unless it was a milestone marking a change of policy or unless it became the occasion for a political crisis, is of too local a significance both in time and in place to have much interest for later generations.

5. THE END OF AN ERA

Pelham's death brought this era of stability to an end. He left no one in whom both the King and the Commons had the same confidence. Newcastle, in some ways his natural successor, was in the House of Lords. There were men of great ability in the Commons, outstanding among whom were Fox and Pitt, but Newcastle's

[1] W. Coxe, *Pelham*, vol. II, p. 207.

[2] In 1745 Pelham cut the Excise on tea to 1*s.* a pound, compensating the revenue with a 25 per cent. tax on sales at the East India Company's auctions, so putting the smugglers out of business for a time. But as a result of war finance the duties began to mount again until by 1783 they stood at 119 per cent.—N. Williams, *op. cit.*, p. 97.

jealousy, which had even resented at times the assumption of authority by the brother he so dearly loved and whose death left him plunged in grief, was hardly likely to concede to them the necessary free hand. Henry Pelham's death was a loss to his friends, a loss to his King, and a loss to his country. The judgment of Archdeacon Coxe, his most solid biographer, was that 'His knowledge was useful rather than extensive; his understanding more solid than brilliant.'[1] Walpole's influence on him had been considerable and Pelham 'was proud to acknowledge that he considered himself as a pupil and follower of Sir Robert Walpole in the science of politics and finance'. He was less ruthless and more conciliatory than his master. There was little about Pelham that put men's backs up, he did not line his pockets with public money, his private life was all it should be. He lacked Walpole's driving ambition; perhaps lacked too his complete confidence in his own judgment. He was less likely to drive brilliant rivals into opposition because of these qualities, and when he died most men of ability were in some ways attached to the government. Because he was in all these ways a less outstanding person than Walpole, his success in these last years is the more illuminating. It was not the triumph of an overriding personality but the confirmation of the mechanics by which the Revolution settlement could be made to work that marks the importance of Pelham's ministry. The years that were to follow underlined this fact. Apart from the last two years of George II's reign, it was not until 1770, when Lord North became First Lord of the Treasury, that these conditions were reproduced.

[1] W. Coxe, *Pelham*, vol. II, p. 301.

10

BRITAIN AND HER OVERSEAS POSSESSIONS
ON THE EVE OF THE SEVEN YEARS WAR

PELHAM's death brought to an end the era inaugurated by Walpole, with its stress on peace and an unadventurous foreign policy. Though the forty years from 1714 to 1754 had by no means been a period of unbroken peace, Britain had been involved in continental wars to safeguard her position in Europe rather than to extend her influence overseas. The claims made by the opposition whigs against Spain in 1739 fell into a different category but the emphasis they put on British freedom in the Caribbean was premature. Moreover their motives, with the possible exception of Pitt's, were as much political as economic. Until the middle of the century most men were content with the share of trade and colonies which had already fallen to England. After 1754 the picture changes. To some extent this was due to the emergence of Pitt, who was prepared to go with the tide of expansion rather than to attempt to stem it in the interests of preserving peace. Nevertheless the fundamental fact was that Britain was stronger than she had been in 1714. Politically she was more stable. Economically her population was beginning to show an upwards surge, while in both industry and agriculture her resources were growing. The same things were happening in her overseas dependencies. They too were expanding and the danger of clashes with their neighbours was rapidly becoming imminent. To understand the position in 1754 it is necessary to stand aside from the main stream of events and to trace developments in her colonial possessions whose fortunes were to influence both British external relations and internal policy in the second half of the century. By the beginning of the century their geographical limits had been roughly defined though Georgia had yet to be added to the American colonies, their characteristics had been sketched in and the whole could be described as a going concern. Variations of climate and of government were many but to English and some extent Scottish merchants a desire for profit was the common factor. Roughly speaking these overseas possessions fell into four groups; the colonies strung along the coasts of North America, where already the development of considerable settlements represented a potential clash between the settlers and the British merchants, the islands of the Caribbean, the trading and slaving forts on the African coast, and the factories of the East India Company in India. All these, though so widely scattered, were integrated into the British economy, making a complex of trading interests with the mother country and with each other.[1]

1. NORTH AMERICA

The oldest settlements were those on the American mainland, but to speak of these as if they were in any sense a unity is misleading. Neither in forms of government, nor in social structure, nor in economic interests were they alike. By the middle of the century Newfoundland, Nova Scotia, New Hampshire, New York, New Jersey, Virginia and the Carolinas were royal colonies, and Georgia was about to become so. Pennsylvania, Delaware and Maryland were proprietary colonies, Rhode Island and Connecticut corporate colonies, and Massachusetts a mixture of corporate and royal. The degree of influence exercised by the Crown depended on the form of government, being greatest in the royal and least in the corporate colonies. Nowhere was it absolute. Indeed, the colonial governor was very largely between the devil and the deep blue sea. The colonists regarded themselves as Englishmen, with all the rights and liberties, theoretical and actual, which the constitutionally-minded Englishman claimed at home. These rights were obstinately maintained by the locally-elected colonial Assemblies. All the older colonies, except Pennsylvania and Delaware, were bicameral and, however the Upper House was chosen, the Lower House represented colonial interests and prejudices. Without its co-operation colonial government could not be financed. Just as George II had on occasions to defer to his faithful Commons, so the colonial

---

[1] L. H. Gipson, *The British Empire Before the American Revolution* (4 vols., 1936) provides a detailed analysis of the imperial problem throughout the period covered by this book. For a shorter treatment consult I. R. Christie, *Crisis of Empire* (1970).

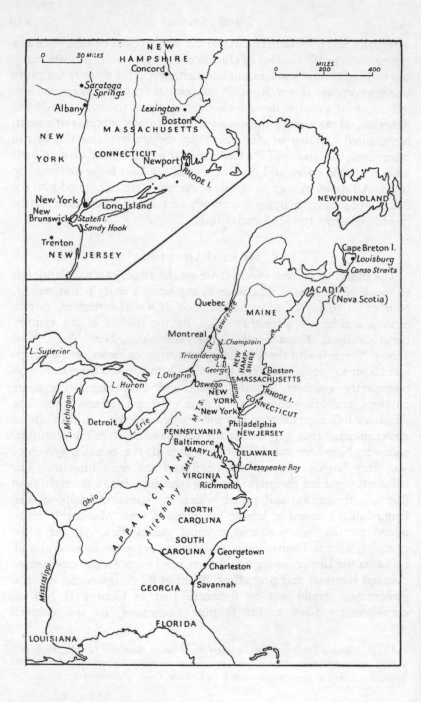

Inset map (upper left):

NEW HAMPSHIRE
Concord

Saratoga Springs

Albany

Lexington
Boston
MASSACHUSETTS

NEW YORK

CONNECTICUT

Newport
RHODE I.

New York

New Brunswick
Staten I.
Long Island
Sandy Hook

Trenton

NEW JERSEY

0   50 MILES

Main map:

MILES
0   200   400

NEWFOUNDLAND

Cape Breton I.
Louisburg
Canso Straits

ACADIA
(Nova Scotia)

Quebec

MAINE

St. Lawrence

Montreal

L. Champlain

Ticonderoga

NEW HAMPSHIRE

L. George

L. Ontario

Boston
MASSACHUSETTS

L. Superior

Oswego

RHODE I.

L. Huron

L. Michigan

NEW YORK

Hudson

CONNECTICUT

Detroit

L. Erie

New York

Philadelphia

APPALACHIAN MTS.

PENNSYLVANIA

NEW JERSEY

Baltimore

DELAWARE

MARYLAND

Ohio

Chesapeake Bay

VIRGINIA

Richmond

Alleghany

NORTH CAROLINA

Mississippi

SOUTH CAROLINA

Georgetown

Charleston

GEORGIA

Savannah

LOUISIANA

FLORIDA

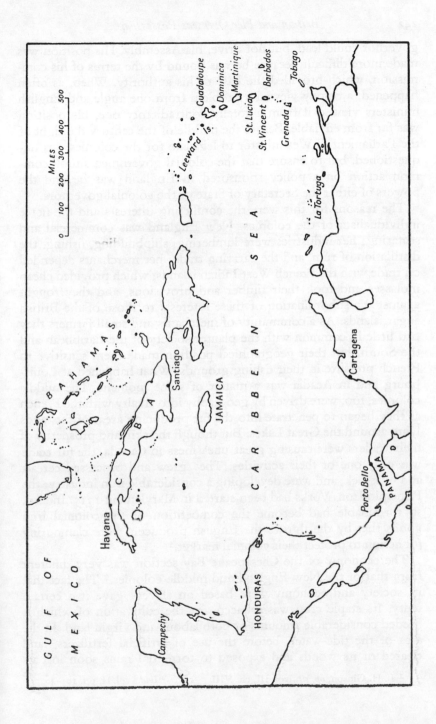

governor could lead, but not drive, his Assembly. His position was made more difficult because he was bound by the terms of his commission, which provided the base of his authority. When, as often happened, a colony viewed a problem from one angle and English ministers viewed it from a totally contradictory one, his position was far from enviable. Before the middle of the century the right of the Parliament at Westminster to legislate for the colonies was unquestioned, but to ensure that the colonial governments took common action on a policy sponsored in England was beyond the powers of either the Secretary of State or the colonial governors.

The reasons for this were the conflicting interests and the fierce individualism of the colonies. New England was commercial and seafaring; her industries were lumbering, shipbuilding, fishing, the distillation of rum, and the carrying trade; her merchants depended on trade with the French West Indian islands, which provided cheap molasses and took their timber and provisions, and they fought against the subordination of these interests to those of the British sugar islands. As a community of merchants and small farmers they had little in common with the planter society of the Caribbean and the South, but their geographical position made them sensitive to French pressure in their fishing grounds. What happened at Louisbourg and in Acadia was a matter of some moment. The middle colonies, too, were driven by geography into rivalry with the French as they began to penetrate into the fur producing areas of the lands lying around the Great Lakes. But though the skill and prosperity of their traders were causing great uneasiness in Canada, the fur trade was only one of their activities. They grew and processed cereals and livestock, and were developing a considerable iron industry: the Principio Iron Works had been started in Maryland in 1715. Indeed, so formidable had become the competition of the colonial iron goods that by the thirties the English producers were clamouring for action to protect their colonial market.[1]

The economy of the Chesapeake Bay section was very different from that of the New England and middle colonies.[2] The fact that its society and economy were based on slavery gave it a certain unity. Its staple crop was tobacco, for the cultivation of which it needed considerable amounts of both labour and virgin land. In the area of the tide-water, before the use of artificial fertilizers, land cleared of its woods and exposed to torrential rains soon lost its

---

[1] L. H. Gipson, *op. cit.*, vol. III, ch. VIII.   [2] *Ibid.*, vol. II, pp. 103–40.

top soil. Three or four years might well represent its active tobacco-growing life. Labour used to cultivate the tobacco plants in the spring and summer could be utilized to clear fresh ground in the winter. Thus most Virginian planters were forced to become land speculators. Because conditions were comparatively humane in the physical sense, they also became breeders of slaves, instead of, like their fellow sugar planters of the Caribbean, being forced to replace their labour force by fresh importations every seven years. Few of the planters were wealthy men; if they were, their wealth came not so much from the profits of the tobacco crop as from land speculation or trade or the practice of law. Few came of gentle English stock. Nevertheless they built on and recreated the English aristocratic tradition. Because of their over-reliance on a single crop they tended to be economically somewhat vulnerable, not so much because of the machinations of English merchants, which must have been considerably checked by the rivalry of their counterparts from Glasgow, as because of the spasmodic saturation of the market after a bumper crop and the constant competition of newly cultivated land. In consequence many Virginian planters carried an almost hereditary load of debt to some English or Scottish merchant house. In some respects the rice growers of South Carolina were more fortunate. The unit of production was less, thirty slaves being an adequate labour force, and their markets were more secure. For it must not be forgotten that though the tobacco planter was protected in the British market, in Europe he had to meet severe Spanish competition.

2. WEST INDIES, AFRICA AND THE SLAVE TRADE[1]

The economy and society of the sugar islands were again slightly different. The most important, Jamaica, lay in the midst of the Spanish islands; by the middle of the century it had a population of some 10,000 whites and 120,000 Negroes, many of whom were raw jungle natives. In consequence the island went in fear of slave risings, and its laws and conditions of life were so harsh that, unlike Virginia, the slave population failed to breed and had to be constantly renewed by importations. This made it an active centre of the slave trade, especially as after the collapse of the Asiento certain contractors got licences to import slaves into the neighbouring Spanish colonies. Its social life, too, was less satisfactory than that

[1] On the Slave Trade see J. D. Hargreaves, 'The Slave Trade', in *The Silver Renaissance*, ed. Natan (1961), pp. 81–102.

of the southern mainland colonies; most of the wealthiest planters seem to have been absentees, there were few openings for the middling sort, and the planters who were in residence made a closed despotic clique.[1] By the middle of the century the competition of the French sugar islands, the devastation of hurricanes, the heavy investment in slaves, and the costs of cultivation when the unit of production was necessarily large, all combined to reduce profits and depress the economy of the island. Nevertheless it continued to be regarded as an important element in the wealth of the mother country. The other islands in British possession were both happier and economically of less significance. Barbados, only 21 miles long and 14 wide, had a pleasant, cultivated social life, as did the Leeward Islands. Nearly 600 miles east of the Virginian coast lay the Bermudas, and to the south-west of them the Bahamas. In the Caribbean, but as yet not finally allotted to any European power, were the so-called neutral islands of Dominica, St Lucia, St Vincent and Tobago. By the middle of the century France and England were both jockeying for position with the object of establishing ownership.

The source of most of the prosperity of both the mainland colonies and the islands was to be found in Guinea. This provided the necessary slaves and was also an attractive market for the rum of New England, for the coarse fabrics exported by the East India Company, and for the trinkets of Birmingham. The leading merchants in this triangular trade were largely drawn from Bristol and Liverpool. Earlier in the century the Bristol merchants had occupied the leading place, but by 1750 when 134 British and some 20 American ships were engaged in the trade, they had been overtaken and passed by Liverpool. The first bank in Liverpool was founded by a group of merchants concerned with the African trade. Inevitably it was a grim business, not so much because of deliberate brutality (for the slaves were valuable merchandise and no captain wanted to arrive with half his cargo dead), as because of the inevitable hardships of a long and overcrowded voyage endured by men whose background made them particularly susceptible to its rigours. Indeed, in some cases the conditions of European emigrants to America can rival if not surpass the horrors of the middle passage. Certainly no Liverpool or Bristol merchant felt the need to blush for the source of his wealth. On Foster Cunliffe's tomb (he owned five slaving ships) is

---

[1] R. Pares, *A West Indian Fortune* (1950), gives a detailed picture of the planter's economy on Nevis.

the epitaph: 'a Christian devout and exemplary in the exercise of every private and public duty'. About 10,000 Africans were required each year. The Royal African Company had had a monopoly of the trade, but it had lost this in 1697, and from the early eighteenth century any merchant paying the requisite fees to the Company could trade. As the Company still had its forts to maintain, after 1730 Parliament had been forced to provide a subsidy of £10,000 a year; but as French traders had established themselves at Anamboe, the best centre of the trade, and were offering nine ounces of gold for each slave as against the eight given by English merchants, the English government had to give further help to the Company. Its financial plight was indeed so desperate that the £10,000 voted by Parliament in 1745 because of the unsatisfactory management of the Company's affairs, had to be rushed out to pay the most pressing claims and save the situation. In June the Duke of Bedford, as Secretary for the Southern Department, asked the Board of Trade to prepare a scheme for the general reorganization of the Company in order to protect and push the interests of the British against the French. There was the usual struggle between those merchants who favoured a strict monopoly and those who favoured a more open trade, but by 1750 the tide of opinion was running against the former. Finally it was decided that all British merchants interested in the West African trade should be incorporated as the Company of Merchants Trading to Africa. All the property of the old Royal African Company was transferred to the new body, which was to be managed by a committee of nine, three from Liverpool, three from Bristol, and three from London. The Company, however, was not to trade in its corporate capacity, though with the dues paid it was made responsible for the upkeep of the forts and trading stations. To deal with the recent French encroachments, early in 1752 Commodore Buckle was sent out in the appropriately named *Assistance* to drive the French from Anamboe.

3. INDIA

Everywhere the same motif of Anglo-French trading rivalry appears, and to this India was no exception. By the early years of the eighteenth century British trade with India was considerable and highly valued. In the first half of this century the East India Company was still a trading and financial corporation, to which the acquisition of territory or the extension of empire made no appeal. What mattered were its trading profits. Its three main dependencies in India were Bombay on the Malabar coast, Madras on the Coromandel coast, and Calcutta. Each of these Presidencies had subsidiary forts dependent on them. Each had its own governor and council, empowered to carry on the day-to-day administration, to make laws and ordinances, though these were to be approved by the directors at home and not to conflict with the laws of England. Also the five senior members and the governor were placed on the Commission for the Peace and charged with the responsibility of holding Quarter Sessions and administering British justice. In addition *zemindar* courts were held to administer Indian law for natives living in the British Presidencies. Local government, as opposed to the direction of its trading activities, in these three cities had, since 1726, been entrusted to a mayor, aldermen and council on the English model. Government was, however, a necessary ingredient in the business of trade rather than of prime importance. What was chiefly asked of the governors was that they should establish such connections and friendly relations with neighbouring rulers as to facilitate the purchase of goods for export and, as far as possible in the face of India's preference for silver, to organize the sale of British manufactures. This two-way traffic was managed through a network of local agents and Company servants, for whom there were also opportunities for private trade. It was by taking advantage of these openings that the Company's servants made fortunes. By the middle of the century all three cities were prospering under the Company's rule. Calcutta, with an estimated population of 12,000 in 1710 had reached 117,000 by 1750; the increase in Bombay, once the more tolerant and flexible Company rule had replaced that of the Portuguese, was equally striking, while Madras numbered some 80,000 in 1746 and if its dependencies are included nearly a quarter of a million. Of these 250,000 people hardly more than 300 were English and of these two-thirds were soldiers. Reasons for the large Indian populations lay not only in the prosperity but in the security which the Company had been able to give. To many wealthy Indians this was a lure of considerable magnitude.

For such prosperity at least two things were vitally necessary. One was a peaceful hinterland in which trade could be carried on. The other was the absence of any over-mighty trading rival. By the middle of the century both these were less well assured than they had been. Even during his lifetime the great Mogul empire of

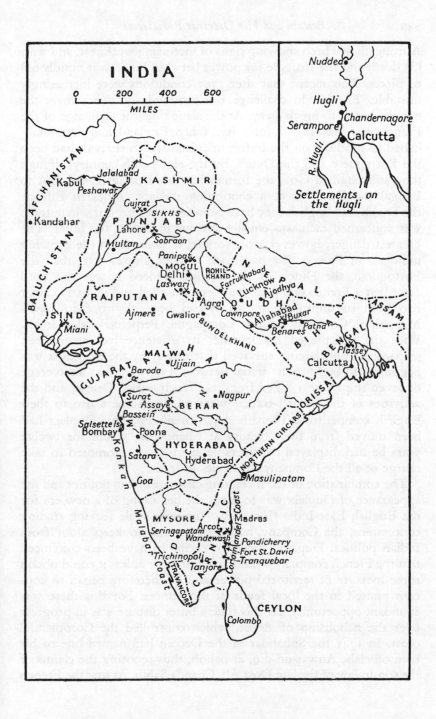

INDIA

0   200   400   600
MILES

AFGHANISTAN

Kabul •   Jalalabad
Peshawar •

KASHMIR

Kandahar •

Gujrat •
SIKHS
PUNJAB
Lahore • × Sobraon
Multan •

BALUCHISTAN

Panipat
MOGUL
Delhi •   ROHIL-
Laswari •   KHAND   Farrukhabad
   Lucknow •   Ajodhya
RAJPUTANA   Agra •   OUDH
     Cawnpore •   Allahabad

N E P A A L

A S S A M

SIND
Miani

Ajmere •
Gwalior •
BUNDELKHAND
Benares •
Buxar •
Patna •
BIHAR

GUJARAT

MALWAH
Ujjain •
Baroda •
Surat ×   Nagpur •
Assaye ×   BERAR
Bassein ×

A R A V A L L I S

BENGAL
Plassey ×
Calcutta

ORISSA

Salsette Is.
Bombay •
Poona •
HYDERABAD
Satara •
Goa •
Hyderabad •

NORTHERN CIRCARS

Masulipatam •

MYSORE
Seringapatam •
Wandewash •
Arcot •
Madras
Coromandel Coast

Trichinopoli •
Tanjore •
Pondicherry
Fort St. David
Tranquebar

Malabar Coast
TRAVANCORE
CARNATIC

CEYLON
Colombo •

Settlements on the Hugli

Nuddea

Hugli •
Serampore •   Chandernagore •
    Calcutta

R. Hugli

Aurungzib had been showing signs of increasing weakness, and with his death and the struggle for power between his sons it rapidly fell to pieces. This meant that after 1707 conditions were increasingly unstable. The Hindu challenge was renewed and everywhere the nabobs began to break away. At the same time the challenge of the French was growing in intensity. When England had first established its foothold on the Indian mainland the chief rivals had been the Portuguese and the Dutch. By the eighteenth century, though they still retained Goa, the former had been outdistanced, but in Bengal the Dutch were a continuing menace. Allies in Europe the Dutch and English may have been forced to be, but where trade was concerned each was equally anxious to outwit the other. The greatest danger, however, now seemed to come from the growing influence of France. She had made a much slower start than the Portuguese, the Dutch or the English. Indeed it was not until 1664 that a French company had been founded and its early career had been so unpromising that it had been absorbed in Law's Mississippi Company as the Compagnie Perpetuelle des Indes. With the collapse of his schemes its existence had again been jeopardized but, having survived that threat, by the thirties it was beginning to build up its trade. Between 1737 and 1742 an average of seven ships a year sailed from its French port L'Orient, and the activities of the French traders were causing some alarm to their English competitors. Then in 1742 Joseph François Dupleix had been moved from their factory at Chanderna, where for twelve years he had displayed considerable energy, and promoted to take charge of all the Company's factories in India.

The combination of the increasing chaos of Indian politics and the appearance of Dupleix was to mark the beginning of a new era for the English East India Company. Hitherto, while seeking trading concessions, the Company had endeavoured to keep aloof from Indian politics. Dupleix, however, seems to have been convinced that the French company would never prosper unless it could obtain some measure of territorial power and he therefore began to concern himself in the local feuds of the princes. For this there was abundant opportunity. At this time a bitter dispute was in progress over the nabobship of Arcot, which controlled the Coromandel coast. In 1741 the Subahdar of the Deccan had named one of his own officials, Anwar-ud-din, as nabob, thus ignoring the claims of the son-in-law of the late Dost Ali, Chanda Sahib. At first the French had recognized Anwar-ud-din and had persuaded him, when hostilities began between England and France in Europe, to inform the English in Madras that all the ships of all foreigners were under the protection of the Mogul. To this attempt on the part of the French to save their shipping from English attacks, the English governor refused to agree on the ground, which was true, that he had no control over what his government did on the high seas and in Indian waters. He did, however, accept the idea of neutrality on land, but in the spring of 1746 a French squadron under Bourdonnais drove away the English ships protecting the coast, and left Madras undefended. The opportunity was too tempting and the French attacked and took the town. Bourdonnais would have been prepared to accept the English offer to ransom the town but the monsoon made him unable to stay on the coast and Dupleix had other views. He determined to keep Madras. He was not, however, the only interested party for, in order to gain the assistance of Anwar-ud-din, he had promised him the town. When it became obvious that he had no intention of keeping his word Anwar-ud-din attacked. The battle that followed was a landmark in Indian history. In it large Indian forces were completely defeated by the small but highly trained body of French troops. It was an indication of what influence the French might acquire, since obviously in the struggle of the princes their help might be decisive. By the Treaty of Aix-la-Chapelle Madras was handed back by the French, but Dupleix's next moves soon made it abundantly clear that he was determined to use the ambitions of Chanda Sahib as a stalking horse for French predominance in the Carnatic.

Even so brief a survey should make it clear how very complex and varied were the problems with which George II and his ministers had to deal. By the middle of the century England, Scotland and even to some extent Ireland were increasing in wealth and were enjoying a higher standard of living. Admittedly this growing wealth was very unevenly distributed. There was much misery and even starvation among the poorer sort in years of high prices. Nevertheless England at least was beginning to move out of a pre-industrial economy. The pressure of the population on subsistence was not too great; increases made in the easier years were being maintained. But the wealth so gained had to be both extended and defended. Each of the merchants pursuing his own private profit, whether it was in the colonial trade, as a slaver, or as an

East Indian stock holder, thrust his own problems, by means of petitions and memorials and addresses by friendly M.P.s, to the notice of the administration. Again and again trade was the connecting link. What happened in the Caribbean, in the Carnatic, on the banks of the Ohio could never happen in complete isolation as far as either ministers or the merchants of the City were concerned. Gradually, however little ministers might desire it, trade and empire were becoming inextricably intertwined. Moreover, because in Canada, in the hinterland of the American colonies, in the Caribbean, on the African coast and in India, our most dangerous rival was France, it was going to prove increasingly impossible to divorce these economic overseas interests from European diplomacy. Even by the time of Walpole's fall some men were beginning to see that this must be so. Though much of the cry for a naval colonial war was, in its early stages, purely factious, designed to embarrass a minister rather than to extend an empire, it still contained the seed of a new conception of England's destiny. The Seven Years War, under the direction of William Pitt, Earl of Chatham, was to tie together the problem of the balance of power in Europe with that of an expanding interest in possessions overseas.

II

'NOW I SHALL HAVE NO MORE PEACE'

1. INTERNAL DIFFICULTIES

GEORGE II's much-quoted remark on Pelham's death, 'Now I shall have no more peace', provides the keynote for the next three years of his reign. Neither at home, where Pelham's death ushered in a period of political instability, nor abroad, where the impossibility of avoiding a new war with France was becoming increasingly apparent, was the old King to know peace. The two problems were closely linked together, for only an efficient ministry enjoying the confidence of both King and Parliament could hope to wage a successful war. Of the two the more immediate problem was the reconstruction of the ministry. Here the major difficulty was to provide for the management of the House of Commons without arousing the fears and jealousies of Newcastle. Though under the first shock of his brother's death the Duke declared that he had no more heart for business, he had been at the centre of the political game for too long to abandon it lightly, and it was taken for granted that he would continue to play a major part. Certainly this was the assumption on which his friend the Chancellor Hardwicke acted when negotiations for filling Pelham's two offices were begun. Newcastle had acknowledged his brother's role as leading minister, but he was not likely to allow anyone else the same pre-eminence if he could avoid it. He therefore went to the Treasury as First Lord. This freed the Secretaryship of State, and also the Chancellorship of the Exchequer, an office by now traditionally belonging to the House of Commons. It also made it imperative to decide how the business of that House was to be managed. As First Lords of the Treasury, Walpole and Henry Pelham had been able to speak with authority. They were able both to explain, and argue in favour of, a policy which in the Cabinet and the Closet they had helped to formulate, and also to distribute that patronage which would give it additional attractiveness to wavering members.

There was no lack of capable men in the Commons, two of whom were of outstanding, though very different, abilities. These were William Pitt and Henry Fox. Pitt had now for eight years been Paymaster, during which time he had for the most part given loyal support to the administration. Pelham and Newcastle had found him useful but, trading on George II's known dislike of him, had kept him out of power. He was now 45 and a sick man. For him the crisis could hardly have come at a worse time. For two years he had been a semi-invalid, suffering ostensibly with the gout, though his symptoms, with their periods of black depression followed by brief intervals of brighter spirits, suggest that the trouble was more emotional and mental than physical. In 1753 he had given up South Lodge and built a house in Bath, which now became his headquarters. He was there in March when Pelham died, and at a disadvantage in that he could press his claims only on paper and through the good offices of friends who were possibly more concerned with their own political future than with his. Fox had less of Pitt's fire, less of his belief in his own and England's destiny, but he was easier to work with. He was a clear, logical debater and, like Walpole, knew well how to persuade men in private. In his own opinion he had 'more judgment' than Pitt. He too, however, suffered from two disadvantages in a bid for high office, a bid which he made by attempting to organize support as soon as he heard of Pelham's death. The first of these was the dislike he had aroused in Hardwicke after the unfortunate debate on the Marriage Act, which now had serious repercussions because Hardwicke was the centre of the negotiations between George II and the politicians; the second was his close connection with the Duke of Cumberland. It was feared both by the Leicester House party and by Newcastle and Hardwicke that if Cumberland controlled the army and Fox the House of Commons, then, should George II die while the Prince was a minor, Fox and Cumberland would have the full resources of the State at their disposal. In such circumstances Leicester House trembled for the position of the legal heir, and Newcastle and Hardwicke for their own.

Fox and Pitt were therefore, for different reasons, unacceptable both to the King and to the clique of leading politicians. Moreover, even if this had not been so, it is clear that Newcastle wanted a docile mouthpiece in the Commons, not a rival who might challenge the ducal influence in the Closet. Pitt was passed over with many protestations of the 'I would if I could' variety; the problem of Fox needed more subtle handling, for George II favoured his appointment as Secretary of State. Fox had accepted this eagerly, but Newcastle had no intention of giving him an independent empire in the Commons and, after his acceptance, made it clear that all patronage would remain with Newcastle. This would have been to clip Fox's wings for, as he protested, it would have been impossible to smooth the path of government legislation and supply in the Commons. 'How', he asked, 'shall I be able to talk to members when some have received gratifications and others not?' He accordingly refused the proffered preferment and gave his reasons in a letter to the Duke of Marlborough. 'To take the office from the Duke of Newcastle on these conditions and observe them would be to be a fool; to take the office from the Duke of Newcastle on such conditions, in order, when I could, to do him mischief, would be to be a knave. I would be neither.'[1] His refusal left the way open for the sort of appointment that Newcastle preferred. The new Secretary was Sir Thomas Robinson, for many years the British ambassador in Vienna. With foreign policy in the hands of Lord Holderness and Sir Thomas Robinson, Newcastle and Hardwicke could count on remaining in effective control.

Pitt was both furious and despondent. He felt doubly betrayed. Legge, a close friend, was given the Chancellorship of the Exchequer, George Grenville was promoted from a seat at the Treasury Board to be Treasurer of the Navy, while Lyttleton became Cofferer of the Household. They had not neglected their own interests during the reshuffle, however unsuccessful they had been in promoting those of the absent Pitt. Newcastle and Hardwicke likewise, for all their protestations, had been broken reeds. The injury would have been less bitterly felt if the new ministers had been men of outstanding ability. Pitt protested that he would have been willing to serve under Fox who looked likely at one time to succeed Pelham at the Treasury; but to be passed over for Sir Thomas Robinson was too much. It may be that the contrast between Pitt and Sir Thomas has been a little unfair to the latter. He was an experienced diplomat,

[1] Lord Ilchester, *op. cit.*, vol. I, p. 194.

well versed in European politics:[1] the French ambassador Mire-poix, when engaged in trying to settle questions relating to English and French claims in the Ohio valley, was to find him particularly well informed as to these regions. But he was out of touch with the House of Commons, and experienced debaters like Fox and Pitt could very easily run rings round him. This, by mutual agreement, they proceeded to do, and the House was soon treated to the edi-fying picture of the Paymaster and the Secretary of War holding up to ridicule their colleague the Secretary of State.

This joint opposition from within the ministry seems to have come as a most unwelcome surprise to Newcastle and Hardwicke.[2] Pitt's share in it was partly due to an event which not even the most cautious politicians could have foreseen. In the early summer depression and despair had Pitt so firmly in their grip, that, faced by what seemed the relentless hostility of the King, he was talking of resigning. In September, almost by chance, he visited Wotton, where Hester Grenville was staying with her brother George. He had known her for some twenty years; when they had first met at Stowe she was a child of nine. In all that time he had shown no great interest in her; now suddenly, overwhelmingly, he fell in love. Her family, to his relief and gratitude, showed no opposition to the marriage in spite of the difference in their age and family connection. By 15 November they were married.[3] Pitt had now someone who believed in him implicitly, who understood him and, as far as any woman could, stood between him and his despairs. He was now also the brother-in-law of the proud and rich Lord Temple, not a mere hanger-on of the 'cousinhood'. Inspired by his new happiness, Pitt's vigour, his certainties, his ambition returned. When Parliament reassembled in November it rapidly became clear that the ministers would have either to come to terms with Pitt or to fight him. The almost obsequious acceptance of the last eight years was over. Newcastle disliked the idea of so formidable a critic

---

[1] Newcastle writing to Hardwicke on 14/25 November 1748 from Holland attributed much of the success of the peace negotiations to him.—*Hardwicke Correspondence*, vol. II, p. 13.

[2] *Ibid.*, vol. II, p. 245. By 4 Sept. 1755 Hardwicke had come to realize that Newcastle would have to give more weight to the minister in the Commons than he had been prepared to concede to Legge and Robinson.

[3] The surprise that this occasioned is reflected in a letter from the Hon. John Yorke to his brother Viscount Royston: 'Who do you think is going to be married,' he wrote.—*Ibid.*, vol. II, p. 137.

in the Cabinet, though he was willing enough to consult Pitt when it suited him. George II equally disliked the prospect of his having access to the Closet. Their best hope lay therefore in the possibility of splitting the alliance of Fox and Pitt by buying off either one or the other, but preferably Fox. Tentative feelers made it plain that Pitt would not be content with anything less than responsible office, and though negotiations with him continued in a spasmodic way, it was to Fox that an offer was finally made of a seat in the Cabinet and on the Board of Regency when the King went to Hanover in April 1755. During the autumn and early spring, when these negotiations had been taking place, relations between Pitt and Fox had remained friendly, the latter taking care to let the former know what was afoot. But by May this surface friendliness had given way to an open breach, the reason for which is obscure. Possibly a private promise made by Fox when he joined the Cabinet to break his connection with Pitt came to the latter's ears. In any case the two men were temperamentally very different, and were not likely to hold together in the face of any great strain. Pitt now turned more and more to Leicester House, becoming friendly with the rising star there, Lord Bute, the nephew of the Duke of Argyll. He remained Paymaster, however, and Newcastle hoped for the best now that he had at least bought off Fox.

2. WAR CLOUDS

And yet the situation could not be described as satisfactory from the government's point of view. There was still no effective control over the Commons: Newcastle had been unwilling to pay either Pitt's or Fox's price for that, and Pitt was still unappeased. Moreover, relations with France were deteriorating rapidly with no corresponding growth of cordiality between London and Berlin. While George II was in Hanover and until Parliament met again in the autumn of 1755, the question of the leadership of the Commons could be shelved. But if by then foreign affairs had taken a turn for the worse, or if it were decided to meet the threat from Frederick II and France by the building up of subsidized allies for the defence of Hanover—a policy favoured by both Newcastle and Granville— it would not be safe to ask for large grants from the Commons unless the administration could depend on keeping its majorities. Parliamentary strategy would have to be adapted to the needs of foreign policy.

The Treaty of Aix-la-Chapelle had left too many issues undecided to usher in a period of tranquillity. Maria Theresa had small reason to be pleased with the 'old system' which, though it had helped to secure much of the Hapsburg inheritance, had done it in such a way as to earn little gratitude for England and none for the Dutch. The only gainers had been Prussia and to a less degree Sardinia. France remained formidable in contrast to her traditional enemy the House of Hapsburg. Frederick II might be an undependable ally, but between them he and Louis XV could dominate Europe as long as Russia did not intervene. In the continuing of this alliance lay the best hope of European peace. Though Frederick II hankered after further expansion at the expense of Saxony, he knew that the risks involved in active aggression were too dangerous to be undertaken lightly. If an uneasy stalemate had been achieved in Europe the reverse was true overseas. Here the increasing rivalry between France and England was becoming more apparent every year. To England France was a threat and a danger. Just before the great wave of inventions, usually summarized by the phrase 'industrial revolution', it seemed as if French industry were outstripping that of England and competing successfully in her traditional markets. France had the advantages of a large population—at least eighteen million as against a possible six; she had tremendous reserves of technical skill, precision and industry, and her workers were commonly supposed to be accustomed to a lower standard of living than their English counterparts. To Britain it seemed as if the French were obtaining a decided superiority in the cod fisheries off Newfoundland, in the production of sugar, molasses, indigo and ginger in the West Indies, in the manufacture of beaver hats and other articles of luxury made from the furs provided by the North American continent.

France in her turn was alarmed by the restless, unorganized expansion of the British colonists. French overseas possessions constituted a heavy drain on her exchequer: neither Louisiana nor Canada was self-supporting. The latter, however, had at least one great asset in the fur trade. This the New York traders were threatening by enticing the Indian trappers from the lower Great Lakes area to Oswego, with its bait of plentiful and cheap goods. This diverted the furs that would have gone to Montreal. In the same way, south of Lake Erie Pennsylvanian traders were penetrating the passes of the Alleghenies and making direct contact with the Indian villages which lay beyond. In the Ohio valley Virginians were staking out claims. This was not a new development; by the late twenties men looking for fresh land had been pushing into the trans-Appalachian region. In 1749 a group of interested persons, including the London merchant John Hanbury, were incorporated as the Ohio Company. In return for this royal grant they were required to build a fort. Further south still, to the north of the Gulf of Mexico, Carolina traders were entering the Choctaw country and weaning these Indians, as they had previously won over the Chichasaws, from their French connections. Everywhere there was friction, from that between Halifax and Louisbourg in the north to that between Virginians and Canadians in the Ohio valley. In the Caribbean and the so-called Neutral Islands to the West Coast of Africa, and between the rival companies in India the story was the same. That force would eventually be used to secure predominance in some, if not in all, these areas was inevitable.

The protagonists were very different. France with its centralized government had probably a clearer view of imperial policy. Its dominions were controlled from Paris in a way in which the English colonists with their self-governing institutions could never be. Every aspect of life and trade was carefully organized along paternal lines. French soldiers, quartered at strategic points, held the whole together. The French colonists might not have the economic wealth of the English, but whereas English governors had to plead and cajole with the separate assemblies, who would only give help if their immediate interests and frontiers were threatened, French government could requisition and command. The differences between the two countries were particularly marked in the brief period between 1748 and 1754. The French government, particularly in Canada, seems to have had a clear idea as to its policy. Limits were to be placed on the expansion of the English, who were to be confined between the Alleghenies and the sea. The rich lands of the Ohio basin, as yet largely unsurveyed, were to be French, and Canada and Louisiana were to be linked. It would have been difficult for either country to make out a cast-iron legal case for the right to these areas. If they belonged to anybody it was to the Indian tribes whose hunting grounds they were. France could base a claim on early exploration, though certainly not on effective occupation. The English colonies could argue that royal charters had conferred on them rights of occupation. Everything was in fact extremely vague since the lands in question had never been surveyed, and even their natural features were a matter of some uncertainty. Indeed, one of the English suggestions in the attempt to avoid a war was that the Ohio lands should be considered neutral territory, open to the traders of either country but governed by neither.

If France was going to act at all there was much to be said for her doing so promptly. Because of the nature of its economy and of the internal policy of the French government, the Canadian population was growing much less rapidly than that of the English colonies. But against small resources of manpower France could balance the advantage of a unified and centrally-controlled policy. Accordingly she took the offensive. The fortifications of Louisbourg were strengthened, and regular soldiers sent out from France. Forts on the isthmus of Nova Scotia were built, since in any future struggle this was likely to be a key area. Acadia had been handed over to Britain by the terms of the Treaty of Utrecht, but had proved an acquisition of doubtful value because French policy had refused to allow the peaceful absorption of its inhabitants.

The colonies most affected by this stiffer French attitude were those in New England—who felt that unless Acadia could be adequately safeguarded their valuable fishing grounds in the Canso straits would be lost—and Virginia. It would be misleading to speak of any colonial government's taking swift action, but by 1753 the latter was awakening to the need to do something. The Virginians had, however, no feeling that the problem was solely, or perhaps even mainly, theirs: it was one of the responsibilities of the mother country. Dinwiddie, their energetic governor, began to press for some action on the part of the British government, and the Lords Commissioners for Trade wrote to Lord Holderness in March 1753 pointing out that 'unless some measures were speedily taken to put a stop to these proceedings and encroachments . . . any further attempts of His Majesty's subjects to make settlements in the interior of America will be effectively prevented'.[1] This was indeed the very heart of the problem. The ministry under Newcastle had often been blamed for the dilatory and ineffective response that it made to such appeals, but the situation was not so simple as historians, benefiting from their knowledge of future developments, have sometimes implied. It was arguable whether an

[1] L. H. Gipson, op. cit., vol. IV, p. 289.

unlimited expansion of the English American settlements was really a vital British interest. To increase her hold on Acadia and secure the northern fishing grounds, or to challenge the growing French influence on the Neutral Islands, might well seem more important. This at least had been done under the inspiration and energetic direction of the Earl of Halifax by the founding in 1749 of the town named after him. On the African coast, too, in 1752 the *Assistance* had been sent to drive away French traders and establish the British, while in India the English Company was taking the initiative; it was the French governor Dupleix who was recalled. The ministry had not been completely indifferent or supine, but to take resolute action in the Ohio valley was a complicated and delicate matter.

The European situation was uncertain. Neither France nor England wanted war, and from the close of the late hostilities commissioners in Paris had been trying to settle boundaries. This was far from easy. Again and again crops up the difficulty of adjudicating on land that was imperfectly surveyed; claims were necessarily vague and wide, yet in years to come they might prove a title to thousands of acres. It was little wonder that the negotiations dragged on and were eventually inconclusive. One cause of their failure was the determination of the French to make no major concessions: the hinterland was to remain French. But this is something that is clearer to historians, with their access to both French and British archives, than it could be to contemporaries. Newcastle and his colleagues became increasingly suspicious of the good faith of the French, but were loath to accept the necessity of another major clash with them. One reason for this lay in the unsatisfactory state of the 'old system' which has already been discussed. War with France might lead to a French attack on Hanover. Should this happen subsidies would have to be paid to German princes to win their alliance and once again England would be dependent on Austrian help. Also, when Lord Holderness, accompanying George II to Hanover in the spring of 1755, seized the opportunity to sound out Dutch intentions in such an eventuality, he found them increasingly inclined to withdraw into a strict neutrality. This situation was enough to breed caution in ministers. In essence, therefore, Newcastle's problem was how to protect the interests of the British settlers while doing nothing that would precipitate a new war in Europe.

3. COLONIAL CONFLICTS

But though Newcastle was attempting to get the best of both worlds he was not prepared to abandon the colonists to their fate, however querulous and almost panic-stricken some of his reported remarks may have sounded. In response to the pressure which Halifax was exerting as President of the Board of Trade, a Cabinet of mid-August 1753 decided that the right of His Majesty's subjects to settle in the interior, and the grants to the Ohio Company, must be protected. Holderness was consequently instructed to write a circular letter to the colonial governors empowering them to repel force with force, though only within the undoubted limits of His Majesty's dominions. To some extent this was a begging of the question, for these had still to be defined. While the English had been looking for a way round the impasse the French had been acting. Having in 1752 annihilated the trading post of Pickawillany on the central Ohio, the new and vigorous governor of Canada, Duquesne, started to build in 1753 a series of forts with the object of dominating the strategic forks of the Ohio. The Virginians had to decide between the alternatives of allowing their pretensions to go by default or taking some more positive steps to protect them. Dinwiddie's first action was the moderate one of sending George Washington, a young Virginian militia officer of good family, to deliver a protest to Fort le Bœuf. When this was rejected Dinwiddie was faced with a difficult decision. It might, perhaps, have been wiser to wait for instructions from England, or at least until he could have organized a larger colonial force; but the first must involve long delays, while the amount of help which might eventually have been sent was problematic. The second meant attempting the almost impossible task of both getting adequate supplies from the Assembly and persuading at least some of the other colonies to act in unison with her. Instead, in the spring of 1754 he decided to send young Washington (he was only 22) forward with a small detachment to build a fort at the disputed fork.

It was an optimistic project in the face of known French determination. The advance party under Ensign Ward, who was entrusted with the preliminary task of building, was overwhelmed and surrendered without bloodshed to a superior French force, which promptly started building their own fortifications there. This was on 17 April. To attack the new French fort, called after the governor Duquesne, was extremely rash; the colonial detachment was too small and deficient in cannon, and there would be no element of surprise. Moreover, the Virginians would be the first to shed blood. Washington, meeting a small body of French troops, attacked; he killed several, including the Ensign in charge, and took others prisoner. French reprisal came swiftly. On 28 June de Villars left Fort Duquesne and on 3 July Washington and his men were forced to surrender their hastily constructed Fort Necessity. This swift sequence of events made the avoidance of war more difficult. After his defeat Dinwiddie, whose rashness in sponsoring the expedition was partly to blame for its failure, appealed for English regular troops. The French had been steadily reinforcing their own army but at first George II was reluctant to send regulars to America. He thought that munitions and officers to train the local militia ought to be assistance enough. Cumberland, however, put his influence on the other side, and even before the news of the surrender of Fort Necessity had been received Newcastle was clear that 'the colonies must not be abandoned, that our rights and possessions in North America must be maintained and the French obliged to desist from their hostile attempts to dispossess us'.[1] Before Parliament met in November, therefore, it was decided to take action along these lines. It was apparently hoped, however, that this need involve no more than a local war. Objectives were to be limited to restoring the position as it had been before the new French aggressiveness of 1749. The new forts were to be reduced and elbow room for expansion secured.

To do this it was determined to send two regiments of regulars to America, and in September Major-General James Braddock was chosen to command them. When Parliament met in November it endorsed this policy by a vote of a million pounds to strengthen the army and navy, and on 25th added a further £50,000 for Braddock's two regiments. He sailed on 15 January and arrived in Virginia on 19 February. Because of the subsequent failure of the expedition his appointment has been much criticized, but at the time it was popular. His record had been a good one; he had fought well at Dettingen and had campaigned in the mountains and glens of Scotland. Though he was a strict disciplinarian he showed genuine consideration for his men and a good deal of skill in the actual handling of the attack against the French. He was certainly not the stupid, hidebound figure that historical legend has tended to paint but, like many

[1] L. H. Gipson, *op. cit.,* vol. VI., p. 54.

eighteenth-century commanders both on land and sea before professional standards and training had crystallized out of the experience of many campaigns, he was not well served by all his officers. If he was at a disadvantage in an Indian ambush so were the Virginian militia that fought with him: the picture of the flexible colonial and the routine-bound English soldier belongs more to American tradition than to history.[1] Even after his defeat and death the colonists showed no disposition to 'go it alone' and were still insistent that a stiffening of British regular troops was essential for success. Nevertheless his defeat and the routing of his army within nine miles of Fort Duquesne was a setback for the English plan of war for limited objectives. More would have to be done if the French were to be pushed back to the position in 1714 and doing more carried with it the danger of spreading the war.

The same tentative approach had been shown with regard to naval affairs. By the autumn of 1754 France was aware that Britain was preparing to send regular troops to America. Morally she had little right to object as it was something she had consistently been doing herself. But with the dispatch of the expedition under Braddock she intensified her efforts to reinforce her troops in Canada. This presented the English ministers with yet another problem. Were they to allow these reinforcements to get through or were they to take the risk of stopping them? Officially England and France were at peace; if the navy were brought into action could the war still be localized? Once again the ministers hoped that it could, so long as the fighting took place in American waters. On 25 March the Cabinet decided to intercept the French transports and just over a month later, on 27 April, Admiral Boscawen sailed. A week later the French left Brest. Again luck was not with the English. It is sometimes hard for twentieth-century readers to remember the difficulties of naval warfare in the days of wooden ships and sail. To keep a fleet in being and at sea at all in bad weather was something of a feat: contrary winds might ruin the most carefully thought-out strategy. Fog and unfriendly weather hampered Boscawen: through no fault of his, most of the French fleet with its transports got through; only

[1] According to the Hon. Joseph Yorke George II said 'that Braddock had neglected the common rules of war, but that he wash'd his hands of it as he did not choose him for that his son had recommended him, and he owned that he had been surprised at it, at the time.'—*Hardwicke Correspondence*, vol. II, p. 285. The King, however, had been reluctant to send any regulars at all, and in consequence may have felt that the results of the campaign had justified him.

a couple of stragglers, the *Alcide* and the *Lys* were captured. To send these troops had been an act of some courage on the part of the French once they knew that the English fleet was at sea, for to enable them to carry the maximum of men most of their ships had been stripped of the greater part of their armament. If caught they would have been an easy prey, but of the 78 companies that were sent only 10 were intercepted. When the news reached London it caused dismay. Hardwicke described it as 'that too little—too much that happened at sea'.[1]

At this juncture Newcastle did not lack courage: he was prepared to order Hawke to attack in European waters. But by then George II with Lord Holderness was in Hanover, desperately trying to control a diplomatic situation which was rapidly getting out of hand, and in his absence the Lord Justices of the Regency Council were unwilling to take so decisive a step. Meanwhile Boscawen kept up the blockade of the French Canadian ports, for though the troops had got through a real blow would have been struck at French naval power if the ships that had brought them could be immobilized. Even here success eluded him. On 24 August De la Motte's fleet managed to slip out of the St Lawrence, followed on 19 September by Admiral de Salvert from Louisbourg. Only the *Esperance*, which had been partially disabled by a storm, was captured on the way home. The one success of the proposed campaign for 1754 had been the surrender of Beauséjour on the Acadian isthmus to New England troops on 16 June, and even that was in no small measure due to the treason of Thomas Pichon who was able to supply the English with invaluable information as to the French internal dispositions and intentions. But the expedition planned against Crown Point and the fort at Niagara had to be postponed until the following year, owing largely to the friction between William Johnson, the Indian agent, and Shirley, the governor of Massachusetts. The only other strengthening of the British position in America came from an act which has been much criticized—the expulsion of the French settlers from Acadia. They were the victims of circumstance and geography. It was essential for the English that they should have loyal colonists on the Acadian isthmus, but while French priests were allowed to guide their flocks their influence was used to keep alive the hope that one day Acadia would again be French. In the struggle to control the isthmus something like a raiding war had

[1] *Ibid.,* vol. II, p. 284.

broken out on the frontier dividing English and French territory. Some Acadians joined the French in these operations and the rest were obviously willing to do so at the first sign of success. This situation was judged too dangerous for the old tolerant policy to be followed. In July 1754 it was decided to remove all Acadians who refused to take an unqualified oath of allegiance to George II and to distribute them among the loyal colonies. Such an operation calls for great administrative skill and ample resources if the minimum of hardship is to be inflicted; however carefully carried out it must cause misery and resentment. The British authorities probably did the best they could, but the details of the story are heavy with suffering and despair. From the point of view of strategy their deportation was justified. One of the French difficulties in organizing campaigns based on Canada was the problem of supply. Acadia had furnished grain and meat for their troops; henceforth these would have to be found elsewhere.

Though something very like open war existed between the French and British in America, with both royal military and naval forces employed, war was not formally declared until May 1756. Apart from the extreme unwillingness which Newcastle showed to do anything to provoke the French in Europe, there were at least two reasons for this. One was the determination of the French not to be forced into action until their fleet had been strengthened. The other was the uncertainty regarding the diplomatic situation in Europe.[1] The clue to subsequent developments lies in the separate interests of the Great Powers. Maria Theresa wanted either to regain Silesia or to receive an equivalent; to her Frederick was still the arch-enemy. England and Holland wanted above all things to preserve European peace, and Kaunitz, the Austrian Chancellor, realized that they were interested only in the safety of the Austrian Netherlands and would never be useful allies against Prussia. George II feared that if war did occur, France, with Prussian aid, would attack Hanover; this was his chief reason for wanting the Austrian alliance. It was with the hope of ingratiating themselves with Maria Theresa that the King and Holderness were busy in 1755 with a futile scheme for getting her son Joseph elected as King of the Romans, thereby ensuring his peaceful succession as Emperor on the death of his father Francis II. But in view of Maria Theresa's lukewarm attitude it

[1] See W. L. Dorn, *Competition for Empire 1740-1763* (1940), ch. 7, 'The Diplomatic Revolution', for a brief summary of the European situation.

seemed necessary also to provide more dependable allies for the protection of Hanover. A subsidy treaty was made with the Landgrave of Hesse-Cassel in June, and concentrated efforts were made to complete a treaty with Russia. In April 1755 Sir Charles Hanbury Williams had been sent to Moscow and by September the terms of a treaty had been agreed upon. It was clearly directed against Frederick II, who on both personal and public grounds was intensely disliked by the Russian Empress Elizabeth. In return for an annual subsidy of £100,000, which in time of war was to be increased to £500,000, 55,000 Russian troops were to be stationed in Livonia, ready to march if either Britain or her allies were attacked. The treaty was plainly defensive as far as England was concerned. It was to apply only to Germany and to European possessions; America and British overseas possessions were specifically excluded in the hope of preventing the fighting between the British and French in those areas from spreading to Europe.

These subsidy treaties had important repercussions on English domestic politics for they posed the question of who was to get the financial proposals through the House of Commons when it met in November. An indication of the difficulties ahead was given by the refusal of the Chancellor of the Exchequer, Pitt's friend Legge, to make the initial payment until authorized by Parliament. Clearly the House must be firmly guided and equally clearly Pitt must if possible be brought to support the proposals. Half-acknowledged negotiations with him had been going on throughout the summer. First old Horatio Walpole had sounded him in April, and to him Pitt avowed his willingness to wait for the Secretaryship and to support government policy, but only on condition that Newcastle informed him fully and in advance of the measures to be adopted. This would have committed the Duke to submitting to too much unpalatable advice and pressure, and he preferred to let the matter drop. But with Hesse subsidies to be approved both he and Hardwicke felt that another attempt must be made. This time Charles Yorke, Hardwicke's son, was detailed for the task. This attempt was no more successful than the last, for on each occasion Pitt's demands became more clear and definite.[1] He was now unwilling to commit himself to support any policy that was not in line with his own views on the situation. On 9 August Hardwicke had a long talk with him in which their divergence of views became apparent.[2] Both agreed that the American

[1] *Hardwicke Correspondence*, vol. II, p. 228.   [2] *Ibid.*, vol. II, p. 230.

and naval war must be supported, but Hanover remained a stumbling block. Pitt's argument was that the Electorate was of no strategic value, that it would be better to let it be occupied, rather than spend on its defence money which was needed for the naval and colonial war, and that it could always be recovered in the peace negotiations. All this argued no support for the subsidy treaties. On 2 September Pitt had a conversation lasting $2\frac{1}{2}$ hours with Newcastle himself but the result was merely to stress the difference in the point of view of the two men.[1] Though Pitt wanted the kind of office in which he had real responsibility, he was not prepared, in order to obtain it, to support a policy in which he did not believe. He preferred to remain at the Pay Office, though in view of the increasing gulf between his opinions and those of the administration it was doubtful, even with the slack eighteenth-century conventions on agreement between colleagues, how long he would retain even that.

With Pitt in this mood it was impossible to leave the seals in the hands of the hapless Sir Thomas Robinson. A typical eighteenth-century reshuffle was therefore arranged. Lord Barrington surrendered the Wardrobe, to which peaceful haven—with the additional gift of a pension of £2,000 a year—Robinson now retreated. Fox became Secretary and Barrington Secretary at War. In spite of his close connection with Cumberland, Fox, who could be relied upon to steer the subsidy treaties through the House, was for this reason preferred to the implacable Pitt. How formidable the latter could be was speedily demonstrated in the debate on the Address, which had approved the subsidies and promised help for Hanover. Mercilessly he criticized the foreign policy of the administration. Geography, he argued, had made Hanover indefensible and what was needed were ships, not subsidies for troops; the only justification of war was the plight of 'the long injured, long neglected, long forgotten people of America'. For once the debate was prolonged into the early hours of the morning and of the twenty-nine speakers who took part sixteen were against the Address. Of these, Pitt, George Grenville and Legge were all members of the administration against which they voted. In spite of their eloquence, to which Fox replied somewhat ineffectively, the new Secretary had done his work well and the motion passed by a large majority. That the rebels could remain in their places was too much to expect. A week later Holderness

[1] *Hardwicke Correspondence,* vol. II, p. 237.

informed Pitt, George Grenville and Legge that the King had no further use for their services.

For a time Newcastle's political manœuvring seemed to have justified itself. Lyttelton was offered, and accepted, the Chancellorship of the Exchequer, Dodington replaced George Grenville as Vice-Treasurer of the Navy. The cousinhood[1] were furious at Lyttleton's defection, and the bitterness of Pitt's feelings poured itself out again and again against Fox, with little practical result. Fox kept both his temper and his majorities and Pitt was left once again to demonstrate the ineffectiveness of eloquence against a well-managed House of Commons. He had lost office and with it his best chance of influencing policy; he had lost his official income, though with great generosity Lord Temple filled some of the gap with an allowance of £1,000 a year till 'better times', and he was once again a voice crying in the political wilderness. It was not a heartening position for a statesman of 47.

4. The Diplomatic Revolution

Meanwhile a startling change had taken place in the diplomatic affairs of Europe, a change which at first sight seemed to have solved Newcastle's problems and made Pitt's sacrifice vain. This was a new and sudden accord with Prussia, a policy which he had always advocated. The Russian treaty, by threatening to immobilize Prussia, had made Frederick II of less use as an ally to France. Kaunitz meanwhile had persistently and skilfully been endeavouring to create links with Louis XV. There was, from the French point of view, much to be said for a change of alliances. Frederick II had proved undependable. Austria, though still a Great Power whose alliance was worth having, was no longer a danger. Moreover, to gain her friendship would smash the 'old system' on which England had so long relied. Nevertheless had it not been for the development in British and Prussian diplomacy, the reversal of alliances, known to history as the Diplomatic Revolution, might well never have materialized. In concluding the Russian treaty ministers merely thought of themselves as underpinning the 'old system', while gaining an additional protection against Frederick II. The new situation, therefore, was one that made him most apprehensive, and he began to

---

[1] *The Faction of Cousins. A Political Account of the Grenvilles 1733-1763*, by Lewis M. Wiggin (Yale University Press, 1958), deals very fully with this aspect of eighteenth-century political life.

think of ways of keeping the war away from Germany. This new attitude gave a fresh twist to negotiations which had been going on between England and Prussia since the summer of 1755 and in which George II had been trying to get Frederick to give him a unilateral promise not to attack Hanover. Previously the latter had felt safe enough to take an independent line, but once the Convention of St Petersburg had been signed in September 1755 Frederick became much readier to listen to the English proposals. As both parties were anxious to avoid a European war they swiftly came to terms. Accordingly the Convention known as the Convention of Westminster, though it was actually signed at Whitehall, came into being on 16 January 1756. The contracting parties promised not to attack one another's possessions and agreed to resist any foreign power who should enter, or attempt to pass through, Germany. By a secret article the Austrian Netherlands were expressly excluded from the treaty.

The consequence of this arrangement seems to have come as a shock to both Frederick II and the English ministers. When Elizabeth of Russia discovered that Britain had no intention of using the Convention of St Petersburg as a preliminary step to an attack on Prussia she was furious, and it was clear that the agreement would never be implemented. Louis XV was equally annoyed for different reasons. He considered that Frederick II, as an ally, had no right to come to terms with England without consulting him. It was in vain that Frederick II pointed out that the Convention of Westminster was purely defensive and that, in deference to French interests, the Austrian Netherlands had been excluded from its scope. Louis's pride was affronted and he was not prepared to forgive. His resentment gave Kaunitz better cards to play, and in May 1756 the Convention of Versailles was signed between Austria and France. Even this success was limited, its aim being neutrality rather than aggression. By its terms Maria Theresa agreed to remain strictly neutral in the war already begun between France and England. In return Louis XV promised not to attack any of her possessions, including the Austrian Netherlands. If one of the contracting powers were threatened or attacked in Europe, the other promised its good offices and, if these were of no avail, limited financial or military help. As in the Convention of Westminster, the war between England and France was excluded, but a secret article provided that if one of England's allies in that war attacked either of the contracting parties the other was bound to come to its assistance. Though the Convention of Versailles had not won active French support against Frederick II it published to the world the fact that the 'old system' was no more. When the United Provinces, very conscious that they certainly could not defend the Austrian Netherlands without Austrian support, offered Louis XV a promise of strict neutrality if he would make it clear that he had no hostile designs against them, even the long alliance of the Maritime Powers was in ruins. The attempts of Newcastle to underpin the 'old system' by both the Convention of St Petersburg and that of Westminster had contributed perhaps more than any one factor to the Diplomatic Revolution.[1] But underneath his lack of foresight lay realities: had the 'old system' been rooted in them it would have survived. The dual function of King and Elector had made its last important contribution to British diplomacy. In four years' time a King was to succeed who described himself with pride as 'glorying in the name of Briton'.

The reversal of alliances need not, however, have led to a large-scale European war. That was something which both England and France were eager to avoid; indeed, both powers considered the new arrangements as enabling them to concentrate on the colonial struggle. Certainly by the spring of 1756 England was expecting some vigorous action from France after the rejection of her demand for the return of French ships captured by the English. As a protection, therefore, the English fleet was concentrated in home waters. Since an invasion was considered too hazardous, France decided to attack Minorca. Of this intention the English ministers were well aware. Information as to French plans and moves kept coming in, so that in March the Cabinet decided to send Admiral Byng with a fleet to the Mediterranean to cover Minorca. He was not, however, able to collect men and supplies until early in April and even then sailed without a full complement and with ships that were ill-conditioned. At Gibraltar he was unable to pick up the additional troops he was supposed to embark, and by the time he reached Minorcan waters Fort St Philip at Port Mahon was already under siege. The governor of the island was in England, the garrison was too small (though it was holding out gallantly under its elderly commander General Blakeney), and Byng had some justification for thinking that without

[1] See H. Butterfield, *The Reconstruction of a Historical Episode* (1951), for an interesting re-assessment.

adequate stores and new troops he could do little. On 20 May he contacted the French fleet under the Marquis de la Glissonière. Byng had one ship more than the French but their gunfire was heavier, their ships were sound and their crews healthy and well disciplined. France had shown considerable control in not striking before she was ready. Now she struck to good effect. With his limited resources Byng fought his ships intelligently, but he was hampered by the precision of his Fighting Instructions, which he feared to ignore, and some of his signals were misunderstood. The result was an indecisive battle. He had good cause to believe that to engage again might lead to a severe mauling of his ships without any corresponding advantage to Minorca. After a council of war held on board his flagship he decided to return to Gibraltar. This course of action had two solid advantages; it kept the fleet in being and it shielded Gibraltar from the fear of attack. The French let him go, de la Glissonière's instructions being to cover Minorca.

The French attack on Minorca was a decisive point in the Anglo-French struggle. At last the fighting was in European waters and could no longer be ignored. When the news reached London England formally declared war. Hostilities, however, were still confined to England and France; the rest of the continent of Europe tossed in an uneasy peace. Minorca was to prove equally important in domestic politics. For a twelve-month Pitt had been thundering, beseeching, taunting, even on one prophetic occasion hoping, that George II would not have Minorca written on his heart, but all his efforts had no effect on Newcastle's majorities. Now it was once again to be demonstrated that an unsuccessful war had the power to destroy majorities and bring down even a minister who had the confidence of the Crown. When early in June a report of Byng's retreat was received from Spanish sources and confirmed before the end of the month by his own dispatches, dismay was widespread and the ministry showed something like panic. The City of London was particularly affected by the news. Minorca was a protection to Britain's Mediterranean trade; moreover, if that sea could be regarded as a French lake the reduced pressure on their naval resources would release their ships for aggressive action in the West Indies. Everywhere went up howls for vengeance, even before Byng's own report had been received. When he landed at Portsmouth at the end of July, having been superseded by Hawke, he was promptly made a close prisoner, pending a court martial.[1] At the time that the administration was losing the confidence of the Commons it was losing also one of its most skilful debaters in the House. This was William Murray. He had never had much stomach for politics,[2] and against his real inclinations, which were for high legal office, he had been brought in to act as a counterweight to Pitt in debate. Often he had been Pitt's butt, but now he demanded the Lord Chief Justice's place, which was opportunely vacant. His self-knowledge was justified. As Lord Mansfield he became one of the great names of eighteenth-century legal history but his loss, coming when it did, was serious for the ministry.

The losses of Minorca and Murray were only the beginnings of the misfortunes which now dogged Newcastle. The next blow came from America with the news that Montcalm, the new French commander in Canada, had swooped down on Oswego and captured it on 14 August. Oswego had great strategic importance for it cleared the way for further French penetration of the west. All the plans made by Shirley, the able governor of Massachusetts, for retrieving in 1756 the disasters of the previous year, had therefore ended in further disaster. Meanwhile serious trouble threatened from Germany. Reports from Berlin seemed to indicate that Frederick II was preparing for military action but, when the British minister there raised the matter in two interviews on 20 and 21 July, the Prussian King was evasively reassuring. So anxious was George II to prevent the spread of the war to Europe that in his capacity as

---

[1] The following squib, which appeared in the *Oxford Journal*, is illustrative of public opinion: 'Advertisement. Whereas the Warehouse of Mr. John Bull, Merchant, situated between the Straights of Gibraltar and the Gulf of Lyons, has been lately robbed of a very large Quantity of Naval Stores and other Effects, by a Parcel of Baboons, owing as he apprehends, to the Treachery or Neglect of either Tom, Jack, George, Philip, Harry, or some other of his Servants. Whosoever can give any certain Intelligence of the Servant who left the Warehouse Door open, and will apply to the Cock in the Pit near Whitehall, or to Jack Ketch'em Esq., at the sign of the Axe and the Block near Great Tower Hill, shall be rewarded with a Piece of the best Superfine Broad Cloth, an Article poor Mr. Bull fears he shall not much longer be permitted to deal in.' Quoted James Townshend, *News of a Country Town* (1914), p. 30. Joseph Yorke, writing to Lord Royston from The Hague on 4 June 1756 said: 'It is clear to me that the French were too strong for him and he seems to have conducted himself perfectly well.'— *Hardwicke Correspondence*, vol. II, p. 295. Later he was inclined to modify this opinion: p. 303.

[2] George III later described him as 'but half a man, timidity and refinement make him unfit for the present turbulent scene'.—*Letters from George III to Lord Bute, 1756–66*, edited R. R. Sedgwick (1939), p. 157.

Elector of Hanover he made a personal appeal to his nephew not to do anything precipitate. On 6 August the Cabinet decided to send an express to Mitchell, the British ambassador to Prussia, to emphasize its point of view. Frederick II's reasons for ignoring this advice and reviving his quarrel with Austria lie outside the scope of British history, though his subsequent actions do not. He waited until it was too late in the year for Russia to move against him; then on 30 August he invaded Saxony after having demanded a passage through the Elector's territory on the pretext that Maria Theresa was massing troops against him in Bohemia. When the news reached England the Cabinet was aghast and the King went so far as to suggest repudiating Prussia's action. The continental war, which Newcastle had so much dreaded and which he had made such frenzied efforts to avoid, had begun.

At home the ministry suffered a final blow with the resignation of Fox. The partnership between him and Newcastle had never been a happy one. Even when the former first took the seals the Duke was comforting himself that 'the King will not suffer Mr. Fox to do anything *even in the House of Commons* without consulting me'.[1] As a result Fox began to feel tricked and excluded from real influence. He also became increasingly alarmed at the unpopularity of the government. The loss of Minorca, the loss of Oswego, the horror of the Black Hole of Calcutta when it became known, were heavy loads for any ministry to bear. Newcastle's actions filled him with suspicion as rumours of his twists and turns to strengthen the administration came to Fox along the political grapevine. First the Duke saw no hope unless Pitt could be secured, then, in reaction, he swung back to the inevitability of Fox. In such circumstances the latter had not the least desire to face the Commons when they met for the new session. He knew that he would have to face the devastating criticisms of Pitt and that his political rear was far from secure. By October he had decided to resign and sent his request to be allowed to do so to George II through Lord Granville on the 15th of that month.

It was at last clear even to George II that Pitt must be secured.[2] Once again, on 19 October, Hardwicke and he met to discuss the

---

[1] Quoted B. Tunstall, *op. cit.*, p. 142.

[2] His unwillingness to do so was again stressed in a letter to Hardwicke, 14 October 1756: 'My opinion is that his Majesty wishes to avoid Pitt and would go a great way to gratify Fox. At the same time if the King could be assured that Pitt would *do his business*, I think he might be brought to take him in.'—*Hardwicke Correspondence*, vol. II, p. 322.

situation. At last Pitt was in a position to present an ultimatum, for such in effect were his five demands, accompanied though they were by every profession of respect and duty towards the King. He made it plain that he would not serve with the Duke of Newcastle, that if he came into office it must be with full access to the Closet, and that he must have permission to reintroduce a militia bill on the lines of one he had steered through the Commons in the last session only to have it rejected by the Lords. The last of his demands arose out of a case that had attracted great public interest. A Hanoverian soldier, stationed at Maidstone, had either by accident or design paid for four handkerchiefs and walked away with six. The result was a fierce altercation as to whether he should be tried by the civil or the military authorities. Finally the unfortunate man had been tried by court martial and mercilessly flogged. Pitt's uneasiness was not at the sentence but because foreign troops were not amenable to English law, and he demanded a further inquiry. He also refused to commit himself not to inquire into past measures in the conduct of the war. Here was something to make the present ministers tremble. Two days later, perhaps not trusting Hardwicke as an intermediary, Pitt took the, for him, unusual step of going to see Lady Yarmouth and through her conveying to the King his views on the kind of administration he envisaged. The Duke of Devonshire was to be First Lord of the Treasury, Pitt and Sir Thomas Robinson to be the Secretaries, Legge Chancellor of the Exchequer, Temple Lord Lieutenant of Ireland, George Grenville Paymaster; places were to be found for the rest of his small band of supporters. To George II this attempt to dictate an administration was an outrageous attack on the King's right to choose his own ministers. It is true that, through the discreet channels of negotiation, the monarch often had to take men of whom he disapproved, but the thing had been decently done. Pitt's demand, put so baldly, was an innovation. When Hardwicke saw him again on 24 October it was to intimate that the King could not accept his five points and the negotiations ended in deadlock. It is interesting to notice that despite the bitter attacks that Pitt had made on his competence in the autumn of 1755 and the spring of 1756, he too now discovered that Sir Thomas Robinson might have advantages as a co-Secretary.

5. PITT STORMS THE CLOSET

After Newcastle and Hardwicke had told the King on 26 October that they could not go on, it became increasingly clear that there was no practical alternative to Pitt. George II did not give in without a last fight; he tried almost every possible combination. Pitt was prepared to serve neither under Fox nor with him; Fox refused to try to collect a ministry without him. Finally the King was forced to send for the Duke of Devonshire, hoping that he would be able to persuade Fox and Pitt to serve together. Now Fox had to pay for having antagonized Pitt by the way in which their earlier co-operation had broken down, just as earlier he had had to pay the price of antagonizing Hardwicke over the Marriage Act. Once again Pitt refused. On his refusal Devonshire was sufficiently a realist to offer Legge the Chancellorship of the Exchequer. After this earnest of his good intentions Pitt agreed to accept the Secretaryship. On 11 November Newcastle formally resigned, and on the 15th Pitt became Secretary. It was not considered by the political wiseacres to be a strong ministry. Pitt's immediate political following was few in number and lacked influence. For once the pasture was too extensive for the faithful flock. The ministry when finally constructed differed very considerably from Pitt's original plan. Like all eighteenth-century ministries so far, it was a mixture of the old and the new. Granville remained President of the Council and Holderness the Northern Secretary, Barrington stayed at the War Office. Pitt did, however, put two of his firmest supporters at the Admiralty: George Grenville again became Treasurer of the Navy and Lord Temple First Lord of the Admiralty, though whether Pitt really increased the chances of naval efficiency by removing Lord Anson to make way for his brother-in-law may well be doubted. Once again the power and the favour were divided. Pitt might have the ear of the Commons, though even there Newcastle was able to hold his friends together; he certainly had not the favour of the King. How long he would retain office in these conditions was a matter of speculation from the time that he kissed hands.

There was indeed little hope of his strengthening his position by any spectacular victory, while as Secretary he must inevitably advocate many measures and work with many men whom he had condemned in opposition. Whether he realized the vulnerability of his position or not, the sense of purpose which produced his proud affirmation to Devonshire—' I know that I can save this country and that no one else can'—drove him on to the insistence that his own measures must be acted upon. This was made clear in the

King's Speech when Parliament met on 2 December. In theory Pitt was not yet Mr. Secretary Pitt, for the ceremony of kissing hands was put off until the first business of the session had been completed. This was because of the awkward provision of 1708 that members accepting a place of profit under the Crown had to stand for re-election. For the business of the session to have been propounded in the absence of Pitt would indeed have been to play Hamlet without the Prince of Denmark. In the Address 'the success and preservation of America' was declared to be the main object of the King's 'attention and solicitude'. Pitt intended there to be no doubt about this. Instead of the old divided interests he promised a new 'resolution of vigour and dispatch'. He also indicated a new English exertion for English ends. The Hanoverians and Hessians were to be sent home and a national militia, rather on the lines of his previously rejected proposals, was to be mainly responsible for home defence in case of invasion. Once the Address was safely out of the way Parliament was adjourned for the new ministers to comply with the need for re-election. In the circumstances Pitt could hardly have stood for his old seat at Aldborough, which was one of Newcastle's boroughs. As, however, Lyttleton had been made a peer on his vacating the Chancellorship of the Exchequer, Pitt was able to stand for his constituency at Okehampton.

It was in many ways a strange ministry. For most of his four months of office Pitt was confined to his bed, his couch, or at least his house at Hayes with gout. He was able to come down to the House only fifteen times: he attended George II in his Closet only six. Whether this was a gain or loss in so far as the royal favour is concerned it is hard to say. George II had described much of Pitt's first draft of the Address as 'stuff and nonsense' and later complained that when he did see Pitt he 'made him long speeches, which possibly might be very fine, but were greatly beyond his comprehension';[1] George II had long made up his mind that he did not like Pitt. Yet in spite of his physical disability Pitt showed a superb control over not only policy-making, but over all the administrative details which would make that policy effective. Perhaps he, too, like Florence Nightingale, subconsciously realized that to conduct a complicated campaign from an invalid's couch saved energy and prevented argument. His achievements are the more remarkable because there were so few members of the ministry

[1] Quoted Tunstall, *op. cit.*, p. 179.

whom he could trust. Holderness, his fellow Secretary, was in close and constant communication with Newcastle and Hardwicke. Temple, though loyal, by his arrogance and lack of tact put everybody's back up, including the King's, and was perhaps almost more of a liability than an asset. In Parliament he and his friends had little borough influence, though against this must be put the extremely interesting fact that the independent country gentlemen, so often described as tories, gave Pitt steady and unconditional support. It is too soon to speak of a revival of a tory party, but the tories in the House found themselves in substantial agreement with Pitt, in so far as they felt that he would spend their money for English ends. To beat France on the sea and to place military power in the hands of a country militia officered by themselves were policies they could understand and approve. He also had the backing and friendship of Leicester House. This was growing more important every year. Prince George was now eighteen; he had his own establishment, a concession most grudgingly made by Newcastle just before his resignation, and not many years could elapse before he became King. In view of later strains it is sometimes forgotten that Lord Bute and Pitt were on very cordial terms during these years; Pitt was his 'Worthy Friend'. But against the favour of Leicester House was to be set the dislike of the Duke of Cumberland, egged on by his crony Henry Fox, who was now determined to pull Pitt down if intrigue, Court influence and pressure subtly exercised on George II could do it.

During the next four months Pitt's major activities were concerned with the American war. Here no quick success could be expected. The situation for which he had now to assume responsibility was supremely discouraging. British naval forces were inadequate, which meant that ships had to be kept at sea until they grew foul and consequently slow, and their crews unhealthy from long confinement and bad food. It is characteristic of Pitt's detailed planning that he included fishing nets in the equipment for his expeditions, so that diets could be varied by fresh fish. Attempts to keep French fleets blockaded and so cut Canada off from reinforcements of men and—perhaps of even more importance—of stores, were bound to fail in such circumstances. From the American colonists little could be expected, since no colony was prepared to exert itself for the common good. It is true that Pitt tried to breathe a new spirit into the governors and their Assemblies by promising that, if they raised the men, His Majesty's government would supply the necessary stores; but their response was more verbal than practical. What the colonists wanted, even after Braddock's failure, were regular regiments to do the fighting and British money to finance the campaigns. As the French were fighting very much on traditional lines with trained troops, there was some justification for the contention that Britain must do the same. Pitt certainly felt the necessity, even while doing all he could to get the colonists to exert themselves in their own interests. Pitt wanted to send an expedition of some 8,000 men but they were difficult to collect. Fear of a standing army, reliance on the hiring of foreign troops, and a limited population on which to draw were all hampering factors. As the Hanoverians, and later the Hessians, had been sent home, Pitt aimed at getting the necessary men by both increasing the strength of existing regiments and raising new ones. His most controversial contribution here was to recruit from the Highland clans, commissions being issued to Montgomery and Lord Fraser, the son of the executed rebel Lord Lovat, for this purpose. To many people the plan seemed rash in the extreme, in view of the doubtful loyalty of the Highlands, but the upshot was to strengthen the British army by men whose fighting qualities were of a very high order. Another factor which may well have eased Pitt's task in attracting more Englishmen to the colours, was that by the middle of the century the upsurge in population was starting; there was a larger margin of manpower on which to draw.

The gap between Newcastle's foreign policy and that envisaged by Pitt was in theory very wide. The first thought in terms of the continent of Europe, though he was more aware of colonial problems and potentialities than some of his detractors have allowed, the second in terms of the empire overseas. Nevertheless, when Pitt came to assume responsibility for the direction of the war he found himself doing many things that in opposition he had condemned. This was partly because he had inherited commitments he could not evade. It was even more because he came to see that his own aims could best be secured by a course of action which, when motivated by other aims, he thought dangerous. To pour out money and men in order to save Hanover because George II was Elector he thought wrong, and there is no reason to suppose he changed his views. To pour out men and money to keep an active enemy of France in the field, even though this expenditure took the form of protection for Hanover was a very different proposition. This is not something which he realized immediately. It took time to educate him into the possibilities of the situation.

When Pitt became Secretary England was already committed to Prussia, who seemed to be an ally of doubtful value. Frederick had invaded Saxony and, when Austria failed to come to its help after the indecisive battle of Lobositz, he treated it as a conquered country. For this he had been put to the ban of the Empire. What was more serious, Louis XV promised two armies of over 100,000 and Russia one of 60,000, and Sweden joined Russia and France. To meet this danger Frederick had only his own army and some 30,000 to 40,000 Hanoverians and Hessians. The threat to Prussia, and to Hanover and Hesse, was great, and before his fall Newcastle had been negotiating with Frederick II for the creation of an army of observation to defend north-west Germany. In his desperation the King of Prussia pressed for vigorous action from England. Pitt's attention was taken up first by the domestic crisis and then by his absorption with his American schemes, but in the spring of 1757 he made one of his few personal appearances in the Commons to move a subsidy of £200,000 for Prussia, though he was careful to add that half this would be saved on expected expenditure by the non-payment of the subsidy to Russia. Already he had come to think that an army which protected Frederick II's flank was of value, because the more deeply France was engaged in Europe the better chance there was of English victories in America.

This decision, which might have been expected to win Pitt approval in the Closet, contributed to his dismissal. George would have favoured neutrality for Hanover if he could have got it. So would his Hanoverian ministers, who realized that the Electorate was being used as a shield for Prussia, rather than being protected by that power. To them the future looked unpredictably dangerous. It was not, however, the major issue of policy but the minor one of the command of the army of observation that precipitated the crisis. Cumberland, almost certainly influenced by Fox, refused to take the command if Pitt, the favourite of Leicester House, were to be left as chief minister of the Crown. The King had been grumbling to Lord Waldegrave for some time about his new ministers. Temple's arrogance in particular had aroused his fury and he was not unwilling to have a good excuse to make a change. The moment seemed opportune in other ways. Pitt's popularity was not what it had been. At sea French fleets had broken the blockade; there was no good news from America. At home the price of corn was high; Pitt had done what he could to alleviate this by allowing foreign corn to be imported and by selling grain cargoes captured from the enemy, but despite his efforts discontent caused by the scarcity was a useful weapon for his opponents to wield against him. Finally he lost some personal popularity by his handling of the Byng trial. This had opened on 28 December amid a storm of hostile propaganda; on 27 January Byng was sentenced to death, though with a strong plea for mercy. Pitt was uneasy at the findings of the Court. He had little sympathy with bunglers but he knew enough to realize some of Byng's difficulties and thought that the late ministers were as culpable as he. Yet to intervene and throw away his own popularity, which was his chief strength against the King, might render him less capable of performing the tasks that lay ahead. Eventually he did decide to act with Byng's friends in an attempt to save him, but these last-minute efforts were abortive in face of Hardwicke's skilful manœuvres and the obduracy of George II. On 16 March Byng was shot on his own quarter-deck and Pitt lost some of his popularity to no purpose.

Less than a month later, on 6 April, he was dismissed. The move was nicely timed to take place after supplies had been voted and before the threatened inquiry into the conduct of ministers over Minorca could be held. Once again the old trick which had worked with Bedford and Sandwich—dismissing the inferior in the hope that the superior would resign—was tried. Temple was dismissed on 4 April. Pitt, however, failed to react as expected. In consequence George II was forced to come into the open by dismissing him too.[1] The next twelve weeks are an illuminating commentary on eighteenth-century political practices. As usual the administration was not dismissed nor did it resign as a body. Legge resigned the Chancellorship of the Exchequer, George and James Grenville followed Pitt out of office. Temple's place at the Admiralty was soon filled by Lord Winchelsea; but Devonshire remained, as did Holderness and Granville. During this protracted period of negotiation

---

[1] This is the occasion on which it is said to have 'rained gold boxes' as corporation after corporation conferred the freedom of the borough on him. In an interesting article P. Langford has shown this publicity to have been a well organized publicity stunt. The number received was twelve, not all of them even from important cities and towns. —See Paul Langford, 'William Pitt and Public Opinion, 1757', *Eng. Hist. Rev.* Jan. 1973.

the administration was therefore limping along without one Secretary and the Chancellor of the Exchequer. Everybody of any political experience, including the King, knew that the way in which these vacancies were filled would determine the future character and policy of the administration. Theoretically the King was free to choose whom he would. There was no unbroken whig party holding him in its toils and forcing unwelcome ministers upon him. But there was a great reluctance on the part of the politicians to accept offices which would carry with them the responsibility for directing the war. There was a pretty general conviction, except among the friends of Fox and the Duke of Cumberland, that Pitt must come back, though there were divergent views as to his possible colleagues. George II, with his elderly contemporary Lord Waldegrave as a go-between, was negotiating madly, trying every possible combination in turn.

By the beginning of June the candidates for office were coalescing into two groups, the friends of Newcastle and the friends of Pitt. On 3 June Bute and Hardwicke, acting in unison, managed to bring Pitt and Newcastle together at Leicester House. Here they were successful in roughing out a basis for compromise, but as the projected arrangements made no provision for Fox, to whom George II thought himself committed, the King refused to give them his blessing. Instead he called on the co-operative Waldegrave to take the Treasury. This had been vacated by Devonshire who, with the intention of easing the negotiations then going on with Newcastle, had consented in May to transfer to the office of Lord Chamberlain. Newcastle's next move showed how deep was his conviction that a stable administration was impossible without Pitt. He used his influence with the docile Holderness to persuade him to resign. Should this not prove sufficient pressure he had six Lords of the Bedchamber in reserve, ready to follow the Secretary's example. When he found both Pitt with his eloquence and Newcastle with his parliamentary following ranged against him, Fox lost his nerve.

By the middle of June George II realized that Pitt and Newcastle it would have to be, and that the royal influence must be confined to making the least disagreeable arrangements possible within that framework. George II accordingly stipulated that Fox must have the Pay Office and Temple some place that did not involve much personal contact with his sovereign. Nobody got quite what he had wanted but the ministry that finally emerged was a reasonably satisfactory compromise. Pitt now became Secretary for the Southern Department, and as Holderness was his colleague this placed him in effect in sole control of foreign affairs and important domestic issues. Newcastle went back to the Treasury with Legge as his Chancellor of the Exchequer. Temple was shelved as Lord Privy Seal, Granville, like the Vicar of Bray, remained in his old office. The two important newcomers on the legal side were Pitt's friend, Charles Pratt, as Attorney-General, and Hardwicke's second son, Philip Yorke, as Solicitor-General. In subsequent ministries the ambitions of these two men were to be important. One of the more satisfactory aspects of this compromise ministry was that Winchelsea gave up the Admiralty and made it possible for Anson to return. He was Hardwicke's son-in-law, but he was an efficient First Lord, and with George Grenville back as Treasurer of the Navy Pitt could feel that a key department was in competent hands. Pitt at last was in a position to push on with his far-reaching plans. He was in control of the chief executive offices and his political rear was doubly protected, first by his popularity in the country which, after its temporary eclipse over the Byng affair, had been fully restored by his dismissal, and secondly by his pact with Newcastle. Once again the power and the favour had been united. Even if George II should die the friendship of Bute and Leicester House seemed to promise a secure future. Pitt at last could turn his undistracted energies to organizing victory.

I 2

PITT'S PINNACLE OF GLORY

1. EARLY DIFFICULTIES

THE situation which faced Pitt when he resumed office might well
have daunted a less dedicated man. From every side news of disaster poured in.[1] Most people thought that a peace on disadvanta-
geous terms would have to be concluded by the end of the year.
There were few who would have dared to prophesy that only a
couple of years separated England from some of her greatest
conquests. Without Pitt the end might have been different, though
it must always be remembered that he had a good hand to play in
spite of having lost the early tricks. Geographically the struggle
can be described as five almost distinct wars. There was the European contest in which Frederick II took the lead. There was the war
on the American continent, with the Middle West and Canada for
its prize. There was the Caribbean rivalry with the acquisition of rich
sugar islands as its bait. There was skirmishing to decide the
dominant power on the African coast. Lastly there was the struggle
between the English and the French East India Companies which
was to decide the future of so much of the continent of India.
Slowness of communications emphasized this five-part character of
the war. Letters from India took anything from six to twelve
months to reach London; orders sent to America could reach the
ports in six weeks but to contact commanders who were up country
was still a lengthy business. There were, however, certain factors

[1] A very full treatment of these years is to be found in L. H. Gipson, *op. cit.*, vol. VI,
The Years of Defeat, 1754-7.

which gave unity to these widely dispersed campaigns. One of these was the strategy of Pitt. From the beginning he saw the war as a whole and fought it as a whole. France was the enemy: to weaken her and to acquire her richest colonies was the object of his policy; this single-mindedness imposed a pattern on the war. Subsidies to Frederick II, attacks on the French coast, campaigns in America, naval expeditions to Africa and India were all interlocked for this purpose.

However brilliant Pitt's strategy and however meticulous his planning, he could have done little without England's financial resources and her naval strength. If the war was fought for trade it was also financed by trade. Contemporaries were staggered by the large sums that somehow were raised to finance allies, equip armies and build ships, apart from the burden of paying large forces in the field and at sea. Pitt, seeing what must be done, had little patience with a cheeseparing policy. Though he abominated waste and raged with fury at any suspicion that funds were being misapplied, for his expeditions he made ruthless demands for money, which he expected Newcastle somehow to provide. For the Duke time had brought a strange reversal of roles. Once he spent on German allies money which Pelham had to find; now the business of supplying a far harder taskmaster than he had ever been fell to him. Often despairing, full of misgivings, at once frightened and petulant, somehow he found the money. Inevitably the burden lay heavily on the English people. The Land Tax stood at 4s. in the pound, heavy duties on malt hit the mass of the people, there were taxes on houses and on windows. Over £11,000,000 was being raised from a population of between five and a half and six million, many of them desperately poor and living barely at subsistence level. The gap between expenditure and taxation was filled by loans. Had the economy not been both sound and expanding it could hardly have been done. Closely allied to Britain's financial and economic strength was her growing naval power. An increasing population provided the necessary seamen and more men to train as shipwrights and craftsmen of every kind. New ships were built; growing investment in the manufacture of brass and copper and progress in the production of iron provided the munitions and the armaments. As sea power grew it became another unifying factor. Once the command of the seas had been gained it was possible to cut off supplies of men and munitions from France to Canada and India, to raid the

French coasts—thereby immobilizing men and relieving the pressure on Frederick II—and to acquire important French possessions both in the West Indies and on the African coast. This pressure could be kept up everywhere, so that France could never conserve her energies and concentrate them on any particular objective. In consequence, each year that the war continued England secured a tighter stranglehold.

In 1757 success still lay with France and her allies. Probably the break in Pitt's tenure of office had little to do with this. Before he was dismissed in April his plans for the year had been made and his orders given. Because of the slowness of communications Loudon was still acting on these orders when Pitt returned to office in June. Before the success or failure of the plans for 1757 was known it was impossible to plan for 1758. Only in the case of Rochefort might earlier planning have led to greater success. The catalogue of failures is soon told. In Canada, where Loudon had been reinforced and a fleet sent under Holburne, Pitt aimed at the capture of Louisbourg and, perhaps with the optimism induced by looking at maps without a personal knowledge of the country, Quebec. When they joined forces at Halifax Loudon had 12,000 troops and Holburne 15 ships of the line. But by then Louisbourg had been reinforced by de la Motte, who lay in the harbour with a force of 18 ships of the line. France's concentration on her navy was paying dividends.[1] It is true that de la Motte's ships were not in good shape and that the capture of Beauséjour and the expulsion of the Acadians had left the French with a perpetual logistic problem. To Loudon, however, an attack in the face of the apparent odds seemed unlikely to succeed and was not made. Something might still have been achieved if Holburne had been able either to bottle up de la Motte's ships or to intercept them on their way home; but a storm disabled his own fleet so that even this was not achieved. As Montcalm had succeeded in taking Fort William Henry, the way lay open down the Hudson to New York. In America therefore the advantage lay with the French; Louisbourg still defended the St Lawrence and the vulnerability of the middle colonies had been much increased.

From Germany the news was equally bad. Frederick II had failed to destroy the Austrian forces, which had based themselves on

[1] For the background of naval strategy in this period, see G. S. Graham, 'The Naval Defence of British North America, 1739–63' (*Trans. Roy. Hist. Soc.*, 4th ser., vol. XXX, 1948).

Prague, and when he attacked Marshal Daun, who was moving to the relief of the city, he was disastrously defeated at Kolin on 18 June. Next month a similar fate overtook the army of observation under the Duke of Cumberland. His situation had in many ways been a difficult one. His freedom of action was fettered by instructions to remain on the defensive. George II was anxious not to widen the breach between himself and Maria Theresa, and more concerned to protect Hanover than to help Frederick II. In addition the Hanoverian chancellery was nervous of acting with Prussian troops, as their King had been put to the ban of the Empire. It was not therefore suprising that Cumberland was defeated by superior French forces at Hastenbeck on 16 July. Under pressure from Hanoverian ministers he then fell back to Stade, where the Electoral archives had been taken for safety. Already Hesse-Cassel and most of Hanover had been abandoned to the French. George II, in alarm for his Electorate, gave Cumberland full powers to treat with the French. The result was the signing of the Convention of Klosterzeven on 8 September. By it the Hanoverian contingents were immobilized and the Hessians and Brunswickers sent home. This exposed Frederick's flank. Moreover, the close alliance between Louis XV and Maria Theresa meant that France now had the use of the ports of the Austrian Netherlands, either to stage an invasion from Ostend or to organize raids on British trade. George II could not even console himself with the fact that Hanover had been saved, for the French occupation proved a heavy burden on its people. Accordingly, faced with the terms of Klosterzeven, the King was furious, declaring that his son had disgraced himself, and, as France failed to observe its terms strictly, it was decided that the Convention should be repudiated.

The final blow for the year came from the failure of the expedition against Rochefort, which it has been suggested was intended to divert the attention of Pitt's tory supporters away from the operations in Germany. Its purpose therefore was at least as much propagandist as military. Beyond this little was achieved. The contractors who were to provide the transport were extremely dilatory; George II insisted on Sir John Mordaunt leading the expedition though, having reached the age of sixty, his present elasticity of mind was less than his reputation for past daring. Finally the winds were contrary. Accordingly little was done apart from the capture of the fortified island at Aix at the mouth of the Charente. By 7 October the great expedition, on which £1 million had been spent, got back to Spithead having achieved nothing concrete.[1]

By the close of the year affairs were looking a little better. In Germany Frederick II's fortunes had touched a new low level with the occupation of Berlin by the Russians on 16 October, but by a magnificent attack on the Franco-Imperial army at Rossbach he won a decisive victory on 5 November. Then, by a forced march of 170 miles in 12 days, Frederick made contact with the Austrians and defeated them at Leuthen, to the west of Breslau, on 5 December. These two victories changed the situation. The Russian army, unable to winter in Prussia, retreated. The French army under Richelieu evacuated Brandenburg; the Swedes left Prussian Pomerania. The Imperial armies withdrew to south-west Germany, and the Austrians relaxed their hold on Bohemia. The future was still extremely precarious, but the present, until the opening of the new campaign in 1758, was safe. These events were beginning to have their effect on Pitt's ideas on policy. After the repudiation of the Convention of Klosterzeven on 28 November the Cabinet, with his approval, had agreed that England should assume the financial burden of the army of observation, which was now to be placed under Ferdinand of Brunswick, one of Frederick's most experienced officers. To that extent England had been committed to play a responsible part in the war against France on the continent. Pitt was also coming to realize that Frederick II could not be allowed to be overwhelmed. Hard bargaining followed between the two Courts. Frederick II wanted English troops and an English fleet in the Baltic. Pitt, with ambitious schemes of his own for attacks on Canada in 1758, in the Caribbean and on the French forts on the African coasts, knew that neither ships nor men would be available. He was, however, prepared to sponsor a subsidy, and by the second Treaty of Westminster it was agreed that Frederick II should have £670,000 per year. Each of the contracting parties promised not to make a separate peace without the consent of the other. In addition, by a special declaration, it was agreed that the army under Prince Ferdinand should be made up to 50,000 and that George, as Elector, would provide another 5,000 at his own expense.

2. PITT LAYS THE FOUNDATIONS FOR SUCCESS

While these negotiations were going on, and in spite of the

[1] P. Langford, art. cit.

discouragements of the previous year, Pitt had been busy in the late autumn and early winter in roughing out his plans for a fresh attack on France's overseas possessions. Again the main operations were to be directed against Canada. Since his first coming to office as Secretary Pitt had put an immense amount of detailed work into acquiring full information as to the local conditions which would mould his strategy. This was for him no new interest. In the years when he had been engaged in the routine work of the Pay Office he had made friends and contacts with people who had knowledge of overseas territories, and were acquainted with the needs of trade and the prospects of its advancement. Out of the welter of suggestions, schemes and information which he had accumulated came his plan for a three-pronged attack on the French position in America. There was to be a full-scale attack on Louisbourg; an advance from New York via Lake George and Lake Champlain to take Crown Point, Ticonderoga, and eventually Montreal or Quebec; and from Philadelphia an expedition to retake Fort Duquesne and re-establish British power on the forks of the Ohio. To succeed with so ambitious a plan it was necessary to secure command of the sea, to overcome problems of transport and supply and, perhaps most vital of all, to pick the right leaders. Tremendous efforts were made to augment the numbers of both ships and seamen:[1] Hawke and Boscawen were able officers. Pitt, with his driving energy and attention to detail, was capable of solving the problems of logistics. The main trouble came when it was necessary to choose commanding officers. George II regarded jealously the fact that he was head of the army, and his views and Pitt's were seldom in harmony. Pitt wanted flair and the power to follow through a decisive punch: if an officer with those qualities were young and without much influence Pitt brushed aside such obstacles to promotion. George II preferred the more experienced commanders; seniority meant much to him and he had an unfailing eye for a mediocrity. He was too good a soldier to appoint a bad man, but too conventional to appoint a first-rate one. In fairness, however, it should be remembered that Pitt's own choices in the early days were not infallibly good. He would have appointed Conway to the Rochefort expedition and thought very highly of

---

[1] The naval estimates for 1757 included one first-rate (i.e. flag) ship and 11 ships of the line, of which 9 were to be put in hand immediately.—K. Fenwich, *H.M.S. Victory* (1959).

Lord George Germain.[1] But, unlike George II, he was at least looking for new and outstanding talent.

Pitt, who had little patience with failures that sprang from over-caution, was determined to get rid of Loudon. In this he followed his familiar tactics of denigrating him in the House of Commons, focusing unpopularity on him and then securing his recall. Whether this was a wise move on Pitt's part at least one distinguished American historian has doubted.[2] Loudon was not a stupid man and he had learnt much from the past campaign. He was familiar with the country and had made his plans carefully to strike at the French before the improvement of weather conditions had made it impossible for them to reinforce their vital spots. His troops had been concentrated for this purpose and Pitt, by altering these dispositions, which involved moving them over vast areas of difficult country, created new problems. Nor could he plead the justification of having a first-rate man to put in his place. Here George II was the stumbling block; with his fetish about seniority he insisted on appointing General James Abercromby, the senior officer then serving in America. Pitt did, however, succeed in sending Lord Howe, in whom he had justifiable confidence, as his second in command; but to supersede Loudon with Abercromby seems a rather useless changing of horses in mid-stream. For the key operations against Louisbourg he was able to make a more satisfactory appointment in the person of Colonel Jeffrey Amherst— a good soldier of a conventional type. He did succeed in taking Louisbourg but his methods were those of carefully placed artillery and the siege train, not the sudden swoop advocated by his brigadier, young Colonel Wolfe. The siege lasted from 7 June until 26 July. The capture of Louisbourg was the greatest success yet scored against France, but it came too late to stage a full-scale attack on either Montreal or Quebec. This might perhaps still have been done if the fall of Louisbourg had coincided with a successful attack on Ticonderoga, which would have held Montcalm's forces. This expedition had, however, proved both unlucky and unsuccessful. The ill-luck it suffered was the death of Lord Howe by a stray bullet, a disaster which might have been avoided if he had been less personally brave and more concerned with his responsibility to keep alive. The lack of success came from Abercromby's mishandling

---

[1] There may have been more justification for this than his behaviour at Minden suggests.   [2] L. H. Gipson, *op. cit.*, vol. VII, p. 108.

of the military position; having hurled his men in vain in a frontal attack against Montcalm's carefully prepared positions, fearing the further mauling of his troops he decided on retreat.

The third expedition was better handled. For the advance against Fort Duquesne Pitt had chosen Colonel Forbes. Born in 1707, Forbes had started his military career as a cornet in the Scots Greys; by 1750 he was a lieutenant-colonel and seven years later he was given the command of the 17th Regiment and attached to Loudon. He had much to recommend him: he knew the country, got on well with the colonials and, having acted as deputy Quarter-Master to the army was thoroughly familiar with the problems of supply. He was unfortunately a sick man and for the most part had to organize this advance from a litter. Only a spirit as indomitable as Pitt's drove him on. Forbes was taking no chances. Previous expeditions against Duquesne had failed for lack of a siege train but, even if they had succeeded, the problem of provisioning the fort and supplying it with ammunition would probably have led to a mere destruction of its fortifications followed by its abandonment. Under Forbes the expedition advanced steadily, making a useable track and bringing up the artillery and supplies. The threat of his methodical and well-supported approach was enough. When he arrived on 24 November he found the fortifications destroyed and the French gone. Once again the English were in command of the vital river fork, and the fear of being cut off from the west was removed. Much was due to Forbes's skilful preparations but there were other contributory factors. One of these was the successful attack launched by Bradstreet on Fort Frontenac. This was rather in the nature of a sideshow due to local initiative than to any careful planning by Pitt. In the previous year Bradstreet had submitted a proposal to Loudon for an attempt on Frontenac which, being of a somewhat unorthodox character, had been rejected. In Pitt's scheme he had been cast for the part of Quartermaster-General in the southern colonies but, as he was busy at the time organizing the building of the boats required for transport on Lake George, Abercromby found himself another Quartermaster-General. Later, after the failure against Ticonderoga, Bradstreet managed to get Abercromby's permission to put his plans into operation. His difficulties were with the terrain and his own men rather than with the French, for he found the fort slightly held and it surrendered on 27 August. With the fall of Frontenac the control of Lake Ontario passed to the English.

The results of the American campaign, if less than Pitt had hoped in his more grandiose moments of planning, were considerable. Though there had been no major attack on the heart of French power in Canada its outposts had fallen. Louisbourg, Duquesne, Frontenac were all in British hands. The pressure on France was beginning to reveal the weaknesses in her position, which were in part due to the character of the French settlements in Canada. These were scattered, the most enterprising of her settlers being trappers engaged in the fur trade. Her agriculture was barely sufficient for her own needs and quite inadequate to support considerable bodies of troops, especially when the able-bodied men were drafted into the army or used as militia. To be able to call on the entire manpower and resources of the colony gave France advantages denied to the English government, faced by the selfish policy of the individual colonies, but more men in the army meant fewer in the fields. The harvests of 1756 and 1757 had been bad and Canadians were on low rations. This made the growing British control of the seas a decisive factor, for supply ships got through only in driblets or not at all, so that the French commander was starved of both provisions and munitions. Shortages also had their effect on the Indians. They had been among the most formidable weapons used against the frontier colonists, both as irregular troops and as scouts. But once the stream of presents dried up, and once the prestige of the English colonists began to revive, the French control of their Indian allies waned. The American colonists too were being gradually brought to take a more active part in the war for their own hinterland. This was mainly owing to Pitt's conciliatory policy towards them. Their Assemblies were no longer expected to find the financial resources, only the necessary manpower: over 25,000 provincial troops were now paid by the home government. Their officers, moreover, were encouraged to assume responsibility through a new order, sponsored by Pitt, which gave them precedence over an officer of lesser rank on the regular establishment. Previously any holder of a regular commission took precedence over any colonial officer; now a colonial captain would rank just below a regular captain but above a regular lieutenant. Nevertheless, in spite of the increased part played by the colonial forces as second-class and reserve trooops, they could not have driven out the French unless the despised redcoats had acted as a spearhead and as assault troops, though the provincial levies had an important part to play.

3. ANGLO-FRENCH RIVALRY IN AFRICA AND INDIA

The news from Africa and India was also encouraging. Aware as Pitt was of the needs of trade, it was to be expected that he would give a sympathetic hearing to the plans of merchant Thomas Cummings for the acquisition of the French trading posts in Africa. But with so many demands on his naval resources all that Pitt could contemplate in the spring of 1758 was an exploratory probe. Accordingly a tiny squadron, accompanied by a small force of marines, sailed under the command of Captain Henry Marsh and Major Mason in March. By acting with speed and audacity they managed to capture Fort Louis, protecting the entrance to the Senegal river, though they were driven back from Goree, which the French held in some strength. The initial results of the expedition had, however, been sufficiently successful, both in the capture of Fort Louis and in the booty which went with it, for Pitt to determine to follow it up. Though it was late in the year another small force, this time under Commodore Keppel, was sent out, and it captured Goree before the end of 1758. This was a valuable acquisition; it increased the area from which supplies of slaves could be drawn, it provided additional gold dust and ivory, and it gave Britain a monopoly of the gum arabic used in the manufacture of silk and therefore vital to France. The harbour, better known by its modern name of Dakar, was a useful base for a power aiming for control of the sea.

India, unlike America and West Africa, hardly came into Pitt's scheme of things. The struggle there was ostensibly between two rival companies striving to dominate trade, not between two rival countries aiming at empire. Though the Treaty of Aix-la-Chapelle had secured the return of Madras to the East India Company, it had not led to a cessation of the intrigues with Indian rulers, backed by the warlike operations of the two companies. The centre of these was the Carnatic. It will be remembered that in 1741 the Subahdar of the Deccan had nominated one of his own officials, Anwar-ud-din, as Nabob, passing over the claims of the late Dost Ali's son-in-law, Chanda Sahib. As relations between Anwar-ud-din and Dupleix had been strained over the possession of Madras, the French now looked to Chanda Sahib as a more likely channel for their influence. Accordingly Dupleix backed his claims to the Nabobship of the Carnatic, and those of his confederate Muzaffar Jang to the office of Nizam of the Deccan, and provided a stiffening of French troops for the critical battle with Anwar-ud-din. The result was a complete triumph for the allies; Anwar-ud-din was killed and his son Mohammed Ali fled to Trichinopoly in the south of the Carnatic. Neither the French nor Chanda Sahib were willing to leave him in possession of such an important and rich city. They therefore followed him south and laid siege to it. The English Company was justifiably alarmed by this growth of French influence and in its turn began to support Nasir Jang, Muzaffar's rival in the Deccan. The events of the next few years were a complex of violence, intrigue and treachery, as the two Companies and their Indian allies manœuvred for position. By the end of 1750 the French position seemed the stronger, though that of the English was perhaps slightly less desperate than it appeared. The French had had to detach large forces under de Bussy to secure the Deccan, and this had left Chanda Sahib to deal with Mohammed Ali. The money required for these expeditions was proving a heavy drain on the resources of the French Company, and at home its directors were growing restive. Perhaps less was needed to tip the balance than is sometimes thought, when in July 1751 Clive decided to march with every available man against Chanda Sahib's capital Arcot. To leave Madras and Fort St David almost denuded of men was a brave decision on the part of its governor Saunders. The well-known story of Clive's achievements is soon told. Trichinopoly was relieved, Chanda Sahib murdered and Mohammed Ali proclaimed Nabob of the Carnatic, before Clive returned to England for reasons of health in 1753. The result was a stalemate; de Bussy, the brilliant fortune-hunting soldier in charge of the French expedition, had established his hold on the Deccan but the English had re-established themselves in the Carnatic. At this point the directors of the French company intervened and in August 1754 recalled Dupleix; they had found the financial burden of his expansionist policy too great a price to pay for his successes. The English directors were equally anxious to return to conditions of peaceful trade, and a treaty based on mutual concessions was arranged between the two companies. By the end of 1754 it seemed as if the struggles of the last fifteen years were over and that a new period of commercial expansion lay ahead.

That this did not happen was due first to events in another part of India and then to the renewal of war between England and France in 1756. The struggle shifted to Bengal. In studying the fortunes of the English East India Company it is easy to forget that a continent was involved. In each of the three main centres of its influence—Bombay, Madras and Calcutta—its problems, *vis-à-vis* the Indian rulers, were different. In the Carnatic and the Deccan the break-up of the Mogul empire had spread uncertainty and confusion so that there politics were a welter of opposing claimants. In Bengal Alivardi Khan, until his death in 1756, had been sufficiently strong to prevent the rivalry between the English in Calcutta and the French at Chandarnagore from breaking into active strife. Had he been succeeded by a man of the same calibre a crisis might have been avoided, though the increasing commercial activities of the English were arousing the jealousies of Indian traders. His nephew and heir Surajah Dowlah was not such a man. He was suspicious of the fortifications which the East India Company was belatedly constructing at Calcutta in fear of a French expedition, and resentful of the way in which its trading practices were defrauding his revenue. When his remonstrances were ignored he marched against the town with a large army and took it. Again fortuitous circumstances played their part. After resisting as long as possible, those English who had not been successfully evacuated by sea surrendered on a promise of good treatment. That they were crammed into the notorious Black Hole of Calcutta was the work of a subordinate, but Surajah Dowlah did nothing to express remorse or even disapproval for the horrors of that night. When the news reached Madras it was felt that their death must be avenged and Calcutta recovered if British prestige were not to be fatally damaged. The situation was tricky, for it was known that war was imminent, and that a French expedition was likely to be sent against the Carnatic to redress the balance of the past few years. Nevertheless it was decided to send Clive, who was now back in Madras as a Lieutenant-Colonel and a member of its Council, with a force to regain Calcutta. Escorted by Admiral Watson, he sailed in the middle of October and in six weeks reached the mouth of the Hugli river. Though fighting against very great odds Clive, with his vigour and skill, made Surajah Dowlah agree to peace and the restoration of Calcutta.

The situation, however, remained tense. War between France

and England made the position of the French at Chandarnagore a threat if, as was expected, de Bussy made a thrust from the Deccan into Bengal. Acting on his own initiative Clive decided that the French settlement must be seized and in March he attacked and took it. His action confirmed all Surajah Dowlah's fears that the French and English between them would turn his territory into a second Carnatic. In view of his enmity it was decided that he must be replaced by a new ruler, dependent upon, and therefore complaisant towards, the English. Surajah Dowlah was not popular with many of his own officials and it was not difficult to find support amongst his own Court for his overthrow. Mir Jafar was selected as his successor and, after an unsavoury period of intrigue and treachery, Surajah Dowlah was defeated at Plassey on 23 June 1757. Mir Jafar was proclaimed and the real control over the rich provinces of Bengal, Behar and Orissa passed to the East India Company.

To Clive, with the picture of Indian disintegration before him, the time seemed opportune to lay the basis of territorial power in that country, and he tried to make Pitt see the scope that the assumption of sovereignty would provide. But Pitt, though delighted with the victories of his 'Heaven born General', was already so deeply committed to his American plans that his resources could be stretched no further; India he preferred to regard as the responsibility of the East India Company. All that he could be induced to contribute to its necessities were four ships of the line, which he sent out under Commodore Stevens to reinforce Watson. These can be regarded as part of his containing policy, for they prevented the French from preying on English merchantmen in Far-Eastern waters and ensured that the French squadrons under Commodore D'Ache were unable to interfere with the movement by sea of the Company's troops. By 1758 this policy of containment had become a major part of Pitt's strategy, and at last the British were scoring some success. On 28 February there had been a naval victory off Cartagena in Spain. On 3 April Hawke triumphed in the Basque Roads. In spite of the failure at Rochefort in the previous year Pitt decided once again to combine naval pressure with further raids on the French coast. By so doing he hoped to pin down French forces which might otherwise be used against Frederick II. Regarded as independent incidents these costly expeditions were failures, justifying the gibe that Pitt was breaking windows with guineas. In June the troops which were landed to attack St Malo, as Pitt intended, returned in July with little to show for the money lavished on the project. In August a new expedition was directed against Cherbourg. Once again Pitt was ill-served by his military commanders; Bligh had little taste or aptitude for his task and his soldiers got badly out of hand. The result was a brutal sacking of the town by drunken troops. Otherwise, beyond destroying the fortifications and the shipping in the harbour, little was achieved, though this destruction did something to lessen France's naval potential. Another attempt was made against St Malo at the beginning of September. Once more the handling of the forces was most incompetent and, as they were intercepted before they could regain the ships, casualties were heavy.

4. PITT AND THE CONTINENTAL WAR

Pitt's policy of forcing France to disperse her forces led to considerable modification in his attitude towards the continental war. In the early stages of the War of the Austrian Succession, and again when in opposition after his dismissal from the Pay Office, his attacks on any help given to Hanover had been outrageously bitter. Even when in office it had been clear that he disliked the payment of subsidies for its protection. When he became Secretary in December 1757 he seemed likely to follow the same policy. All his energy had been thrown into organizing the colonial and naval war and he showed little disposition to give Frederick II the help for which he was pressing. When he returned to office in June 1757 there is evidence that his views were beginning to change. The Treaty of Versailles had given France dangerous facilities in the Austrian Netherlands, where the use of Ostend was a constant threat to English shipping. After the disastrous Convention of Klosterzeven Pitt was prepared to take the army of observation into English pay; in April 1758 by the second Treaty of Westminster Frederick II had been promised a substantial subsidy. Eventually Pitt was to declare that the continental war had been a vital factor in securing Britain's dominant position in the New World. In this there was much outward inconsistency. His enemies pointed out that Pitt in office was as tender of Hanoverian interests as any minister of the Crown. Pitt was perhaps never over-troubled by the need to appear consistent, but there is truth in his argument that the difference between his post-1758 policy and that of previous ministers was one of emphasis. They had placed all their faith in the diplomacy of the 'old system' and their major energies in securing the safety of Hanover, which was not an English interest. He, on the contrary, was putting purely English interests first, trade was to be secured by an all-out attack on our greatest rival, France, and the major effort was to be made on the seas, in America and in the West Indies. Everything that distracted France from putting forth her full strength in these areas was worth while, whether it was attacks on the French coasts, the blockading of French harbours, or the subsidizing of the enemies of France. Also he could not help but realize that if Hanover were overrun his earlier argument, that it could be brought back at a subsequent peace, might have unfortunate results for his policy of imperial aggrandisement. As it was Minorca would have to be redeemed. Might not Louisbourg, or even Canada itself not have to be surrendered to win back Hanover for the English King? Though his interests remained purely English, he had now come to see that those interests and the safety of Hanover were not necessarily opposed to each other, and his policy became adjusted to this conviction. In Europe the fortunes of the opposing forces swayed to and fro. Ferdinand of Brunswick proved himself a good and steady commander of the army of observation; his aim was to clear the French troops out of Hanover and push them first back to, and then over, the Rhine. Again it was largely a matter of supplies, and Ferdinand gained a useful initial success when at the beginning of the spring campaign in 1758 he had managed to seize Verden and drive the French behind the Aller and Weser rivers. This success was sufficient to allow Pitt to become slightly more involved in the continental war. In response to requests from the Prince he sent a small squadron under Holmes to cruise off the mouth of the Ems, to prevent supplies getting to the French up that river. When, as a consequence of this combined military and naval pressure, the French evacuated the town of Emden, Pitt finally agreed that it should be held by British troops. This was an important landmark. By the spring of 1758 Pitt had become converted to the need to play some part in the struggle that was taking place in Germany. In that year the House of Commons under his leadership voted £1,200,000 for the maintenance of the army of observation. The early results were encouraging, for Ferdinand succeeded in clearing the French out of Westphalia, Hanover, Brunswick and Hesse and at Emmerich on 27 March drove them over the

Rhine. On 23 June came his victory at Crefeld. That was followed by a further involvement of England in the continental war, for at last, in response to repeated requests that England should furnish men as well as money, five regiments of horse and four of foot were sent out under the Duke of Marlborough and Lord George Germain to reinforce Ferdinand. By this action Pitt recognized that large-scale containing operations on the continent were an essential part of his worldwide struggle with France.

In the latter part of the year Ferdinand was less successful, for a French counter-attack reoccupied Hesse and took Cassel; however, he still managed to hold Hanover and Westphalia. This meant that Frederick II's flank was secure and that he could concentrate his energies and his troops against Russia and Austria. Without such assistance it is difficult to see how he could have survived, superb soldier as on occasions he showed himself to be. The year 1758 was still critical for him. Though he cleared the Austrians out of Silesia, two Russian armies were threatening the new Mark of Brandenburg. It is true that after the battle of Zorndorf on 25 August they withdrew to Poland, but Prussian casualties had been heavy. Nor was Frederick able to relax, for he had to dash south to where the Austrian and Imperial forces were again threatening Saxony and Silesia. Here the Prussians were badly defeated at Hochkirk on 13 October. The Austrians, however, failed to make much use of their victory and Frederick, in spite of his defeat, was able to relieve Neisse and so hold Silesia. By the end of the year the Prussian King was therefore still in possession of his loot, Saxony and Silesia, but his twin enemies had not been decisively defeated; they would have to be repulsed again next year.

5. THE YEAR OF VICTORIES

The campaigns of 1759 were likely to be critical both overseas and on the continent, though for very different reasons. Overseas English prospects were bright; for Frederick II in Germany it was a problem of survival. In America it was at last possible to plan the striking of a decisive blow. It was characteristic of Pitt's strategy that this was not to be confined to the possessions of the French in the North. Their possession of well-placed islands in the Caribbean, combined with their control of the mouth of the Mississippi, made the danger of a thrust from the south a possibility. Martinique in particular, lying as it did to windward of the prevailing Trade Winds and with its excellent base of Port Royal, would always be a potential danger to English shipping and commerce in those waters. The importance of the West Indian trade can hardly be exaggerated because from it came a considerable amount of the financial resources of the City. Whatever the demands of other theatres of the war, some naval strength had always to be provided to protect the merchantmen who supplied the islands with the additional food, timber and goods that they required, and to transport their precious crop of sugar to Europe. The capture of Goree at the very end of 1758 was a shrewd stroke against the French sugar islands, for it had been a chief source of their necessary slaves. Pitt was never content to nibble at the fringes of French power, and once Louisbourg had fallen he began in earnest to plan an attack on the island of Martinique. Thus the policy of a twofold attack was again adopted. In the north Amherst was to advance on Canada either by Lake Champlain and Crown Point or by the Hudson; he was to seize Fort Niagara, thereby completing the British control over the waters of Ontario, and advance against Quebec or Montreal as circumstance offered. It was from this direction that Montcalm expected the British attack to come, but Pitt's plan was a combined military and naval operation along the St Lawrence. In the West Indies a similar joint operation was to be launched against Martinique, and this left the English base of the Barbadoes in the middle of January 1759.

That year was to be the famous 'year of victories'. To Pitt must go a great deal of the credit, though not, as is sometimes assumed, all of it. His contribution was a threefold one. His had been the co-ordinating mind which had gathered information from many sources and welded it into a coherent strategy. It was his meticulous attention to the details of supply which not only collected transports and troops but saw that they had the necessary equipment and stores. Often imperious and unreasonable over other people's difficulties, he forced men to do and provide things which hitherto they had considered impossible and impracticable. Thirdly he had chosen his commanders with skill, though considerably hampered by George II's intense personal interest in this field. Amherst was a compromise choice, but he was a sound, if hardly dashing, soldier. Wolfe, though only 32, Pitt succeeded in placing in charge of the vitally important attack on Quebec.[1] For the West Indian expe-

[1] Recent research has thrown a good deal of light on the details of the Quebec

dition, though he was forced to accept the elderly General Hopson, he did provide an excellent second in command in the person of Colonel Barrington, who, when death carried off his aged superior at a timely moment, took charge of the expedition with fortunate consequences. The result was a series of successes which, if they did not quite come up to Pitt's most sanguine hopes, were still very substantial. By 25 June Wolfe and Saunders, who was in command of the naval forces, were in position before Quebec. If the French under Bougainville had not managed to slip up the river in the early spring, bringing not only stores but an intercepted letter which revealed the British plan of campaign, they might have had the advantage of surprise. As it was, a wearying period when each side was jockeying for postion intervened and reduced Wolfe to extreme despondency before his successful attack on the heights of Abraham on 13 September. On the 17th Quebec surrendered. The fall of Quebec was not, however, the end of French power in Canada; the French still held Montreal, for Amherst's advance had been slower than Pitt had anticipated. His methods were those of the professional soldier; no undue risks were taken and the artillery was prudently and methodically handled. It was to organization rather than improvised inspiration that the surrenders of Fort Niagara, Ticonderoga and Crown Point were due, the main body of the French retreating before his superior forces. It was not therefore until 31 July that the English were in possession of Crown Point, and not until October that they could be said to be in control of Lake Champlain. The West Indian expedition also had not quite the success that Pitt had hoped. Martinique proved too formidable to overrun, but the wealthy island of Guadeloupe was secured, largely owing to the skill and daring of Barrington.

That Pitt pushed on with his attacks on the French in Canada and the West Indies was a tribute to his steadiness of nerve, for at home the situation was threatening. On the continent both Frederick II and Ferdinand were in difficulties, while England herself was threatened with invasion. In France Pitt was now matched by a man with something of his own vision and drive, for in November 1758 Bernis had been replaced by Choiseul. The result was a greater con-

campaign. C. P. Stacey, *Quebec, 1759: The Siege and the Battle* (1959), is very critical of Wolfe's ability as a commander and assigns much of his success to luck, to the quality of the troops he commanded and to the co-operation of the navy. R. Reilly, *The Road to Fortune: The Life of Major-General James Wolfe* (1960), takes a more favourable view.

trol and a more realistic handling of French policy. French help to her allies was curtailed in tacit recognition of the fact that England, not Frederick II was her enemy, and that the major French efforts in Germany must be directed against the army of observation under Ferdinand. If Hanover and Hesse could be captured and held, France would have something of value with which to bargain for the return of her lost overseas possessions. There he was forced to admit that the initiative once held by France had passed to Britain; both in Canada and in the West Indies only a defensive role was possible. By the beginning of 1759, the French trading posts had already gone and in India Lally's siege of Madras had had to be raised with the arrival of Admiral Pocock's fleet. It might, however, still be possible to strike at the very heart of the great British octopus, thus destroying at one blow the strangling grip of all its tentacles. Choiseul turned therefore to the organization of an invasion of Britain. If it did not succeed it would at least have the merit, or so he hoped, of keeping English men and ships tied down in the same way that Pitt's policy of raiding the French coasts had immobilized those of Louis XV. The plan, which like most foreign intelligence eventually fell into Newcastle's hands, was to concentrate fifty thousand troops along the coast of the Austrian Netherlands, using Ostend, and along the northern coasts of France. From Brest a further twenty thousand were to make a diversion by attacking the Clyde, and there was to be a large-scale raid of Ireland led by the famous privateer Thurot. These plans, however, as Pitt was well aware, depended on the French obtaining at least the temporary command of the Channel. The Mediterranean fleet under de la Clue was to leave Toulon, evade the British and join the Brest fleet. Only when that operation had been successfully accomplished would the danger of invasion be imminent.

Because he did not believe this to be likely Pitt refused to be stampeded by other men's fears into changing his plans. Newcastle characteristically was much more nervous. For Pitt to denude the country of troops for colonial campaigns and fill the gap by calling out the almost amateur militia, put a great strain on his faith and his judgment. Pitt's reliance on the navy proved completely justified. His intention had been to blockade the French ships in their home ports and for this purpose Boscawen had managed to keep his fleet at sea off Toulon and Marseilles during the summer months. If England had had enough ships to arrange for sufficient relieving squadrons then, despite the hazards of wind and weather, a close blockade might have been maintained. But since this was not possible the time came when Boscawen had to return to Gibraltar, his nearest base, for refitting and supplies. This was the opportunity for the French under de la Clue to leave Toulon. They had still to get through the Straits of Gibraltar without being seen, which de la Clue unsuccessfully attempted to do by night. Within three hours Boscawen was at sea and next morning the fleets were engaged. When finally four of the Frenchmen tried to find safety in the neutral Lagos Bay, Boscawen followed them into Portuguese waters and burnt two and captured the other two. Pitt later apologized to Portugal but the Toulon fleet was no longer in being. This put the entire responsibility for covering the invasion on the Brest fleet. Like de la Clue, Conflans, its commander, managed to evade Hawke, and slip out but, thanks to British intelligence, Hawke knew that his orders were to make for Quiberon Bay to pick up the transports. On 20 November Hawke found him and followed him into the rocks and shoals of that treacherous bay. Four French ships were destroyed before darkness made further fighting impossible; next day Conflans ran his flagship aground, one ship sank, the rest scattered and Hawke was left to continue a victorious patrol of the Channel. The fear of an effective invasion was over.

6. Neutral Rights at Sea

Choiseul's second device, that of embroiling England with the neutral nations of Europe, was more subtle and less easy to counter. Because the use of her sea power was one of England's strongest weapons against France, relations with neutral maritime powers were bound to be strained. It was a major part of Pitt's policy that French trade must be destroyed, and the communications between her and her overseas possessions cut. As this policy exerted more and more pressure on France her statesmen inevitably tried to use neutral shipping to ease it. This made the interpretation of international rights of neutral shipping of vital importance. Neutrals claimed that free ships meant free goods and that, apart from the recognized contraband of war—troops and their equipment and munitions—French goods could legally be carried in neutral ships.[1] To concede this would have been to permit so many leakages in

[1] For a full discussion of these and kindred problems consult R. Pares, *Colonial Blockade and Neutral Rights, 1739–63* (1938).

Pitt's economic blockade as to make it all but valueless. Instead, England claimed that enemy goods remained enemy goods even if carried in neutral bottoms. Also, by the so-called Rule of 1756, it was contended that no neutral had the right to engage in wartime in any branch of commerce from which in time of peace they had been excluded. This claim was of the utmost importance. Eighteenth-century commerce had been forced to adapt itself to a framework of prohibitions by which the trade between colonies and the mother country was forbidden to outside powers unless based on special treaty arrangements. What England demanded was that regulations which held good in peacetime should hold in wartime also. This, in practice, meant that as France reserved the right to the trade of her colonies for French ships in peace she had no right to relax this rule because it suited her, and permit Dutch or Swedish or Spanish or any neutral to engage in the trade. These rights England enforced by holding up and searching neutral ships suspected of carrying French goods. It is perhaps slightly ironic that Pitt, who had declaimed with much bitterness against the right of search when exercised by Spain in the late thirties, should now be enforcing it not only in the confined water of the West Indies but wherever the British flag flew. For instance, ships from Genoa and Tuscany in which the French tried to keep their Mediterranean seaborne trade alive were searched and their cargoes seized. By such actions French trade was destroyed but neutral opinion much inflamed.

Searches by the navy were not the only hardship which the smaller maritime nations had to face. There was also the threat of the privateers. These half-auxiliary naval forces were a bugbear to commerce. Though they were licensed by the country in whose service they were, their profits came from their captures. This, as had been the case with the Spanish *guarda costa* in Walpole's day, hardly encouraged the most scrupulous care in the searching of ships and the seizing of cargoes. Even if, later, an English prize court declared the capture unjustified, and ordered restitution to be made, much damage might have been done and much hardship, perhaps even violence, suffered. It was natural for neutrals to protest and bear resentment. England's difficulties *vis-à-vis* the neutrals were further complicated because they were also both her customers and the suppliers of certain vital goods. She could hardly have fought a prolonged naval war without the naval stores which came from the Baltic countries. Her trade with Russia was extremely important to her; so was that with Sweden. Both these countries were at war with Frederick II and England had to go warily if their enmity were not to be transferred to herself. She had no wish to drive the Danes, with their strategic position on the Sound, or the Dutch into hostility. Even less did Pitt wish to antagonize Spain, whose naval power, combined with that of France, might have tipped the scales in the latter's favour. In the Mediterranean, too, drastic action might, in the same way, drive Naples, Sardinia, Tuscany and Genoa into collaboration with France. England's very success was therefore creating new difficulties which seemed likely to be augmented when in August 1759 Charles of Naples became King of Spain on the death of his half-brother Ferdinand. His dislike of England was well known, and Spanish grievances against England, which the coolness between the Bourbon powers after the Peace of Aix-la-Chapelle had made less dangerous, were, in his energetic hands, likely to be used effectively in the diplomatic game.

The news from the European fronts during the *annus mirabilis* was considerably less satisfactory than that from overseas. It is true that Frederick II was still in possession of Silesia and Saxony with their revenues and resources, but the demands of the war both on his manpower and on his finances were beginning to cripple his efforts. All that he dared to undertake in the early part of the campaign was a series of sudden drives directed at destroying the supplies of his enemies rather than at a military defeat of their troops. Ferdinand, too, found himself faced by considerable pressure from the French forces. Early in the year they had captured Frankfort-on-Main and were threatening Hesse, Cassel and Hanover. For the protection of Hanover Ferdinand constructed a series of strongpoints near Minden. Here, on 1 August, a decisive battle took place which both saved Hanover and forced the French to relax their hold on Hesse. The wisdom of strengthening Ferdinand's army with a British contingent was amply justified, for everyone agreed that the British infantry fought magnificently and made a major contribution to the much-needed victory. Less could be said for the cavalry under Lord George Germain. Though repeatedly ordered by Ferdinand to charge and complete the rout of the enemy, he refused to do so: pique rather than cowardice explains his action. On this occasion, at least, Pitt had made a mistake in his man, whose recall and subsequent cashiering were to have further unfortunate results for him. Though Minden saved the situation in west Germany, its effects on the continental campaign as a whole were reduced by the disasters that almost overwhelmed Frederick II. The Russians advancing from Poland invaded Brandenburg, defeated one of Frederick's generals at Zullichau on 23 July, and captured Frankfort-on-Oder; and on 13 August, aided by an Austrian contingent, they inflicted a heavy defeat on Frederick in person at Kunersdorf. His military chest and his magazine were seized and at first he regarded the blow as a fatal one. Had the roles been reversed it probably would have proved so, but the Russians and the Austrians were mutually suspicious. The former, in need of supplies, retired to their own frontiers and Frederick II was able to gain his second wind. Though he held his own for the rest of the fighting season, Daun took up his winter quarters in Saxony, and Frederick was more than ever dependent on the help he gained from his English subsidy and the protection of Ferdinand's army at his rear.

England, too, in spite of her victories, was feeling the strain of the war. It is difficult to know how popular it had ever been, except in the moments of wild rejoicing and hope when the news of victories had been received.[1] Newcastle and his friends had tried to avoid it until the very last minute. As handled by Pitt it had been popular in the City. Much of it was financed by loans which gave wealthy business men opportunities for profitable investment; its fruits were an expansion of trade, the capture of fresh markets and the opening up of fresh sources of supply. The years 1758–61 were a period of economic activity and general prosperity. For the country gentlemen the picture was less rosy. In the early stages of the war they had supported Pitt, believing that in him they had found a statesman who would fight the naval war of tory tradition, and not pour funds into Germany. Even so, a Land Tax of 4s. was a heavy burden to bear year after year. When the war started the annual revenue was something just under seven millions; by 1759 it had been stepped up to eight and a half. Newcastle, who was responsible with Legge for raising it, felt that the limit had been reached, that additional supplies for a prolonged struggle could hardly be found. In the country districts the first attempts to enforce the new Militia Act, by which a local force, chosen by lot and officered by the local

---

[1] The original declaration of war seems to have been popular. *The Oxford Journal*, 29 May 1756, reported that 'on the like Occasion there never appeared a more general Joy on the Face of every True Briton in hopes of once more humbling a perfidious Enemy, ever restless to disturb the Tranquillity and interupt the Commerce of this Kingdom.'—Quoted J. Townshend, *op. cit.*, p. 30.

gentry, were to train for two days a week, and be embodied and paid like regulars if an emergency arose, were met with riots and resistance. Later, when the threat of a French invasion hung over the country, it became more popular, but its popularity waxed and waned with the imminence of that danger.

7. RISING DEMAND FOR PEACE

By 1760 there was a persistent, if half muffled, demand for peace from people who did not share Pitt's sweeping vision of an empire trade. Now that England had control of the sea and so many French possessions were in her hands, she was in a position to conclude a good peace. The argument that it would be even stronger if the French could be driven out of Canada, and the strategically desirable island of Martinique taken, seemed to many people to be tempting Providence. Moreover, in Europe the army of observation under Ferdinand was still facing superior French forces, while Frederick II's chance of emerging victorious from the struggle seemed slim. If the war went on until Pitt's colonial ambitions had been satisfied, it looked as if the continental campaigns would prove a sink down which English money and manpower would be poured in increasing quantities. This situation caused deep divisions in the Cabinet. While the position had been desperate, Newcastle and his friends had shown loyalty of action, if not always of words, in supporting Pitt's schemes. At times their loyalty and patience had been sorely tried. Because he mistrusted his colleagues and was contemptuous of their ability, Pitt endeavoured to supervise and control every aspect of policy; the movements of fleets, the planning of campaigns, the handling of neutrals were all in his hands. So confident was he of his own opinions that he was prepared to criticize and wreck the financial schemes of the Treasury, or to frame legislation on legal points without consulting the Solicitor-General. He had to be both omnipotent and omniscient. Never strong, since he became Secretary he had driven himself without respite, except that given by a happy married life. He was living on his nerves: it is not surprising that he was an impossible colleague.[1]

[1] On 9 April Newcastle wrote pathetically to Hardwicke, 'Mr. Pitt flew into a violent passion at my saying we could not carry on the war another year; that that was the way to make peace impracticable and to encourage our enemy: that we might have difficulties but he knew we could carry on the war, and were one hundred times better able to do it than the French; . . . In short there was no talking to him.'—*Hardwicke Correspondence*, vol. III, p. 244.

The events of 1760 were to underline the divergence between Pitt and his colleagues. His chief fear was that they might enter into secret negotiations for peace before the final necessary conquests had been made. With plans for these he pushed on as rapidly as possible. In Canada the main objective was Montreal; not until it had been taken could the British hold over the St Lawrence basin be considered secure. In this, his major objective for the year, Pitt's plans, carried out by the methodical Amherst, were completely successful. On 8 September the town, entirely surrounded and with its garrison hopelessly outnumbered, surrendered; Canada passed into British hands. In India the war brought further successes, though these owed less to Pitt's plans than to the men on the spot. All that he had been able to send in response to the East India Company's desperate appeals were some troops under Colonel Eyre Coote, which arrived towards the end of 1759. With their help the French General Lally was decisively defeated at Wandewash, which he was besieging, in January 1760. Little now remained to the French but Pondicherry, for after de Bussy was recalled from the Deccan an audacious expedition, dispatched by Clive from Bengal and led by Colonel Forde, had seized its capital Masulipatam and expelled the French from that region. Even so, Lally held out until January 1761, waiting vainly for naval help from the French island base of Mauritius, which the French feared was to be the subject of a British attack. The year 1760 had therefore seen two enormous blocks of territory brought within the sphere of British influence, though officially the gains in India lay in the destruction of French power and its replacement by a system of Indian client rulers rather than in an addition, as in Canada, to the dominions of the Crown.

To have gained so much was a justification in Pitt's eyes for the continuance of the war. 1760 had also seen Pitt converted into a wholehearted supporter of the continental campaigns, fearing that without the assistance of English men and money the German front might collapse and release French forces, before Canada had been secured and Martinique attacked. To effect this, additional German troops were taken into British pay, and the number of British troops under the Marquis of Granby, who had displaced the disgraced Sackville, was raised from ten to twenty thousand. To Pitt's previous supporters, and above all to Leicester House where any apparent tenderness to Hanover was anathema, this reversal of his earlier and much publicized mistrust of a continental war caused bitter criticism. The lack of success in Germany during 1760, in spite of the reinforcements, gave his critics additional ammunition. Both Frederick II's struggles against the Austrians and Russians, and those of Ferdinand against the French, were indecisive and by the end of the year neither side seemed any nearer to a conclusive victory. Against the manpower of his enemies Frederick, for all his tactical skill, could do nothing but hold them at bay. Public opinion in Britain, therefore, contrasting the successes in Canada and India with the failure in Germany, came more and more to regard that war with distaste. The cry was for a separate peace with France. Frederick's popularity, which had been high as a Protestant hero after Rossbach, had disappeared, and the continual expenditure in Germany seemed to many people to be throwing good money after bad. In the military stalemate it seemed as if only a new approach to the problem could break the deadlock.

In such circumstances it is hardly to be wondered that 1760 was a difficult year for Pitt. He was no warmonger, in the worst sense of the term, and the strain of the ultimate responsibility for its conduct was wearing him down. In the previous year his frayed nerves and imperious temper had been shown up in the ridiculous business of his brother-in-law's Garter. Lord Temple had set his heart on this gratification for his pride, but it was one which George II, who disliked Temple intensely, was loath to give. Temple had little claim to so high an honour, and his elevation must disappoint men with more claim. For a time George II held out and in November 1759 Temple resigned his office of Privy Seal. He was coaxed back by colleagues terrified that Pitt might resign also and leave them with the war on their hands. Pitt made the Garter a personal matter, the only thing that for all his tremendous services he had ever asked, and next year, when two vacancies occurred in the Order, Temple got his Garter. It is difficult sometimes to remember that he and the understanding, sympathetic Hester Pitt were brother and sister. Because Pitt knew that his colleagues were more and more attracted to the idea of a negotiated peace, he was forced to exploit their fear of his bitter tongue and remorseless energy to drive them on. In his eyes the spectre of a compromise peace now was far more frightening than the burden of continuing the war for another year or two. Almost everything that France valued must be in British hands before the peace conference. Only in this way could

Pitt have so many counters with which to bargain that he could keep all those conquests which were vital pieces of Britain's future commercial jigsaw. While France remained victorious in Germany and still kept Minorca, Britain would have to give back too much to secure a peace. But, if the war with France was to be continued as a vital British interest, then the German war could not be allowed to collapse. Frederick must be supported, not only from motives of honour but, still more, from those of policy.

Such were Pitt's views even in the face of the disappointing results of the summer campaign in Germany. In spite of the lukewarm attitude of most of the ministers he was therefore pressing on with his schemes against France. He hoped that after the fall of Montreal British military and naval resources could be switched to the West Indies. There Martinique was the supreme prize, but if the lateness of the season did not make a full-scale attack on it practicable, it might be possible to seize St Lucia, with its fine harbour, and Dominica. In order to increase his pressure on France and relieve hers on Germany, he also reverted to the notion of another formidable raid on her coasts. This time the objective was to be Belleisle. Though of little value except from a strategic point of view, because of its position off the French coast, the French would have to buy it back at any price. It would therefore be an extremely useful conquest to exchange for Minorca, whose return to Britain in any peace was a *sine qua non*. Most of the Cabinet, including Anson, were against the attempt so late in the year. Hawke, as commander of the western squadron, gave an unfavourable opinion, and George II, who had at first been in favour of the scheme, was won over to oppose it. Whether Pitt would have succeeded in the teeth of so much opposition will never be known. Suddenly, on 25 October, George II died, and his death altered the whole complexion of events. The change in Pitt's views on the continental war had brought the two men much more in sympathy; George III was likely to look at things very differently.

In the last three years Pitt had done great things. There was much substance in his proud boast, 'I know that I can save this country and that nobody else can.' The machinery for waging war was badly designed and desperately uncoordinated. Only a minister prepared to welcome responsibility and to ride roughshod over departmental limitations could provide the necessary unity. And who among the politicians of the day had the personality and conviction to do this but Pitt? He alone had the imagination to see the pattern of things to come and to inspire other men with his vision and to drive them on with relentless pressure. He had fused a neglected navy and an inadequate army into a force capable of defeating the unified command of France. Even the German war and the King's concern for Hanover had been made to serve his overriding purpose. When George II died, Scottish disaffection had been partly abated by the enrolment of the Highland regiments, colonial pride had been soothed, and Englishmen had been given new fields for expansion. It was no mean record.

13

THE ACCESSION OF GEORGE III

1. Differing Interpretations of its Importance

CONTEMPORARIES were well aware that the entire political scene could be changed by the accession of a new King. To suppose otherwise would render nonsensical the pattern of the last two reigns, in which the opposition to the ministers of the day had clustered round the heir to the throne. The question which men were asking in October 1760 was—how great would that difference be? What were the intentions of the new King? On the answer to this question historians have failed to agree, though at one time one answer, at another a different one has held the field. All, however, would agree that the question is an important one which affects the whole framework of eighteenth-century history and must influence the interpretation of the events of the next few decades. It is impossible to provide a narrative of the early years of George III's reign and ignore the personality, intentions and background of the King.

American, and until recently, British historians have had a tendency to malign George III as immature, obstinate, intellectually limited and the victim of a mental instability that resulted in recurring fits of insanity. He was 'the mad king' whose defects of character played a major part in the loss of the American colonies. Recent research has greatly modified this picture. It is true that when George III ascended the throne he was an inexperienced youth of twenty-one, and that his mother's desire to protect him from the temptations of contemporary society, combined with his grandfather's determination not to allow him any role in politics made the society over which he was now the ruler unknown territory. The man on whom he relied for guidance, his ex-tutor and 'dearest friend', Lord Bute, was unfitted for this task in that not only did he lack political experience and any gift for leadership, he also lacked nerve and a grasp of realities. In addition he had no capacity for handling men. He and the King were twin babes in the dangerous wood of politics. For a time the young King's devotion blinded him to Bute's deficiencies, causing him to act on his advice even when this went against his own opinion. To this many of the early difficulties of George III's reign can be attributed. In later life the King was to show himself to be no mean politician and a ruler who could face a crisis with courage, and who, in the face of odds persisted, often in devious ways, in doing what he thought to be right and his duty to his country, which he conceived was to uphold the Revolutionary Settlement as he understood it. Within this acceptance there is no evidence that he ever desired to undermine Parliament or to usurp its authority. Nor was he as intellectually limited as the nickname 'Farmer George' might imply to modern ears. He was a great collector of books, spending lavishly from the Privy Purse to build up that great library now housed in the British Museum and still known as The King's Library; he contributed financially towards the project of the Royal Academy, as the name implies. Nor was he concerned only with the Arts. He collected scientific instruments, had his own observatory and gave the astronomer Herschel a pension of £200 a year. According to one of his latest biographers George III has good claims to be regarded as 'the most cultured monarch ever to sit on the throne of Great Britain'.[1] Recent research has also given a new interpretation of his so called 'madness', arguing that George III was not insane in the sense of being a man of unstable temperament capable of being pushed over the edge of sanity by emotional stress and strain but that he suffered from an obscure physical complaint known as Porphyria, so called because of the red colour imparted to the urine during attacks.[2] Essentially this condition was caused by changes in the metabolism of the body, which produced symptoms such as pains in the chest, weakness in the limbs, digestive troubles, volubility of speech, restlessness and in its later and more severe stages delusions and other signs associated with insanity. It can be argued that this new diagnosis is interesting rather than historically important. To argue thus is to ignore the light which it throws on

[1] J. Brooke, *King George III* (1973), p. xv.
[2] I. Macalpine and R. Hunter, *George III and the Mad Business* (1969).

George III's personality. The behaviour of a well balanced and
basically intelligent man thrown off balance for brief periods for a
specifically physical cause presents the historian with a very different
picture from that of a mentally and emotionally unstable ruler. It is
one which appears to fit the general pattern of George III's life, both
public and private, in a way which the earlier diagnosis fails to do.

The versions nearest in time to George III tend to be sympathetic
towards his problems, if not always towards his solutions.[1] They
picture the late King as having been very much in the grip of the
great whig magnates, who had usurped many of the royal powers
and made his active intervention in politics, except in the limited
spheres of the Bedchamber and the army, largely ineffectual.
George III, they assert, was not content to play so passive a role
and was determined to regain those powers which the Revolutionary
Settlement had left him. In this there was at least as much love of
country as of self-aggrandisement, for he had been sickened and
shocked by the extent to which corruption had been used to cement
and retain political power. Connection and party he equated with
this system of parliamentary management, and in its place he
wanted, by ending the political proscription of the tories, to make
it possible for men to be chosen as individuals and not because of
their 'connection' to serve the King as ministers.[2] There is no
accusation that George III was aiming at an unconstitutional revival
of royal power, or in any way challenging the Revolutionary
Settlement. To this he was completely loyal, but he was determined
to free the monarchy from the stranglehold of a few great political
families, so that the balance of the constitution could be preserved.
Corruption must go, partly because it was the means by which the
ruling clique had maintained its power, partly because it was morally
objectionable.

By the mid-nineteenth century a much less favourable gloss was
put on George III's actions. There was considerably less sympathy
for, and understanding of, the role which it was alleged he had wished
to play. By then the need of the monarch to act through ministers
who were fully responsible to Parliament, and especially to the
House of Commons, had come to be accepted constitutional doctrine.
Anything that had prevented or held up this development was,

---

[1] H. Butterfield, *George III and the Historians* (1957), pp. 41–50.

[2] Dr. Samuel Johnson, *The False Alarm* (1770), described him as 'a King who knows
not the name of party, and who wishes to be the common father of all his people'.

almost inevitably, regarded as a retrograde step.[1] The terms 'whig' and 'tory' and 'party' meant very different things in 1760 and 1860, but Victorian historians were inclined to assume that the conditions with which they were familiar prevailed equally at the earlier date. To them George III was putting the clock back: he was returning to earlier, less desirable, methods of government. By attempting to free the monarchy from the control which the whig ministers had exercised in the latter years of George II's reign he was, they argued, acting unconstitutionally and endeavouring to reintroduce arbitrary government. This was the whig, as opposed to the earlier, more sympathetic, tory interpretation of the events of 1760.

More recent research, associated with the names of the late Sir Lewis Namier and his school, has deepened the understanding of this critical period by making available a more detailed study of the structure of politics. Using this material it is possible to argue that the Revolutionary Settlement left the Crown in such an ambiguous position that the only way of making our 'mixed form of constitution' work with reasonable smoothness was for ministers of the Crown to enjoy both the 'power' of the Commons and the 'favour' of the Closet. If the King were 'in toils' because of this, so were his ministers. If he was often forced to bow to circumstances so were they. Half the intrigues of the time were intrigues for the favour of the Closet: in the struggles in the Cabinet between Newcastle and Pitt the royal wishes were often a trump card. The picture of a King reduced to being a puppet in the hands of his ministers is not really in accord with the facts as revealed by a detailed study of the closing years of George II's reign. In such circumstances a royal campaign to regain powers which had never been lost would have been pointless. Nor can George III be accused of destroying responsible government which, as the nineteenth century was to interpret the term, did not exist. In any case such elaborate explanations were unnecessary. When a young, untried, but vigorous King succeeded one who was old, tired, and the victim of habit, it was natural that there should be changes of personnel and outlook. What gave the accession of George III its importance was not the immediate political events of 1760, or any deep-laid schemes on his

[1] J. Brewer, 'The Misfortunes of Lord Bute', *Historical Journal*, March 1973, argues that the doctrine of ministerial responsibility was already coming to be accepted: the King had a right to appoint ministers but must act through them and the balance of the constitution was upset by the appointment of a personal friend like Lord Bute.

part, but the lack of an heir to the throne. There was now no reversionary interest around which disappointed politicians could rally, and, lacking a constitutional figure-head, they were forced to elaborate new views of the constitution and fabricate a new plot to justify their resistance to administration. According to this interpretation it was not design but a series of unforeseen developments which led to a crisis, and to the raising of new political issues.[1]

In brief outline these are the three schools of thought which have attempted to interpret the importance of the accession of George III. Of the three the whig interpretation, at least in its crude form, can be most easily dismissed. Recent research makes it difficult to argue that the royal actions were unconstitutional, though George III's choice of Bute as his chief minister was politically rash in view of the latter's lack of previous experience. The other two explanations can be regarded as each containing certain vital pieces of the solution without being a complete answer to the problem. Opinions will continue to differ as to how far George II was 'in toils' according to the emphasis that is laid on different pieces of evidence. A study of George II's anguished remarks when in the middle of a political crisis, to which his own obstinate prejudices had often contributed a great deal, must produce a picture of a king bullied and badgered into submission by a political machine in which he is almost a mere decoration. On the other hand a detailed study of day-to-day administration, or even a different phase of the same political crisis mirrored in Newcastle's correspondence, will show a king by no means powerless, even when he grew old and weary.[2]

There is still room for differing interpretations as to the scope of the changes George III intended to make. Was he merely determined to get rid of ministers whose views on policy were not his, believing with some justification that many people, both in and out of Parliament, would agree with him that peace was now in the country's best interest? Or did he genuinely wish to cleanse government of those corrupt accretions which seemed to degrade public life? His background and personality suggest certain clues, though they cannot provide complete answers. Carefully and even rigidly brought up by his mother, he had little but theoretical knowledge of the

---

[1] See the Introduction to R. R. Sedgwick's *Letters from George III* . . ., pp. xi–xix, for a stimulating discussion of the importance of this point.

[2] See J. Owen, 'George II: a reappraisal', in *Statesmen, Scholars and Merchants: Essays presented to Dame Lucy Sutherland*, ed. Bromley, Dickson and Whiteman (1973).

outside world. He had indeed something of the simplicity of a child who divides the world into 'good men' and 'bad men'; he tried to be a 'good man' himself. From that it was an easy step to believe that those who differed from him were 'bad'. To the end of his life he never either understood or forgave ministers who disagreed with him. In addition he had no reason to like either Newcastle or Pitt. For the greater part of his career the enmity between George II and his son had forced Newcastle to be the enemy of Leicester House. Pitt's record had been more mixed, for politicians in opposition were its natural allies. Moreover, after Frederick's death in 1751, Pitt had championed the cause of the Princess of Wales, as against the Duke of Cumberland, over the question of the Regency bill. In the crisis of 1757 Bute, now the close friend and adviser of the Princess and after his majority Groom of the Stole to her son, had given what support he could to Devonshire's ministry, and had taken a useful part in the negotiations leading to the coalition of Pitt and Newcastle. Unfortunately for Pitt, these good relations had not continued. He had no intention of allowing Bute to fulfil the role of political mentor, for which he was inclined to cast himself, and he was unable, through no fault of his own, to persuade George II to let his grandson take any active part in public life, either civil or military.

Apart from personal rancour, differing views on policy played their part. Leicester House had carefully dissociated itself from the pro-Hanoverian policy of the late King, and Pitt's insistence on a colonial and naval war had been very much to their liking. In 1758 Bute had written to him: 'greater thanks are due to you, my worthy friend, for the revival of that courage. . . . Valour was despised, America neglected, and you left singlehanded to plead the cause of both.' But when Pitt became converted to the need of sustaining the German war, this had seemed to them a betrayal of earlier convictions for the sake of Closet favour. Both George III and Bute, therefore, had substantial personal reasons for wanting to get rid of Newcastle and Pitt when the political situation seemed favourable. But during the early months of the reign, with a new Parliament to be called and the threads of the complicated business of running the war to be gathered together, this was impracticable.

Had George III and Bute any purpose beyond this? Did they really dislike the way in which interest and influence had entwined themselves in and out and through the structure of politics, and wish to replace it by some system which was less open to the charge of corruption? There are strong indications in their personal correspondence that this was so,[1] and it was noted that 'the language of the Court' had changed. In the first few years of the reign the Court publically aligned itself with an attack on 'those odious party distinctions'. *The Auditor*, reputed to be Bute's own paper, speaks of 'the late revolution at Court', and stresses the need to free the Crown from the encroachments made upon it by ministerial power. The implication certainly was that, by the misuse of their position, ministers had secured an unconstitutional hold over the King, and that the cause of the purity of public life and the freedom of the King to choose the best men available, stood or fell together. Whatever George was trying to do he was not trying to do it secretly,[2] and he obviously expected the support of 'good men' in his campaign.

The characters of Bute and George III make it probable that the propaganda they were circulating was something more than a smoke screen. What they were saying in the early sixties is what the opposition had been saying since the days of Walpole. With monotonous regularity independent members, or opposition members, had introduced place bills into the Commons with the sole purpose of lessening the means of corruption at the disposal of ministers. The points put forward by the Prince of Wales when he was trying to rally support before the surprise election of 1747 are interesting in this connection. He declared that 'it is his Intention totally to abolish for the future all Distinction of Party . . . to take away all Proscriptions from any Set of men whatever, who are Friends to the Constitution'. He also promised a bill 'to exclude all Military officers in the Land Service under the degree of Colonels of Regiments, & in the Sea Service under the degree of Rear Admirals, from sitting in the House of Commons'. He also promised to institute an inquiry into 'the great Number of Abuses in Office'.[3] Such views were part of the political jargon of Leicester House; whether believed or not they had been trotted out, in season and out of season, by enemies of the

---

[1] R. R. Sedgwick, 'Letters from William Pitt to Lord Bute 1755–58' (in *Essays presented to Sir Lewis Namier*, 1956). It is interesting to notice that Pitt was apparently familiar with these pre-accession dreams. On 20 June 1758 he wrote to Bute: 'May my noble friend's honest labours in planting the seeds of moral virtue never be frustrated and may the reviving country reap the happy fruits of a Prince, train'd to love his people enough to wish generously to reform them.'

[2] *Ibid.*, p. 50. In the middle of November 1760 George III wrote to Lord Bute: 'If I do not show them that I will not permit Ministers to trample on me, then my subjects will in time come to esteem me unworthy of the Crown I wear.'

[3] Quoted J. Owen, *op. cit.*, p. 313.

Court; young George must have absorbed them almost from the nursery. To his friend Bute also they had an obvious appeal. His intentions were good; he took an idealistically high view of the functions of the King; he was capable of being mesmerized by high-flown sentiments. Both he and George III, having been excluded from any genuine familiarity with the day-to-day practices of government, had little idea of the delicacy of the machine and the perpetual need to compromise. There is nothing improbable in the suggestion that they hoped to secure greater purity in public life and thought this could be done by smashing the party connections which hampered the King in his choice of ministers.[1] But just because they were so unfamiliar with practical politics, it is equally probable that they had little or no conception of the magnitude of the task they were attempting. They were 'new brooms'; they intended to sweep clean, without realizing that it would be necessary first to build a new house to attain the standard they desired. The task to which they had dedicated themselves was one beyond their capabilities. Perhaps it was beyond anyone's if the Revolutionary Settlement was not to be scrapped. Through bitter experience George III found that he, too, had to accept the framework of politics as he found it and work within it as his grandfather had done.

2. THE ASCENDANCY OF BUTE

The most immediate problem was the policy to be adopted over the war. From the beginning of the reign, when in his speech to the Lords in Council assembled George III had alluded to the war as 'bloody and expensive' and, under pressure from Pitt, had altered it in the printed version to 'an expensive but just and necessary war', it was clear that the great war minister and the young King were at variance. George III was certainly not prepared for peace at any price: he seems to have approved of the naval and colonial war. But his prejudices against the German war were too strong[2] for him to have the least sympathy with Pitt's policy of reinforcing Ferdinand of Brunswick and providing subsidies for Prussia. Until, however, he

[1] R. Pares, *George III and the Politicians* (1953), p. 61: 'But he designed a change of system too, in that he meant to do his duty better than George II had done it; and in this sense it is fair to say that the new reign differed intentionally from the old, that the drift of the constitution in a certain direction was now deliberately arrested with a sharp jerk.'

[2] R. R. Sedgwick, *Letters from George III . . .*, p. 28. On August 1759 he wrote of 'that horrid Electorate which has always liv'd upon the very vitals of this poor country'.

had strengthened his hold over the political machinery, and until the increasing burden of the war had given additional vigour to the demand for a reasonable peace, he could do little.

The first step was to gain control of the political machine. By the middle of the eighteenth century it had not yet become obligatory for the King to consult his Cabinet: he could still act through the minister whose department was concerned. But in time of war, when it was necessary to consult the Secretaries of State, the First Lord of the Treasury and often the First Lord of the Admiralty, before a complicated expedition could be equipped and launched, to ignore the Cabinet would have been extremely difficult and to reject its united advice even more so. It was therefore vital that it should contain at least one minister on whose loyalty George III could rely implicitly. For this task there was nobody available but the faithful Bute. During 1759 Lord Holderness had passed on a good deal of Cabinet news to Leicester House, but he was too committed to the old gang to be completely serviceable. Therefore, though the formal offers of Newcastle and Pitt to resign were politely rejected, on 15 November Bute was made Groom of the Stole. George III's intentions in making this appointment are clear from Bute's oft-quoted remark to Temple that he was not 'a bare Groom of the Stole. The King will have it otherwise.' George III would have preferred more decisive action—to arrange for Holderness's resignation, so that Bute might have been given the vacant Secretaryship; but this Bute himself had negatived.

No further changes, either in policy or in persons, were likely until after the election of a new Parliament. So far electioneering for this had been very languid because, though the present Parliament was due to expire under the Septennial Act in the autumn of 1760, no one had expected its life to be long enough to make any effort to secure election. This was because of the provision that a new Parliament should be called within six months of the accession and as George II was then seventy-seven no one expected its life even to approximate to the customary seven years. The accession of a young King in October 1760 changed the situation overnight and electioneering grew brisk.[1] Even so it was a perfectly normal election. As usual the real battles took place over nominations; only 48 out of a total of 315 constituencies went to the polls. In accordance with George III's campaign for purity, no money was issued directly from

[1] Sir Lewis Namier, *The Structure of Politics*, p. 159.

the Treasury for electioneering purposes, but this fact becomes less impressive, except as a proof of royal intentions, when it is realized that the sums spent in this way were never very large; in the election of 1754 they had amounted to only £30,000.[1] The more usual methods of creating a government majority—gratitude for past favours and expectations of those to come—continued as before. Also, though Bute and George III took considerable interest in the nominations, Newcastle was still left to manage those boroughs which were dependent on the votes of Customs or Excise men. Indeed, in the end, in spite of Newcastle's agonized fears, the King only put forward three names, and not more than twelve M.P.s appear to have owed their seats to Bute's direct influence.[2] It was in other ways that George III made it clear that he was the effective fountain of honour, as when he appointed five Lords of the Bedchamber without consulting Newcastle. The new House of Commons was very like its predecessors and there was nothing to mark it out as a first fruit of a revolution at Court. In March 1761 George III further strengthened his personal hold over the administration by arranging that Holderness should retire and so allow Bute to take over the important office of Secretary. Legge, for whom the King had little liking, was replaced as Chancellor of the Exchequer by Lord Barrington, Charles Townshend taking the latter's place as Secretary at War and, as George III did not want to antagonize Pitt, whose relations with Bute were cold and formal, James Grenville was made Cofferer of the Household in an attempt to mitigate his disapproval of the recent changes.

3. NEGOTIATIONS FOR PEACE

With a new Parliament chosen and Bute installed as one of the Secretaries of State, it was possible to consider ways and means of bringing about an acceptable peace. The spring, with new campaigns opening, was always a critical time. In January Pitt had succeeded in getting the King's consent to the sending of an expedition under Keppel to seize Mauritius, a project held over from the previous year. He also instructed Amherst to detach 2,000 troops to be used in the naval attack on Dominica and St Lucia, if it seemed possible to do so before the hurricane season broke. With these schemes already under way and the hope of a successful attack on Belleisle,

---

[1] *Ibid.*, p. 164.
[2] Sir Lewis Namier, *England in the Age of the American Revolution* (1930), pp. 175-6.

Pitt, while ready for negotiations, had no wish for them to be concluded before he had the anticipated bargaining counters in his
hands. Also he still hoped that there would be time for a new attack
on Martinique. Pitt wanted peace but only on his own terms.
Choiseul also was coming to think that peace was in France's best
interests.[1] Frederick II, too, was in favour of negotiations between
England and France. His situation had grown steadily more desperate as his resources dwindled, and he hoped that, her major quarrel
settled, France would cease to give Austria much help and would
evacuate those Prussian territories which she now held. In return for
these advantages and the continuance of England's financial help,
Frederick II was prepared to welcome a separate peace. In England
the rising demand for peace was illustrated by the success of Israel
Mauduit's pamphlet *Considerations on the Present German War*,[2] which
said all the things that Pitt now repudiated. With Bute and George
III holding very similar views, with Newcastle despairing of raising
funds for another year of global war, and with the Duke of Bedford
convinced of the unwisdom of pushing France too far, the prospects
of a successful negotiation seemed good.

Choiseul took the initiative in March 1761 by suggesting that, if
France and England opened separate talks and thus prepared the
ground, a general congress of all the combatants might be called
with some hope of success. The basis he proposed was that each
country should remain in possession of conquests made before
certain fixed dates, and that there should be a mutual restoration of
any places taken after them. This principle is that of *uti possidetis*.

---

[1] 'He was anxious to secure peace as rapidly as possible, as he felt the knife at his
throat.'—A. von Ruville, *William Pitt, Earl of Chatham* (1907), vol. II, p. 361. For a
very clear discussion of the determining factors behind the negotiations see vol. II,
pp. 362–7.

[2] Israel Mauduit, *Considerations on the Present German War* (1760): 'We have now no
les an option to make, than whether we will lavish away five millions a year in
Germany, without a possibility of doing that, or England any good, and annually run
the kingdom ten millions in debt; until it shall be at length exhausted, and unable to
defend either; or whether we will realize to this nation a revenue of five millions a
year for ever, at our enemies expence; and totally disable France hereafter from raising
a Maritime power, which can ever be in any degree formidable to Britain.' A contemporary described Mauduit as a Blackwell Hall trader, 'once a dissenting teacher, a
fellow of the Royal Society, & much esteemed by the best persons of it; one of the
first rank in Lord Willoughby's Sunday night Club of Divines, Philosophers &
Scholars at large. A man of fortune enough to live as he likes, wanting neither place
nor pension.'—A. Hartshorne, *Memoirs of a Royal Chaplain 1729–63, Correspondence of
Edmund Pyle D.D., Chaplain in ordinary to George II* (1907), p. 339.

Obviously everything turned on the fixing of these vital dates for the various theatres of war. France suggested 1 May 1761 for Europe, 1 July for Africa and the West Indies and 1 September for the East Indies. Pitt, though prepared to accept the principle, was not prepared to accept these dates, as he was busy with plans for the conquest of Martinique and Belleisle. As Choiseul would not agree to negotiate alternative ones, it was arranged that the *uti possidetis* formula should be dropped and instead each country should exchange representatives and attempt to hammer out acceptable peace terms. These negotiations were to prove abortive; even so they were extremely important because indirectly they brought about the resignation of Pitt.

Though his views with regard to the German campaigns had altered, his fundamental aims had remained unchanged. France was still the enemy; every advantage that could be wrung from her for the benefit of British trade must be insisted on in the peace treaty. But though the commercial element in the City was behind Pitt, many of his colleagues were not. To Newcastle and the moderates, appalled by the expenses of continuing the war and assuming that France was apparently prepared to make substantial concessions, Pitt's intransigence seemed unreasonable. The Duke of Bedford and his supporters went further. They argued that to strip France of too many of her possessions was unwise, that so great a country could not be kept in a permanent state of commercial inferiority, and that too harsh a peace would only breed future wars. The attitude of Bute and of George III fluctuated with changing circumstances. For propaganda purposes, if for nothing else, they had to have as good a peace as possible; they could not allow Pitt to stand alone in the public eye as the sole guardian of Britain's interests. But their opposition to the continental war seems to have been grounded in real, if rather emotional, conviction, and their attachment to the idea of peace was genuine. As a consequence Bute and his master practised what in modern language might be described as 'brinkmanship'. In the negotiations which followed, Bute was prepared to back Pitt against his more pacific or cautious colleagues until it was clear that further pressure would have the effect of making France ready to break off the negotiations. From that brink he drew back, whereas Pitt was prepared to go forward, even if the consequences were a breakdown of the negotiations and the extension of the war to Spain.

Two of the most difficult problems for discussion were the conditions for ending the German war, and the fishing rights off Newfoundland and in the St Lawrence. In Germany, France wanted to regard any enemy territory she had seized, whether Hanoverian or Hessian or Prussian, as bargaining counters to be set against Britain's colonial acquisitions. It was therefore against her interests that the colonial and continental wars should be treated as if they were two separate issues. In particular Choiseul was anxious to retain for France a share in the fishing rights of the St Lawrence, even though he was prepared to let Canada go. These rich fishing grounds were of great economic importance. The fish, caught by the fleets that sailed from Europe every year, after being salted or dried, were one of the most valuable commodities for sale to Mediterranean countries with their large Catholic communities. In the pre-war period both French and English fishermen had used the banks off Newfoundland, but France alone had fished the Gulf of St Lawrence. Pitt wanted to secure the monopoly of both these areas for Britain. This would have spelt ruin for the fishing ports of Normandy and Brittany, and to the great commercial interests which had been built round them. France would have to be desperate indeed before any such clause was written into a peace treaty signed by her.

Choiseul's new proposals were not unreasonable. Minorca would be exchanged for Guadeloupe, Marie Galante and Goree; Canada would be ceded after a careful delimitation of her frontiers. France would also be prepared to give up her German conquests. But in return Choiseul demanded that French fishing rights be restored and Cape Breton handed back as a base for her fishing fleets. These terms were considered at Cabinet meetings on 24 and 26 June. It is important to notice how fully George III consulted his Cabinet on these occasions. It was well understood that Bute was acting as the King's mouthpiece but there was no attempt to burke discussion. There was considerable give and take on both sides in the early stages of the discussions, and the opposition that Pitt had to meet was by no means confined to the Closet. At times Bute was his only ally. Nobody was willing to surrender Cape Breton, or to embark on the diplomatic quicksands of attempting to define Canadian boundaries,[1] but on the issue of the fisheries the division

---

[1] In a *Letter to the People of England on the necessity of putting an Immediate End to the War* (1760), it was argued that England had better give up her West Indian conquests

of opinion in the Cabinet was clear; to exclude France from all her ancient fishing grounds seemed to most ministers too drastic. Even so the reply sent to Choiseul was extremely stiff.

In view of the uncompromising attitude of the British Cabinet Choiseul was forced to weigh further concessions against the possibility of continuing and extending the war. Since the accession of Charles III in Spain the two Courts had grown closer together. Spanish grievances against England were not purely imaginary. Her trade had suffered from British stiffness in enforcing her claims to a right of search, claims which the proximity of Spanish possessions to the area of conflict in the Caribbean made very inconvenient. There was also the old dispute over the right to cut logwood in Honduras. Pitt had been conscious of the increasing strain between the two countries and had, for him, returned conciliatory answers to Spanish complaints. Choiseul was not therefore without diplomatic resource if England, under Pitt's leadership, continued adamant. On 13 July Choiseul made a last attempt at a settlement which, while it made certain further concessions, stood firm on the Newfoundland fisheries and Cape Breton. London was, however, in even less of a mood to agree than before, because on 20 July news had been received of the fall of Pondicherry and the capture of Dominica. Also the final arrangements for the attack on Martinique were well advanced. Losing hope of reaching an accommodation with the British ministers, Choiseul made it clear that France did not stand alone by ordering de Bussy to present two memorials to Pitt. The first of these suggested that Spain be asked to guarantee any peace made between England and France, on the ground that she too had grievances against England.[1] In particular an old and frivolous Spanish claim to share in the fishing rights off Newfoundland was used to involve her in this much disputed issue. The second memorial concerned the German war. In it Austria assented to a separate peace between France and England, but only if she

rather than Canada, otherwise she would give 'Occasions in a few years for another War' as even if France should 'give up their long since projected schemes of elbowing our Colonies and of edging down by degrees to the Sea Coasts' yet the settlers and traders on the spot 'at the first Temptation of any considerable Profit, the advancing Borderers will insult each other! Their complaints will be heard by their respective Sovereigns and the two nations involved be again in a ruinous and bloody war.'

[1] A. von Ruville, *op. cit.*, vol. II, p. 382, points out that 'a very ominous feature was the fact that it introduced the Spanish points of complaint into the Anglo-French negotiations'.

were allowed to keep her own conquests from Prussia and if no further help were given to Frederick II.

The serious issue raised here was that of Anglo-Spanish relations. To invoke the good offices of a country actually at war with Britain in order to force the discussion of Spanish grievances was a distinctly unfriendly act. Far from being intimidated, the first reaction of the English ministers was to reply with an ultimatum, which was handed to Choiseul on 29 July and which again pressed for the full acceptance of the earlier British terms. From this point Choiseul seems to have despaired of concluding peace on any terms which France could accept and to have turned to Spain, though until this help could become effective the negotiations were allowed, nominally, to continue. France was now committed to Spain and eleventh-hour British concessions were too late to save the negotiations.

The latter stages in these discussions are therefore of more interest for their effect on domestic politics than for their influence on international relations. The Cabinet had a couple of stormy meetings on 13 and 14 August when a request by de Bussy for a personal interview was debated. Finally it was decided that the request should be granted, but the terms in which Pitt notified de Bussy of this decision were far from conciliatory. When the more pacific members of the Cabinet tried to soften some of the expressions of this communication Pitt retorted that he would not allow his draft to be 'cobbled'. So irritated were Devonshire and Bedford that they determined to attend no more meetings. Up to this point Bute had supported Pitt but he was not prepared to risk the chance of peace for the sake of the St Lawrence fisheries. Indeed, earlier he had declared that if British firmness on this point proved unavailing he intended to give way. He now threw his weight on to the side of Pitt's opponents and in the Cabinets of 19 and 20 August the latter found all his colleagues against him. It was then at last agreed that French fishing rights in the St Lawrence should be restored, together with some small base (not Cape Breton) which would make the concession a practical proposition. As a further gesture the fortifications of Dunkirk were only to conform to the less onerous conditions of Aix-la-Chapelle. This reply was sent on 27 August.

4. PITT'S RESIGNATION: THE MINISTRY RECONSTRUCTED

The differences of opinion between ministers were genuine and not the fruit of a political intrigue. Though Pitt had been difficult and dictatorial on many occasions, neither Bute nor Newcastle wanted to drive him to resign: he was still necessary for the conduct of the war. Nor was there thought to be much hope, in spite of Newcastle's wishful thinking, of ultimately avoiding a war with Spain. Pitt was for bold and dramatic measures. His advice, which in the teeth of the royal wishes he insisted on presenting to George III in writing, was for the immediate recall of Bristol, the British ambassador, and the issuing of orders to the fleet to pounce on the Spanish treasure ships on their way from the Caribbean. By one swift blow he hoped to destroy both the Spanish fleet and its war chest, and so dispose of the vital help that France planned to gain from this new Family Compact, which had in fact been signed on 15 July, though the English ministers could not be certain of this. Acting on an intuition did not commend itself to the Cabinet as a whole; they preferred the diplomatic respectability of proceeding by the conventional formulas towards the outbreak of war to Pitt's more robust strategic realism. To take the offensive, and so add another enemy to their problems before it was clear that Spain was really committed to war, seemed politically and morally an indefensible step. The Cabinet meeting of 2 October made it clear that either they must give way to Pitt or he would resign. It was in the course of this Cabinet that he made his famous statement that 'Being responsible I will direct, and will be responsible for nothing I do not direct.'[1] In a narrow sense these words can be interpreted as responsibility to the King and the direction of his own office as Secretary; in a wider sense they were a challenge to the constitutional practices of the day. Pitt was claiming for himself as minister powers of the most sweeping kind against the united opinion of the Cabinet.

The situation in which George III and Bute now found themselves was one of great difficulty. Either they had to let the great war minister go, knowing that any failure on their part to manage the remainder of the war successfully, or to get a good peace, would make the House of Commons very difficult to handle, or they had to accept his views on Spain. It took courage to let Pitt go, though to retain him on his own terms would not necessarily have avoided a political crisis. Devonshire and Bedford were in revolt against his views; Newcastle and his friends might well have refused to go on supporting a policy which they so much disliked. It was, indeed,

---

[1] Quoted B. Tunstall, *op. cit.*, p. 305.

almost impossible for Bute and George III to reverse their policy, even if they had wished to do so. If, however, Pitt's resignation postponed the necessity to take a decision on war with Spain, it produced a crop of new problems. The chief of these was who was to have the vacant Secretaryship? The number of effective and trained politicians was always small. The new Secretary must be able to work with others. He must be able to manage the Commons and answer Pitt in debate. He must also be reasonably acceptable to the rest of the ministers. Henry Fox had the ability but was mistrusted and unpopular;[1] for him to have succeeded Pitt would have produced an unpleasant impression. Bute inclined to George Grenville; to choose Pitt's brother-in-law to succeed him was on the surface a slightly surprising choice. George Grenville was not a likeable person; he was pedantic, mentally rigid, and like his elder brother Lord Temple who had just resigned the Privy Seal in sympathy with Pitt, extremely self-opinionated. But against this must be set administrative ability, sound understanding and a grasp of detail. His own ambition was to become Speaker of the Commons, and most historians are agreed that he would have filled the office admirably. Bute wanted him as Chancellor of the Exchequer, for which his personal qualifications would have well fitted him, but Newcastle opposed this and it was decided to offer him the Seals. Family loyalty precluded him from accepting the somewhat embarrassing offer, but he agreed, while keeping his office of Treasurer of the Navy, to undertake the leadership of the Commons. This made it possible to choose the new Secretary from the Lords, and Lord Egremont, distinguished for little beyond the fact that he was Grenville's brother-in-law, was appointed. Once these arrangements were completed, Bedford, who was a member of the effective Cabinet but had not previously held office, now succeeded Temple as Lord Privy Seal. In private conversations with Fox a bargain was struck by which he agreed either to give active support or to maintain a tactful silence, whichever should be required of him. This was necessary because of the underlying friction between him and Grenville. Thus Bute made reasonably sure that when Parliament met on 13 November 1761 the Commons would be controllable, even if Pitt should go back on a promise, given at the time of his resignation, and attack the administration with his old venom.

[1] Hardwicke had earlier described him as 'a bad, black man' and 'a dark and insidious genius'.—*Hardwicke Correspondence*, vol. II, p. 69.

By the middle of November Pitt's popularity stood as high as ever. There had been a brief eclipse after his resignation when it was known that he had accepted a peerage for his wife with descent to her children, and a pension of £3,000 a year for himself and any two other lives. The royal intention on making this award has been open to a good deal of criticism, and has often been regarded as a clever trick to discredit Pitt by making it appear that he, too, had his price. The fact that his resignation and these grants were both announced in the *Gazette* for 9 October gives some colour to this supposition; certainly Newcastle told Hardwicke that it had been deliberately done. But both George III and England owed Pitt a vast debt, and at a time when pensions were the normal way of providing for the retirement of politicians, Pitt received a little under rather than over the norm. To have done nothing for Pitt would have been openly ungracious, though no doubt Bute was alive to the fact that every favour accepted from the King would make later attacks less dangerous. In any case, if a trap was intended it failed to close on its victim, for once Pitt had avowed in a public letter to Beckford, his sounding board in the City, that the cause of his resignation had been difficulties over Spain, Mr. William Pitt and Baroness Chatham were reinstated in the public regard. The fear that Pitt might make difficulties for the administration in the Commons did not immediately materialize. Indeed, it was when the grant of a million pounds for the German war was being debated that Pitt, defending the measure, made his famous statement that America had been conquered in Germany.[1]

The combination of a rather complicated pattern of events was, however, once again bringing the strategy of the German war under fire. Though the Cabinet had not been prepared to act on Pitt's conviction that Spain was on the point of joining France in open warfare, Bute did not intend to stand supinely by without taking some steps to resolve that uncertainty. A Cabinet of 23 October instructed Bristol to demand assurances of the non-offensive nature of the Franco-Spanish compact, and when these were not forthcoming the English ministers decided that war was inevitable. This was declared on 2 January 1762.[2] By now the Spanish treasure

[1] 'Had the armies of France not been employed in Germany they would have been transported to America. . . . America had been conquered in Germany.'—*The Parliamentary History of England*, edited W. Cobbett (1806), etc., vol. XV, p. 1266.

[2] By 12 January George III was writing of 'this unhappy tho' just Spanish War'.—*Letters from George III . . .*, p. 80.

fleets were safely in their own ports and the strategic advantages that Pitt had aimed at lost. In other respects the situation was favourable in spite of the increased burden of a fresh war. One of Pitt's last acts had been to arrange to send Rodney with naval reinforcements to the West Indies. Martinique had been taken in January, St Lucia, St Vincent and Grenada followed shortly after, and the British forces in the area were available for an attack on the great Spanish possession of Havana, which fell in August 1762. In the same way British forces already in the East Indies received reinforcements and orders to attack Manila in the Philippines. Though these latest successes came when Pitt was no longer organizing the war, the responsible departments knew what had to be done, the navy and the army had had training in co-operation, and by an almost reflex action victories continued to be won. But even victories have to be paid for, and in addition a Spanish attack on Portugal opened up another front, though Lisbon was never in serious danger. These additional expenses gave fresh ammunition to those men who disliked the German war. It was in these circumstances that the renewal of Frederick II's subsidy came up for review. In January 1762 the death of Elizabeth of Russia introduced a new factor. Frederick II now had in the new Tsar, Peter III, a warm admirer instead of a determined enemy. Suddenly the whole diplomatic picture changed, and it was natural that the British ministers should revise their ideas on the German war.

Newcastle had always supported it, Pitt had become convinced of its necessity, but Bute and the King had been anxious to get out of it as soon as they decently could. The expenses of the Spanish war seemed to provide an excuse for this. When the problem was raised in the Cabinet early in January 1762, it was decided to warn Frederick II that with her new burdens England would have to curtail her expenditure on the German war, and that in his own interests he should make peace with his enemies on the best terms he could.[1] When, therefore, the news of Peter III's accession reached London in February, it confirmed the direction British diplomacy was already taking with regard to the German war. The problem now was that of deciding where the new economies had best be made—at the expense of the army of observation defending Hanover, or by discontinuing the subsidy to Frederick II.

[1] On 5 February 1762 George III wrote of 'obliging that *proud, overbearing Prince* to see he has no safety but in peace'.—*Ibid.*, p. 81.

The subsidy treaty was an annual one which ran from April to April. If it were renewed Britain would be committed to continuing the war until April 1763. In addition by the treaty both sides had bound themselves not to make a separate peace without the consent of the other. By not renewing the treaty Britain would both save money and regain her freedom of action. Faced by these alternatives Bute adopted a policy of compromise. He would continue to keep an army in British pay for the defence of Hanover and to protect Frederick II's flank, but on a less ambitious scale than previously. Secondly, before renewing the subsidy treaty, he would make it plain that English money would be available in future only to enable a satisfactory peace to be made, and not for the prolongation of the war for Frederick II's personal advantage. As by his general conduct the latter made it clear that he had no intention of conforming to the English terms, Bute informed Newcastle on 12 April that he intended to withhold the subsidy. Newcastle was greatly distressed by this decision, but it did not drive him into immediate resignation. That point was reached when Bute revealed his intention of drastically curtailing British expenditure in Germany. Newcastle considered that two million was the least that the House of Commons should be asked to grant as a war credit, one for the defence of Portugal, one for the German war. Bute told him that he meant to ask for one million only. When his decision had been endorsed by the Commons, the old Duke felt he could no longer go on. He went to see George III on 14 May and formally resigned ten days later. It was the end of the old firm, for with Newcastle's resignation Hardwicke also ceased to attend Cabinet meetings.

This gave George III the opportunity to place his 'dearest friend' at the head of the Treasury. Bute seems to have been personally reluctant to assume a responsibility which involved managing a divided cabinet and concluding the controversial peace negotiations, but finally agreed to do so. This meant that his previous office of secretary of state had to be filled, which was not easy. The only man of sufficient weight available was George Grenville, and from Bute's point of view he was far from ideal. The fact that the other secretary was Lord Egremont, Grenville's brother-in-law, would give the new secretary more influence in the Cabinet than seemed desirable. As Anson, who had been a sick man for some time, died in June, his place was given to Lord Halifax, who now became a member of the inner Cabinet. Grenville's promotion had left the Treasurer-ship of the navy vacant and this was given to Barrington, of whose political career it could certainly be said that 'each man in his time plays many parts'. Sir Francis Dashwood,[1] an eccentric of wide interests (he was a member of the notorious Medmenham Society) but with no qualifications for a successful Chancellor of the Ex-chequer, was nevertheless appointed to that post.

5. THE PEACE NEGOTIATIONS RENEWED

By the spring of 1762 Bute was once again engaged in peace negotiations with Choiseul. War had hardly beeen declared on Spain before letters began to be secretly exchanged between the two men through the medium of de Viry, the Sardinian ambassador in London. This was before the resignation of Newcastle. The suggestions put forward by Bute, with the approval of Newcastle and Hardwicke, were that the French should be allowed to share in both the coveted fishing grounds, and be given the use of the small islands of St Pierre and Miquelon as bases for their fishermen; Goree was also to be restored to France. It was proposed to deal with the German problem by the stipulation that, once peace had been concluded, the help either gave to their late allies should be purely financial. The basis for a resumption of negotiations having been laid, on 29 March Bute suggested in a full Cabinet that the time had come to reopen formal peace talks. This was agreed. Though the war had been going well for England, Bute's attitude encouraged Choiseul to hold out for better terms than the military situation of either France or Spain warranted; he was particularly anxious to retain St Lucia, the largest of the Neutral Islands, with its superb harbour. As a bait, therefore, to induce the Cabinet to give way on this point, Choiseul intimated that France would be prepared to make a separate peace without waiting for Spain if that country should prove obdurate. To secure this, Bute thought the surrender of St Lucia would be worthwhile. Other ministers were more mistrustful, and it was only after prolonged discussion that it was decided to return St Lucia only if France pledged herself to use her utmost endeavours to persuade Spain to be a party to the peace treaty and promised to give her no further help should she refuse. Early in September the Duke of Bedford went to Paris to conclude the preliminaries on the lines now settled. But Bute's

[1] Betty Kemp, *Sir Francis Dashwood* (1967), takes a more favourable view.

difficulties were not yet over. When Bedford forwarded the draft treaty on 24 September it contained no mention of any compensation for the return of Havana, which had been captured by Pocock and Albemarle in August 1762. Bute was so anxious for peace that he was prepared to accept the treaty as it stood, but he was faced by the outright defiance of Grenville and Egremont. They argued that if England restored Havana she should receive as compensation both Puerto Rico and Florida; Bute thought that if compensation were demanded then Florida was sufficient. This dispute throws an interesting light on the working of the Cabinet and the relations between the King and his ministers. Grenville and Egremont had been sufficiently influential to rally the rest of the Cabinet against Bute, and neither he nor his royal master had been prepared to ignore its united opinion. The discussion was therefore postponed until the meeting on 4 October. In the meantime the recalcitrant Secretaries were called into the royal presence and subjected to considerable pressure. Even George III's personal intervention made no impression on them; the result was a head-on clash on policy between the King and his ministers in which the latter refused to give way. George III had not, however, exhausted his resources. The Cabinet which had been called for 4 October never met. George III and Bute decided instead to remove Grenville from the key position of Secretary and make other arrangements for managing the Commons. Once again the able, unscrupulous Fox was considered. The offer of the Seals he declined from prudential reasons, but he did agree to take over the leadership of the House and in this capacity attended the Cabinet meetings; Halifax and Grenville then changed offices. Bute was at last master of his own Cabinet, and the manner of his becoming so is an interesting commentary on the royal power to appoint and dismiss ministers.

6. The Peace of Paris

The negotiations with France and Spain were then completed without further incidents. Bute, having reasserted his authority but conscious that parliamentary opinion, fanned by public comment, would be opposed to handing back Havana without an equivalent, informed Bedford that this would be demanded. The final terms were then discussed at Cabinet meetings held on 22 and 25 October and the preliminaries were signed in Paris on 3 November. Bute and George III were well aware that when the terms came before Parliament they were likely to be bitterly criticized by sections of both

Houses. Pitt was certain to criticize them as falling far short of those on which he would have insisted. There was also the possibility that Newcastle, Hardwicke and Devonshire might act with him, at least in opposing those concessions which had been made after they had ceased to attend the Cabinet. Fearing this, Bute had made various attempts during the summer to draw Newcastle again into the orbit of the administration. He had made it clear that the Duke's attendance at the Cabinet would be welcome and that an office, though not his old one, was his for the asking if he would support the peace. Newcastle, with more firmness than might be expected, resisted these overtures, and Devonshire, by way of making his position clear, refused a summons to attend a meeting of the Council. George III was furious and told Bute that he intended to dismiss the Duke from his office as Lord Chamberlain. Accordingly when Devonshire presented himself at St James's the King sent a curt message by a page refusing to receive him, whereupon the Duke immediately handed over his wand of office. This insult to a great whig peer caused the resignations of his brother Lord John Cavendish, of Lord Bessborough and, shortly after, of the young Marquis of Rockingham. The royal reaction was to strike Devonshire's name off the list of privy councillors.

Parliament met on 25 November and on 9 December the preliminaries were laid before it. It was clear that Pitt would oppose them in the Commons; this he did, though he was obviously a very sick man, in a speech of over three hours. Though the House listened to him attentively only 65 voted against the preliminaries while 319 voted for them. In the Lords they were voted without a division in spite of speeches by Newcastle and Hardwicke against them. It is usually assumed that their swift passage was to be attributed to the skill of Henry Fox and the funds and patronage put at his disposal. Certainly great care was taken to manage the House, though Horace Walpole's account of the affair seems to have been both highly coloured and inaccurate.[1] But it may be doubted if that is the whole explanation. England had become weary of the war, the financial burden had been great and peace was popular. If England had not got as much as Pitt would have demanded, she had still got a great deal. All Canada and Cape Breton were hers, together with the hinterland behind the American colonies. In that area everything for which she had originally contended had been

[1] Namier, *Structure of Politics*, pp. 182–4.

obtained, and for the colonists the way to the west was open. In the West Indies she gained Grenada, Dominica, St Vincent and Tobago, in Africa Senegal. In India, though on the surface the two companies returned to the position of 1749—that is, before Dupleix's conquests—the predominance of English influence was to prove decisive; this was particularly true of Bengal, where Clive's conquests, not being against the French, were retained. In Europe, England had regained Minorca; France had evacuated and restored the territory she had conquered in Hanover, Hesse and Brunswick, and she had evacuated both the Prussian possessions, which she had occupied, and also Ostend and Nieuport, which she now handed over again to her ally Austria. From Spain, who had now no option but to make peace, England secured Florida, potentially dangerous because of its threat to British shipping going to the West Indies, and in addition secured the recognition of her long-contested rights to cut logwood in Honduras. Spain also restored everything she had taken from England's ally Portugal and agreed to renounce any claim to share in the Newfoundland fisheries. To many people British gains in the peace treaties with France and Spain appeared satisfactory.

On the other hand a great deal taken from both countries had been given back. The French were still to share in the fishing rights both off Newfoundland and in the Gulf of the St Lawrence, and for this purpose they had received the two islands of St Pierre and Miquelon. In the West Indies France was practically as strong as ever, because she had recovered Martinique, St Lucia, Maria Galante and Guadeloupe. Over the position in the West Indies feelings were mixed. Pitt, viewing the problem from the angle of strategy, was deeply disturbed; to him Martinique and St Lucia were ideal bases from which new French attacks could be launched against the British islands and should never have been left in French hands. To the British sugar planters there was much advantage in having the prosperous French sugar islands the other side of a customs barrier. In Africa, Pitt declared, to have restored Goree, with its fine harbour, was to subject Senegal to a perpetual threat. Britain's behaviour to her late ally Frederick II was also open to criticism. Though she had insisted that territory taken from her other allies should be evacuated and restored to their original owners, in the case of Frederick, France was bound to evacuate but not necessarily restore her conquests. With a little sharp practice this might have led to their being occupied by her late ally Austria.

The debates in Parliament brought out very clearly the fundamental difference of opinion that divided the supporters and opponents of the Peace of Paris. Pitt and his followers in the City regarded France as Britain's chief enemy and most dangerous trading rival. Therefore not to have taken everything she could to secure her future was madness. Though the burdens of the war had been great, Britain, with her fleets controlling the seas, made great trading profits and could have carried on the struggle longer than France. Bute and Bedford argued otherwise, adopting a viewpoint that was in some ways more modern. If, as Bedford argued on occasion, France was left with an intolerable sense of grievance it could only lead to a fresh war. If British naval predominance seemed to threaten the freedom of the smaller maritime powers eventually they would be driven to banding together against her. The essence of statesmanship was to take what was essential to British safety but no more: it was better for the health of Europe that France should remain a great power. If the proof of the pudding is in the eating Pitt was more of a realist than his opponents. The moderation they displayed failed to gain French friendship and in the war of American Independence she took her revenge.

There is less substance in the charge that Bute had behaved shabbily to Frederick II. Though he had been useful in diverting French resources it is arguable that, had neither France nor England been entangled in a continental war, the greater economic resilience of the latter might still have triumphed over the greater manpower of the former. In addition to the payment of his subsidy Britain had at great expense kept the army of observation in the field. This had been of the greatest help to Frederick in that it prevented his being attacked in the rear and enabled him to deal with Austria and Russia. When the subsidy was finally withheld it was because, once the threat from Russia had been removed, Frederick was patently intending to use it to continue the war and smash Austria, which was no part of British policy. Moreover, it is not the case that even after Bute asked the House for one million instead of two in April 1762 the forces under Ferdinand were completely starved. Under general appropriations large sums were still provided for the German war and Frederick had every opportunity of making a satisfactory peace. In so far as he could, Lord Halifax, the new Secretary, used his good offices to secure a settlement which safeguarded Prussia's interests. Spain had more to complain of in the peace terms than had Frederick, though France showed a last minute consideration for her late ally by transferring Louisiana to balance the Spanish loss of Florida. It was a significant gift. By handing over the mouth of the Mississippi to Spain France finally renounced her ambitions to dominate the mainland of America. Pitt's work had been done and the west at last lay open for colonial development.

14

THE SEARCH FOR A STABLE
ADMINISTRATION

1. Bute's Resignation: The Grenville Administration

WHETHER George III is to be regarded in the traditional whig view as an eighteenth-century Machiavelli, skilfully playing on the weaknesses of his antagonists, or as a well-intentioned but inexperienced young man floundering among circumstances too difficult for him, the dominating impression of the first ten years of his reign remains one of unstable administrations and shifting political groups. This appearance of mere political intrigue is deceptive; the decade is of fundamental importance. One strand in the pattern of events then woven was the clash of personalities and personal ambitions: Newcastle's pathetic clinging to the hope of office, Pitt's neurotic megalomania, Rockingham's insistence on aristocratic influence, Burke's spinning of constitutional theories, the obstinate determination of the King to do his royal duty as he saw it. The second thread came from the changing economic circumstances- of the post-war period. The East India Company was assuming new territorial responsibilities, for which neither its past history nor its existing machinery of government fitted it. In America growing wealth and growing nationalism were combining to pose new problems in imperial relations. At home new wealth, created by expanding trade, by better agriculture, by more efficient industry, was creating new classes, less and less content with traditional political arrangements. In this decade new standards of responsibility for the government of India, which culminated in the India Act of 1784, new forces mobilized against the Old Colonial System, which contributed to the recognition of American independence in 1783, and a new radicalism in politics, associated half-accidentally with the cry of 'Wilkes and Liberty' were all taking shape.

Basically George III's problem remained the same as his grandfather's: to secure ministers acceptable both to Parliament and to himself. Though he has been accused of deliberately splitting his opponents and breaking them one by one, like sticks from a bundle, it would be truer to say that in his search for a stable administration ministry after ministry broke like rotten sticks in his hand, unable to sustain the weight of this double role. Lord Bute could never be a complete answer to this problem because of his lack of parliamentary support and his personal unpopularity. Nor had he the temperament to enjoy the rough and tumble of a political fight, or to endure the constant pinpricks of being in a minority in the Cabinet. Once the peace treaties had been steered through Parliament Bute lost his nerve and, apparently fearing for his life at the hands of the London mob stirred up by his political enemies, resigned on 8 April 1763.[1] Partly because of circumstances, and partly because of personalities, the business of reconstructing the ministry was not easy. Bute's experience had shown that it was necessary to appoint to high office men who may be described as professional politicians. These, partly as a result of the long Newcastle-Pelham supremacy, were in short supply and had the additional disadvantage of being encumbered with group connections and loyalties.

An attempt was made to secure Pitt, but his resentment against his late colleagues was too great to allow him to act with any of them. Newcastle and his friends would only have come in as a group, but, apart from this disadvantage, George III did not want them. Much against his personal inclination Bute then suggested approaching Henry Fox and when, after toying with the idea, Fox refused, Bute next proposed George Grenville. Both men seem to have assumed that he would raise no objection to the continued close co-operation between the King and his 'dearest friend', though the memory of his obstinacy over the question of Havana should have disabused them of any belief in his pliability. This false assumption on their part was to have serious political consequences. It bred in George Grenville a deep resentment against Bute and long after the latter's influence

[1] Brooke, *op. cit.*, pp. 100–1.

with the King had vanished both Grenville and the Newcastle-Rockingham connection were haunted by the spectre of Bute as 'the minister behind the curtain', and shaped their political conduct accordingly. George III tried to reconstruct the ministry in such a way as to restrict Grenville's influence over it, but because he was indispensable and knew it they were only partially successful. They had hoped to remove Lord Egremont, Grenville's gluttonous brother-in-law, from his office of Secretary, replace him by young Lord Shelburne,[1] at this time a protégé of Bute's, and compensate Egremont with the Presidency of the Council, which Lord Granville's recent death had rendered vacant. To this Grenville would not agree, and finally Halifax and Egremont were left as the two Secretaries, the Admiralty was given to Sandwich, in the hope that the Bedford group would continue to support the administration, and Shelburne went to the Board of Trade. Bedford, however, disliking the very narrow base of the new ministry, resigned the Privy Seal.

2. THE WILKES AFFAIR

Most people seem to have considered the new ministry as a stop gap, not likely to endure long. The King did not like Grenville, the friends of the Duke of Newcastle were his opponents, and he had earned the bitter enmity of Pitt for his desertion of the 'cousinhood'. If therefore he, by some blunder of ill-considered action, should provide the politicians in opposition with a topic on which they could unite and carry Pitt with them, he might expect trouble. This opportunity was very soon provided by the affair of John Wilkes. Though most people had welcomed the end of the war, Bute's opponents had managed to whip up a virulent attack, both vocally and in the press, against the peace. Of this campaign the notorious article in No. 45 of the *North Briton*[2] was an extreme example. John Wilkes, the owner and editor of the paper was M.P. for Aylesbury. He was a man of strong personality, a fighter by instinct and, in spite of a middle-class, mercantile background, the

---

[1] Two recent appraisals of Shelburne as a statesman and reformer, including details of his early political career are to be found in John Norris, *Shelburne and Reform* (1963), and P. Brown, *The Chathamites* (1967), pp. 67–108.

[2] The *North Briton* was founded in 1762 to attack the administration, and from the beginning Wilkes, as co-editor with Charles Churchill, had done so with audacious brilliance. For details of his career see G. Rudé, *Wilkes and Liberty* (1962) and C. P. C. Trench, *Portrait of a Patriot* (1962).

friend of men like Sandwich and Dashwood. Like them he was a member of the secret and reputedly licentious Medmenham Society. At first sight he hardly seemed to be the stuff of which martyrs, even political ones, were made. He had attached himself to Temple and the tone of his journal, which first appeared in June 1762, was in consequence anti-Bute. In his speech from the throne George III had described the peace as 'honourable to my Crown and beneficial to my people'. Wilkes took advantage of the accepted constitutional convention that the speech was not a personal expression of the King's opinions but the work of his ministers, and attacked it in No. 45 as 'the most abandoned instance of ministerial effrontery'. By the date of its publication, which was 23 April, Bute had resigned, but Grenville, Halifax and Egremont had all been members of the Cabinet during the final peace negotiation;[1] nor could they pass over in silence the veiled insult to the King. It was therefore decided to issue a general warrant for the arrest of the authors, printers and publishers of the offensive article. This was done under the authority of Lord Halifax as Secretary of State by a general warrant, a procedure which had developed under the Licensing Acts of Charles II and James II and which, despite their lapse in 1693 had continued without the question of their legality being raised.[2] General warrants were a convenient way of proceeding against a group of printers and publishers as no specific names were required. Philip Carteret Webb, Solicitor to the Treasury, assured Halifax that such warrants were sufficiently hallowed by precedent to be legal. It was less clear whether parliamentary privilege extended to seditious libel. Charles Yorke, the Attorney General, was of the opinion that it did not. Accordingly the administration went ahead.

In doing so they landed themselves in a situation which was to have important repercussions on English political life for years to come. They had also provided the opposition with a cause for which to fight. Wilkes was arrested, interviewed by the two Secretaries, and committed a close prisoner to the Tower. Immediately the opposition championed his cause; Temple moved for a writ of *habeas corpus* in the Court of Common Pleas, where Pitt's friend Charles Pratt was Lord Chief Justice. Pratt's views with regard to liberty were whiggish and in his Court, if anywhere, Wilkes was

[1] It is easier to follow the sequence of events if it is remembered that 45 *North Briton* appeared on 23 April, on the 26th the general warrant was ready, on 3 and 6 May the case was heard before Chief Justice Pratt.

[2] See I. R. Christie, *Myth and Reality*, p. 199.

likely to get a favourable verdict. In London, where Pitt's close associate Alderman Beckford was influential,[1] Wilkes's cause was taken up with great enthusiasm, an enthusiasm stimulated by the fact that he was to prove himself a first-rate showman, using every art of publicity to parade his wrongs. When therefore on 6 May Sir Charles Pratt discharged him on the ground that parliamentary privilege covered all offences except treason, felony and a breach of the peace, his release was greeted with wild rejoicings. Wilkes now became a popular hero. There was little that ministers could do until Parliament met, but unfortunately neither Grenville nor George III had the wisdom to realize that having stirred up a hornet's nest their best course was to let it settle again without further provocation. Instead they decided to start a prosecution for seditious libel in the Court of King's Bench, presided over by the more reliable Lord Mansfield.

Though the King and Grenville were in accord over Wilkes he failed to win the royal confidence.[2] They did not work easily together and the King spent the late spring and summer in political probes to find an alternative. His first attempts were to detach Lord Hardwicke from the opposition and to persuade him to accept the vacant Presidency of the Council. This would at least have introduced another element into the Cabinet, leaving Grenville in a less dominant position. Hardwicke, however, refused to be separated from his friends. When another attempt was baited with the suggestion that one of the great Court offices might be bestowed on Newcastle, Hardwicke made it plain that neither of them would come in without Pitt, with whom they had lately been reconciled. Attempts to negotiate with Bedford and Pitt were no more successful. Bedford had no objection to acting with Pitt, but suspected that Bute might still remain the minister 'behind the curtain'. Pitt refused to enter

---

[1] Beckford was an interesting character. Miss L. S. Sutherland, *The City of London and Opposition to Government, 1768–74* (The Creighton Lecture in History, 1958, p. 9), summarizes his career as 'Beckford, when he first stood for the City, was a man of some note and experience in parliamentary opposition . . . he was the first politician of some experience outside the City to see its value as a backing for his personal power. . . . As Pitt's supporter he played the chief part in forging the links between the City and the great war minister; and in and after his mayoralty he encouraged their support of John Wilkes, though there was even then no love lost between the two men.'

[2] 'Lord B. once told Mr. J. that the original cause of the King's displeasure with Mr. G. was the violence he used in endeavouring to extort everything from him.'— N. S. Jucker, *The Jenkinson Papers 1760–66* (1949), p. 399. See J. Brooke, *op. cit.*, pp. 105–9 for an analysis of the relations between Grenville and the King.

an administration which contained Bedford because of his attitude over the Peace of Paris. After these failures George III seems to have resigned himself to the situation. Then on 21 August Egremont died. He had never been much more than an outwork of Grenville's power and his death was important only in that it gave the King another opportunity to reconstruct the ministry.

This time, through Bute, he opened direct negotiations with Pitt, whose conduct since his resignation had rekindled some of the regard with which George III had once held him. Apart from his opposition to the Peace of Paris Pitt had kept himself aloof from all factious opposition and connection; if he came in it would be as an individual not as a member of a group. At first the conversations went well. On 27 August it was apparently agreed that Pitt should return to his old office as Secretary, with Charles Townshend as his colleague. Newcastle was to be Lord Privy Seal, Hardwicke Lord President, his young friend the Marquis of Rockingham was to have the Admiralty, and Devonshire was to be restored to his old office of Lord Chamberlain. There would have been much to be said for this arrangement. It would have reconciled the King and the Newcastle whigs without fettering him. Moreover, Pitt showed compliance with the royal wishes that places should be found for some of Bute's friends and relations. The one stipulation on which he did insist was that no one should hold office who had been directly responsible for the hated peace treaty. Apparently Pitt thought that this meeting had been decisive. To his surprise, and to the chagrin of Newcastle, when Pitt saw George III two days later the whole atmosphere had changed. Where the King had seemed all co-operation and compliance, he now spoke of his honour being involved, abruptly breaking off the conversation with the remark, 'Well, Mr. Pitt, I see this won't do.' Why George III changed his mind has never been quite clear; Pitt himself was surprised and baffled. One interesting suggestion is that his stand against anyone who was responsible for the Peace of Paris may have alarmed the King for Bute's sake.[1]

The result was to leave George III more than ever at the mercy of Grenville. Shelburne, who had played an active part in the late

[1] D. A. Winstanley, *Personal and Party Government 1760-66* (1910), pp. 176-83. On 10 April 1763 George III had written to Bute: 'I can never receive the Ds of New. and Dev., men who would have ruin'd my D. Friend if they could, my honour and my real friendship for the best of men make that impossible.'—*Letters from George III* . . . Here too the stress is on his honour.

negotiations, felt forced to resign. Lord Mansfield, too, asked to be excused from attending the Cabinet. These vacancies had to be filled and the ministry strengthened, if it were to carry on. The various attempts of the last few months had shown that the best hope of doing this lay in attracting the Bedford group, one member of which, Lord Sandwich, was already at the Admiralty. Bedford, approached once more, agreed to accept the Presidency of the Council, Lord Sandwich was promoted to the vacant Secretaryship, Lord Egmont became First Lord of the Admiralty, and Shelburne's office was filled by Lord Hillsborough. This turned out to have been an unlucky choice, for Hillsborough's handling of American affairs was far from happy. In this way the vacancies were filled, but whether the administration was much strengthened is problematical: the Cabinet was now divided into two groups, Grenville and Halifax, and Bedford and his friends.

When Parliament met on 15 November the most controversial business was the Wilkes affair. Neither Grenville nor George III was prepared to let the matter of the 45 *North Briton* drop. At the beginning of the session Lord North, in one of his first contributions to the political conflicts of his age, moved that No. 45 was 'a false, scandalous and seditious libel'. In order to bring it within the limits of treason it was also stated in the resolution that it was likely to excite the people to 'traitorous insurrections against his majesty's government'. This was carried by 237 votes to 111. It was in many ways an important debate, both for its consequences and for the light that it shed on contemporary political groupings. It is often suggested by champions of Wilkes, and by sympathizers with the whig position, that its result was due to the royal influence over the placemen in the Commons, and that it represented a truckling to that influence. Undoubtedly the influence of the Crown was thrown against Wilkes; the way in which the debate was introduced left no doubt as to the royal wishes. But many of the independent members of the House must have felt with the King and his ministers that No. 45 was indeed a 'false, scandalous and seditious libel' and been quite willing to see it condemned as such. The clamour that the London mob had raised of 'Wilkes and Liberty' was no recommendation to them.[1] The debate was also interesting in that it

---

[1] Between 1763 and 1774 there was a series of bad harvests. As a result the price of food was high and there was considerable rioting and disorder among the poor. Signs of social insubordination, even when unconnected with political issues, always tended to rally the property-owning classes behind the government.

revealed the difficulties and divisions of the opposition. Here a conflict of personalities and personal ambitions was entangled with matters of principle. [1] The opposition—or, if the term is preferred, the 'outs'—were, like the administration, divided into two groups. On the one hand were Newcastle, Hardwicke, Devonshire, Rockingham; on the other, Pitt with his few followers, and Temple. Newcastle, who knew the political game thoroughly, was convinced that without a close alliance with Pitt there was no hope of making a significant reduction in the government's majorities. Accordingly throughout the summer he had been anxiously cultivating more friendly relations with him, and endeavouring to find common ground on which concerted resistance to ministers might be offered.

It was a difficult task. Pitt still accepted the political convention that organized opposition was faction. Though all politicians paid lip service to this theory, practical men like Newcastle knew that, without continuous attack by men who acted together as a group, ministers who held the confidence of the Crown could never be unseated. To this difference of outlook was added the clashing interests of friends: Charles Yorke and Sir Charles Pratt both had the Woolsack as their ultimate ambition. The former was the second son of Lord Hardwicke; he had been Attorney-General in the Grenville administration until, extremely reluctantly, he had been persuaded by family pressure to resign in the interests of a united oppposition. Sir Charles Pratt, before whom Wilkes had appeared in Common Pleas, was the friend of Pitt. This rivalry, with each side pressing its own candidate, was further complicated because when Yorke had been Attorney-General he had advised the ministry that seditious libel was not covered by parliamentary privilege. This difference of opinion on a legal matter made it very difficult for Wilkes's supporters to act in concert. In the relevant debate Pitt supported the view that seditious libel was covered by parliamentary privilege; Yorke, though now out of office, supported the government in accordance with his previously expressed judgment. Yorke's life, torn as he was between the political interests of his friends and family and his own legal ambitions, was from this

---

[1] Pitt to Grafton, 5 Nov. 1765: 'All I can say is this; *that I move only in the sphere of measures*. Quarrels at Court, or family reconciliations shall never vary my fixed judgment of things. Those who, with me, have stood by the cause of liberty and the national honour upon true revolutionary principles will never find me against them, until they fall off, and do not act up to those principles.'—*Autobiography and Political Correspondence of Augustus Henry, third Duke of Grafton*, ed. Sir William R. Anson (1898), p. 61.

time a long-drawn-out tragedy of indecision and frustration. Pitt's declaration in the course of the debate that he stood alone was a signal of hope to the administration and of despair to the Newcastle whigs.

In dealing with Wilkes the ministers were further strengthened by the use they were able to make of his private life. Women and wine and scurrilous verse, if not song, had played a considerable part in it. In particular a parody of Pope's *Essay on Man*, entitled *Essay on Woman*, the tone and contents of which took full advantage of eighteenth-century freedom of expression, had been privately printed for circulation among his friends. To it had been appended notes purporting to be by Bishop Warburton. By somewhat dubious means the ministers had got hold of a copy, which they now used in a clever smear campaign to destroy the reputation of the popular hero. On the ground that the *Essay* libelled Warburton, Bishop of Gloucester and a member of the Lords, Sandwich drew their attention to the matter. It was a remarkable scene. Everyone knew Sandwich's own reputation in such matters, and that he and Le Despenser, the title revived for Dashwood on his elevation to the peerage as a reward for being one of Britain's most incompetent Chancellors of the Exchequer, had been close cronies of Wilkes at Medmenham. The spectacle of Sandwich solemnly reading out with shocked horror to an eagerly listening House obscenities at which he may well have laughed at earlier and more convivial gatherings, did his own reputation no good, however great the damage he inflicted on that of his quondam friend. It has, however, been suggested that Sandwich had some justification for his apparent disloyalty in that a No. 46 *North Briton*, containing a virulent attack on Sandwich which the latter as Secretary of State had probably seen, had first been printed and then destroyed by Wilkes when the warrant for his arrest had been issued. Whatever Sandwich's motives the House duly voted the Essay 'a most scandalous, obscene and impious libel'. Outside the House this did Wilkes a great deal of harm. Because social conventions in the eighteenth century permitted a frankness of expression and behaviour not to be experienced again before the emergence of the so called 'permissive society', it is often forgotten that the *Essay on Woman* was as unacceptable to the decent, solid substratum of the middling sort as it would be today to the attackers of pornography.[1] It became more difficult to cham-

[1] B. G. Martelli, *Jemmy Twitcher* (1962), pp. 64-6.

pion Wilkes in public after Sandwich's revelations. Wilkes was also in personal difficulties. He had been involved in a duel with another member of the House, Samuel Martin, in which he had been seriously wounded. He was therefore unable to attend the debate on parliamentary privilege and seditious libel. As the motion so vitally concerned him it was postponed once to give him time to recover. By the 23 December, however, when he was still unable to be in his place, it was decided to proceed with the question without him. As usual the ministers had a comfortable majority, but for once the opposition found itself acting in harmony, for Charles Yorke, as well as Pitt, thought the discussion should have been put off once more. Unfortunately this harmony was brief indeed, for on the motion, which was debated the following day, Charles Yorke spoke as violently for the motion as Pitt attacked it. From an opposition so divided the ministers had little to fear. The result was a foregone conclusion: it was affirmed that seditious libel was not covered by parliamentary privilege. Yet even in these unhappy circumstances Newcastle and his friends did gain one valuable recruit, for General Conway voted against the motion, as he had done against the earlier one denouncing No. 45 as a seditious libel.

Wilkes was now liable to prosecution in the courts and in face of this threat he slipped away to France at the end of December. While he was in Paris visiting his daughter his health broke down, and he sent this as an explanation to the Speaker of the House when he did not return to oppose the motion for his expulsion in January 1764. The ministers supposed that they had now disposed of Wilkes, but they were in fact nearer to defeat than they had ever been, for at last the opposition found one aspect of his case on which they were all united. This was the question of general warrants. In the case which Wilkes had brought against the Under-Secretary Wood, Pratt had declared general warrants illegal and had awarded £1,000 to Wilkes. The opposition now decided to raise the matter in Parliament. For once there was no legal difference between them. Yorke declared that he had not seen the general warrant which had been used against the printers and publishers of the 45 *North Briton*, and that it had not had his approval. In consequence both Newcastle's friends and Pitt were able to act together. This was, however, to some extent flogging a dying horse: legal opinion was swinging against their use and when the Opposition brought the matter before Parliament in 1764 George

Grenville had himself declared that if the Courts did not curtail the practice, which was at the moment *sub judice*, he would not oppose the introduction of a law to do so.[1] On the motion to adjourn the debate the ministry only just scraped home by ten votes. It is an instructive occasion. For once all the main members in opposition were in agreement and the debate had been carefully organized; but that is not the entire explanation. The unity between Pitt and Newcastle could not have produced such a marked drop in government votes unless by their arguments they had been able to convince the independent members. To argue that the influence of the Crown was enough to carry the earlier measures against Wilkes by such a large majority, means explaining also their failure to achieve the same result over general warrants. Probably the earlier successes of the government and their near failure on 15 February were both due to the prejudices of the independent members. They did not approve of Wilkes or respect him as a man and what he had written seemed to many of them outrageous. Equally they were always suspicious of ministerial power and the misuse of the executive. They liked general warrants as little as they liked standing armies, and expressed this dislike by the votes they gave.

Newcastle and Pitt, acting in conjunction, were never to be so near success again. Some of the blame for their failure to follow up their success may be attributed to their own bad tactics. Hardwicke died in March, and all the energies of his friends were diverted to securing the Chancellorship of the University of Cambridge, which, he had held, for his son Lord Royston, who was opposed by Lord Sandwich. But even if there had not been this distraction it is difficult to know what they could have done. It was not possible to go on discussing general warrants and whipping up feeling over them for ever, as they were to discover when they tried to follow this course later. Nor was it easy to discover another cause which would appeal so greatly to the independent members that they would either be regular in their attendance or vote against the King's ministers. The administration might lack outstanding figures like Pitt, it might be unpopular with the City and the mob, but it was perfectly competent to carry on the daily routine of government unless George III was prepared to plunge again into the work of reconstruction. Also George Grenville shone as a Chancellor of the Exchequer, particularly in comparison with some of his predecessors. His budget,

---

[1] I. R. Christie, *Myth and Reality*, p. 203.

introduced on 9 March 1764, was a popular one in that he made a
point of not increasing taxation.[1] So long as the King was content,
and the country gentlemen were content there was really very little
that Newcastle could do. Moreover, the breach between him and
Pitt was widening once again. Pitt was disgusted that the attack had
not been pressed home; physically he was badly in need of a rest,
and the bequest of the country estate of Burton Pynsent in Somerset,
worth some £3,000 a year, which came to him under the will of Sir
William Pynsent, engaged his attention. For the next two years he
played little part in politics. The opposition did, however, gain a
new recruit in General Conway who, as soon as the session was over,
was dismissed from the Bedchamber and the colonelcy of the Royal
Dragoons for his votes in the debates on Wilkes and general warrants.[2] Shelburne, because he was not prepared to assent to the
curtailment of parliamentary privilege, was dismissed from his office
of aide-de-camp to the King, and Calcraft, the army agent, lost his
post as Deputy Commissary General. With Hardwicke dead, Charles
Yorke still hankering after the Great Seal, Charles Townshend
calculating his future chances, and Pitt in semi-retirement, George
Grenville could look back, despite the hazards of February, with
some satisfaction over the past session.

The political scene was not to remain calm for long. In the early
spring of 1765 the King became seriously ill. Rumour suggested 'a
decline', or in modern usage consumption. There was no suggestion,
later fostered by historians, of mental illness; what was feared was
death not insanity. It was for this reason that after his recovery it
seemed prudent to make some legal provision for a Regency, in view
of the fact that if George III should die young he would only leave
an infant son to succeed him. Unfortunately difficulties arose over
the terms of the bill. For family reasons George III did not want to
name the Regent in the proposed act, wishing to reserve that right
to himself. Grenville, always suspicious, took this as an indication
that the King meant to insert his mother's name, with the intention
that should he die Lord Bute, through her, would once again
dominate the political scene. Nothing apparently was farther from
his mind. The Hanoverians were obsessed by a fear of a 'wicked

---

[1] S. Maccoby, *English Radicalism, 1762–85* (1955), suggests that the government pam-
phleteers were assiduous in getting it a good press and that it was bitterly attacked by
opposition writers as mere window dressing. David Huntley, who published 'The
Budget' in September 1764 was a friend of Rockingham's.

[2] This was on 19 April, the day that Parliament was prorogued.

uncle' re-enacting the role of Richard III and the Princes in the Tower, and as a consequence George III was anxious neither to name his brother, Edward Duke of York, nor to cause trouble by pointedly excluding him. Unfortunately Grenville was ignorant of the King's real motives and persuaded him to accept an amendment in the House of Lords worded in such a way as to exclude the Dowager Princess. When later George III realized the slight that inadvertently he had allowed to be offered to his mother he asked Grenville to re-insert her name when the bill was debated in the Commons. Grenville demurred and made difficulties, which proved to have been quite unnecessary, for Lord Northington, the Chancellor, easily arranged for a private member to move the necessary amendment, which was accepted without a division. Over the ministerial handling of this matter the King was justifiably annoyed; he showed less interest and no disapproval over an Act that was to have much graver consequences. This was the Stamp Act, which Grenville proposed in February 1765. It was accepted by most members as a sound measure. Not its passing but its repeal was to be the subject of acrimonious debates, and its substance is probably better discussed then. When it passed few people realized that it was to be a landmark in the relations between Great Britain and her colonies, whereas sagacious politicians might well have regarded the affair of the Regency bill as likely to herald another attempt on the part of George III to get rid of his ungracious ministers.

This was made in May. Even before the crisis of the Regency Bill the King's uncle, the Duke of Cumberland, an able and experienced politician, who however had been under something of a cloud since the unfortunate episode of the Convention of Klosterzeven, had been summoned to Court and asked to sound out the opposition on the possibility of forming a new administration. Grenville's attitude over the Regency Bill had made George III even more anxious to get rid of him but Cumberland's first efforts to find a replacement were wrecked by Pitt's unreasonable demands and attitude. The result of this failure was to place the King in an almost impossible position. He had made his dislike of his ministers so plain that they were almost ready to resign in a body: if they did, George III, owing to Pitt's unhelpfulness, had no one with whom to replace them. He had therefore, almost as a suppliant, to ask them to remain in office. They consented but on their own terms. These included the dismissal of Henry Fox, now Lord Holland, from the Pay Office and, what

George III minded more because he felt that his honour was involved, the dismissal of Bute's brother, the Hon. James Stuart Mackenzie, from the Privy Seal of Scotland, which the King had promised him for life. To accept these terms was a personal humiliation, but George III had no choice; he could find no one else to head an administration. George Grenville was not good at forgiving; neither was George III. The former was determined to teach the King a lesson but, unfortunately for his own political future, the moral which George III drew from it was that he must not fail again.

Once more he turned to Pitt, requesting him that despite the gout he would wait on the King at Buckingham House. On this occasion the direct conversations between the two men were amiable. George III realized that he would have to make concessions and agreed to meet Pitt more than half-way. General warrants were to be condemned, Pratt was to be Chancellor, policy towards America, where by now the resistance of the colonists to the Stamp Act had aroused Pitt's sympathies, was to be more conciliatory, and if possible an alliance was to be made with Prussia and Russia. Pitt in return showed himself complaisant towards the royal wish to reinstate Mackenzie, and was obviously unwilling to heap personal humiliations on the King or to surround him with men whom he disliked. Moreover, both George III and Pitt agreed on the fettering action of connection; representatives of the great whig families were to be restored to office, for the practical reason that Pitt had no large personal following of his own and the whigs were the nearest political allies to whom he could look for fellow ministers. But, to make sure that they came in as individuals and that the administration should not be dominated by them, Pitt asked, and the King agreed, that Temple should take the Treasury. Pitt was to have his old office as Secretary. So far there had been no direct negotiations with Newcastle and his friends, for both Pitt and George III felt sure of their co-operation and, after the failure of May, the King was not willing to offend Pitt's touchy self-regard by negotiating with anyone else until he had been secured. The ministry, if it were formed, was to be unmistakably Pitt's. There was unfortunately one man who objected to this predominance—Temple. Possibly because he realized that Pitt would be the real first minister, ostensibly because he argued that Pitt's health would not permit him to take an effective share in the management of the Commons, Temple refused to take the Treasury. For George III it was a bitter blow, because

Pitt professed himself unable to accept office without his brother-in-law. His reasons for this decision are not clear. Though he owed Temple both gratitude and affection, neither of these forbade his taking office without him. In fact there was frequent strain between the two men which Hester Pitt had to smooth over. Nor was Temple of outstanding ability: on the contrary he was often dictatorial and difficult. It has therefore been argued that Pitt's dependence on Temple was not so much personal as strategic. By now it had become an accepted convention that the First Lord of the Treasury was the head of the administration. Pitt was not prepared to undertake the burden of the Treasury himself and without Temple he may have felt that the new ministry would have been too much under Cumberland's influence. Whatever his reasons George III made desperate efforts to make him change his mind, even calling him 'My Friend' and alluding to his own 'present distress'. Pitt wrote back with 'a heart overflowing with duty and gratitude', but still refused to come in without Temple. The King's position was now, if possible, worse than ever; he was determined not to ask Grenville to stay on, even if the latter would have consented to do so. Once again he turned to his uncle for help in forming a new administration. With Grenville and the Bedfords in opposition and Pitt standing aloof this was a matter of some difficulty: experienced politicians were in short supply.

3. THE ROCKINGHAM ADMINISTRATION[1]

Cumberland's choice for the First Lord of the Treasury was the Marquis of Rockingham, by whose name the ministry is usually known though in reality and in the opinion of contemporaries the Duke himself, until his death in October 1765, was its directing and dominating mind: he was 'the head and soul of it all'. He attended Cabinet meetings, though he held no office, and no major decisions were taken without prior consultation with him. Rockingham accepted the role assigned to him with genuine reluctance and surprise. He had no natural aptitude for the political game. He suffered from an almost total inability to speak in Parliament, where he rarely opened his mouth, he was deficient in political nerve when faced by a crisis and he was too indolent and unpunctual ever to be a good man of business. Nevertheless he could act with a certain obstinate resolution once his mind was made up, though too frequently he was obsessed with anti-Bute prejudices and with the

[1] For a recent appraisal see Paul Langford, *The First Rockingham Administration* (1973).

determination to preserve his own reputation for consistency at all costs to display that opportunist flexibility which the political situation demanded. Only in the particular circumstances that confronted George III, even in the conditions that prevailed in eighteenth century English politics could such a man have been asked to fill so onerous an office, for which neither he nor his abilities really fitted him. Only in the conditions that prevailed in eighteenth-century English politics could such a man ever have attained to an office of such responsibility, for which neither his ability nor his experience really fitted him. A sense of what he owed to his position had driven him into political life[1]; his power was essentially territorial. He had wide estates in Ireland and was one of the great Yorkshire landowners: in 1761 his estates were estimated to produce a rent roll of £24,000 a year. His interests were those of a country gentleman. Arthur Young, describing him as one of the great improving landlords of the North, declared that he 'never saw the advantages of a great fortune applied more nobly to the improvement of a country'; and it was typical of his outlook that his early parliamentary activities should have been concerned with the championing of the interests of the Yorkshire wool-growers. He was devoted to the Turf and an active member of the newly-formed Jockey Club, as well as being deeply involved in the promotion of the Doncaster and York race meetings. It was characteristic both of him and of his age that much important political business was transacted at his table and on the racecourse. In these ways he was a representative member of the aristocracy on which whig principles had conferred the responsibility of political power. His father had been a supporter of the Newcastle-Pelham group, to whom he had owed his advancement in the peerage, and young Rockingham had been *persona grata* to both the elderly Duke and the ageing King. It was from such sources that his influence was derived; his political experience before he found himself functioning as First Lord of the Treasury had been limited to the office of a Lord of the Bedchamber and the Lord Lieutenancy of the West Riding. The first post he had resigned as a protest against George III's action in striking out the

---

[1] G. H. Guttridge, *The Early Career of Lord Rockingham, 1736–65* (1952), p. 47: '. . . howsoever unsuitable I might be for that office from my health and inexperience in that sort of business, yet I thought it incumbent on me to acquiesce in the attempting it, rather than throw any fresh confusion into the negotiation, which had but too many difficulties without my adding to them by a refusal which my own private ease and comfort would no doubt strongly have inclined me to'.

name of the Duke of Devonshire from the list of his Privy Councillors, and from the second he was dismissed in the purge that
followed Newcastle's opposition to the Peace of Paris. His deficiencies were to some degree to be corrected by the lucky recommendation of Edmund Burke as a suitable man to become his private
secretary.[1]

Such was the man who at the age of thirty-five became the first
minister of the Crown. Apart from the aged and querulous Duke of
Newcastle, who became Lord Privy Seal, and whose advice was
generally ignored by his young colleagues, none of the new ministers
had held high office previously. General Conway, an honest likeable man with a paralysing capacity to see both sides of any question,
had only acted as secretary to the Lord Lieutenant of Ireland before
assuming the dual roles of Secretary and Leader of the House of
Commons, a task for which he lacked the requisite firmness. The
other Secretary, the Duke of Grafton, was even younger than
Rockingham, and like him a keen member of the Jockey Club.
Dowdeswell, who went to the Exchequer, was by contrast at least
a sound politician and good man of business. Charles Yorke was
finally persuaded to return to his old office of Attorney-General on
the promise of the Woolsack within the year, but in general the new
men appointed to the lesser offices were an undistinguished team.
Mediocracy and inexperience were not the only difficulties with
which Rockingham had to contend: he could command the loyalty
of only a part of the administration over which he presided. Though
many of the 'Old Whigs' who had suffered in the political purge of
1762–63 were re-instated or compensated, and though Grenville's
closest associates had been removed that nucleus of the ministry
whose political loyalty had always been to the Crown rather than to
Grenville, still remained. Lord Egmont continued at the Admiralty,
Lord Northington retained the Lord Chancellorship. Both these

---

[1] Burke's opinion of his new employment, contained in a letter written to Charles
O'Hara, 11 July 1765, was: 'I have got an employment of a kind humble enough; but
which may be worked into some sort of consideration, or at least advantage; Private
Secretary to Lord Rockingham, who has the reputation of a man of honour and integ-
rity; and with whom, they say, it is not difficult to live.'—*The Correspondence of Edmund
Burke*, vol. I, 1744-68, edited by T. W. Copeland (1958), p. 211. Since its foundation
in 1758 Burke had been editor of the *Annual Register*, but because of the contemporary
prejudice against journalists he never formally admitted his connection with the paper.
For a scholarly scrutiny of the evidence consult T. W. Copeland, *Edmund Burke: Six
Essays* (1950), ch. 3.

men, together with many of the lesser office holders who had been allowed to retain their places in spite of the 'Old Whigs' drive against Bute and his friends, represented a potential danger in that they neither liked Rockingham's views nor owed him any personal allegiance. With this weak and divided team Rockingham had to face the powerful opposition of the Grenvilles and the Bedfords. Without political allies he and his friends were neither strong enough nor numerous enough in Parliament to do this successfully. Nevertheless during the first months of their administration their position was relatively secure. George III was prepared to give them his full, if not personally enthusiastic, support, while Cumberland's authority was sufficient to keep both wings of the administration together. With his death the situation changed.

Rockingham could no longer rely on the members who were coming to be known as 'the King's Friends' and whose political affiliations were rather with Bute's previous administration. Political realism would have dictated that Rockingham now made some concrete move to secure their support. A judicious distribution of offices and above all an offer to re-instate Mackenzie in his old office of Privy Seal for Scotland would have gone far both to achieve this and to strengthen their influence in the Closet. Unfortunately for the success of his administration the Marquis's prejudices were too strong, moreover to make a firm alliance with men whom in opposition he had condemned smacked of inconsistency. Instead he placed his hopes on securing the co-operation of Pitt. From the beginning of the Rockingham administration ministers had been obsessed by the conviction that this must be done. Grafton indeed had only joined the ministry on this condition; Conway too was a Pittite. Every attention had been paid to the 'Great Man'; his opinions had been sought on many occasions and in every way they had angled for his favour. Because he could see little chance of forming an alternative administration George III gave his consent to negotiations being opened in January 1766 but he was irritated and annoyed and though he continued to support the ministry he did so with increasing coolness. Yet the ministry had to deal with a crisis that was rapidly becoming serious in America—a highly contentious issue in which they found themselves in disagreement both with the King and, though on different grounds, with Pitt. Dissensions within and difficulties without were to make the ministry's life a short one. But though short it was not unimportant because to it fell the handling of the American colonial dispute. This was a legacy from the previous ministry, which had persuaded Parliament to approve Grenville's Stamp Act in order to obtain from the American colonies some contribution to the heavy expenses which extended responsibilities were bringing to the mother country.

4. THE STAMP ACT

When the Seven Years War came to an end few people realized that a new era in British colonial history was beginning. By 1763 the American colonies had reached the point of maturity at which they were no longer incapable of managing their own affairs. The Peace of Paris had taken the burden of fear from them, for the remaining Spanish settlements constituted no danger. They began to regard themselves as largely the authors of their own salvation and it was now that the American legend grew of incompetent British leaders and valiant colonial troops. This feeling of independence and self-sufficiency was fostered by their growing prosperity. Unfortunately this increasing wealth was to play a considerable part in bedevilling their relations with the mother country. Since much of it could be attributed to the success of the late war it seemed reasonable that the colonies should make some contribution to the new burdens of empire. Though the French had been driven out, British statesmen were convinced that America could not be left without some degree of military protection. In taking over the French claims to the hinterland, the British had taken over the problem of Indian relations in those areas.[1] In spite of the proclamation of 1763 which had promised to respect the claims of the Indians beyond the Appalachians, suspicion had driven the tribes into a great revolt. Clearly if control was to be maintained over restive Indians and reluctant French settlers there must be garrisons stationed at strategic posts. As Britain had borne the greater part of the expenses of the late war and had even appropriated £1,150,000 between 1756 and 1763 to re-imburse colonial governments for their expenditure, it seemed a little hard if she had to go on incurring expenses that were primarily for American interests.[2] Yet the problem of how to divert some of the stream of American prosperity without causing more than minor friction was to prove insoluble.

This was because of the way in which the colonies had been

[1] See I. R. Christie, *Crisis of Empire*, pp. 23–6.

[2] B. Donoughue, *British Politics and the American Revolution* (1964) points out that this had been an important issue since the mid 1750s.

fitted into the British economy. From their beginnings they had been intended as a stimulant to British trade and an important factor in the economic self-sufficiency at which she aimed. In this there was a less degree of exploitation, in the sense in which modern opinion uses and condemns that word, than is always realized. Though major British interests were paramount there was no intention of riding roughshod over colonial interests; the two economies were often dovetailed together with considerable patience and skill. If colonial products were deliberately directed to British markets they received preferential treatment there, by way either of lower duties or of bounties. If the requirements of the colonists had to be met from the products of English industry there were few markets in which, in view of the expansion of British industry in the eighteenth century, they could have been bought more cheaply. The very prosperity of America is proof that the trade laws were far from intolerable. In 1763 this relationship was accepted on both sides of the Atlantic; it was, though in a more liberal form than some, the normal pattern of mother country-colony relationship of the eighteenth century. Such a control of imperial trade inevitably meant a good deal of legislation which was largely financial in character. Some of this was concerned more with direction than taxation; for instance, certain commodities, such as tobacco, rice, molasses, rum, naval stores, beaver skins and other furs, could be sent only to England. Though such a canalization of important products was of advantage to British merchants it was not directly a financial measure. Much of the manipulation of trade was, however, effected by the imposition of duties, though the primary reason for these was not supposed to be revenue but the securing of a balanced and self-sufficient economy for the empire as a whole. As such it was accepted by the colonists. Money required for internal administration was granted by the Lower Houses of the colonial legislatures, though this might include such items as the payment of the governor's salary and other governmental functions. There was therefore a clear distinction in the minds of the colonists between what the Parliament at Westminster might do and what was the business of their own Assemblies in the matter of raising funds.

To Grenville fell the task of trying to ease the strain of the post-war years on the British taxpayer. The bitter resistance to the Cider Tax of the previous year had illustrated the difficulty of finding any fresh source of revenue which could be tapped without social tumult. If money could be found from American sources it would ease the situation considerably. At first Grenville looked only to a more effective use of the laws of trade. Here there was a good deal of slack which could be taken up, for the Customs duties, owing to extensive smuggling, were not yielding anything approaching the sums that they should, particularly in the New England colonies. If smuggling was a constant leak in the English revenue system it was a gaping hole in the American. Officials were often non-resident and their American deputies were notoriously venal. The Molasses Act that was supposed to regulate the trade between the New England colonies and the French West Indies was very largely ignored. Even during the crisis of the late French wars, when the success or failure of campaigns often turned on questions of logistics, trading with the enemy went on wholesale. Pitt exhorted colonial governors again and again to use all their efforts to stop it, but so deeply was the merchants' prosperity bound up with the practice that not until he used the ships of the navy to cut off and round up ships with illicit cargoes, and the Vice-Admiralty courts, which acted without a jury, to condemn them, did he get the contraband trade under control. Once wartime restrictions and efforts were relaxed, smuggling operations on the old scale began again and in New England, New York and Pennsylvania legal imports dropped sharply. Grenville's immediate reaction was to tighten the administration of the Customs in America and order the ships of the navy in those waters to use their best endeavours, which would be sharpened by the hopes of forfeitures of the captured contraband, to stop the trade. As by now smuggling had become almost a prescriptive right of even respectable merchants, news of these orders was received with both alarm and anger.

From the point of view of smooth imperial relations it was unfortunate that Walpole's Molasses Act was also due to expire. In view of Grenville's obvious determination to enforce the trade laws a widespread colonial campaign was started to demonstrate that the heavy duties imposed by the Act, namely 6*d*. per gallon for molasses, 9*d*. for rum and 5*s*. for a cwt. of sugar, were ruinous and if enforced would both strike at the manufacture of rum and prevent those people who now sold New England its necessary molasses from buying from them the provisions and lumber which were the foundation of the colonists' foreign trade. The campaign was skilful and probably influenced Charles Townshend, who was then First

Commissioner at the Board of Trade in place of Shelburne, to suggest that in the new act the duty should be reduced from 6*d*. to 2*d*. per gallon for the vital molasses. Against such a reduction, however, the British planters in the West Indies were certain to protest, as giving them too little protection from unfair competition. There was some justification for their attitude, for not only were the French islands subsidized by their home government but, as they were not allowed to export rum or molasses to France for fear of the injury it might do to the consumption of brandy, they had to dispose of their molasses, which was a by-product of their sugar manufactory, wherever and at whatever price they could. The Sugar Act in its final form attempted to strike a balance between all the different interests. The duty on molasses was lowered to 3*d*. a gallon and the New England distillers protected by the prohibition of foreign rum. To compensate the West Indian planters for this lower protection, foreign sugar imported into a colony was now to pay not 5*s*. but £1. 7*s*. o*d*. per cwt. Duties were also imposed on foreign wines, coffee, indigo and pimento, and on various East India Company fabrics. As some indigo was produced by the Southern colonies, they too were receiving a measure of special consideration. By these provisions Grenville hoped to raise about £45,000 towards what could be regarded as purely American expenses. On rational grounds the Sugar Act can be described as carefully thought out and fair but, because it was meant to be enforced, it met vigorous protests. The duty was declared to be penal and the intention of evading it was widely expressed. A committee of the Massachusetts House of Representatives went so far as to protest that the act was an infringement of the right of British subjects to assess their own taxes. Plainly American opinion was going to be highly critical of any further moves in this direction.

The sugar duties, even if successfully enforced, were not expected to bring in enough revenue to be an adequate contribution towards the cost of colonial defence, and it was known that Grenville was already considering other methods of raising the money. Among the suggestions put forward was one for a Stamp Act. The idea was not a new one. It had been part of the English fiscal system since 1694, and on more than one occasion in the intervening years it had been suggested that it might be extended to the colonies. As soon as the idea had been brought forward, in one of a series of resolutions submitted to the Commons on suitable means for raising money for the American establishment, there had been so many protests from Americans in London and from the colonial agents that Grenville had thought it wiser to hold the measure over for further consideration and fuller discussion. It was not therefore included in the Revenue Act for 1764, but it was clear that, unless some alternative suggestions came from the colonists in the interim, Grenville would go ahead with the scheme. It was certainly not pushed forward in any thoughtless spirit of bravado. Responsible Americans in London were aware of the fairness of the request that the colonies should make some contribution, beyond that of the much evaded laws of trade, to their own defence. But when it came to a discussion on how this should be done, though there were many suggestions there was no agreement. As a way of reconciling American rights with British needs one of the proposals was that the American colonies should themselves request His Majesty's Parliament to levy a Stamp Duty. In reply Franklin, the influential colonial agent for Pennsylvania, pointed out the extreme unlikelihood of the colonies doing any such thing, and in his turn suggested that if the government would ask for a specific sum for the purpose of defence, and authorize the calling of a colonial Congress to devise means of raising it, the practical needs and the theoretical rights inherent in the situation might be reconciled. In this connection, too, the possibility of the colonies' sending representatives to sit in the British Parliament was discussed; the conclusion reached was that the practical difficulties were almost insurmountable, while the number of American members would be too small for them to be in anything but a permanent minority. Therefore, despite protests from America, where the colonial press early became vocal on the subject, the Stamp Act seemed as good a solution to the problem as any; in February 1765 resolutions to this effect were moved in the House and in March it became law.

Though the majority of the members of both Houses were entirely favourable it did not pass without some criticism, and some voices were raised in warning. Colonel Barré, while not denying the right of Parliament to impose it, questioned its wisdom and urged the rejection of the measure. But even the Americans in London, of whom there were always a certain number engaged in business or pleasure, though they knew the Act would be unpopular, were taken by surprise at the amount of resistance it aroused. The government had done its best to make the measure as little burdensome as possible. In particular, the act had been framed in such a way that the money paid for the stamps would not be taken from the country, which was always chronically short of sterling to pay its overseas debts, but would be used to defray the expense of the American garrisons. They thought, therefore, that though there would be grumbling it would die down, and Americans of good standing in the colonies, who would certainly have refused to become involved if they could have seen the consequences, agreed to act as distributors of the stamps. They, like the home government and the members of Parliament, failed to realize that a major crisis was impending. They were all soon disillusioned.

The American reaction falls into two clearly marked types. One was the moving of official resolutions and the preparation of petitions by the individual colonial Assemblies. The other was violent mob action against anyone whose name had been linked with the hated stamps. Both soon came to be underlined and reinforced by the refusal of American merchants to pay their debts to British importing houses, and by a general boycott of British goods. That colonial opinion was deeply aroused was clear; nor was it without justification in so far as the method of raising money through internal taxation by an act of British Parliament was an innovation. However carefully the Act was drafted to minimize the burden, and however reasonable the cause for which it was imposed, it was an infringement of what all Americans regarded as the inalienable privileges of all British subjects, namely that money should be granted to the Crown by elected representatives only. In other ways they were prepared to recognize the right of the imperial Parliament to make regulations for the general ordering of trade, since it was realized that, for this, one over-riding authority was necessary. They were prepared, too, to recognize a large degree of control over their own internal legislation. Colonial acts which in any way infringed the British common or statute law, or which were held to be against the interests of other American colonies, were regularly submitted to the Privy Council. Only after they had been carefully vetted by the Lords of Trade, who then made representations to a committee of the Privy Council which then reported formally to the whole body, were such acts allowed or disallowed. In addition, appeals from the colonial courts came to the Privy Council. But, though on occasions individuals and special interests might be hurt by this power, so carefully was it generally exercised that the system worked smoothly.

Even against this degree of interference, however, there had been more criticism after the peace, particularly when it had been used against smuggling and to strengthen the local executive. What was even more significant was that attacks on the claims of Britain, whether vocally in the various Assemblies, or by lawyers like Otis defending a popular case, or in the press, were becoming more and more popular. The resistance offered to the Stamp Act had had its precedents, but these had been scattered and intermittent. The campaign against it clarified half-formulated opinions; though the measure itself was later repealed the issues that it raised remained.

In official protests the Virginian House of Burgesses may be said to have led the way when Patrick Henry, who in the courts had already attacked 'the bondage of the people who were denied the privilege of enacting their own laws', now moved resolutions which in arresting language expressed extreme views on the rights of the people of Virginia.[1] Though these went too far for the House of Burgesses to accept them in their entirety, the four resolutions which the House did pass and forward to England made it quite clear that constitutional issues of fundamental importance were being raised.[2] What was quite as significant is that Patrick Henry's original resolutions were widely circulated and as widely approved. Massachusetts's action was outwardly more decorous, but in some ways even more alarming, for it was decided to call a general congress in New York in the following October to consider a united petition against the Stamp Act.

The action of the Massachusetts mob was less restrained. On 14 August serious rioting broke out. The effigy of Andrew Oliver, who had been appointed stamp distributor for Massachusetts was first hanged and then burnt and his house broken into by the mob. Next day, as the officials plainly either would or could do nothing to protect him, he resigned his office to save both his property and his family from further violence. The riots in Boston were a signal for similar demonstrations elsewhere, so that one after another the

---

[1] *English Historical Documents*, vol. IX, p. 669.

[2] Soames Jenyns, *The Objections to the taxation of our American Colonies by the legislature of Great Britain briefly consid'd* (1765), points out '. . . every *Englishman* is taxed, and not one in twenty represented: Copyholders, Leaseholders, and all men possessed of personal Property only chuse no Representatives; Manchester, Birmingham and many more of our richest trading Towns send no Members to Parliament consequently cannot consent by their Representatives, because they chuse none to represent them; yet are they not Englishmen? or are they not taxed?'

unfortunate stamp distributors were forced publicly to resign. In Boston itself the disorders culminated in the partial destruction of the house of the Lieutenant-Governor, Thomas Hutchinson, not because he had supported the Stamp Act but because he had been closely associated with the drive against smuggling. After so much violence the attitude of the Congress, when it met in New York on 7 October, was reassuringly moderate.[1] There was certainly no encouragement given to wild talk, and the allegiance and loyalty of the colonists to the Crown were carefully stressed. Nevertheless, though their language was restrained, its members stated clearly their sense of grievance in the imposition of the recent heavy duties, and claimed that the Stamp Act infringed their rights as British subjects to pay no taxes without representation. A further grievance was the provision that cases concerned with the act should be tried in the Vice-Admiralty courts, which denied the right to be tried by jury. By 1 November, when the Act was to go into effect, it was clear that American opinion was determined to defy it.

This was the extremely difficult situation which the Rockingham ministry inherited when it assumed power. To persist with the enforcement of the obnoxious act was to run the risk of civil war within the empire and to accept a serious dislocation of trade. On the other hand, to repeal it was yielding to violence, and perhaps opening the door to further American demands to manage their own business. Unpopular as the trade laws were becoming, how long would America be content to accept the British version of their common good? Though the showdown had come belatedly, neither George III nor his ministers were under any misapprehension as to the seriousness of the occasion. In the King's own words it was 'undoubtedly, the most serious matter that ever came before Parliament'[2] and he added in a spirit of prophecy, 'it requires more deliberation, candour and temper than I fear it will meet with'. Men in public life found themselves seriously divided on this issue, and ministers were uncertain what line to take. In this confusion of opinion the Speech from the Throne, when Parliament met on 17 December, was non-committal, though Grenville, as might be expected, wanted to move an amendment expressing 'our just resentment and indignation' at what was happening across the Atlantic. Private discussions held between ministers failed to clarify

[1] *Eng. Hist. Doc.* vol. IX, p. 672.
[2] B. Dobrée, *Letters of George III* (1935), p. 33.

the situation; the Cabinet of 27 December showed that its members were divided between plans for modification and the determination to press for total repeal. In such circumstances Rockingham was most anxious to know Pitt's views. A lead from the latter would have been received almost as the pronouncement of an oracle, so anxious were the ministers to entice him to support them. But when Thomas Townshend was sent to Bath to sound him, the oracle refused to speak, except to the King or in Parliament.

When Parliament reassembled on 14 January 1766 the position was fluid. The idea of giving way in the face of colonial resistance was repugnant to George III, but Rockingham seems to have become convinced of the necessity for repealing the contentious Act. Petitions from ports and towns whose trade had been affected by the colonial non-importation agreements had been pouring in since early December and there is some evidence to suggest that Rockingham, far from being unsympathetic, was encouraging them. Because King and ministers were divided on this issue the Speech from the Throne gave no clear indication of future policy towards America. With the position so nebulous the stage was set for one of Pitt's dramatic appearances. He now declared himself on 14 January in a way that he had refused to do when his advice had been asked privately in December. Characteristically, he at once both supported repeal and dissociated himself from the men who were working for it. By declaring himself 'single and unconnected' he destroyed any hope that Rockingham still cherished that he might strengthen their administration by supporting it. He did, however, support their practical policy of repeal by declaring that though the government of Great Britain was 'sovereign and supreme in every circumstance of government and legislation' yet 'taxation is no part of the governing or legislative power'. Moreover, in reply to Grenville's defence of the measure he had sponsored he made his famous pronouncement that 'I rejoice that America has resisted'. Emboldened by the knowledge that Pitt agreed with their policy, though he refused to act with them to effect it, the Rockinghams now decided to introduce a bill for the repeal of the Stamp Act.

It would not, however, be correct to say that in so doing the ministry was slavishly following the lead given by Pitt. Rockingham, who had always shown himself sympathetic to the merchant community and to the woollen manufacturers of Yorkshire, had become convinced of the economic necessity for the repeal of the Stamp Act

for the sake of Britain's own prosperity though it is likely that both
he and his contemporaries were placing too much emphasis on
purely political factors. The years 1763 and 1764 had seen a postwar
boom, but by the autumn of 1765 this was followed by a postwar
depression in most of Britain's markets, augmented by bad harvests.
That no formal decision to repeal had been taken before the 14
January was due not to any lack of conviction on Rockingham's part
but to the disunity within the Cabinet. Yorke and Northington
preferred modification, as did the King himself, and it was only by
slow degrees, influenced by the prospect of unemployment and
disorder, that they could be won over to accept outright repeal. This
was as far as even Rockingham was prepared to go; there was
certainly no disposition at this stage to accept Pitt's denial of the
right of Parliament to tax the colonies, and as early as 27 December
the idea of affirming in some way British sovereignty over the colonies
had been under discussion. The repeal of the Stamp Act was never
intended to prejudice the fundamental rights of the Mother Country:
the Declaratory Act which accompanied it was as much Rockingham's policy as the removal of the stamp duties.[1]

Even with Pitt's support the repeal of the Stamp Act was unlikely to have an easy passage through either House. If American
opinion had been aroused, so had British. Grenville and his friends
were all in favour of a strict enforcement, even by arms if necessary.
In the Lords, Temple, taking an independent line, spoke against
repeal, and he, with Bedford and Bute, made a strong group against
concession. Though in order to facilitate its passage ministers spread
the idea that the King favoured repeal, this was not strictly true, as
George III himself made clear. He accepted repeal because his
ministers insisted that it was necessary, but personally he would have
preferred modification. A debate which took place in the Lords on
10 February made it plain that if repeal were to be carried at all it
would have to be accompanied by the strongest affirmation of British
sovereignty. It was in these circumstances that on 21 February
General Conway, who had never liked the Stamp Act, asked leave
for permission to bring in a bill for its repeal. The debate was tense.
It was not until the morning of the next day that the motion was
carried by 275 to 167. On 4 March the bill, accompanied by a
Declaratory Act, based on the two resolutions moved by Grafton in
the Lords on 10 February, to the effect that the British legislature

[1] See P. Langford, *op. cit.*

had the authority to bind every part of the empire and that the colonists were 'emphatically subjects of Great Britain' survived its third reading. In the Lords the resistance was tough and bitter. Repeal was only carried by 34 votes; in contrast only five peers voted against the Declaratory Act. Ministers have been often criticized for their unwisdom in coupling their concession with the latter measure, but such critics rarely explain how, without some such reassurance, they would have succeeded in removing the Stamp Act from the statute book. The Rockinghams seem to have felt that there was something sinister about the resistance they had encountered: 52 placemen had voted against repeal in the division in the Commons on 26 April without receiving any sign of the royal displeasure. George III's response to this ministerial discontent was that, though he had acted as a constitutional monarch in taking his ministers' advice, he was not prepared to use his personal influence to persuade men to vote against their consciences. This incident was to have further repercussions in that it seemed to prove to the Rockinghams the existence of a group of politicians known as 'the King's friends' through whom George III could work to thwart ministers of whose policy he disapproved.

Recent research has dissipated the fog of sinister legend with which nineteenth-century historians were apt to surround this group. It seems to have been composed of men who were becoming more and more like embryonic civil servants and less and less like active politicians. But, because effective administrative offices were in a state of transition, the men who filled them were torn by divided loyalties. On the one hand eighteenth-century political convention required that a man should show adequate loyalty to the patron to whose influence he owed his office. On the other, the demands of administrative efficiency required continuity in office, which could only be secured by a willingness to support whatever ministers enjoyed the royal confidence. Where a conflict occurred between these opposing concepts of duty, office holders (such as the Under Secretaries to the Treasury or to the Secretaries of State) valuing permanent tenure looked more and more to the permanent head of the executive, the King, and took their lead from him. The career of Charles Jenkinson well illustrates their personal dilemma.[1] The second son of a country gentleman, young Jenkinson had his own way to make. He was fortunate in attracting the interest of Lord

[1] See N. S. Jucker, *op. cit.*, Introduction, for details of his career.

Harcourt, for whom he did a good bit of unpaid 'devilling' and who eventually introduced him to Lord Holderness. Finally Jenkinson attached himself to George Grenville who, in the brief period when he and Lord Bute were well disposed to one another, persuaded the latter, when he became Secretary of State in March 1761, to take Jenkinson as Under Secretary in his department. When his new chief went to the Treasury Jenkinson resigned his official position to become Bute's private secretary. On the latter's resignation in 1763 Jenkinson was created one of the joint secretaries to the Treasury, where his old patron, George Grenville, had now become First Lord. Then, as the rift between Grenville and George III became wider and wider, Jenkinson was faced with two loyalties which rapidly became irreconcilable. To add to his difficulties, in the 1761 Parliament he had been chosen to represent Cockermouth on the interest of Sir James Lowther, who was afterwards Bute's son-in-law. He was therefore both doubly bound to the Bute interest and expected to further the interest of Sir James Lowther, who was an insatiable seeker after patronage for his own friends and clients. For men so situated the question of political allegiance can never have been easy. Nevertheless the common interest which they shared with the Crown in efficient administration made them increasingly ready to desert a political patron for a royal master.

Even so, the votes given by the placemen against the repeal of the Stamp Act were not necessarily due to any disloyalty of George III to his ministers. When he said that he was not prepared to ask men to vote against their consciences he was probably stating the situation correctly, for to concede to the colonists a victory won by sheer defiance was extremely distasteful to many members.[1] In the Commons the pressure of commercial interests, combined with the influence of Pitt and the electoral strength of Rockingham and his friends, had been sufficient to carry repeal. But it was not a popular measure, and it did nothing to strengthen the ministerial hold over Parliament. Conscious of their weakness they tried again and again to win over Pitt. His answer always was that he would serve with Rockingham, Conway and Grafton, but that Newcastle must go and Temple, if he wished it, be given office. With the struggle over repeal at its peak, Rockingham tried again, and once again Pitt refused. By so doing he helped to bring about the fall of the discredited ministers, for Grafton, who had only taken office in the hope that Pitt would be

[1] R. Pares, *George III and the Politicians*, p. 108.

persuaded to join the administration, resigned at the end of April.

5. THE MINISTRY RECONSTRUCTED UNDER CHATHAM

The days of the Rockingham administration were almost over. Having failed to win the support of Pitt, and having refused to strengthen the ministry after Grafton's resignation by allying themselves with the Bute connection, Rockingham's political credit was sinking fast. By early May George III decided that they were now too weak to provide him with a stable and viable administration. Rockingham's insistence that the Duke of Richmond, whom the King personally disliked, must succeed Grafton as the new Secretary of State did nothing to improve George III's confidence in his ministers but made no material difference to the situation.[1] The King had already decided to begin negotiations for a new ministry. Meanwhile he allowed his present one to continue until he could secure Pitt and until some suitable occasions for their dismissal should occur. Neither was long in coming. Lord Northington was both actively prepared to co-operate in the royal plans and genuinely opposed to the line which the Rockinghams were proposing to take over the problems posed by the acquisition of Quebec and its French settlers. Over the latter he first refused to attend cabinet meetings and when this did not force Rockingham's hand he resigned. As by 9 July George III felt sure of Pitt, Rockingham and his friends were dismissed that day. Their tenure of office had been brief but not uneventful. The American problem had temporarily been shelved and, partly though vainly in the hope of pleasing Pitt, the clauses to which he had objected in the Cider Tax—involving the searching of private premises—had been repealed; a resolution of the House had declared general warrants to be illegal unless sanctioned by act of Parliament, and, if used against a member of the House, a breach of privilege. The ministry of Pitt which followed, and from which so much was hoped had, in some ways, a less satisfact-ry record.

This time the negotiations between Pitt and his King proceeded smoothly.[2] Pitt still asked that Temple might be offered the Treasury

---

[1] George III to Bute, 12 July 1766: 'I withstood it until I found that they meant to retire if this did not happen; I therefore permitted it yet declared to them that I did so merely as a proof that I did not want to change my administration, but that I did look upon it as a measure that they themselves would repent of.'—*Letters from George III.*

[2] For an exhaustive study of the political situation between 1766–8 consult J. Brooke, *The Chatham Administration 1766–68* (1956); on which the following pages have been largely based.

but made it clear that his refusal would not, on this occasion, be made a reason for breaking off the negotiations. Because of his over-whelming pride, which would not accept the second place in any administration, he did refuse, and in his place Pitt suggested the Duke of Grafton. It was an unfortunate choice. The young Duke lacked application to business and was of limited intellectual capacity.[1] That Pitt should have advocated his appointment is an interesting commentary both on his own character and on his political position. He was susceptible to the flattery of Grafton's devotion, and because he deliberately disavowed connection and party as instruments of political life, when appointed to office he had no trained and reliable henchmen to act as his lieutenants. George III found this a great relief. Holding these views, and because of the paucity of his following, Pitt was prepared to accept the old administration as the basis for the new one. Lord Northington resigned the Great Seal to Camden, for whom Pitt at last was able to secure this coveted office, and took instead the Lord Presidency of the Council with a sweetener of a pension of £4,000 a year on retirement. Camden's promotion so offended Charles Yorke that he resigned his office of Attorney-General, and carried his brothers, Lord Hardwicke and John Yorke, back to the Rockingham camp. Conway, also an admirer of Pitt, remained in his old office of Secretary of State, merely transferring from the Southern to the Northern Department.

---

[1] After his resignation in 1770 Grafton wrote of his feeling of being 'released from business, and from an office which was peculiarly irksome to me'.—*Grafton Autobiography*, p. 256.

15

THE FAILURE OF THE CHATHAM ADMINISTRATION

1. EARLY PROBLEMS

WHEN George III finally secured the services of Pitt in July 1766 he must have felt that he had at last reached a genuine oasis in his search for a stable administration. His new minister, whatever his other disadvantages, was at least free from the fetters of 'connection': he was the minister of the King's own choice rather than one forced on him by political necessity. As such George III was prepared to give him his full confidence and to co-operate with him in every way in building up his control over Parliament. Here, though he lacked the cohesive strength of firm political alliance, Pitt could depend on the support of the independent members, relieved to find a first minister in whom both they and the King had confidence, and also on that of the City and trading elements. Outwardly Pitt's ministry promised to be a firm and successful administration, sympathetically in tune with the new elements in the economy and in society. Yet in two years it was to have bungled the reconstruction of the affairs of the East India Company, aroused a storm of passionate resistance to British colonial policy in America, and created a new crisis over Wilkes. The oasis proved a mirage; the search for stability was to consume four more years.

From the beginning, in spite of the royal support and the great name of Pitt, the ministry suffered from major weaknesses. The first of these was Pitt's decision to accept the office of Lord Privy Seal and to direct his administration from the House of Lords as Earl of Chatham. His action is understandable; an earldom was a special

mark of the royal favour, both gratifying his pride and proclaiming
the King's confidence in his new minister. His health was making it
increasingly impossible to face the strain of the Commons, and
hitherto the office of Lord Privy Seal, with its combination of dignity and lack of pressure of business, had only been held by a peer.
Nevertheless on this, as earlier on the occasion when his wife had
become Baroness Chatham, Pitt paid the price for his own over-
ostentatious incorruptibility. What in other men would have been
considered normal, in Pitt was regarded as a breach of faith.[1] This
loss of popularity might easily have been purely temporary if the
Earl of Chatham had proved himself to be as great a minister as
Mr. William Pitt. Various factors prevented it. One was undoubtedly
his breakdown in health which left the actual direction of business
to the Duke of Grafton. The weakness of the administration in the
Commons was equally fatal. Had Pitt remained there, even if his
health had only permitted him to take part in important debates,
his authority, combined with the backing of the Treasury, would
have enabled him to gain the support of the independent country
gentlemen and to manage the placemen.

With both the First Lord of the Treasury and Pitt in the Lords the
old difficulty of managing the Commons revived. This was intensified by the personalities of the leading ministers in that House. Few
men were less suited to manage their fellow members by the methods
customary at that time than Conway, the leader of the House.
Sensitive and honourable, driven by his conscience and concerned
with the appearance of his actions, he had an instinctive dislike for

---

[1] The press abounded with squibs and lampoons, of which the following selection
contained in *A Genuine Collection of the several pieces of Political Intelligence, etc.*, printed
for Thomas Butcher, Print seller, London, 1766 are typical. 'To be disposed of, considerably under Prime cost, the Stock in Trade of a late eminent Patriot, consisting of a
large Assortment of confident Assertions, choice Metaphors, Flowery Similies, bold
Invectives, pathetic Lamentations, specious Promises all little the worse for wear. The
Reason for their being Sold is that the Proprietor has retired, and has no further use
for them.' Another announced that 'The Pitt, a *first Rate*, being much damaged in the
Head in a *late Cruise* on the Coast of Scotland, is being *paid off and laid up at Chatham.*'
A third breaks into verse,

> Shall P--t to sacred Freedom late so dear,
> Like shifting Pulteney Sink into a Peer!
> Shall Britain's Boast, the Great, the Good, the Wise,
> Quit his firm hold, and learn to temporize?
> Then Patriot Virtue's but an empty Name.
> P--t, Gr---lle, B-te and B--d, much the same.

a 'job', which made it difficult for him to 'oblige' a friend. He was essentially a soldier and an administrator; as a political manager he was neither efficient nor happy. The other outstanding minister was Charles Townshend, the new Chancellor of the Exchequer.[1] He was Grafton's choice and Pitt had only agreed to his appointment with reluctance. For this reason he was not originally a member of the Cabinet. Because in addition he would have preferred to remain in his more lucrative office of Paymaster he was prepared to be difficult. In any case his character was such as to make him an unreliable colleague. No one denied his brilliance; he could hold the House spellbound by his eloquence and his wit. Unfortunately he was too often intoxicated by his own cleverness and was capable of political irresponsibility. Had Pitt remained the head of his own administration he might have led him; it was a task beyond Grafton.

Because of his weakness in the Commons it would have been good tactics on Chatham's part to have strengthened his administration by coming to terms with one of the opposition groups. This he seems to have realized, for he made an attempt to win over the Bedfords in October.[2] They, however, demanded more in the way of offices than Chatham could offer unless he was prepared to dismiss some of the Rockingham connection who still remained in the administration. This would have been an act of doubtful wisdom since at the moment the Marquis and his friends were prepared to behave with friendly tolerance towards the new administration. When Parliament met on 11 November it did not seem as if Chatham would have to face much criticism in spite of the failure of the negotiations with the Bedfords. In the hope that these would be renewed in the near future they were prepared to be complaisant, while Rockingham and his friends were unwilling to make difficulties because of Conway. The only serious opposition threatened to come from Grenville. With incredible political clumsiness Chatham had, within a few weeks, united the Bedfords, the Rockinghams and the Grenvilles into something very like a regular opposition. As so often in the eighteenth century the trouble arose from men not measures. Chatham wanted to give the Treasurership of the Household to an adherent of his own, Thomas Shelley. This would have involved the removal of Lord Edgcumbe, who was a member

[1] Sir Lewis Namier, *Charles Townshend, his character and career* (Leslie Stephen Lecture, 1959, pp. 2–15).

[2] See J. Brooke, *op. cit.*, ch. II, for a detailed analysis.

of the Rockingham group. Rather unimaginatively he tried to compensate Edgcumbe with a place in the Bedchamber, a less honourable appointment. In doing so he was transgressing one of the canons of eighteenth-century politics: to shuffle men from office to office was perfectly permissible but the compensation must be adequate and honourable. Edgcumbe was affronted, and as Chatham refused to make concessions, or even to take a suggested way out of the difficulty which would have saved Edgcumbe's face, Rockingham persuaded seven of his friends to resign from the administration. These were the Duke of Portland, Lord Bessborough, Lord Scarborough, Lord Monson, Saunders, Keppel and Meredith. Disgusted and disillusioned by Chatham's disregard for goodwill, Rockingham hoped that Conway would follow his friends out of office. Had he done so it would have placed the administration in an almost impossible position in the Commons. Loyalty to the King made him stay on, but from this time the constant aim of the Rockinghams was to secure his resignation.

In such circumstances the wisdom of securing the Bedfords was apparent. Nor were they unwilling to negotiate now that Chatham had seven places, including that of First Lord of the Admiralty, to offer. Unfortunately for the success of the negotiation he advised the King to give the Admiralty to Sir Edward Hawke without even discussing the appointment with Bedford. This may have been a consistent act on the part of two men who hated 'connection', but it showed a lack of political realism. By the beginning of December, therefore, all hope of accommodation with the Bedfords was over; the administration would have to struggle on alone. This mishandling of the political situation may have been due in part to Chatham's health. His gout had once again been troublesome, forcing him to spend much of the summer in Bath, and on his return to London he had shown himself difficult and arrogant.

2. THE EAST INDIA COMPANY

As usual his mind was obsessed with large schemes, in the forefront of which was a reorientation of British foreign policy, and a determination to put the affairs of the East India Company on a satisfactory basis. In both cases there was a good deal of justification for taking action. Choiseul's obvious endeavours to strengthen France's military and naval forces implied, to any realistic student of foreign affairs, that he was not willing to accept as final the setback which France had received at the Peace of Paris. In the Baltic, too, the growing power of Russia, that 'great cloud of power in the north', might soon come to constitute a real threat to British Baltic interests. To Chatham it seemed imperative to renew the closest links with Prussia. In India also by 1766 a complicated situation had developed. One effect of the East India Company's changed status from a mere trading corporation to a considerable territorial power had been to involve it much more deeply in parliamentary politics. Its new wealth and extended patronage made influence over it attractive to the politicians, while within the company personal feuds and opposing policies among the directors, faced with new responsibilities and opportunities, made them welcome political allies in their internal struggles for power. Any attempt therefore on the part of the administration to interfere in Indian matters was likely to produce immediate repercussions in Parliament.

The immediate reason for governmental interference in the affairs of the East India Company was financial.[1] After Clive's return to England things had not gone well in Bengal. The Company's servants were out of hand, and private trading, to an extent that both damaged its profits and made it hated in India, was producing every kind of disorder. By 1764 Clive's supporters in the Company were demanding that he should be sent back to deal with the abuses which had developed in his absence. This was done, and as a result the East India Company took over the direct financial administration of Bengal. This was expected to be tremendously profitable and a wild boom started in East India stock. The result of this widespread belief in the enormous wealth of the Company had considerable repercussions on English politics. The pressure of war debts was heavy and the country gentlemen were increasingly restive under a peacetime Land Tax of 4*s*. In addition there was the fear that this wealth might further corrupt political life as new men, who had made their fortunes in India—in current slang 'the nabobs'—used their riches to secure seats in Parliament. Rumours abounded of fantastic prices to which their competition had forced the cost of a seat; so did the tales of a House of Commons swamped by them. These fears seem to have been wildly exaggerated, but to a government hard pressed to service its loans and finance its day-to-day expenses the new opulence of the East India Company

[1] For a detailed account of the first parliamentary interference in the affairs of the East India Company see L. S. Sutherland, *op. cit.,* ch. VI, pp. 135–77.

appeared to offer a fresh source of revenue. On this point Chatham and his heterogeneous ministry apparently agreed. Controversy arose over the methods to be employed to divert this golden stream to the Treasury. To Chatham, with his love of dramatic schemes and grandiloquent phrases, the correct procedure was to launch a direct attack on the right of the Company to enjoy the revenue from the new territorial rights which Clive's victories implicitly, and his new reforms in Bengal explicitly, had conferred upon it. It could be argued with some justice that these had been originally obtained by the help of the naval and some military forces provided by the Crown, and that they were incompatible with its character as a trading company. Chatham does not, however, seem to have contemplated taking over the direct administration of Bengal, a task for which English governmental resources would have been quite inadequate. His aim was the more limited one of claiming the right to do so and, once this had been confirmed by Parliament, coming to some agreement with the Company as to the contribution it was prepared to make to the Treasury. Townshend and Conway, though equally eager to secure the money, favoured a less direct attack. By holding the threat of a parliamentary inquiry over their heads they hoped to induce the directors to begin negotiations which would lead to their making a substantial contribution to the Treasury. This would by-pass the complicated issue of deciding on their territorial rights and not raise the difficulties which a frontal attack on the Company would involve. This division of opinion between ministers was important both in relation to the affairs of the East India Company and because it materially weakened the administration.

As a result of this clash of views the subsequent handling of the matter falls into two parts. The first was dominated by Chatham's determination to hold the projected inquiry as a preliminary to any negotiations. The second was concerned with a series of negotiations between members of his Cabinet—in particular Townshend, Conway and Shelburne—and the directors which ended in a temporary agreement between them. The first stage of the battle opened when Chatham entrusted a motion asking for 'an enquiry into the state and condition of the East India Company' to Alderman Beckford. If Chatham valued good relations with the Company it was not a happy choice. Beckford was a champion of the lesser London merchants and profoundly antagonistic to the great monopolistic corporations. When this motion was introduced on 25 November Rockingham's friends and the Grenville group, as the upholders of the rights of chartered companies, opposed it. Townshend too was noticeably lukewarm in its defence. Nevertheless it was carried by 129 to 75.

The directors took advantage of the Christmas recess to open negotiations with the administration. On 6 January 1767 Grafton received their first proposals. Chatham's reaction to them was hostile. This was to be expected, as the whole negotiation flouted his plan to determine the Company's right to any territorial revenue. He was, however, no longer in London. Gout had driven him back to Bath and when he tried to return for the meeting of Parliament on 16 January it forced him to return to Bath and take to his bed. He was therefore unable to enforce his authority when the matter was discussed by a Cabinet on the 21st. Instead, he wrote querulous letters to Grafton, reiterating that the question of right must be settled first, but giving him little practical help in securing this object. In his absence Townshend seized control of the situation. The proposed inquiry was postponed several times while the directors' proposals were examined by the Cabinet, finally it was fixed for 6 March. Chatham did not get to London until the 2nd, and when he arrived he was both mentally and physically a sick man in no state to discipline the energetic Townshend or conciliate the wavering Conway.[1] George III wrote optimistically to him, 'now you are arrived in town every difficulty will daily decrease'.[2] Events were to prove otherwise. Chatham did make one effort to get rid of Townshend. He hoped to replace him at the Exchequer by the comparatively obscure Lord North. He, however, was unwilling to undertake the responsibility and in the apathy of depression Chatham let things take their course.

The conclusion of the matter might have been smooth had it not been for the activity of the stock jobbers. Since the taking over of the diwani, which had given the East India Company control over the finances of Bengal, speculation in its shares had been heavy.

---

[1] Burke's impression was that Chatham was at this time 'incapable of forming any rational plan, and is above communicating even his reveries to those who are to realize and put them in execution. . . . In this great matter of the East India Company, not one in the House knows what the plan or design of administration is. Most people believe that they have never conceived anything like one.'—*Burke Correspondence*, vol. I, April 1744–June 1768, edited by Thomas W. Copeland (1958), p. 303.

[2] *The Letters of George III*, 7 March 1767, p. 47.

By the autumn of 1767 the profits of some well-organized financial rings depended on there being a rise in the dividend. To this the directorate, who were aware both of the burdens which the Company had to carry and of the delusive nature of some of its apparent sources of wealth, were unwilling to consent. Also they realized that the appearance of prosperity, which such an action would imply, was strategically most unwise when they were actively negotiating for favourable terms with the ministers. The lure of an increased dividend was, however, more than the Court of Proprietors could resist; in September 1766 it was raised from six to ten per cent. Not content with their victory the bulls got a further advance to twelve per cent. Such effrontery was too much for the House. A motion was introduced to limit the Company's right to declare a dividend above ten per cent. Also, as the majority for the recent increased dividend had been created by the splitting of large holdings of stock into faggot votes, this practice was now made more difficult by the provision that the £500 worth of stock which was necessary to qualify for a vote must have been held for at least six months. In vain the directors tried to ward off this direct interference in its internal affairs by an offer of £400,000 a year for the next two years, accompanied by a private understanding with Townshend and Conway that they, in their turn, would oppose the unwelcome legislation. The interim agreement to pay the £400,000 was accepted and the need for the parliamentary inquiry shelved, but Conway and Townshend within the Cabinet, and Rockingham and his friends in opposition, tried in vain to raise the limit on the dividend to twelve and a half per cent. Opinion within the House had little sympathy for either stock jobbers or nabobs. For the next two years there was a lull in East India business but by 1769, when the temporary agreement expired, it once again became a storm centre of controversy.

It is an interesting and instructive episode illustrating how little control Chatham had over the ministry that bore his name. The solution he favoured had been deliberately sabotaged by Townshend, abetted by Conway, yet he took no action against them. The final agreement was even the work of his own protégé within the administration, Lord Shelburne, who had used his influence with the Company to secure a negotiated financial bird in hand in preference to Chatham's nebulous visions. Even more important was the fact that the affairs of the East India Company had been brought into the forefront of politics. This place they were to occupy intermittently until Pitt's India Act of 1784. Even the hamstrung inquiry sponsored by Chatham had produced some very disquieting revelations of what was happening in India, and a precedent had been set for parliamentary interference in the internal affairs of the Company. The future was to show that it was not possible to leave to it the responsibilities which the Peace of Paris and Clive between them had forced it to assume.

3. THE AMERICAN COLONIES

More serious in its ultimate consequences was Charles Townshend's handling of American problems, though even here it is possible to argue that he acted as 'a junior partner of the inevitable'. The repeal of the Stamp Act had failed to put the clock back. It was not so much that the Declaratory Act was resented, for most Americans considered it to be a mere formal piece of face saving, as that the earlier crisis had forced men to think and speak and write about their relations with the mother country, and views, once given expression, could not be smothered by the negative action of repeal. As a consequence, on both sides of the Atlantic public opinion remained suspicious and sensitive, and actions which before 1763 would have been accepted without comment were now subjected to critical scrutiny. Almost immediately friction, though in a milder form, reappeared. By the Quartering Act of 1765 British troops marching through, or quartered in, a colony where there were no barracks, were to be housed in unoccupied houses, or barns or outhouses and supplied with such necessities as firewood, candles, vinegar, salt, bedding, cooking utensils and limited quantities of small beer or cider at the colonies' expense. When General Gage, commander-in-chief in America, asked the governor of New York to make the necessary arrangements for his troops, the Assembly first ignored the request and then passed a bill of its own providing for a curtailed list of supplies. This they did, not because they had any objection to the presence of the troops, which indeed were welcomed as a shield against the warlike Six Nations on their frontier, but because they regarded the request as the thin end of the wedge of taxation without representation. In England their action was regarded as a piece of defiance to a reasonable request by a legal authority and was resented accordingly. Even Chatham spoke of 'the spirit of infatuation' that had seized the colonists, and had plainly little realization of the new channels into which American aspirations were flowing. In Massachusetts trouble arose out of Conway's demand, made as Secretary of State, that the victims of the anti-Stamp Act riots should be compensated for the damage they had suffered. After long discussions as to whether the colony as a whole should shoulder the burden, or whether Boston should foot her own bill, it was decided to comply. Unfortunately for better relations, the Massachusetts Assembly linked its payment with the grant of a 'free and general' pardon to the rioters. This usurpation of the royal prerogative of mercy the English ministers were forced to declare inadmissable.

Such incidents illustrate the infinite possibilities for misunderstanding, and the growing sense of irritation on both sides. It is against this background that Townshend's financial duties, and his new administrative measures for tightening up the Customs, must be studied. It was not an easy task to raise an adequate supply from a House that already considered the country heavily overtaxed. On 26 January 1767, in a debate on the army estimates, Grenville pressed, though without success, for the transference of some of the financial burden to the American taxpayer. The importance of the debate lay in the fact that Townshend showed himself not unfriendly to the idea. Encouraged by the obvious sympathy of much of the House, he gave his approval to the principles that lay behind the Stamp Act, made mocking nonsense of Chatham's distinction between internal and external taxation, and promised at a later date to bring forward proposals of his own. When on 27 February Dowdeswell, the ex-Chancellor of the Exchequer, successfully carried a motion reducing the Land Tax from 4*s.* to 3*s.*, Townshend received an additional incentive to go ahead with his scheme in order to find new sources of supply to fill the gap. In attacking the Stamp Act Pitt had declared: 'We may bind their trade, confine their manufactures, and exercise every power whatever, except that of taking their money out of their pockets, without their consent.' Townshend now proposed to use this distinction to levy duties at the ports on glass, lead, paper, paint and tea. The revenue raised by this nominally 'external taxation' was to be used to defray British expenses in America. The sum itself was not great, being estimated at about £40,000 a year, which would not go far to fill the gap of £500,000 left by the reduction in the Land Tax.

From the financial point of view the resulting relief to the British

Exchequer was not commensurate with the risk of disturbing
normal trading relations between Britain and her already suspicious
colonies. To the Americans these taxes represented a new attempt,
lightly disguised by a verbal quibble, to impose taxes without
representation. The result was an immediate storm of protest.
Behind it was an element of genuine fear and dismay, for Townshend, not content with imposing new duties, was taking steps to
see that machinery for their collection was effective.[1] This was to
touch the colonists on one of the sensitive spots of their economy,
their dependence on wide-scale smuggling and Customs avoidance.
Hitherto the administration of the American Customs had been
entrusted to four Surveyors-General who had been under the
control of the Board of Commissioners in London. Because of their
subordination they had been unable to give final and ruling decisions,
and American merchants had grumbled at the delays that a reference
to England entailed. Townshend now set up an American Board of
Commissioners, co-ordinate with those in London and responsible
only to the British Lords of the Treasury. From the American point
of view this disadvantage outweighed the advantages of quick
decisions, for the new commissioners were empowered to appoint
their own minor officials, searchers, tide waiters, collectors, sur-
veyors, clerks, etc. Since the commissioners were to act in close
conjunction with the Admiralty Courts, the safeguard of trial by
jury could be by-passed. This new administration of the Customs
made the business of smuggling more difficult and expensive, though
owing to the strength of public opinion and the lack of American
co-operation, Townshend's reforms were less effective than he had
hoped and Americans had feared.

Apart from financial considerations the colonists disliked the
objects on which the surplus revenue so raised was to be spent.
This was to make 'a more adequate and certain provision for
defraying the charge of the administration of justice and the support
of civil government in such provinces, where it shall be found
necessary'. Hitherto the fact that funds for these purposes had come
largely from the grants of the colonial Assemblies had given them
a large measure of control over officials who were, in theory, the
legal guardians of the authority of the mother country. In reviving
the issue of taxation Charles Townshend has been accused of acting
with great political irresponsibility, the assumption being that his

[1] *Eng. Hist. Docs.* vol. IX, p. 702.

motives were mere financial expediency and a love of the applause of the Commons. Recent research has, however, suggested a more respectable explanation and attributed to him 'a steadiness of purpose with which he has not been credited'.[1] According to this view the raising of additional revenue was not the main purpose of his policy, which was to secure such independence for British officials as to make them the effective instruments of British authority in the colonies. Even as a junior member of the Board of Trade he had been instrumental in sending instructions which had endeavoured, though without success, to secure a permanent provision for the salaries of the governor, judges and other officials of the colony of New York.[2] Now, as Chancellor of the Exchequer, he was using finance to achieve the same object, which made his actions a much greater threat to American liberties than if they had genuinely been inspired by a desire to lighten the burdens of the British taxpayer. In resisting them Americans were showing a sound political instinct.

4. THE MINISTRY RECONSTRUCTED

To contemporary politicians the interest of the late spring and early summer of 1767 lay not in the failure to grapple with the East India Company's new responsibilities nor in the prospect of renewed trouble in America, but in the obvious internal weakness of the administration. It was clear that unless it was strengthened it would collapse from a combination of its own weakness and the pressure of a temporarily united opposition. July therefore was taken up with the busy manœuvres of politicians attempting to detach at least one of the opposition groups by an offer of places in the administration. It was the old technique, and the interest derives from the clash of opposing objects between Rockingham and the King. The former's experience in 1765 had soured his relations with George III in so far as Rockingham had felt let down by the latter's failure to discipline those members who had refused to vote for the repeal of the Stamp Act. Earlier suspicions that Bute had continued to act as 'minister behind the curtain' after his resignation had hardened into a belief in the existence of a double cabinet, one official, the other secret and exclusive, within which all genuine power resided. It was this fear that made the Rockinghams insist that they could only accept office

---

[1] Sir Lewis Namier, *Charles Townshend*, p. 17.   [2] *Ibid.*, p. 29.

if they had a monopoly of power and that, in order to secure this, it was vital that Rockingham should come in as a party leader entrusted with the formation of the new administration. Furthermore, to achieve this it was essential that on all important matters the party should adopt a common line and that, because of their belief in a double cabinet, the royal influence over Parliament should be curtailed by cutting down the royal weapon of patronage. George III, while he was prepared to appoint Rockingham to high office, was equally determined to make his choice unhampered by 'party' or 'connection'. He wished to strengthen not to replace his present ministry. Of the three opposition groups he was determined not to have George Grenville and Temple, whom he found most uncongenial on personal grounds. The possibilities, therefore, were either the Bedfords, or Rockingham and his friends. Grafton appears to have preferred the former, George III the latter. For this the King had two reasons, one positive, the other negative. The key to the continued life of the administration was still Conway. Without him to manage the Commons and balance Townshend the administration must inevitably fall to pieces. George III would then have had to take Rockingham on his own terms. If, however, Conway could persuade his friends to take office on the King's terms both these difficulties would disappear. Even if the negotiations failed they might still have served the useful purpose of convincing Conway that it was the obstinacy of his friends rather than the unwillingness of the King which excluded them from office. Bedford on the other hand would do nothing to placate Conway and might insist on places being found for Grenville and Temple. On 2 July preliminary conversations took place with both groups, as a result of which it was decided to go ahead with an attempt to secure the Rockinghams.

In the interviews and letters which followed there was some very pretty manœuvring for position.[1] Rockingham, blinded perhaps by wishful thinking, chose to assume that he had, or soon would have, the royal mandate to form a new administration. On this assumption he went ahead with negotiations for a comprehensive ministry which would have included the Bedfords and even found places for some of the followers of George Grenville. This was the very last thing that George III and Grafton desired, for a ministry constructed on so broad a bottom, and held together by connection,

[1] J. Brooke, *op. cit.*, pp. 162–217.

would have had little need to depend on royal influence for its control over the Commons. At the same time the Court hardly dared to show its hand by refusing outright to grant Rockingham the royal audience, which would have recognized his pretensions to form an administration *de novo* because Conway by 22 July was threatening to resign. From this dilemma George III was saved partly by Conway's wavering loyalties and infirmity of purpose, partly because when it came down to precise details Rockingham's hopes of a comprehensive administration began to fade. Too late he found that the co-operation of George Grenville, which he thought he had secured, was hedged about by unacceptable provisos, concerned with the American colonies. Grenville was determined that any ministry that had his support must affirm in the fullest manner British sovereignty over them; Rockingham was equally sensitive to any implied criticism of his repeal of the Stamp Act. Accordingly by 25 July all hope of a comprehensive administration was over. Meanwhile Conway had found a characteristic compromise. He resigned his salary but continued in office, so making it clear that it was not greed but his duty to the King that had influenced his decision to remain.[1]

George III had now no objection to taking the Rockinghams into his administration. This offer was refused. From the point of view of practical politics it would have left Rockingham in the same weak position as that in which he had found himself in 1766, and would have conflicted with his own conception of the Rockinghams as a political party of which he was the head. He must come in as First Lord of the Treasury or not at all. On the surface, therefore, the ministry remained in much the same condition after the negotiations as before them. This, however, was not so. Conway had at last thrown in his lot with the Court, shattering Rockingham's dream that he would resign and so bring down the administration. Accident also helped Grafton: Charles Townshend died suddenly in August and was replaced by Lord North, a man of very different temperament. North had been a junior lord of the Treasury in 1759 and, though he had resigned on the creation of the Rockingham administration, Chatham had made him Joint Paymaster and had tried to persuade him to accept the Chancellorship of the Exchequer when

---

[1] Burke's bitter comment was: 'Conway stays in, as a Scotch warming Pan, to keep the Bed in a comfortable State for those who hate and despise him.'—*Burke Correspondence*, vol. I, p. 339.

Townshend had first started to get out of hand. Though almost grotesquely ugly, North had the personal charm that made men forget his appearance, and a wit that made them welcome his company. In the early stages of his career no one thought of him as a candidate for high office but he soon showed a capacity for managing the House of Commons. At last George III had an alternative to Conway, which strengthened Grafton's position considerably.

The royal prospects were further improved when it became clear that there was no real danger of the administration's having to face a united opposition in the new Parliament. The old Duke of Newcastle, whose last chance of returning to office seemed to depend on it, did all that he could to revive the shattered alliance. Rockingham was at last persuaded to give up the unreliable Conway and to work with the Bedfords, and when Parliament reassembled in November it looked as if the opposition groups had papered over their cracks. George Grenville soon destroyed this apparent harmony. In a bitter speech he attacked the American policy of the Rockinghams. Bedford, through Weymouth, protested that his friends could not be responsible for what Grenville said but Rockingham, both hurt and annoyed, brushed their protests aside. Plainly it did not augur well for a joint opposition. Certainly the Bedfords did not think so, for almost immediately they made overtures to the Court. If they could be secured, George III's immediate problems would be solved and Grafton could carry on. In these circumstances he was not disposed to haggle over the terms, which were Cabinet office for Gower and Weymouth together with a place for Rigby: they were willing for the remainder of their followers to be accommodated later. The negotiations were, however, complicated by Grafton's desire to use the reshuffle to drive Shelburne to resign. This seems to have been due more to his personal unpopularity than to any considerations of policy, but as he was more closely attached to Chatham than any other member of the Cabinet he could not be abruptly dismissed. It was therefore decided to create a new Secretaryship of State for the Colonies, which had hitherto been part of the sphere of the Secretary for the Southern Department. With the growing complexity of colonial issues there was ample justification for this. Moreover, the advantages of the scheme included the possibility that Shelburne, who was Secretary for the Southern Department, would feel affronted and resign. In this Grafton failed. Shelburne decided to remain as Chatham's personal watch-dog in the Cabinet. The new

Secretaryship went to Lord Hillsborough. As, however, Conway had been anxious for some time to resign, Grafton was able to meet the demands of the Bedfords by giving the Northern Department, which he had vacated, to Lord Weymouth. Sandwich had to content himself with the office of joint Postmaster-General; Rigby became joint Vice-Treasurer of Ireland, and was promised the Pay Office later. By these accessions George III was able to strengthen the ministry considerably, but it was no longer the administration that he and Chatham had planned, because the Bedfords had come in as a united group. Also, though Chatham remained as its nominal head, the new ministers had little patience for his sympathy with the colonists' views, and in their less conciliatory approach lay the seeds of further trouble.

5. John Wilkes Reappears

The more immediate problems which the administration had to face were concerned with John Wilkes. Until the autumn of 1766 he had remained in exile, but when Grafton and Chatham returned to power he had hopes, in view of their earlier championship of his cause, that the government might relent towards him. As ministers of the Crown they were placed in a difficult position; George III was not disposed to forgive and neither of them cared to force his hand. As a consequence Wilkes received temporizing answers and little encouragement. His reaction was to publish an open letter in December 1767, in which he denounced Chatham as 'a proud, insolent, overbearing and ambitious man', and to return to England in February 1768.[1] What was worse, he stood in the general election of that year as a candidate for the City of London. He was more popular with the City mob than with the City electors and was unsuccessful. But because of the long drawn out nature of elections previous to Representation of the People Act 1918, he was able to stand for Middlesex, where he was returned at the head of the poll. The mob was exultant and for two nights London's streets rang with the cry 'Wilkes and Liberty'. His election raised grave legal and political issues. Could a man who was an outlaw and who, in his absence, had been convicted of seditious libel take his seat in the Commons? Wilkes determined to get rid of these liabilities. He surrendered to his outlawry which, when he appeared before Mansfield,

[1] L. S. Sutherland suggests that his return was forced upon him by the need to escape from his creditors in France.—*The City of London and the Opposition, etc.*, p. 13.

he argued was technically invalid. He might have spared his eloquence; Mansfield with Gilbertian logic argued that as Wilkes had surrendered to his outlawry, instead of waiting to be arrested, the case could not be tried. A technicality of this kind was easily remedied; Wilkes was duly arrested and committed to prison. When the case was again argued before him on 7 May Mansfield postponed giving judgment. As Parliament was prorogued on 21 June, no one knew during the recess whether Wilkes was an outlaw or not, and the ministers decided that the question of what to do about him had better be held over until the new session. By that time the situation had been clarified to the extent that King's Bench had reversed the sentence of outlawry but had refused to quash his conviction for seditious libel. For this he was sentenced to twenty-two months imprisonment with a fine of £1,000, and ordered to find sureties for his good behaviour. When Parliament met in November ministers at least knew the legal position: Wilkes was no outlaw but he was serving a term of imprisonment for seditious libel. Their problem was to decide what to do next.

6. THE RESIGNATION OF CHATHAM

Before Parliament met, a fresh crisis faced the administration: Chatham resigned. For this Grafton and the King were jointly but inadvertently responsible. As snubs and slights had failed to drive Shelburne to resign, they finally decided on the drastic step of dismissing him. As they realized that this might alienate Lord Camden, Chatham's other close friend in the ministry, they approached the matter with caution and attempted to get in advance Camden's acquiescence if not his approval. Grafton also tried to sound Lady Chatham, in an interview on 9 October, as to her husband's probable reaction. Though Chatham had been incapacitated for so long from taking any share in public life, neither George III nor Grafton wanted to lose the prestige which his name gave to the administration. Unluckily for their plans Chatham, whose illness was dispersing, mustered enough decision on 12 October to ask for permission to resign. He gave as his reason the state of his health, but this had been poor for so long that the reason was not entirely convincing even to those who most wished to believe it true. His resignation was followed by that of Shelburne, who thus narrowly avoided being dismissed, and of Barré; Camden and Granby decided to remain in office. Grafton at last was the titular as well as the real head of the ministry, but its reconstruction left him the prisoner of the Bedfords rather than its effective head.

Chatham's resignation could make little difference to day-to-day administration or even to the formulation of policy. Nevertheless, in the wider field of politics, it was important. While he had been the nominal head of the ministry George III could persuade himself that the bogy of faction and party was being held at bay. But with Chatham's resignation even the illusion of an administration headed by a great national figure in whom the King had confidence, and composed of men who had been chosen for personal rather than party reasons, could no longer be accepted. Such reality as it had had, even in the beginning, had been a brittle thing. Chatham required followers not colleagues, and from the early days of the administration it had been clear that the individuals, unconnected as they were by party ties, were not disposed to find harmony in subordination to his views. Had he retained his vigour he might have dominated them and given some unity of policy to the Cabinet. As it was, the vagaries of Townshend, the indecision of Conway and the weakness of Grafton were hardly recommendations for the royal anti-party views. Nevertheless the new situation was not basically unfavourable to the Court. If Chatham had been lost Rockingham had failed to storm the Closet and force on George III a comprehensive administration not of the King's choosing. If he had been obliged to take in the Bedfords as a group, their views on America were in harmony with his own. Conway also had been retained, and in Lord North, George III had a leader in the Commons on whose loyalty and resources he could rely. In addition the difficult Shelburne had been replaced by the more tractable Lord Rochford. In all these ways the ministry had gained in coherence and strength.

7. AMERICA AND WILKES

The threat of future danger lay in the fact that Chatham might decide to act with the Rockinghams. Health had been his excuse for resignation, but this had been bad for so long that even his summoning enough energy to resign might be a prelude to recovery. If this should be so, how would he review the actions of the administration which had once been his? Already there were threats of further difficulties from Wilkes and from America, and the present ministers were hardly likely to find solutions along lines favoured by Chatham. It is true that his position was not so formidable as when he stormed the Closet as a younger man. In time of peace he was deprived of his strongest card, his undoubted gift for leadership, and the Lords never responded to his eloquence as did the independent gentlemen of the Commons. Also the gulf between him and the Marquis of Rockingham was deep; they were still divided by the personal ambitions of Camden and Yorke. Their temperaments were poles apart. Rockingham was touchy of his dignity, sensitive to charges of inconsistency, seeing himself as the guardian of whig and aristocratic principles, and he thoroughly disliked Chatham's appeals to popular feeling and his friendship with City demagogues like Beckford. Chatham was arrogant, insensitive to other men's difficulties, inconsistent and dramatic, driven on by hidden furies and urges, and yet inspired by flashes of prophetic insight and sympathy that made him able to touch the hearts, as well as to inspire the actions, of men. Even so, political adversity makes strange benchfellows, and should they combine there were certain weaknesses in the ministry which it would not be difficult to exploit. Those members of the Cabinet who were not bound to each other by connection were particularly vulnerable to pressure from outside. Conway still felt the pull of his old friendship with Rockingham, Camden might well respond to the influence of Chatham.

This was the situation when Parliament met in November 1768. The events of the next few months were to make the lack of leadership and of judgment painfully clear. In a little more than a year, under the twin pressure of fresh American troubles and a new eruption on the part of Wilkes, Grafton was forced to resign, though this was due more to his own uncertainties than to either the skill of the opposition or a genuine lack of support for government policy in Parliament.

In the autumn of 1768 America seemed a more pressing danger than Wilkes, now serving his sentence for seditious libel. Townshend's revenue duties, combined with his reorganization of the administration of the Customs, had once again aroused the Americans to fury. Resistance was strongest in the port of Boston. This was due in part to the fact that the new Commissioners had their headquarters there, in part to the fact that the port was slowly losing its old commercial pre-eminence. Had times been better agitators might well have found less receptive audiences for their oratory. Once again an attempt was made to revive the non-importation agreements which had proved so effective a weapon against the

Stamp Act. Economic action could, however, be a two-edged weapon, hurting American merchants as severely as their British counterparts. Nor had the American merchants identical interests: it was always difficult to organize common action between those of the various colonies. In such circumstances resistance might once again have died down had it not been for the hardening of public opinion against the mother country stimulated by the outpourings of the press. In the early stages of this literary campaign the 'Letters of a Farmer in Pennsylvania to the Inhabitants of the British Colonies' played an important part.[1] The author was John Dickinson and the first Letter appeared on 5 November 1767 as a protest against the act for suspending the legislature of New York. The second Letter attacked the Townshend duties. In the course of his argument the distinction between internal and external taxation was swept away: 'Impositions for raising a revenue may be hereafter called regulations of trade: but names will not change the nature of things'. In writing in this way Dickinson was still very far from advocating revolution or a renunciation of allegiance. Indeed, he exhorted his readers to 'behave like dutiful children who have received unmerited blows from a beloved parent. Let us complain to our parent; but let our complaints speak at the same time the language of affliction and veneration.' To inflamed American opinion his letters appeared a mild though firm statement of their case; to British opinion, in spite of their respectful tone, they read more like an incitement to rebellion.

From the British point of view worse was to follow. In February 1768 the Massachusetts Assembly decided to send a circular letter to the other Assemblies denouncing the Townshend duties as a violation of the principle of no taxation without representation. As by their previous actions they had made it perfectly clear that Americans considered such representation as neither practicable nor desirable, this argument was perhaps somewhat disingenuous, but in the circumstances most effective. In it Massachusetts was not only challenging the rights of the British Parliament, she was also inciting the other colonies to follow her example. No government so defied could sit back and take no action. Hillsborough promptly ordered Governor Bernard to instruct the House of Representatives to rescind the resolutions on which the circular letter was based and to

---

[1] S. E. Morison, *The American Revolution, (1764–1788) Sources and Documents*, contains a useful selection from these letters.

repudiate it under threat of dissolution. Under the same threat t :
other Assemblies to which it had already gone were ordered not to
receive it. When these instructions arrived late in June, Bernard,
as might have been expected, failed to secure the compliance of the
House, and that gathering was duly dissolved. It could not, however,
be expected that a new House of Representatives would be any more
amenable, and meanwhile the circular letter had been endorsed by
New Hampshire, Virginia, Maryland, Connecticut, Rhode Island,
Georgia and South Carolina. At the same time an inopportune demand by the Commissioners of Trade that duties should be paid in
specie, always in very short supply and therefore a tender spot in the
colonial economy, had secured the backing of the merchant community for the non-importation agreements, though even then
Virginia did not join until the following year. By the summer of 1768
British authority in Boston was almost non-existent; Customs officials
were tarred and feathered in the streets and every attempt to collect
duties, even those of long standing, was resisted. In the circumstances
Hillsborough did what any Secretary of State would have done in
England: he called in the military. On 1 October troops under Major-
General Gage landed in Boston. To the people of that port it was a
further infringement of their liberties; to British ministers it was the
elementary duty of restoring order. In this immediate objective it
was successful. For a time the threat of violence as opposed to civil
disobedience was averted.

As a topic of parliamentary importance American affairs were
temporarily to be eclipsed by Wilkes. Early in the session a friend of
his in the House, Sir Joseph Mawbey, presented a petition on his
behalf asking for redress of grievance. As the ministers had already
burnt their fingers once and were now in some doubt as to the best
line to take, they prudently let it lie on the table until late in January.
For Wilkes to be ignored was fatal and his next step seemed deliberately designed to provoke the ministers. For this to some extent
circumstances were favourable. The last few years had been a period
of considerable distress. By October 1767 a bad harvest had pushed
up the price of food so that in the speech from the throne Parliament
had been asked to consider the 'distresses of the poorer sort'. In the
May of next year *The Gentleman's Magazine* was beginning to report
food riots; in London glass grinders and journeymen tailors were
demonstrating and on the Thames coalheavers and sailors were at
each others' throats. Everywhere there were reports of looting,

rioting and social unrest. That Lord Weymouth should instruct the Middlesex magistrates not to hesitate to use the troops to maintain order in the absence of a civil police force, was an understandable precaution; it was the normal practice. It was, however, politically unfortunate that these powers had been used to break up a pro-Wilkes demonstration on 5 May, and even more so that five or six people had been killed. Wilkes, with his usual luck and resource, had managed to secure the text of Weymouth's letter, which he published on 8 December in the *St. James's Chronicle*, annotated with his own acid and exaggerated comments. His interpretation was that the letter revealed a deep-laid government plot against the liberties of the people. Once again in popular eyes 'Wilkes and Liberty' were synonymous terms. This provocative action, when his petition for redress of grievances was due to be heard by the Commons on 27 January 1769, could only mean his realization that it was bound to be rejected and that attack was the best means of defence. Even in face of this provocation Camden was inclined to press for pardon for Wilkes's past offences as the most effective way of dealing with him, but the rest of the Cabinet were for sterner measures. Wilkes had at least ensured that they should not ignore him.

As Weymouth was a member of that House, the Lords were the first to take action. They voted Wilkes's introduction to the now famous letter 'an insolent, scandalous and seditious libel'. They communicated this resolution to the Commons, where North moved that that House should concur. Here he ran into resistance. The Commons never much liked taking action which smacked of dictation by the Upper House, and it is illustrative of the divided views in the Cabinet that it was Conway, backed by Dunning the Solicitor-General, who protested that the Commons must first examine the evidence for themselves. Burke and Grenville for the opposition took the same line. In response to these protests witnesses were heard on 19 December and further action delayed until the debate on Wilkes's original petition on 27 January. The debate lasted three days and the petition, as was expected, was dismissed. The way was now clear, and on 2 February Wilkes's notes on the Weymouth letter were debated. Called to the bar of the House, Wilkes was openly defiant, glorying in his authorship of the obnoxious comments, and adding to his offences by describing Weymouth's letter as a 'bloody scroll'. Thinking that he had delivered himself into their hands, the ministers now moved that the publication should be voted an 'insolent, scandalous and seditious libel'. In vain Grenville pointed out that even so it was no concern of the Commons, as it was not a member of that House who had been libelled; once again his opinion was disregarded.

To condemn Wilkes was only the prelude to more serious and more controversial action. On 3 February Lord Barrington moved that he be expelled from the House, in which he still represented Middlesex. In supporting the motion the ministers were displaying an animosity and a lack of realism which were to bear bitter fruit, as Grenville again prophesied. Speaking against the motion he stressed the illegality of combining four separate charges into one omnibus condemnation, warned the House that Wilkes would be re-elected, and that inevitably a contest would follow between the House and the electors of Middlesex. Grenville's speech was not without effect; the independent members had a genuine respect for his solid arguments and convictions. But in their dislike for Wilkes most of them were at one with the Court and Barrington carried his motion by 82 votes. The rest of the story is soon told. On 16 February Wilkes was re-elected. Subsequent action was further complicated by an interpretation of a rule of the House that a member so expelled could not take his seat during the current session. Without rescinding this rule the House could not go back on its verdict. However unwise Grenville had considered the original expulsion, both he and Conway, who had also opposed it, now felt bound to vote against Wilkes's re-admission during the remainder of the current session. On the 17th Lord Strange moved that Wilkes was incapable of being elected to the present Parliament; the farce was repeated again in March. It was a sequence of events which might have been repeated at regular intervals throughout the session, and when in April, for the fourth time, Wilkes was elected for Middlesex, it was felt that somehow that dilemma must be solved. This led the House into an action which could fairly be described as an attack on the liberties of electors, for they declared his opponent Luttrell duly elected, though he had only managed to poll 296 votes as against the 1,143 given to Wilkes. Here at last was a topic on which all the opposition groups could combine. This was not, however, its sole importance. Concern over the Middlesex election touched off the elements of a new radicalism which seems to have been smouldering in the ranks of the popular party in the City at least since 1756.[1] The

[1] For an analysis of early radical movements in the City of London see L. S. Sutherland, *art. cit.*, and G. Rudé, *op. cit.*, chs. viii and x.

affair of Wilkes gave an opportunity for the expression of deeper discontents with the prevailing political system of privilege and limited representation. Wilkes himself was never a parliamentary reformer by conviction, though later he found himself forced to sponsor that cause, but the agitation associated with his name gave men who were—men like Beckford and John Sawbridge—an opportunity to whip up support for their views, in the City and even, briefly and to a less degree, in the country at large.

The other vulnerable spot in the policy of the administration was presented by America. Though the physical resistance of Boston had come to an end with the arrival of Gage and his troops, the non-importation agreements were becoming increasingly effective. To wear British goods, or enjoy British luxuries, was an unpatriotic act, and great pains were taken and skill displayed to create among American women a united opposition. Even more fundamentally dangerous was the tone of the press and of political speeches. Public opinion was solidly ranged against the payment of duties; though open defiance, and even the manhandling of Customs officers, was a frequent occurrence, witnesses could never be found, juries would never convict. The troops were too few for effective policing, and because they were the constant butt of jibes and obstruction their nerves became frayed. The surprising thing is not that there was such an incident as the Boston massacre but that there were no more of them. By the end of 1768 it was clear that any hope of a revenue from the colonists to relieve the British taxpayer must be given up for ever. It was no longer a matter of what duties they would pay but whether they would continue to accept British sovereignty at all. In the late spring of 1769, therefore, the Cabinet had to decide what to do about Wilkes and how to deal with American resistance. Townshend's duties, by provoking non-importation agreements and stimulating the production of colonial manufactures to replace those habitually bought from Britain, were inflicting considerable harm on the British economy. Yet it was generally felt that the sovereign rights of the Crown over America must be reaffirmed; to withdraw the duties in response to violence would be a denial of that authority. Even those persons most friendly to America had no desire to encourage colonial independence. Men like Chatham still professed to see a distinction between the right to tax, which they held to be no essential part of government, and the right to legislate which still resided in the Crown. When Chatham declared that he was glad the Americans had resisted he was speaking in this limited sense; unlike the Rockinghams, he had never reconciled himself to the idea of American independence. The ministerial problem at this point was largely one of strategy. They had to decide whether more harm would be done to the permanent links between Britain and her colonies by retaining the Townshend duties than by once again retreating and repealing them. What they did in a Cabinet held on 1 May was to make a compromise which was to have fatal results. They decided to repeal all the duties except that upon tea. For this decision, in a desperate effort to save face, they adduced commercial arguments which could deceive nobody. Tea was kept as a symbol of British authority; it was to prove a signal for its final destruction. Opinion in the Cabinet had been much divided and the tea duty was retained by only one vote.

Even by the middle of 1769 George III had good reason for viewing the future with some apprehension: his ministry was weak and divided and in their handling of Wilkes and America had provided two topics of major importance on which opposition groups could concentrate. If these could so weaken the control over the Commons that the existing ministers could no longer do the royal business in Parliament then George III would be forced to give office to Grenville, Rockingham and his friends, and Chatham, whose inopportune resignation had cost him the King's regard. But if the situation looked threatening to George III it was not altogether plain sailing for the opposition. Between each set of men there were serious differences of opinion; common ground had to be sought with ingenuity, and when it was found all-round self-restraint would be vitally necessary. It was a task made no easier by the death of Newcastle in 1768, which deprived the Rockingham whigs of his great political experience, though it may have improved their chance of collaboration with Chatham.

8. OPPOSITION TACTICS

At first, however, the fact that Rockingham and Grenville found themselves in agreement over the Wilkes affair made the prospects of joint action rather better. In London feeling was running high against the ministers, whipped up by the vitriolic, mysterious *Letters of Junius*,[1] even before the final affront of Luttrell's election.

---

[1] His identity has never been authoritatively established but the general assumption is that Junius was the pen name of Sir Philip Francis, later the deadly enemy of Warren

On 21 February this was given practical expression at a meeting held at the London Tavern by Wilkes's supporters. This meeting is of something more than passing interest, for it saw the inauguration of a new society, 'The Supporters of the Bill of Rights'.[1] This was the first of those notable societies which were for more than fifty years to play a prominent part in the struggle for parliamentary reform. The forging of this weapon in defence of liberty was, however, still in the future; the immediate object of the society was to protect existing rights enjoyed under the constitution against the high-handed infringements of the administration. Once again it was 'Wilkes and Liberty' under a new guise. On 9 May a great political dinner, held at the famous Thatched House Tavern and attended by both Rockingham and Grenville and some seventy of their supporters, proclaimed to the world that the two men were prepared to act together at least over this issue.

This was the situation when Chatham began to come out of his retirement. When he attended the Levee on 7 July and afterwards had a private interview in the Closet, political circles buzzed with rumours. Whether his attendance was prompted by the courtesy which Chatham always paid to the person of the King, and what expectations, or plans, lay behind it, it is impossible to say. Chatham seems to have given no indication of any desire to return to political life. Nor did he give George III any reason to suppose that he approved of Grafton's policy in his absence, or that he would be willing again to join a ministry which included his erstwhile supporter. Chatham and the King had at least one quality in common: they neither of them forgave easily men whom they considered had failed them, and they made few allowances for the cause of that failure. Plainly after this interview the King discarded Chatham: they never met again. Rockingham also seems to have viewed Chatham's political resurrection with modified rapture. As an ally he might be of great value in bringing about the fall of the ministry, but neither man was content to subordinate himself to the other. This made the organizing of an effective campaign extremely difficult.

Hastings. Dr. Johnson's comment was that 'While he walks like Jack the Giant-Killer in a coat of darkness, he may do much mischief with little strength.'—*Thoughts on the Late Transactions respecting the Falkland Islands*, 1770, p. 120.

[1] Its original purpose was to secure funds from supporters with which to buy off Wilkes's creditors, though it afterwards played an important part in the development of eighteenth-century radicalism.

Moreover, their fundamental attitudes towards political problems were different.

This difference of outlook was sharply underlined when in 1770 Edmund Burke produced his controversial *Thoughts on the Cause of the Present Discontents.*[1] In it 'party' is deliberately proclaimed 'a good thing'. George III is blamed not so much for his policies as for his challenge to a wise and beneficent pattern of government. In it Burke gave a new dignity to 'party' as a political concept. To him it was 'a body of men united for promoting by their joint endeavours the national interest upon some particular principle in which they are all agreed', rather than a group held together by personal connections and interests. In his opinion the Rockinghams were such a party. *The Cause of the Present Discontents* was a piece of superb political propaganda. Whether Burke's claim can be substantiated, whether the Rockingham whigs differed from other contemporary political groups in any essential way has been hotly debated. Yet if to have a mental image is eventually to shape yourself in conformity with it, then the Rockinghams were not quite as other political groups. Vague and fluctuating though the numbers who accepted the Marquis's leadership were, it is possible to distinguish some sixty in the late 1760s, around eighty in 1780 and as many as 150 in the brief Fox–North administration. Despite their weakness, a weakness increased by their refusal to accept the political realities of their day, over this period the Rockingham whigs do seem to have been developing a structure somewhat more coherent than other opposition groups.[2] Pragmatically the Bedfords knew that by acting together their bargaining position was strengthened. Burke's pamphlet produced a moral basis for what had long been the practical aim of all politicians, namely to get as much of their own way with as little royal interference as possible. Also, now that opposition groups could no longer rally behind a Prince of Wales in order to attack the King's ministers, it was convenient to have a respectable principle for which to fight. This the new concept of party provided.

For the administration the prospect looked bleak when Parliament reassembled on 9 January 1770. Burke's controversial pamphlet

1 Writing to Richard Shackleton, 6 May 1770, he described it as 'the political creed of our Party' declaring that it 'will explain to you the Grounds of our proceedings.'— *Burke Correspondence*, vol. II, July 1768–June 1774, edited L. S. Sutherland (1960), p. 136.

2 On this point see I. R. Christie, *Myth and Reality*, pp. 27–53 and A. S. Foord, *op. cit.*, p. 344.

had not yet appeared to emphasize the different conceptions of the constitution held by the attacking groups, and in Wilkes's expulsion they had a topic on which they could all unite. Also at last the breach in the 'cousinhood' had been repaired: Temple, Grenville and Chatham were once again on good terms. Even so the danger lay not so much in the possibility of a defeat in the Commons as in certain weaknesses within the ministry on which the opposition might play. Camden was returning to his old allegiance to Chatham, and Granby, that popular soldier, was inclining the same way; so in the Commons was Dunning, the Solicitor-General.[1] If enough resignations could be brought about, so that the King could not fill the vacancies, it would be necessary for him to come to terms with Chatham and Rockingham. Chatham started the offensive by moving an amendment to the Address which condemned the handling of the Wilkes problem. It was his first speech in the Lords since his illness and some of the old fire was lacking, though when he intervened later in the debate it was with more effect. In the Commons Dowdeswell moved a similar amendment. Neither was carried, though Dowdeswell secured 138 votes. What was important, however, was that Camden in the Lords, and both Granby and Dunning in the Commons, voted against the government. It was a sign for the resignations to begin. Dunning led the way, followed by Beaufort, Manchester, Huntingdon and Coventry, who gave up posts in the Household, Sir George Yonge, Sir Percy Brett and Jemmy Grenville and finally by Granby. Camden, George III decided after such insubordination in supporting the amendment, must go. And so at last, most bitterly, came to Charles Yorke the fulfilment of his life's desire. On 12 January, at the King's express desire, Grafton offered him the Great Seal. He was far from well at the time and the decision was an agonizing one to make. Without a Chancellor it was doubtful if the King could hold out against the opposition attacks; to accept therefore was to betray his friends the Rockinghams. Yet to refuse was to lose forever the distinction he most coveted, for even if George III succumbed to the Rockinghams there was still Chatham's partiality for Camden to be overcome, and George would never forgive Yorke if he failed him now. Miserably torn between his friendships and his profession he vacillated for some days. Eventually he surrendered to a personal appeal from the King himself and accepted the Seal. Three days later

---

[1] For details of his career see P. Brown, *op. cit.*, pp. 231–321.

he was dead, probably from physical causes accentuated by the strain of the last few days, though rumour suggested suicide.

Two days later still, on 20 January, Rockingham moved a resolution to take into consideration the state of the nation. The speech in which Chatham supported him is something of a landmark in that it contained one of the first serious suggestions that a reform of Parliament was the only remedy for the ills of the age; he wanted a greater proportion of genuinely independent members in the House. To secure this, accepting the prevalent but possibly incorrect view that the county members were independent while corruption and patronage lurked in the boroughs, he advocated that the county representation should be increased by an extra member for each county. It was not a proposition likely to commend itself to the Rockinghams, who preferred to see a reduction in the offices in the gift of the Crown which could be used to influence votes given in the House, and Chatham seems to have flung it out in the course of the debate somewhat casually. For a time no more was heard of it, but later, when once again a respectable member, Wilkes was to raise the question of parliamentary reform in the House.

For a little time longer Chatham and Rockingham were too full of hope to allow their differences of outlook to divide them. On 25 January in the Commons Dowdeswell moved a cleverly worded motion 'That this House, in the exercise of its judicature in matters of election, is bound to judge according to the law of the land, and the known and established law and custom of Parliament.' Sentiments so impeccable, they argued, the House would find it difficult to repudiate; yet to carry the amendment would be to condemn by implication their ignoring of the Middlesex electors. In this crisis North showed his parliamentary ability by moving an amendment stating that the expulsion of Wilkes was agreeable both to the law of the land and to Parliament. Even so his amendment was carried by only 44 votes in a full House. The opposition whigs were jubilant: never had they been so near to success. Two days later it seemed as if it were fully theirs; on 27 January Grafton lost his nerve and resigned. Their hopes were short lived for Lord North, coming to the rescue of his King, accepted the Treasury.

16

DOMESTIC SUCCESS AND COLONIAL DISASTER

1. The Failure of the Opposition

ONCE again it was to be demonstrated that stability could only be secured by a minister who had the confidence both of the Commons and of the Crown. North seems to have had little ambition. What kept him for twelve years as head of the administration was the insistence and persistence of the King. At times North appears almost like a puppet held in position by George III's manipulation of the twin wires of Jenkinson and Robinson. One quality he shared with Walpole and Pelham: he was a good House of Commons man. He was aware of members' prejudices and was able to play both on them and on their loyalties. Though as a colleague he could be difficult,[1] irresolute of purpose and without the power to animate and direct to a common cause his co-members of the Cabinet, in handling the Commons as a body his touch was sure. It took the disasters of the American war to break the partnership of North and George III. But for twelve years more the world was to be shown that while the Commons was composed only partly of active politicians and partly of independent gentlemen, that while the patronage of the Crown was at the service of the administration, and that while the King and his chief minister were in concord, nothing which even a combined opposition could do could shake the ministerial majority in either House. To do that a national crisis was required.

[1] John Robinson's relations with Lord North in the early part of 1780 illustrate the latter's unfortunate manner in handling individuals. See I. R. Christie, 'The Political allegiance of John Robinson, 1770–1784.' (*Bulletin of the Institute of Historical Research*, XXIX, 1956).

Divergent points of view soon became apparent when Rocking-ham and Chatham found that they would have to carry on the offensive. Basically the Marquis disliked what he regarded as the democratic element in Chatham's strategy. This rift between the two men was made evident when in March 1770 Beckford, who was now Lord Mayor, presented a remonstrance to the King. This, though emphasizing the Middlesex election, was really a recapitu-lation of grievances and was barely civil in tone. Many members resented his affront to the King, and Sir Thomas Clavering moved that the offending document together with the King's reply, be laid before the House. In the subsequent debate the assistance which the Rockinghams gave to their Chathamite allies was so lukewarm as to advertise to the world their dislike of Beckford's petition. The Loyal Address was carried by a large majority, and Chatham was bitter about the lack of support which Rockingham's friends had afforded. If by his handling of this petition North was able to play on the loyalty of the country gentlemen and their dislike of the upstart City democrat, he was equally skilful in giving way to their wishes over disputed elections. As everyone knew, these were never settled with any reference to the rights of the case, and were always regarded as a trial of strength between the adminis-tration and opposition groups. George Grenville, who by now had attained something of the stature in the House of an elder states-man, was to make one of his last contributions, and perhaps his most useful, to the statute book. This was a bill providing for the hearing of disputed elections by a select committee which could admit evidence on oath, rather than by a committee of the whole House—the practice hitherto.[1] North did not oppose the motion, which he knew would be popular with independent members, who thought well of Grenville and ill of ministerial corruption. It was therefore passed as a temporary measure in 1770 and made per-manent in 1774. By the Easter recess it was clear that North's skill in depriving the opposition of good fighting topics was bearing fruit; the ministry was much stronger than it had been at the beginning of the year.

Patriotism and the national welfare were the twin banners under which both Rockingham and Chatham claimed to fight, but their behaviour over the affair of the Falkland Islands, when Parliament

---

[1] Pitt said 'This happy event is the dawn of better times.' *The Chatham Correspondence*, edited W. S. Taylor and J. H. Pringle (1838–40), vol. IV, p. 332.

reassembled in November 1770, can only be described as completely factious. This crisis blew up during the summer recess. The Falkland Islands had been originally claimed by Spain, but, remote and infertile, had promised to be of little use to anyone.[1] As, however, trading activities became more expansive, and as stations where ships could refit were useful in times alike of peace and war, in 1748 England had planned to send an expedition to the islands. Spain had protested; England had refused to accept her protest, but the expedition had not sailed. In 1764 Choiseul had taken possession of the most easterly of the islands and founded a settlement called Port Louis. This, with memories of the Seven Years War fresh in men's minds, spurred on the British government to seize one of the western islands, and found Port Egmont. In face of Spanish protests Choiseul, to whom Spanish friendship was of more importance than an obscure settlement in the Pacific, withdrew. Port Louis was now occupied by Spain and renamed Port Soledad. Friction developed in November 1769 between the representative of the British government—Captain Hunt who was stationed off Port Egmont in the frigate *Tamar*— and the Spanish authorities. The former met Spanish protests at the British occupation with threats to eject the Spaniards from Port Soledad itself. How seriously the threats of the hot-tempered captain influenced the Spaniards is not clear. What is certain is that after Hunt had sailed for England, five frigates based on Buenos Aires forced the English garrison to surrender Port Egmont.

This display of force on the part of Spain, however sound her theoretical claim to Port Egmont might be, was an insult which no British administration could ignore. Clearly it constituted a threat to the general peace of Europe, for to demand reparation and an apology might spark off a general conflict. Everything depended on whether France was prepared to back Spanish claims. In these difficult circumstances the Cabinet acted with an admirable combination of firmness and caution. Lord Weymouth, Secretary for the Southern Department, demanded that the action of the local Spanish governor, Buccarelli, be disavowed and that Port Egmont be restored; he could indeed ask no less. But at the same time he was careful to inform France of the steps England was taking, in the hope

---

[1] Dr. Johnson described it as 'a colony that could never become independent, for it could never be able to maintain itself', in *Thoughts on the Late Transactions, etc.*, p. 80. When writing of independence he was clearly thinking in economic not political terms.

that she would exercise a moderating influence over her ally. Meanwhile James Harris, the British *chargé d'affaires* in Madrid, saw Grimaldi, Spain's chief minister, who, after temporizing, proposed a settlement which fell short of the British demands. When Parliament met, the situation was therefore one of some delicacy. Ministers had to act firmly enough to vindicate British honour without driving France to the support of Spain. But the very suspicion of Spanish aggression was enough to provoke Chatham to unreasoning fury. In a speech delivered on 22 November he described England with considerable exaggeration, as 'an injured, insulted, undone country' and he castigated the administration for not having put it on a warlike footing as soon as Hunt had returned in the previous June with his news of friction over Port Soledad. The impression he gave was that there was nothing he so much desired as to drive this country once more into war with Spain.[1]

It is difficult to analyse the forces which urged him on. Spain he had always considered as the national enemy, along with France. His earliest triumphs against Walpole had been won in his agitation for a Spanish war, though later he came to see how much there was to be said for Walpole's handling of the problem. His own resignation in 1761 had been forced upon him by the refusal of the Cabinet to declare war immediately on Spain. Moreover, if war did break out, once again there might be a national call for Pitt. It is difficult to believe that he seriously thought that England's interests demanded war. Yet if this was not his genuine belief his behaviour, and that of the Rockinghams, was deplorable, because by their criticisms of the unpreparedness of the country they were making successful negotiations almost impossible. As at the same time they were continuing to harry and distract the administration over the stale Wilkes affair, and were raising new issues over the law of libel, it certainly looks as if hatred of Lord North and George III was their prime motive.

By the middle of the month the chances of saving peace were considered small by most people. Spain felt that she also had a case; she expected England to pay some attention to the provocation which she had received from Captain Hunt, and she did not

---

[1] Dr. Johnson, who was called upon to answer the attack made by Junius on the ministerial handling of the crisis, wrote, with some justification, 'He is an enemy to the ministry, he sees them hourly growing stronger. He knows that a war at once unjust and unsuccessful would have certainly displaced them, and is therefore, in his zeal for his country, angry that the war is not unjustly made, and unsuccessfully conducted.'— *Op. cit.*, p. 124.

want to renounce her final rights in the islands. Also, though Choiseul had at first used his influence for peace he seemed to be swinging round to the idea that French interests would be best served by backing Spain. Then on 16 December the crisis was intensified by the resignation of Lord Weymouth, who wanted a tougher line while the rest of the ministers were reluctant to take steps which they feared might precipitate the outbreak of war. Refusing to panic, George III and North now transferred Rochford from the Northern to the Southern Department.[1] Equally unintimidated by Spain, a Cabinet held on the 19th decided to recall James Harris from Madrid. This decision proved to be embarrassingly precipitate. Louis XV, who was engaged in domestic quarrels with the French Parlement, refused to endorse Choiseul's warlike attitude and dismissed him on 24 December. Without an ally Spain was forced to give way; the danger of war was over.

The weakness of the Rockingham-Chatham opposition soon became increasingly obvious. The number as well as the quality of anti-government members had been seriously diminished by the death of George Grenville in November 1770. At the same time Chatham lost his mouthpiece in the Commons through the death of William Beckford. Gradually the old faces of the heroic middle years of the century were beginning to disappear. Also, once again, Chatham and Rockingham found themselves without a good fighting topic on which they could agree. They continued to make attacks on the handling of the Falkland Islands crisis, but such criticism was unlikely to gain them votes, for it was difficult to make reasonable men believe that a negotiation which had avoided a war without loss of national dignity was a matter for the overthrow of an administration. The stand which they took over the interpretation of the law of libel was morally more justifiable. In the earlier trial of Wilkes for seditious libel Mansfield had laid it down that the decision as to what constituted a seditious libel was a matter for the judge. The jury could only decide as to its printing and publication. This ruling was obviously one of great legal and political importance. The law of libel was intricate, and juries were composed of men unversed in the law and probably full of prejudices; to leave to them difficult legal points, even with the direction and help of the judge,

---

[1] But see John Calcraft to Chatham, 18 December 1770. 'There is great alarm, and very great disagreement amongst the ministers. His Majesty is sick, was bled on Sunday, and had no levee yesterday. In times past, these were certain symbols of anxiety and changes.'—*Chatham Correspondence*, vol. IV, p. 60.

might produce verdicts which, in the legal aspect, were very un-satisfactory. On the other hand, in a time of political controversy, to deprive a man of the protection of his fellow citizens, sitting as a jury, when the whole weight of the administration was against him was to jeopardize the liberty of the subject. It was this issue which gave the case of Woodfall and Almon its importance. A devas-tating, and anonymous critic of the government, the 'Junius' already mentioned, was causing considerable trouble to North and George III. One of the most virulent of his *Letters* appeared in the *Morning Advertiser* of 9 December 1769, and the administration decided to prosecute. As, however, the identity of the writer could not be discovered, only the printer Woodfall and the publisher Almon[1] could be arrested. In his direction to the jury Mansfield again gave the ruling that the decision as to whether what they had printed and published constituted a seditious libel was a matter for the judge, not for them. Both Chatham and Rockingham agreed that this question was one of vital importance and that it should be raised in Parliament as concerning the liberty of the subject. Un-fortunately for their chances of successful co-operation they favoured different approaches. The basic trouble was the old rivalry between Mansfield and Camden, who had disagreed with the former's interpretation.

Chatham wanted a complete vindication of Camden's views and pressed for a committee of the House to inquire into the administration of criminal justice. Rockingham thought it wiser to concentrate on getting an act which would secure to future juries the right to decide whether a publication was libellous. This pro-cedure would have the great advantage of by-passing the problem of the legal arguments contained in past rulings. Their disagreement soon became apparent, the subsequent debates in the House being largely a series of arguments between the two wings of the oppo-sition.[2] It was clear that the government was never in the slightest danger. After this public confession of weakness and disunity, only the most stalwart of Rockingham's personal cohorts could feel that

[1] Almon had been prominent in the early attacks on Bute and with the backing of opposition politicians had set up as a bookseller in Piccadilly. In 1767 he had started the *Political Register*.

[2] Chatham wrote 'I trust this compound of tyranny and folly will meet with the re-ception from the public which such a task master deserves. However, I will keep down rising sensations so justly founded . . . the constitution, however, I will not sacrifice, even to union.' *Ibid.*, vol. IV, pp. 103–4.

there was any purpose in continuing their parliamentary attacks. Chatham, weary and disillusioned, did not even trouble to attend Parliament when it met in January 1772. Yet however factious the behaviour of the Newcastle-Rockingham whigs had been since the resignation of the old Duke in 1762, and however mixed their motives in opposing the Crown, they had some solid justification for their disquiet which was not purely personal. The affair of the No. 45 *North Briton* had shown George III resolute to stifle comment and ready in doing so to employ methods which were questionable. In their handling of the Middlesex election the ministers had put themselves in an impossible position; they had been driven to ignore the rights of the electors and to put a resolution of the House of Commons on a par with a statute.[1] In the case of Woodfall and Almon there had been a similar attempt to stifle public opinion by a drastic use of the law of libel against political writers.

In the same session a somewhat undignified struggle took place over the publication of parliamentary debates. In the bitter conflicts which preceded the fall of Walpole the Commons had declared that the publication of its debates was a breach of privilege, though reports of speeches still appeared in the press—under fictitious names and in an imaginary assembly. By 1771 these accounts of debates were being used in such a way as to belittle ministers; opposition papers made very little attempt to disguise their intentions. The Commons, always sensitive to criticism, instructed their messenger to arrest the printers and publishers of the offending reports. Wheble and Thompson were then arrested within the confines of the City of London and, being brought before the City Aldermen—one of whom was Wilkes, now free from prison—they were promptly discharged on the ground that their arrest infringed the privileges of the City. Wilkes and his friends were in a position to carry the war into the enemy's camp, for the messenger of the Commons was committed to prison by the Lord Mayor for having attempted to execute in the City a warrant which had not been backed by a City magistrate.[2] In retaliation the Commons then committed the Lord Mayor and one of the aldermen, who were

---

[1] *Letters of Junius,* 8 Aug. 1769: 'What was law yesterday is not law today; and now, it seems, we have no better rule to live by than the temporary discretion and fluctuating integrity of the House of Commons.'

[2] Only a City magistrate could issue the necessary warrant for an arrest within its boundaries.

also members of Parliament, to the Tower for contempt in arresting the messenger of the House. Immediately their case was taken up by the opposition, and Rockingham, Portland and Burke all paid them propaganda visits. As, however, the House's right to commit to prison extended only to the end of the session, the prisoners, after being the heroes of the London mob, were released as soon as Parliament rose.

The government had a measure of justification for much of its action against freedom of speech since 1763. Again and again the abuse and misrepresentation to which it had been subjected went beyond the limits of fair comment. Nevertheless it is possible to argue that George III and his ministers were using their influence over the House in a more dangerous way than their predecessors had done. Perhaps never before had London's public opinion beaten so bitterly, and with so little effect, against the walls of Parliament. Again and again it had seethed with fury. Political riots were a commonplace; frequently Bute, North, sometimes even the King himself, were hissed in the streets. Past opponents may have been muzzled by similar methods. Walpole had prevented the publication of parliamentary debates and imposed a censorship on plays in an endeavour to muzzle his critics; but there had not been the open defiance of public opinion and the open overriding of the rights of electors which had marked the last ten years. The fact that many members of the Commons were in sympathy with George III made the situation even more dangerous, because a common dislike of Wilkes and Junius and all that they stood for gave him the support of solid country gentlemen whose votes were not for sale. Prejudice may well have been an even more influential factor than corruption in suppressing distasteful comment and in asserting the rights of the House against its electors.

Whatever the cause, by the end of 1772 it seemed that victory lay with Lord North[1] and that the worst of his difficulties had been overcome. The opposition had fallen apart; the old topics were threadbare and North was careful not to provide them with new ones.[2] For a time at least Chatham had turned his back on the world

---

[1] cf. Chatham's comments to Shelburne, *Chatham Correspondence*, vol. IV, pp. 332–3.

[2] Burke refused to share this pessimistic view. *Burke Correspondence*, vol. II, p. 309. The future was to justify Burke's optimism while leaving open the question as to what would have happened had the American War of Independence not provided them with a heaven sent 'Occasion'.

of politics, which he had always found distasteful when there was
no immediate cause for which to fight. Rockingham carried on a
routine, ineffective opposition, in which it is impossible to know in
what proportions an obstinate adherence to principle and personal
vanity were mixed. Such an opposition had little to offer the independent members, who in any case had no reason to be ill-content
with North. In particular he possessed one quality which always
appealed to them—a flair for finance. Even in his first budget as
Chancellor of the Exchequer he had impressed his colleagues by
his gift for lucid exposition.[1] Like Walpole and Pelham he was a
competent and successful head of the Treasury. Had there been
no American war to deflect him North might have gone down in
history as one of the outstanding financial reformers of the eighteenth century. Even as it was the younger Pitt built on the foundation which he had laid.

In 1772 George III and Lord North could hardly be expected
to realize that they were merely experiencing the calm before the
storm. In Europe, British reputation stood high. This was not solely
because of the military prowess, the economic resources, the successful political direction which had been revealed in the Seven
Years War. For Europe was not only attracted by the success of the
British way of life; she was impressed by the intellectual vigour of
the victorious islanders.

Of course, this interest was not new. After the triumph of Queen
Anne's reign, after the decline of the prestige of the monarchy of
Louis XIV, there had been a comparable interest. Voltaire and
Montesquieu had both come to England to learn lessons for their
own country and the *Letters on the English* and *The Spirit of the Laws*
spread the fame of English liberty. Voltaire was an effective popu-
larizer of the doctrines of Newton which were driving those of
Descartes out of the schools and academies of Europe. Though
Voltaire could only half comprehend the English admiration for
Shakespeare, he was well fitted to appreciate Pope and Congreve,
Swift and Bolingbroke. The novels of Richardson were admired,
wept over, imitated; *Gulliver* and *Robinson Crusoe* entered into the
general European heritage. In what it was still reasonable to call 'the
Republic of Letters' English had not replaced French, but it was far
more necessary to learn English than it had been. Both Louis XVI and
Danton had a respectable knowledge of the language. In translations

[1] J. E. D. Binney, *op. cit.*, p. 263.

most of the ideas of the English and Scottish enlightenment found their way all over Europe. Hume and Gibbon were Parisian figures as well as ornaments of Edinburgh and London. The fame of Adam Smith in Glasgow reached Moscow. And these were only the most famous names. Much of the architectural glory of St Petersburg and its palaces was due to the great Scottish architect Charles Cameron; horse races in the English style and men's clothes in the style of the English gentry were imitated by such great figures in the aristocratic society of Europe as the Duc d'Orleans. The next two decades were to tarnish this glory: the English political system extolled by one Swiss, de Lolme, was denounced by another, Rousseau.

2. East India Company Problems

In the early years of Lord North's ministry the affairs of the East India Company seemed to present a more pressing problem than British relations with the American colonies, where the repeal of the Townshend duties, except that on tea, had led to a temporary slackening of tension. After 1763 the Company's administrative machinery, which had been adequate for the needs of a trading corporation, began to develop glaring weaknesses under the strain of handling its new responsibilities. After Clive's victories, and the assumption of wide responsibilities for the handling of the revenue of Bengal, native rulers were no longer strong enough to control the activities of the Company's servants in India. That a man should acquire a private fortune by individual trading, in addition to that carried on for the Company in its corporate capacity, had long been one of the perquisites of service in India. Previously, though individual cases of trickery and fraud had taken place, such activities had been kept within the bounds of what the eighteenth century considered decent. Now extremely ugly tales of exploitation and greed trickled back to England, where such public opinion as there was began to turn against the Company. This was due to several entangled causes. Wealthy 'nabobs', as men who had acquired fortunes in this way came to be called, were bitterly resented by those sections of society who suffered from them. In addition many people were genuinely disturbed by what they heard. Finally, when the administrative chaos in the Company seemed to threaten its dividends, sections of the Court of Proprietors began to clamour for some measure of reform. Ministers also were coming to realize that they could not hope to avoid some involvement in East Indian affairs.[1]

Hitherto the relationship between the Company and the Crown had been almost purely financial. As one of the 'monied companies', the East India Company had been an integral part of the financial structure of the City. Also, because of its wealth, whenever the charter became due for renewal, the government of the day had been able to secure considerable sums for the Treasury. But though Chatham's attempts to review the whole question of the Company's right to its territorial revenue had been hazy in conception and skilfully sidetracked by Charles Townshend, he had at least realized, with one of his characteristic flashes of foresight, that in future the Crown could not confine itself to being a mere receiver of money in return for periodical renewals of the Company's charter. Public money had been used to finance its conquests and public opinion was beginning to demand that the Crown must exercise some oversight in the way in which they were administered. George III showed genuine concern over the need for some reform, but the motives of his ministers were not merely altruistic. The internal weakness of the Company and its divided counsels encouraged speculation in its stocks. This in turn led to a series of financial crises which disturbed the smooth working of the London money market. There was also the further danger that a weakly aggressive policy in India itself might lead to fresh outbreaks of fighting with native rulers, which France might use to re-establish her own political strength there. If that happened the Crown could not stand idly by. Once again public money would have to be spent on armies and fleets. In this way circumstances were gradually driving ministers to realize that whether they were content to work through their influence over the directorate, or whether they obtained legislation for the purpose, they must assume some measure of control over the Company's more important actions.

The first necessity was to carry out reforms within the Company. Without this it was impossible either to check the worst abuses of its servants in India or to strengthen its financial structure at home. Unfortunately feuds within the Company made it almost impossible to do this. Investigations were certain to uncover scandals, while reforms would curtail private opportunities to make money. To safeguard themselves individuals grouped into factions behind prominent directors, each pledged to protect the interests of his own

---

[1] For full details, summarized in the following pages, consult L. S. Sutherland, *The East India Company, etc.*, chs. VII, VIII, IX.

clique. The constitution of the Company lent itself only too well to this kind of intrigue. A holding of £500 stock conferred a vote in the Court of Proprietors, which was responsible for the annual election of the directors; and the General Courts, which were called to approve policy, became the battleground of the contending factions. In these struggles the device of vote-splitting was increasingly employed. Proprietors of large blocks of stock would fictitiously split them into units of £500 and distribute them among their supporters in order to create the necessary majority for their policies in the Court of Proprietors. Ministers in their attempt to exercise some measure of indirect control over the affairs of the Company were forced to engage in similar practices; on occasion the balances at the Pay Office were used for this purpose. The employment of such subterranean methods marks the transition between the indifference of the Crown to the policy followed by the Company and its assumption of a real measure of responsibility. Though Townshend had ruined Chatham's wider plans, the settlement negotiated in 1767 had been merely an interim one designed to give time for a fuller investigation. Two years later it had been followed by another temporary agreement. This, too, showed comparatively little awareness of the immensity of the problems which the extension of the Company's territories had created. Even so it had seen the beginning of a new kind of interference in its affairs. In future, in order to check the wild speculation in its shares which had marked the past few years, its dividends could not be raised above 12½ per cent without parliamentary sanction. In addition it had to supply the Treasury with certain financial information. Events were soon to show that such control was not enough. By 1772 its affairs were in such disorder that the Company was on the verge of bankruptcy and it was forced to approach the Treasury for a loan. These were the circumstances which forced Lord North to introduce his Regulating Bill. By it he hoped to secure some measure of reform to check the worst of the Company's weaknesses until the renewal of its charter in 1780 provided a better opportunity for a thorough reorganization. This, North was aware, would require more thought and longer preparation than the immediate necessities of the present crisis would permit. It is not fair therefore to regard the Regulating Act as a measure of fundamental importance which failed. It was a stop-gap measure. Nevertheless it marks a milestone in the assumption of public responsibility for British rule in India.

In order to give some unity to the Company's actions in India, because the slowness of communications often made it necessary to take important decisions on the spot without instructions from home, overriding authority was given to a Governor-General in Bengal. To prevent the abuse of this authority he was to be forced to act with a council of four, whose decisions, if he were in a minority, he could not overrule. In addition, all incoming dispatches from India were to be submitted either to the Treasury or to the Secretary of State. In framing these provisions there had been no intention of ignoring the legitimate interests of the Company. The government nominated as the first Governor-General Warren Hastings, a trusted servant of the Company, who since 1772 had been struggling to improve the administration in Bengal. Richard Barwell also represented its interests. The other three members of the council were intended to act as watch-dogs for the Crown. It had not been easy to find suitable candidates, and the final selection of General Clavering, Colonel Monson and Philip Francis was to prove disastrous for the smooth working of the scheme. At this time ministers had full confidence in Hastings and expected that their nominees would work harmoniously with him; that they failed to do so was due to personal ambitions and animosities. At the same time an attempt was made to strengthen the control of the directors by preventing the creation of fictitious votes; £1,000 was to be the minimum qualification. This it was hoped would make it less easy to build up factions within the Court of Proprietors. When the bill became law North might well hope that he had solved with some adroitness a difficult problem, without either splitting his own Cabinet or giving opportunities to the opposition.

3. THE GROWING CRISIS IN AMERICA

In America, too, by 1772 the situation was not unpromising. The removal of all the Townshend duties except that on tea, which after some deliberation had been kept as a symbol of the authority of the British Parliament, had eased the position in the colonies. Though the extremists had wanted to continue the non-importation agreements until the tea duties had also been removed, the majority of the American merchants were ready for a compromise. As men of property they viewed with apprehension the increasing power of the politicians and the use that they were making of the mob to enforce their views. In spite of the temporary stimulus of the Boston

Massacre, which ironically took place on the very day that North was proposing to the Commons to repeal the Townshend duties, the colonists' united front was beginning to crumble. By the middle of 1770, after serious internal feuds, New York broke away and the collapse came quickly. By 1772 it seemed as if the crisis were over. That it was sparked again into life was not entirely the doing of the British authorities. Only if they had accepted what in fact, if not as yet completely in theory, was the American contention, namely that every kind of British authority must be withdrawn, could peace have been permanently restored. While the British continued to try to enforce the laws of trade, and for this purpose made war on the smuggler, incidents were bound to occur. Such was the burning of the *Gaspee* in June 1772.[1] Engaged in chasing some smugglers, she had run aground. In that helpless condition, though she was a ship of the royal navy, she had been boarded, her commanding officer seriously wounded, and the ship finally burnt. No government could accept such a challenge to its authority, and the British reaction was to set up a commission of inquiry to collect evidence and to send the suspects to England for trial, as it was clear that no local jury would convict. In this they completely failed. Though the identity of the raiders was widely known no evidence could be collected, and the commission was in consequence completely helpless. What is more, the action of the government in setting up the inquiry was regarded as but one more infringement of the British on American rights; in Virginia, Patrick Henry and Jefferson got the appointment of a standing committee of the Assembly to inform itself by what right the court of inquiry had been set up. Once again the movement of protest spread, and at the invitation of Virginia other Assemblies set up similar committees. In such an atmosphere the determination of the home government to create a Civil List in Massachusetts, and to pay the governor and the judges from the Customs revenue was yet another grievance. So long as these officials were paid by colonial funds, raised by the Assemblies, they could be controlled by the threat of the loss of their salaries.

Already the problem, viewed in the framework of eighteenth-

[1] Describing this incident a Rhode Island collector of Customs wrote to Admiral Montague: 'So farewell Gaspee! Farewell justice! I am prepared for the consequences, I know what they will be: here is an end to security to government servants, here is an end to collecting a revenue and enforcing the Acts of Trade.'—*The Private Papers of John, Earl of Sandwich, First Lord of the Admiralty, 1771-1782*, edited by G. R. Barnes and J. H. Owen (1932), Vol. I, p. 53.

century politics, was extremely intractable. To expect the British ministers and the British King to concede what was virtually independence, even of commercial regulations, within the formal framework of sovereignty was to expect something so revolutionary in concept as to be impossible of acceptance. Though opposition speakers, in attacking the administration, showed great sympathy with the colonists' point of view, they were aware of the possible consequences of provoking them still further and even Chatham was totally opposed to the grant of independence. Indeed, in his last speeches in the Lords, while putting forward hazy and impractical ideas for a reconciliation, his main effort was to oppose the defeatist talk—current, as always, during an unsuccessful war—that independence would have to be granted. Yet if every assertion of British rights were to throw the Americans into a ferment of near-revolt, how could the relations between them and the mother country ever regain the normality and stability necessary for their mutual advantage? The problem looked utterly different according to the side of the Atlantic from which it was viewed. Suspicions once aroused are not easily put to sleep; every action taken by George III and his ministers seemed a sinister extension of British tyranny, while in England each colonial protest or riot seemed a further piece of disloyalty and even treason. To take no action for long enough to allow colonial feelings and suspicions to subside might have been prudent, but to execute such a policy required a deeper insight into the causes of the friction than could be fairly expected of North's ministry. Even the sympathy of the opposition was based on a misreading of the situation; such problems once raised cannot be solved by even the most masterly inactivity. By the time that Lord North had become First Lord of the Treasury the damage had been done.

Nevertheless it can hardly be denied that he blundered into fresh American trouble through failing to realize the probable American reaction to his proposal that the East India Company send its tea directly to America instead of bringing it first to this country. The Company, far from being the financial asset which had been expected to result from the taking over of the administration of Bengal, was by 1773 in serious financial difficulties. Its English warehouses were crammed with unsold tea for which, in the face of smuggling activities and the falling-off of the official American demand, it could find no market. The normal pattern of trade was for the tea to be brought to England and then re-exported to the colonies. North's proposals were intended to help the Company by allowing it to export directly to America. The Townshend duty would still have to be paid but this was inconsiderable, and the Company would have been able to undercut the smuggled tea which was so widely drunk there. The plan, however, would have cut across the interests, both legitimate and illegitimate, of many colonial merchants. To the trader who had bought tea through the usual channels, and who was storing it until the agitation against tea drinking had died down, the proposition was disastrous; he would now have to sell his tea at a loss owing to the new lower prices. The man who had smuggled tea would also be hit, though to a less degree as he had paid no duty on it; even so, legal tea would be cheaper than the price at which he could sell. Such practical considerations were enough to range the commercial interest behind the campaign of the politicians, to whom the whole arrangement seemed a trap to entice them, with the bait of cheap tea, to concede the British right to levy external duties at the ports for revenue purposes. Everywhere determined efforts were made to organize the boycotting of the tea, but Boston went further. Determined to subject its citizens to no temptation, a gang of men, lightly and almost insolently disguised as red Indians, boarded the tea ships and threw their cargoes into the water.[1] This was the famous Boston Tea Party. Once again an act of defiance had been committed which could not be ignored.[2]

Both the American and the British handling of the new crisis showed an increasing toughness. After the passing of the Stamp Act, Rockingham and his colleagues had drawn back in some dismay before the violence of American resistance. Resistance to Townshend's duties had produced a similar retreat, with only the tea duty left as a symbol of the British right to impose taxation. In both cases leniency had brought merely a temporary calm, and George III and North had some reason to suppose that to give way again would settle nothing. However long the sleeping dogs were left to lie,

[1] A. M. Schlesinger, *Prelude to Independence* (1958), points out that 'John Brown, one of the leading merchants, not only organized the destruction but took part in it personally.'

[2] 'Few campaigns have ever scored a more brilliant success.'—*Ibid.*, p. 169. It appears, however, that the destruction of the tea was not part of the original programme; it grew out of the special situation at Boston and at first both that port and the rest of the American colonies, feeling that they had gone too far, greeted it with 'a stunning silence' (p. 182).

at the first word of command they bared their teeth as sullenly as ever. Viewed from the American side of the Atlantic it seemed as if the English ministers were perpetually probing to find a weak spot in their defences, ready to withdraw when resistance became too damaging to their commerce, but maintaining consistently their challenge to American liberties, Nor was it ever possible to go back to the *status quo* before the last crisis. Each new episode led to the formulating of new arguments and revealed a little more the incompatibility of the colonists' conception of their liberties with the traditional views of British sovereignty held by the Crown. By 1773 American extremists had gone a long way towards talking themselves and their fellow countrymen into an acceptance of the idea of independence. In 1773, it is true, few responsible statesmen were prepared to admit that this might be the only workable solution; but the idea was already in the air, permeating men's thinking more than most of them realized. The third crisis was to make explicit what was already implicit in their minds; already the colonists were half-way along the road to nationhood.

4. ENGLISH POLITICIANS AND AMERICAN RESISTANCE

It is unlikely that George III and his ministers realized this. Even if they did, they could have had no sympathy with such aspirations. The measures which they took to deal with Boston insubordination were severe but not, in their eyes, nor in the eyes of the majority of M.P.s who gave substantial majorities to their policies, unjustified. Other towns had refused to accept or to permit the distribution of the tea, but Boston's open defiance seemed to mark it out for special treatment, more particularly as the town authorities refused to pay compensation for the loss. The tea had gone overboard on 16 December 1773; on 18 March 1774 a bill was introduced to close the port of Boston until it should pay compensation to the East India Company.[1] In spite of the protests of the small Rockingham clique the bill passed its third reading on the 25th without even dividing the House; its passage through the Lords was equally swift and easy, and on the 31st it received the royal assent. Bills in April and May remodelled the government of Massachusetts, abrogating some of its chartered privileges and bringing it more under royal control. At the same time provision was made for the

---

[1] *Eng. Hist. Docs.*, vol. IX, p. 780.

quartering of troops in America where their presence might be needed in districts unprovided with barracks In the colonies this legislation was bitterly resented. The Port Act meant economic ruin for the inhabitants of Boston, while the other acts invaded their cherished privileges. If, however, the British ministers had hoped to cow Boston and to intimidate other colonies into obedience by their severity they had miscalculated: the general reaction was to unite in support of the victimized city against what in American parlance became known as the 'Intolerable Acts'. Colonial resistance was further stimulated at this time by the passing of the Quebec Act.[1] This dealt with what on the surface was a Canadian rather than an American problem. After assuming the sovereignty of Canada the government had been continued for some time on a provisional basis, but this was not intended to be a permanent arrangement. The Quebec Act was designed to give Canada a new constitution. In it a fairly imaginative attempt was made to combine English conceptions of law and government with the French traditions of the majority of the inhabitants Thus the old French civil law was retained, the Roman Catholic religion was recognized, and the Church was even given the right to continue to collect its tithes. Because, however, the French had had little experience in self-government, instead of an elected Assembly the governor was assisted by an appointed legislative council of twenty-two persons. Moreover, this system was extended to the French-speaking settlements in the valley of the Ohio and the Illinois country.

To the Americans the provisions of the Quebec Act seemed fraught with danger. Before the Peace of Paris French Canada had been a continual threat to American westward expansion, and even to the security of the original colonies. It was the fear of French aggression perhaps more than anything else which had made the protection by British troops so vitally necessary, and it was the lifting of that threat which had made the events of the last ten years possible. Now it looked as if it were to be revived in a new way. The French inhabitants were to be reconciled to their new masters by the recognition of their Roman Catholic faith and Church—a faith and Church deeply distrusted in America, and particularly in the neighbouring New England colonies. Moreover, the power of

---

[1] R. Coupland, *The Quebec Act. A Study in Statesmanship* (1925), p. 122, is of the opinion that 'no more for its effects, therefore, than for its motives as they bore on other colonies can the Quebec Act be condemned'.

their feudal superiors over the Canadian peasantry was also recognized. This, combined with the absence of any provision for an elected legislative assembly, seemed to imply that the ministers in London would be able to dispose at will of the resources of Canada. The extension of this act to cover western lands which the Americans regarded as their natural hinterland, seemed a further threat. Accordingly, when the Massachusetts Bay House of Representatives called on the other colonies to send representatives to a general congress in support of American liberties the response was swift. On 5 September the representatives of all the colonies except Georgia met in Philadelphia in what was to be known as the first Continental Congress. The attempt to punish Boston looked like being the prelude to open war.

At this stage George III seems to have had little doubt that, though force might have to be used, it would be effective, and he carried his ministers with him. Not all the English politicians were similarly blind. The Rockingham whigs had consistently opposed the passage through both Houses of the various 'Intolerable Acts'. Again and again Fox and Burke, Barré and Dowdeswell, stressed not only the American case but also the virtual impossibility of subduing their resistance if it should come to an armed conflict. On 26 May Chatham had made one of his rare appearances in the Lords to protest against the severity of the administration's measures against Boston,[1] and on 17 June he rose to attack the Quebec Act with unmeasured invective. Neither the King, nor his ministers, nor the Lords, nor the Commons were disposed to listen, and a motion to repeal the tea duty and attempt to put back the clock, though supported by all the arguments of Edmund Burke, was rejected by 182 to 49 on 19 April. For their only too accurate prophecies of

[1] In a letter written 20 March 1774 to Shelburne Chatham had made his position in this matter very clear: 'Perhaps a fatal desire to take advantage of this guilty tumult of the Bostonians, in order to crush the spirit of liberty among the Americans in general, has taken possession of the heart of government. . . . Boston, I hope and believe, would make reparation, for a heinous wrong, in the tea cargo; but to consent quietly to have no right over their own purse, I conceive the people of America will never be brought to do. Laws of navigation and trade, for regulation not for revenue I should hope and believe, America, once at ease about internal taxation, would also acquiesce under, and friendly intercourse be again opened; without which we, not they, shall be undone.'— *Chatham Correspondence*, vol. IV, pp. 337–8. This extract is important first because it makes both the sympathy and the limitations of Chatham's position clear, and secondly because it shows how rapidly the swift progress of events was creating a gulf between it and American public opinion.

future woes Chatham and the Rockingham whigs have received much praise from historians, but it must be remembered that their contribution to the problem was essentially negative. They hoped by refraining from provocation to be able to return to an earlier relationship which in reality had already been smashed beyond repair. They were sympathetic because they disliked George III and North and because their own political past was associated with the repeal of the Stamp Act; they thought of the liberties for which the colonists were struggling as the liberties of Englishmen, not those of independent Americans, and failed to see that they were incompatible with the older traditions of sovereignty. They had no more a new vision of empire than George III. Indeed he, rather than the whig opposition, was being realistic when on 11 September he wrote to North, 'The die is now cast, the Colonies must either submit or triumph.'[1]

If the King was being realistic his realism was of a dangerously superficial kind in that he was also being extremely short-sighted. The opposition speakers were wiser than he in stressing the unlikelihood of a British victory. It was idle to suppose that Britain could exert anything like her full strength in campaigns fought in America. The first difficulty lay in the physical impossibility of keeping in touch with the progress of the fighting and adapting policy to meet changing circumstances. The Atlantic crossing never took less than a month and bad weather might delay ships so seriously that two, or even in extreme cases three, months elapsed between the writing of a letter in London and its delivery to the commander in America. Many of the disasters which subsequently overtook British schemes can be traced to this factor alone. It is true that these difficulties had not prevented successful campaigning against France during the Seven Years War, but then the situation had been essentially different; France had suffered from the same disadvantages, while England had benefited from the inspiration and organizing power of Pitt and from the support of the colonists. In the new contest North, who was not a good organizer and whose heart was not in the struggle, failed to give cohesion to the direction of policy and Lord George Germain,[2] who suc-

[1] B. Tunstall, *op. cit.*, p. 447.

[2] As long ago as 18 December 1770 Chatham, writing to Calcraft, had observed: 'I consider that Lord George Germain is becoming every day more and more important to the public: his abilities are certainly good.' Pitt, more generous on this occasion than many of his contemporaries who continually taunted him with that unfortunate episode,

ceeded Dartmouth as Colonial Secretary in November 1775, though not without ability was a very inadequate substitute for Pitt. Apart from the difficulty of distance, geography also made the planning of a campaign a hard task. Communications between colony and colony were bad. America had no capital, for even the meeting of the Continental Congress at Philadelphia conferred no strategic importance on Pennsylvania's capital. To capture Philadelphia or Boston or New York was not to inflict a fatal blow. Nor had America a connected system of vital communications which, once held, could operate as a stranglehold on its economic and military activities. In addition, the terrain itself was often most unsuitable for the successful employment of regular troops. What looked a reasonable route to men who only studied maps in London, in practice meant the hazard of trackless forests, of rivers running through narrow gorges, of hilly and even mountainous country in the north, and of forests, swamps and wide estuaries cutting deep into the countryside in the south. There were also great potential international dangers in getting bogged down in a colonial war. France and Spain had too many grudges against England not to be tempted to take advantage of her difficulties if the struggle with the colonists should be prolonged or unsuccessful. Because they had drawn back over the Falkland Islands it would be unsafe, as the whig opposition pointed out, to assume that they would not attack in more favourable circumstances.

In view of these difficulties and dangers it might have been wiser, as Fox, Burke and Chatham argued, not to assert unenforceable rights. In the early stages of the struggle none of these men envisaged American independence as a desirable thing. To have accepted the situation might have retained the nominal sovereignty of the Crown over the colonies. Whether such a sovereignty would have been worth having in eighteenth-century eyes, or whether the whig opposition realized how meagre in practice it would have been, may well be doubted. It would at least have avoided fighting a war which England could hardly have hoped to win and which in the end was to range France and Spain against her. George III was probably

had decided to overlook his behaviour at Minden.—*Chatham Correspondence*, vol. IV, p. 64. Most historians, including his latest biographer A. Valentine, *Lord George Germain* (1962) are critical of his handling of the war but P. Mackesy, *The War for America*, writes: 'He was not a great war minister, yet both as an administrator and planner he had much to commend him' (p. 516).

right in supposing that if he wanted to exercise genuine authority in the colonies he would have to take stern measures. Not all his ministers, however, thought that a frontal, military attack was the best means of forcing American compliance; economic weapons could be used against the colonists as well as against this country. Without doubt the non-importation and non-consumption measures which were immediately adopted against British goods by the Continental Congress injured British merchants, but if the colonists could be prevented from getting alternative supplies from elsewhere their standard of living would be severely hit. Lord Barrington urged the use of naval power to institute a blockade of the American ports and leave economic distress and the long, slow pressure of attrition to do its work.[1] After 1770 the non-importation agreements had gradually been abandoned; they might be again as merchants found their livelihood gone, and as everywhere shortage of manufactured goods pressed down the standard of living. Whether such a policy would have achieved the desired results may again be doubted. Naval blockade was a difficult art and the American coastline was long. We could, however, almost certainly have held such ports as Boston, New York and Charleston to act as bases, which would have made the task easier. But whether such treatment would have produced more than a temporary restoration of authority is questionable.

That George III and his advisers should not have realized this is in many ways understandable. The whole conception of rebellion and independence was so outrageous and so foreign to their way of thinking that they could not bring themselves to believe that more than a handful of the American people were behind the resistance with which they were faced. To the end of the war they remained convinced that the loyalists were in a majority, held down temporarily by a violent minority and only waiting to be rescued by the royal troops. The idea was less fantastic than it seems to-day. It has been estimated that at the beginning of the war they may have comprised a third of the population. New York, New Jersey and the peace-loving colony of Pennsylvania were regarded askance by

---

[1] J. C. Miller, *The Triumph of Freedom 1775–1783* (Boston, U.S.A., 1948), points out that in the early stages of the struggle the colonists were desperately short of guns, powder and all kinds of munitions of war. Had England been able to cut off the trickle of foreign supplies which they were getting, American resistance might have collapsed before it had been fully organized.

the other colonists as 'enemy's country'.[1] In the north many of the gentry disliked the more democratic element which the rebel leaders seemed ready to encourage in the New England states, while in the south dislike of the semi-aristocratic leadership of the greater planters confirmed many lesser men in their loyalty to George III. Nor were all the nominal supporters of the rebellion prepared to die in the last ditch for it. Many people tried to remain uninvolved, giving a nominal allegiance to whichever side controlled the area in which they lived and making their profit out of selling supplies indiscriminately to either army, though with a preference for the English so long as they paid in hard cash rather than in the rapidly depreciating Congressional money.[2] In such circumstances the English ministers could easily persuade themselves that not one-third but two-thirds of the colonists were loyal at heart. And even had they realized that the majority of the colonists were prepared to fight they might well have doubted their ability to do so. Whatever American propagandists may have said both then and later, the fighting between 1754–63 had been done largely by regular soldiers; the majority of the colonial militia had reached no more than the standard of second-class troops. The first year of the new war was to show how pitifully inadequate the military resources of the Americans were.[3] There was a great shortage of capable officers, little belief in the value of professional discipline, and almost total ignorance of military tactics. When faced by English and German soldiers using the bayonet the militia promptly ran away; and as Congress had failed to grasp the need to enlist its regular army for longer than a year at a time, military service was treated as a civil contract in the sense that when the year was up the enlisted men went home. At critical moments Washington was in considerable doubt as to whether he was likely to have an army at all. His position as commander-in-chief was made more heartbreaking by the fact that Congress had inherited the whig fear of a standing army. Frequently it refused to take him into its confidence, and invariably it underpaid its troops. Since to this must be added a crippling shortage of supplies, rifles, powder and shot, George III had some justification for thinking that a few successful engagements might end the unnatural rebellion with which he was faced.

[1] Not all the colonial propaganda was pro-independence: though less in volume, that of the loyalists was cleverly conceived and well executed. *See* P. Davidson, *Propaganda and the American Revolution, 1763–1783* (1941), p. 315.

[2] For this background see J. C. Miller, *op. cit.*, ch. IV.   [3] *Ibid.*, ch. IX.

There is no doubt that in 1775 and 1776 the majority of Englishmen, both those who were reasonably well informed and those who reacted in ignorance and prejudice, approved of the strong line that the government took. On 25 August 1775 Sandwich, writing to Admiral Graves, informed him that 'the nation (except some factious and interested opponents) are in a manner unanimous in their resolution to crush the unnatural rebellion that has broken out in America by force of arms, which to our great concern we now find to be the only expedient left'.[1] That this was not mere wishful thinking is borne out by Camden's sad comment: 'Who could have imagined, that the ministry could have become so popular by forcing this country into a destructive war and advancing the power of the Crown to a state of despotism?'[2] It has been suggested that one reason for this popularity lay in the fact that with the end of the Russo-Turkish war in 1774 there had been a sudden European demand for British manufactures. As a consequence, except for those merchants to whom American planters and business houses owed money, there was less reliance on the colonial market. It is perhaps significant that Manchester, Lancaster and Liverpool all sent loyal anti-colonial addresses, while the older centres of the American trade, Bristol and London, acted with the opposition. Even Lord North could hardly have pointed out that recruiting was slow— not because of the unpopularity of the war but because of the flourishing state of trade—if there had not been at least some justification for his statement.[3] With the majority of public opinion both in Parliament and in the country at large behind him, it would have been surprising if George III had adopted any other course than the one he followed. In view of the divisions both between and within the American colonies, their notorious slowness to arm and their lack of military stores as well as military experience, an American victory was by no means a foregone conclusion. The British mistake, viewed at least from the angle of short-term policy, was that they struck neither swiftly enough nor hard enough.[4] American independence owed much to Sir William Howe, the English commander. Regarding the struggle almost in the light of a civil war,

[1] *Sandwich Papers*, p. 70.   [2] *Grafton Autobiography*, p. 279.
[3] S. Maccoby, *op. cit.*, p. 217.
[4] G. S. Graham, 'Considerations on the American War of Independence', *Bulletin of the Institute of Historical Research, 1948–50*, p. 23, and see P. Mackesy, *The War for America* (1964) who argues that had Britain struck hard in the early stages and kept the initiative she might have crushed the American resistance (pp. 510 *seq.*).

wanting to beat the Americans, but not too much lest resentment might spoil future hopes of reconciliation, Howe allowed his interpretation of the situation to impede still further his irresolution and slowness in making war. By so doing he gave Washington time to organize a more effective resistance and by defeating him again and again, but always in slow motion, taught him and his troops at last to defeat the royal forces. This in 1775 George III could hardly have been expected to foresee. His folly lay not so much in supposing that there was a good chance of beating the Americans in the field, and reducing them by harrying their trade, as in supposing that a victory of this kind could restore the old relations between them and the mother country. Had the King won, it was highly probable that he would have demanded his pound of flesh. If he had, American submission could only have been temporary and the whole circle of revolt and repression must have started again. The strength of the opposition whigs was that they had more realization of this fundamental dilemma.

5. THE EVE OF WAR

Nevertheless the actual outbreak of fighting did not occur until the skirmish at Lexington on 19 April 1775. Few people, beyond a small group of extremists in America and possibly George III himself wanted war, and the approach of the majority of the colonial leaders towards it was extremely hesitant. The intervening months were therefore occupied by both sides making their position clear in the hope that their opponents would see the danger-signal and give way. The British measures were largely confined to the ostensible punishment of Boston, where Thomas Gage, commander-in-chief of the army in America, was now made governor of Massachusetts. His real authority was, however, confined to the areas controlled by his redcoats, and he was soon aware that any attempt to enforce it outside Boston itself would start the struggle which he, as a practical soldier, viewed with far more misgivings than the administration in London.[1] Again and again he sent home reports stressing that many troops and much equipment would be required if the colonists were to be subdued. The only result of his warnings

---

[1] These views were apparently not shared by Major Pitcairn, who had been sent out to reinforce Gage and who was afterwards mortally wounded at Bunker's Hill. On 14 February he wrote: 'all the friends to government are of opinion that vigorous measures at present would soon put an end to the rebellion'.—*Sandwich Papers*, p. 57. See also P. Mackesy, *op. cit.* p. 510 *seq.*

on the majority of the ministers was to make them critical of Gage himself. Meanwhile the Continental Congress was making a last effort to hold its extremists in check, and to create a basis for negotiation with England. The proposals of 14 October, however, show how far even the moderates had advanced along the road of practical independence. Though prepared to concede the theoretical right of the mother country to pass legislation enforcing a general commercial code on the whole empire, it specifically denounced the acts passed since 1763 as detrimental to 'the life, liberty, property of the people of the colonies'. This was followed by a petition to the King which, while showing verbal loyalty to his person, made it clear that his prerogative must in America be exercised in accordance with Americans' conceptions of their rights and liberties. As these rather dubious overtures were accompanied by non-importation and non-consumption laws and by appeals to both the older and the new colonies in the Caribbean and Canada for support, to George III they savoured rather of treason than of conciliation.

By the end of January 1775 the Cabinet had decided to send additional troops to Gage and on 2 February an address moved in the House of Commons described Massachusetts as being in a state of war. Requests from ministers for additional funds for the army were readily granted in spite of the protests of opposition speakers. Though the new Parliament which met in January was plainly in general agreement with the King, without the exercise by him of any marked influence, Chatham and the Rockinghams continued to fight a rearguard action, not made any easier by the fact that the former blamed the passing of the Declaratory Act by the latter for many of the present evils. In January Chatham moved that the British troops be recalled from Boston, arguing that by so doing American fears would be assuaged and that in any case the military conquest of America was impracticable. In February he introduced a bill of his own into the Lords which was rejected by 61 votes to 32. Even had it been accepted, however, it is unlikely that its terms, with their underlining of British fundamental rights, combined though those were with generous concessions on specific points, would any longer have contented the now almost revolutionary feeling across the Atlantic. The efforts of the opposition therefore merely encouraged American resistance by suggesting the divisions of opinion at home, without really being able to bridge the gap between the contending points of view. North did, however, make one last effort. On the 20th he pushed through his Conciliatory Resolution;[1] by it any colony which was prepared to contribute towards the common expenses of empire and provide a civil list for the payments of its civil and judicial officers was to be assured that Parliament would make no attempt to levy any kind of internal tax for revenue purposes, and that even those collected for the *bona fide* purposes of regulating trade should be handed over for the use of the colony in question. The proposition was less innocent than it appeared. Though outwardly conciliatory, if the colonists had agreed to make permanent provision for a civil list they would have given up their only means of controlling the royal officials, namely the power of the purse.[2]

6. MILITARY OPERATIONS IN AMERICA

In Boston Gage received the news of the Conciliatory Resolution by the same ship which brought earlier instructions from the Colonial Secretary ordering Gage to use force if necessary and informing him that additional reinforcements were on the way. Six days later, thus admonished to be more active in upholding rights, Gage sent an expedition, which marched via Lexington, to seize military stores which spies had told him the colonists were accumulating at Concord. During the last months of the uneasy peace the colonists had not been idle: everywhere revolutionary assemblies had been supplanting the legal legislative and administrative machinery of the individual colonies. Everywhere, too, militia had been drilling and preparing for the struggle which few people now hoped to avoid. When, therefore, the British troops left the shelter of Boston they found their way blocked by American patriot militia at Lexington. Who fired the first shot has never been clearly established; at the time each side accused the other. After a skirmishing fight the redcoats got through to Concord and destroyed what stores the rebels had not been able to remove, though on the way back they were subjected to attack and ambush in which the British lost 273 as against 95 Americans. In terms of modern battles, or even of those in contemporary Europe, such losses were inconsiderable, but throughout the following war the numbers of troops engaged were always small, and it must be remembered that every British soldier killed had to be replaced by another trained

---

[1] *Eng. Hist. Docs.*, vol. IX, p. 877.
[2] I. R. Christie, *Crisis of Empire*, p. 96.

man, not easy to find, who had to be transported across the Atlantic. Had the losses been even the balance would still have been against Britain. The armed clash at Lexington, suitably embroidered with atrocity stories of plunder and rape, would have been sufficient to ensure the rejection of North's would-be conciliation gesture— even if the Americans had trusted it, which they did not.

Even so, the moderates, headed by John Dickinson, author of the *Letters of a Pennsylvanian Farmer* which had once seemed so revolutionary, struggled to find some compromise which would retain the links between America and the Crown. It was still just possible for them to regard Parliament rather than the King as their oppressor, and in the second Continental Congress, which had met in May 1775, a final Olive Branch Petition was voted in early July, appealing to George III to protect their rights against the attack of the British Parliament. Few people expected any success from the move,[1] and during the late spring and early summer the Congress was busy improvising some kind of national administrative machinery. Funds were provided by printing dollar bills, which it was intended that the state legislatures should redeem later in proportion to their population, and, after some discussion, it was decided that the army so raised and paid should be placed under the command of George Washington. On 23 July the continental troops, as those under the control of the Congress of Philadelphia were called in contrast to those in the employment of the individual states, left under his command for Boston, now rather loosely invested by colonial militia. Even before their arrival a certain amount of fighting had taken place round Boston. Reinforcements, with three major-generals—Howe, Clinton and Burgoyne—to assist General Gage, had arrived late in May. They had not, however, felt strong enough to attempt a reconquest of the interior until fresh troops had arrived. Meanwhile the colonial troops had endeavoured to make the British position within the town untenable by establishing themselves on one of the small hills dominating it. The most suitable for this purpose would have been Bunker's Hill, but for some obscure reason the hill they attempted to fortify was Breed's Hill, though the ensuing engagement is usually known as the battle of Bunker's Hill. The enterprise itself failed, but the British losses in recapturing the hill were heavy, and the men could be ill spared. Thereafter nothing decisive happened until the follow-

---

[1] The extremists were anxious that it should fail.

ing spring; then, partly owing to British lack of forethought, on 4 March 1776 the Americans dug in on the Dorchester heights overlooking the town. Once artillery had been placed there the British position became impossible and Howe, who had replaced Gage on 10 October, decided to evacuate. The attempt to punish Boston had therefore merely led to its loss; in the immediate future the British were forced to rely on Halifax as a base.

If the British failed to hold Boston the Americans equally failed to reconquer Canada. That they should attempt to get possession of it was to be expected. Though the governor, Sir Guy Carleton, was a successful and capable official, it was known that some of the troops under his command had been detached to strengthen the garrison in Boston. Also it was hoped that both the older French settlers, and the newer ones of British stock, might be won over to the colonial cause. The hopes proved largely illusory. If the French Canadians felt little affection for the British, they equally had little cause for active discontent. In the coming struggle they remained for the most part indifferent. At first the Americans met with some success. Ticonderoga, the key to the approach via Lake Champlain, was seized without much difficulty on 10 May. Encouraged by this, after some indecision on the part of Congress, it was determined to push on to Montreal. A late start, difficulties due to the terrain and the stubborn resistance of the fort of St John delayed the American advance until 2 November. As, however, Carleton was unable to defend the city with the small force under his command the Americans entered Montreal on 13 November. Carleton made his difficult way back to Quebec. There he was able to hold out until a relieving force arrived from England in May 1776. The American forces were too few to carry the fortress by assault and they had suffered severely from the hardships of a winter campaign.[1] With the arrival of British reinforcements they had no alternative to a retreat. Having failed to take Quebec it was decided to evacuate Montreal also. By June 1776 Canada was once more clear of American troops.

That the fighting between the spring of 1775 and that of 1776 had been so inconclusive must be attributed, at least in part, to the need of both sides to prepare themselves for more extensive operations. It was not until the end of May (1775) that the news of the clash at Lexington reached England, and Gage's official dispatches

[1] These hardships were largely due to the failure of Congress to provide adequate supplies and the indifference of the local Americans. *Eng. Hist. Docs.*, vol. IX, pp. 221–5.

were not received until two weeks later. Not until June therefore was the Cabinet seriously engaged in discussing the best way to raise the large forces which would obviously now be required. It was then decided that regiments should be taken from Gibraltar and Minorca (a dangerous move if Spain should determine to attack), that fresh troops should be raised from the Highland clans, and that new drafts should be recruited in England. By the winter it was clear that such sources would be insufficient, and treaties were made with the smaller German princes to hire mercenary troops from them to use in America. A lack of available superfluous manpower at home made some such arrangement necessary, but the use of the Hessians—which, because of the numbers employed, became a generic name for the German troops employed—widened the breach between George III and his rebellious subjects and left lasting bitterness behind it. These military measures were accompanied by an intensification of the naval blockade. In February 1775 the Newfoundland fisheries had been closed to New England vessels and Newfoundland had been forbidden to trade with any colony except the West Indian islands. In the following November a Prohibitory Bill established a more complete naval blockade. Instead, however, of leaving this to exert its slow pressure, as Barrington urged, it was decided to use the newly collected forces in a determined attempt to break American resistance.

In face of the mounting threat of the British attack, Congress was forced to define its own position. The outcome was the Declaration of Independence. The tide of public opinion had been turning in this direction ever since Lexington. In January Tom Paine had published anonymously his famous pamphlet *Common Sense*. In it, in vigorous prose well laced with abuse which fitted the mounting tempers of the moment, he had put the case for independence. Had not men's minds already been prepared by past events for the ideas he so eloquently propounded, its influence must have been much less. But coming at the moment that it did, it forced people to face the issue and to accept the fact that the logical outcome of their actions must be a separation from Britain. Perhaps one of its greatest contributions to this cause was to make it seem desirable rather than something to be deplored. Such was the demand for copies that 120,000 were printed in three months. Not everyone was prepared to accept its arguments, and in resistance to its thesis the Loyalists also began to define their position. In such circumstances the debates in the state assemblies or conventions, which had replaced the traditional legislatures of the colonial days, were protracted and bitter. It was in these bodies that the critical decisions were made, for though a motion was introduced in Congress in favour of independence on 7 June, in this matter delegates could act only in accordance with instructions from their own states, as the thirteen colonies now began to describe themselves. Pending this approval a committee was appointed to draw up a Declaration of Independence; this famous document was in effect largely the work of Thomas Jefferson. By 2 July agreement had been reached and, with New York abstaining but approving, the delegations from the individual states passed a resolution that 'These United Colonies are, and, of right, ought to be, free and independent states: that they are absolved from all allegiance to the British Crown, and that all political connection between them, and the state of Great Briain is, and ought to be, totally dissolved.' They were proud words; now there could be no going back on either side. Two days later, on the famous 4 July, they were approved by Congress.

The interest of the next five years lies in the military attempts of the British to break down American resistance and to force the colonies to return to their allegiance. Had British resources in supply and in manpower been swiftly concentrated and used with the daring that Pitt had used them against the French, there was a bare chance that this might have been done. The Americans had to build up their army and organize their commissariat with little experience to help them: to get any army, and most of all an amateur army, into the field takes time.[1] Had they never been permitted to get past the preliminary stages, had armies been smashed as soon as formed, it is just conceivable that George III might have been successful. All this, however, presupposed a quality of direction which neither the politicians at home nor the commanders in the field possessed. The time taken to formulate plans, to get the approval of them by London, to transport the necessary men and stores, was a fundamental difficulty. Above all, though Howe and Clinton were capable commanders and Burgoyne had imagination,

[1] J. C. Miller, *op. cit.*, stresses the almost impossible position of Washington as a commander of troops who had only enlisted for a year, so that his armies were always disintegrating; while the militia constantly ran away when faced with a bayonet charge. See pp. 161-2 for particular instances.

Howe was too slow, too reluctant, in view of the difficulty of replacing his losses, to take risks; Burgoyne, as his nickname 'Gentleman Johnny' implied, took too many. The caution of the one and the enterprise of the other were to have disastrous effects. At home military success or failure was woven into the fabric of political life. At first the little group of Rockingham whigs and the remnants of Chatham's following, notably Shelburne and Camden, protested to deaf ears. George III was determined to go on, ministers like Sandwich and Germain were in complete agreement with him, North stifled his doubts with his loyalty, and the independent members of the House felt that the colonists' behaviour was outrageous and must be punished. Had he been successful, the King's hold over the machinery of government and over his Parliament must have been strengthened, a fact of which the opposition were well aware, so that to them British victories became a threat to British freedom. Military defeat, on the other hand, meant a loss of confidence in everything for which George III had stood. To follow political fortunes at home it is therefore necessary first to study the campaign of the American war.

The plan for 1776 was to reinforce Carleton with 1,000 men, so that he could drive the Americans from Canada (which was done) and then move down towards Albany. Howe, with the main force, was to seize New York and, acting in conjunction with Carleton, who it was now hoped would be advancing southwards, cut off New England from the rest of the colonies and so break its resistance. As, however, these operations could not be begun until the summer it was decided to send Clinton, with 3,000 men and a supporting fleet under Admiral Parker, to combine with the loyalists of the South and strike a swift blow at the southern colonies. On paper it was not an unpromising scheme which, if successful, might have disrupted American resistance. In the preliminary business of collecting and dispatching men and supplies Germain showed great energy, but in America much less was achieved than had been hoped for. The expectation that Clinton would receive decisive assistance from the loyalists in South Carolina was ruined because they rose prematurely and were suppressed before the British arrived. Without allies on shore Clinton failed even to make an attempt to take Charleston, and he sailed back with nothing accomplished to join Howe who, on 12 July, had reached Sandy Hook from England. Staten Island, which was unfortified, was occupied as a base for operations against New York, which Washington, with a rather sketchy army, was preparing to defend. Though speed was essential if he, with his 10,000 continentals and doubtful supporting troops, was to be dealt a decisive blow which could be followed up before the onset of winter, it was not until 22 August that Howe began serious operations. At first, having the advantages of superior numbers, of well trained troops and of mistakes on Washington's part, he forced the Americans to evacuate Long Island. On 12 September Washington withdrew from New York. Once again Howe failed to follow up his victory. Not until 9 October did he begin to push Washington back again, and establish the British winter quarters at Trenton and Bordentown in New Jersey. If the object of a commander is to seek out the enemy and destroy him Howe's first campaign was a failure; Washington's army was still in being.

This was forcibly demonstrated on 26 December, when Washington suddenly attacked the Hessian and English forces stationed at Trenton. It was not a major engagement, but they were taken by surprise while recovering from their Christmas celebrations and driven from the town. In spite of the fact that the Americans were not strong enough to hold it once Cornwallis appeared with fresh troops, and that Washington failed to take Bordentown, the propaganda effects of the victory were considerable. Also it had military advantages in that it enabled Washington to establish himself on the hills of Morristown. As this constituted a threat to Howe's flank the British withdrew to New Brunswick. By the end of the year Howe's best chance of crushing colonial resistance had been lost. This the British apparently failed to realize. The capture of New York was hailed as the first step to victory and plans for a vigorous campaign in 1777 were in active preparation. Here a mixture of slow communications, vacillation between alternative plans and personal rivalries, led to a major disaster before the end of the year. Five days before Trenton, Howe sent off details of an ambitious plan, which would, however, have involved his having at his disposal an army of some 35,000 men. As he doubted, rightly, whether these would be available, for it meant reinforcements to the extent of some 15,000 men, three weeks later he sent another plan of more modest dimensions. This suggested marching with 10,000 men to Philadelphia, partly because the loyalists were considered to be numerous in the area, and partly because, as the seat of the Congress,

Philadelphia was assuming some of the functions of a capital city. Some troops would be left to hold New York and Rhode Island, and another 3,000 be detached to operate on the Hudson and strengthen a projected thrust from Canada down towards Albany. The first plan—which had provided for careful co-operation between the Canadian thrust and the forces based on New York in order to cut off the New England colonies, as well as an attack on the South—was rejected as already it was clear that the additional troops could be raised only with difficulty, and in a letter of 3 March Germain gave his approval to the second plan. It was only some weeks later that he also sent Howe, for his information, a copy of the instructions previously sent to Carleton, ordering him to advance from Canada. As Howe was now committed to marching most of his troops to Philadelphia there were some dangers in the scheme, for should the forces advancing from Canada find themselves in difficulties, the main army would be too far off to give much assistance and the 3,000 tentatively allotted to co-operate with them might be insufficient. Personal rivalries now contrived to produce further complications. Carleton and Germain were on bad terms, which did not promise well for co-operation, and when Burgoyne, ambitious for a leading role, arrived back in London he persuaded Germain and George III that the command of an army based on Canada should be given to him. Meanwhile Howe, before he had received Germain's dispatch of 3 March, put forward yet another plan by which he proposed to go to Philadelphia by sea with 11,000 men, leaving 4,700 in New York under Clinton and another 2,400 in Rhode Island. By this new plan there was no force, except that provided by the local friendly loyalists, to act with the forces under Burgoyne.

Here was matter for confusion. It is true that Howe did write to Canada explaining his change of plan. When this third set of proposals was received in London Germain seems to have been aware of the weakness inherent in dividing the available forces in America, because he wrote to Howe exhorting him to finish the Pennsylvanian adventure quickly in order to be at hand in New York if his forces were needed. Though this letter was dated 18 May it was only received by Howe on 16 August while he was at sea on his way to attack Philadelphia. This story of changing plans, of slow communications, of a lack of overall control is interesting because of the light it throws on the inadequacy of the British government to wage war in such circumstances. The rest of the story can be more briefly told. In so far as his own limited objective was concerned Howe was successful. He landed early in September, defeated Washington, who had planned to defend the city, at Brandywine and on the 25th entered Philadelphia. But though defeated and driven back once again, Washington's army was not destroyed and, in appalling conditions of hardship throughout the winter, managed to hang on at Valley Forge some 20 miles away. On the face of it a British triumph, the taking of Philadelphia had little practical effect on the campaign, so that Americans have suggested that it was rather Philadelphia that took Howe, pinning down British forces than the other way about. Meanwhile the disaster that was always implicit in the plan overtook Burgoyne. At first all went well. He arrived in Quebec on 6 May and with a force of about 9,500 officers and men and 138 cannon moved against Ticonderoga, which the Americans evacuated on 7 July. Then, though he was only 70 miles from Albany, his difficulties began. He was short of horses, the 50 cannon he still kept with him and his too abundant equipment proved encumbrances. The Americans took every advantage of the difficult country through which he had to move, by felling trees and releasing floods. Meanwhile St Leger, with a supporting British force which was moving down from Oswego, was defeated and failed to get through. By 20 August Burgoyne's position was already precarious. By the end of September he was very short of food, by 13 October his army was surrounded, and on the 15th he surrendered at Saratoga. Against this disaster the capture of Philadelphia was of little value and Howe sent in his resignation. In May 1778 Clinton succeeded him in what was now an all but hopeless task.

The surrender at Saratoga had important repercussions both at home and on foreign relations.[1] To ministers it emphasized the immensity of the task they had undertaken and underlined the warnings of opposition speakers that it might well prove to be beyond England's resources. Though few people were yet prepared to accept with Charles James Fox the fact that independence was inevitable, politicians were beginning to count the cost of a long war, and to wonder if a negotiated peace, which fell short of

[1] P. Mackesy, *op. cit.*, (p. 510), argues that Saratoga need not necessarily have been decisive. The King also described it as 'very serious but not without remedy' (quoted J. Brooke, *op. cit.*, p. 184).

independence but which conceded much that had hitherto been refused, might not be the only practical course to take. In particular North, to whom Saratoga brought confirmation of all his earlier doubts, began to think in terms of resigning. At the same time it brought the prospect of foreign intervention perceptibly nearer. From the very beginning of the conflict France had been interested, and even before the close of 1775 had been sending agents and providing supplies surreptitiously to the colonists. Vergennes, her foreign minister, was anxious not to commit France until it was plain that the Americans had the strength to continue the struggle, but as early as March 1776 he was sounding Spain as to the possibilities of joint action against England. Though the Americans were ready to welcome the financial aid which, under the guise of a commercial company, both France and Spain began to provide through Caron de Beaumarchais in May 1776, it was not until after the Declaration of Independence that they began to turn in any formal way for help to France. The break with tradition was for them, too, a formidable one and the lurking fear remained that France, having helped to destroy the British hold, might revive her old claims to their valued hinterland. Once, however, Congress had committed itself to independence, French help became of vital importance and three commissioners, one of whom was Benjamin Franklin, were sent to Paris to negotiate for recognition.

This was not easily obtained, for both Vergennes and Louis XVI realized that to recognize the independence of the colonies must lead to European war. Before they committed themselves they were understandably anxious both to make sure of Spanish support and to be confident that the colonists would not come to terms with Britain and thus leave them with a European war on their hands. Therefore French readiness to recognize fluctuated with American chances of success. In August 1776, after the British failure off Charleston, Vergennes seemed prepared to do so; then came the loss of New York and he drew back. Though Franklin was personally popular in Paris, he and his colleagues achieved little beyond sympathy throughout the summer of 1777. It was not until the news of Saratoga was received that France at last felt sufficiently sure to act. Indeed, in view of the change in the British attitude, delay seemed more dangerous than recognition, for if the Americans, despairing of securing foreign allies, were tempted to accept the more conciliatory terms which everybody now felt must be offered by George III, then the opportunity to revenge themselves for the failure of the Seven Years War would be lost. On 17 December, therefore, Vergennes indicated verbally that France would recognize the new United States, though Louis XVI did not give his final agreement until 6 January 1778. By 13 March the British were formally notified that France had recognized the United States and a week later the three American commissioners, Deane, Franklin and Lee, were received in audience at Versailles. Spain refused to take similar action. With some justification she was doubtful of the wisdom of recognizing the claims of colonial rebels in the New World and she did not, in fact, do so until after they had been recognized by Britain. Nor was Spain anxious to involve herself in a war with England unless she was confident that France would give full backing to her claims. It was not, therefore, until April 1779 that she joined France by the Convention of Aranjuez in return for the agreement that she should receive Gibraltar and Minorca.

While these negotiations had been taking place the English ministers had been reluctantly considering the need for a fresh approach. The news of Saratoga had been received in London on 2 December while Parliament was still sitting. Shattered by the disaster Chatham rallied his remaining energies to speak three times within the next ten days. The theme of all three speeches was the need to abandon the use of force, which again and again in striking phrases he declared could never be successful in a country like America, to recognize the justice of the colonial causes and, while making the most generous concessions to her short of independence, to concentrate on the menace which he realized would come from France. The motion to adjourn Parliament until 20 January in spite of the gravity of the situation was one that filled him with dismay. He had, however, one ally among the ministers and this was North himself. As a level-headed student of the possible, and a financier who hated the squandering of money on military and naval enterprises when the whole financial administrative machinery at home needed overhauling, North had never been an enthusiastic supporter of the war, though he had little sympathy with the colonial cause. Nothing but George III's tenacity and his own sense of loyalty had kept him in office so long. Now his threats to resign became more urgent; if he were to remain, at least he must be allowed to see what conciliation could do. On 17 February North put his plan, to which he had received the reluctant consent of the King, before the Commons. The terms he now offered were very much those that would have satisfied the majority of Americans before, or even in the lull after, Lexington. He proposed to repeal the Townshend duty on tea, the Massachusetts Government Act and the Prohibitory Act, and to send commissioners to negotiate. These men were to have extensive powers. There was to be no refusal to negotiate with Congress or any other revolutionary body. They were to have power to sign an armistice, grant pardons and suspend any legislation relating to America that had been passed after 1763. In putting this programme before the House he acknowledged that coercion had failed and that France would probably soon declare war.

Indeed, it seems that through his spies he had already had news of the signing of the treaty between the United States and France on 6 February.

7. FRENCH INTERVENTION

The formal notification of recognition was made by the French ambassador on 13 March and a few days later Lord Stormont, the English ambassador in Paris, was recalled. Everyone knew that war between England and France could not be long delayed. North was conscious, perhaps over-conscious, of the weakness of the ministry. Certainly he felt that it was quite inadequate to the tasks in front of it. Since the previous August Sandwich had been stressing our naval weakness in face of a possible French attack. There simply were not enough ships to patrol American waters, convoy troops and supplies, protect trade and defend England herself against invasion.[1] For this state of affairs North, with his refusal to overstrain the finances, was to some extent responsible. The fact that Sandwich had acted with great shabbiness towards Wilkes, and that his private life called for moral censure, did not necessarily make him a bad First Lord of the Admiralty. With inadequate resources and an antiquated system he probably had done as well as any other politician would have been likely to do. Certainly the Admiralty had been the goal of his political ambition and there is no doubt of his keen personal interest. Enthusiasm will not, however, make up for a lack of seaworthy ships, nor can large addi-

[1] Between 1763 and 1778, 97 ships of the line had been struck off the effective list and only 54 replacements built. Ships laid up were neglected and left unprotected against rain and snow, with the result that rot set in and they became beyond repair.—K. Fenwick, *op. cit.*, p. 37.

tions be made to a navy in a few months. In the spring of 1778 England would be undeniably weak at sea. North felt no confidence in his own ability to impose a pattern on the direction of the war. Moreover he realized that war on a large scale would once again revive the demand for Chatham. His return to office might also help to make the Americans, whose cause he had so long championed and with whom he had previously worked so successfully against France, more inclined to receive favourably the commissioners who were to re-open negotiations with them. Here North found his power to persuade or influence George III too small. It had not been easy to get him to agree to conciliatory negotiations, and the employment of Chatham once again he refused to contemplate. He would, he said, 'rather lose the Crown I now wear than bear the ignominy of possessing it under their shackles'. He therefore refused to send for Chatham or even to see him. The utmost that North could get from his royal master was permission to see if he could persuade Chatham and Shelburne to join a ministry that remained nominally North's.

With this grudging consent North did attempt to open up negotiations through William Eden and Shelburne, but it was soon clear that Chatham would never be gained on such terms. North continued to plead and the King to deny until the death of Chatham on 11 May put an end to the argument. Like so much of his life its closing scenes were dramatic. While the flurry of negotiations was going on, the Rockingham whigs had come to the pragmatic and uninspired conclusion that all Britain could now do was to cut her losses. Events in America had gone too far for any solution but independence; meanwhile France, and possibly Spain, were a more serious and immediate menace. Sound policy therefore required that Britain recognize the new United States, try to win back as much of their goodwill as possible by an eleventh-hour friendliness, and concentrate on reviving trade and commercial links with them. In this way something might be saved from the wreckage and Britain be able to turn her entire strength against her old French enemies. On 7 April Richmond intended to move a motion embodying such a policy. To Chatham such suggestions were a denial of everything that he had ever stood for with regard to the colonies. Though he had been struggling with an attack of gout, and was so frail that he could never have assumed the responsibilities of office, even if George and North had agreed on this issue, he managed to take his place in the Lords in order to oppose Richmond's motion. It was his last speech, his last attempt to save the empire he had helped to create and rally it against his old Bourbon foe. When he rose again to reply to Richmond he collapsed and was carried from the Chamber; on 11 May he died at Hayes, which he had so much loved. With no Chatham on whom to call for even the assistance of the shadow of his name, at the King's earnest request North agreed to carry on.

Even if Chatham had lived it is unlikely that the Americans would have agreed to negotiation on the terms offered. The commissioners did not arrive in Philadelphia until the beginning of June, when the treaties of friendship and alliance with France had already been ratified by Congress. By this time no one, beyond the ranks of the loyalists, had any trust in George III and it was widely felt that if, at the eleventh hour, America gave up the French alliance and returned to its traditional allegiance it would be defenceless against any double-dealing on the part of Britain, once the continental armies had been disbanded. Moreover, by June 1778 the military situation was looking more promising. Washington had managed to hang on in spite of the hardships of Valley Forge, and, on orders from Germain, Clinton, now in supreme command, was busy evacuating Philadelphia. In its answer of 17 June, therefore, Congress refused to treat on any other basis than the acknowledgement of independence and the withdrawal of all British troops. On demands so fundamental the commissioners had no power to treat; the war would have to be fought out until either victory or exhaustion made one or other of the combatants alter his policy.

In the end the French fleet was to prove the determining factor. On land stalemate seemed more probable than a clear-cut victory, for while British ships could control American coastal waters British troops could hold such ports as New York or Newport or any other that they might capture. While they held the ports their armies on land could be reinforced; they could harry and raid and perhaps strike even more decisive blows. Yet until the continent had been cleared of English troops America could not build up a normal economic life. The fighting of the next few years was to demonstrate that the English armies were not yet beaten. Out of stalemate, without French help, might have come not the kind of negotiated peace that George III would have liked but at least one which would have recognized his formal sovereignty. The events of the years between the evacuation of Philadelphia and the surrender at Yorktown are therefore important, though they can be briefly told. Not all Clinton's forces were evacuated by sea; they were too numerous for that. But, after indecisive fighting at Monmouth Court House, the American forces failed to prevent those making the overland march from getting through to New York. At first also it seemed as if the threat from the French navy had been over-estimated. D'Estaing, arriving from France just after Admiral Howe, with the convoy from Philadelphia had reached New York, attempted with the help of Washington to take the town, and failed. A similar result followed an attack on Rhode Island. After two failures the Frenchmen sailed to the West Indies, where they had vital interests to push against the British. Even their presence there, however, was of some advantage to the rebels; it lessened the pressure which the British fleet could exert against their own long coastline and, by diminishing the protection which it could give to British merchantmen, it afforded more openings to the American privateers.[1] Even in the early days of the war the damage which they had done to British commerce had been considerable. American historians estimate that between March and December 1776, 342 British ships had been captured, and that the total in 1777 had been 464. New England had a long tradition of seamanship fostered by the Navigation Acts. If, however, the Americans had a weapon of offence in their seamen and their ships, they were also vulnerable to British attacks of a similar nature. Throughout the war the damage suffered by merchantmen on both sides was heavy.

The defeat at Saratoga and the entry of France into the war meant that any hope of a quick victory, following a knockout blow, had to be abandoned. When this was clear Germain ordered Clinton to evacuate even New York if necessary, though he was to retain Newport as a base if it was at all possible. With the forces thus released he was to ravage the coasts of New England, attempt an invasion of Georgia, where the loyalists were thought to be strong, and provide troops for an attack on St Lucia. As D'Estaing failed in his attempt against New York it proved unnecessary to give up that city, which remained the main British base for the rest of the war. The other part of the plan Clinton put into piecemeal

[1] Prominent among these was Captain Paul Jones. For an account of his activities consult Rear Admiral S. E. Morison, *John Paul Jones* (1960).

operation in the following months. In December the expedition was sent against Georgia. It was brilliantly successful, for Savannah was taken on the 29th and exactly a month later Augusta also fell. With Georgia again in British hands hopes in London began to rise. The organizing of raids, too, harassed the rebels. The command of American coastal waters made it possible to ravage and destroy towns on the seaboard, while inland raiding parties of tories and Indians based on Niagara and Detroit spread devastation along the western frontiers. The Americans for a time seemed literally to be between the devil, in the shape of the Indians, whose atrocities often merited that description, and the deep sea. Though in the south the British failed to take Charleston in the spring of 1779, the French fleet, which had been summoned to the help of their allies, equally failed to drive the British from Savannah and once again sailed back to the more congenial waters of the West Indies. Cheered by these successes, at the end of December Clinton felt strong enough to sail south with some 8,000 troops in order to put the plans against South Carolina into operation. Again, though not quite so rapidly, fortune smiled on the British and Charleston was captured on 8 May. As 5,000 men and a considerable amount of equipment were also taken this represented a substantial success. Now South Carolina as well as Georgia was in British hands, while the raiding in the north and middle states was inflicting widespread damage. Finally, an attempt to break the British hold on South Carolina was defeated at Camden by Lord Cornwallis, whom Clinton on returning to New York had left in command at Charleston. Everywhere by the winter of 1779-80 the American prospect was depressing. Nor was the situation made any easier for Washington by the hardships which the officers and men of his continental army suffered. Paid in depreciated paper dollars and often short even of food, while more fortunate members of the community were making money out of the inflation, it is a tribute to their patriotism that his army did not melt away completely.

But though George III felt more confident and, after the general election of 1780, was still able to keep both his majorities in the Commons and his First Lord of the Treasury, mistakes on the part of the British commander and last minute naval help from France were in 1781 to alter the entire picture. After his victory at Camden Cornwallis had turned against North Carolina, hoping to bring that state also under British control. Here the Americans had managed to check him at King's Mountain, but after being joined by reinforcements in January 1781 he again pressed forward. Though he won another victory at Guildford he was forced to realize that he had not sufficient force to hold North Carolina, even if he could conquer it. It was now that he made his fatal mistake. Knowing that British troops were creating a diversion in Virginia he decided to move the main body of his forces there to join them and to concentrate his efforts against that state. Once again this split British forces in America, which were now strung out from Charleston to New York. Nor was he successful in dealing with the patriot forces within Virginia itself. Clinton in New York was aware of these dangers and tried to make Cornwallis change his plans or at least send most of his troops back to New York. Cornwallis won this battle of bickering and fortified his position at Yorktown. If a French fleet superior to the British force should appear he was trapped. If Clinton was aware of this so were the Americans, who repeatedly urged their allies to dispatch such a fleet. In response to their entreaties de Grasse sailed from Brest for the West Indies in the spring of 1781, informing his allies that he would reach the Chesapeake in August. Washington seized the opportunity this plan offered to hem in the British army. Removing his colonial troops and the French expeditionary force from New York he marched south. The combined manœuvre was brilliantly successful. At sea the British relieving squadron was defeated and on 19 October Cornwallis was forced to surrender with the 7,000 men under his command. It was the end of any real hope that the British could do more than hang on to their remaining bases until the politicians could negotiate a peace. The most that could now be hoped for was to stave off a French attack on the West Indies and to defend Britain itself against the threat of invasion. From the point of view of George III the situation was equally desperate. Since Saratoga and the entry of France into the war his administration had tottered from one crisis to another. Now the end could not be long delayed.

17

THE INFLUENCE OF
THE AMERICAN WAR OF INDEPENDENCE
ON DOMESTIC POLITICS

1. EFFECT OF THE WAR ON POLITICAL GROUPS

THOUGH the metaphor must not be pushed too far there is some justification for regarding the American War of Independence as the watershed that divides eighteenth- from nineteenth-century England. Certainly after Saratoga Anglo-Irish relations began to take another direction and even more after Yorktown the slogan 'measures not men' began to assume some political reality. The year 1772 can well be considered as seeing the final flowering of the eighteenth-century constitution. George III was, as he intended to be, the head of his own ministers, choosing them yet acting with and through them in conjunction with a loyal and co-operative Parliament. Through Lord North his relations with the Commons were easy; corruption and influence alone will not explain the harmony between them and the King. The opposition groups, weak and divided, were as voices crying in the wilderness and events seemed unlikely to make straight their path before them. In 1772 there was very little indication of the humiliations to come. Yet by 1782 a revolt of the independent members of the Commons had forced North to resign and George III, much against his will, to appoint Rockingham as First Lord of the Treasury in his place.[1]

The vital factor responsible for this dramatic change was the American War of Independence. The fortunes of that struggle provide the necessary clue to the situation which developed at

[1] See L. Namier, *Country Gentlemen in Parliament: Crossroads to power* (1962), p. 45.

Westminster between 1772 and 1782; at no time was the impact of war on English domestic politics greater than during these years. In 1772 the prospects of North's administration seemed good. The months following Grafton's resignation had seen several interesting new appointments. The first of these was that of Edward Thurlow who replaced Dunning as Solicitor-General in March 1770.[1] Thurlow was a rising barrister who had made a parliamentary reputation by defending the ministry's action over Wilkes and arguing its case in favour of the control of juries in libel actions and of the press. On George Grenville's death in November of that year his followers under Lord Suffolk decided to come to terms with North. When, therefore, Lord Weymouth rather unexpectedly resigned the Secretaryship in the course of the Falkland Island crisis a considerable rearrangement of places, with the aim of strengthening the administration, was possible. In the course of this, Thurlow, who had been connected with Lord Weymouth and who showed signs of resigning with his patron, was promoted to the place of Attorney-General. The vacant office of Solicitor-General was then accepted by Alexander Wedderburn. Definitely a careerist, he played his hand without much regard for either principles or reputation, except that of being a dangerous man if thwarted. Above all he understood the value of opposition and even more how to blackmail an administration by the threat to oppose. Though he had come into Parliament under the patronage of Lord Bute (Wedderburn, too, was a Scot), during the crisis of the Middlesex elections he had attacked the government and, applying for the Chiltern Hundreds, had resigned his seat for the Ayr Burghs. Immediately he became the hero of the opposition whigs. Clive found him a seat, and his new associates toasted him with enthusiasm at the Thatched House Tavern, that scene of so many whig dinners. In the next eighteen months he had shown what a skilled and formidable debater he could be, clashing frequently both in the Commons and in the courts with Thurlow. The new appointments turned them into colleagues but they were uncongenial yoke-fellows, disliking one another and being rivals for the same prize, the Woolsack. Nevertheless from the administration's point of view they were a notable addition to its debating strength in the House.

---

[1] Robert Gore-Brown, *Chancellor Thurlow. The Life and Times of an Eighteenth Century Lawyer* (1953), provides a readable account of his career.

An even more interesting recruit was Charles James Fox,[1] Lord Holland's second and beloved son. When only nineteen he had been elected as member for Midhurst in March 1768 and, in spite of his minority, allowed to take his seat. From the beginning both his eloquence and his personality had made a great impression on the House. This eloquence had been placed at the disposal of Lord North, for young Fox was a staunch supporter of Luttrell against Wilkes, and an extravagant defender of the rights of the House of Commons against the electors of Middlesex and the City of London in the person of Crosby its Lord Mayor. So exuberant had been his attack that even Wedderburn, still a member of the opposition group, was discomforted by him in debate. North was fully alive to the value of his support, for if the opposition groups were weak in numbers they possessed some formidable speakers. He therefore persuaded George III—though he disliked young Fox's disorderly way of life and hated his father—that he must be secured. Accordingly he became a Junior Lord of the Admiralty in 1770. It was characteristic of the man that two years later he resigned his office in order to lead an attack on the Royal Marriage Act of 1772. To do so was to flout the known wishes of the King. George III had been extremely annoyed by the recent marriages of the royal Dukes: Gloucester had married Lady Waldegrave and Cumberland Mrs. Horton. He was determined in future that no member of the royal family should marry without the monarch's consent and insisted on legislation being carried for this purpose. It was not a popular measure. Just as in 1719 the Peerage Bill had been resented by the gentlemen of England who saw their chances of enoblement vanishing, so now it was declared that if the measure became law it would prevent their daughters from marrying the royal princes. Nevertheless, in face of the King's determination the bill passed. The resistance it encountered was not, however, completely fruitless, for by an amendment the prohibition did not apply after the age of twenty-five. For good measure, and as an act of filial piety, Charles James Fox now tried to modify Hardwicke's original Marriage Act. Speaking brilliantly, he even secured by a majority of one vote leave to introduce his measure in April 1772, though that was the extent of his success. To North he seemed too dangerous as an unattached member, and by December of that year he had

---

[1] For details of his career see Loren Reid, *A Man for the People* (1969), and J. W. Derry, *Charles James Fox*; and, for a shorter assessment, I. R. Christie's essay in *Myth and Reality*, pp. 133–44.

again been brought into the government fold by the offer of a seat at the Treasury. As the wits remarked, he knew as much about raising supply as any man in the kingdom! The jibe was not without justification for in the next year his father paid his son's debts to the reputed amount of £140,000.

Fox was to prove an acquisition of doubtful value. His brilliance was unquestioned but he showed himself to be headstrong and unaccommodating, unattractive qualities for a ministry which had had its share of awkward situations and which now only wanted to be left to get on with its task of government in peace. When, therefore, Fox attempted to commit North to still another round with the printers and the press, both he and George III decided that he was more of a liability than an asset and on 24 February he received his congé in the famous note: 'Mr. Fox, His Majesty has thought proper to order a new Commission of the Treasury to be made out, in which I do not see your name. North.' In this way the connection between Fox, afterwards to be one of his most formidable critics, and North was broken just when America was again becoming a dominant issue. It was an issue on which Fox was as yet entirely uncommitted. Everything in his past had indicated an intolerant championship of the rights of the House of Commons, and it is fascinating though unprofitable to speculate what his attitude would have been had he still sat on the Treasury benches. In his new circumstances he soon found himself acting with the opposition, a co-operation facilitated by his personal friendship with Edmund Burke. It was during these years that 'The Club' of which Dr. Johnson was the leading deity was acting as a focus for what was most brilliant and stimulating in ideas and in the arts in London. Founded in 1764, ten years later it had become something of an institution to which any man would consider it a high honour to be elected. Garrick, Gibbon, Sheridan, Adam Smith, Boswell, Burke all enjoyed this distinction, and the fortnightly meeting, which took place in various coffee houses while Parliament was in session, made a wonderful talking shop, the more stimulating because views on politics were far from unanimous. Johnson himself told Goldsmith that he would not talk to Burke of the Rockingham party. It was a tribute to the quality of his mind and the breadth of his interests that Fox was elected to this body in 1774.

The revival of the American problems after the Boston Tea Party on 16 December 1773 recreated the clash of active political opinion in Parliament. 'Wilkes and Liberty' was an outworn theme, the attacks of the opposition on the handling of the Falkland Islands dispute had been purely factious. It was obvious that both the Rockinghams and the Chathams were opposing for the sake of trying to bring down the King's ministers, never too respectable an object in the eighteenth century. The cause of the Americans gave them a genuine principle on which to fight. It is interesting to trace the various paths by which these champions of the colonial cause came to hold their opinions. Chatham had for the colonies something of ʰhe passion of a creator. As the director of the triumphs of the Seven Years War he had secured for them opportunities of expansion which held infinite prospects of future prosperity. His personal popularity with them was great, his confidence in them unbounded. If through other men's mishandling, this great prize of empire which he had helped to bestow on Great Britain were lost, then his life-work would be destroyed. Never a man who cared greatly for money in the sense that he felt any obligation to cut his coat in accordance with the financial cloth, to him the danger of losing the allegiance of the colonists to save the price of a few regiments of soldiers was inconceivable stupidity. Rockingham and his friends had reached sympathy with the Americans by a rather different road, one to some extent pointed out by political accident. It was no concern over America which had persuaded the Marquis to take office in 1766, but because of the outcry against the Stamp Act the question of its repeal became one of the most difficult problems which he had to handle. In deciding to support this line of action it is probable that Pitt's known views, and the desperate need that the Rockinghams had for his support, were at least an important, possibly a decisive, factor. Once, however, they had taken their stand on repeal, they were in a sense committed to a pro-colonial approach, especially as Rockingham valued his reputation for consistency.[1] Even so, at the time of the Townshend duties they showed little realization of the seriousness of the step which the Chancellor of the Exchequer was taking, or of the repercussions which were likely to follow. Their activities were more concerned with detaching Conway and bringing the administration down than with

---

[1] *Memoirs of the Marquis of Rockingham*, edited by George Thomas Keppel, Earl of Albemarle (1852), vol. II, p. 303: 'I cannot vary from opinions and principles which afford me the pleasing recollection and infinite comfort of not feeling *self accused*, of having *abetted* the systems in this reign which have brought on all the national calamities.'

saving American liberties. Yet because politics continued to range them against the King, and because of his inflexible attitude towards American resistance, they came, as men will, to have a deeper conviction of the value of the principle for which they were fighting. Nor was this mere self-deception; there was much that could be argued on the side of the colonists, just as there was much justification for the British point of view. What their previous political history had ensured was that they should approach this new crisis from an angle sympathetic to the American viewpoint. From this it was an easy step to a genuine conviction that ministers were handling it disastrously. Moreover, Burke was an Irishman, well acquainted with the less happy aspects of English rule and aware of the resistance and tensions it might set up. He was also the colonial agent for New York.

The sympathy the Rockinghams had with the cause of American resistance was not shared by the majority of members in either House. When the ministers determined on the strong measures of closing the port of Boston and remodelling its constitution until compensation should be paid for the destroyed tea, they got the required legislation easily. Neither Burke on 19 April nor Chatham on 27 May could make any dent in the ministerial majorities. When in the next February Chatham brought forward his own plan for conciliation it was denied even the courtesy of a second reading. In March, though Burke's speech in favour of conciliation rather than force contained verbal gems such as 'a great empire and little minds go ill together' and the famous description of the ties of liberty 'which though light as air are strong as links of iron', it was equally unsuccessful in winning members' votes. Even the adherence of Fox to this small band had no apparent result. So matters remained until the disaster at Saratoga gave the opposition more solid ammunition than lectures on political theory and prophecies of disaster. In the intervening years the position of the government seemed sound.[1] The general election in 1774 had, as might have been expected, returned a friendly House, and by 1776 Rockingham and his friends, in spite of the protests of Fox and even Burke, decided that it was useless to continue to take an active part in parliamentary business until times changed. By 1777 Burke had come to agree

[1] Sir George Savile to Rockingham 15 Jan. 1777: 'We are not only patriots *out of place*, but patriots out of *the opinion of the public*. The repeated successes, *hollow* as I think them, and the more ruinous if they *are real*, have fixed or converted ninety nine in one hundred'—*Ibid.*, vol. II, p. 305.

with his chief that there was nothing further to be done. In such circumstances, since the prospect of a forlorn hope, a gambler's chance, stimulated rather than discouraged him, Fox and a few friends battled on alone. By so doing he gained in stature and in leadership. The Fox of 1777 was a very different man from the near youth who had defended the rights of the Commons against Wilkes. Liberty was becoming his rallying cry and he was entwining colonial success and domestic freedom in one unbreakable rope. To him a colonial success was not a national disaster but the only real security for the preservation of the rights of Englishmen.[1] It was not a view which commended itself to a House of Commons whose estates were burdened with a heavy land tax for the prosecution of the war.

Fox was not destined to struggle on for long alone. At the end of 1777 came the news of Burgoyne's surrender at Saratoga; immediately the whole scene changed. For the first time the certainty of a long struggle, and the possiblity of European war and ultimate defeat, faced the Commons.[2] North, who had justifiably little confidence in himself as an organizer of victory, was more anxious than ever to resign. George III remained obdurate; North must remain at the Treasury and if Chatham and his friends were prepared to accept office on this condition then reluctantly he would give his assent. But while North had been hoping that the Americans might be brought to agree to a reversal of their Declaration of Independence by an eleventh-hour change in policy, another section of the opposition had come to realize that such a solution was unlikely. Americans they had never recognized as enemies : they were British subjects defending a common right to liberty; war with France was a different matter and into that war they were prepared to put all their energy. But this, they argued, meant detaching America from her new French friends, which could hardly be done

---

[1] On hearing of the capture of Long Island by the British troops he wrote to Rockingham of 'the terrible news from Long Island' and continued; 'Above all, my dear Lord, I hope that it will be a point of honour among us all to support the American pretensions in adversity as much as we did in their prosperity, and that we shall never desert those who have acted unsuccessfully upon Whig principles, while we continue to profess our admiration of those who succeeded in the same principles in the year 1688.'—*Memoirs of the Marquis of Rockingham*, vol. II, p. 297.

[2] 'It may now, whatever it was in the beginning, be a matter of doubt, whether any superiority of power, of wealth, and of discipline, will be found to over-balance such difficulties' (i.e. those of distance and the terrain).—*Annual Register*, 1777 (printed 1778), p. 176.

without conceding her claim to independence. Thus, as George III prepared reluctantly to consider reconciliation and the abandoning of practical control for the sake of retaining a theoretical sovereignty, the Rockingham whigs moved to the position of accepting what they had come to feel was inevitable. It was in opposing Richmond's motion to this effect in the House of Lords that Chatham made his last speech on 7 April. On 11 May he died.

2. WEAKNESS OF THE ADMINISTRATION

His death in some ways simplified the political scene. There was no one now to relieve North of his burdens, for an attempt to reconstruct the ministry under Lord Weymouth by taking in Rockingham and his friends and Fox, and dropping Germain, Sandwich and North himself broke down. In the circumstances North felt impelled by his loyalty to carry on,[1] and in July Thurlow, now one of the strongest personalities in the Cabinet, a man liked and trusted by the King, was promoted from being Attorney-General to the Woolsack. It was the best the King could do, since he was determined not to surrender to the opposition, which now, with a real issue on which men could not help having decided opinions, was beginning to develop into the party of Burke's earlier dreams. From this point the political struggle became clearly one between this incipient Rockingham party and the King himself. The differences in opinion between them were clear-cut. The Rockinghams believed in party as a foundation of political life; they stood for the recognition of America and the salvaging of as much commercial well-being as could be secured, by ending the bitterness of what they regarded as a fraternal conflict. George III in contrast believed, as he had always believed, in his right to choose his own ministers, and in his personal responsibility for maintaining his sovereignty over the empire. In the conflict between them the House of Commons was at once the field on which they fought and the prize for which they contended. Whichever could win the adherence of the independent members could claim the victory.

In such circumstances the ministers were likely to be judged by their success or failure in the war. The two key officers were there-

---

[1] See J. Brooke, *George III*, p. 193: 'It is time to scotch the legend that North was no more than a tool of the royal will who continued to retain his place only because of pressure from the King. . . . He wanted at the same time the pleasures of office and the pleasures of retirement.'

fore Lord George Germain, who was responsible for the handling of the American war, and Lord Sandwich at the Admiralty. Both were unpopular, perhaps unfairly so, and regarded as liabilities by their colleagues. The episode of Minden when, as Lord George Sackville, Germain had been 'disobliged' to the extent of disregarding Brunswick's orders, had left a faint aroma of cowardice around his name, which his opponents used to undermine his reputation. Fox blamed him for the disaster which had overtaken General Burgoyne at Saratoga, and by 1778 the House had very little confidence in him. To Sandwich was attributed every misfortune that overtook the navy.[1] This bitterness was intensified after the part which he played in the court martial of Admiral Keppel. The circumstances were these. Keppel, a popular officer, was in command of the fleet intended for the defence of this country against the French. On 27 July he came in contact with the French off Ushant. The engagement was indecisive and Keppel blamed Sir Hugh Palliser, who commanded his rear, for having disobeyed a vital signal. Palliser in turn criticized Keppel's conduct of the battle and demanded a court martial. Unfortunately politics intervened to give bitterness to the subsequent proceedings. Keppel was by connection one of the Rockingham whig group; Palliser belonged to the Court faction. Though in the court martial both men were acquitted, in the fleet, and certainly in the anti-government press, it was maintained that Keppel had been unjustly charged because his friends were not supporters of the government.[2] As many of the best serving officers were connected with the Rockinghams and their friends, the whole episode made a serious rift between the Admiralty and the fleet. In the crisis of 1779, when a French invasion seemed imminent, the Admiralty had to rely on a 'dug-out', Sir Charles Hardy, because so many younger men were unwilling to accept a command while Sandwich remained at the Admiralty.[3]

[1] There was apparently little foundation for these charges. In 1771 Sandwich 'was by his experience and knowledge of naval affairs, better fitted to be First Lord than any other statesman in either House'.—*Sandwich Papers,* p. 13.

[2] Sir Hugh Palliser and Keppel had been friends of twenty years' standing, and it was Palliser who had recommended the appointment of Keppel in spite of his whig connections. Their friendship was not, however, able to withstand the strain of the political situation.

[3] *The Annual Register,* 1781 (3rd edition, 1800), reported that his death in the middle of May 1780 caused a fresh crisis: 'the discontents which had so long prevailed in the navy kept several of our best officers from the service'. He was succeeded by Admiral Geary, another retired officer.

Other factors beside the unpopularity of these two men helped to weaken the ministry.[1] Within its ranks there was little unity and less direction. As the situation grew more difficult North became increasingly afflicted by paralysis of the will. His business, he protested, was the Treasury; what other ministers did was no concern of his. The result is that Cabinet business was neither properly prepared nor adequately discussed, and vital decisions were not taken until it was too late for them to be effective. The letters of George III and Thurlow, perhaps the two most effective men responsible for administration, are interlarded with complaints of his tardiness and irresolution,[2] while much of the King's so-called backstairs influence sprang from his efforts, exercised through subordinates like Jenkinson now Secretary at War, and Robinson, the Secretary to the Treasury, to sustain North's morale. A minister whose desire to evade further responsibility was almost driving him to a nervous breakdown, in charge of a govenment in which so much of its effort was put forth to maintain it in office in order to direct a war in the success of which it did not believe, was obviously likely to find himself facing a series of crises. In consequence the year 1779 was one of almost intolerable strain. The ministry looked like falling to pieces and new recruits were difficult to find. There was a very real threat of invasion from France. Ireland seized this moment of English weakness to secure the redress of some of her own grievances. Finally, the discontent of the landowners with the burden of expenses and lack of success was utilized by the Rockingham and Fox opposition to mount a most formidable offensive against the ministry in the House of Commons.

3. THE INVASION THREAT

During the summer of 1779 the country was faced with the threat of a combined Franco-Spanish invasion.[3] Hitherto Spain had hesitated to join the war against England but by mid-June her fears had been overcome. England was wretchedly prepared to face this addition to the naval strength of her enemies. All the ships she could muster were desperately needed in American waters. The

---

[1] See H. Butterfield, *George III, Lord North and the People 1779-80* (1950), for a full discussion of these.

[2] cf. Sandwich to George III in Sept. 1779, *Correspondence of George III*, edited by the Hon. Sir John Fortescue (1927-8), vol. IV, p. 435.

[3] See A. Temple Patterson, *The Other Armada* (1960), and R. B. Morris, *The Peace Makers* (1965), ch. 2.

country was short of shipwrights and neither the necessary men nor the necessary ships could be produced in a matter of months to meet a sudden crisis. For this, Sandwich was not to blame. The navy had been badly neglected before he became First Lord of the Admiralty in 1775; since then he had done his best with limited financial resources. Had the French been able to mount an effective invasion it might well have succeeded. Subsequent debates revealed that the defences of Plymouth were deplorable; for instance, there were guns but no powder, and the gun carriages were so weak that they broke down if attempts were made to move them. Most of the regular army was in America, yet the ministers could not agree among themselves on a measure to double the militia, and the main reliance was placed on the raising of volunteer regiments. As the only shield against the prospect of invasion was a weak fleet under the command of the elderly Sir Charles Hardy, who inspired little confidence in his officers or the men he led, it is understandable that few people shared their King's robust optimism that the French would be repulsed. Hardy's handling of his problem was inglorious, and for a time the combined enemy fleets dominated the Channel;[1] but storms and the facts that they too were ill-found and riddled with disease prevented their taking any effective action. By the autumn the immediate danger was over, though it might easily become serious again in the following year. Elsewhere the events of the summer had increased the strain on England's naval forces. Though Britain, after the entry of France into the war, had managed to keep control of American coastal waters, her position in the West Indies was less happy. A French force based on Martinique had taken Dominica and, though the British did succeed in capturing St Lucia, the French also seized St Vincent and Grenada. Moreover, the entry of Spain into the war meant threats against Gibraltar and Minorca; unless communications could be kept open and the garrisons supplied and reinforced neither could be held.

During this critical summer the administration had been limping along with only one Secretary of State. Suffolk, who, it will be remembered, had brought George Grenville's followers back to the government fold after the latter's death, died in March 1779.

---

[1] He had, however, only 37 ships of the line against the combined French and Spanish fleets of 66 and his ships were in very bad condition. Though the fleet felt humiliated, Hardy was probably wise in deciding to keep his force intact, as until it had been destroyed the French dared not risk an invasion of England.

The problem of filling his vacant office was greatly complicated by the ambitions and intrigues of Wedderburn, Eden and Carlisle. North, threatened by unpleasant consequences on every side, took refuge in procrastination. It was not until nearly the end of October that Lord Stormont was appointed. Meanwhile fresh trouble was threatening. Lord Gower, the President of the Council, was on the verge of resigning. His ostensible reason was the failure of the government to deal with serious trouble which had developed in Ireland, but it was suspected that his resignation was part of a plot of the Bedfords to overthrow Lord North. If Thurlow, Weymouth and Carlisle in the Lords, and Rigby, who was Paymaster, in the Commons, all resigned, the chances of reconstructing the ministry under North would have been slim. Hardly had Stormont been appointed when this threatened crisis developed. Lord Weymouth, the other Secretary, resigned. It seems to have been to prevent Thurlow from following his erstwhile patron that George III with considerable political cunning now used him to negotiate a broadening of the base of the administration. This failed, but the King secured his object in that Thurlow did not resign.[1] Finally Hillsborough was appointed to Weymouth's vacant place and Lord Bathurst became Lord President of the Council. With so many vacancies to fill there could be no question of allowing either Germain or Sandwich to go. The leading actors therefore remained as before with an even weaker supporting cast. Meanwhile the parts they had to play were not made any easier by events in Ireland, and by a dangerous union between the opposition and discontent outside Parliament which showed itself in the Yorkshire movement at the end of the year.

4. THE IRISH PROBLEM

Of the likelihood of trouble in Ireland the government had had long warning. Ireland had too many genuine grievances against England for the American revolt not to have had some effect on Anglo-Irish relations. These grievances were partly economic, partly religious, and partly constitutional. To understand them it is

[1] As early as 24 January 1779 Fox was pointing out to Rockingham the unwisdom of declaring that 'you will never have anything to do with any Ministry, that is *not entirely* of your own framing'.—*Rockingham Memoirs*, vol. II, p. 372. While on 16 Dec. 1779 George III wrote to Thurlow: 'none of my Ministers can after this trial advise me to change my Government totally, and to admit Opposition without any terms'.—Sir John Fortescue, *op. cit.*, vol. IV, p. 522.

necessary to look briefly at the social and religious structure of Ireland, and to fit it into the economic doctrines which dictated the commercial policy of the empire. The basic fact was the fear which a Protestant England felt for a Roman Catholic Ireland. Because of it, though the attempt to root out Catholicism by active persecution had been abandoned, savage penal laws had converted Roman Catholics into second-class citizens. They could not be members of Parliament; after 1727 they were not even allowed to vote. They could not be members of corporations, serve on the commission for the peace, practise at the bar, possess arms, join the army or the navy. They could not acquire any interest in land for more than thirty-one years, nor own a horse worth more than £5. In order to encourage conversion to Protestantism, and to prevent the growth of large estates in Roman Catholic hands, these were to be divided equally on the death of the owner—unless his eldest son turned Protestant, in which case he succeeded to the whole. Though Roman Catholics were excluded from Trinity College, Dublin, at least in theory, they were forbidden to send their children overseas to acquire a liberal education at a foreign university. Many of these disabilities they shared with their co-religionists in England, and in both countries the enforcement of the penal laws was very lax except in so far as it affected political influence and the holding of office. But the parallel is essentially a false one. In Ireland Roman Catholicism was the religion of the majority; there the penal code had the effect of encouraging the absentee landlord by concentrating large estates in Protestant hands. In the same way it resulted in the concentration of political power on an even narrower base than in contemporary England.

On this narrow basis Ireland had nominally a good measure of self-government. The authority of the King was represented by the Lord Lieutenant, though it was not until the sixties that he was expected to remain in permanent residence. The legislature, modelled on the English one, was divided into a House of Lords and a House of Commons. In the former were 4 archbishops, 12 bishops, 35 earls, 45 viscounts and 35 barons. Some 300 members sat in the Irish House of Commons; there was no limit to its legal life (until the passing of the Octennial Act in 1768), except the death of the King. Their tenure up to this date was semi-permanent and in the reign of George II one Parliament lasted for thirty-three years. Unlike the English, the Irish Parliament was only called every other year.

As in England, the King had his permanent Civil List but the additional money needed was granted for two years at a time. The legislative freedom of Ireland was further limited in ways which were partly legal and partly imposed by the same opportunities for management as existed in England. The most important of the legal restraints was the statute of Drogheda of 1495, more usually known as Poyning's Law, which prevented business being discussed in the Irish Parliament without the authorization of the Privy Council. Also in 1719 a Declaratory Act had formally reserved to the English Parliament the right to pass laws binding on Ireland. For example, though there were 12,000 troops on the Irish establishment they were controlled by means of a Mutiny Act passed by the English Parliament. These provisions were sufficient to secure an English victory if a head-on collision took place between the two countries, but were not intended to be the normal machinery for keeping the policy of the two kingdoms in alignment. For this the familiar technique of management was employed. In the first part of the century it was customary for the Lord Lieutenant and the administration in Dublin, which in his absence was entrusted to the Lords Justices, to come to terms with a few powerful figures among the Irish dignitaries, known as undertakers. These men, in return for favour and some influence over policy, undertook to provide a stable basis for administration. When, however, Townshend became a resident Lord Lieutenant in 1767,[1] he took over the apportioning of patronage, and with it the direct responsibility for securing pliable majorities in the Irish House of Commons.

The economic and social structure which sustained this constitutional framework was shaped in part by the religious divisions of the country, and in part by the system of commercial regulation to which it belonged. A succession of revolts had transferred much land from the Catholic Irish to the Protestant English. Absentee landlords were one of the curses of Ireland: men like Rockingham and Hillsborough had extensive estates from which they drew large rents. Being absent and alien and Protestant they had little sympathy for their tenants. In England the improving landlord was a familiar

---

[1] This was part of an implied bargain by which the Irish military establishment should be raised from 12,000 to 15,000 to give the British administration extra reserves for colonial defence, and in return the Lord Lieutenant was to reside continuously and the duration of Parliament be limited.—V. T. Harlow, *The Founding of the second British Empire, 1763–93* (1952), p. 512.

figure; wherever good agricultural practices and decent accommodation for the labourer were to be found these were probably his work. In Ireland circumstances combined to discourage the same developments. There the peasantry were exceedingly poor, and their poverty made them brutal and ignorant. The widespread use of the potato meant that a large population, relative to the available acreage, could be maintained at a bare subsistence level. Because the population was relatively large and even a small potato patch would support a family the competition for land was fierce. Further competition came from the graziers who raised cattle for the flourishing provision trade. Sheep were reared for their wool; corn was another cash crop. The results were rack-rents, which left the tenant no capital for improvements, and a fragmentation of holdings which were too small for the application of better methods. With neither land nor capital available a vicious circle of misery was all but inevitable.

Economic subordination to England hindered the development of compensating activities which might have attracted labour from the land into industry. English manufacturers were jealous of Irish competition, both in the home market and overseas, arguing that the low standard of living in Ireland would enable Irish goods to undersell English ones. Since 1699 Irish wool, woollen yarn and cloth could be sent only to England, where they were burdened with heavy duties, though in 1737 these were removed from yarn. Ireland was not allowed to develop a glassmaking industry, and the manufacture of silk was obstructed. Linen on the other hand was encouraged, as it did not compete with an important English industry. As early as 1704 the colonial market in linen which might even be sent in Irish ships had been thrown open. By the middle of the century it was Ireland's most important industry. But with this exception Ireland did not benefit under the Navigation Acts. Scotland, as part of the price of Union in 1707, had secured full participation in the colonial trade, and by the middle of the century Glasgow merchants were making excellent use of this concession.[1] Yet in spite of the difficulties which hampered her, certain sections of Irish society were achieving a modest prosperity in the second half of the eighteenth century. Irish woollens found a market within its own borders, for the numbers of those who could afford the

[1] J. H. Soltow, *'Scottish Traders in Virginia 1750–75'* (*Econ. Hist. Review*, 2nd ser., vol. XII, no. 1, August 1959).

English cloth were limited. Nor was all the Irish cloth of poor or coarse quality. Though much coarse cloth was exported, especially to Wales, the disturbances which broke out in Tiverton in 1750 were caused by the merchants of the town importing worsteds from Ireland. Also, though English graziers had got an act as early as 1663 preventing the export of fatstock from Ireland, a profitable trade in provisions had been built up with the colonies. For the Irish middle-class Roman Catholic to whom, like the English Dissenter, the professions were barred, there were therefore some opportunities to make money in trade and manufacture. Moreover a great deal of smuggling added a certain amount of elasticity to the economy. Travellers from England, like Arthur Young, and native Irish writers and commentators record the noticeable improvement which marked the second half of the century. Such improvement was, however, confined to a very narrow circle. The misery of the peasantry seems to have been as great as ever. Rural outrages and illegal associations, such as the Whiteboys, were endemic; without the presence of the military order could hardly have been preserved or taxes collected.

Even this limited prosperity seems to have encouraged a new national consciousness among the Protestant Irish. Though they still remained extremely hesitant about removing the burden of the penal code from their Romish countrymen, by the seventies a reforming party was coming into being. This aimed at securing the same rights for the Irish Parliament as those which the English one had obtained in 1689 and campaigned for greater freedom within the framework of the laws of trade. This movement was stimulated by two events in 1776. One was the appointment of the Earl of Buckinghamshire as Lord Lieutenant. The other was the American Declaration of Independence. Buckinghamshire was to show himself sympathetic to Irish needs. To him it seemed that prosperity would make Ireland a useful partner rather than a dangerous rival; increased industry in Ireland would stimulate increased imports from England and both countries would benefit. When examining the Irish position he used his own spectacles rather than those usually worn in England. This meant that when Ireland was stirred by events in America to attempt some amelioration of her own situation she had the advantage of an official channel of communication between Dublin and Westminster that was friendly.

The American revolt encouraged this movement in Ireland in

two ways. From the beginning sympathy for the cause of the colonists was general, partly because the Irish regarded them as the victims of the same type of exploitation from which they also suffered, partly because even in the eighteenth century many Irish emigrated to America. At convivial political dinners such toasts as 'Our fellow subjects in America now suffering persecution for attempting to assert their rights and liberties',[1] were popular. This sympathy was soon sharpened by economic distress. The outbreak of war meant that the important and profitable Irish trade in provisions to the colonies was placed under an embargo. This helped to spread distress, for Ireland, with so many eggs in so few baskets, could not afford to see even one of them destroyed. North personally was inclined to be sympathetic; indeed, since the accession of George III, the passing of the Octennial Act in 1768 and the practice of requiring the Lord Lieutenant to reside, he had shown a new sensitiveness towards Irish problems. Under his leadership, therefore, five resolutions were carried in the English House of Commons on 8 April 1778; these, if implemented, would have gone a long way to meeting the Irish contention that English commercial restrictions were stunting Irish economic development and depriving her of prosperity. Resolutions, however, merely express the opinion of the House, and sometimes its emotional rather than considered opinion, and have no authority outside its walls. In this case they served to warn every vested interest in England which feared Irish competition. Protests poured in. English prosperity had also been hit though not so severely, because she had more reserves of economic strength on which to draw, and with the war to finance North dared not antagonize English and Scottish merchants and manufacturers. Finally, after hopes had been raised—always a dangerous action—the only concessions to be embodied in a statute were those to include Irish-built ships in the provisions of the Navigation Acts and to encourage Irish fisheries by the payment of bounties.

With such concessions Irish commercial interests were not prepared to be satisfied[2] and other events were soon to place in their hands a formidable weapon with which to back up their claims for greater commercial freedom. This was the rise of the

[1] R. B. McDowell, *Irish Public Opinion* (1944), p. 43.

[2] At a gathering in Dublin held in April 1779 a non-importation agreement, based on the American precedent, was agreed upon.

Volunteer Movement. Once France had entered the war against Great Britain the question of defending Ireland against a possible invasion had to be faced. The regiments usually stationed in that country and paid by the Irish taxpayer were nearly all abroad; indeed, this had already created a minor problem in those districts where agrarian misery was a perpetual threat to order, so that even before there was any fear from France local bodies of middle-class Protestants had begun to organize for mutual protection. When the fear from France became a reality, an almost spontaneous movement to form volunteer companies for local defence appeared among them. Buckinghamshire was anxious that this policy should be officially adopted and the officers receive commissions, as was often done in raising emergency companies of volunteers in England. This the ministers in London were unwilling to contemplate. In Ireland, however, the movement went on, Buckinghamshire turning a blind eye and excusing himself on the ground that with Irish opinion so inflammable it was the only policy which he could follow. The result was that everywhere bands of Protestant Irish were drilling; by May 1779 Buckinghamshire put their number at 8,000. By February 1782 they were estimated at 40,000 when delegates from 143 corps attended the Congress at Dungannon. There is nothing to indicate that the original aim of the volunteers was other than its ostensible reason—the defence of Ireland against the French. The facts that it coincided with the clamour for free trade, which came to dominate Irish public opinion in 1779, and that this cause was taken up by the Rockinghams in the English Parliament gave it its peculiar importance. On 11 May the Marquis moved an address asking for information about Anglo-Irish trade. This debate was notable for two reasons. The first was that, in the speech supporting his motion, Rockingham stressed the kinship between the movement which was still in its early stages in Ireland with that which had led ultimately to the American war. Irish grievances he indicated were genuine, and he suggested that, if treated as unimaginatively as the Americans had been, the volunteers might turn from resisting French aggression to resisting British oppression. From this time the opposition groups made the Irish case their own. The second important aspect of this debate was that Lord Gower, the Lord President, made a conciliatory reply in which he promised that something should be done to improve Ireland's economic position. Since by October no action had been taken, Gower made this the reason for his resignation, though nobody believed it to be his only one.

To discuss Irish grievances at all was to open Pandora's box. Economic were closely allied to constitutional restrictions, as Fox made plain when he spoke on a motion asking for the prorogation of Parliament to be deferred until Ireland's difficulties had been discussed and some remedy for them proposed. From questioning the right of the English Parliament to impose trading restrictions it was only a short step to questioning its entire authority to legislate for Ireland. Once again the hard-worked doctrine of natural rights was invoked to undermine English legislative power over the sister kingdom. What nature had given, the British Parliament could not take away. No attempt was made to find remedies for Ireland's distress before Parliament was prorogued, but ministers began to bestir themselves to the extent of asking Buckinghamshire to collect and send to them the considered opinion of prominent Irishmen. This in the late spring and early summer he did, and the result was the forwarding of a formidable mass of papers to London. Here they remained for weeks unconsidered. Even before Parliament had been prorogued, North, in a speech on 23 May, in contradiction to the line taken by Gower, had disclaimed any intention, or indeed ability to satisfy Irish demands. By the time Buckinghamshire had collected and forwarded the necessary material on which a policy might have been based there was no minister with the inclination or the leisure to study it. Between March and October North's attention was wholly focused on the difficulties of reconstructing the administration after the death of Suffolk and with the threat of the French invasion. In these months, too, his nervous state was such that even George III, helped by the combined efforts of Jenkinson and Robinson, could hardly bring him to a decision on matters which they thought more vital than Ireland. Meanwhile from the Lord Lieutenant and from John Beresford, one of the commissioners for revenue in Ireland, came alarming accounts of the state of that country. Public opinion was being increasingly inflamed by speeches, the press and the writers of pamphlets, and the growth of the volunteer movement was making it increasingly dangerous. Though the Treasury was empty, and there was no money to put the country into a state of defence against the French fleet now cruising in the Channel, the Lord Lieutenant and his officials dared not summon, as the English ministers suggested, a special session of Parliament. Unless they had some concrete suggestions to lay before it they knew that it would be extremely difficult to handle. Yet in spite of almost despairing appeals from Dublin that the English minister should indicate some policy with which they might meet Parliament, North and his colleagues did nothing. Jenkinson, alarmed by the Irish situation, made a précis of the Irish material, but in vain, for he could not persuade North to read even that.

The result, when the Irish Parliament did meet for the new session on 12 October, was, as might have been expected, a new crisis. Members refused to be put off with the vague generalizations which were all that the King's Speech contained, and moved an amendment 'That it is not by temporary Expedients but by a Free Trade alone that this Nation is now to be saved from impending Ruin'. That it should be carried without a division because government supporters in the House realized the impossibility of opposing it, showed even ministers in London that the problem of Ireland could no longer be shelved. If any doubt had still been possible on this point events in Ireland in November would have dispelled it. In that month popular disturbances reinforced the patriot opposition in the Irish Parliament to such an extent that neither Buckinghamshire nor his chief Secretary, Sir Richard Heron, was able to prevent the carrying of the Short Money Bill. By this the necessary supplies were granted not for the normal two years but for six months only. Meanwhile in the English Parliament Rockingham, Fox and their friends were using the dissatisfaction in Ireland as a major weapon against North and his colleagues. For once they were all united, even Shelburne joining in the attack, though it was Fox who took the most extreme position; he declared that he approved of the 'manly determination' which 'flies to arms in order to obtain deliverance' and thereby incited the Irish volunteers to active rebellion. Under such pressure the government gave way, to the joy of the Irish but to the somewhat ungenerous discomfort of the English opposition groups. What North had refused to concede either to reason or to persuasion he now gave in order to break the link between the parliamentary opposition and the Irish patriots. By the middle of November minutes of information and material dealing with Irish trade were at last hastily studied. By 13 December North was able to lay his proposals before the English House of Commons. By these Ireland was to be allowed to export all manner of woollen goods, or goods in which wool was used, glass and glassware; she was also to be allowed to share equally in the trade with the British colonies in America and the West Indies. Perhaps in no other way than by a threat of violence at a time of emergency could these concessions have been obtained. British vested interests were bitterly opposed to them, as is illustrated both by their earlier successful attack on North's proposals in 1778 and by the younger Pitt's failure to introduce any adequate measure of free trade between the countries in 1785. Other less materially interested persons deplored the step, for it removed out of English hands what, carefully managed, might have been used as bait for a union between the two countries. This solution had already been discussed privately during the crisis of 1779, but it was felt that, however, desirable in theory, it would have been so unpopular with the Irish as to be impracticable.

Meanwhile North's concessions conciliated patriot opinion for a time. Concessions in trade could, however, be regarded only as a temporary stop: constitutional issues once raised could not easily be reinterred. Between the end of 1779 and 1782, when North resigned, a campaign of steadily increasing weight and authority, both in the Irish Parliament and in the country at large, agitated for the repeal of Poyning's Law and the Declaratory Act, and the recognition of the complete legislative independence of the Irish. This to English ministers was an unwelcome development, and the Lord Lieutenant received peremptory orders to prevent such legislation being brought forward. He soon discovered that it was easier to open flood gates than to close them. The technique of public meetings, press campaigns and, if need be, riots and violence to reinforce parliamentary action had been too successful to be given up easily, especially when the growing numbers of the volunteers made it clear that a discontented Ireland might be a dangerous Ireland. Torn as he was between his instructions from London and his own realization of the strength of the movement which he was supposed to extinguish, Buckinghamshire's health and nerves began to suffer. In 1780, after the suppression of the Gordon Riots in London and the news that British troops had conquered Charleston had given North's administration a little prestige, he was replaced by the Earl of Carlisle with Eden as his Chief Secretary.

North's concessions had, however, given him a brief breathing space and even a little transitory popularity in Ireland which enabled him to concentrate his attention on a dangerous co-operation between the gentlemen of Yorkshire and the parliamentary opposition.[1] The origin of the movement is obscure. Undoubtedly there was much discontent and unorganized dissatisfaction in the country caused by the lack of success in the American war. Opposition speeches in Parliament and anti-government writers were skilful in spreading an impression of inefficiency, mismanagement and outright corruption. With so little success for so much expenditure it was not difficult to contrive that such ideas should soak into the consciousness of the ordinary country gentleman. But the fact that plenty of inflammable material is lying about will not produce a blaze unless somebody sets it alight. There must have been considerable activity behind the apparently spontaneous movements of the autumn of 1779 which culminated in the Yorkshire movement at the end of the year.

5. THE PETITIONING MOVEMENT[1]

In Middlesex discontent with the government had been endemic ever since the trouble over Wilkes, and in a by-election in the autumn of 1779 an attempt had been made to manufacture a fresh crisis, which should give the electors of Middlesex once again an excuse for declaring that a corrupt House of Commons had ignored their rights. This move had failed to generate the necessary heat, owing to its very skilful handling by North. Though their immediate tactics had been foiled, the Middlesex troublemakers had no intention of giving up their campaign. Instead they expressed their intention of holding a meeting on 20 December 'to maintain and support the freedom of elections', and the press was full of indications that other counties were also preparing petitions on this subject for presentation to Parliament. The rights of electors, however, which they were unable to dramatize at that moment by the production of a *cause célèbre*, seemed unlikely to win much popular support. Then early in December various letters in the press began to indicate a growing concern for the waste of public money. From this point it was the freeholders of Yorkshire that took the lead, perhaps appropriately. Late in November the Reverend Christopher Wyvill, who owned considerable property in that county, acting

---

[1] For the Petitioning Movement consult H. Butterfield, *George III, Lord North and the People* (1949), and I. R. Christie, *Wilkes, Wyvill and Reform* (1962).

in concert with a few friends, discussed plans for a mass meeting of Yorkshire freeholders to protest against this waste. By the end of the month the idea was being more widely canvassed, likely adherents were being approached, and a meeting of the freeholders at York was fixed for 30 December. As a consequence the freeholders of Middlesex decided to postpone their meeting, originally arranged for the 20th, until the upshot of the northern meeting was known.

There seems to have been no connection at first between the Yorkshire movement and the parliamentary group of the Rockinghams,[1] though the section of the press that was friendly to the opposition was clearly in sympathy with the Middlesex agitation. Even the first rumblings of discontent in the north, and its suggesttion of a mass meeting of freeholders were, however, soon seized upon as offering a favourable subject for attack. It was indeed particularly suited to the needs of opposition members: it had the supreme advantage of uniting all the various connections within Parliament. On this issue Rockingham and Shelburne and Fox could, or so it appeared at the outset, act harmoniously together. In the autumn session of 1779 their parliamentary attack had been increasingly focused on the royal influence over policy. It was widely known that all George III's personal convictions were behind the refusal of his ministers to regard the struggle with the colonists as lost. Though their criticism was nominally directed against North this was due solely to the convention which made it impossible to hold the King personally responsible. Equally it was realized that if the independent members could be persuaded to withdraw their support from North it was most unlikely that the King could find another administration prepared to support the present royal policy in the House. So far, in spite of the difficulties which had faced the ministers in 1779, the efforts of the opposition groups to undermine their authority in the House had produced little result. Convinced as Fox and Burke and Rockingham were that the present trend of British policy was disastrous, such blindness on the part of the majority of the Commons was comprehensible to them only in terms of corruption. It was therefore understandable that they should stress those elements in the management of public business that could most easily be explained in terms of an undue exercise of

---

[1] Sir George Savile, a representative of one of the great territorial families of England and one of the M.P.s for Yorkshire, was, however, an old and close friend of Rockingham.

royal influence. How far they believed their own assertions of grow-ing influence it is difficult to judge, but they were not justified by the facts. In 1761 there were some 250 placemen as opposed to 200 in 1780; in the former House of Commons the administration had had some 30 boroughs more or less under its control, in the present one these had sunk to 22 and this reduction appears to have been a continuing process.[1] But whether justified or not, an attack on the misuse of public money was always sound political strategy. It was always popular with the country gentlemen, and as the financial arrangements were so chaotic the administration was rarely able to produce a reasoned defence to be made against the criticisms of opposition speakers. Indeed, so deplorable was the state of the administration of public finance that it has been suggested that Burke's attack, though carefully timed to take advantage of the wider movement in the country as a whole, was not wholly political in its aims and that, whatever his motives in moving his original motion on 15 December, he did become genuinely convinced of the necessity of reform.[2] Certainly North, as head of the Treasury, agreed with him on the need to overhaul the administration of the finances, and his suggestions for the setting up of a committee which should first collect information and then make concrete proposals, proved in the long run far more effective than Burke's proposals which, because they were part of a dramatic political crisis, have received more publicity.

In spite of Burke's claim to an interest in economic reform, the Yorkshire movement in its early stages had little connection with Parliament, though Sir George Saville, one of the members for Yorkshire, became closely connected with Wyvill. At the great meeting held in York on 30 December it was the gentlemen of Yorkshire who were speaking, not the politicians. Very little attention was paid to such of the local magnates, including Rocking-ham, who attended. Had this meeting been merely an isolated gesture of protest, though it would have filled the press with news and comment and might even have given the administration a temporary moment of alarm, its importance would have been only

[1] I. R. Christie, 'Economical Reform and the "Influence of the Crown" 1780' (*The Cambridge Historical Journal,* vol. XII, no. 2, 1956, p. 147).

[2] J. E. D. Binney, *op. cit.,* pp. 270–1. For the opposing view see I. R. Christie, *art. cit.,* 'The saving of money is but a secondary object. The reduction of the influence of the Crown is the first.'—p. 144.

temporary. What gave it its significance was the way in which an inner ring of radical thinkers used it in order to sketch out the basic framework of an organization which they came to claim was more representative than Parliament itself of the people of England, using that term in the eighteenth-century sense of the solid property-holders, not 'the mob'. The accounts of the meeting make it clear that its organizers had this ulterior motive in mind. After long debate and many speeches the petition was accepted with only one adverse vote. When the attendance was already thinning, a second resolution was presented and passed, to the effect that a committee should be appointed 'to carry on the necessary correspondence for effectually promoting the object of the petition and to support that laudable reform and such other measure as may conduce to restore the Freedom of Parliament'.[1] This resolution was the beginning of a fairly widespread petitioning movement, and other towns and counties adopted the same method of voicing their discontent. The movement must not, however, be regarded as completely spontaneous. Eighteenth-century petitions were the work of local men of importance. Where opposition influence was strong they appeared; where ministerial influence was dominant resolutions critical of the petitions were passed. The nature of the petitions did not, however, make them less of a challenge to the administration.

Though the petitioning movement was originally the child of the radicals rather than of the politicians, one of the politicians of the day was to play a great part in it. This was Charles James Fox. He first became associated with the movement to organize a petition in Wiltshire, and from his showing on that occasion was asked to act as Chairman to the Committee of Correspondence which was set up at Westminster.[2] Associations were to him one of the most useful weapons that could be used against the royal influence. In America and Ireland they had proved how dangerous they could be to established institutions. By 1779 the mere word had already acquired a seditious flavour. Fox's connection with the Westminster Committee gave him a platform for the expression of radical ideas which soon went far beyond the very modest reforming activities of the Rockingham whigs. Thus scarcely had the opposition groups come together before they began to split again as Rockingham and Burke gradually came to stand for a purging of

---

[1] H. Butterfield, *George III, Lord North, etc.*, p. 205.

[2] Fox had been proposed as a candidate for the next election and was returned for Westminster in 1780.

the royal influence to leave a Parliament dominated by the aristocracy, while Fox came to think in terms of a more democratic
representative system. Burke wanted economic reform, Fox a
reform of the franchise. The gulf is wider than it looked at first
sight; eventually it was to break the friendship between the two
men. At first, however, it seemed as if the two movements might
be run in double harness.

The situation in the spring of 1780 was both complex and confused, and outwardly the ministers seemed very near to defeat. In
the House of Commons the Rockingham whigs, with Burke as
their leader, made partially successful efforts to secure some measure
of economic reform. On 11 February he made his great speech on
the subject, cataloguing almost to the point of absurdity the various
capacities—King, Prince of Wales, Duke of Lancaster and so on—
in virtue of which George III was entitled to separate households
and separate officials, all of them, it was implied, merely burden-
ing the kingdom unnecessarily and providing the means of corruption. On 23 February, the ground having been so prepared,
Burke introduced his bill for 'the better Regulation of his Majesty's
Civil Establishments',[1] the clauses of which were hotly debated in
committee during March. Meanwhile outside Parliament Wyvill
and his most confidential colleagues were planning an association
on a national base which should aim at securing a careful scrutiny
of public money, the addition of a hundred county representatives
to Parliament (thereby strengthening what was considered to be the
most independent element in the House), and annual Parliaments.
In order to hold the petitioning movement together, and to formulate plans for a national association, it was decided to hold in
London a meeting of deputies elected by the local committees of
correspondence. By so doing one branch of the Yorkshire movement seemed to be coming into the open as an advocate of semi-
revolutionary ideas. Indeed, it seems to have hoped that the
authority of the London congress of deputies, being based, as they
claimed, on the most respectable public opinion in the country,

---

[1] I. R. Christie, *art. cit.*, points out that 'it appears that the number of placemen
reached a peak in 1761, which was never again to be approached'. By 1780 they had
shrunk by a fifth and there is no evidence that George III and North were using Court
offices to pack the House. It was for this reason that Burke preferred to sponsor an
Establishment Bill rather than a Place Bill; the new line of argument adopted was that
the war had so greatly extended the scope of government patronage that that distributed
by the civil list must be reduced.—pp. 146–7.

might supersede the moral authority of Parliament, and reduce that institution to the level of a rubber stamp for its own decisions.

Here were conditions for cross-currents. Certainly Rockingham and his associates had no desire to see the authority of Parliament reduced; they wanted to see aristocratic influence increased at the expense of that of the Crown. Controversy over such points almost split the Westminster Committee, and for a time Fox seems to have followed a moderate and restraining policy in his dual capacity as its chairman and a prominent parliamentarian. He was anxious to curb the authority of the King, but reluctant to subject prospective Members of Parliament to advance pledges or tests to support the programme of the association in return for the votes of its members. By April, therefore, the attack on the King, for so in essence it was, was breaking into two, one stressing the need of economic reform to preserve members from corruption when elected, the other demanding radical changes in the composition and duration of the Commons itself. For a time this parliamentary opposition pressed the ministers hard. Burke's proposal to abolish the third Secretary of State, the office held by the unpopular Germain, was only defeated by 208 votes to 201. On 13 March the proposal to abolish the Board of Trade, where a post as President had finally been found for Carlisle, was actually carried against the government by 207 votes to 199. When, however, it came to touching the King's own establishment by abolishing the Treasurer of the Chamber, the feeling of the House was against him and the clause was defeated by 211 votes to 158. By the end of March it was clear that economic reform, as a practical weapon against the Court, had broken in the hands of the Rockinghams.[1]

The petitioning movement nevertheless still held potentialities for danger, though the General Assembly of Deputies, when it met on 11 March, was numerically disappointing to its promoters, deputies from only 12 counties and 8 boroughs appearing. However radical the impulse behind the petitions might be, the procedure itself was not illegal, and it was therefore incumbent on the House to make some show of answering, or at least of examining those

---

[1] Rockingham's dislike of the vague platform of the reformers and his preference for Burke's more concrete proposals which he calls 'certain and immediate' is well expressed in a lengthy letter to Mr. Pemberton Milnes, dated 28 February 1780. He proved correct in his conclusion that 'there are so many visionary schemes and expedients by *ways of reforms on float* that a *general* confusion and disagreement will ensue'.—*Rockingham Memoirs*, vol. II, pp. 395–400.

petitions that had been received. Here the opposition were able to win a famous battle, though Lord North won the war. As parliamentary time was running out it was decided that 6 April should be set aside for their consideration by the whole House sitting in committee. The presentation of the petitioners' case was opened by Dunning, one of the most respected and able lawyers in the Rockingham ranks. In his speech he said that he proposed to condense the essence of the complaints into two resolutions which, if the House approved, he would follow up with more practical suggestions for means of redress. The first of these resolutions was the famous one that 'It is the opinion of this committee that the influence of the Crown has increased, is increasing and ought to be diminished.' Ministers had not expected the attack to take quite that form; they were unprepared and the resolution was carried by 233 votes to 215. It was immediately followed by others of a similarly critical character; for once the opposition were getting the ball and they intended to score as often as possible while the game favoured them. Fox, by moving that the resolutions should be immediately reported to the House, completed the victories of the day. North, with his usual habit of immediate despair, thought that the end had come at last. So did many of the opposition; but they were wrong.

The weakness of the parliamentary opposition—Rockingham, Shelburne and their respective friends in the Lords; Burke, Dunning and Fox in the Commons—was that though they could express the common dissatisfaction in generalities, either they had no practical programme to suggest or their remedies went further than the majority in either House was prepared to go. They could win victories of prestige by carrying motions against the administration, but when they attempted concrete reforms they lost votes. For instance, Lord Crewe's bill for disenfranchising revenue officers, who—it was notorious—had to vote for government-sponsored candidates, was defeated on 13 April by 224 votes to 195. The next day the bill disqualifying men with government contracts from sitting in the House of Commons, which the ministers had thought wiser not to oppose in that House, was defeated in the Lords.[1]

---

[1] The number of members who held government contracts in 1761 was 37. In 1780 it was 11; this number, however, was abnormally low. In 1778 and again in 1781 it was 15, but even this represents a considerable shrinking from the 1761 figure.—I. R. Christie, *art. cit.*, pp. 145–7.

Further, a recess until 24 April, necessitated by the ill-health of the Speaker, Fletcher Norton, gave the administration a short breathing space and incidentally allowed the Rockingham coterie to attend the Newmarket races with a clear conscience. When Parliament reassembled, both sides of the House recognized that the events of the next few days would be decisive and mobilized their full strength. Dunning took the offensive and moved a resolution that the House should present an address to the King, asking that Parliament be neither dissolved nor prorogued until 'proper measures had been taken to diminish the influence, and correct the other abuses, complained of by the petitions of the people'. Such an address would have been too reminiscent of the Long Parliament to be acceptable to any House not on the verge of revolt against the authority of the Crown. Its acceptance would have been an act of a very different nature from the approval given to Dunning's earlier motion. Independent gentlemen were willing to deplore the increase of royal influence, meaning thereby ministerial influence. This did not mean that they were prepared to dictate to the King when he should exercise his royal authority, any more than previously they had been willing to interfere in the running of the royal household when called to do so by Burke. The motion was negatived by 254 votes to 203, and with its rejection the attack of the opposition was broken. Once again North, sustained and encouraged by George III, had triumphed.

The Yorkshire movement was also spluttering to its end. It, too, had suffered from divided councils, with Wyvill at first taking the more extreme position and Fox, in his capacity as a member of the Commons, attempting to moderate Wyvill's programme. By the late spring of 1780 these roles had been reversed. In the course of his campaign Wyvill had come to realize the value of aristocratic support, of which at the beginning he had been suspicious. To gain this it was necessary to placate Rockingham and his associates, who shrank from the idea of annual Parliaments. Wyvill therefore attempted to modify his original demands and came out in favour of triennial Parliaments. This failed to win the Rockinghams and alienated his own supporters. As many idealists turned politicians have done, he fell between two stools. In the meantime the Westminster Committee became the last stronghold of the men who saw in parliamentary reform the only cure of the political ills of their day. Into this cause Fox, disgusted by the failure of the parliamentary opposition, threw himself with fresh enthusiasm. Though what the Committee did could have little effect, what it said was important because it publicized a more democratic theory of representation than the accepted one which based representation on property: only men who 'had a stake in the country' were entitled to the franchise. Now the Westminster Committee stressed the fact that every man had his own modest stake in the country in which he lived; he, too, had to pay taxes and serve in the militia. 'Every man', they proclaimed, 'has an interest in his life, his liberty, his kindred, and his country.' From this they deduced that every adult man had also the right to vote for the choice of the M.P. to represent him. And to back their arguments history was ransacked for examples, torn from their context and in fact ludicrously unhistorical. The ideas that the Westminster Committee formulated were not the product of their own original thought; radical writers and thinkers in the previous decade had already been blazing the trail.[1] What happened in the late spring of 1780 was that these revolutionary ideas were thrust under the notice of people and made a talking-point. Ideas which only won a tardy acceptance a hundred years later had little chance of acceptance by the property-conscious electorate of the late eighteenth century. If the petitioning movement and the parliamentary campaign of 1780 had more than a transitory importance, it was an importance conferred on it by later development and not because of any immediate consequences which flowed from them.

6. THE GORDON RIOTS

By the summer the position of Lord North's ministry was much stronger. This was principally due to two events. The first was the Gordon Riots,[2] which influenced respectable opinion to rally round authority in the face of mob disorder. The second was news of the military successes in Georgia and Carolina, which seemed to hold out renewed hopes of a British victory in America. The Gordon Riots are an interesting episode which throws a good deal of light on eighteenth-century conditions and opinions. Their origin lay in the Roman Catholic Relief Bill of 1778. Though after the accession of William III there had been little attempt to enforce the full rigour of the penal laws, legally Roman Catholics remained in a highly

---

[1] Major Cartwright's pamphlet *Take your Choice* was published in 1777.

[2] For a full and vivid account consult Christopher Hibbert, *King Mob: the Story of Lord George Gordon and the Riots of 1780* (1958).

vulnerable position. By the second half of the eighteenth century educated public opinion had ceased to fear them; after the failure of the '45 there had been no real danger of a Stuart restoration, and to a society familiar with the Grand Tour the Pope had become less of a bogy. To those prepared to take an oath of allegiance it seemed unreasonable to refuse the ordinary civil rights of a citizen, though there was still little disposition to entrust them with full political rights. The result of these convictions had been an easy passage through both Houses of the necessary legislation. When, however, it was proposed to pass similar legislation for Scotland the response was immediate and violent. In that Presbyterian country the traditional hatred of the Roman Church was still bitter, and early in 1779 a Protestant Association was formed to resist any attempt to ameliorate the position of the Roman Catholic section of the community. In Edinburgh and Glasgow dangerous riots broke out, and, with the magistrates unfavourable to the idea and no adequate force on which to rely, the ministers decided to leave the Scottish Protestant hedgehog alone. In February 1779 a similar Protestant Association was formed in London and in November of that year Lord George Gordon, who had earlier been prominent in the Scottish movement, was asked to become its President. In the May of the following year it was determined to present a monster petition against the Act, praying for its repeal. The association's widespread support from the lower classes in London well illustrates the continuance of bigotry and superstition among them. The same waves of fear and dislike which earlier had made Newcastle ready to repeal the Act for the naturalization of the Jews, and which had beaten, though vainly on that occasion, against the reform of the calendar, were once again to be manifest.

On 2 June Lord George Gordon, accompanied by a huge crowd of petitioners very much under the sway of his unbalanced oratory, presented his petition to the Commons amid scenes of considerable disorder. Eighteenth-century London was full of wild, brutal and lawless elements who could easily be incited to violence. On such occasions a lust for the destruction of property would seize the milling crowds, so that respectable citizens hastened home to guard their houses and even their persons from violence. For over a week on this occasion London seemed at their mercy.[1] On the day which

---

[1] *King Mob*, pp. 101–2, for a graphic description of the attack by the mob on Langdale's distillery in which the now drunken rioters were burnt to death. Langdale was a Roman Catholic who owned one of the largest distilleries in London.

was appointed for the presentation of the petition some 60,000 persons assembled in St George's Fields, Southwark, and from there marched to Westminster. According to one bystander they seemed to be composed of decent citizens rather than a mere concourse of the usual mob, but their behaviour in Palace Yard while the debate on the petition was proceeding was extremely turbulent. Not till 11 p.m. were the Guards able to clear a path and get departing members out in safety. This demonstration was in part due to the fact that the consideration of the petition had been postponed until the following Tuesday. In the intervening days a good deal of sporadic rioting took place, during which Roman Catholic chapels were destroyed and dwelling houses damaged. In the course of this destruction five rioters were committed to Newgate, a fact which was later to have important consequences; but in general the authorities seemed strangely supine about coming to the rescue of the mob's victims. When, in face of the threatening attitude of the crowds which had once again gathered in Palace Yard for the consideration of their petition, it was decided to postpone it once again until Thursday, the riots took on a fresh violence. On that night Newgate itself was sacked and set on fire and all the prisoners, not merely the five rioters, set free. This was not the only incident. Lord Mansfield's house was set ablaze, his possessions looted, and his valuable library and manuscripts destroyed, because he had been known to favour the Catholic Relief Act. The next day, Wednesday, was one of terror with widespread destruction; the Fleet prison was attacked and this general onslaught on gaols was a characteristic feature of the whole episode. An attempt was even made to seize the Bank of England, though to save this citadel of finance the City authorities and regular troops, which had now been called in, organized a successful counter-attack. Though rioting continued on Thursday, by then the troops were in control. By the 9th everything was over and Lord George Gordon on his way to the Tower.

There seems little doubt that this outburst of violence made men more inclined to rally round the accepted order. To see London and Southwark in flames affected other people besides Horace Walpole. Moreover, though religious fanaticism sparked off the conflagration, and the wretched and vicious elements which made up the dregs of London's society no doubt loved destruction for its own sake, it has been suggested that behind the No Popery slogans there was a considerable amount of social bitterness.[1] The destruction and violence were not concentrated in those areas where the poorer Irish Catholics lived and worked but against the well-to-do. There was 'a groping desire to settle accounts with the rich, if only for a day', which explains the number of hitherto respectable working men who afterwards stood their trial for their part in the disorder. If this is so it is not surprising that, remembering the horror of the week, propertied people drew back from any proposals which seemed to threaten the established order; this had suddenly become precious in their eyes. This, and the better news arriving from America, gave the ministers a breathing space in which to reorganize the basis of their authority.

---

[1] G. E. F. Rudé, 'The Gordon Riots: A Study of the Rioters and Their Victims' *Trans. R. Hist. Soc.*, 5th ser., vol. VI, 1956).

18

SOCIAL AND ECONOMIC DEVELOPMENTS

NEVERTHELESS by 1780 England was a very different country in which to live from the England which had reluctantly accepted the Hanoverian George as her King. Internal peace and political stability had brought an increase in wealth and prosperity. Eighteenth-century wars had been fought on European or colonial soil. They had been a burden which an expanding economy had carried without undue strain while the demands which they had created for ships, for munitions, for the equipping and provisioning of armies and of fleets, had provided additional incentives for production. Overseas conquests too had increased both monopoly markets and the control of valuable tropical products. In every sphere there had been growth and expansion. By 1780 England was turning her back on the past and looking to the future; already in 1776 the Declaration of Independence had crashed through the traditions of the past while in the field of economic thinking the publication of Adam Smith's *The Wealth of Nations*, in the same year, attacked the mercantilist theories which up to then had governed the relationship between Britain and her overseas possessions. While George III had been struggling with problems of government and with the intractable issues of America and Ireland, men of no political importance had been laying the foundations of a new Britain which was to become 'the workshop of the world'. Though, in the absence of any official census, accurate figures are lacking, the population had started its steady upward climb. There were more people who could be productively employed, more people to be fed than when he had come to the throne in 1760. In industry there had been a breakthrough in the techniques that were to make mass production possible in both textiles and heavy industry. Improved transport was binding the country together, both socially and economically, in a way that had never been possible before. Though the hierarchical organization of society had as yet been hardly challenged it allowed sufficient flexibility and social mobility for new groupings to take place. The middling sort were finding new ways of making money, the labouring poor more varied employment. It was in 1776 that Major Cartwright, a lone voice crying in the wilderness, proclaimed the right to manhood suffrage. In other ways, too, men's mental attitudes were changing. New theories of education were in the air, Wesleyanism was helping to promote a greater religious and moral awareness in the lower social strata, in the upper the stirring of Evangelicalism can be discerned. For many people life was more prosperous, less gross and openly materialistic than when the House of Hanover had begun its rule. Though superficially the picture may seem the same the four countries that together made up Great Britain and Ireland had altered considerably as far as their domestic economy, their social nuances, and their mental attitudes were concerned. In all these changes it was England with her greater resources that led the way.

1. AGRICULTURE

In agriculture the story is one of progress but not of steady profit. Between 1730 and 1750, except for the years 1739–42, harvests were good. Grain supplies seem to have outrun demand and prices were low. This benefited the industrial worker and the rural labourer, the first because of the lower price of food, the second in addition because of the increased demand for labour caused by a heavy harvest. In 1732 it was reported that 'the labouring people lived well'. For farmers the position was less attractive: wage bills were high and profits low. The husbandman, with his tiny holding, particularly in areas where arable farming predominated, found his small surplus inadequate to meet his rent. In spite of a large export of grain, on which the statutory bounty was paid, there was much complaint among the farming community. Landlords found rents hard to collect; arrears became common. How far this depression acted as a spur to improvement, local variations in climate, in soil and in costs make it difficult to determine. It was easier for farmers working the light soils of southern England to meet falling prices by employing new methods to increase the yield per acre than for those living on the clay lands of the Midlands. Here the tendency was to enclose for pasture. But enclosure by act of Parliament, which was such a feature of the second half of the century, was as yet a mere trickle. Not until after the deplorable harvest of 1753, when grain prices began to show a sustained tendency to rise, were there more than ten enclosure acts in an average year. If the arable farmer was depressed by low prices the pasture farmer too had his troubles. Between 1734 and 1748 meat prices were very low, though to some extent these were offset by the high price of wool and tallow. In the drought of 1740 cattle died for want of grass; in 1745 they died from foot and mouth disease. It was not until 1757 that the worst was over. During these years the number of sheep sold at Smithfield seems to have risen but they too were subject to many hazards. When rainfall was excessive they developed foot-rot on undrained land; when it was deficient they starved for lack of grass.[1] As a result of these disasters the price of meat, too, was rising by 1754.

During these difficult years the landlord who wanted to keep his farms let to tenants who could afford to pay their rents had to do more and not less for them. On estates like those of the Cokes of Norfolk, even early in the century, tenants were given long leases and bound by farming covenants to farm along progressive lines; the improving landlord who sank capital in farm buildings and the large farmer who rented six, seven, eight or even nine hundred acres, were not peculiar to the second half of the century.[2] As a more detailed knowledge of estate management becomes available, belief in any dramatic 'agricultural revolution' becomes more and more difficult. To recognize the contributions made to improved farming by many landlords in the first half of the century is not,

---

[1] See T. S. Ashton, *Economic Fluctuation in the Eighteenth Century* (1959). Ch. I discusses the effect of weather on the national prosperity. Eighteenth-century writers often took as dismal a view of the English climate as their descendants; witness the following verse:

> All is extremes, no temperate medium found,
> The last year delug'd, and this burns the ground;
> Too much, or none, or sun, or rain is giv'n.
>
> *The Drought*, 1740

For a detailed survey of price variations and other factors affecting agricultural prosperity see A. H. John, 'Agricultural Change' in *Studies in the Industrial Revolution* (1960), ed. L. S. Pressnell.

[2] R. A. C. Parker, 'Coke of Norfolk and the Agrarian Revolution' (*Ec. Hist. Rev.*, 2nd ser., vol. VIII, no. 2, December 1955).

however, to deny the traditional picture of their activities in the second. Agriculture, like any other industry, was influenced throughout the century by the demand for its products and the supply of capital necessary for its needs. The marked growth in the population, which seems to have begun its slow avalanche in the 1750s, and the increased national resources which were coming from trade and industry inevitably swelled the demand both for food and for the raw industrial materials produced on the land. At the same time that demand was increasing available supplies were restricted by a series of indifferent harvests from the 'sixties onwards. Though high food prices were a disaster to the growing number of persons who depended on wages they were a boon to the landowners and to the farmers. The former could now demand higher rents while the farmers made higher profits. It became economically viable to bring land into cultivation which had previously been unremunerative because it was badly situated or of poor quality, or to increase the yield on good land by more intensive farming. As a consequence it became more profitable to finance enclosure bills, both for the open fields and to bring common land into individual ownership. Though the great spate of such bills came in the last decade of the century under the twin pressure of war and poor harvests the movement was well under way by 1784. To dwell too exclusively on the social craze for improved farming in the latter part of the century tends to obscure the fact that, like any other industry, agriculture had to consider its costs and was subject to fluctuations. Even the most aristocratic of farmers was not unaware of the profit motive. In June 1770 the Duke of Richmond wrote to Edmund Burke: 'Among all our Misfortunes we have one Comfort, and that is as fine a prospect of a Plentifull year as ever was known. . . . I wish you could come and see my Saint Foin improvements on a Hill before not worth half a Crown now worth a Pound an Acre!'[1] Yet if there were solid financial reasons why the great landowner was anxious to improve his land, there were also other, more psychological reasons why he busied himself with agricultural affairs. In the same letter Richmond also wrote 'The Farm is smiling, amidst the Frowns and gloomy aspects of Politicks. After all tis the best Trade to stick to. Tho' one can do less good, one is liable to do less mischief. The pleasures are less owing to Vanity, and it gives you Health which the other Hurts.' Such interests and enthusiasms were widespread;

[1] *The Correspondence of Edmund Burke*, vol. II, ed. L. S. Sutherland, pp. 142–3.

Burke himself was a keen farmer and wrote, with a zest one might not have expected from the author of *The Cause of the Present Discontents*, 'the Horse hoe, for all sorts of Garden Crops that you bring into the field, is a glorious thing'. This enthusiasm was not shared by all the farming community, nor did enclosures necessarily lead to the adoption of more intensive farming methods. While prices remained high the benefits of individual ownership were substantial enough to provide a reasonable livelihood even for old-fashioned farmers. This remained true until the postwar depression of the next century; it would be a mistake to assume that by the time Pitt became Prime Minister the majority of farmers were already switching over to the new techniques, as the perusal of Arthur Young's *Tours* will demonstrate. Nevertheless, though it was long adying it would probably be true to assert that the old agrarian pattern, both socially and technically, had received its mortal wound.

2. Heavy Industry

Industry too was moving into a new world of power-driven machinery and mass production though, as in agriculture, the process was piecemeal and haphazard. In spite of Walpole's conviction that the prosperity of the country was best served by peace, war, with its increased demands, had stimulated rather than retarded the adoption of new methods. In the earlier part of the century much of this activity had been concentrated on the mining and smelting of copper and the manufacture of brass. Copper was needed for coinage and for many domestic uses such as pots and pans and other consumer goods. By mid-century Birmingham was developing as a centre for the manufacture of buttons and buckles and similar articles. In 1762 the industrialist Mathew Boulton had moved to his famous Soho works near Birmingham, where by 1775, in conjunction with the inventor James Watt, he was beginning to manufacture the first effective steam engine. Meanwhile in the forties in Sheffield Benjamin Huntsman was discovering how to make cast steel by using coke instead of the traditional charcoal. Until the War of Jenkins's Ear stepped up demand, the advance of the iron industry was less spectacular, though it had been suggested that its stagnation, attributed to the lack of charcoal, has been over-emphasized.[1] Under

[1] M. W. Flinn, 'The growth of the English Iron Industry 1660-1760' (*Ec. Hist. Rev.*, 2nd ser., vol. XI, no. 1, August 1958), points out that it was not so much the scarcity of charcoal as high costs that slowed down its development.

wartime demand it grew rapidly. Stimulated by the expanding markets, the Darbys of Coalbrookdale[1] were seeking desperately for a more effective way of making pig-iron by smelting with coal. In 1748, the year of Aix-la-Chapelle, they were successful in so far as the iron that they made could be used by locksmiths, and chain makers and nailers. Freed from dependence on charcoal, the Darbys were able to produce iron of this quality more cheaply, and between the wars iron became increasingly the raw material of a wide range of secondary products. When large-scale war again broke out in 1756 the expanding industry was ready to meet the new emergency, and considerable capital seems to have been invested in new blast furnaces. In 1760 there were only seventeen of them in Britain, including the famous Carron works in Scotland, but the production of an economically viable steam engine capable of creating an effective blast guaranteed the triumph of the new techniques for making pig iron. Furnaces now began to concentrate round the coalfields, giving the industry a new geographical coherence. This was a half-way house in the mass production of iron. The alliance between iron and coal was only completed in 1783 when Henry Cort patented his famous puddling process which freed the manufacture of iron for the smith and the machine maker from its dependence on charcoal and ushered in the new 'Iron Age'.

War and trade were jointly responsible for a considerable expansion in shipbuilding. The Navigation Acts required all ships which qualified as British to be built in British or colonial shipyards. Certain important trades were confined to such ships, and even in nonprotected branches alien ships paid higher duties. These regulations meant that the great ships employed in the East India trade, the slavers for the African coast and the ships used in the trans-Atlantic trade were the products of English and colonial shipwrights. To New England the industry was of great importance for it was one of the means by which she was able to earn enough to pay for the imports which she needed from Britain; and this demand for imports stimulated British industry still further. In time of war the pressure on the shipbuilding yards became still greater, for many vessels were seized or destroyed by privateers or enemy frigates.[2] In the

---

[1] Arthur Raistrick, *Dynasty of Ironfounders* (1953), gives a very detailed account of the activities of this firm, based upon their business papers.

[2] R. S. Ashton, *Economic History, etc.*, gives the number of ships seized by the Spaniards between 1739–42 as 337. *The Annual Register* for 1760 (1789 edition), p. 111, gives the figure for that year as 32 in March, 47 in April, 80 in May.

early years of a war losses of this kind were always severe, though they were to some extent balanced by prizes taken from the enemy. In time of war, or of threatened war, a good deal of naval construction was undertaken. The independent members of the Commons were usually in favour of a naval rather than a continental war, and it was easier to get additional money for the navy than for the army. Between 1714 and 1763 the size of the navy doubled, though to read some of the contemporary speeches in the Commons one could imagine that no minister of the Crown was ever prepared to spend a penny on it. This demand for ships, whether merchantmen or men of war, created further demands for such articles as sails, ropes, anchors and chains, all of which stimulated industry, particularly along the Thames and in the vicinity of docks and shipbuilding yards. The impact of war on the textile industries is less clear. Those areas which concentrated on heavy woollen cloth suitable for army uniforms stood to benefit; and boom conditions in other industries released funds for personal consumption which may have stimulated demand at home. But as a great export industry depending on foreign markets the woollen and cotton manufactures probably responded best to peaceful trading conditions, though it must be remembered that without a powerful navy and an aggressive trading policy British merchants might have been able neither to obtain the necessary raw materials nor to secure the entry of British goods into valuable markets.

3. THE TEXTILE MANUFACTURERS

The first half of the eighteenth century is marked by the increasing importance of the cotton industry and the establishment of factories for the throwing of silk. To some extent the development of the former had been hampered in the home market after 1721 by the jealousy of the woollen manufacturers, and overseas it had to compete against the Indian materials exported by the East India Company. Though as early as 1701 the woollen interest had secured the prohibition of the wearing of Indian prints, until 1721 Indian cottons printed in England had been exempt. After that date no printed cottons except muslins, neckcloths, blue calicoes and fustians might be worn in England. Lancashire ingenuity found a loophole in the exemption granted to fustian: they claimed that the material made of a linen warp and a cotton weft came within this description and, when an act of Parliament of 1736 upheld this interpretation, printed fustians, almost rivalling the Indian printed materials, became one of Lancashire's leading commodities. There was of course no restraint placed upon the goods that were made for export, but here they came into competition with the goods of the East India Company. Had they been able to capture it there was a great market for gaily-woven and dyed cloths on the African coast, such commodities being much in demand by the native slave dealers. Unfortunately for Lancashire the Indian dyes were better and brighter and the Indian stuffs lighter. There was, however, a brief period in the middle of the century when it looked as if English checks might supplement those of India. But this was chiefly due to the confusion in India during the closing years of the War of the Austrian Succession and the years of nominal peace that followed. The Company had failed to export enough of the cottons beloved of the African buyers and between 1748 and 1763 the gap was filled by Lancashire goods. The advantage gained could not be retained, and in face of the renewed exports of the East India Company the attempts of the Lancashire men to build up a large and permanent market on the West African coast failed.[1] There was, however, a considerable market for fustian in Ireland, on the American mainland, and in the West Indies and in the last two for checks, though the field slaves wore the tougher German linens. In the early part of the century the export of Lancashire goods to Europe was slight; not until the seventies, when the new cotton velvets and allied fabrics provided popular lines, did this side of the trade become important. Even so, though it had not yet attained anything like the proportions which it was later to reach, by the middle of the century Lancashire was an active and progressive industrial area. In addition to the manufacture of fabrics made of cotton, and of cotton and linen, calico printing, both on native and on Indian materials, had reached a high standard. Tapes and small wears were being made on the Dutch looms, and though mechanical defects prevented them from making a profit, Wyatt and Paul had already experimented with mechanical spinning.

In the neighbouring county of Derbyshire, too, there was much activity. Sir Thomas Lombe's original silk-throwing mill at Derby, with its intricate machinery driven by water power and tended largely by women and children, was a true factory as the late eighteenth century would have interpreted the term. By the middle of the century there were similar establishments at Macclesfield, Stockport,

[1] For further details see A. P. Wadsworth and J. de Lacy Mann, *op. cit.*, p. 118.

and other towns. Silk weaving, which was still concentrated round Spitalfields, was less buoyant; smuggled French silks were its major competitor and the English industry knew prosperity only in those years when England and France were at war.

In technical improvement the spinning of cotton and wool lagged behind until the 'sixties. Until then both were dependent on the domestic spinner using the traditional wheel. Much time was lost collecting the yarn from a multitude of scattered homes and after the invention of Kay's flying shuttle, which increased the productivity of the weaver, and which was being increasingly used in the 1750s and '60s, the demand for yarn far exceeded the supply. Early experiments, including those of Lewis Paul, who had invented a successful carding machine in 1748, were failures, but, probably in 1764, Hargreaves produced his spinning jenny by which one spinner could operate eight spindles. When his invention was patented in 1770 the number had grown to sixteen and by 1784 to as many as eighty. The early jennies were hand-driven, they were easy to operate and not expensive to buy, and within ten years the whole process of spinning had been revolutionized. As in the iron industry the early breakthrough only applied to a section of the manufacture; the thread was not strong enough for the weft of the weaver's web. This deficiency was filled by Arkwright's water frame, patented in 1769; ten years later Crompton's mule improved the quality of the yarn still further. The result was a headlong expansion of the cotton industry; wool was not quite so satisfactorily adapted to the new methods in the early stages. Nor was it only a matter of increased productivity; the whole organization of the industry was undergoing a fundamental change. As the spinning jennies grew larger they could no longer be driven by hand, and Arkwright's water frame had always required power. This in the early period was supplied by water, which of necessity destroyed the domestic character of the industry. Everywhere old buildings, often corn mills, along the banks of northern streams, were adapted to house the new machinery. Spinners were becoming full-time workers; in textiles the factory age had begun, though the application of power to weaving remained experimental until the nineteenth century.

4. TRANSPORT

Industrial developments of the magnitude that marked the first half of the century were bound to have repercussions on the rest of the economy. The increased demand for coal led to the sinking of new pits. Areas which had hitherto been in something of an economic backwater, like South Wales, now began to attract capital and population. In the Midlands too, where the expense of transporting coal had made it uneconomic to develop new pits unless there was some considerable local demand, the same stimulation was at work. Just as the increased demand for yarn in the cotton industry encouraged men to struggle with the problem of mechanical spinning, so the new emphasis on mining, whether of copper in Cornwall or of the coal with which it was to be smelted, encouraged the evolution of devices to make deeper mining possible. It was to meet the perennial problem of flooding, which had ruined so many hopeful Elizabethan mining projects, that Savery and Newcomen had evolved their steam pumps. The manufacture of these in turn provided yet another outlet for the energies of the iron masters. The demand for cannon meant more coal, more coal meant more steam pumps, more rails for the coal waggons to run on, more pit props for merchants to import from Norway. In the same way the growth of the cotton industry meant more cotton to import from the Levant and the East, more flax from Ireland. All this activity, particularly in heavy commodities like coal and copper and iron, called for better transport. Here the interests of the farmers and the miners and the manufacturers all coincided. As population thickened near the coalfields, or round towns like Manchester and Birmingham which were coming to dominate and direct local economic activities, it provided new markets for meat, for grain, for dairy produce—markets too valuable to be neglected when agricultural prices were low. It is not surprising therefore that the early part of the eighteenth century is studded with schemes to improve roads and rivers.[1] In most cases the impetus was local. Landowners wanted a better outlet for their produce; mine-owners or iron manufacturers wanted improved facilities for handling heavy goods. Areas like the industrial districts of Lancashire wanted easy access to the ports through which they brought in their raw materials and re-shipped their finished products. Even a clothing town like Stroud was petitioning in 1730 for a bill to improve the navigation of the Stroud water. In such an atmosphere schemes for improving the navigation of adjacent rivers or for making turnpikes

[1] For fuller information about the latter consult T. S. Willan, *River Navigation in England 1600–1750* (1936), pp. 28–51.

became numerous. In the seven years of peace between 1749 and 1755, when heavy industry was still expanding rapidly under the impetus of the late war and the prospect of its early resumption, there were 153 such bills before Parliament. But, though much was done to improve rivers and roads, geography prevented the former, and lack of technical knowledge the latter, from being made adequate to meet the new demands.[1] Something more drastic was needed; in 1755 the making of independent cuts to improve the navigation of the Sankey Brook for easy transport between Liverpool and Manchester was half-way towards the construction of an artificial waterway.[2] Four years later the Duke of Bridgewater began his famous canal from Worsley to Manchester. The Canal Era had opened. The success of the scheme won immediate and numerous converts. Canals laboriously dug by armies of 'navvies' could never be constructed quickly, and it must be a matter for admiration that by 1772 it was possible to go by the new inland waterways from Bristol, that great port of the West, to Hull on the east coast. Five years later Liverpool and Manchester had been connected with the same system. Even Pitt, when he fought to protect and extend British trade, can hardly have guessed how rapid and how extensive would be the growth to which his victories had contributed.

The benefits which resulted from this great improvement in transport were not confined to trade and industry; there were also important social, and even political, repercussions. When George I had become king Britain was little more than nominally a political entity in that it was legislated for by Parliament and ruled, in theory, by the King and his ministers. But in no other way was the country one. Regionalism prevailed. England was full of provincial capitals; East Anglia looked to Norwich, Yorkshire to York, the South-west to Bristol and Exeter. Each provided the administrative, social and

---

[1] It has been calculated that the typical load carried or drawn was: a packhorse ⅛ of a ton, stage waggon on soft road ⅝, on macadam roads 2 tons, in barges on rivers 30 tons, on canals 50 tons. These figures illustrate the pressing need to improve transport. A. W. Sheraplon, 'The Engineers of the English River Navigations 1620–1760' (*Trans. Newcomen Soc.*, XXIX, 1953–5, p. 25).

[2] T. C. Barker, 'The beginning of the Canal Age in the British Isles' (*Studies in the Industrial Revolution*, 1960, ed. L. S. Pressnell), points out that Berry's pioneering achievements in constructing the Sankey Brook navigation have been considerably underrated by historians. See also A. W. Sheraplon, *art. cit.*, p. 34, 'Too often the work of his contemporaries is thought to have been without precedent in England. Actually the canal continued and developed traditions already established by the river navigations.'

economic centres. Counties were governed by local people in name of the King, which is one reason why at times the central government carried out purges, replacing doubtful Lord-Lieutenants and magistrates by men on whose loyalty they could rely. The Hanoverians could not leave the counties to the control of Stuart wellwishers, Walpole needed whigs in key positions because the power of the central government was very limited. With better transport not only goods but people and ideas could travel more freely. London newspapers with their news and advertisements could reach a wider reading public; fashions in clothes, furniture and even architecture could spread more rapidly. As roads improved and coach services multiplied and became faster it was easier for the middling sort to travel both for business and for pleasure. Slowly, very slowly, something like a national consciousness was beginning to emerge.

5. SOCIAL DEVELOPMENTS

Greater physical mobility and greater variety in economic activity must of necessity produce greater changes in the structure and balance of the society that experiences them, though such changes are less easy to pinpoint. Not every section of society is affected in the same way and at the same time; moreover, social habits and ways of thinking remain when the conditions that gave rise to them have already vanished. Power may be ebbing from one section and flowing towards another while tradition still gives the old pre-eminence to the first. This was happening to English society in the late eighteenth century. Though agriculture still remained the basis of the national wealth the interests of the landowner could no longer be protected to the exclusion of those of the merchant and the manufacturer. Greater wealth was flowing into the hands of both these classes and the fact that social pressure was still forcing much of it into the purchase of estates did not cancel out the fact that increasing opportunities of augmenting the national wealth were coming from industry and trade. Increased opportunities for money making and the increased sophistication of life meant an increase in the numbers of the 'middling sort' and the professional groups closely connected with the new sources of wealth. Contemporary memoirs give the impression of a new degree of sophistication and of solid comfort, as well as a new elegance in the domestic arrangements of such people. Both in London and in the provinces the well built and attractive houses in which they lived were multiplying. Local craftsmen were furnishing them from the designs of Chippendale and Hepplewhite. Circulating libraries were opening to cater for the increased leisure of their women folk. Between the gentry and the new type of the middle class, if one can begin to use that term, the gap was narrowing, particularly where the professions were concerned; between them and the craftsman and artisan it was widening.

This does not mean that the poor were getting poorer. Indeed the contrary seems to have been the case. Though income gaps were widening between different sections of the community all were benefiting to some extent by the increase in productivity and trade, and it seems likely that by 1784 the growth of the population had not yet placed the man with only his labour to sell at a serious disadvantage. Until the 'sixties, except for a few crisis years, harvests had been good and the price of food low, leaving the average worker with a little over to spend on consumer goods and able to afford something above the subsistence diet to which he was still driven in years of bad harvests; he was eating better bread and, to the horror of his betters, developing a liking for tea. With the increase in national productivity opportunities for the skilled worker were increasing both in the traditional crafts and in new ones. More middle class meant a greater demand for tailors, for shirtmakers, for cabinet makers, for printers of news sheets and books, and indeed for all the crafts that supplied their needs in the traditional ways. Better roads meant more work for coachmakers and for harness makers, more work for ostlers and coachmen; canals meant not only a demand for manual labour but also for the men who designed and built the long boats and made the locks. Moreover, opportunity was not confined to the traditional crafts. Men were needed to make and service the new machines, to supervise the operation of blast furnaces, to build the new spinning mills and to work in them. Nor were these opportunities confined to men. Women too were being drawn into the new industries in so far as they provided a large part of the work force in the new spinning mills. To modern readers the chance to work twelve hours a day tending a power-driven spinning jenny may not seem an improvement on the past, nevertheless it did mark the beginnings of a new independence from the family. For men and women alike a new type of worker who was neither a craftsman, nor a manual worker, nor a labourer on the land but a factory hand was adding a new element to what had once been the far less undifferentiated 'labouring poor'.

Among the older craftsmen, at least in London, the degree of literacy, fostered by the Charity School movement, had always been surprisingly high and, with the new openings in the industrial North and Midlands more men began to acquire some measure of education, though their numbers were a trickle compared with those of the self-educated, politically conscious trade unionists of the early nineteenth century. It is difficult today to imagine how low the standard of life of those below the status of the skilled worker was, how brutish, ignorant and violent the poor, especially the urban poor, were. Conditions in the country were bad but, though poverty was often extreme, it was less demoralizing: agriculture has its own disciplines for producing a minimum of responsibility; the land has to be tended, the beasts fed, the cows milked. But in town and country alike conditions made it difficult for the mass of the people to live by any strict moral code. Overcrowding made every kind of sexual laxity almost normal. Extreme poverty made thieving and bullying the only alternatives to starvation. Overcrowding, poverty, and ill-health together with monotonous food and over-long hours of work, often found compensation in drunkenness, in a love of brutal sports, and in a violence that broke out again and again when the pressure became too great. It was a hard, harsh world for the mass of English people, and one singularly devoid of pity. Disease, violence, early or sudden death were too common. Men were hanged for food rioting: children were hanged for petty thefts. The old proverb that one might as well be hanged for a sheep as a lamb was bitterly true.

Property-possessing England tried to protect itself by making the theft of property as serious as the taking of life; by repression—by prison, the pillory, the whip and the gallows—it tried to secure some measure of social discipline. The means at its disposal were inadequate for the task. The parish constable, the informer, even the Bow Street runners of Sir John Fielding, between them could provide only a very wide-meshed net in which to catch crime. A horrifying number of individuals were confined in unspeakable gaols, then hanged or transported in conditions that make the modern reader wince, but so many escaped that the deterrent of the penal system hardly acted. Gambling and drink were both eighteenth-century vices. The thief gambled on not being caught, drank to drown his fears, and killed to avoid capture. Yet many of these men, women and children were pitiable objects, the product of evil social conditions which had given them no chance. Discipline from without could do no more than contain the evil, and the eighteenth century seemed to lack those resources which could lead to the cure imposed by self-discipline.

6. THE IMPACT OF JOHN WESLEY

The man who, perhaps more than any other individual, sought the solution through inner discipline was John Wesley, and for him it was a by-product in the business of saving souls. Perhaps that is the explanation of his success. Eighteenth-century England had not been devoid of sober, earnest, religious men and women who had been deeply distressed by the misery and vice they knew existed around them. The Society for the Reformation of Manners, the tremendous enthusiasm put into the Charity School movement, are manifestations of their concern and their zeal. They had seen in religion the solution of the problem and, by checking vice and training the young to read, they had hoped to raise the labouring poor to the level of God-fearing citizens. They had taught their pupils to read the Bible and *The Whole Duty of Man*, they had clothed them and trained them in habits of industry. But love, either divine or human, had not been a vital ingredient in their programme. This is not to belittle the good work that was done. The education given to poor boys was the beginning of a career that raised them above the squalor of destitution and in a world of expanding economic opportunity enabled them to achieve a modest respectability. Nor was the Church always unmindful of its social obligations; there was many a good country clergyman who, like Parson Wood-forde, kept a friendly eye on his flock.[1]

But Wesley brought something quite different—a promise of individual salvation, an inclusive creed not, like the Calvinist, an exclusive one. The way of salvation was open to all not merely to the predestined and those who had the learning and education to understand the requirements of the Christian faith. The most ignorant, the most wretched of creatures had the spark of faith within them by which they could be justified. Men and women for whom society had no regard were told, 'God loves *you*, Christ has redeemed *you*.' Here was the offer of true equality, here was the appreciation

---

[1] See *The Diary of a Country Parson 1758–1802* (1924–31), ed. J. Beresford, for a vivid and detailed account of the life of a country parson. The original diary is in five volumes but a shortened version is available.

of personal value. It is difficult to-day to recreate the impact of that message on a generation of men and women to whom the rational approach of the eighteenth-century theologian could have made little appeal, even if they had been able to understand it. Religion to too many people in the eighteenth century had come to be a sort of social cement. Wesley was concerned with the individual soul. What he had to say was what many of the poor and oppressed must, however unconsciously, have longed to hear.

The steps by which John Wesley became the apostle of the poor were something which he could hardly have foreseen when, returning to Oxford in 1729 to comply with the terms of his Fellowship at Lincoln College, he became closely associated with the small group of undergraduates, of which his brother Charles was already one, nicknamed by their scoffing contemporaries the Holy Club. They were in no sense social reformers but rather men who were seeking spiritual peace. The call to social service came out of their religious convictions. To visit the captive was a Christian duty and, almost accidentally, in August 1730 Charles and John began visiting prisoners in the Oxford gaol. At first the brothers thought their call lay in missionary work and on 14 October 1735 they left for Georgia 'to save souls', as John wrote. The next three years were a chequered, frustrating interlude, and by 1738 they were back in London. On the return voyage John Wesley had come under the influence of a group of Moravians and on 14 May he had gone rather unwillingly to a meeting of theirs in Aldersgate Street. For some time he had been torturingly aware of an inadequacy within himself, but on that night the conviction of forgiveness and salvation rushed over him. From this point he burned with an overmastering longing to bring to all men the happiness he had found. He wanted to rekindle the flame in the Anglican Church, not to leave it or alter it, and to the end of his life he clung to the creed in which he had been ordained. But the congregations of the London churches in which he preached had no desire to be saved by Wesley's methods. They found his appeal emotional, his theology with all that it implied, distasteful. Again and again the Journal records that he was told, 'Sir, you must preach here no more.'[1]

The next step was taken when he turned to the people outside

---

[1] *The Journal of the Rev. John Wesley, M.A.* (Everyman edn. 1906) 28th May, 1738: 'I was roughly attacked in a large company as an enthusiast, a seducer, and a setter forth of new doctrines.'

the regular congregations. Here again the step was taken with reluctance: the innovation of open-air preaching was not his. In March 1739 he received an invitation from George Whitefield, an invitation which he hesitated to accept without the judgment of the lot,[1] to go to preach in Bristol. In his Journal he confessed 'I could scarcely reconcile myself to this strange way of preaching in the field',[2] but two days later, on 2 April, he recorded 'I submitted to be more vile and proclaimed in the highways the glad tidings of salvation, speaking from a little eminence in a ground adjoining to the city, to about three thousand people.' His career as an open-air preacher had begun. It gave him a mobility which he could have attained in no other way, it gave him congregations too large to have been crammed into any parish church, and it won for him the attention of the labouring poor who could gather in an open space to hear the word of God but who would hardly have dared to take their dirt and their rags into a church. Increasingly it gave the growing disapproval of the Established Church no means of muzzling Wesley. When churches shut their doors to him he preached to still larger congregations outside. His activity was prodigious, his journeys averaging well over 4,000 miles each year. What this meant in hardship and endurance his Journals reveal. Wherever he was needed there he went, ignoring atrocious roads and foul weather. At Placey, a little village near Newcastle 'inhabited by colliers only, and such as had always been in the first rank for savage ignorance and wickedness of every kind', it was the custom on Sundays to meet 'to dance, fight, curse and swear, and play at chuck ball, span-farthing, or whatever came to hand';[3] he therefore set out one April day in 1743 though 'The North wind, being un- usually high, drove the sleet in our faces, which froze as it fell, and cased us over presently. When we came to Placey we could very hardly stand.' As soon as they were a little recovered he went into the market square and preached. A crowd soon gathered and both then and again in the afternoon in spite of the wind and the snow gave 'earnest heed' while Wesley called on them to 'repent and believe the gospel'. Such episodes were repeated again and again.

If the labouring poor responded to his teaching the reaction of the Established Church and of respectable society against it was almost

---

[1] John Wesley believed that the divine will could be discovered by opening the Bible at random and seeing on what passage his eye alighted.

[2] *Journals*, March 1739, p. 184.   [3] *Ibid.*, April 1743, p. 240.

as pronounced. The fear and dislike he aroused was both social and theological. Distrust of large gatherings of the labouring poor was deep seated, the assumption being that nothing but riots, disorders and disaffection were likely to come from them. The facts that Wesley's crowds were well behaved, that his own allegiance to the Crown was intense, and that he would have struggled with all his strength against an attack on the social structure of his day, were unable to combat these suspicions. That large crowds could be up to no good and that the men who controlled them did so for sinister motives were accepted axioms. It is interesting to notice that Wesley was accused of being an agent to the Pretender; on 20 March 1744 he was asked to take an oath of allegiance and against Popery, and until the danger of the rising was over the charge in one form or another appears repeatedly.[1] Social mistrust was reinforced by theological dislike. Neither to the Deism of the educated nor to the Calvinism of the Dissenter could his appeal to justification by faith be anything but abhorrent. They disliked the oratory of his preaching with its twin emphases on the torments of hell and the comfort of salvation, they disliked its popular appeal and they disliked the substance of what he had to say. Again and again the very gentry who feared the mob organized mobs against him and magistrates failed to interfere to quell riots against the Methodists. In 1744 the area round Walsall, Wednesbury and Darlaston was the scene of very bad riots. There, in February, to quote from the Journal, 'The mob . . . assaulted, one after another, all the houses of those who were called Methodists. They first broke all their windows, suffering neither glass, lead, nor frames to remain therein. Then they made their way in; and all the tables, chairs, chests of drawers, with whatever was not easily removable, they dashed in pieces. What they could not break, as feather beds they cut in pieces and strewed about the room. William Sitch's wife was lying in; but it was all one; they pulled away her bed too and cut it in pieces.'[2] Many people were beaten and assaulted as well as robbed of most of their possessions. Just as later the mob was used against the Papists in the Gordon riots, and against Priestley in the Birmingham riots, so now it was used to break up Wesley's meetings and intimidate his followers. The object of the persecution mattered little to the brutal, ignorant elements that made up its numbers: it was enough that for once authority was willing to give licence to destroy and

---

[1] *Ibid.*, March 1744, p. 460.   [2] *Ibid.*, February 1744, pp. 454–5.

to loot. Yet against Wesley himself even such mobs were singularly ineffective. Again and again by his personality he quelled violence and outfaced danger, so that those who came to destroy often stayed to listen and, even if they refused to accept his offer of salvation, they let him go in peace. It is a remarkable story and one which no student of eighteenth-century England can ignore.

Its effect on the society of the day has been much debated.[1] Fervent admirers of Wesley have claimed that the moral regeneration of the lower orders started with his work, that it was he who strengthened the loyalty of the masses, making them more impervious to the lure of the French Revolution, and set them on the road to being useful, industrious citizens instead of being ignorant, brutal and drunken. Against this view his detractors have emphasized the almost hysterical nature of his influence, the weeping and shrieking and physical agony experienced both publicly and privately by those who were most moved by his preaching. They have stressed his acceptance of the superstitions of his age, his belief in witches and apparitions, all the non-rational elements in his character. They have stressed, too, his autocratic control over the organization he built up and have given publicity to his sobriquet 'Pope John'. In face of extravagant claims and bitter denunciations it is worth while to attempt to summarize some of the things which stemmed from the Methodist movement in so far as they are likely to have influenced the mass of the people. In the first case it seems fair to say that to many of those working in remote places—colliers and quarrymen—and to those huddled in the growing iron or cotton towns, he brought a knowledge of religion which otherwise would not have come their way. If he had not ridden out to them through wind and hail the colliers of Placey would not have been called upon to repent. That religion was the concern of everybody, not merely of the socially respectable, was perhaps his most important contribution to the making of a more civilized working class.

His contribution did not, however, stop there. A man who accepted salvation accepted responsibilities with it. Above all he accepted discipline—the discipline of a regular life with its obligation to routine religious expression and self-criticism, the discipline of hard work so that he might acquire a competency to lift himself and his dependents above destitution and still leave something over

[1] R. F. Wearmouth, *Methodism and the Common People of the Eighteenth Century* (1945), ch. 2, pp. 217-38.

for charity towards those in greater need. The Methodist was to forsake worldly pleasures, not only the grosser ones of drinking and gluttony, but even indulgence in frivolous conversation. Methodists were to be serious people, wasting time as little as they wasted money, always instant in prayer. Even the poorest were expected to make some contribution to the expenses of the society and the needs of the destitute. In 1740 the Bristol society decided to levy a penny a week on its members to clear the debt on their modest meeting house in the Horsefair. London followed their example and the penny a week contribution became the foundation of the Methodist societies. Constantly, too, collections were made for special emergencies or for those in some special need. Methodists were also encouraged to undertake works of charity as a group. Members were appointed to visit the sick, and in London Wesley set up a dispensary for the poor. Later in the century, towns like Bristol and Leeds organized the Strangers' Friend Societies, to help those who were friendless and away from home.

All this called for organization and, since most Methodists were humble people, it gave men, and women too, opportunities for managing their own societies which was bound to breed a new initiative and self-respect. Groups of twelve were organized into a class, with a leader who was responsible for collecting their pennies at the weekly meeting and supervising their religious welfare. Each local society had its own officers. Its great work of preaching had to be entrusted to laymen for lack, in its early days, of ordained ministers. The full-time preachers were, like Wesley himself, itinerant, covering large areas and supervising and stimulating the life of the local societies. Others were local preachers, men who worked at their trade all the week and took services on the Lord's Day. Most of these men had little in the way of formal education; they were preaching to congregations whose experience of life was their own; no social gulf divided them from their flock. All these class leaders, these trustees, these preachers had to be provided by the working class; and by their need to organize their Society they gained the experience which later was to help them to run trade clubs and even political societies. Many of the nineteenth-century groups that studied Tom Paine copied the class organization of the Methodists with their penny subscription and their class leader.

Too much, however, must not be claimed for the Methodist movement. More people listened to Wesley than were converted by him, and the numbers who became members of the Society, sharing in its responsibilities and developing within its opportunities, were limited. It has been calculated that during its first thirty years the Society increased by something rather less than a thousand a year: during its second thirty it seems to have increased by two thousand a year. By the end of the century the Methodists numbered over a hundred thousand in a population of nearly nine million. Such figures can, however, be misleading. It was in the industrial areas of Yorkshire, Derbyshire, Staffordshire and Durham, as well as in Cornwall, that the membership was strongest. Here the metaphor of the leaven in the lump may well be applied. Though the Methodists were few in number their example and influence over fellow workers must have been considerable. By their lives they were setting a new standard of working-class behaviour and to the extent that the Methodists were sober, God-fearing, honest and industrious, indulging in no excesses, not dealing, even in Cornwall, in smuggled goods, provident in money matters, they contributed to the social amelioration of the labouring poor. To some extent, too, the work of John and Charles Wesley in arousing a social conscience must be recognized. Because they were concerned with the saving of sinners they visited gaols—braving the fevers of Newgate and accompanying their converts to the gallows' foot— and they exposed the evils of those hells before the days of John Howard. Pity for the friendless and destitute, fellowship for the criminal, were concepts which the Wesleys made part of their living Christianity. This emphasis on active benevolence must be weighed against the charge that the Wesleyans were often narrow and ignorant in their outlook and that Wesley's appeal to the poor of his age was the appeal to a neurotic streak in a people who, because life was violent and death an ever-present threat, found a relief from tension in the constant juxtaposition of hell fire and salvation. To some extent this may explain the strength of Wesley's appeal to the uneducated but, if stress is to be put on the violence of dramatic conversion and the intensity of religious experience and outpourings in class, stress must also be placed on the self-discipline, industry and sobriety that the Methodists demanded of their members. It is reasonable to assume that, both for the country and for the individual, the good which Wesley achieved more than balanced any harm that he may have caused.

19

PEACE OVERSEAS AND CONFLICT AT HOME

1. FALL OF LORD NORTH'S MINISTRY

THE years that lay between the spring of 1780 and that of 1784 comprise a period of great interest, partly because of the swift flow of events and partly because of the political and constitutional implications which these revealed. Within this short space of time Yorktown fell; North resigned; Rockingham, after his brief hour of triumph, died; American independence was granted; the arch enemies Fox and North formed a parliamentary coalition; and the young Pitt fought his way to political power. This rapid sequence of events tended to act as a forcing-house for future political and constitutional developments. The elections of 1780 and 1784 were far more influenced by political considerations than had earlier been the case. The opposing points of view of the King and the opposition over the American question were strong enough to divide the Commons into what, at a superficial level, almost looked like two parties. Finally the coalition of Fox and North was able for a short time to force George III to lose the minister whom he preferred and accept a whole administration which he definitely disliked. For these few years then it is possible to see something of the pattern of the future: they contain the brief and tentative success of everything that the disorganized opposition whigs had been struggling to achieve since 1763. Then in 1784 the success of the King and the Treasury in the elections restored everything to its eighteenth-century norm. Once again the old formula was found to work, and a minister, in the person of the younger Pitt, who had the confidence of both King and Commons, entered upon a long period of almost unchallenged power. For years yet, George III was 'to do for his country what it had not yet the means of doing so well for itself'.[1]

The opening scenes in the drama of these years were concerned with the decision to dissolve the existing Parliament in the autumn of 1780. Though by the summer the pressure against the ministers had eased and the worst of the crisis appeared to be over, the behaviour of the independent members of the Commons during the past few months had been disquieting. If the King's business was to be carried on smoothly it was clear that the authority of his chosen ministers over the House would have to be strengthened. By the end of March Robinson was already discussing with his crony Jenkinson the desirability of holding a general election in the autumn.[2] This would give an opportunity for fresh bargains, fresh negotiations and, it was hoped, a strengthening of the ministerial majority in the House. The apparent revolt of the independent members in support of Dunning's resolution in April made George III concur in this opinion. North, as usual, was more hesitant. The decision to dissolve, though certainly not unconstitutional, would be unpopular as a breach of the normal practice of allowing Parliaments to run for their full seven years. By the end of June, however, fortified by the more favourable-seeming situation, North too came over to this view. In addition he seems to have hoped that the ministry could be strengthened by a coalition with the Rockinghams, which would have made the problem of securing a favourable House much easier. Of the various opposition groups, the Marquis certainly represented the most moderate and, as opposed to Lord Shelburne, he had placed all his influence and authority at the disposal of the government in the suppression of the Gordon Riots. To attempt to strengthen the ministry in this way on the eve of an election was the normal eighteenth-century practice. An election was not an attempt to sound public opinion or to substitute one set of ministers for another; it was an opportunity, by bargains and negotiations with a limited number of men who had borough influence, to secure a solid core of ministerial supporters in the Commons. For this purpose the alliance with the Rockinghams would have been invaluable.

This North failed to secure. Rockingham's terms made it clear

[1] R. Pares, *King George III and the Politicians*, p. 207.
[2] I. R. Christie, *The End of North's Ministry, 1780-82* (1958), deals with this crucial period in great detail and should be consulted.

that genuine differences on matters of public policy divided him and his friends from the Court. Only if George III were prepared to recognize the possibility of having to concede independence to the American colonies, and to accept a programme of 'Economical Reform', would Rockingham consent to join the administration. Nevertheless Robinson, who as Secretary to the Treasury must be regarded as the King's most trusted and well-informed election manager, seems to have calculated, over-optimistically, that in the new House the government would have a considerably increased majority. As success was thought to depend on leaving the opposition groups as little time as possible to organize their resources, the determination to dissolve remained a closely guarded secret. While Robinson was endlessly engaged in tabulating political information as to the probable composition of the new House, ministers ostentatiously retired to their country houses for the summer recess. When the news finally leaked out on 30 August that Parliament was to be dissolved on 1 September there was dismay and confusion among the opposition leaders.[1] Nevertheless the result of the election was disappointing for the Court. By 1780, much as the country gentlemen disliked the idea of admitting defeat and conceding American independence, they were growing heartily tired of wartime taxation, possible government corruption and apparent government mismanagement. This was reflected in an increase in the number of county members unfriendly to the administration. In the previous Parliament twenty-six had figured as friendly in Robinson's lists; in the new one only fifteen were so counted. Clashing views over America and economic reform may also have increased the number of constituencies which actually went to the polls. In the Parliament of 1761 these had been forty-nine for Great Britain and forty-two for England; in the general election of 1780 the figures were eighty-six and sixty-eight.

Though from the point of view of the Court the election results had been unsatisfactory, there was no reason for ministers to be unduly anxious when the new Parliament met on 31 October 1780. Indeed, Rockingham and his friends seem to have had little hope of converting a majority of the Commons to their way of thinking about the war, and to have felt that the most effective way to embarrass the government would be to concentrate on the need for economic reform. Even this they were not strong enough to do until

[1] *Ibid.*, p. 44.

after the Christmas recess; too many of their potential allies, the country gentlemen, were extremely irregular in their attendance until the more serious and interesting business came up for discussion in the spring. North therefore, despite his habitual fears, had little difficulty in securing a majority of 212 to 130 for the Address which pledged the government to prosecute the war with vigour. When Parliament reassembled on 23 January the most difficult matter to be handled was the projected declaration of war against Holland. Here the ministers had considerable justification for taking so drastic a step, but it was justification which for diplomatic reasons it was impossible that they should plead. This apparently rash extension of our enemies did therefore give the opposition an opening for attack.

Though by good luck rather than effective leadership England had survived the naval and military crisis of 1779 her position was still precarious. America absorbed most of her military strength and for supplying her troops there it was essential that she should keep naval control of American waters. At the same time she had to defend her own shores against attack. For this dual purpose she had insufficient ships, which made it essential that she should prevent naval stores from reaching the shipyards of her enemies. Here Dutch and English interests clashed. The former argued that the Anglo-Dutch treaty of 1674 had left them free to carry most types of naval stores to countries at war with England. On the other hand British ministers maintained that by the treaties of 1678 and 1716 the Dutch were pledged to give her military and naval aid if she were attacked by another power. The British contention was quite unrealistic, for if Holland had attacked France and Britain had been forced to go to her assistance, British difficulties would only have been increased; but it made a good arguing point. By 1779 the impasse was such that the Dutch were convoying their merchantmen and Britain was insisting on her right of search. The delicacy of the situation in putting the British case before Parliament lay in the attitude of Russia. Early in 1780 Catherine II had committed herself to the view that a neutral flag covered the goods its ships carried unless they had definitely been recognized as contraband of war by a treaty between the carrying and the searching power. In pursuance of this interpretation of the rules governing the right of search Russia was prepared to head and sponsor a League of Armed Neutrality. For Britain any such interpretation was blunting of one of her main weapons against France, and as such was quite unacceptable. If, however, she interfered with Dutch shipping and Holland formally joined the League of Armed Neutrality, then there was the risk that England might find herself at war with the whole League. The problem which faced the ministers was to find a quick and reasonably adequate cause for declaring war on Holland before she had joined the League. If this could be done she became an enemy, whose shipping we had the right to attack witnout any reference to the problem of neutral flags making neutral goods. Luckily for the ministers, papers which showed that negotiations were taking place between the Netherlands and the American rebels fell into their hands, thus making an ostensible cause of war. Nevertheless, because of the need for haste, the official case was thin and full of gaps which could not be explained. In announcing to the reassembled Parliament on 25 January that a state of war existed between Britain and the United Provinces ministers were plainly vulnerable to opposition criticisms.

Though opposition speakers including Burke were able to ask pertinent and potentially embarrassing questions, North seems to have had little difficulty in persuading the House that the war was 'just and necessary', for his majority on the crucial division was 180 to 101. Nor was the opposition much more successful when, after the attendance of the country gentlemen had been secured by a call of the House, it once again raised the question of economic reform. It is true that, uncertain of his strength and possibly depressed by Robinson's calculations which this time turned out to have been over pessimistic, North allowed the first reading of Burke's bill to go through on 15 February, but on its second reading on the 26th he secured its rejection by 233 to 190 votes. After that it was clear that the administration was in no danger, though the opposition did stage further routine attacks on the terms on which North had raised a loan for the provision of supply and on the lavish expenditure of public money. Even the news which arrived in June of the failure of Cornwallis to maintain control in North Carolina, in spite of his barren victory at Guildford Court House, failed to make any real impact on the administration's majority, though it gave Fox ammunition for a telling attack. By now, many of the independent members had left a stinking London for the delights of the countryside, and Fox could only collect 99 votes against the 172 who supported the government. Therefore, though the American war was plainly going less well than the news of the previous year had promised, there was as yet little sign of a major revolt against the King's policy of its vigorous prosecution. Ireland too seemed quiet, and equally to George III, to Lord North and to Rockingham the autumn session, which had been fixed for 27 November, promised to be uneventful.

Two days before this date the arrival of the news of the surrender of Cornwallis at Yorktown completely transformed the situation. Even so it took a little time for its full impact on the political scene to become apparent. Both the opposition and the ministers had to readjust themselves to the changed circumstances. On 12 December there was a lively debate in the course of which North, in a speech of studied vagueness, attempted with some success to produce a formula which would cover almost any future policy. From what he said it was clear that there would be no immediate pulling out, but equally clear that large-scale expeditions designed to reconquer the interior of America would now be abandoned. With this members had to be content when the House dispersed for the Christmas recess on 20 December. North's position was extremely difficult. It is probable that by the end of the year he had come to the personal opinion that peace would have to be made with America on the basis of conceding independence; to this George III was as obstinately opposed as ever.[1] Opinion within the Cabinet was clearly divided; Lord George Germain shared the royal diehard attitude but, with varying degrees of conviction, most of the ministers seem to have sided with North. To agree that peace must be made was, however, to touch only the fringe of the problem. Even if Britain offered immediate and unconditional independence would the American Congress be prepared to desert her allies? If, on the other hand, holding forces were left in America while the main effort was exerted against France and Spain, would a victory over the Bourbon powers force America to accept more moderate terms? Or, if the struggle against the European coalition proved unsuccessful, could England use American bases to bargain for more favourable terms from her Bourbon enemies? Before Parliament reassembled in January both the ministerial and the opposition groups had to come to some conclusions on these points,

[1] See J. Brooke, *George III* (p. 220): 'It was not pride that made King George reluctant to recognise American independence but concern for the commerce and prosperity of Great Britain.'

and had then to persuade the independent members that their own solution was the wiser.

Moreover, North's position was further complicated by the political conventions of his age. He was in a very real sense the King's minister and, though he could resign rather than carry out a policy of which he disapproved, he knew, and George III knew, that to do so meant handing over the direction of affairs to Rockingham or Shelburne or Fox. Both on personal grounds of loyalty to the King and because he distrusted the ability of these men to secure a satisfactory peace, delaying tactics, until the pressure of events forced the King to modify his obstinacy, might well appear the wiser course. Meanwhile North had something of a ministerial revolt on his hands. In an administration of nonentities Dundas,[1] the Lord Advocate—a man of considerable weight and power and one who had little liking for lost causes or for going down with the ship if the judicious sacrifice of an unpopular colleague or policy would avoid shipwreck—had come to be an essential member. In his eyes the safety of the ministry demanded the dismissal or resignation of both Germain and Sandwich—the former because, while he remained responsible for the American colonies, no one would believe that any real change in policy was possible, the latter because of the ill-luck which had dogged the navy, thus making Sandwich a useful scapegoat for the mistakes of the administration. With these views Rigby concurred. When Parliament reassembled it was clear to North that he must either let Germain go or lose both Dundas and Rigby. The second course he dared not take, partly for fear of losing their parliamentary following and partly because of their skill in debate. On 31 January, therefore, Germain was replaced by Welbore Ellis whose main qualification for office was his willingness to assume it.

When Parliament met, Dundas's wisdom in wishing to get rid of Sandwich also was soon demonstrated. On 24 January Fox moved for an inquiry into naval administration. In so doing he had chosen his ground cleverly. In the previous session much had been made by opposition speakers of Sandwich's failure to build up naval strength; Sandwich now expected to have to meet the same sort of attack. He was indeed anxious to do so for he had a not unjustified

---

[1] Cyril Matheson, *Life of Henry Dundas, 1st Viscount Melville* (1933).

belief that his record could be defended.[1] Perhaps Fox was of the same private opinion, for he deliberately concentrated on the management of the naval war. Here again the fault lay not so much with the Admiralty as with the Cabinet as a whole. A large proportion of the navy had been used for convoy and transport duties, leaving insufficient ships for the blockading of enemy ports and for preying on their commerce. In addition the higher naval command was bedevilled by politics, so that capable officers either refused to serve or did so only with reluctance and distrust. The outcome was a long tale of naval frustrations. With such material Fox was able to make a telling, if unfair, attack, and in spite of very careful preparation and the briefing of supporters beforehand, the government was only able to defeat the motion by 205 votes to 183. It was not an auspicious beginning to the session. What from the point of view of the administration was particularly alarming was that members normally regarded as friendly were either abstaining from voting or were even supporting opposition motions.

Encouraged by their success, the opposition now turned from men to measures, switching their attack from Sandwich to the general management of the American war, with special emphasis on the steps to be taken for its termination. In pressing home this attack Conway, whose long record of pro-American memories made him a suitable person, took the lead. On 22 February a motion that an address be presented to the King against continuing the war for 'the impracticable purpose of reducing the inhabitants of that country to obedience by force' was only lost by one vote. On 27 February an almost identical motion was carried by nineteen. It was now clear that either the ministry would have to be strengthened or North would have to go. In consequence a flurry of negotiations took place, with the hope of dividing the opposition by taking in some of its less extreme members. Despite the efforts of Thurlow these were unsuccessful, and North became convinced that if he could avoid resigning until George III had found someone to replace him it was as much as he could do. Even the King was coming to realize that it was vain to try to ignore Rockingham as the prospective First Lord of the Treasury. He, with the entire

[1] George III wrote of his 'unremitting ardour to effect whatever you undertake'.— *Sandwich Papers*, p. 102. Sandwich was continually pressing on North the need to strengthen the fleet, a step he was reluctant to take because of the expense involved.— *Ibid.*, pp. 216, 334, 351, etc.

opposition behind him, made it clear that he would only accept office if he were given a free hand with regard to American independence, were permitted to implement Burke's programme for economic reform, and if his colleagues were men in whom he had confidence.[1] Only a complete realization that the country's business could now be carried on by no one else could have driven the King to accept such terms. Against them he fought to the last, even contemplating abdication. Finally the declared determination of a group of country gentlemen to withdraw their support convinced even his obstinate mind. On 20 March he gave a reluctant consent to North's resignation. In a crowded House, tense and prepared for the final kill, North just managed to announce it before the motion for his removal could be put by Lord Surrey.

2. THE SECOND ROCKINGHAM ADMINISTRATION

The prospect before the new administration was a forbidding one. It was clear that it could expect nothing but the coldest, most official support from the King. Nor were the members united among themselves. Only the chairmanship of Rockingham kept the peace between Fox and Shelburne. Temperamentally the two men jarred on each other. Though each could be regarded as 'forward looking' in his political creeds, Fox, influenced by his association with the Westminster Committee, seemed to look beyond 'the people' as the eighteenth century understood the term, to the mob. Shelburne's views were less flamboyantly expressed, and because he had some of his old leader's deference for the person of the monarch, George III found him less offensive. In the months that followed he could therefore depend on a greater measure of royal support. Finally, though he had not been able to save many of his old ministers, Thurlow remained Chancellor, to the disappointment of Dunning, who had to be content with the Chancellorship of the Duchy of Lancaster and the title of Lord Ashburton. This gave George III one loyal servant to act as his ears and his mouthpiece in the Cabinet.[2]

The Secretaryships, which went to the two rivals, were for the first time divided according to function not geography. Fox became

---

[1] Feeling that at last Rockingham held all the cards Richmond wrote to him: 'For God's sake, your own and the country's sake, keep back and be very coy . . you must soon see all at your feet in the manner you would wish, and with the full means to do what is right.'—*Rockingham Memoirs*, vol. II, p. 446.

[2] On 27 March 1782 George III wrote to North: 'At last the fatal day is come, when

Foreign Secretary, Shelburne Secretary for Home Affairs. The rearrangement was logical but the division of business on this occasion unfortunate for the smooth handling of the imminent peace negotiations; neither man was in full control of them because colonial affairs fell within Shelburne's department. The other major appointments of the ministry formed to liquidate the war were Camden (President of the Council), Grafton (Lord Privy Seal), Richmond (Master of the Ordnance), Lord John Cavendish (Chancellor of the Exchequer), Keppel (First Lord of the Admiralty), Conway (Commander-in-Chief); Burke became Paymaster. This appointment is sometimes attributed to aristocratic prejudice against giving high office to a man of little social standing, but it may well have been due to his own temperamental unsuitability. The fire-eating Colonel Barré became Treasurer of the Navy. These appointments illustrate the cleavage within the Cabinet. Shelburne could look for the support of Grafton, Camden and Ashburton, Fox that of Rockingham himself, Richmond, Keppel and Lord John Cavendish.

To a Cabinet so divided fell the task of prosecuting the war with sufficient vigour to secure a peace which should at least fall short of the disastrous. It was not an easy one. Though public opinion is inclined to forget the fact, and to expect miracles, a change of men can have little immediate effect on the fortunes of war. As in agriculture, changes of policy take time to mature. The previous crop has to be reaped, new seed bought, and new crops not only planned but planted and given time to mature, before it can be known whether the new men are indeed wiser and more farsighted than those whom they have replaced. When some miracle of success comes soon, as with Rodney's victory at the battle of the Saints,[1] good luck rather than good management is the deciding factor. There is little to indicate that Keppel was a more efficient head of the Admiralty than Sandwich had been, though it is true that his position was made easier because he was personally popular with the navy and could

the misfortunes of the times and the sudden change of sentiments of the House of Commons have drove me to, of changing the Ministry, and a more general removal of other persons than, I believe, was ever known before. I have fought to the last for Individuals, but the number I have saved, except My Bedchamber, is incredibly few.'— *Sir John Fortescue, op. cit.*, vol. V, p. 421.

[1] This was fought on 12 April 1782. The Saints were some small islands between Dominica and Guadaloupe. The victory saved Jamaica from the threat of invasion and left the smaller islands held by the enemy at the mercy of the British navy.

depend on the loyal co-operation of his officers. The position when he took over was alarming. The declaration of war on Holland in 1780 had put still more strain on English sea-power, though the immediate consequences had been encouraging. In India the Dutch factories of Trincomalee and Negapatam had been taken, and in the West Indies St Eustatius, the island of Demerara and Essequibo. But this handful of successes proved to be of short-term value only. After the shattering capitulation at Yorktown, which was due to the paucity of England's naval resources in American waters, the Dutch islands were rapidly reconquered. In addition the British lost St Kitts, Nevis and Montserrat. In European waters things had gone equally badly. Though Gibraltar was still holding out, Port Mahon in Minorca had been forced to surrender in February 1781. With so little on the credit side beyond the obstinacy of Gibraltar, which might yet fall, and the previously mentioned victory of Rodney, which had re-established British naval power in West Indian waters, Fox and Shelburne were likely to find themselves in a weak bargaining position when faced with the responsibility of conducting negotiations for peace.

Fresh trouble was also threatening from Ireland, where the calm produced by North's concessions had proved to be of short duration. Irishmen were very conscious that what England had given under duress she could take away when the pressure on her lessened. The only effective barrier against a reactionary policy seemed to them to be to secure an immediate statutory recognition of the legislative independence of the Irish Parliament. This was the line adopted by Grattan who, though he had only been a member of the Irish Commons for four years, had taken over the leadership of the reformers after Flood, their previous chief, had accepted a government office. On 19 April 1780 he introduced a motion which, though impeccably loyal in its language, affirmed that the royal authority in Ireland could be exercised only in conjunction with the Irish Parliament. This would involve the repealing of Poyning's Law and the repudiation of those legal rights and political con- conventions which gave English ministers formal machinery for controlling the Irish Parliament. So great was the obvious sympathy of the Irish Commons, even of those members who were commonly supporters of Government House, that it was thought safer to move the adjournment of the debate rather than to risk a defeat on the motion itself. North and his colleagues were much disconcerted and ready to blame Buckinghamshire for having lost control of the situation. The next move of the reformers was to press for an Irish Mutiny Bill. This was a clever, backdoor manœuvre to force some recognition of Irish legislative independence from the English administration. In time of war a Mutiny Act, on which army discipline depended, was an absolute necessity. Otherwise there could be no control over desertion, which was common. When, therefore, the Irish courts refused to recognize the English Mutiny Act as binding in Ireland, the English Cabinet was forced to choose between having no legal control over the army in Ireland and allowing the Irish Parliament to pass its own Mutiny Act.

Faced with this dilemma it was decided to allow the Irish to pass a Mutiny Act but to stipulate that, unlike its English counterpart, which was an annual measure, it should be passed in perpetuity. Buckinghamshire failed to secure this; the Act when passed was valid only for two years, though with a proviso for its regular re-enactment. In view of the Lord Lieutenant's warnings as to the inflammable state of Irish feeling, reinforced by the knowledge that there were 40,000 Irish volunteers under arms, North and his colleagues hesitated for some time before returning the bill to Dublin with the objectionable proviso omitted. Though there was grumbling and discontent, the crisis which Buckinghamshire had expected did not materialize; the truncated bill was accepted. This seems to have decided North and Hillsborough, who had been growing increasingly distrustful of Buckinghamshire's conciliatory attitude towards the Irish reformers, to manœuvre him into offering his resignation. He was replaced by Lord Carlisle, with Eden as his chief Secretary. These two appointments promised to give North more dependable men in Dublin and solve the problem of finding suitable places for Carlisle and Eden, who ever since their return from America had been difficult and awkward to handle. For a short time it looked as if his hopes would be fulfilled. When in October Grattan asked leave to bring in a new limited Mutiny Bill he was defeated by 177 votes to 33. But if government influence in the Irish Commons was too strong for Grattan, he could still rely on dangerous forces outside the House. In February 1782 a Convention of Volunteers met at Dungannon and gave a solid backing to his demands, and English ministers could not fail to be aware that the country as a whole was getting once more very near to the point of revolt. Indeed, by the end of March Carlisle too was writing to suggest that retreat might be necessary. This was the situation which faced Rockingham and his colleagues when they took office. The men who had sympathized with Ireland and America were now to be put to the test.

With regard to Ireland little time was given to them. When they assumed office Grattan had already given notice of his intention to move a motion in favour of Ireland's legislative independence, and they found that he was not prepared to postpone this because his friends Rockingham and Fox had come to power.[1] In the circumstances it was difficult for them to do anything but advise the King to accede to the Irish demands. Accordingly Shelburne in the Lords and Fox in the Commons proposed the repealing of the Declaratory Act of 1719, and on 27 May the Duke of Portland, who, in the new arrangements had replaced Carlisle as Lord Lieutenant, informed the Irish Parliament that the King would not oppose a modification of the hated Poyning's Law nor the introduction of a two-year Mutiny Bill.[2] Once again there was an outburst of gratitude and the Irish Commons voted a considerable sum, £100,000, for the British navy and allowed England to use for foreign service 5,000 of the 12,000 men on the Irish establishment. Soon, however, suspicion began to mar the brief honeymoon and the fear revived that what England had given she might again recall. Before this fresh climax came to a head Rockingham was dead and Shelburne was the most powerful man in the ministry. Deeply involved in the negotiations for peace with America and Spain, he had neither the inclination nor the opportunity for another tussle with Ireland. Flood, who had now taken over the Irish leadership from Gratton, had the satisfaction of securing a formal renunciation of the rights of the Parliament at Westminster over that at Dublin. In less than a year after North's resignation therefore, Ireland, though acknowledging the sovereignty of the British Crown, was made responsible for the full management of her own internal affairs and became an equal partner of the sister island. In the same year the last of the savagely punitive penal laws against the civil rights of the majority of the Irish Roman Catholics also disappeared from the

---

[1] For a brief account of the political campaign consult V. T. Harlow, *op. cit.*, pp. 525–6.

[2] H. Butterfield, *George III, Lord North, etc.*, pp. 381–2. Duke of Portland to Edmund Burke, 21 April 1782: 'if resistance or half measures are adopted, I cannot and *will not* answer for the consequences'.—*Rockingham Memoirs,* vol. II, p. 471.

Irish statute book. At last there seemed some chance that Ireland might settle down to a period of growing prosperity and that increasing wealth, by solving also some of her social problems, might make her a more contented land. Too soon, however, Irish politicians came to realize that legislative independence was little more than a façade so long as the Lord Lieutenant—by patronage, influence, and the arts of parliamentary management—could still exercise an effective control over the Irish Parliament. The remedy seemed to be the reform of the Irish House of Commons; by the summer of 1783 a movement for this was in full swing.

Whether the Irish politicians would have reached this conclusion for themselves, uninfluenced by English example, it is impossible to say. Since the petitioning movement and, above all, the activities of the Westminster Committee had given publicity to the ideas of earlier, obscure reformers like Jebb and Cartwright, there had been a growing movement in England both for the curtailing of the royal influence over the House of Commons and for a widening of the basis of representation. These aims were by no means linked or advocated by the same people. Indeed, one of the weaknesses of the reformers was that they were not agreed among themselves. Fox and Shelburne, divided though they were by personal mistrust, agreed that some measure of enlargement of the franchise was necessary. Burke shrank in horror from any attempt to alter the structure of the House of Commons. He wanted to abolish offices which were a brake on the efficiency of government or a means of influencing votes, but he did not want to abolish sinecures which could be used to reward men for public service or provide for their retirement. Burke was good to his friends, and to his family as the eighteenth century would understand the term, and he found little incongruity in pleading the cause of economic reform in the Commons and trying to get the rich sinecure of the Clerk of the Pells for his own son at the same time. It was royal not aristocratic influence to which he objected. Rockingham, as was typical, adopted a half-way position. He favoured economic reform but was prepared for a modest measure of parliamentary reform also.

From a ministry so composed some action along progressive lines was to be expected. Though it was unusual for an administration to commit itself in advance to any particular policy, Rockingham on assuming office had made it a condition that the King would agree to the introduction of bills similar to those formerly introduced by Burke and Crewe as part of the opposition's campaign for economic reform. Proposals for such bills were consequently included in the speech from the throne when Parliament met after the Easter recess. In the course of the session bills disenfranchising revenue officers and excluding government contractors from the House of Commons became law. Burke's own bill was less far reaching than his proposals of 1780 had been. Even in its more modest form sinecure offices to the extent of some £70,000 were extinguished. Though well intentioned, it has been described as the bill of a politician rather than the work of a man with practical financial experience.[1] Nevertheless, though defective in many ways because the problem was more complicated than he and his sympathizers realized, it was an important landmark in the history both of the Commons and of public finance.

The administration assumed a more non-committal attitude towards parliamentary reform. It was almost impossible, in view of its composition and of eighteenth-century precedents, that it should do anything else. Rockingham had asked for no such mandate from the King and was aware that motions of this kind would expose the divisions among the ranks of his followers. The most the small group of would-be parliamentary reformers could hope was that the influence of the Treasury would not be used against them and that an opportunity might be given them to try to win over the uncommitted sections of the House. The man deputed to ask leave to move the motion was young William Pitt,[2] who was commonly counted among the friends of Lord Shelburne. He was Chatham's second son and had always been intended for a political career. Chatham himself had been unhappy at Eton and his son had been privately educated, a common eighteenth-century practice; he had gone up to Cambridge at the age of fifteen. As so many gentlemen did, he had then kept his terms at Lincoln's Inn, and had practised, though briefly, on the Western circuit. In the general election of 1780 he stood for Parliament. With that lack of disbelief in his own powers which was habitual to him, he chose to stand for Cambridge, where his age and want of experience were no doubt responsible for his failure to secure election. He was, however, soon provided for by Sir James Lowther, who secured his

---

[1] J. E. D. Binney, *op. cit.*, pp. 119–20.
[2] On William Pitt consult J. Ehrman, *The Younger Pitt*, vol. I (1969).

return for Appleby. Pitt took his seat in January 1781, making his maiden speech a month later in support of a motion of Burke's for the reform of the Civil List.

As his early parliamentary career had been thus closely associated with the reformers, he was a fitting person to move a proposal for the appointment of a committee of inquiry into the possibility of a 'moderate and substantial reform'.[1] The importance of his speech lay partly in its competent eloquence, partly in the picture which he drew of the inadequacy of the present system. In the debate he was well supported by Fox, who had long been committed to the same cause, and by Sheridan. Their combined arguments carried considerable weight: the motion was lost by only 20 votes, 141 in favour to 161 against. But, even though the French Revolution had not yet poisoned men's minds with a fear of democracy, the memory of the Gordon Riots was still with them. Moreover, the mass of the independent members were averse to change: the present system represented with fair accuracy the England they knew and the society in which they moved. A motion which Pitt also supported, for shorter Parliaments—an inspiration long cherished by opposition speakers since the passing of the Septennial Act—was lost by the much more impressive majority of 88. Plainly the main mass of members were yet in no mood for substantial reform in any shape. They did, however, accept a motion to expunge from the journals of the House the record of Wilkes's expulsion and the Middlesex election, an object for which the former had been striving ever since he had been allowed to take his seat. For the rest, the reformers had to be content with attending meetings at the Thatched House Tavern, where Major Cartwright was organizing support for his 'Society for Promoting Constitutional Information'.

3. THE PEACE NEGOTIATIONS [2]

Far more important than any question of reform, or the justification of the long Rockingham struggle on behalf of Wilkes, was the conclusion of peace with America and her allies. Until the death

---

[1] The Duke of Richmond had earlier bargained with Rockingham for a committee of inquiry into parliamentary reform as a condition of supporting the administration.— *Rockingham Memoirs*, vol. II, p. 482.

[2] For details of the negotiations from the American angle see J. C. Miller, *op. cit.*, ch. XXIX, or J. R. Alden, *The American Revolution* (N.Y., 1954). From the British imperial angle consult V. T. Harlow, *op. cit.*, chs. VI and VII; D. B. Horn, *The British Diplomatic Service, 1689–1789* (1961), pp. 174–5.

of Rockingham on 1 July, the position was greatly complicated by the fact that the negotiations with America were managed by Shelburne and those with France and Spain and Holland by Fox. After that date the resignation of Fox left Shelburne in virtual control of both, and the peace, when made, must be regarded as his peace. When Rockingham succeeded North, the position had looked exceedingly discouraging, but to some extent outward appearances were misleading and divergent aims among England's enemies held out hopes that skilful diplomacy might still manage to drive a wedge between them. The difficulty in Franco-American relations was Spain. Eager though she was to regain Gibraltar and Minorca, her statesmen thoroughly disliked an alliance with revolutionaries. Also in America itself her interests clashed with those of the colonists. Spain had not abandoned her hope of establishing herself in strength on the mainland, where she already held Louisiana. In 1780–1 she had seized the British colony of West Florida and was anxious, by obtaining a strip of territory east of the Mississippi, to prevent further American pressure to the west. In America, therefore, a strong Spain must always be a dangerous neighbour to the colonists. If they were to have the opportunity for expansion, for which they had been struggling since 1748, the Mississippi must be recognized as the minimum western boundary which they would accept, and the right freely to navigate that river was essential to them. By 1782 John Jay, the American representative in Madrid had realized that Spain was likely to be a stumbling block to American aspirations. It was also becoming clear that where the interests of Spain and America clashed, Vergennes would back the former while paying lip service to the latter. When Shelburne with the authorization of the Cabinet sent his private agent Oswald, the rich West African merchant, to start exploratory talks with Franklin, it was hoped that these internal strains might work out to Britain's advantage. At the same time Fox sent Thomas Grenville, the second son of the late George Grenville, to start discussions with Vergennes. British ministers still had some assets with which to bargain. The reassertion of British naval supremacy after the battle of the Saints meant that her remaining bridgeheads in America could be reinforced. Gibraltar also was still holding out under General Elliott, having been reprovisioned late in 1779 and again in April 1781. The last furious assault took place in September 1782 when the fall of the fortress would have exercised a decisive effect on the peace negotiations. Once again a relieving fleet, this time under Lord Howe, managed to get through. After this success, though the siege continued in a half-hearted manner until the conclusion of the preliminaries of peace in February 1783, the fortress was never again in serious danger.

The fate of Gibraltar had not been decided before Rockingham's death, but the general pattern of the peace was already clear. On the English side there was no longer any hope of reconquering the American colonies. Minorca had gone and the French had strengthened their territorial position in the Caribbean. British trade was further threatened by the commerce raiders of France, Holland and Spain and by the defensive alliance of the Armed Neutrality. The allies of the colonists on the other hand had nothing about which to be complacent. Attempts to invade England had come to nothing. In August 1781 Admiral Hyde Parker had in a tough, indecisive battle off the Dogger Bank so mauled the Dutch fleet that it was subsequently of little use to Holland's allies. After the Battle of the Saints Britain had regained control of West Indian waters. Also the financial strain of the war was beginning to tell on France, who, by the beginning of the eighties, had little inducement to continue a long war. America had won *de facto*, and saw a reasonable chance of securing *de jure* her independence. In such circumstances there was considerable will to peace among all the combatants, though this did not prevent the negotiations from being tough and protracted.

The interest in the first weeks centred on the conversations between Franklin and Oswald and Grenville, for though the American Congress had appointed a commission of five to negotiate a peace, only Franklin was in Paris before 23 June, when he was joined by John Jay; John Adams did not arrive until October. The divisions in the Cabinet were important and help to explain subsequent events. So long as Britain did not recognize the independence of the Americans Shelburne would continue to be responsible for the negotiations with them. Once, however, the colonies became a foreign country responsibility for both sets of negotiations would pass to Fox as Foreign Secretary. Both men had therefore a public and a private interest in the policy which they followed. Shelburne did not want to concede American independence in advance of a general peace treaty, because it would leave Britain with no bargaining counters; it would also cut him out of the negotiations. Fox, in contrast, wanted to separate the interests of the colonists from those of the French, so that by cutting her losses on the American continent, England could concentrate all her efforts against the Bourbon powers. This course of action would also have the advantage to him of putting him in sole control of the final peace negotiations. Therefore, though both ministers were prepared to make generous concessions to split Congress from its allies, their programme for the timing of these was different. That Franklin should use the situation skilfully was only to be expected from a man of his experience; while refusing to keep Vergennes in the dark he listened to both Oswald and Grenville and made his counter-proposals in turn. One of these was to play a considerable part in Fox's subsequent resignation.

Franklin was probably indulging in a little diplomatic kite-flying. He knew that Shelburne was very reluctant to sever every tie between Britain and her erstwhile colonies. To avoid this it was essential, he assured Oswald, that England should make generous concessions now. Among other things he suggested as desirable, though it was not one of his essential demands, that Britain should cede the whole of Canada to the new United States and agree to free trade between the two countries. To the latter suggestion Shelburne was favourably inclined but knew that he could not hope to gain the support of the Commons for the proposition. The former he recognized as so unrealistic that, when Oswald wrote to him, repeating his conversation with Franklin, he did not even report the incident to the Cabinet. When, however, it came to Fox's knowledge he affected to believe that it was only one more instance of Shelburne's duplicity. He complained repeatedly that Shelburne's handling of the negotiations was making their success impossible, and by the end of June he was threatening to resign. Whether he would in fact have done so is uncertain, for the major political crisis of Lord Rockingham's death was superimposed on the minor one of the quarrel between the two Secretaries. At the early age of fifty-two Rockingham died on 1 July.

4. Reconstruction of the Ministry under Lord Shelburne

The death of Rockingham made the existence of two groups within the Cabinet painfully clear. That Fox and Shelburne would continue to work together was not possible when the death of the nominal head of the administration made it necessary for the formal precedence to be given to one or other of them. It was well known that given a free choice George III would choose Shelburne. Though when he had assumed office Fox had become a reformed character, developing gifts of industry of which his friends had hoped rather than believed him capable, forsaking the gaming table and pouring his undoubted talents and energies into his new career, George III still disliked him. Yet to a man of Fox's temperament, to have a man like Shelburne placed over him was intolerable. Moreover, and this was a practical consideration, he knew that Shelburne would have the backing of the Closet. Therefore, as Rockingham's friends were in the majority in the Cabinet, Fox fabricated yet another elaboration of constitutional doctrine—that the choice of a new first minister lay with that body rather than with the King. This was an extension of the use that he and his friends had been making of the Cabinet machinery since North's resignation. The relations between the Cabinet and the King were still fluid and undefined. The general practice seems to have been for a head of a department to bring important matters for which he was responsible to the royal notice. Then, if both King and minister thought it desirable, the advice of the Cabinet would be taken. Certainly George III thought himself entitled to ask for the joint advice of his ministers in this way, and he frequently availed himself of it. But this did not mean that he recognized the right of his Cabinet to discuss officially matters which had not been laid before it by the royal command; to offer advice that had not been asked was still constitutionally impertinent.[1] Nevertheless, in the last three months there had been an increasing tendency for the Cabinet, under the promptings of Fox, to poach on the prerogative in this way. When George III asked Shelburne to form a ministry, his Rockingham colleagues made it clear that though he might have the royal confidence he had not got theirs. Instead they suggested that he should suggest the Duke of Portland as acceptable to the majority of the Cabinet. This Shelburne did, only to have the proposal firmly rejected by the King. Fox therefore resigned, though he obscured the issue somewhat by declaring that it was his mistrust of Shelburne's handling of the peace negotiations which had driven him to this step.

[1] R. Pares, *King George III and the Politicians*, pp. 153-4.

Even his friends doubted his wisdom and only a handful of them —his brother-in-law Fitzpatrick, Portland himself, Lord John Cavendish, Edmund Burke and Sheridan—followed him into retirement. The Duke of Richmond was against it and persuaded his friends to stay in office. In so doing he was both conforming to established constitutional practice and refusing to produce a political crisis in the middle of the peace negotiations. The gaps were filled with surprising ease largely by persons of no marked personality. Thomas Townshend and Lord Grantham became the new Secretaries of State, Earl Temple replaced Portland as Lord Lieutenant of Ireland. One appointment, however, was of considerable interest, for Shelburne offered the Chancellorship of the Exchequer, vacated by Cavendish, to his old chief's brilliant son, William Pitt. His refusal to accept subordinate office earlier was amply justified, for at the age of twenty-three he became virtually the leader of the House of Commons, no sinecure when he would have to meet the combined eloquence of Fox, Sheridan and Burke. Thus reconstructed and with its weakening rivalries eliminated, the ministry under the leadership of Shelburne was able to give its undivided attention to the securing of the peace. The next few months were to see rapid progress.

5. The Peace of Versailles

By 5 October 1782 a draft treaty had been approved in Paris and was ready for submission to the British Cabinet. Though this was to take effect only when peace had been made between France and Britain, so that the new United States had not technically made a separate peace, their action meant that the French could expect little advantage from prolonging the war. There was, however, still some delay, for the draft terms sent to Shelburne were not entirely acceptable. By them Canada was to remain British but with boundaries that excluded the territory between the Great Lakes and the Ohio, whose annexation to Canada had been one of the provisions of the hated Quebec Act of 1774. America was to have access to the fisheries and Britain to be allowed freedom of trade and navigation on the Mississippi. Extremely progressive clauses on free trade were included. In the past their mutual trade had been of the greatest importance and an attempt was made to salvage this by a provision that Americans and British were to enjoy equal rights in navigation

and commerce in the dominions of each country. This would have
thrown the trade of the West Indies open to America as in former
times. It is interesting to speculate what might have been the result
had this clause been accepted and implemented.

Whatever Shelburne's private predilection for the commercial
arrangements advocated by Adam Smith he knew that such provisions would never be accepted by the British House of Commons.
Also, encouraged by the British success in revictualling Gibraltar,
he thought that it might be possible to secure some favourable
rectification of the proposed Canadian boundaries, and having the
pressure to be expected from British merchants in mind, he wanted
to obtain a promise that private debts owing to British subjects
should be accepted as still valid. He was also anxious to get better
terms for the loyalists, who were now faced with confiscation and
ruin. It was not therefore until 30 November that the final draft
was signed. In it Shelburne did secure some concessions. The
boundaries of Canada and the United States were slightly altered in
favour of Britain. Private debts were to be recognized as valid. The
commercial clauses were replaced by the recognition of the unrestricted character of the Mississippi. But for the unfortunate loyalists,
on whom George III and Germain had pinned so many of their
hopes, and whose activities had caused such intense local bitterness,
only a vague phrase, recommending individual states to revise their
confiscatory laws, was obtained. On this point American opinion
was adamant. This was one of the criticisms of the preliminaries
of peace subsequently made by Fox and North. Shelburne, however,
convinced that he could get no better terms, accepted these limited
concessions and turned his energies to bringing about the general
peace which would make them operative. In little more than two
months this had been done; the preliminaries of peace were signed
on 20 January 1783.

Its terms provided a bitter contrast with the Peace of Paris but
could not fairly be described as disastrous. St Lucia was handed
back to France and Tobago ceded to her; but Dominica, Grenada,
St Vincent, St Kitts, Nevis and Montserrat were all restored to
Britain. In Africa, where France received Senegal and Goree, the
balance was tipped in her favour, though Gambia and Fort St James
were guaranteed to England. In India once again French commercial
establishments were restored and some outstanding matters of
dispute with France were settled in her favour. Her rights in the

Newfoundland fisheries were fully confirmed and the two small islands of Miquelon and St Pierre, which she had been allowed to use as bases for her fishing fleet by the earlier treaty, were now ceded in full sovereignty. At last, too, the irritating stipulations about the fortifications of Dunkirk, which had bedevilled Anglo-French relations for so long, were given up. Spain came out of the struggle with some spoils, though not all that she had hoped for. Minorca and West Florida remained hers, and England ceded East Florida; but she failed to get Gibraltar. As on many previous occasions, suggestions were made for its surrender in return for a suitable equivalent. It was a question on which the Cabinet was divided. Both Shelburne and the King seem to have been in favour of letting it go, but Richmond and Admiral Keppel fought for its retention. Public opinion, too, after its long defence, would have been loudly vocal in condemning such a step. In return for the concessions Spain agreed that Providence and the Bahamas, which had been briefly in her possession, should be recognized as English possessions. She also guaranteed the much-disputed right of the British to cut logwood in Honduras Bay. Holland, for whom the war had been unfortunate, signed a separate treaty. Here again the basis was a mutual restoration of conquests, except that England kept Negapatam in India. The definitive Treaty of Versailles was signed on 3 September 1783.

6. The Coalition of Fox and North

Though the treaty was substantially the work of Shelburne he was by this time no longer in office. He had been forced by the manœuvres of his parliamentary rivals, Fox and North, to resign on 24 February. Shortly afterwards the spectacular coalition of Fox and North proved strong enough to force itself into office under the nominal leadership of the Duke of Portland. The prominence which this short-lived ministry has received, both from contemporaries and from historians, seems to have been due more to its dramatic character than to its constitutional significance. The structure of politics at the time indeed made some odd combinations of personalities almost inevitable. The genuinely political groups in the Commons were three in number. Lord Shelburne's personal following was small, but he could depend on the administrative members in the House, and he had the support of the Closet.

The other two were composed of those members who, for one reason or another, had given their allegiance to either Fox or North. Fox had inherited the leadership of the ex-Rockingham group, though not all of them had retired from office on his resignation; and his links with these men, combined with his personal charm, were sufficient to give him a respectable following. North, too, had retained the loyalty of many of those who had accepted his leadership when he had been in office. Neither man, however, could hope indefinitely to keep his following unless there were a prospect of returning to office. Eighteenth-century politicians had no objection to a short sojourn in the wilderness provided that the promised land of office was well in sight and the road to it reasonably clear.[1] Both Fox and North would have been very bad politicians, which they were not, if they had stayed inactive and let their followers drift away from them. Action did not, however, necessarily imply coalition with each other. It was clear that Shelburne's administration was beginning to break up. His personal failure to establish easy relationships with his colleagues was to some extent to blame. Even Pitt, who stood by him until the end, was careful not to include him in his own ministry when the time came for him to form one. But in addition to this, politicians have little liking for being connected with an unpopular peace. Richmond, who had opposed Shelburne in the Cabinet, ceased to attend its meetings in January; while Keppel resigned outright. So did Lord Carlisle, the Lord Steward. Then when Carlisle was replaced by the Duke of Rutland, Grafton took offence at Shelburne's failure to discuss the matter at a Cabinet, thus providing another instance of the way in which the Cabinet was attempting to nibble away the right of the King to play an active and personal part in politics. He too resigned, while Conway, as usual, was wavering. That so many of Fox's friends should have resigned in so short a time is suggestive. In this undermining and breaking away, events were following the normal eighteenth-century pattern; it was clear that if George III wanted to retain Shelburne's services the ministry would have to be strengthened by taking in one or other of the opposing groups.

The choice was not an easy one for either George III or Shelburne. At first there seemed to be a preference for North, if his following could be secured without having to pay too high a price by bestowing office on its leader. But without Cabinet office North was not

[1] R. Pares, *King George III and the Politicians*, p. 81.

to be had. Reluctantly George III allowed Shelburne through Pitt to approach Fox. Here the impediment was the rivalry between them: Fox had resigned rather than serve under Shelburne. Now, once he had found out from Pitt that his rival was still to continue at the Treasury the negotiation came to an abrupt end. Further attempts made through Dundas to come to some terms with North made no impression, and it was clear that the Court had failed. The reason for this soon became apparent. In the debates on the preliminaries of peace on 17 February 1783 Fox and North supported one another in attacking them, with the result that, though they were carried in the Lords by 13 votes, in the Commons they were defeated by 224 to 208. On the 21st the now united opposition carried a vote of censure by seventeen votes, 207 to 190. These two adverse votes made it clear that Shelburne could not continue to do the King's business in the House, and on the 24th he resigned. George III's distress was very great, and Thurlow described him as 'the most miserable man in the kingdom'. True to his nature, he made every attempt to avoid surrender to this pair of political buccaneers, but the number of suitable politicians available was pitifully small. His major hope was that young Pitt would consent to try to form a ministry, and between Shelburne's resignation and the royal surrender to Fox and North on 1 April, George III made every effort to persuade him to do so. In this he failed. Pitt took literally the biblical advice that before going to war one should weigh one's resources against those of the enemy. Carefully and methodically he studied the allegiance and probable behaviour of every member of the House, much in the way that Jenkinson and George III were wont to do before a general election. The result was not encouraging, and Pitt preferred to reserve his energies for a more favourable occasion. Politically he was wise. A very few months were to justify him, but it left the King without any practical way of escape, though he even tried such unlikely candidates for the Treasury as Thomas Pitt and Lord Temple. On 31 March Pitt too resigned, and the new ministers kissed hands on 2 April.

The coalition of Fox and North has been widely condemned as an unprincipled act. George III called it 'the most daring and un-

---

[1] As early as September 1782 Robinson was worried about his future behaviour, and in a long letter in which he deplored any attempt on North's part to storm the Closet he wrote: 'To entertain any idea of making terms now or to have any bargains made in my opinion ... would surely not do you honour.'—I. R. Christie, *The Political Allegiance ...*, p. 116.

principled act that the annals of this kingdom ever produced'. There is a sense in which the charge is true. In 1782 George III had been forced to take ministers whom he disliked because the independent members of the Commons had come to the conclusion that his present ministers could not and would never attempt to make a realistic peace. It was a genuine revolt of the opinion of the House. The new coalition was something different. The peace which was now being discussed had been ardently desired and was probably the best that could be obtained. Though Fox could justify from his own past speeches the continuance of the war against the Bourbon, and North his insistence on securing better terms for the loyalists, few people thought that dislike of the treaty was the genuine cause of their joint attack on it. It was in fact a successful attempt to storm the Closet by a skilful use of political faction. In essence there was little that was new in the manœuvre: the sense of outrage lay in the barefaced way in which it had been carried out, and in the personalities involved. As yet the right of the King to chose his own ministers was generally accepted as constitutional, and though the right of Parliament to refuse to support those ministers, where they judged their continuance in office detrimental to the national well-being, was also accepted, the exercise of this right for faction and not of necessity was still of dubious constitutional propriety. Yet the fact remains that a coalition of some sort, either Shelburne and North, or Shelburne and Fox, or Fox and North, was unavoidable if the administration was to secure an adequate majority in the Commons. Given the attitude of the King and the personality of Shelburne there was considerable concealed pressure in the situation to bring about what on the surface seemed a surprising personal combination. It was in essence an old technique used with a new lack of inhibitions.

Of the two, the behaviour of Fox is the easier to understand. He disliked both George III and Shelburne and had little wish to spare them any humiliation or leave them any power. His brief period of high and responsible office had only increased his appetite for it; it had been just long enough to convince both him and his friends of the reality of his talents for it. Furthermore, to him there was no particular objection to working with North. There was no personal animosity between them, for Fox's parliamentary attacks had been only nominally against North, and in reality against the King. He had, moreover, little respect for the sanctity of constitutional conventions, and had long shown himself adept at an interpretation that could further his immediate political plans. Lord North's conduct is more difficult to explain. When in office his responsibilities, combined with his realization of his own inadequacies, at times seem to have driven him to the verge of a nervous breakdown. He was bound to the King, who had paid his debts in 1777, by ties of gratitude as well as friendship. His sight was beginning to trouble him; in a few years he was to go blind. Why should he wish for office? Was he egged on by his followers, anxious once again to enjoy the spoils of office? Was he dominated by the stronger will of Fox? Or had office become such a habit that life without it seemed incomplete? There is some evidence that this was so. In spite of the fact that over the last years he had frequently begged to be allowed to resign, and that on one occasion the King had agreed to release him at the end of the session, when it came to the point he had clung to office. Moreover, his sense of gratitude to the King must have been blunted by the shabby way in which the latter had held him responsible for an election debt contracted in 1780.[1] Fox on the other hand was willing to agree that for the time being nothing more should be done about economic reform and that each group was to take its own line on parliamentary reform. This agreement to differ over what are now considered fundamental problems is sometimes taken as a proof of the essential unscrupulousness of the coalition. This is hardly fair. The differences between Burke and Fox on parliamentary reform were quite as deep as those which divided Fox and North, but no one suggested that this was any reason for their not acting as colleagues in Rockingham's administration.

Though this administration is always known as the Fox-North Coalition its nominal head was the Duke of Portland. He now assumed the mantle of Rockingham and became First Lord of the Treasury. The two new friends took the key office of Secretary—Fox, as was to be expected, taking the Foreign Office and North being responsible for domestic affairs. The other appointments are not of particular interest. Cavendish returned to the Chancellorship of the Exchequer, Burke to the Pay Office, Keppel to the Admiralty. As Fox refused to have a personal adherent of the King in his Cabinet in the shape of Thurlow the Lord Chancellorship was put in commission. Where Fox's innovating influence was felt was in the claim which Portland made to fill up the minor offices of the

[1] See I. R. Christie, *Myth and Reality*, pp. 183–95.

administration without reference to the King.[1] Fox and his friends were now claiming that the King, once the composition of the Cabinet had been laid before him and had gained his acceptance (however forced that might be), had no further right to meddle in the junior appointments made by the ministers who had his official approval. If they could carry their point, as in this case they did, the control of the Cabinet over their subordinates could become a reality and the influence and patronage of the Crown would be to that extent diminished. Not surprisingly George III made it plain from the beginning that if his ministers could differentiate so sharply between the personal and the official wishes of the monarch so could he. His actions made it clear that he had no personal regard or respect for those men whom, in his official capacity, he had called to office. This he showed by refusing to exercise in favour of any of their friends the as yet undoubted prerogative of creating peers. For the next few months events were dominated by the determination of Fox and North to stay in office and by that of George III to get rid of them, and the struggle took on all the drama of a personal vendetta.

Contrary to popular belief George III had no desire to reduce his ministers to puppets. In the past twenty years on many occasions he had given loyal support to men for whom he had little personal liking and had accepted advice from them which he found uncongenial. George III appears genuinely to have believed in the constitutional doctrine that stressed the need to preserve the balance between Parliament and the executive, and there is no evidence to suggest that he ever planned to undermine the former. From his point of view Charles James Fox was behaving unconstitutionally in attempting to reduce the Crown to 'the appearance of power only'. But probably he would never have encroached so blatantly, nor the King defended his prerogative so resentfully, if the political struggle between them had not been based on a personal vendetta. George III had two reasons for his aversion to the younger Fox's father, Henry Fox, Lord Holland. One was his reputation for jobbery and corruption; the other concerned Lady Sarah Lennox, for whom George III as a young man had felt a decided partiality. Henry Fox's hopes of political influence through a royal alliance had been destroyed when the young King had married Princess Charlotte of Mecklenburg but the Town buzzed with rumours and George III suspected that Fox

<hr />

[1] R. Pares, *George III and the Politicians*, p. 123.

would still have viewed with complaisance the installation of his niece as the royal mistress, and was indeed even scheming to this end, if thereby his own political influence might be secured. To the King, whose ideas were strictly moralist, such an idea was disgusting, and that Fox should have entertained it made him a *persona non grata*. Therefore, though for his services in steering the Peace of Paris through the Commons in 1763, George III had raised Fox to the peerage as Lord Holland, the latter had never enjoyed the royal favour, never succeeded in transforming his barony into the earldom which he so much coveted. In consequence the feud between the House of Holland and the House of Hanover continued, accentuated by the fact that, possibly from pique in the first instance arising out of his dismissal, the younger Fox had joined the attackers of the administration's policy over America. In the debates over this troubled issue Fox had lost no opportunity of attacking the King, so that by 1783 the vendetta was more bitter than ever.

The element of ill will between the two men was further strengthened by the fact that once again the recurring pattern of animosity between the King and the Prince of Wales had flared up. This had happened too consistently for mere clashes of temperament to explain it, but in this particular instance such a clash probably exacerbated it. George III was a sober, hardworking man, dedicated to duty, devoid of personal extravagance; on his accession, as a matter of principle, he had surrendered the hereditary revenues in return for a Civil List of £800,000, a sum that was to prove inadequate for his legitimate expenses. His domestic life was both happy and respectable and, unlike both his predecessors and his successor, there were no royal mistresses. George, Prince of Wales, was a complete contrast. By 1783, when he came of age, he had already accumulated debts of some £60,000; he was a man of fashion and pleasure; he gamed; he had mistresses. George III could never have approved of such a son, any more than later Queen Victoria and Prince Albert approved of the future Edward VII as a young man. The king attributed much of the blame for his son's lapses from grace to Charles James Fox who, like most politicians in opposition, had cultivated the Prince and in the process had converted him into a friend and a boon companion. As the Prince was now twenty-one the time had come to settle the matter of his parliamentary allowance. In pursuance of an earlier promise, therefore, Fox now proposed to the House of Commons that this should be £100,000 a year. George

III agreed with reluctance. When, however, the cabinet belatedly decided that the Commons would object to having to find so large a sum at a time when taxation was already high difficulties arose. The Duke of Portland suggested that apart from the revenues of the Duchy of Cornwall, Parliament should only provide £38,000 and that the other £50,000 could come from the Civil List. George III, with some justification, was furious that Fox, a minister of the Crown, should have put the interests of the Prince of Wales before those of the King. Though eventually a compromise was reached over the question of the Prince's allowance the way in which Fox had handled it drove yet another nail into his political coffin.

Though this awkward matter was successfully handled Pitt, Dundas and their friends were able to exploit with considerable skill the inconsistencies which the political pasts of Fox and North afforded. When a new loan was raised by the old system of private allotment, which Fox had attacked so bitterly when in opposition, Pitt was quick to comment on his changed opinions. His tactics seem to have been to lessen Fox's influence over the reformers by placing him in a position where he either had to soft pedal his former views or risk estranging North and his friends. For instance, when Pitt again brought forward his scheme for parliamentary reform it was defeated by a majority of 144, chiefly composed of North's friends. Though such differences of opinion were normal in eighteenth-century administrations this defeat did at least emphasize, as it was meant to do, that Fox the reformer had chosen strange political bedfellows. What was still more embarrassing was the matter of Burke and the Pay Office.

When the question of economic reform had first been discussed seriously in the Commons, North, who was genuinely interested in administrative efficiency, had proposed the appointment of commissioners to investigate and report on the handling of public money, and to suggest better ways of keeping accounts, so that more reliable information might be available for the House. In the course of their investigations, which extended over several years, the commissioners discovered that two Pay Office officials, Powell and Bembridge, had been guilty of irregularities to the extent of £48,000 in settling up Henry Fox's accounts. Colonel Barré, who was Paymaster at the time of this discovery, promptly dismissed both of them. With the fall of Shelburne's administration Burke returned to the Pay Office and reinstated them. His action caused a storm in the Commons.

It was a gift to Pitt and his friends, for it both threw doubt on the genuineness of Burke's campaign for economic reform and stressed in a pointed manner the source of Fox's fortune. Burke, defending his action, argued that he needed the help of both men in the reforms in which he was at the moment engaged, that it was the system which was responsible for the irregularities and that to victimize individuals would be unfair. Powell, he declared, had been insane ever since the strain of his examination by the commissioners, a fact somewhat difficult to reconcile with Burke's earlier statement that the process of reorganization would be facilitated by the reinstatement of both men. Burke was notoriously soft-hearted where his friends were concerned, and there is some evidence to suggest that Powell may have helped the Burkes in earlier speculations in the West Indies, while Bembridge was a friend of Richard Champion, who was a friend of Burke. In May Powell committed suicide.[1]

7. THE INDIA BILL AND ITS ANTECEDENTS

None of these issues, either singly or in combination, was capable of arousing sufficient opposition in the Commons to be a real danger to ministerial majorities. The problem of India was very different. This was a responsibility which the ministers had inherited and which they could have hardly evaded, though they seem to have given it their serious attention only during the summer recess. To understand Fox's East India Bill, which was to bring about the destruction of his ministry, it is necessary briefly to survey the affairs of the Company since the passing of North's Regulating Act in 1773.[2] That measure, which had been tentative and experimental, was designed to give the government some indirect control over the Company, and so to remedy the worst abuses of its rule, without either taking over the responsibility for its administration in India, or interfering with the management of its trade. Inevitably the method adopted ran into difficulties. Though the Governor-General had been nominated in the Act, and though there were now three ministerial appointees on his council, ministers had still largely to

---

[1] J. E. D. Binney, *op. cit.*, pp.153–5.

[2] For a full account of the background and provisions of this Act consult L. S. Sutherland, *The East India Company, etc.*, chs. 10–13.

work through the machinery of the Company. This had involved building up the same kind of influence within it—and by much the same methods—as ministers employed to create parliamentary majorities. It was essential to secure a majority of friendly directors and, because their decisions on controversial issues had to be confirmed by the General Court of Proprietors, to organize a party of government supporters among the holders of East India stock. This was largely the task of the indefatigable Robinson. The initial aim of ministers was the apparently modest one of sustaining the financial strength of the Company, so important for the stability of credit in the City, of checking abuses, which both undermined this and also disturbed public opinion, and of keeping Indian questions out of Parliament. Events in India were soon to show that only on the surface could such hopes be deemed modest, and that the machinery set up by the Regulating Act was quite inadequate for such purposes. Indian problems were hideously complex; communications between Bengal, Madras and London were desperately slow and remote control was almost impossible. In order to introduce some unity of policy into the Company's Indian administration it had been necessary to give the Governor-General in Bengal authority over Madras. The weakness of the Regulating Act lay in the provisions which made the Governor-General subordinate to the majority of his council. This, however much in accord with eighteenth-century fears of a strong executive, was in practice to prove unworkable.

Already by June 1775 disquieting dispatches were being received reporting that Warren Hastings, the Governor-General, was at odds with the nominated council. How far the clash was one of personalities it is difficult to assess. Hastings had a profound knowledge of India, and had grown dictatorial under the burden of his responsibilities. Before the arrival of his new colleagues he had already done much to bring order into the administration of Bengal, and his experience of realities made him impatient of criticism. Of the new arrivals Philip Francis was ambitious, jealous and able to dominate his colleagues, Monson and Clavering. Moreover their own position was ambiguous. They were expected to work with Hastings but were also expected to reform abuses and check malpractices. Hasting's personal ambition did not lie in the accumulation of a large personal fortune and his energies were absorbed by the problems of administration; but he was not squeamish as to the activities of his friends. Indeed, no one who had worked long in India and had had to work with whoever of the Company's servants were available, could be over nice in this matter. Though his own hands were comparatively clean according to eighteenth-century standards, those of many of his friends and associates were not. To them the activities of the reformers constituted a dangerous threat. This clash of interests was bound to lead to friction on the council. To North and his colleagues the situation was disturbing. Once it was clear that the enmity between Hastings and his council was irreconcilable, their solution was to use ministerial influence with the directors to get Hastings recalled. In this they failed. Though the directors were persuaded to fall into line with the government's wishes the Court of Proprietors was not. Among the holders of East India stock there were too many people whose interests would have suffered if the reformers had their way, and it was easy for them to manufacture resentment at this attempt to interfere in the affairs of a chartered company. Though at one time ministers hoped that Hastings's resignation might be secured by a friendly negotiation, this too failed to materialize. In the meantime Hastings's position was improved by the death first of Monson and then of Clavering, and ministers, unable to unseat him, came to give him their grudging support.

This apparent acquiescence did not mean that North's administration had been satisfied with this solution. On the contrary their men of business, Robinson and Jenkinson, had been busy collecting information and studying the principles on which any thorough reorganization of the Company's affairs would have to be based. By 1778 Robinson's initial plan was so far advanced that it was able to serve as a basis for discussion for the next three years. Yet in spite of the time and thought given to the problem, all that Lord North's government produced was another interim measure in 1781. Once again a major reorganization was shirked. This was hardly surprising. After 1778 the attention of ministers and the King alike was largely taken up first with the American and then with the European war. Under the stress of these years, when the administration seemed in almost daily danger of falling to pieces, when Ireland was a more pressing problem and England itself in danger of invasion, it is not to be wondered that so thorny but not apparently so desperate a question should be shelved.

But though temporarily ignored by ministers it was becoming a matter of interest to the opposition. The name of Edmund Burke is so closely associated with his attack on Warren Hastings that the almost accidental way in which the Rockingham whigs became interested in Indian affairs is often forgotten. In the beginning it was a matter of connection and politics rather than one of moral conviction, and arose out of the Pigot affair. The appointment of Lord Pigot to be governor of Madras had been the work of the opposition within the Company; to ministers he was a *persona non grata*, whose quarrels they were unlikely to support. Once in India his policy towards the native rulers had not been liked by either Hastings or the nabobs. The result was that he became the victim of a palace revolution engineered by discontented members of the Company in concert with the Nabob of Arcot. When ministers showed no sign of taking up his case the Rockinghams raised the matter in Parliament. Hitherto Francis had had little success in interesting Burke in the wrongs which he alleged Indians to have suffered from Hastings's rule, but now the need to defend Pigot swung the Rockinghams into attacking both Hastings and the Indian policy of the North administration. Early in 1781 they moved for the appointment of a select committee to investigate reports both of friction between the executive and judiciary in Bengal and of the unpopularity of the judiciary there. On this committee, largely owing to North's slackness, they obtained a majority. This gave them a useful platform for their views. In April alarming news reached London that Hyder Ali had invaded the Carnatic and reached the gates of Madras, and that a French fleet was cruising off the Coromandel coast. The government, now alive to the folly of allowing the Rockinghams to monopolize the ear of the House on Indian business, appointed a strong secret committee on the causes of the war in the Carnatic. Dundas, already one of the administration's coming men and soon to be recognized as an expert on Indian affairs, was its chairman, and the already wellinformed Jenkinson a prominent member. This time ministers were taking no risks.

Both committees were still in existence when the Fox-North coalition forced its way into office, with the result that the rivalry between them had kept the Indian problem constantly before the House. As was to be expected, when Dundas's committee laid its proposals before the Commons, Fox and North secured their rejection. They dare not, however, rest content with a purely negative attitude. Neither the affairs of the Company, which was once again on the apparent brink of bankruptcy and begging for help from the Treasury, nor the by now passionate interest of Burke would have allowed this. They were therefore forced to introduce their own India Bill—the bill which led to the fall of the coalition.

George III was not prepared to play the unconstitutional tyrant, but he was determined to get rid of Fox and North as soon as it was politically possible. The controversy connected with the new bill gave him his chance. The essence of the new measure was to make a sweeping transfer of power from the Company to seven commissioners, who were to hold office for four years. Nine assistant commissioners were to be responsible for the management of trade. The vulnerable spot in these proposals from the political angle was that the commissioners were in the first instance to be nominated in the act, and only subsequently appointed by the Crown. As Fox and North dominated the Commons, the original nominations were naturally made from among their own friends and supporters. In consequence the whole arrangement could be, and was, attacked as a gigantic job. The patronage of the East India Company was reputed to be vast and it was argued that all of it would be used to secure the continuation of the coalition. In this their political opponents were probably attributing more deeply laid schemes to Fox and North than they in fact harboured. By 1782 it had become clear to every man who had given any attention to the matter that the affairs of the East India Company and those of the state were so closely entangled that the Crown must assume some responsibility for the fairness, stability and morality of the Company's rule, and for the soundness of its finances. Conditions in India dictated that good government must be strong government; slow communications meant that the man on the spot must be free both to take decisions and to enforce them. To politicians reared in the old whig tradition of distrust of the executive and fear of too strong a Crown, this presented an almost insoluble problem. Dundas, who was a realist and an administrator, might be prepared to entrust the Governor-General with sweeping powers, but Burke, who was neither, was not. With the precedents of the last years behind them neither he nor Fox could sponsor a bill which conferred extensive patronage on the Crown; for this reason the commissioners must be nominated in the act. Nor with their mistrust of untrammelled power could they confer its immediate exercise on the Governor-General; therefore he must be controlled by Commissioners in London.

This parliamentary control might be good 'whiggery'; it was not practical politics. The control of commissioners in London would have created great administrative difficulties, and once the ministers who had appointed them were no longer in power, they might have found themselves, like an American Senate after the election of a new President, at political loggerheads with the new administration. It was, however, because of its supposed rather than its genuine weakness that George III was able to use its unpopularity so effectively. Inevitably it was much disliked by the directors and Court of Proprietors of the Company. Also the influence of the invaluable John Robinson was no longer available to North, as he disapproved of his coalition with Fox and their subsequent policy. Even so, in the Commons Fox had little difficulty in carrying his bill. It was in the Lords that a stand was to be made. On 11 December George III gave Lord Temple his famous permission to let it be known that whoever voted for the bill was no friend of his. Had there not been a considerable and well-organized dislike of the bill, as an attack on the rights of a chartered company, and a suspected 'job' of the first magnitude, even the royal intervention would hardly have been effective. Nor probably would it have been made. But in the circumstances it was sufficient to bring about a decisive defeat on 17 December. The King lost no time. On the night of the 18th Fox and North were ordered to deliver up their seals of office through their Under Secretaries.

The importance and constitutional propriety of George III's active intervention is a point on which historians differ. It has been described as marking the political and constitutional climax of the reign because 'the conflict was a struggle not merely for power but between rival views of the constitution'.[1] On the one hand King George stood for what can be described as the policy of the 'broad bottom' by which the Crown still played an active part in selecting ministers and in the process ought not to be fettered in the choice by party or connection. On the other hand Fox and North were fighting for an administration for a ministry dependent not on the Crown but solely on a majority in the House of Commons, views which foreshadowed the political thinking of the nineteenth century

[1] John Cannon, *The Fox and North Coalition* (1969), p. ix.

rather than the contemporary situation. To one historian, writing in the whig tradition, George III's action was 'indefensible according to both the constitutional theory and practice of the day'.[1] This judgement has been criticized. Apart from the theoretical question whether the Crown 'can ever behave unconstitutionally' it has been argued that eighteenth-century monarchs had never felt any necessity to conceal their opinions on public matters and that in addition in this particular instance, as a majority of peers were probably ignorant of the King's wish to see the bill defeated, some such declaration of the royal wishes was necessary, and that his action can more accurately be termed 'devious' and even 'unscrupulous' than constitutional.

8. THE TRIUMPH OF PITT

The younger Pitt also can be accused of disingenuous behaviour. His public image was that of a man who stood aloof from the normal intrigues of political life, a reputation which was to stand him in good stead in the months to come. Recent research has shown that not only was he well aware of the influence the King intended to exercise over the Lords, but that he had actually required some such public proof that the King would stand by him if he undertook to form a new administration. Pitt never took political risks if he could insure against them; it was not until the invaluable John Robinson, who had broken with North over his coalition with Fox, was able to produce an analysis of the support Pitt could expect in the Commons when backed by the King that he agreed beforehand that he would take office on the dismissal of Fox and North. Pitt also knew he would have every possible support from those experienced politicians, Dundas, Robinson and Jenkinson. Therefore, though he had a difficult game to play, he also knew he held some good cards. Otherwise, as on previous occasions, he would probably not have consented to take office. For Pitt youth and rashness were not synonymous.

On 11 November he kissed hands as First Lord of the Treasury and Chancellor of the Exchequer. The immediate problem was to provide him with an administration. It was necessary to scrape the barrel to find enough politicians of any standing to accept office. This task was made still more difficult by the resignation of Lord Temple, who was to act as leader in the House of Lords, on 22

---

[1] *Ibid.*, p. xiii.

December. His motives are obscure but were not apparently the outcome, as was formerly suggested, of pique at not receiving a dukedom for his services. Faced as he was by the bitter enmity of Fox and North, who still commanded a majority in the Commons, his precipitate resignation may have sprung from a sudden fear of impeachment. In consequence Pitt's cabinet was not impressive. Tommy Townshend, now Lord Sidney, became Home Secretary, and Carmarthen took the Foreign Office. Gower was President of the Council, Rutland the Privy Seal. Thurlow, who at least had experience, courage and brains, returned to the Lord Chancellorship, and Howe made a respectable First Lord of the Admiralty. Richmond accepted the office of Master of the Ordnance and soon re-entered the Cabinet. Most of Pitt's support, as was inevitable, came from the Lords, and in the Commons he, with the assistance of Dundas, who now became Treasurer to the Navy, had to battle on alone. In this list of ministers there is one noticeable omission. Shelburne was not given office, though late in 1784 he was raised a step in the peerage as Marquis of Lansdown. The letters that passed between the two men were friendly but cool. They contain no hint of Pitt the young disciple sitting at his master's feet. On the contrary, by what they do not say, they convey the impression that Pitt was deliberately emphasizing his own political independence. For this there were good reasons. As Shelburne's Chancellor of the Exchequer Pitt had been a loyal colleague but he had not found Shelburne easy; nobody did. Moreover, a combination of Shelburne and Pitt in the same administration might have led to doubts as to where the real authority lay and these were doubts that neither Pitt nor George III had any intention of encouraging. Also it was clear that no administration could contain both Shelburne and Fox and by not including the former Pitt left the way open for a future reconciliation with the latter. At the moment there seemed little chance of this. Fox was furious at his dismissal; he still retained a majority in the House of Commons and he was in a position to make Pitt's task one of great difficulty when Parliament reassembled on 12 January 1784.

Once again, and in a more dramatic form than ever before, the conflict between the 'power' and the 'favour' was to be fought out. That Pitt had the latter was made clear by the almost immediate creation of four new peerages, that mark of the royal favour which George III had so ostentatiously denied his late ministers. While, however, they could keep their majority in the Commons the 'power' still remained with Fox and North. Fox's problem was twofold: how long could he keep it and what use he should make of it. His retention of it was threatened from two directions. The King might decide to dissolve Parliament or, even in the present House, Fox's supporters might drift away and re-form round Pitt. Both self-interest and constitutional theory dictated such conduct. To storm the Closet as blatantly as Fox and North had done was to claim a right to force ministers on the King which conservative opinion was unwilling to concede. Moreover, once it became clear that Pitt would not easily be driven into resignation, it became politically dangerous to persist in opposition. It was the old story of majorities crumbling into minorities, when it became obvious that new hands would dispense the loaves and fishes. If, however, George III decided to dissolve Parliament, Fox realized that with the full force of the Treasury against him he was unlikely to return to Parliament with any majority at all. He had therefore to do his best to prevent this step being taken. His only hope was to keep the present House of Commons in being, prevent Pitt from carrying on the King's business and so force him to resign. This, however, in the last resort meant the refusal of supplies, if Fox dared to take this step and could induce the Commons to follow him. If, however, George III was driven too far he might dissolve; the refusal of supplies might well prove a two-edged weapon.

When Parliament reassembled, the first clash, apart from the debates on the state of the nation, was over a new India Bill which Pitt introduced on 14 January 1784. On the second reading, which took place on 23 January, it was thrown out by 222 votes to 214 amid shouts of 'resign' hurled by the opposition at Pitt. From his point of view the division was not unpromising; the opposition majority, which had been over a hundred when he first took office, was down to eight, a clear indication that the tide was now running strongly in Pitt's favour even in the Commons. In the country, too, supports on which Fox had firmly relied were beginning to crumble. The fierce fight which he made to avoid appealing to the electorate was necessary for his own parliamentary strategy and popular with members, who certainly did not want to face that expense when they had counted on another three years of security; but it consorted ill with his previous demands for annual Parliaments. In consequence the remnants of the democratic movement turned against him. On one occasion the electors of Westminster shouted him down and a wave of addresses, thanking George III for having dismissed him, began to pour in. Pitt, like his father, received the freedom of London in a gold box. How far such addresses can be considered as a proof of a real swing in public opinion is difficult to say. The influence of the East India Company in stirring up the City, and that of other chartered bodies, cannot be ignored, nor can the desire of many owners of parliamentary boroughs to jump on the new band-wagon before it was too late. But however produced, the effect of the addresses was to encourage Pitt to hold on.

Meanwhile a certain section of the House was trying to arrange an accommodation between the two rivals. To many of the independent members the old dream of a broad-bottomed administration as a panacea for all political strife had not lost its attraction, and at a meeting at the St Albans Tavern late in January fifty-three of them decided to work for such a solution. Neither of the principals was enthusiastic, but nobody, not even the King himself, thought it politic to turn down the suggestion out of hand. Whereupon some pretty political manœuvring took place. Fox declared himself not unwilling to act with Pitt, but he insisted that first the outrage done to the constitution must be repaired by the latter's resigning. Pitt in turn professed himself willing to consider a coalition with Fox and his friends, North having voluntarily stood aside, but he refused to resign in advance or to commit himself to unknown arrangements. While these negotiations were going on with Fox and the Portland whigs, the former was still carrying resolution after resolution against Pitt in the Commons. Fox did, however, shirk taking the vital and decisive step of cutting off supplies, preferring rather a policy of threats and postponements. For instance, the second reading of the Mutiny Bill was put off until 23 February and then until 9 March. Meanwhile a last effort was made to get George III to dismiss Pitt, since it was clear that the hope of returning to office via a broad-bottomed administration was illusory, and that Pitt would not resign. On 1 March an address to the King asking for the removal of his ministers was carried by only 12 votes. A week later a long representation of the illegality of Pitt's retention of office only scraped home by one vote. It was the end of Fox's control of a majority and was widely accepted as such, a recognition marked by the passing of the long-postponed Mutiny Act without further resistance from the opposition.

The dissolution of Parliament on 25 March was the last episode in the drama. George III was not content to build up a working majority round Pitt in the existing House; he intended to destroy the foundation of Fox's power. In this he was definitely using the right to dissolve as a political weapon in a way in which it had not been used before. Robinson's careful calculations had indicated that the position was favourable and the results justified his judgment. Over a hundred of 'Fox's Martyrs'[1] lost their seats, and even Fox himself in spite of the blandishments of Georgiana, Duchess of Devonshire, was only returned as second member for Westminster. How much of his defeat can be ascribed to a genuine repudiation of him by the electors it is difficult to say. Certainly the Treasury took no risks; the pattern of the election was the familiar one of sounding out the proprietors of boroughs, and creating from their ranks the raw material of a parliamentary majority. To say that .public opinion, even in the eighteenth-century sense of the word, swept Pitt back into office would be patently untrue. Yet if in some ways the election followed the traditional pattern of the past, in others it indicated future developments. Political issues were beginning to rise from the local to the national level, and Fox's record was made the target of a widespread propaganda campaign. Though the coalition in its form can be regarded as merely one of a series of similar eighteenth-century arrangements, the personalities had made it something more to contemporaries. Many people seem to have felt that it genuinely was 'a scandalous alliance', while others who looked for Court favour were very ready to spread the same opinion. Certainly Wyvill and his Yorkshire friends felt a keen sense of betrayal that Fox, their late ally, should have deserted them for North. The main wave of feeling against Fox, however, seems to have been aroused by his India Bill. Whatever its real intentions and real results would have been, even responsible men seem to have felt that its effects would be to transfer a dangerous amount of patronage to Fox. With such resources, plus the control of the Treasury, it was argued that when the next election, due under the Septennial Act in four years' time, took place, it could only confirm Fox's power, and that the limitation of the initial right to appoint could easily be extended. In savage cartoons that had a wide sale,

---

[1] M. D. George, 'Fox's Martyrs: The General Election of 1784' (*Trans. R. Hist. Soc.* 4th ser., vol. XXI, 1939).

he was depicted as Carlo Khan riding on an elephant, master of the wealth of the East. Against such a background the action of the King in dismissing Fox and North and entrusting the administration to the unsullied Pitt, could reasonably be described as saving the constitution. Even in the eighteenth century such widespread and bitter propaganda was not without its effects. It is true that the number of voters was limited, and that many of them were so tied by local interests, loyalties and influence that their opinions could have little effect on their votes. But this was not true of some of the open constituencies, or even in some of the counties. Moreover, the patrons of boroughs were free to take their own line, even if the nominal electors were not, and they were susceptible to the prevailing climate of opinion. Contemporaries regarded the election as a landslide: George III and Robinson seem to have been surprised at the extent of their success. Atmosphere is something that is difficult to recapture. The number of contested elections and the number of new members returned may seem to show little significant variation from the past. Nevertheless, in the tone of the press, in the placards and in the cartoons there are genuine echoes of a political contest of a new type. If most men who voted for the administration candidate would have done so in any case, this does not mean that in 1784 they were not more than usually willing to do so. If public opinion did not greatly influence the final results, at least it would appear actively to have approved of them. Even this was something new.

Yet in another sense the essence of the election was its conservatism. Once again it reaffirmed the right of the King to chose his own ministers and Fox's novel constitutional doctrines were repudiated. Once again the 'power' and the 'favour' were united and, though the historian can see that the Crown had made its last great effort, for many years to come the partnership between Pitt and George III was to be a more equal one than most nineteenth-century historians realized. Bitter differences on policy during the American War of Independence, and bitter personal rivalries, out of which were born new constitutional doctrines, proved for a decade a forcing-house for the growth of something like a party system. But once the political climate was again more nearly normal, this somewhat feverish growth could not be maintained. Its roots survived to sprout again when conditions became more favourable, but in the early years of Pitt's ministry Henry Pelham, had he returned, would have found nothing very unfamiliar in the way in which the administration was carried on. Only if he had read the works of Adam Smith and visited the new industrial areas of Lancashire, the Potteries and the Black Country would he have realized that a new England with new interests and new capacities was coming into being. Beyond her shores the same thrust into the future was apparent. While American and British men between them were destroying the old empire, the explorations of Captain Cook were indicating the possibilities of a new one. In 1788 the first settlement was made at Botany Bay in Australia. It was not at Westminster that the shape of things to come was most evident when the new Parliament met on 18 May 1784.

NOTE ON BOOKS

The majority of books which a student approaching this period for the first time would be most likely to consult have already appeared as references in my footnotes which, as I explained in the Preface, have been used as a running bibliography. For convenience' sake, however, I have re-listed the main ones here, together with some comment which may help readers to select their further reading according to their needs and interests.

1. BIBLIOGRAPHIES AND GENERAL BOOKS

The most exhaustive bibliography for the period as a whole is still J. Parellis and J. D. Medley, *Bibliography of English History, The Eighteenth Century 1714–89* but as this was published in 1951 it does not contain the latest books published on the subject. For the period after 1760 students will find I. R. Christie, *British History since 1700* (1970), which is a select and therefore more manageable bibliography, an invaluable source of information. J. B. Williams, *A Guide to the Printed Materials for English and Economic History 1750–1850*, is more specialized and is now somewhat out of date as it was published in 1926 and should be supplemented by I. R. Christie's bibliography, which has a section on this aspect of the period, and by the excellent reviews and lists of recent publications contained in *The Economic History Review*. In the same way the *Annual Bulletin of Historical Literature* published by the Historical Association and the reviews contained in its publication *History* should be used as a means of keeping up to date. In addition, both for their notes on books and articles and for the wealth of illustrative material that they contain, the relevant volumes of *English Historical Documents* should be consulted. These are vol. IX, *American Colonial Documents to 1776* (1955), edited by Merrill Jensen, and vol. X, *1714–83* (1957), edited by D. B. Horn and M. Ransome.

There is no outstanding book that covers the period as a whole. For the reign of George III the volume in the Oxford series by J.

Steven Watson, *The Reign of George III* (1960), is lively and readable and incorporates the results of research up to the date of its publication. It also contains a comprehensive bibliography. For the first half of the century the second edition of Basil Williams's *The Whig Supremacy 1714–63* (1962) in the same series should be consulted. For a factual account of the major aspects of colonial development J. A. Williamson, *A Short History of British Expansion* (1922) is still useful.

2. BOOKS ON SPECIAL ASPECTS

For social and economic history the articles in *The Economic History Review* referred to in my footnotes are worth consulting. A good general background is provided in the first part of P. Mathias, *The First Industrial Nation: an Economic History of Britain 1700–1914* (1969). T. S. Ashton, *An Economic History of England in the Eighteenth Century* (1955) is full of interesting comment and stimulating suggestions but does presuppose some background knowledge of the subject. Both fact and comment are well blended in Phyllis Deane, *The First Industrial Revolution* (1965) which, however, only deals with the latter part of the century. T. S. Ashton, *Economic Fluctuations in England 1700–1800* (1959) provides a background to politics that is too often ignored by students of political and constitutional history. There are useful essays on this borderline territory between politics and economic history in *Statesmen, Scholars, and Merchants* (Essays presented to Dame Lucy Sutherland), edited by Bromley, Dickson and Whiteman (1973), and, more purely economic, in *Studies in the Industrial Revolution* presented to T. S. Ashton and edited by L. S. Pressnell (1960). *The Cotton Trade and Industrial Lancashire* (1660–1780) by A. P. Wadsworth and J. de Lacy Mann (1931) gives a full and authoritative picture of the background of the new industrialism. For books dealing with other special industries consult either the bibliography by I. R. Christie, or that contained in Phyllis Deane's *The First Industrial Revolution* (1965), as the output in recent years has been too considerable to list here. A good summary of English trade is to be found in *English Overseas Trade* (1957) by G. D. Ramsey. Social history also has been attracting a good deal of attention recently. A stimulating book, which slots the cultural background and social development of the century into its political history and which therefore would make an ideal backup to this present volume is J. Carswell, *From Revolution to Revolution, 1688–1776* (1973). Rather earlier is E. N. Williams's lively and authentic *Life in Georgian*

England (1962). My own *English People in the Eighteenth Century* (1956) is also intended to provide a picture of the social structure of eighteenth-century England. More specifically on certain aspects are G. E. Mingay, *English Landed Society in the Eighteenth Century* (1963), M. G. Jones, *The Charity School Movement: a study of eighteenth-century puritanism in action* (1938), my *The English Poor in the Eighteenth Century* (reprinted 1969), and the volume on *The Old Poor Law* (1927) contained in the mammoth work of Beatrice and Sidney Webb's *English Local Government from the Revolution to the Municipal Reform Act* (1906-29), which is a mine of information on this aspect of English history. On London, apart from books and articles referred to in the footnotes, see M. D. George's classic work on *London Life in the Eighteenth Century* (1935), my *Dr Johnson's London* (1968), and George Rudé, *Hanoverian London* (1971); his *The Crowd in History 1730-1848* (1965) contains some interesting comparisons between England and France in this period.

The last twenty years has seen a great deal of important work on constitutional and political history. Much of the initial impetus for this was provided by Sir Lewis Namier, *The Structure of Politics at the Accession of George III* (1929, revised 1957) and by his *England in the Age of the American Revolution* (1930), though this latter title is slightly misleading as the book deals largely with the early years of George III and was planned as the first of a series which was never written. These two books made it necessary to examine the whole basis on which eighteenth-century history had been written. In the 1950s historians like R. Walcott, *English Politics in the Early Eighteenth Century* (1956), assumed that the conditions described by Namier applied also to the earlier part of the century, but in the last few years this view has been challenged by G. Holmes, *Politics in the Age of Queen Anne* (1967), and by J. H. Plumb, *The Growth of Political Stability in England, 1688-1725* (1967), both of whom show convincingly that at this time party rivalries continued to play a major part in English political life. A publication of outstanding importance, particularly to persons engaged in research in this period, is the *History of Parliament*, two sections of which cover the period from 1715 to 1790, the first by R. R. Sedgwick, *1715-54* (1970) and the second by John Brooke, *1754-90* (1964), which provide very useful surveys of the House of Commons as well as detailed sketches of constituencies and biographies of members. Another useful addition to parliamentary history is A. S. Foord, *His Majesty's Opposition,*

1717–1830) (1964). More specialized studies, arranged chronologically, are J. H. Plumb, *Sir Robert Walpole*, vol. I: *The Making of a Statesman* (1956) and vol. II: *The King's Minister* (1960). J. Carswell provides an authoritative account of this complicated episode in *The South Sea Bubble* (1960). J. B. Owen, *The Rise of the Pelhams* (1957), deals with the period 1742–47 in great detail. In addition to the work of Namier the introduction by R. R. Sedgwick to *The Letters of George III to Lord Bute* should be consulted. The most recent contributions to the latter part of the reign are P. Langford, *The First Rockingham Administration* (1973), J. Brooke, *The Chatham Administration 1766–68* (1956), I. R. Christie, *The End of Lord North's Ministry* (1958), and J. Cannon, *The Fox and North Coalition* (1969), written very much from the whig point of view. Other aspects of the reign are dealt with in I. R. Christie, *Wilkes, Wyvill and Reform* (1962), and *Myth and Reality in Late Eighteenth-Century British Politics* (1970), H. Butterfield, *Lord North and the People* (1949), and also *George III and the Historians* (1957), while R. Pares provides a stimulating commentary on the whole reign in *George III and the Politicians* (1953). Much illustrative material and excellent commentaries on it will be found in E. N. Williams, *The Eighteenth-Century Constitution 1688–1815* (1960).

There is no very recent biography of William Pitt, Earl of Chatham; Brian Tunstall's *William Pitt, Earl of Chatham* (1938) should be consulted. More work has been done on the second half of the reign, with considerable concentration on George III himself. I. Macalpine and R. Hunter, *George III and the Mad Business* (1960), have dealt exhaustively with the nature of his recurring periods of mental confusion, and their findings have been widely though not universally accepted. Two full-scale biographies of the King, as a man as well as a sovereign, both of which re-assess him in a very favourable light, are J. Brooke, *King George III* (1972), and S. Ayling, *George the Third* (1972). J. Ehrman, *The Younger Pitt*, vol. I: *The Years of Achievement* (1969), provides a fascinating picture of that part of his life covered by this volume. Earlier lives of Charles James Fox have been superseded by Loren Reid, *A Man for the People* (1969), which concentrates on his role as a parliamentary orator, and J. W. Derry, *Charles James Fox* (1972). C. P. Chenevix Trench has produced a readable study of Wilkes in *Portrait of a Patriot* (1962). A. Valentine, *Lord North* (1967), though extremely detailed, has little fresh to say; probably students will find J. Cannon's *Lord North*, published by the Historical Association, a shorter reliable assessment of that statesman. In general the Historical Association's journal, *History*, and the pamphlets published by the Association provide short up-to-date re-assessments of both current historical problems and personages on which students can rely. A recent study of Lord Shelburne, J. Norris, *Lord Shelburne and Reform* (1963), concentrates on that aspect of his career; P. Brown, *The Chathamites* (1967) contains useful material on both Shelburne and Dunning. Sir Lewis Namier and J. Brooke, *Charles Townshend* (1964), provides an interesting assessment of his career.

In the field of foreign affairs B. D. Horn, *Great Britain and Europe in the Eighteenth Century* (1967) provides a very useful book of reference; because British relations with each country are dealt with separately there is inevitably a certain amount of repetition and each chapter should be read as background when required: Chapter 2 should be consulted by any reader anxious to understand *The Machinery for the Conduct of Foreign Policy in the Eighteenth Century* which is very illuminating. With regard to British overseas possessions Dame Lucy Sutherland, *The East India Company in Eighteenth-Century Politics* (1952) is outstanding. For British relations with her American colonies before 1776 the standard work is L. H. Gipson, *The British Empire before the American Revolution* (14 vols., 1936 onwards); this provides a detailed analysis of the imperial problem throughout the period covered by this book; vol. II deals with the Southern Plantations and the Caribbean Islands; vol. III. with New England and the Middle Colonies; vol. IV is devoted to the zone of international friction; see also the same author's shorter *The Coming of the Revolution 1763–1775* (1956). For an up-to-date and concise treatment students will find I. R. Christie, *Crisis of Empire* (1970) provides a useful and manageable summary. The opposing attitudes of British and American politicians on colonial issues in the early 1770s are discussed in B. Donoughue, *British Politics and the American Revolution* (1964); for the actual campaigning and its problems see P. Mackesy, *The War for America* (1964). R. B. Morris, *The Peacemakers* (1965), gives an exhaustive and detailed account of the peace negotiations from the American angle. For imperial history after 1763 see V. T. Harlow, *The Founding of The Second British Empire* (2 vols., 1952–64). Other important, somewhat specialized books are J. M. Beattie, *The English Court in the Reign of George I* (1967), which deals with the Court as an institution and instrument of political power; N. Sykes, *Church and State in England in the Eighteenth Century* (1934), and S. Maccoby, *English Radicalism 1762–85* (1935). On finance there are two important books, P. G. M. Dickson, *The Financial Revolution in England 1688–1756* (1967), and J. E. D. Binney, *British Public Finance and Administration 1774–92* (1958). For the period as a whole Sir William S. Houldworth, *A History of the English Law*, vol. X (1938) is both illuminating and stimulating, with a scope much wider than its title might suggest.

This note on books is in no sense exhaustive. I have made no mention of the many standard editions of eighteenth-century correspondence, but the reader who is interested in consulting these will find complete references to the most important in the footnotes. Many of these provide an insight into the political and social life of the century which cannot be obtained in any other way. Nor should the pleasure and profit to be obtained from a study of the poets, novelists and painters of the age be forgotten. Pope and Fielding, Hogarth, Reynolds and Gainsborough transform an impersonal record into a human chronicle.

INDEX

543

Index 545

Frederick, Prince of Wales: marriage of, 162–3; and election of 1747, 186, 188, 316; relations with George II, 221, 232; death of, 234

Frederick II of Prussia: and War of Austrian Succession, 184–5, 203–4; 212–13; and Seven Years' War, 297, 303–4, 307; and subsidies, 295, 328, 334

Fur Trade, 256

Gage, General Thomas, 376, 421–4, 426
Gambia, 515
Garrick, David, 443
Gaspee, the, 410
Gay, John, 166
General Warrants, 339, 346, 349
Gentry, description of, 30–2
Genoa, 198, 217, 303
George I (1714–27): personality, 78; and Hanover, 79–80; foreign policy, 94–5, 99, 131; and his ministers, 102, 112, 114; and Prince of Wales, 121; and von Platen marriage, 137; death, 148
George II (1727–60): accession, 148–9; and Hanover, 223; views on foreign policy, 134, 148; on War of Polish Succession, 174; on War of Austrian Succession, 185–7, 194–6, 200–1; relations with Walpole, 132, 188–9; reconstruction of ministry, 1742, 193; and Pelham, 203–8; dislike of Harrington, 235; and Pitt, 210–12, 275; and, Temple, 307; and Army appointments, 287; death, 308
George III (1760–1820): conflicting views on, 310–17; and Bute, 315–18; and election of 1760, 318–19; early political problems, 325–6, 340–1, 348–9; and Newcastle, 328–9, 332; and nervous breakdown, 347; and Stamp Act, 363; and American resistance, 412–21; views on party, 447; and opposition, 451; election of 1780, 495; and Yorktown, 499; reconstructs ministry, 502, 513; dislike of Fox, 513, 515, 521–2; and Fox North Coalition, 517–18; and Prince of Wales, 522–3; and India Bill, 528; and the younger Pitt, 530
George, Prince of Wales, and Fox, 522–3
Georgia, 17, 171, 182, 438
Gibbon, Edward, 406, 443
Gibson, Edmund, Bishop of London, 105, 166
Gideon, Samuel, 225
Gin drinking, 164, 229–30
Glasgow merchants, 243, 454
Gordon, Lord George, 469–72
Gordon Riots, 469–72
Goree, 291, 298, 515
Gower, 1st Earl of, 209–10

Gower, 2nd Earl of, 451: and Ireland, 457
Grafton, 3rd Duke of (1735–1811), 352, 366–7, 369, 380–3, 396, 503, 517
Granby, Marquis of, 395
Grantham, Lord, 253–4, 266, 514
Granville, John Carteret, Earl (1690–1763): early career, 116; Secretary of State, 130; rivalry with Walpole, 136–40, 152, 159, 187; again Secretary of State, 194; foreign policy and War of Austrian Succession, 195–204; minister behind the curtain, 205–13; fails to form government, 214; President of Council, 235, 272, 274; death, 338
Grenada, 328, 333, 450, 515
Grenville, George (1712–70): early political career, 200, 202, 205, 209, 226; Treasurer of Navy, 253; dismissed, 267, 273, 279, 281, 326, 329–31; First Lord of Treasury, 337–8, 340, 346–8; and Stamp Act, 355–6, 361; Revenue Act, 357–8; and Wilkes, 339, 342, 380; and disputed elections, 398
Grenville, James, 319
Grenville, Thomas, 510–11
Guadeloupe, 299, 322, 333
Guildford Court House, Battle of, 498
Guinea, 244
Gyllenborg, Count, 95

Habeas Corpus, suspension of, 203
Halifax, Charles Montagu, Earl of (1661–1715), 44, 73
Halifax, George Montague Dunk, Earl of (1716–71), 259–60, 329, 339–40, 342
Hanau, negotiations at, 197, 204
Hanbury, John, 257
Hanover: and British politics, 79–80; and Northern War, 115–21; and War of Austrian Succession, 195–6, 201; and Seven Years' War, 277, 285
Hanover, Alliance of (1725), 146
Hanoverian troops, 200, 205, 211
Harcourt, Lord, 365
Hardwicke, Earl of (1690–1764): 159, 193–4, 204–9, 263; and peace negotiations, 219; and Marriage Act, 230–1; and Pitt, 265, 272–3, 276, 327, 329, 332, 343; death, 346
Hardy, Sir Charles, 448–50
Harrington, 1st Earl of (1690–1756): Secretary of State, 147; and War of Polish Succession, 174, 184, 189–90, 205, 209, 213, 219–20; dismissed from Ireland, 235
Harris, James, 401
Hastenbeck, battle of, 285
Hastings, Warren, 409, 525–6
Havana, 331